D1281343

Typography and Graphic Design

Roxane Jubert

Typography and Graphic Design

From Antiquity to the Present

*Forewords by Ellen Lupton
and Serge Lemoine*

Translated from the French by
Deke Dusinberre and David Radzinowicz

Flammarion

In memory of Marion Sauvaire

To Peter Keller

The author would like to thank in particular: Julie Rouart, commissioning editor of the collection, for her energy and open-mindedness; Peter Keller for his invaluable assistance and for sharing his expertise in this domain; Serge Lemoine for showing such enthusiasm during the supervision of the thesis from which the present volume emerged; Andy Stafford and Isabelle Ewig for their invaluable friendship.

Gratitude is also due to all those who have become involved with or who encouraged this work in many different ways: Albert Boton, Joëlle Carreau-Labiche, Bernard Cazaux, Roger Chatelain, Jacqueline Chevalier, Françoise Courbis, Jean-Pierre Criqui, Wim Crouwel, Christian Debize, Francis Dumas, Marsha Emanuel, Emmanuel, Claude Eveno, Francis Freisz, Pierre Fresnault-Deruelle, Friedrich Friedl, Karl Gerstner, G. †, Françoise Giroux, André Hatala, Hans-Jürg Hunziker, Gérard Ifert, Francine Jamin, Marc Jimenez, Pierre Jullien, George Henry Katz, Robin Kinross, Jadette Laliberté, Sylvie Lavaud, Jean-Philippe Lenclos, Sandrine Maillet, Victor Margolin, Massin, Hans Eduard Meier, Rudi Meyer, Jan Middendorp, Didier Moiselet, Bruno Monguzzi, L. M. †, Jean-Michel Palmier †, Arnauld Pierre, Sylvie Pouliot, Christian Rondet, Margo Rouard-Snowman, Béatrice Saalburg, Dimitri Salmon, Robert Schenck †, Helmut Schmid, Bertram Schmidt-Friderichs, Anouk Seng, David Steel, Niklaus Troxler, Jan Van Toorn, François Vermeil, Jean Widmer, the personnel at the École Nationale Supérieure des Arts Décoratifs, and my former teachers.

*At the outset this study benefited from a research grant awarded by the FIACRE
(Fonds d'Incitation à la Création)/French Ministry of Culture.*

Ouvrage publié avec le soutien du Centre national du livre – ministère français de la culture.
This work is published with support from the French Ministry of Culture, Centre National du Livre.

Contents

Foreword

Ellen Lupton

Curator of Contemporary Design, Cooper-Hewitt, National Design Museum, New York City;
Director, Graphic Design MFA Program, Maryland Institute College of Art; writer and graphic designer.

Dan Friedman once asked, "Is graphic design pervasive throughout society, or is it virtually nonexistent?"* Friedman, who was one of the leading figures of the New Typography movement of the 1970s and 80s, was thinking about the curious way in which graphic design relentlessly inscribes the surfaces of daily life, leaving its mark on cereal boxes, movie tickets, screen savers, junk mail, pop-up ads, package inserts, and innumerable other mundane, even noxious, bits of messaging. At the same time, graphic design is a discipline that seeks a meaningful, critical engagement with its own cultural language and with the institutions of modern life. Understood from this second perspective, graphic design is a narrower phenomenon, influencing but a minor current in the rushing stream of media. Graphic design is everywhere, yet nowhere. It is commonplace, yet specialized. It is global and public, yet it turns inward to its own community of makers.

The same can be asked of design's history. Does graphic design encompass the entire sphere of mark-making, or is it a specific discourse anchored by the invention of reproductive media and printed letters in the modern era? This ambitious book, written by the distinguished French art historian Roxane Jubert, draws a long, inclusive line around design's evolution, reaching back into prehistory and pulling ahead into the stunningly complex practices of our own time. Yet while taking this broad view, Roxane Jubert has nonetheless set limits to her subject, allowing it to take shape against the impossibly vast and cluttered field of visual communication.

The story begins with a look at the ancient non-verbal representations made in the caves of present-day France and Spain over 20,000 years ago, and it chronicles the invention of writing systems in Mesopotamia, China, Greece, Egypt, and elsewhere. But the focus of this book is the alphabetic universe of the West, where a concise phonetic code became the medium for preserving, transmitting, marketing, and transgressing the intellectual materials of Western modernity. The story thickens with detail as it enters the twentieth century, when graphic design finally emerged as a professional discipline, yielding an approach to public communication that fanned out across the world.

Many threads emerge and reconnect across the pages of this book. We see the rise and fall of governments and empires, the invention and spread of technologies, the articulation and embodiment of philosophies, and the rich, human contribution of individual designers, printers, and typographers. But the story that asserts itself again and again, page after page, is the evolving life of the letter. We see the alphabet emerge as a supremely efficient technology for encoding the spoken word, and we see it triumph as an object well-suited to mass production (1452, fig. 66). We see typography take hold of Renaissance thought and creativity, pulsing outward from commercial centers like Venice into the widening marketplace of the literate world (1500, fig. 96).

The letter became theoretical, discovering its own body in the writings and diagrams of Albrecht Dürer (1525, fig. 100) and Geofroy Tory (1529, fig. 108). It submitted to scientific analysis in the diagrams of Louis XIV's Imprimerie Royale, seeking finality in the pristine mesh of a gridded plane (1692, figs. 127–8). Abandoning perfection in the nineteenth century, printed letters plunged into a lurid world of color and variation. The alphabetic body assumed bizarre new proportions and costumed itself in outlandish ornaments. In lithographic advertisements, words became objects whose physical presence was unmatched by the products they promoted (1889, fig. 179). Such excess inspired reform, and the critique of mass culture came to define modern design as a principled, self-conscious discourse (1896, fig. 185). New forms of lettering evolved in resistance to popular media; birthed inside the castle walls of the fine press movement, they inexorably influenced commercial production (1900, fig. 257).

Whereas letters in the Renaissance and Enlightenment lived chiefly in the pages of the book, the Industrial Revolution pushed typography out onto the street. The modern city became encrusted with signs, from the commercial (1850, fig. 157) to the corporate (1909, fig. 251) to the civic (1916, fig. 440). Responding to the convergence of typography and urbanism, the Cubists—followed closely by the Futurist, Dada, and Constructivist avant-gardes—depicted modern life by aggressively incorporating the disjunctive, indigestible husk of lettering into the pictorial image (1912, fig. 265). Buildings became signs (1924, fig. 376), and new architectures were built entirely from letters (1927, fig. 285).

* Interview with Ellen Lupton, 1994, in *Mixing Messages: Graphic Design and Contemporary Culture* (New York: Princeton Architectural Press and Cooper-Hewitt, National Design Museum, 1996), p. 167.

Out of the experiments of the avant-garde came utilitarian strategies that were informed by modernist aesthetics and a critical stance towards mass culture. The designer emerged as a practical visionary equipped with a bracing new formal language and a sense of social purpose. Such ideas spoke through the publications and practices of the legendary Bauhaus (1925, fig. 362) and were codifed as the "New Typography" (1928, fig. 362), preparing the ground for design's professionalization in the post-war period.

Today, the letter continues to see itself in new ways. Since the mid-twentieth century, typography's body became dematerialized, its massive mechanical apparatus transformed into the film and light of phototypesetting and the vectors and pixels of digital production. The modular assembly of the digital letter provides the functional basis of post-industrial media (1972, fig. 750) as well as a matrix that invites astonishing formal manipulations (1997, fig. 757). Typography's digital grain is not entirely new, however; fascist spectacles in Germany (fig. 454) and Italy (1937, fig. 483) coalesced out of thousands of human bodies, each serving as a pixel subordinated to an overwhelming message. Typography is a medium of oppression as well as liberation; its power has been unleashed anew on the Internet, where battles are being waged today to exploit and control its potential, politically as well as commercially.

Writing has always been tied to power and wealth. The alphabet and other forms of writing were invented to serve some mix of everyday utility and ritual formality. Early scripts met the needs of commerce as well as law and religion, helping merchants, makers, and tax collectors account for the flow of goods. While the symbols inscribed laboriously in the tombs and monuments of ancient kings are works of art, the fragments of routine commercial life are equally crucial relics of design's history. The static inscriptions of the memorial aspire to last for millennia, while the fast-moving marks of daily transactions are fleeting.

In modern times, everyday communications rush by, assaulting the senses before quickly disappearing. Labels, trade cards, and posters often survive only because they are printer's samples that have never actually circulated—they were never glued to a can, pasted to a fence, or sent through the mail. Eventually, some of these artifacts acquire the uncanny status of "ephemera," interred in a library folder or a museum box, where they are captured in time and yet still marked as passing, as temporary, their right to endure cast in perpetual uncertainty. This book builds a home for the discourse of graphic design and typography, providing a framework for understanding what we see and make today and how it connects to a rich field of accumulated practice. It is hard to imagine going forward without access to what is documented inside these covers.

Foreword to the French edition

Serge Lemoine

President of the Musée d'Orsay, Paris. Professor at Université Paris IV, Sorbonne.

Typography and France: two worlds, two entities that seemed incompatible. With a handful of exceptions, in the twentieth century, typography and graphics—the art of composing letters, words, and texts, and of laying them out—and their relationship to drawn images, never found a rightful place in France. This is all the more astonishing in the country of Henri de Toulouse-Lautrec, the creator of the modern poster who, in his works based on paintings, was instantly able to find the right relationship between the image, simplified and expressive, and the text, reduced to a minimum. Moreover, with *La Revue blanche* and *L'Assiette au beurre*, journals on which the finest artists collaborated (including Lautrec himself, in addition to Bonnard, Vuillard, Vallotton, Denis, Villon, Kupka, and Steinlen), at the onset of the twentieth century France possessed all it might have needed for success in a fledgling domain that was to become so rich in possibilities. Admittedly, France had not experienced an artistic movement of the scope of Arts and Crafts in the United Kingdom, and the genius of Hector Guimard was not able to express itself as Henry Van de Velde's did in Belgium or more especially in Germany.

Beside the work of Gallé and Majorelle, there is nothing resembling the Austrian Wiener Werkstätte, nor *a fortiori* the Werkbund in Germany. States of mind in France seem to have been unconducive to groundbreaking typographical design. There was, however, Stéphane Mallarmé and the revolutionary typesetting of his poem *Un Coup de dés… ,* and although it had no repercussions in France, Marinetti and the Italian Futurists drew on its radical design, and were soon followed by the Dada artists and poets. From the "1900"-style poster prevalent in France, the chosen genre of those who followed Jules Chéret, such as the distinguished figures of Eugène Grasset and Alphonse Mucha, no determining trends emerged. More significant events were afoot in Germany with the development of the *Sachplakat* and the masterly creations of Lucian Bernhard, Ludwig Hohlwein, and Hans Rudi Erdt, which had dramatic consequences in their own country and soon in Switzerland. For their part, in France, Sonia and Robert Delaunay sought to move from art to its application in advertising, but the results of their efforts were limited.

A new phase kicked off after World War I. The period from 1918 to the middle of the 1930s proved innovative and productive in the fields of typography, graphics, and the poster. It was largely marked by the ideas of such major painters as Piet Mondrian, Theo Van Doesburg, Alexander Rodchenko, and El Lissitzky, and had centers predominantly in central, Northern, and Eastern Europe. Piet Mondrian, who lived and worked in France, was the dominant figure in the Netherlands: it was within the movement of De Stijl and with the theory of Neoplasticism that Van Doesburg evolved a new typography whose culmination was the cover to the second series of the review *De Stijl* (begun in 1923): sans serif type, asymmetry, the importance attached to blank space, lettering laid out horizontally and vertically and placed on the periphery, two colors, black and red—all in the service of a perfect equilibrium. Still in the Netherlands, Piet Zwart and Paul Schuitema began to emphasize photomontage.

In the Soviet Union, from the very start of the 1920s, Constructivism was the predominant force, finding expression in typographical creations by Rodchenko, the expert in photomontage, and El Lissitzky, who remained marked by Suprematism: granted permission to leave his native land, he worked in Berlin, Hanover, Cologne, and Zurich, and became the leading propagandist of this type of art in the west. The Vhutemas school went as far as to teach these novel techniques, devoting itself to the applied arts envisaged from the point of view of the reigning Communist ideology.

The situation in Germany was initially conditioned by the irruption of Dada, and the extraordinary progress in typography achieved by Raoul Hausmann with his poem-poster, *FMSBW*, and on the cover of the first number of the review *Der Dada*, to which should be added the decisive inventions of John Heartfield in the area of photomontage. The impact of Neoplasticism and Constructivism also proved crucial: with the arrival of László Moholy-Nagy from 1923, it began to percolate through the Bauhaus. Fundamental work was untaken that affected lettering, page-setting, and the creation of printed materials, including the book—as shown by the series of *Bauhausbücher*—and the poster (see the one for Kandinsky's jubilee exhibition in 1926 by Herbert Bayer, for instance).

But Germany is not just the Bauhaus, and in many other cities workshops were springing up run by artists such as Walter Dexel, Willi Baumeister, Max Burchartz, and Jan Tschichold (one of the principal theorists of the New Typography), and Kurt Schwitters, who founded the Ring Neuer Werbegestalter, where one could meet among others Cesar Domela and Friedrich Vordemberge-Gildewart.

Czechoslovakia at the end of the 1920s was not far behind, through the work of Karel Teige, the author of *Abeceda*, one of the most beautiful books of the time for its decorated initials, and Ladislav Sutnar. Poland, too, saw innovations in typography, and Mieczyslaw Szczuka, Henryk Berlewi, Henryk Stazewski, and Wladyslaw Strzeminski came to the fore, applying their ideas in typographical designs.

These activities were evidence of a veritable liberation from the forms of the past, and the result was the creation of a wholly modern visual language. France remained on the margins, though it benefited from the career of Cassandre, one of the greatest poster artists of the first half of the twentieth century. His style, deeply inspired by Le Corbusier and Ozenfant's Purism, made its impact in original compositions, audacious simplifications, an aptness of abbreviated form and the intrinsic poetry of his images, while the effects of repetition used in his three-part poster, *Dubo Dubon Dubonnet*, amalgamated time and space. Next to Cassandre, Charles Loupot and Jean Carlu and, to a lesser extent, the more familiar figure of Paul Colin, add to what was a glowing poster environment where pictorial criteria remained paramount.

Such works, however, give a false idea of a situation made still worse by the onset of the Art Deco movement, whose backward views also made inroads in typography. In France, scarcely an innovation emerged in the field of the alphabet, which since the eighteenth century had remained wedded to the principles of Firmin Didot and of page-setting *à la française,* with a single axis of symmetry and the use of capitals remaining endemic. Cassandre himself created an alphabet, Bifur, which remained underused. This was in marked contrast to the situation elsewhere in Europe: in Germany Herbert Bayer, Joost Schmidt, and Paul Renner were revolutionizing the art of lettering with the assistance of the printers' corporations, no less.

The review *L'Esprit nouveau* set up by Le Corbusier and Ozenfant is symptomatic in this respect: it is undoubtedly the most significant publication of the time in terms of its ideas, but its page-setting remains traditional and banal, unlike, for example, *Das neue Frankfurt*, whose Constructivist layout was by Hans Leistikow, a Bauhaus student.

Similarly the inside pages of the journal *Minotaure*, with sumptuous covers designed by the likes of Picasso, Masson, Dalí, and Ernst, show scant typographical interest—like Surrealist publications as a whole.

Able to fall back on a continuous history from the 1920s, Switzerland came into its own after 1945, with major creations by Otto Baumberger, Ernst Keller, Niklaus Stoecklin, Herbert Matter and, already, Max Bill. Adopting Concrete art and basing themselves on the teaching of the Kunstgewerbeschule in Zurich and Basel, inclined to theory and supported by trade and industry, Swiss typographers, the majority of whom were artists (Max Bill, Richard Paul Lohse, Carlo Vivarelli, Emil Ruder, Armin Hofmann), created a functional style entirely rooted in economy of means and formal rigor and making systematic use of the grid, as one of the masterpieces of the period, Vivarelli's poster *Für das Alter*, demonstrates. This state of mind endured for several generations, with Josef Müller-Brockmann, Karl Gerstner, Marcel Wyss (for instance, the review *Spirale*), and continues up to today. Its equivalent can be found in Germany, with the creation of the school at Ulm, the Hochschule für Gestaltung by Max Bill, where Otl Aicher, Friedrich Vordemberge-Gildewart, and Josef Albers all taught and from which one of the greatest poster artists of the 1960s emerged, Almir Mavignier.

The United States also entered the scene at this time, with Paul Rand, Lester Beall, and Will Burtin, whereas Mehemed Fehmy Agha, Alexey Brodovitch, and Alexander Liberman, the latter coming from Paris, had been active as art directors on fashion magazines from the 1930s, revolutionizing the art of composition.

France at the time saw the reign of Raymond Savignac, most appreciated for his good nature and humor, a factor that conditioned the extraordinary success of many Swiss graphic designers who came to settle in Paris and who made an impact in many different fields: Adrian Frutiger, who a created the Univers type, and who worked for the Paris Métro and the airport at Roissy, Bruno Pfäffli, who designed catalogs and posters for museums, Peter Knapp, who became art director for *Elle* magazine, and Jean Widmer, who oversaw *Jardin des modes* and designed freeway signage, before Ruedi Baur set up in France. Meanwhile Roman Cieslewicz from Poland composed catalog layouts for the Centre National d'Art Contemporain and soon after for the Centre Georges Pompidou. Switzerland, Germany, and the Netherlands continued to innovate in this field, while in France the Grapus agency won the competitive tender for the logotype of the Délégation aux Arts Plastiques.

Since the era of Cassandre, Loupot, and Carlu, where are the quality French posters? What book has really made an impact in the history of graphic design? One might even add, since these things are interdependent: what postage stamp, what corporate identity has been influential?

In these conditions it is surely significant that no book has been published in France on the subject, while Karl Gerstner and Markus Kutter brought out their *Die neue Graphik* back in 1959 with a specialized Swiss publisher, Niggli, a fundamental history of graphic design that is in itself a masterpiece of layout. At the same time, from 1958 to 1965 there appeared in Zurich a periodical overseen by Richard Paul Lohse, Hans Neuburg, Josef Müller-Brockmann, and Carlo Vivarelli—*Neue Grafik*—whose form was as exemplary as its contents. Meanwhile in 1969 in London, Herbert Spencer issued *Pioneers of Modern Typography*, a noteworthy publication in spite of its modest presentation, and which has been repeatedly reprinted since. In 1971 in Zurich, Josef Müller-Brockmann and Shizuko Yoshikawa published their summa on the art of the poster, *Geschichte des Plakates/History of the Poster*, with a layout that was a triumph of graphic design, not forgetting, in 1986, *Geschichte der visuellen Kommunikation/A History of Visual Communication*, by Müller-Brockmann alone.

In France, however, the few works published on the subject, including dictionaries, are translations, some adapted, while the second edition of Alain Weill's book *L'Affiche dans le monde*, appearing in 1991, finally afforded an international account of the question. No books. No exhibitions. No equivalent to the Kunstgewerbemuseum in Zurich or the Stedelijk Museum in Amsterdam. In Paris, a latecomer, the Musée de l'Affiche, opened only to immediately close again. Later, much later, it was replaced by the Musée de la Publicité, inaugurated in 1999, whose program, concentrating on cultural history, centers on business partners, such as Air France or Pastilles Valda. This is equally transparent from the few major exhibitions organized in Paris on the theme of "design," where the same status was granted the Perrier water bottle as Rietveld's blue-and-red chair, while a brand like Monsavon was preferred to Jan Tschichold's creations for the Phoebus-Palast.

One can then only continue to dream of a major show on Cassandre (the earliest dates back to 1950 at the Musée des Arts Décoratifs in Paris) or Dutch graphics, which one can imagine dividing into three sections: the 1920–1940s, with Van Doesburg, Van der Leck, Huszár, Zwart, and Schuitema, not forgetting Wijdeveld and the review *Wendingen*; after 1945, with Willem Sandberg; and from 1970 onwards, with Pieter Brattinga, Jan Van Toorn, Wim Crouwel and the Total Design agency (which employed Jean-Louis Froment at the CAPC, Bordeaux) and Karel Martens, and which would show how the history of this art lives on in that nation and how it has acquired a real visual culture of its own.

In this context, a book concerning the history of typography and graphic design by a French author brought out by a French publisher comes as both as a relief and a welcome surprise: congratulations are due to its originators, Roxane Jubert and Éditions Flammarion.

Roxane Jubert was a student under Jean Widmer at the École Nationale Supérieure des Arts Décoratifs, Paris. She is also an art historian and presented a doctoral thesis, which I had the honor to supervise, at the Sorbonne. She works as a graphic designer and teaches at the ENSAD and at Université Paris IV. She is thoroughly acquainted with the subject, covering a broad chronological sweep that emphasizes the history of writing and the creation of the most important alphabets with their various characteristics.

She lays special stress on the period from the end of the nineteenth century to 1914, though she does not forget to offer an account of the extraordinary lettering Edward Johnston created for the London Underground in 1916. She also explains in detail the decisive interwar period, as well as introducing creations by Gustav Klutsis and addressing the role of Charles Peignot, providing a convincing analysis of the crucial turn that France neglected to take in the 1920s. (Already in 1930, when Heinz and Bodo Rasch's work *Gefesselter Blick*, published in Germany, listed the names of the twenty-six greatest graphic designers of the time, not a single French one appeared.)

Roxane Jubert's study then turns to the second half of the twentieth century, considered from every aspect, before going on to present-day developments in typography and the new practices thrown up by computing technologies.

A salutary text. An essential overview. A hope for the future.

Ts-ang Chieh, the legendary inventor of Chinese
script, c. 3500 BCE. A Chinese legend ascribes the
invention of characters to Ts-ang Chieh.
Endowed with two pairs of eyes one above
the other, he was able to take in the sky and
the earth in a single glance, and is supposed to
have invented writing while simultaneously
observing celestial bodies and marks left by
living creatures. (*Portraits of some of the
principal Chinese who made themselves famous*,
Bejing, 1685.)

Introduction

graphikos:

— concerning the art of lettering or drawing;

— concerning the action of writing; concerning the art of script and composition; concerning painting.

type (typo-, -type, -typy) :

— from Latin *typus*. "model, symbol";

— from the Greek *tupos*, "imprint, mark; written character," from *tuptein*, "to apply, strike."

Typography and Graphic Design is an account and exploration of visual communication through the centuries, concentrating on the nineteenth and twentieth centuries, with an outline of earlier periods.

"During the twentieth century, graphic design has developed to become simultaneously an identifiable element in contemporary culture and an economic motor of prime importance." (Massin). "More than any other form of visual culture, graphic design is inescapable." (Paul Jobling and David Crowley). In France, the domains in which signs are created and produced would be advanced by the existence of a consolidated and better inter-related sector of research, a sector which would benefit from a recognition of its position as an entity in itself. Such a development is abundantly justified by the omnipresence of graphic design in our everyday environment, which has persisted through the twentieth century (and is still more in evidence today thanks to digital technology). Significant too, is the openness of graphic design to multidisciplinarity, and its inextricable connections with the arts. The intermediary position of graphics in the arts hierarchy is something of a quandary—*a fortiori* when it is contrasted with fields as varied as architecture, photography, cinema, the book, writing, or even technology generally.

The present volume stems from research begun in 1993 at the École Nationale Supérieure des Arts Décoratifs in Paris and continued under the umbrella of a doctoral thesis for the department of art history at the University of Paris IV, the Sorbonne. As its focus tended to extend gradually back in time, the thesis turned into a broad historical overview presented in the form of an outline or a series of landmarks indicating the main lines of development rather than a formal written history.

The origin of this study sprang from a drive for historical comprehension. The absence of specific training programs has been raised elsewhere, notably in 2003, Steven Heller noted in *Print* magazine that "arguably the biggest void left by graphic design education programs is a critical awareness of design history." The adoption of the long view entails an approach that attempts to reflect the singularities and complexities of the topic, to discover or to rehearse its various phases, paths, turning-points, affiliations, associations, and ruptures in its eventful history. The desire to grasp its extension in time has necessarily resulted in limitations, while focused examination of specific areas and case studies (a certain number of in-depth analyses are the subject of parallel publications) has been eschewed.

This work should be considered as a foundation rather than as a conclusion, to be enriched, refined, studied from all angles, and corrected where necessary. This position is based on the knowledge that there is a need for general histories and for the development of research into the field. English, American, German, and Swiss contributions make up some of the principal general works that offer a vision of graphic design and its history that is wide-ranging, varied, precise, with a multidisciplinary and global viewpoint.

Publications devoted to the history of graphics and/or typography offering panoramic views and fundamental studies include:

—for graphic design: *Die neue Graphik. The New Graphic Art. Le Nouvel Art graphique* (Karl Gerstner and Markus Kutter, 1959), *Geschichte der visuellen Kommunikation* (Josef Müller-Brockmann, 1971), *A History of Graphic Design* (Philip B. Meggs, 1983), *Graphic Design. A Concise History* (Richard Hollis, 1994), *Graphic Design. Reproduction and Representation since 1800* (Paul Jobling and David Crowley, 1996), *Clean New World. Culture, Politics, Graphic Design* (Maud Lavin, 2001), *Graphic Design History* (Steven Heller and Georgette Ballance [eds.], 2001), *Le Design graphique* (Alain Weill, 2003);

—for typography, writing, and lettering: *La Lettre d'imprimerie. Origine, développement, classification* (Francis Thibaudeau, 1921), *Die Schriftentwicklung/Le Développement de l'écriture* (Hans Eduard Meier, 1959), *Schriftkunst. Geschichte, Anatomie, und Schönheit der lateinischen Buchstaben* (Albert Kapr, 1971; English trans. *The Art of Lettering. The History, Anatomy, and Aesthetics of the Roman Letterforms*, 1983), *La Civilisation de l'écriture* (Roger Druet and Herman Grégoire, 1976), *Typographic Communications Today* (Edward M. Gottschall, 1989), *Anatomy of a Typeface* (Alexander Lawson, 1990), *Modern Typography. An Essay in Critical History* (Robin Kinross, 1992), *Twentieth Century* Type (Lewis Blackwell, 1992), *A History of Writing. From hieroglyph to multimedia* (general editor, Anne-Marie Christin, 2001).

Among these publications, the list of which is far from exhaustive, Philip B. Meggs' vast summum, appearing in the United States more than twenty years ago in 1983 (the year of the First Symposium on the History of Graphic Design at the Rochester Institute of Technology), and updated in 2006, has been acknowledged as a groundbreaking achievement.

There emerges, with respect to the vast array of works devoted to the history of visual expression, a certain number of diverse factors. Some volumes proposing pithy if essential overviews focus on the twentieth century, sometimes running back into the end of the nineteenth. Visual material tends to be plentiful (as shown by, for example, the work *Typo: When Who How* by Friedrich Friedl, Nicolaus Ott and Bernard Stein), a situation further enhanced by the increasing number of volumes in which illustration predominates.

The domain of the poster is also well represented and has been amply studied. In certain countries, publishing and research have profited from impetus from universities (as in the activities of certain American university presses and in research undertaken in association with the Department of Typography and Graphic Communication at the University of Reading in England). Moreover, certain figures in typographic creation and graphic design have contributed actively to the written culture of their field, sometimes with a historical focus; Jan Tschichold's published output has in this respect been highly significant, running to dozens of books and nearly two hundred articles and other texts, including, in the period 1925–35, *Elementare Typographie, Die neue Typographie, Foto-Auge/Œil et photo/Photo-eye* and *Typographische Gestaltung* (in the twentieth century, this category also covers works by Eric Gill, Paul Rand, Emil Ruder, Otl Aicher, Massin, Ellen Lupton, J. Abbott Miller, and many others besides). For the most recent period, one should also not forget the extremely rapid development and sheer abundance of information and texts on the topic posted on the Internet.

As regards writings in French, awareness of graphic design and typography has been singularly enhanced by numerous studies originating in related or closely allied fields. These analyses often offer essential reading in more than one respect and benefit from an advanced level of research. As instances of what are sources of very varied kinds, mention might be made of exhibition catalogs such as *Art & publicité 1890–1990, Poésure et peintrie, L'Aventure des écritures*, pieces in *La Naissance du livre moderne, Peinture et poésie*, various publications by the Centre d'Étude de l'Écriture et de l'Image in the University of Paris VII, or again contributions from historians such as Laurent Gervereau.

As abroad, written culture and the state of historical knowledge and research in France concerning typography and graphics have been tackled many times over the last few decades, by practitioners as well as by art historians, critics, journalists, and pedagogues. There are still gaps to fill in the history of graphic design before it can constitute a branch of science with its own specific areas of research, reflection, and demarcation with an international scope. For the time being, it seems that the culture marshaled often originates from personal, self-taught conceptions (such as those dispensed, for example, by a number of teaching professionals in art schools).

Graphic design has benefited from a promising surge in interest. New initiatives are taking form (exhibitions, round tables, encounter groups), often devoted to current or recent phenomena, providing a fillip to the field and placing it firmly in what has become a transnational context. Such impetus would clearly gain from an upswing in publishing activity (essays, reviews, anthologies, reprints, translations, or other specific publications), by the development of research structures (and of a correlative pedagogy), by the organization of conferences—and more especially by increased visibility and analysis generally.

If graphic design and typography are to coalesce into a field of study in their own right, forming a branch of research that treats them as its primary object of investigation, they cannot be considered separately. They present natural and sometimes fundamental links with a considerable number of other practices and forms of creation—the visual arts, photography, design, creative writing, architecture, urban structures, and so on.

A broad survey also means taking account of where the field borders on or overlaps with the history of the book, the press and the media, of script, technology, propaganda, and so on. Moreover, stress is regularly placed on the fact that the position of typography and graphic design in history—beyond the question of the forms, images, and letters they are concerned with—has become interwoven with artistic and cultural issues, such as the development of the relevant crafts, technology and industry, as well as with the social, political, religious, and economic context (factors which prove more or less relevant and/or influential depending on the situation and era under consideration).

If existing histories of graphic design and typography, whatever periods they cover, constitute the essential reference point for the present investigation, equal interest is here shown to graphic design and typography, resulting in a balanced approach that pays respect equally to the two terms, while adequate room has also been allocated to an account of the creation of typefaces. (Conceptions on the matter vary widely, with some, following Wim Crouwel's example, erecting typography into the cornerstone of graphic design). Except for general and thematic works, several other sources of documentation and information have proved of crucial importance: the consultation of monographs from very diverse sources, the use of countless articles in periodicals and other specialized documents, as well as the use of a particular form of oral culture, through contact with experts and specialists, and with researchers, creators, and international publishers.

Special effort has been made to date the various tendencies, texts, and events. Many sources fail to agree and imprecision often subsists, while the investigation of certain dates has called for much laborious verification and crosschecking (for example, the date of birth of Claude Garamond). A certain number of uncertainties and doubts linger, in particular concerning facts in remote history (for instance, the portrait usually associated with the name of Gutenberg), and the spelling of proper names is sometimes erroneous. From a different perspective, tackling such a long period makes it possible to gauge the difficulties of dating, as well as to track over time centuries-old forms such as typographical characters.

The arrangement of this book into its constituent parts derives from a chronology based initially on major historical divisions. This has since been reworked in the light of specific cases and liberally enriched with other viewpoints depending on the material, though the intention is not to establish a hard and fast explanatory principle of a trans-historical nature. Each of the six parts interconnects various points to form a unit. The broad historical sweep has made it possible to face up to (sometimes only to glimpse) the polymorphism of typography and graphic design and to offer appraisals of a number of their parameters, and occasionally to juxtapose and contrast them on comparative lines.

Essentially, our itinerary keeps to the West, crisscrossing Germany, Italy, France, Great Britain, the Netherlands, Switzerland, the United States, Russia, Poland, Hungary, and Czechoslovakia. The first part also touches on Asian inventions, Chinese and Korean in particular, which were fundamental to certain developments in typography and graphic design. It should be noted that non-Western practices remain to be explored and the study of Far Eastern scripts and the writing of other graphic cultures casts light on regions and patterns of creativity that are all the more insightful as they are likely to call into question many of our preconceptions and prejudices.

The first part of this book offers a brisk overview of prehistory and antiquity, before embarking upon an outline of the Middle Ages and modern times. It also highlights a number of landmarks in the development of archaic lettering and graphics, and notes the relevant medieval contributions, before examining Gutenberg's technique up to the late eighteenth century. The fifteenth century witnessed the shift from manual inscription to mechanized process, by means of which script morphed into typography. The decisive elements in this respect were letterpress, paper, and the reproducibility of the written word by means of movable type. The classic period to the end of the eighteenth century developed a tradition based on expertise and on step-by-step technical evolution. The first phase of this history is then dominated by the book, script, and typography.

The second part covers the nineteenth century, when the context of graphic and typographical production was completely reorganized and practices were transformed by the Industrial Revolution, the mushrooming of new-found techniques, and the diversification of forms and media. While various outlets and supports were becoming ever more current, the progressive elimination of illiteracy and the emergence of mass communication resulted in a totally altered landscape. The sectors of graphic design and typography were both widened and more cogently defined by a host of phenomena: the soaring number of typefaces, galloping mechanization, the rise of the press and publishing, the birth of the "modern poster," etc. The second half of the century saw new perspectives open up in the wake of upheavals in the pictorial arts and the spectacular emergence of the color poster in the cityscape, as well as other factors.

The third part deals with the first third of the twentieth century. While avant-garde practitioners embarked on ever more visible transformations, expertise and experiments were the theater of vital interchange and the cross-fertilization between artistic and cultural practices gained in intensity. The Futurist "typographical revolution" prolonged into Dada and Russian Futurism. The Great War, which by and large steered the poster and other forms of visual communication down other routes, also had an impact on avant-garde graphics. From the end of the 1910s, construction and rationalism accelerated the search for viable forms.

The fourth section of this book dwells over the problematic period of the 1930s and World War II—a watershed characterized in certain places by the cultural stranglehold of totalitarianism. Managing to pursue its activities in a handful of places, the avant-garde was exiled en masse, causing a step-change in the geographical landscape that saw the United States occupy the central role. Meanwhile, in Europe, graphic design was dragooned into the service of dictatorial regimes hell-bent on exerting control over their "image." Against this backdrop—while the attitude of creators fissured into exile abroad or at home, resistance, confrontation with propaganda, compromise, or collaboration—typography branched out into new channels. World War II accentuated these phenomena, sparking off a new phase in the serviceability of graphic design.

A fifth section covers the postwar period around the 1970s. Thirty boom years saw the graphic and typographical scene in the West completely redrawn. Movements, outlooks, and trends quickly propagated, with the most meticulous graphic design existing cheek-by-jowl with practices intent on a more relaxed attitude or a return to manual expressiveness. Wartime visual communication was thus succeeded by less severe forms. Making the most of the fruitful explorations of preceding generations, this was an era of a more rounded professionalism, of developing education structures, and of the establishment of international publications and associations that imparted fresh dynamism to graphic design and typography, which resulted in still further specialization. It was during this period that graphic design, global design, business identity, signage, and environmental design became entities in their own right.

A sixth and final part considers the final third of the twentieth century, from the protest and underground movements of the 1960s and 1970s to the most recent period marked by the shift from the mechanical to the digital. It has been no easy task to identify this ever-increasing number of trends and practices with exactitude. Nevertheless, certain general proclivities do appear revelatory of the specific traits and heterogeneity of the prevailing situation and of the current creative environment. The era of noisy protest that started in the 1960s spawned new graphic forms. While the "New Wave" marched on, the ultimate decades of the twentieth century were marked, it seems, by leanings to "deconstructivism" and a contemporary eclecticism. From the middle of the 1980s, the emergence of digital technologies fostered a reconfiguration of organization and practices. This ongoing transformation has given rise to new preoccupations accompanied by significant expansion in the scope of graphics and typography.

This history maintains several viewpoints — "axes" such as graphic design/ typography, the arts/technology, the arts/crafts, industry/ craft, experimentation/ propaganda, group movement/ marginality, success/ failure, and so on—all dichotomies whose pertinence will depend on the given topic. As far as possible, this book reflects the divers facets of the history of graphic design and typography, including the role of technology; the impact of politics; the importance of international interchange, encounters, and relationships; the role of the patron, and of teaching and training; the effect of texts (in particular those by exponents themselves, from trail-blazing essays and/or reconsiderations of age-old and fundamental questions); the importance of reception and dissension; and the dark, tragic face of history, and the resulting disparities between the lengths of certain careers or the extent of an individual's corpus. Certain media and aspects of visual communication are scarcely dealt with here, and clearly another history might, for instance, have allotted more place to popular graphics, to anonymous creation, to expressions of protest, to graffiti and tags, to official inscriptions, to everyday forms of advertising, to the illustrated book and graphic illustration, to the comic strip, to graphics for the screen (cinema, television, digital film), to signage—or to little-known facts and phenomena concerning areas which history has tended to overlook, such as creations by women and, of course, non-Western civilizations.

In the attempt to throw fresh light on various aspects, the present investigation maintains a broad field of vision that allows comparisons and confrontations to be drawn and relationships to be established between seemingly remote factors. In aiming to improve progressively the understanding of such a wide history, our study combines in-depth comprehension and synoptic vision by way of a supranational standpoint and a concern with a raft of disciplines. The extension of and interconnections between the disciplines of knowledge and the historical viewpoint, and consciousness are a reflection of visual experience. They engage with cultural history—a fact that should be borne in mind at a time when digital technology has made the practice of typography and graphic design available to a far wider public.

From antiquity to modern times

Archaic signs, figures, and writing

"The development of pictograms, hieroglyphics, syllabaries, alphabets, and other symbolic representations
of language [...] constitutes the event—or more exactly the sequence of events—that separates history,
in the ordinary meaning of the term, from prehistory." [1]

Paul Needham

"It is surprising [...] to note how the myth of the verbal origin of writing persisted for so long [...].
What primarily characterizes the structure of writing is its mixed nature: not only because its system is based
simultaneously on two registers—that of the word and that of the script—but also because these registers
are themselves fundamentally heterogeneous with respect to one another [...]. Would it not be [...] more logical
to presume it was the graphic act and not language that provided the resources and motivations necessary
for the emergence of writing? Indeed, it constituted an already composite medium that associated the spatial support
for a given form and material with figures inscribed thereon which, as such, remained alien to it." [2]

Anne-Marie Christin

Marks, proto-inscriptions, and ante-historical signs

Since remotest times, archaic diagrams, images, inscriptions, and proto-scripts constitute a major record, marking the passage of humanity and its successive societies. They bear witness to and bequeath fragments of memory, traces, and signs that retain considerable mystery as to their origin, significance, and raison d'être (art, shamanism, commemoration, communication, divination, magic, mnemonics, mythology, mythography, and ornamentation, as well as relationships to the afterlife and to ritual and symbolism).

These representations took shape at the intersection between belief, power, expression, gesture, material, and technology. Subsequently, a host of identifiable factors joined forces in fashioning both texts and images, associated with the geographical, economic, social, cultural, and political context, as well as individual, intentional, subjective, and socioprofessional aspects.

To our way of thinking, prehistoric signs, images, inscriptions, and motifs— on walls and objects, as well as other supports and materials—constitute an embryonic state of script and the graphic that foreshadows the advent of writing. The interpretation of cave art and of ancient artifacts, drawings, notches, and other marks remains fraught with difficulties. It has given rise to various explanations and assumptions that have been revised, enriched, and undermined in the light of fresh discoveries, of improvements in dating methods, of new methodologies, and so on.[3] Thus the old conception of an art and of representations that would have developed from simple forms towards complex ones, from primary abstract signs to stylized and sophisticated figurations (or, contrariwise, explanations that start from the pictographic writing and go on to abstraction[4]) has been much debated.

If it is indeed improbable that the precise point of origin of human inscription shall ever become known (one only has to recall that some of the media concerned may well have perished over time), instances of simple marks—parallel lines, series of striations and notches—do appear in the Mid-Paleolithic, in Africa, for example. The beginning of the Upper Paleolithic saw the appearance of abstract markings comprising a series of lines, dots, concentric circles, and so on. One notched bone incised with a series of points or cupules has been interpreted as a device for noting the phases of the moon corresponding to a lunar calendar dating to some time between 35,000 and 20,000 BCE. Likewise, outlines and drawings dating from 30,000 BCE (the Aurignacian) attest to highly elaborate animal representations, in particular on wall surfaces.

1

2

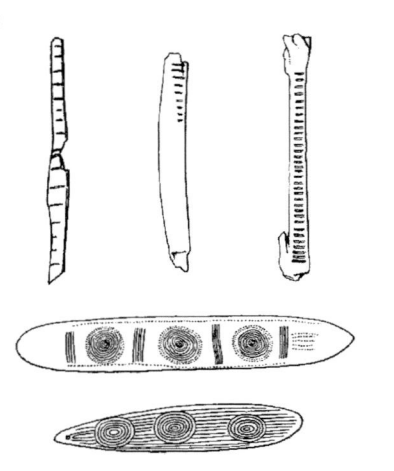

1
A sequence of incisions on animal bone, found in the Dordogne (France), 30,000–20,000 BCE. The incisions are believed to have been used to record the phases of the moon (interpretation open to debate).

2
Above: Paleolithic bones incised with a series of lines or cupules. Below: pieces (*churinga*) of carved stone and wood with abstract patterns, Australia.

3

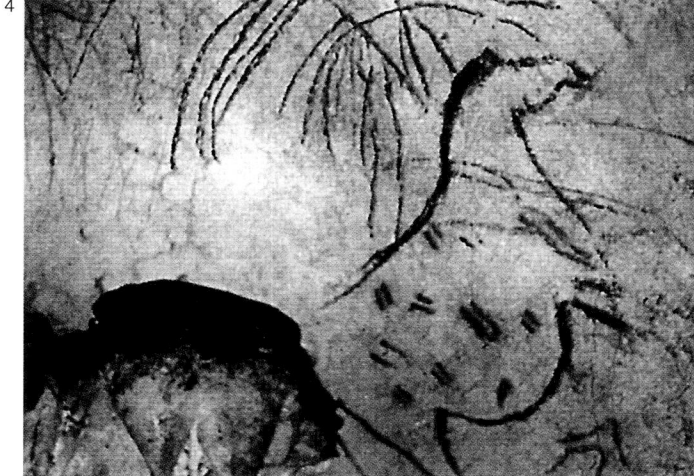

4

5

6

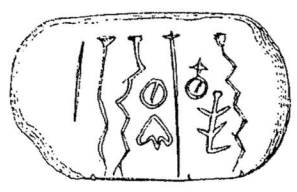

7

3
A large dotted sign, Spain (Chufin Cave, Cantabria).

4
Painted pregnant mare, Spain (Pileta Cave).

5
Painted framed quadrangular signs and dotted lines, Spain (El Castillo cave discovered in 1903).

6
Engravings and incisions showing symbols, animals, and dots, France (Dordogne and Hautes-Pyrénées), c. 30,000 BCE.

7
Grooves, abstract signs, broken lines, and animal figures carved on basalt pebbles, Syria (Jerf-el-Ahmar), c. 10,000 BCE. Among the oldest known pictograms, interpreted as "proto-writing."

"Pre-graphical figures",[5] archaic inscriptions, age-old figures, and signs thus display demonstrable heterogeneity and diversity, covering as much diagrammatic forms (up to and including the most synthetic) as images conveying a sense of reality. Such ancestral graphic forms predate by several tens of thousands of years the birth of the script itself (defined as a set of signs that are spatially organized, meaningfully arranged, and function as a code to record a language). Usually situated during the second half of the fourth millennium BCE, the formation of writing symbolically marks the shift from prehistory (or, more precisely, from proto-history, understood as the period concerned with events immediately prior to the appearance of writing) to antiquity.

Antiquity—the constitution and development of writing

Primitive forms of art and visual expression can take the form of parietal paintings or drawings, of notches and incisions, or of sculpture. Incised and carved signs—prior to the constitution of written forms identified as such—have been described as "proto-writing." Inaugurating a new type of inscription, from the outset writing conveyed an iconic dimension. In effect, "everywhere, the image seems to have been at the origin of writing."[6]

Associated with the onset of antiquity, the appearance of writing coincides with pre-urban organization in the Middle East accompanying the formation of built environments (such as Uruk in Lower Mesopotamia and Susa in Elam), and the development of the city-state and of civilization generally. "Mankind has adopted four principal methods of preserving traces of information or of communicating them: pictograms, sign-words, syllabic signs, and the alphabet."[7] Pictograms, ideograms, hieroglyphics, logograms, phonograms, determinatives, grammatical elements, syllabic, monosyllabic, consonant and alphabetical forms, are the names associated with the signs vehicling the varieties that occur according to nature and function. Owing to the complexity of (and occasional overlap between) these divers systems, they have fuelled intense debate.

The first known scripts appear in Mesopotamia, in the Middle East, and in Egypt around 3300–3200 BCE, well before the alphabet (and for this they are known as "pre-alphabetical"). Mesopotamian pictographic writing dates from 3300 BCE (with cuneiform developing towards 2800); known as Sumerian, it was probably widespread over a vast zone of the Near East. At the same time, around 3200, Egyptian hieroglyphics appeared, with a system split into three main categories of signs: logograms, phonograms, and determinatives. Over the course of the following millennium, about the sixteenth to fourteenth centuries BCE, there emerged the Proto-Sinaitic, Proto-Canaanite, and Ugaritic writing systems, which signal the passage to the alphabetical form (cuneiform in the last case).

Round about the fourteenth century BCE Chinese script appeared, a form characterized as

8

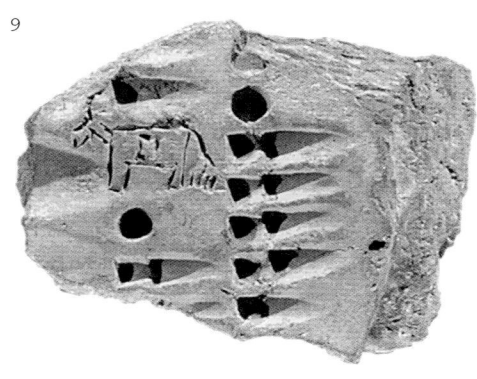

9

8
Pictographic pre-cuneiform tablet, clay, Lower Mesopotamia, c. 3100 BCE. Approx. 1 ³/₄ × 1 ¹/₂ in. (4.5 × 4 cm). Shows number of cows (angle topped by a curve) and sheep (cross within a circle).

9
Fragment of a large Proto-Elamite tablet, Susa, Iran, c. 3000 BCE. Pictogram with circles and notches representing figures.

"ideographic."[8] This probably preceded the Phoenician alphabet (eleventh century BCE) by a few centuries. This latter will lead, *inter alia*, to the Greek (eighth century BCE or before) and Latin alphabets (seventh to sixth centuries BCE). Then, in the space of the millennium that straddles the dawn of the Common Era, there came Square Hebrew, several forms of Indian script, the Pre-Columbian systems of Mesoamerica, Runes, the Ethiopian syllabaries, the Coptic, Arabic, and Armenian alphabets, etc.—as well as lesser-known scripts, such as Meroitic in Africa and Ogamic in Ireland, which may present intriguing graphic forms. Comprised of logograms, phonograms,[9] or other types of signs, the written forms appearing before our era show notable richness and complexity in form, nature, function, and operation. Some have remained undeciphered to date. Generally speaking, they betray links with a number of preceding images and signs (the figuration of objects or living beings, various representations, symbols, outlines and glyphs, abstract marks, regular or ordered sequences of incisions, etc.).

From the point of view of their characteristics and ramifications, the heritage of ancient writing systems to the history of graphic inscription is considerable. For Sumerian writing on clay, for example, notation was initially schematic (a cross within a circle stands for a sheep). Commonly named pictograms, these figures number between several hundred to one or two thousand. They gradually morphed into cuneiform (with syllabic notation)—a simplified set of lines obtained by impressing the triangular tip of a reed-pen into the clay according to a fundamentally abstract idiom.

The very much later writings of Pre-Columbian Central America are rooted in representing images whose signs range from the figurative to the abstract. There, the script can be painted: the iconic dimension of the text is such that Pre-Columbian manuscripts have been qualified as "picture-texts," and as such are supremely representative of the primal interlock between text and image. Later still, the writing of the Aztecs reflects some particularly original factors: "contrary to other known pictographic systems, in the Mesoamerican, color constitutes a minimal element of the underlying system: they are pronounced (each possesses a phonetic value) and the syllables of their names combine with those belonging to other elements."[10]

The appearance of specifically phonic systems reproducing the sounds of the language directly presented a great potential for a writing system.[11] The Ugaritic cuneiform alphabet discovered on the north Syrian coast is one of the first known notations of this kind. Encompassing around thirty signs, it is attested from the fourteenth century BCE and has been characterized as Proto-Phoenician. The script of the Phoenicians,[12] often cited as the springboard for a number of alphabetical systems (including those presently employed in Europe), dates from the eleventh century BCE. Some of its letters appear very similar to our own. Comprising twenty-two letter-consonants, the Phoenician alphabet is written right to left, often in black or red ink on stone. The inscription on the sarcophagus of Ahiram, king of Byblos, is a prime example of a consonant system that remained current to the third century CE.

If a significant role can be assigned to the Phoenician coast (today Israel, Lebanon, and Syria), a not dissimilar form of graphic notation—one whose signs, few in number, represent sounds—gained the fringes of the Mediterranean around 900 BCE, giving rise to various alphabets. The Greek variant borrowed from earlier forms, and from 800 BCE added for the first time vowels to consonants, using for the purpose those Phoenician consonants superfluous to Greek dialects. In the seventh or sixth century BCE there appeared archaic Latin inscriptions inherited from Greek via Etruscan script that branched out into systems based on the Latin alphabet.

The universe of writing

From antiquity on, certain specific aspects of writing associated with signs emerged, such as direction and punctuation. Direction of reading varies according to place and time. Phoenician is written right to left, while Greek came up with several variants: right to left, left to right,

10

Cuneiform writing, Sumerian tablet, Lower Mesopotamia, c. 2360 BCE. Length 3 in. (73 mm). Each phrase is inscribed in a compartment.

11

Flat stamp for imprinting foundation bricks (placed into the walls). Lower Mesopotamia, nineteenth century BCE. Molded then baked earth.

12

Phoenician alphabet comprising twenty-two signs. From left to right: Ahiram, Mesa, Classical.

13

Fragment of an inscription on the sarcophagus of King Ahiram in Byblos, end of the second millennium BCE. Regarded as the oldest document bearing an inscription in the Phoenician alphabet (inscription discovered in 1924).

14

Comparative table of twenty-one letters from various alphabets (incomplete). From left to right: Proto-Sinaic, Phoenician, Aramaic, Greek, Southern Arabic, Latin.

15

Greek stone inscription in *boustrophedon*, c. 500 BCE.

and *boustrophedon* (in alternate directions). These three orientations were still in use by the time the first Latin inscriptions arrived. At a later stage, and according to an idiosyncratic principle, the script of the Uighurs went so far as to differentiate the direction of inscription from that of reading.

As regards punctuation, various practices had already become prevalent by the course of the first millennium BCE. If, in Greek and Latin texts (in particular, ancient Greek manuscripts), words may be noted one after the other in a long uninterrupted succession of signs,[13] a restricted system of punctuation was established that appears on Roman monuments, in Greco-Latin manuscripts, and even in graffiti. They are essentially points placed at the bottom, in the middle, or at the top of the line according to the strength of the punctuation required (these signs were to evolve as they mutated or altered in value). Other forms of separation occur, such as vertical lines segmenting Semitic inscriptions or paragraph marks on papyri written several centuries before the Common Era

The genesis of writing is accompanied by many myths and legends. Ancient civilizations often believed that their earliest scripts emanated from a divine or royal source. The Egyptians, for example, came to ascribe the invention of writing to the god Thot (a

16

personification of knowledge and language), while Sumerians alluded to the sovereign of the city of Uruk, Enmerkar. As regards Chinese writing, a text from the first century poetically records how Ts-ang Chieh (attached to Emperor Huangdi, seventeenth to sixteenth century BCE) was meant to have come up with the ideogram while observing tracks left by animals. His "two pairs of eyes" enabled him to look simultaneously at the sky and the earth and he was inspired in his invention by traces left by birds or tortoises as well as by celestial bodies (the moon and stars). Legend has it that his discovery made the sky and the earth tremble and the gods weep for an eon. As for the Greeks, they ascribed the introduction of Phoenician letters into their regions to the legendary hero, Cadmus. Through its links to the sacred and the supernatural, even at its origin writing could be regarded as harmful. Thus, foretelling of the risks associated with its practice, the Egyptian god Amon is supposed to have lamented: "This art will produce oblivion in the soul of those who learn it because they will cease to exercise their memory."[14]

16
Oracular inscription, China, sixteenth to eleventh century BCE. Incomplete tortoise plastron. Height 4¼ in. (11 cm). Inscription over four columns, read bottom to top.

The earliest forms of writing are rich and diversified in the manner in which they invent and incorporate graphic signs, in their mode of operation, and in the motivations associated with the media they constitute. Depending on geographical location, culture, or other factors, these forms can carry out the most diverse functions and pursue various aims: they can bolster memory, serve an economic purpose, fulfill needs of a practical or material order (listing, enumerating, inventorying, calculating, counting, and so on), to express power, institute laws, or ensure communications (including with the sacred and the world beyond); they may form part of a ritual, as an intrinsic component in divination; they may honor the dead, broadcast the oracles, accompany or disseminate magical practices, take on a symbolic dimension, preserve preexisting literary writings, become imbued with poetry, etc. In the course of the second millennium BCE, for instance, writing could just as readily be associated with oracular inscriptions or divinatory practices in China as used to record recent collections of laws and official inscriptions enacted by the powers that be in Mesopotamia. In one famous example, the Code of Hammurabi (1792–1750 BCE) is both a monument of Babylonian literature as well as one of the very earliest legal compendiums. Standing more than six and a half feet high, this stone stele promulgates the laws of the kingdom. To an extent, it also serves as a code of good conduct intended to promote social cohesion, and each city would possess its own version of the stele erected on the public square. Other similar inscriptions can be regarded as an archaic form of "poster."

In antiquity, writings were already being preserved, and from the third millennium BCE collections of texts were compiled in Mesopotamia and Egypt. The works gathered together in

17
Rolled, inscribed papyrus scroll, Egypt,
Ptolemaic period, third to second centuries BCE.

18
Limestone seal, Egypt, fifth or sixth centuries CE.
The relief is inked before being imprinted onto
the papyrus. Incisions containing traces of red
ink; reversed so as to obtain an impression the
right way up. The only known relief of this kind.

the seventh century BCE under the impetus of Assurbanipal, an erudite king of Assyria, comprise one of the most important ancient libraries known and covered a vast number of cuneiform tablets—although literature was proportionally underrepresented and a certain number of items appear in more than one copy.

If written culture was now being archived, ancient peoples seemed unconcerned with tackling mass illiteracy. Knowing how to read and write remained a business for initiates. In Mesopotamia, its practice was the subject of a specific training program and its scribes belonged to an elite. In Egypt, too, the act of writing was the prerogative of scribes, while in the Greek and Roman cultures the roles of copyist and public reader were the preserve of slaves.

It seems that the rate of alphabetization remained low in both Greece and the Roman Empire from the seventh century BCE to after the start of the Common Era. As an indication, "some individuals in some cities were able to read and write" in Greece towards the eight century BCE; "without any doubt a higher percentage in democracies than under other regimes and in centers of trade than in remote rural regions."[15] Particularly in the urban environment, it may be that the number of men taught reading and writing reached some 20 percent during the first century.

With the birth of writing naturally appeared archaic reading media, as well as the ancestral artifacts that eventually led to the book. Egyptian papyrus scrolls were in use by the third millennium BCE. Stuck together and then rolled, papyrus sheets were written only on the recto. Assembled in this manner, they number among the earliest illustrated books to have come down to us. In China, forms predating the book were inscribed upon an extensive range of materials, including tortoiseshell and strips of bamboo, while the rolls of silk employed later attained impressive lengths.

According to the nature of the support used and the practices and requirements concerned, ancient writings can run to a large number of volumes and incorporate various surfaces and spaces in different ways. Addressed to the eye, these supports naturally adopted formats related to the proportions of the human body, to its gestures, field of vision, and stature. In the Middle East, clay tablets measuring a few inches along the side were worked and written in the palm of the hand. The handling and size of a scroll, too, derive from the time both of its manufacture and its consultation. As for a stele such as the Code of Hammurabi, it alludes schematically to the dimensions of an outsized human body.

In antiquity, scripts, graphic signs, figures, and images appeared on many different materials, including wood, clay, stone, slate, bone, shell, textile, brick, and animal skin. From the most durable to the most perishable, their properties and characteristics affected both the forms of the support and the script concerned. The flexibility of papyrus allows successive

leafs to be stuck together into a long strip that can be rolled up. In it, image is closely related to writing and distributed in dense and regular columns of text. The Prisse Papyrus is regarded as the oldest known Egyptian book. Dating to approximately 1900 BCE, it initially appeared as a roll more than twenty-two feet long. Already, and as on many other Egyptian inscriptions, the papyrus features a text inscribed in black punctuated with red (a scattering of color that recurs in script and typography in the present day). Probably one of the first colors to be used in prehistoric times, red is documented in various scripts and graphic artifacts of antiquity, in Phoenician inscriptions as much as on red-ink Egyptian seals from before the Common Era.

Greco-Roman forms of writing

Public inscriptions intended to be viewed and read developed in Greco-Roman antiquity. As the population at large was relatively illiterate, Greek and Roman proclamations were largely oral, a state of affairs that, for congruent reasons, persisted up until the Middle Ages. At the same time, however, archaic forms of inscription and illustrative announcement were very widespread (sometimes in the form of painted lettering), serving to promote shows or advocate various political agendas. In Greece, swiveling wooden panels—*axons*—were used to convey information of every kind, to promulgate official pronouncements, to publicize advertisements, and to announce public games and sporting events (such as gladiatorial combats).

Similar supports existed in the Roman Empire. Such texts, painted on wooden panels or directly onto house walls, can concern laws or regulations, political information, electoral "posters," programs of cultural events (festivals, circuses, etc.), as well as messages from private individuals and others (such as an appeal for the recapture of an escaped slave, or advertising a horse sale). Known as *alba* and sometimes subdivided into separate segments, these wooden panels were originally whitewashed, like walls. Official pronouncements and information were inscribed in black and often in red or red ocher, painted on with a brush. A large number of these inscription-posters (electoral in particular) have been unearthed in Pompeii. As with inscriptions on Egyptian papyri, the color red was used for emphasis. Exposed to public view at the busiest points in the city, the Roman *album*, like the Greek

axon, can be regarded as a support comparable to the modern poster.

Throughout Greco-Roman antiquity, supports for texts and images appear to increase significantly in number—or at least they seemed to gain a certain prevalence in the public arena. In addition, the practice of the handwritten book and other text-bearing articles persisted, though, due to its fragility, little of this material has come down to us. If the book became an everyday article in Rome towards the first century CE, other bearers of written information are also recorded there. One such case is the weekly and daily press that appeared prior to the Common Era. The *acta diurna* (acts of the day) thus carried current affairs, topical events, dispatches and military communiqués, cultural programs, personal announcements, etc. Genuine little handwritten newspapers, they appeared each week in around ten thousand copies produced by some three hundred slaves. The press, the book, and the public pronouncement were joined by other forms of writing: inscriptions in lapidary capitals (sometimes on monumental stones), graphics or signs appearing on store fronts, and marks, heraldic emblems, and other marks of identification.

There also survive illustrated poems, adapting the composition of the texts to forms with images. Ancestors of the *calligramme* (picture-poem), similar games using alphabetical script and the image are attested towards the fourth to third centuries BCE (identified as the work of Dosiadas, Theocritus, and Simmias).[16] Throughout antiquity, many supports and

19
Bronze plaque imitating a writing tablet bearing an alphabet, writing exercises, and a dedication, fourth to third centuries BCE. From the sanctuary of the goddess Reitia at Este.

20
Young woman reading a *volumen*, fresco in Pompeii (detail), first century CE. In Rome, the book was becoming a familiar item.

21
Electoral "poster," Pompeii, before 79 CE. *Rustica capitalis* painted in red ocher on a house. The largest letters are approx. 19 3/4 in. (50 cm) in height.

22
PΕΜΒΑ
OTAVAϟM
ODIOYϟΜΕN
ATOϹANAϟTA

23
CORNELIVS·LVCI
VS·SCIPIC·BARBA
TVS·CNAIVOD·PA
RYFHQVGXKMZ

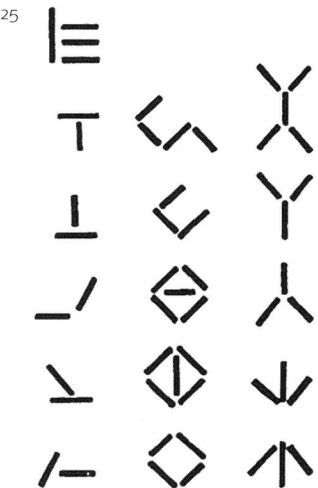

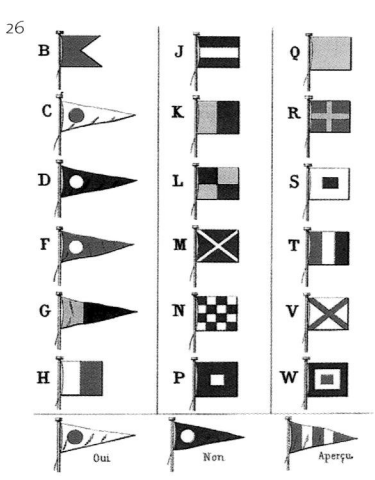

22
Greek lapidary lettering (originally read *boustrophedon*), Latin text, fifth century BCE.

23
Roman lapidary lettering, second century BCE.

24
Graffito, ancient Greek inscription on a vase of the Geometric style, c. 700 BCE.

25
Owners' marks on pottery, sixth to fifth centuries BCE.

26
Plate showing signaling flags, c. 1900. Flags for communication at sea using a code based on shape and color. The use of maritime flags and banners dates from at least the first or second millennium BCE.

forms associated with graphics and writing emerged. The genesis of various types of text and image are rooted in these remote times, when they already acquired the dimensions that determine the ways in which they are still displayed and read today. So it is that ancient signs and forms of expression reveal the growth of the alphabet system, of diverse types of punctuation (related to page layout and visual division), of the use of ink and color, and of the manufacture and use of paper. These ancient practices reveal archaic forms of the book, of the poster, of the public advertisement, and of the newspaper; the principle of printing in ink (see, for instance, the traces on objects dating from the second millennium BCE or the Egyptian seals with red ink in use from the second century BCE on); as well as picture-poem games, monumental inscriptions, and even—and once again before the Common Era—gatherings and collections of writings in the form of libraries. Certain ingredients and characteristics constitutive of the graphic act such as it is understood today already existed in part: the relationship between text and image (interaction, play, overlap, dissociation, etc.); composition, the layout of the text, the page, and the empty space; rhythm, organization in lines, columns, and rectangular surfaces; the role of color; and the impression, appropriation, and diversification of various supports.

At this early stage then, ancient supports and inscriptions already display the exceptional range of written signs and of forms of visual expression, from their communicative dimension to the more mysterious aspects of the visible world.

The Middle Ages:
graphic design as cottage industry

27
Medieval scribe, woodcut, Paris, 1526.

The practices of writing and of image-making, already very advanced in antiquity, met with fresh transformations during the medieval era, some of which built into the foundations of current (typo)graphic forms. The visual richness and daring of illuminated manuscripts, together with changes in the shapes of Latin lettering, number among the most important innovations in medieval art, writing, and graphic design. First and foremost though, probably one of the principal phenomena resides in the centralization of written culture, which in the Middle Ages retreated to religious enclaves, as well to other privileged forums such as the libraries of great princes. Around the fifth century CE, writing, teaching, and scholarship moved into the Christian monastery. Consequently, the art of the manuscript entertained a necessarily close relationship with the Church.

Medieval pictorial language centers on religious painting, on sacred and mythological themes. If the concept of art at the time designated a variant of craft, of practical and technical skill, the period also favored the reproduction of preexistent models. The essence of creation stemmed from the divine, the artist only affirming himself as a creator in his own right during the Renaissance.[17] For the time being, knowledge proceeded from faith, while the know-how required for writing was vouchsafed to religion, whose prerogative it would remain for nearly a thousand years.

The opulence of the medieval book made it a luxury item, accessible by and large only to a well-read and well-heeled minority. Men of religion and learning who had mastered Latin (the domination of the Latin language in writing dates back to the fall of the Roman Empire following its Christianization in 325) were called *literati*. As distinct from this lettered elite, to the European population as a whole—to the *illitterati*—such a written culture was alien. This state of affairs persisted until the thirteenth century when the monasteries lost their exclusivity over the written word and a noticeable if still limited rise in literacy took place (the elimination of mass illiteracy occurred only in the nineteenth century).

Since medieval peoples remained largely ignorant of reading and writing, communication with the public relied on the spoken word. Having rung for attention, town criers could transmit various kinds of messages, including, among others, private announcements, royal edicts, and official communiqués. Once proclaimed, the information may then have been plastered on the walls of the city or village. Traders would also shout out the virtues of their wares, as some still do today. The voice of the medieval crier thus constituted a genuine form of advertising and publicity.

If advertisements and announcements of the time were partly aural in nature, promotion could also be visual—as on shop- and stall-signs, as well as in other marks of identification (the armorial bearings of the Later Middle Ages representing a distinct graphic phenomenon). To attract the eye, these supports would in all probability resort to illustration and symbol in preference to text.

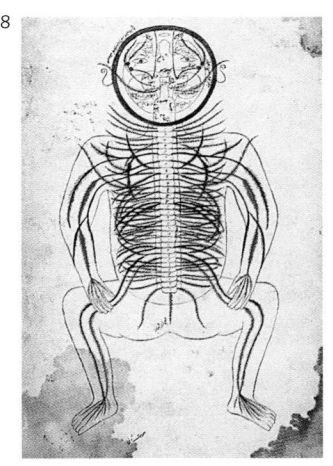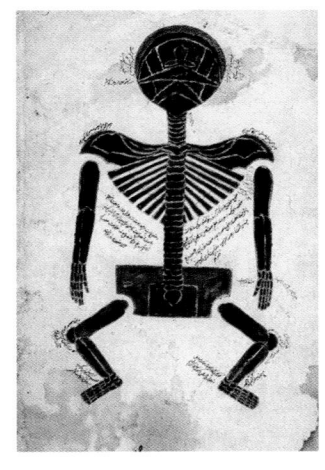

28
Anatomical plates (nerve endings and human skeleton), Arabic manuscript, thirteenth century.

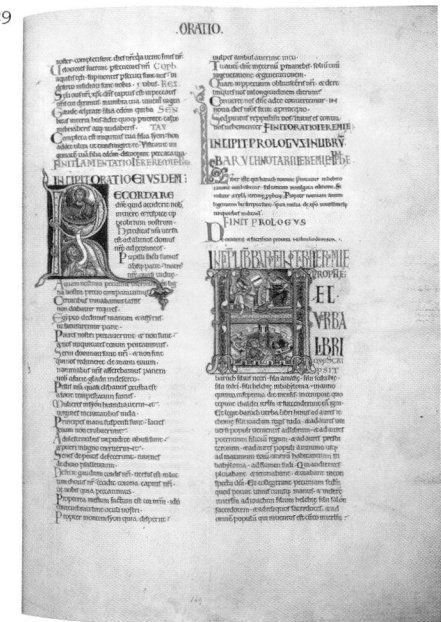

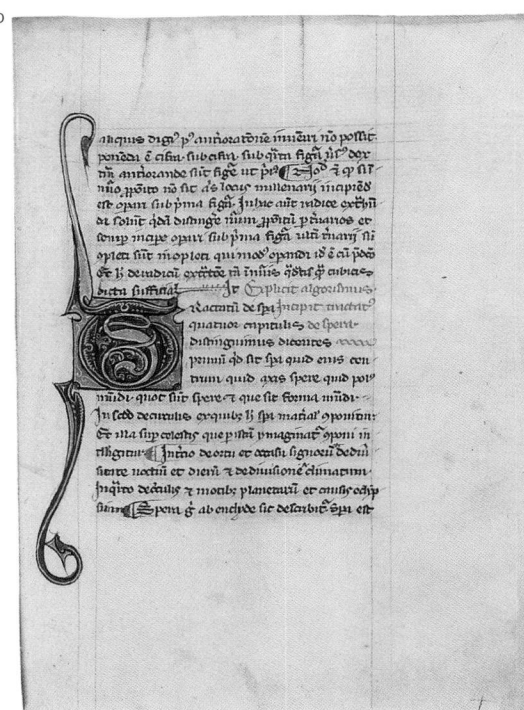

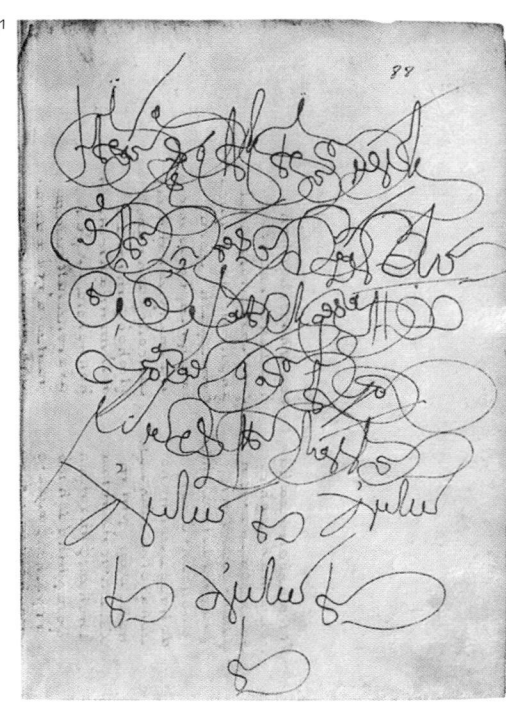

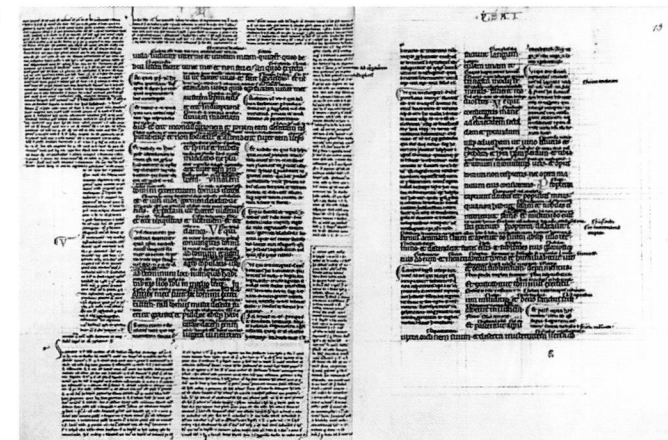

29
Page from the Winchester Bible, Great Britain, twelfth century.

30
Ugo Cappellarii (scribe), medical texts, Paris, c. 1280.

31
Monocondylic script ("without lifting pen from page") in red ink. *Arithmetical Treatises*, Byzantium, 1350–75. 8 × 5 $^1/_2$ in. (20.6 × 14.2 cm).

32
Book of Isaiah with Glosses, France, first quarter of the thirteenth century. Two levels of commentary are organized around the main text; an ordinary explanatory gloss (written in the spaces between the line or in an external column), and a gloss on the gloss.

The book as handwritten object

If official proclamations and popular announcements were pronounced or written for the public sphere, the book flowed instead from the religious domain. It is there that it was inscribed and preserved, belonging henceforth to a domain reserved primarily for ecclesiastics and nobles. The form of the book as we know it was generally accepted by the beginning of the Middle Ages. Invented at the beginning of the Common Era, the manuscript book called the *codex* gradually replaced the ancient roll or scroll—the *volumen*[18]—with its utilization gaining ground between the second and fourth centuries. Thus constituted, the book gave rise to the page as a basic module, as well as to the unit of visual space concomitant on the page or double page. Just as certain incunabula (block-books) can be based on manuscripts, the page layout of an early codex might well be inspired by the graphic composition of the scroll. One or two columns of text are arranged over the page, with the presence of any image being closely associated to the written word. If the combination at the outset often appears rather dense and close-knit, the book soon underwent a series of transformations in the Middle Ages and continued in the Renaissance. Over time, the role of the margin became more coherent, textual separations became more visible, and the image acquired a measure of independence with respect to the written component.

If an ancient codex might be made from wooden slats bound together, a medieval book is manufactured from leaves folded, assembled into signatures, and sewn. At the beginning, the sheets were made of parchment, an animal skin especially treated for writing before being made into volumes.[19] The flexibility of this material, which gradually ousted papyrus, endowed the book with characteristics that we still recognize today. Transformed in its aesthetic nature, the book-object represented a new form of support, together with its own materials and structure, handling and consultation, etc. Manufactured by this method, it could be conserved with relative ease, a quality that fostered the transmission of the manuscript heritage, in marked contrast to numerous writings of antiquity (notably Greek and Roman) that have long since

33
Latin palimpsest: uncial (among the first Roman uncials on parchment), *De re publica*, end of the fourth century, obscured by a text of the eighth.

34
Progressive development from capital to minuscule.

35
Italian and Merovingian scripts from the early Middle Ages. Dating, top to bottom, from: 504, 876, seventh century, eighth century.

disappeared as their supports offered little resistance to wear and tear.

The composition of a medieval manuscript depended on the conjunction of expertise that was accumulated, implemented, and transmitted by monks. Copyists, illuminators, parchmenters, miniaturists, and bookbinders pooled their skills, working in one and the same "writing-" or "script-shop," the *scriptorium*. They were peerless craftsmen who created often dazzling works, and their brilliance and skill in combining text, image, initial, and ornamentation spawned a treasury of masterpieces, major landmarks in the development of the book as well as in the history of graphic design.

Paintings, owing to their form, had been poorly conserved in scrolls, but with the codex, miniatures (fine paintings used as illustrations) and illuminations could make their entrance into the space of the book. The place allotted to the image and the dimension of calligraphy contributes greatly to the magnificence of these volumes. Although dated by the style of their script, their materials, their mass, or the wear they have suffered, many of these works evidence ideas in the graphic and visual fields (page layout, composition, the association between text and image, the way the space is occupied, rhythm, interplay between scripts, abbreviated variants, detailing, etc.) that remain astonishingly modern and strikingly original today.

At the preparation stage, the medieval book already reflected an advanced degree of organization. Upstream, scribes scored vertical and horizontal lines, known as "ruling," to form a grid for the page layout. Thus prepared, the book was ready to receive the main visual ingredients of its composite pages: illuminations, miniatures, calligraphy, decorative initials and other markers, interlace, and various other species of ornament. Illumination endowed the book with the brightness and color of a picture.

The letters themselves, often decorated, present a wealth of diversity. Devoted to religious expression, the medieval manuscript also gives full rein to the human imagination. The function of the ornamented initial, which arose around the fourth century CE, is patently to attract attention and afford pleasure to the eye. It also achieved the specific aim of marking articulations in the text. One of the central contributions of the medieval period was the historiated letter, a hybrid of writing and drawing that formed within the space of the initial genuine illustrations comprising human figures or animals relating to the contents of the text.

Other distinctive signs include the heading and red lettering (initials, paragraph marks, introductory lines, titles, etc.). As the repertoire of punctuation marks remained under development, graphic organization constituted a powerful tool for visually punctuating texts, combining "the importance and richness of major indicators (illuminations, capitals) [with] the sobriety of internal signs."[20] As the scrutiny of one manuscript makes abundantly clear: "The hierarchy of illuminations is impressive: large titles with miniatures, one large initial per column, capital letters ringed in red after the stops, red loops for certain letters, etc. If the text is clear, this is not on the 'sentence' level, but across larger divisions of the text that constitute the harmony of the page."[21] The tenor of the text relies on its calligraphic form, which, with the illuminations, provides the work with its overall tone.

Over the course of the early centuries of the Middle Ages, European writing workshops tended to privilege letterforms inherited from the Romans. Scribes and copyists thus appropriated Roman majuscules, such as the *capitalis rustica* (rustic capitals), and instituted the use of the *capitalis quadrata* (square capitals).[22] They also made abundant use of Romans uncials and half-uncials (semi-uncials), with a vast number of religious writings bearing uncial scripts. Ascribed to the Romans of the fourth century, and probably formed during the two preceding centuries, bookhand is characterized by a more supple form of the Roman capital. Of a slightly later date, uncials are presumed to have originated in the fifth century. Associating forms of what now call capital and small letters, it seems to have been one of the first mixed alphabets. As in Roman minuscule, the extenders of a half-uncial can be clearly

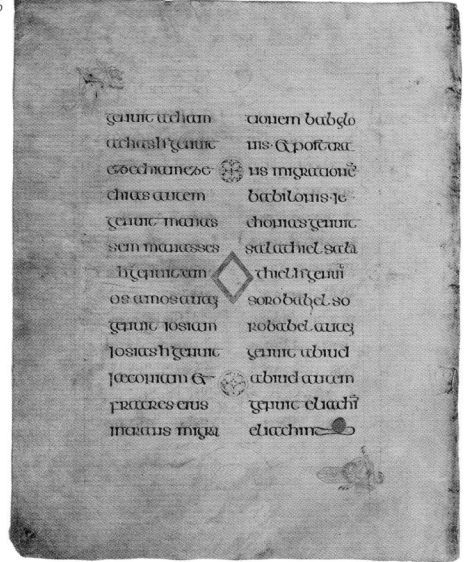

36
Unfinished page from *The Book of Kells* showing the order in which the pigments were applied, c. 800 (f. 30v).

37
Page from *The Book of Kells*, c. 800 (f. 114v).

38
Latin picture-poem taken from an Anglo-Saxon manuscript of the tenth century.

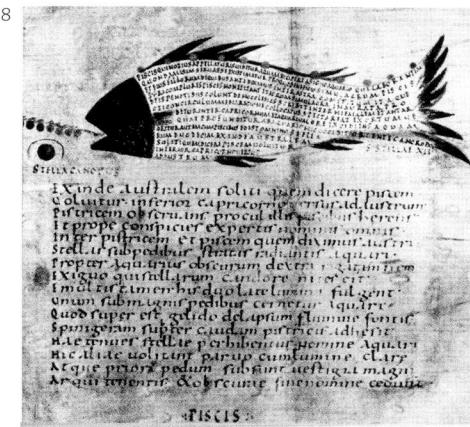

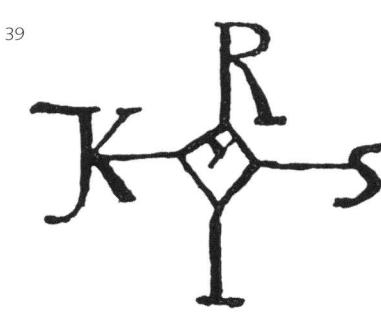

39
Charlemagne's monogram (742–814).

delineated. The now cursive script is increasingly fleet, flexible, and rounded. The uncial was transmitted to Ireland at its conversion to Christianity and by the eighth century the arts of the book and of penmanship had been raised to their zenith by Irish monks. In the British Isles generally, script adopted special forms, including Anglo-Saxon and Irish minuscules, which accentuate the serif. Playing a notable role in the transformation of the decorated letter, Celtic art was to prove especially influential on European book craft. Illuminated manuscript-making from the British Isles, especially from Ireland, around the eighth century, boasts exceptional works, such as the world-famous *Book of Kells* (c. 800) and the *Book of Durrow* (late seventh century), as well as the *Lindisfarne Gospels* (c. 698) and those of St. Willibrord. The freedom of the illustrations and the stature of the text in these volumes combine with a wealth of ornamentation or with complex Celtic motifs. Calligraphied in Irish half-uncials, these works are regarded as masterpieces of the art.

Script reform under Charlemagne

At the very moment the Irish manuscript was reaching its apogee, other script styles were taking shape, in particular in Germany and France. Since the legibility of the script could be compromised by almost undecipherable regional idiosyncrasies, at the end of the eighth century Charlemagne undertook important measures to unify European scripts and thus ensure the conservation of the book. His reign (768–814) is marked by decisions designed to stabilize a kingdom that was swelling into an immense empire. If the king himself was illiterate (according to his biographer, he learnt how to read and write only late in life), his decisions nonetheless had a major impact on both the preservation and the appearance of the book. To push through these reforms, he surrounded himself with European scholars from Italy, England, and Spain, and many decisions were enacted regarding language, writing, and the book. By compelling the use of Latin, Charlemagne restored the language while, by founding new teaching establishments, he provided a fresh impetus to education. Various directives stipulated that manuscripts be copied in accordance with a revised style of presentation, a measure that applied to texts of every nature. Carolingian writing workshops

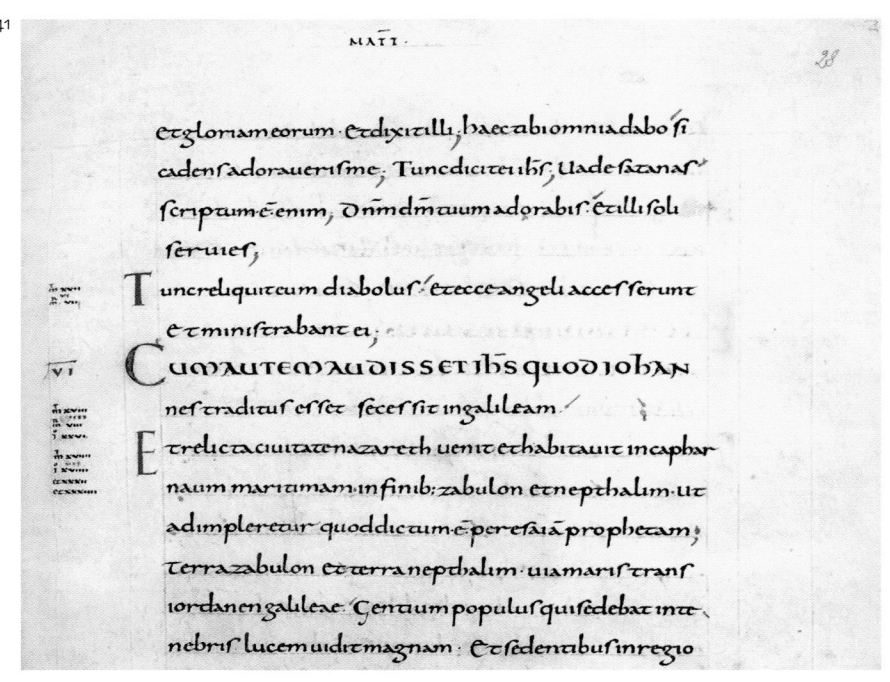

40
Carolingian minuscule, France and Germany. Dating, top to bottom, from: c. 800, beginning of the ninth century, eighth century, c. 993.

41
Carolingian script, Prüm Gospels, manuscript written at Tours, ninth century.

thus found themselves faced with the awe-inspiring task of safeguarding the Greek and Latin texts of antiquity and conserving the vernacular literature of the first centuries of the Common Era. Charlemagne's reign also witnessed reforms concerning how language was to be written down, which, among other measures, prescribed adjustments to syntax or punctuation. By the final decades of the eighth century, standardized writing practices had been propagated over vast swathes of Europe.[23] It was an event that marked a fundamental turning-point in the history of writing, instigating practices and aesthetic outlooks that proved extraordinarily durable.

To implement the "unification" of script, Charlemagne had summoned a scholar monk from England, Alcuin of York. In all probability, it was he who was charged with developing and disseminating a specific style of writing already employed in certain *scriptoria*. The measure consisted in halting the fragmentation of European script types, some of which, at least to our eyes, border on the illegible, and replacing them with a newly instituted, model form.

As its starting point the script took the half-uncial, the Anglo-Saxon minuscule, and Irish script. Regarded since as a historical milestone, the result is usually designated by the name "Caroline" (from the Latin, *Carolus*, "Charles," i.e., Charlemagne)—Caroline minuscule, Caroline letter or script, or Carolingian minuscule. From the standpoint of our reading practices, the Caroline displays little complication in form and presents a particularly readable letterform. The signs can be readily detached from each other; the characteristic outlines and the up- and downstrokes appear clearly. Certain letters, such as the "A," conserve definite traces of the uncial or half-uncial. Caroline script already features many elements or characteristics that have been handed down to present-day writing, including a basic outline very close to contemporary small letters, sentences introduced by a capital, the main text in small letters, the insertion of blanks (which do not yet correspond, however, to a regular spacing between words), the use of punctuation (of which the period), and so on.

In inscribing capitals, initials, titles, and other priority entities for reading, monks used Roman capitals as well as the *rustica* or uncial (employed for this purpose until the twelfth century). The simultaneous and demarcated use of a dual capital/miniscule alphabet is thus one of the main contributions of Carolingian script.[24] The association of the minuscule form of Caroline with capitals inherited from Roman examples thus heralds the historical advent of a dual alphabet that has remained in use since that period. Because they are easily distinguished, capital letters also function as punctuation. According to Alcuin, "the copyist has to distinguish meaning by marks [various signs of punctuation], which make the text more 'beautiful.'"[25]

It was during the Middle Ages furthermore that the alphabet acquired other novel punctuation signs. If the medieval comma and stop (variously declined) were in everyday usage, it would seem that quotation marks only appeared around the seventh century, the semicolon in the eighth, and the question mark and dash during the following century. Many practices were invented and clarified, as witness the monk "Hildemar, a punctuation mark theorist, [who] already in 840 was employing three different question marks."[26]

From the ninth century on, the form of the Caroline letter gained ground throughout the monasteries of Western Europe. In the north of Italy, in England, and in Spain, it became the

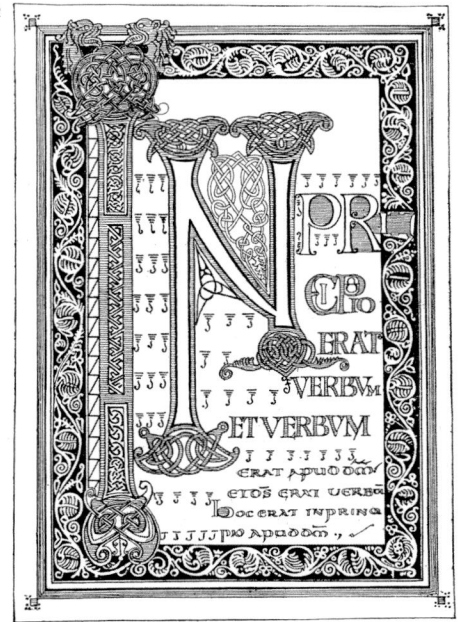

script of reference. After the death of Charlemagne in 814, his son and grandson succeeded him at the head of the Carolingian Empire, prolonging until the end of the ninth century policies that benefited both writing and the book. Caroline endured, remaining prevalent until the twelfth century, spreading and advancing without undergoing many noteworthy alterations. Once again, however, the script was gradually colored by local idiosyncrasies. The initial model for the Caroline fissured into alternatives, some of which were to lead ultimately to forms of the Gothic.

In parallel to transformations in script, the practice of calligraphy and copying also underwent significant developments in the ninth and tenth centuries. Henceforth, the majority of monasteries, abbeys, cloisters, and churches were to house a scriptorium of their own. For nearly five centuries, books and education were to be the monopoly of the clergy. By restricting literary work and knowledge to a certain category of the population, the Early Middle Ages created an aesthetic of opulence around its written culture, through its scripts and their iconic dimension, and through page layout and the presence of the image. These centuries represent a key period in the history of the graphic, focusing on the book, on the creation of scripts, and on a sumptuous corpus of illustrated artifacts.

Changes in the twelfth and thirteenth centuries

In the early centuries of the second millennium, breaches were opening up in the feudal world and, by the twelfth and thirteenth centuries, social, economic, and political upheavals had vastly shifted the focus of cultural life. As the population moved to the cities, so written knowledge tended to leave the confines of the monastery, cloister, or castle. The monastic school went into decline and the culture of the book underwent a process of secularization. The period around the thirteenth century is marked by the expansion of the universities that had grown up in Western Europe during previous centuries. With Bologna, Oxford, Cambridge, Paris, and Salamanca among the first, they quickly multiplied and in their wake came intellectual life and scholasticism. In parallel, though still in a very limited manner, literacy levels were gradually rising in Europe.

A certain number of phenomena testify to how the written word, the book, the text, and writing were acquiring new roles and functions in society. Merchants and bankers now exchanged economic and political news and views by means of handwritten sheets that circulated from city to city. Another significant event: in the fourteenth century, Charles V the Wise, regarded as a champion of the arts and letters, founded the French Royal Library. Under his auspices, a considerable number of major texts were translated into French.

As readers were becoming less and less confined to specific locales, the readership was also gradually broadening. Previously the preserve of men of the Church and aristocrats, the book was now accessible to a middle class, to literate merchants, as well as to teachers and students in the universities. Reading to oneself also became more widespread, as an adjunct to reading aloud, which had been the general practice since antiquity.[27]

Slowly leaving the monastic realm, the book trades now formed into guilds within secular workshops. It was a reorganization that implied a degree of job demarcation, entailing notable transformations in the processes of book manufacture. Efforts to fulfill the increasing demand for texts linked to an upsurge in patronage, and a tendency to simplification and standardization in writing succeeded the astonishing diversity of types hitherto deployed.

Formation of the Gothic and Humanist scripts

These transformations were accompanied by a new dawn in artistic expression. Between the twelfth and thirteenth centuries, initially appearing in architecture, the Gothic style took root in the manuscript, and miniatures, decorations, and scripts adopted new forms. Gradually Gothic lettering ousted the Caroline, which had already been gradually losing ground for half a millennium. One other notable factor arose: original texts in books were being

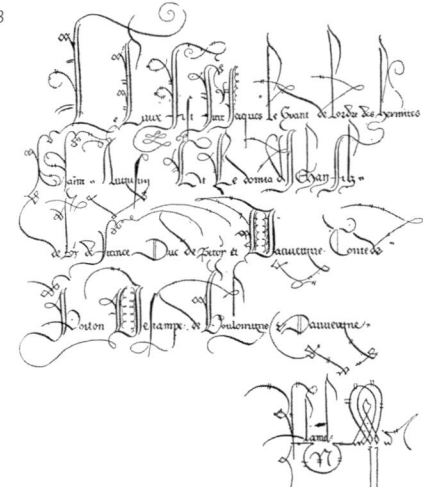

43
Specimen of a florid Gothic capital (the origin of the "grotesque initial"), 1490.

44
Antiphonar, Carmelite choir book, Mayence, c. 1432. Calligraphy and illumination on parchment, 22 ³/₄ × 16 in. (58 × 41 cm).

45
Traditional Bastard Gothic, manuscript taken from a book belonging to Emperor Maximilian I, c. 1467.

46

46
Example of Humanistic script, fifteenth century. The form may be compared to the corresponding type, the Roman. Characteristics of this script include: the relatively flat attack of the curve of the n (generally rounder), the loop of the e, the bowl of the a, and the special shape of the g.

enriched with lengthy commentaries that might entail various zones of writing and levels of reading. Wherever the page became denser, neighboring texts could be distinguished by variations in size, position, hierarchy, fullness, proportion, nesting, intercalation, etc. Though remaining relatively tightly knit, the columns of text were slowly gaining room to breathe. Graphic and decorative elements drew attention to the material's connective tissue, signaling, for example, cross-references from one text to another. Sentences now took shape around the capital and the full point (stop), while word spacing (some words being divided by hyphens) became more regular. Various means were developed to guide, pace, or orientate reading. Textual transitions were pointed up by visual cues, the use of the stop as a punctuation mark underwent continuous renewal, a rich palette of abbreviated signs formed, and leaves were now more frequently paginated. Additionally, the alphabet was extended with Arabic numerals, which had arrived in Europe around the twelfth century.

Current by the thirteenth century, the practice of Gothic script was deployed in very different styles depending on geographic area and chronological period. In certain regions of Western Europe, in Germany and in the north of France, it displays narrow and lengthened forms, with very angular minuscules. This version of Gothic possesses a strong orthogonal structure, varying and multiplying the same modules along the entire line. Baptized Textura, it was employed primarily for copying holy writ and legal documents. Gothic lettering as used in the south of Europe (in particular in Italy, Spain, and in the south of France) takes the name *rotunda*, or "Round Gothic." Its forms are broad and generous, presenting a number of links with Caroline. Relatively readable to modern eyes in comparison with other subspecies of Gothic, it can be found in conjunction with the most highly decorated forms. Many other families of Gothic script were to appear, such as Fraktur (in Germanic lands) and Schwabacher.[28]

The expansion of Gothic script was accompanied by countless variants. Thoroughly developed by the end of the fourteenth century, it was extensively used in Germany, England, and France. International in scope and predominant in various arts, in the manuscript the Gothic style attained its apogee, spawning a host of masterworks. The celebrated *Très Riches*

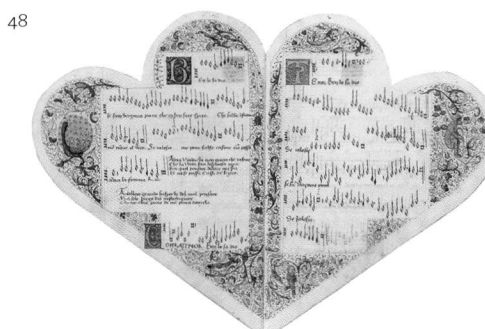

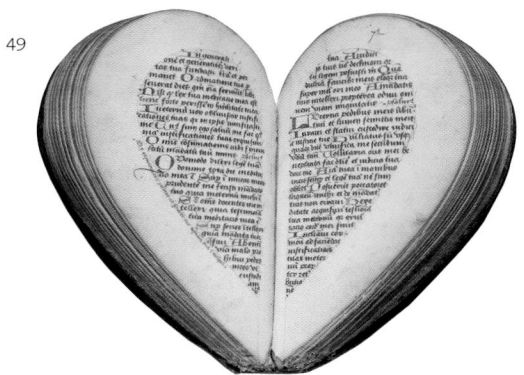

Heures du Duc de Berry, for instance, complete with its painstakingly detailed paintings, was compiled between 1413 and 1416 by the Limbourg brothers.

While Gothic lettering was still widely used, the beginnings of the Quattrocento witnessed the flowering of a very different form of script. Referred to by the term "Humanist," its forms are associated with the spirit of the Renaissance. The earliest specimens apparently arose in Italy in the very first years of the fifteenth century, in 1402–03. If the Humanist script is reminiscent of Italian Round Gothic, it takes direct inspiration from the Caroline minuscule and the Roman capital. In the course of their studies of Classical Greco-Roman literature in manuscripts copied by the Carolingians, Humanists believed they were handling authentic works of antiquity, the probable reason for their dubbing this new script, *lettera antiqua*. In its turn, Humanist (Humanistic) script was a watershed in the formation of the Latin alphabet. Spreading rapidly in Italy, by the second half of the fifteenth century it was serving as a model for typefaces. With precedents such as the lapidary capitals of Roman antiquity and the Caroline of the Early Middle Ages, the Humanist script remained the predominant template for modern written forms for more than six hundred years.

The close of the Middle Ages

If script was undergoing significant mutations, in the Late Middle Ages miniature and illumination remained major pictorial forms, with the book the chief medium of painting. During the fourteenth century, the relation between text and image in the volume continued to progress. Illustrations abound on every page, enhancing the splendor of the book and its iconic value. "Text and image combine to turn the book into an art object and the page into an authentic, carefully framed, if small-sized picture. Such illustrative treatment became still grander in fifteenth-century Psalters, Books of Hours, Gospels, and secular works whose magnificence embellished aristocratic and ecclesiastical libraries alike."[29]

Book illustration was soon to reflect Renaissance art and sometimes the image gained a degree of independence from the written area. Illustration, with the manuscript as a prime vehicle of its expression, sometimes relegated the script to the background, becoming less decorative and more realistic. Now distinct from the text and having flourished remarkably in the book up to the end of the Middle Ages, the painted image was to be increasingly the focus of easel painting.

Other transformations, just as fundamental, awaited the arts of the book in the fifteenth century. With the growing use of printing (in woodcut, in particular), followed by the reinvention in the West of movable-type composition, text and image were less and less dependent on a cottage industry, and, aided by a wide range of devices, started out on the journey to mass reproduction. Bookhands, scripts, and penmanship were gradually ousted by typography, thereby laying the foundations for what has been called "mechanical graphic" or "the art of impressure."[30] Similarly, illuminations and decorations were to yield the field to monochrome engravings that were sometimes hand-colored.

Though never actually killed off, the scriptural and pictorial arts of the manuscript (drawing, calligraphy, painting, decoration, etc.), which dated back to antiquity and which had enjoyed an extraordinary proliferation in the Middle Ages, now witnessed the advent of a technique with which it could not, quantitatively, hope to compete. Inextricably bound up with the logic of its production, typeset text may forfeit facets of the special charm of the handwritten book (richly illustrated and often so free in composition and ornamentation), but it also paved the way for fresh aesthetic departures.

Techniques and materials:
paper, printing, and composition

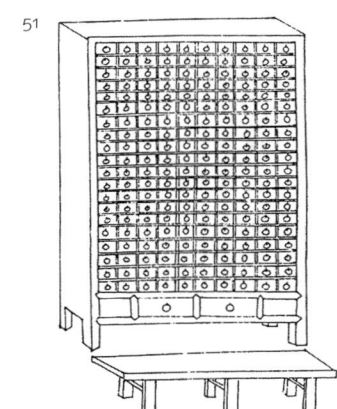

50
Stamping on paper of a sutra engraved on stone drawn by Gongquan Liu, May 8, 824.

51
A stand with pigeonholes for storing Chinese characters (wooden movable blocks from the imperial printing works in Beijing), after Jin Jian, China, seventeenth century. The characters, arranged in radicals according to the number of lines, are sorted in twelve cupboards each provided with two hundred drawers divided into eight compartments.

52
Manual setting of forms with movable characters, as in Jin Jian, *Wuyingdian juzhenban congshu chengshi*, China, eighteenth century.

The pioneering role of Asia

As the cradle of a certain number of trailblazing inventions relating as much to the manufacture of materials as to technical processes, Asia played a key role in the history of the mass reproduction of text and image. Additionally, well before the question of reproduction arose, fledgling forms of writing had appeared on the fringes of the Asian domain: archaic inscriptions and seal impressions from the fourth millennium BCE have been found over a vast Middle Eastern region straddling Mesopotamia and Persia. It was similarly in the Middle East that alphabets such as Ugaritic and Phoenician were forged. In conjunction with other systems devised in earlier eras, the alphabet provided a new functional platform for writing.

On the practical front, the principle of alphabetical notation was crucial to typography. Due to its restricted number of signs, letters can be manufactured in quantity and arranged in boxes of a handy size (if the Phoenician alphabet is composed of twenty-two letter-consonants, the visual signs of Chinese amount to thousands or tens of thousands of character forms depending on the linguistic level concerned).

Paper, printing, and typography in China

As regards the invention of materials and processes relating to printing, China, and Asia more generally, stands in the vanguard. It was there that xylography (woodblock printing) and movable-type printing were invented—roughly five hundred years before these twin techniques developed in the West, with the first known dated printed book going back to the ninth century. It was there, too, that the first paper was manufactured more than one thousand years before it made its way to Western Europe. An enduring tradition has ascribed its invention to Cai Lun, tracing it back to the very beginning of the second century. "In 105, Cai Lun, a senior official attached to the imperial court, describes with precision a process for manufacturing paper from mulberry-tree fiber which was referred to for centuries to come. By replacing strips of bamboo, wood, and silk alike, paper thus became a medium for writing, with major repercussions on the development of written civilization in China (on its culture, government, etc.)."[31] Cai Lun is supposed to have improved the manufacture of a material whose existence is attested in China from the second or third century BCE at least, and which was also used, for instance, for making furniture.

Independently of paper, the invention of the press and of movable type both represent essential stepping-stones on the road to reproducing text and image. One of a number of age-old means of impression, stamping makes it possible to make repeated imprints of a pattern on an incised surface. In a primitive form of the process, it consists of applying a previously dampened sheet of paper to an engraved medium, thus preserving the imprint in ink. The Chinese used this process widely, in particular to reproduce inscriptions on stone steles. If the method may have already been employed in the Han period (third century BCE to the third century CE), the earliest stampings attested in China date from the seventh century. The earliest such imprint known today, obtained from a stele reproducing a piece of calligraphy,

53

54

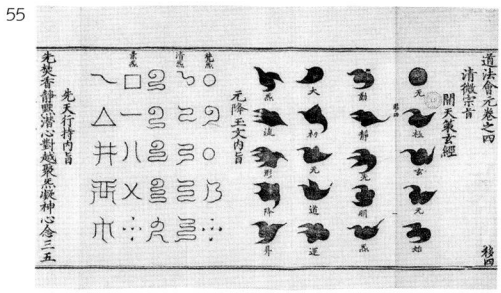

55

53
Movable type in Uighur, carved pear-wood, thirteenth to fourteenth centuries, found in China. Height of the characters: ¹/₂ in. (1.3 cm).

54
First known dated printed book. *The Diamond Sutra*, China, 868. Chinese woodblock scroll reproduced by Wang Chieh from carved wooden boards.

55
Illustrated woodblock publication, *Zhengtong Daozang*, Tao Canon of the Zhengtong era, China, Ming Dynasty, 1444–45 edition. Oblong concertina-fold books (gold silk cover, five-panel cardboard cases covered in gold silk); 13 ³/₄ × 5 in. (35 × 12.8 cm). Five columns per folded panel, twenty-five columns per sheet, seventeen characters per column. Successively: special forms of characters and their decipherment; a series of talismanic characters broken up with their explanations; talisman separated.

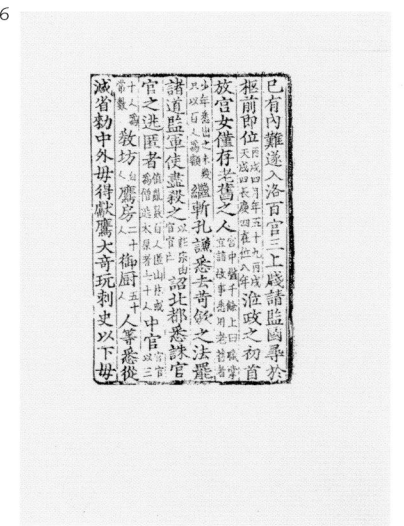

56

56
Korean letterpress using movable characters, *Shiqishi zuan gujin tongyao*, "Extracts from the seventeen dynastic histories," 1412.

is a scroll entitled the *Inscription of the Hot Spring* (10 ³/₄ × 57 ³/₄ in. [27 × 144 cm]) whose colophon records the date 653.

The block-book was yet another principle created in China. Wooden boards or metal plates engraved with texts and images, inked and then rubbed on a sheet of paper, can be used to reproduce printed pages in quantity. These constitute the earliest forms of xylographic—woodblock impression—practiced in China in the eighth century and becoming widespread in subsequent periods. A similar technique allowed for the production of the first printed books, in the shape of scrolls, such as the famous *Diamond Sutra*, the first dated example known. Dating back to 868, this Chinese woodblock book is a scroll reproduced by Wang Chieh from carved panel boards. Though the technique was already prevalent in China, Wang Chieh numbers among the very first printers known. In addition to the Chinese, the Koreans had a significant hand in a number of inventions. Moreover, quite apart from the development of processes of impression, the written or printed support as such foreshadowed many types of publication of future eras—such as the early issuing, around 800 in Beijing, of a monthly periodical.

Other Far Eastern developments ushered in techniques that mark a step-change from current methods of printing—most notably, the principle of movable type. If the tools were new, however, the guiding principles harked back to processes in use even before the Common Era, since seals and stencils had long ago rendered "printing" viable. The techniques developed to mint ancient coins (struck with the punch from at least the seventh century BCE, in India as well as in the Hellenistic domain) led the way to processes that were eventually to allow the reproduction of typographical characters.

A Chinese text from the end of the eleventh century mentions the existence of blocks of characters made out of terracotta: the experiments of the Chinese blacksmith, Bi Sheng, number among the very first in this direction. Between 1041 and 1048, he is supposed to have carved characters out of clay, baked them in a fire, and then assembled them onto an iron bed specially constructed for the purpose. The printing surface obtained thus prefigures, in some respects, the system Europeans were to devise some four hundred years later. Following Bi Sheng's example, the technique of movable type was improved thanks to the choice of a different material (it is possible besides that he himself attempted to manufacture characters in wood). Other printers continued his experiments and carved characters in wood that could be then pared with a blade, measured, adjusted in size, and arranged in wooden storage boxes. To be truly complete, however, a set would require from thirty thousand to a hundred thousand characters, or even more.

In a text of 1313, the printer Wang Zhen[32] describes the manufacture of the characters carved on wood that he was using at the end of the thirteenth century, a technique similar to that adapted around the same time to Uighur script. If, in 1395, a Korean publication obtained from this type of character set could be reproduced in hundreds of copies, there had surely been many other models, earlier still, based on similar processes. Like clay, however, wood is not a particularly suitable material and proved delicate to use. Type was only to discover solidity and longevity with the introduction of molten metal. It should be stressed that such characters were indeed employed in Korea, perhaps for the very first time, where they were used to print several publications as early as the 1230s, before becoming current in subsequent centuries.

Printing and typography in Europe
Paper, woodblock, and movable type

For long a closely guarded secret, paper manufacture gained a foothold in the seventh and eighth centuries in the area around Samarkand in Central Asia, from where it spread to the Arab world in the space of a few decades. In their turn, the Arabs introduced it into Sicily and Spain, where it was manufactured from the mid-twelfth century. Thence, between the twelfth and fourteenth centuries, the material arrived in Italy, France, and latterly in Germany and England; it arrived later still in Russia and in America.

In the West, paper is made from rag,[33] and paper mills were set up to transform it into the end product. The written word thus acquired a new medium that was far less costly than parchment (a volume of average size in parchment might necessitate about fifteen animal hides). Parchment was in regular use since the first century and remained current until the fifteenth century, after which time it was rapidly supplanted by paper (whose flexibility facilitates folding and shaping), a medium that soon played a key role in the expansion of printing and typography. However, paper, contrary to a relatively widely held belief, is not a necessary precondition for letterpress, and it is intriguing to note that some of the first incunabula[34] combine leaves of printed parchment and paper.

If it is indeed the case that paper arrived in the West from Asia at the end of a steady advance along the Mediterranean, the work of Gutenberg, his predecessors, and his associates seems nevertheless to have been a reinvention. Furthermore, the type he used was far smaller than that manufactured in China and Korea from the eleventh century. In Europe, as in China, xylographic printing (from a relief-engraved matrix) precedes at least by a few centuries the development of movable type. In Italy, engraved woodblocks were already being used to print patterns on cloth by the twelfth century. It is a technique that was also prevalent in India, where wooden stamps were famous for the quality and finesse of their printmaking. It seems that after Italy, woodblock printing then spread to Germany, France, and other countries in Europe during the thirteenth and fourteenth centuries. The process was in particular employed for reproducing religious images, playing cards, calendars, and other printed items.

Similarly manufactured using xylographic techniques, the first known printed books in the West date from around 1420–30. The first specimens of woodblock incunabula to be found in the Netherlands and Germany (*Blockbücher* or block-books), were obtained by rubbing from engraved and pre-inked wooden boards. This is a laborious process and production costs are high. Given the wear and tear meted out to the wood as it is pulled, the "print-run" for such works (often containing from thirty to fifty pages) does not generally exceed about fifty copies (to increase this, the boards have to be recut). Texts and illustrations are engraved on wood, separately or in combination.

57
Paupers' Bible, block-book, Germany, second half of the fifteenth century.

58
Playing cards, queen of clubs, Lyon (?), end of the fifteenth century. Stencil-colored woodcut on paper, 4 × 2 1/2 in. (10 × 6.7 cm).

In these conditions, it is not rare to find one and the same image the subject of more than one reproduction, with a sole illustration used on several occasions in various contexts, following a practice that endured for some time. For instance, the same engraving representing an overall view of a city center could be used in turn to illustrate the towns of Mainz, Lyon, Naples, or Bologna, and reemployed moreover over many years. Thus, "in the *Chronicle of Nuremberg* (Koberger, 1493), the repeated use of 645 blocks provides 1,809 illustrations, the same depiction even being deployed to illustrate two different cities."[35] A further example from a late sixteenth-century publication shows a view of the Seine in spate illustrated by an engraving representing Venice, a document moreover already in existence for more than a century. At various times and in diverse circumstances, one and the same picture can thus reappear in several volumes, here as a title page or frontispiece, there as an illustration. This particularly revealing phenomenon even affects the face of Gutenberg himself: "No authenticated portrait of [Gutenberg] has been preserved. The first known likeness appeared in Basel in 1565, nearly one hundred years after his death, in a work by Heinrich Pantaleon dedicated to the great men of Germany. A few pages further on, in accordance with the cost-conscious habit of the time, the same engraving is employed to illustrate another personage."[36]

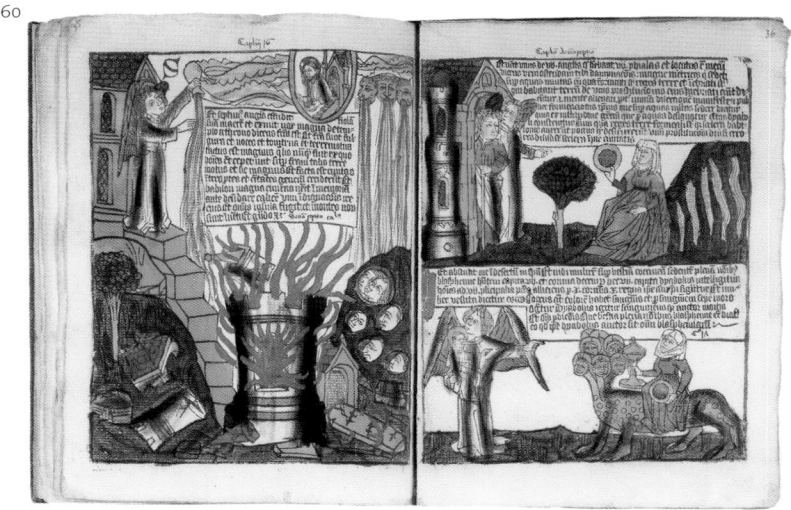

It may be that movable type meets with precedents in Europe prior to the invention ascribed to Gutenberg. Already in the thirteenth century, and possibly before, initials and ornaments were engraved on wood or metal and transferred to the manuscript by stamping or rubbing (for example, the relief impression of drop initials). The letter or motif was printed in a single tint and the design left for coloring by hand. It seems though that the manufacturing principle behind movable type was already in use to create certain initial letters cast in metal in a mould. Before the existence of the press, bookbinders used engraved movable metal letters for imprinting on covers. Even in the sixteenth century, the attribution to Gutenberg for inventing movable-type printing was called into question. A Dutch text of the period points to Laurens Janszoon (alias Coster, an inhabitant of Haarlem, died c. 1440) as the father of wooden and molten-metal movable type in Europe. Janszoon is supposed to have learnt of the existence of characters from Asia, whose manufacturing principles he is said to have adapted to the letters of the Latin alphabet between 1420 and 1430. Using movable type, he may even have printed on sheets and assembled them in the form of a book. If Coster's precise contribution remains hard to appraise, the town of Haarlem for one has erected two statues to perpetuate his memory. It even seems that he also had a part to play in the remarkable development of woodblock printing at the time, in particular in respect of the Dutch volumes obtained by this process. If the occasional attributions of the invention to him today are couched in more or less legendary and scarcely credible terms, the idea that he was something of a precursor has survived for several centuries and has its roots in several venerable texts. One of these, published in 1588, describes Coster as

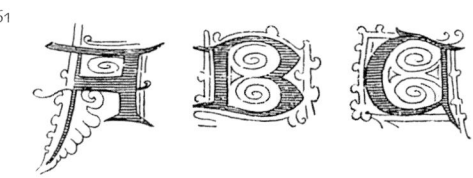

59
Four colorings of the same engraving, reproduced in *Histoire de la nature des oyseaux*, Paris, 1555 (comparison by H.-J. Martin). "No homogeneity is discernable between the various copies that present more or less the possible states ranging from being rapidly smeared with watercolor to being painstakingly painted with gouache. [Coloring] is not undertaken by the printer and remains the affair of the owner, who can thus leave the mark of his own reading in his book."

60
Apocalypse, block-book, fifteenth century.

61
Stamped initials, examples taken from a manuscript in the Vatican and a manuscript from Laon, thirteenth and fourteenth centuries. Used to speed up the work of the copyist, the letters are engraved on wood or metal and then transferred by rubbing or pressing and illuminated subsequently.

the "man to whom should be restored the fame, at present usurped by another, of having been the inventor of the whole art of printing."[37] It is besides conceivable that Gutenberg's work was influenced by woodblock printing and by Dutch examples.

The Gutenberg circle: towards the mechanization of writing

62
Portrait of Laurens Janszoon (alias Coster), holding a letter A in his left hand. Printer at Haarlem (Netherlands), born c. 1370. Some ascribe the invention of movable-type printing to him.

63
Supposedly imaginary portrait of Johannes Gutenberg (from which most depictions of the printer are derived). Copper engraving by André Thevet, Paris, 1584. According to Kapr "as all the other depictions of Gutenberg, this one is pure invention."

"The art of writing artificially."[38] This expression of the period perfectly encapsulates the end result of the processes associated with the "Gutenberg era," during which they were devised and perfected. Born at Eltville close to Mainz, probably between 1393 and 1404 (and dying in 1468), Johannes Gensfleisch zur Laden zum Gutenberg—known as Gutenberg—was German and German-speaking. His contribution to printing and typography is well documented and many texts proclaim him to be "the inventor of printing," or the "inventor of typography." Several printing techniques existed well before his time, such as woodblock (and the printed book, too, thanks to this technique), and it is probable that experiments were being undertaken at the time, outside Gutenberg's entourage elsewhere in Europe. If the advances attained by Gutenberg and his team are unlikely to have created typographic printing *ex nihilo*, they nevertheless proved of the utmost importance. Gutenberg is regarded as the first to have successfully employed movable-type printing in Europe, the technique of typesetting developing in his own workshop. It appears that before he turned to printing, he was not unacquainted with the use of the press, but it is by no means certain that he had previously been a goldsmith or jeweler, as is often alleged. It is probable that he devised the printing press at the end of the 1430s.

Hitherto, from ancient Chinese stamps through to carved boards reproduced by rubbing or simple hand pressure (block-printing), processes of impression had remained purely manual affairs. In designing his printing press, Gutenberg turned to the principle of the wooden press with a vertical screw of the type used for wine and oil. He had a wooden press made that was still operated manually but that incorporated nevertheless an embryonic form of mechanization. Two key factors are fused in this technique: the possibility of multiple pulls and a not insignificant acceleration in rate of impression. On a purely practical level, several

64
Printing press employed for typographical composition using movable type, c. 1500. Hand-press made entirely of wood (including the screw). The engraving has the mark of Josse Bade, bookseller-printer from 1503 to 1535.

operations are necessary prior to printing. The array of characters comprising the printing surface (named the "form" or "forme") is laid out over a horizontal galley. After inking, a sheet of paper or parchment is placed over the form. Activated by a bar that rotates an endless screw made of wood, the platen descends, pressing the paper firmly against the type. In spite of the tools deployed, from which full mechanization will subsequently derive, the process of printing remained essentially a handicraft.

Though paper was not indispensable to printing, in fifteenth-century Germany it was still a rare material and that used by Gutenberg's workshop was imported from Italy where it was in comparatively common use. Paper was to prove essential, for subsequent developments, since it is cost-effective in large quantities and its natural properties, such as regularity of grain and flexibility, made it a medium particularly well suited to printing. A complementary innovation was the invention of a special ink whose complex composition allowed him to print in black on both sides of the same leaf. Up to that point, leaves in volumes could only be printed or written on a single side, as inks had a tendency to seep through manuscript and block-book pages alike.

Gutenberg is presumed to have started out trying to produce movable type around 1440, although many of the materials necessary for the tools to create letterpress were not yet in place. To achieve his aim, Gutenberg gathered around him jewelers and goldsmiths, though it is also likely that he had acquired personal knowledge of working in metal and other substances. After years of arduous work, however, the centerpiece of the typesetting technique was slowly taking shape.

65

(Fragment text in Gothic script, image of printed Sibylline Book fragment)

65
Fragment from a *Sibylline Book*, among the
oldest Western letterpress printing known.
Doubtful attribution and dating; perhaps from
Gutenberg's workshop, c. 1453–54.

(Gothic script specimen for caption 66)

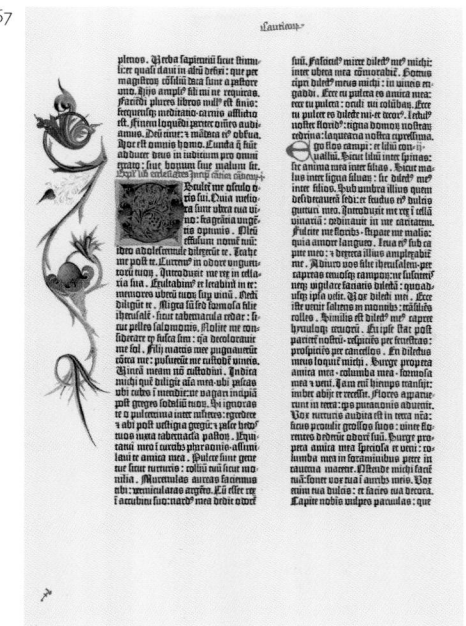

The development of mobile type comprises three phases. The first consists in engraving in relief at the end of a hard metal punch a reversed character (capital and small letters, digits, punctuation, ligatures, abbreviations, pi-sorts, etc.). The second occurs when the punch is struck into a matrix made of a softer metal. The sign then appears indented at the base of the matrix, which then serves as a mould. The final stage consists in casting an alloy into the matrix that, on taking its imprint, thus becomes a character. Now ready for composition, the letters and signs thus obtained can supply as many copies as required of the master (the engraved punch).

The endurance of the above process through the centuries stems from the properties of the materials employed. The alloy used for the purpose is composed of 80 percent lead (together with antimony and tin) and outstripped the limits imposed by characters in clay or wood (and even xylography), which were more fragile, harder to reproduce, and more prone to wear. One indication of this is that the Mainz workshop is supposed to have cast no less than an estimated one hundred thousand types. With the development of movable type, Gutenberg's equipment at last combined all the elements necessary for letterpress printing: letters and signs that could be reproduced in quantity, a suitable ink, sufficient amounts of support (parchment or paper), and the printing press.

The earliest incunabula

Around 1450, in order to obtain the necessary plant and the means to realize his ambitions, Gutenberg secured sizable loans, one of which was funded by Johannes Fust, a moneylender and trader from Mainz. As a guarantee, Gutenberg found himself bound in the event of nonpayment to cede his workshop, presses, and characters to Fust. The two men thus formed a partnership, establishing the workshop that became the first productive typesetting printing plant. Gutenberg had for his part already put his equipment through its paces. The earliest attested proofs come from the 1440s, in particular between 1449 and the very beginning of the 1450s, and it is from this latter period that a fragment of the *Sibylline Book* dates, one of the first Western examples of typographic printing (considered the oldest and discovered in 1892). About 1450, Gutenberg's presses also prepared several editions of Donatus, a standard Latin grammar that numbered among the most widely distributed texts of the epoch.[39]

A second loan from Fust allowed Gutenberg to print the famous *42-line Bible*, usually designated as "B42," a "work [...] conceived rather like a manifesto for the new technique."[40] Printed in Mainz probably between 1452 and 1455, this Bible appeared in two volumes pulled in some two hundred copies on parchment and on paper. The work was realized by a team numbering a score or so craftsmen combining engravers, founders, typesetters, ink manufacturers, printers, and booksellers (publishers). Based on the "Golden Canon"[41] of medieval manuscripts, the layout of B42 comprises two columns with ample margins. The piece possesses many qualities characteristic of the more harmonious illuminated manuscripts. The printed surface, for example, has been found to be proportional to the surface of the sheet in a ratio of approximately 3:4.[42] Both horizontally and vertically the page is divided into nine. Among many other interesting particularities, less obvious but surely equally essential to the functioning of the whole and also to be found in manuscript work, the height of the text column corresponds to the breadth of the leaf. In B42, both for ornamentation and the development of the type, Gutenberg was similarly inspired by calligraphied books. Textura, a frequent script for religious texts, was common in Germany, and it was this that served as the initial model for the creation of letterforms, although, if hot-metal fonts were at the outset Gothic, a very different shape of letter was quickly to come into existence, inspired by Humanistic bookhands.

As regards color, the first impressions were made using black ink. Already, in B42, however, a second printing with red ink was tried out in certain places of the text corresponding to

66
Johannes Gutenberg, type for the *42-line Bible*,
Mainz, c. 1452–55.

67
Gutenberg, page from the *42-line Bible*, known
as B42, Mainz, probably printed between 1452
and 1455 (specimen from the Burgos Library).

headings. In this work, as in many other incunabula, some areas were left free of all print and set aside for penmen or illuminators. Although some of these voids were never actually filled, others were—as in the past—completed with drawings or paintings, titles, initials, punctuation, illuminations, ornamented words, and other polychrome decorations.[43] Thus, the earliest printed books owe much to manuscripts (in terms of illumination, composition, letter style, proportion, etc.), but are characterized all the same by a number of other traits, such as line justification.

Johannes Fust and Peter Schöffer: the growth of printing

At the outset, the typographical experiment can be considered as much for its technical prowess as for its aesthetic component. With the 42-line Bible, Gutenberg's workshop went beyond the testing phase and attained unprecedented production levels. Now typeset, the printed book was on the brink of outdoing handwritten copying. At this point in his career, however, and just as Gutenberg's life's work was primed to attain its goal, he was beset by serious financial hardship. A lawsuit brought against him by Johannes Fust in 1455 forced him to give up a proportion of his printing plant. Gutenberg, however, managed to start up the business again and new printings left his workshop, including, possibly, the *Catholicon* in 1460, a publication that if he had a hand in preparing, he may not have printed. The *Catholicon* (a Latin dictionary-cum-grammar of more than seven hundred pages and with a print-run of some three hundred copies) called for characters of reduced size, most probably the smallest faces yet employed in printing. Moving away from purely Gothic type, this letterform also contains the beginnings of a new offshoot: while preserving the Gothic imprint, it also heralds a primitive form of Roman, occasionally designated by the term Gothico Antiqua.

Breaking with Gutenberg, Fust then took over the entire material of the print-shop. Having lost the collaboration of the great initiator, Fust could nonetheless benefit from his successful and already conclusive research, and he began working with Peter Schöffer (who went on to marry his daughter, Cristina). Before joining the workshop in Mainz, Schöffer had been an ecclesiastic and a penman at the Sorbonne. Thus possessed of both expertise and material means, Fust and Schöffer's printshop met all the conditions it needed to pursue Gutenberg's findings. With a slightly different aesthetic approach, they made improvements, and their earliest work, the *Mainz Psalter*, left the press in 1456 and 1457. Though in the midst of his lawsuit with Fust, Gutenberg also played a part in bringing out this edition of the Psalter.

Though various tests had been essayed beforehand, it appears that this collection of the Psalms marks the true inauguration of color printing.[44] The initials, in blue and red, were printed together with the black text in a single pull. Each ornamental letter is composed of two woodcuts inset one within the other and inked. The Psalter is also apparently the first book to be issued with a colophon,[45] which explains the work in the following manner: "The present book of Psalms decorated by the beauty of the capitals and rubrications was made thanks to the invention of a mechanical way of printing and fashioning characters without writing with the quill in any way whatsoever."[46]

The use of woodcuts for the impression of these initials had repercussions on style, moreover. As regards the main text, the Psalter is composed in large characters of approximately one centimeter in height, so that the various members of the choir can follow the same copy. The two fonts employed in this work were probably bequeathed to Johannes Fust by Gutenberg. The complete array numbers some nearly five hundred different signs overall, that is to say twice the total deployed in the 42-line Bible. After the Psalter, Fust and Schöffer's workshop continued to bring out exceptional works, especially religious texts, the dominant genre in publishing and amounting to approximately

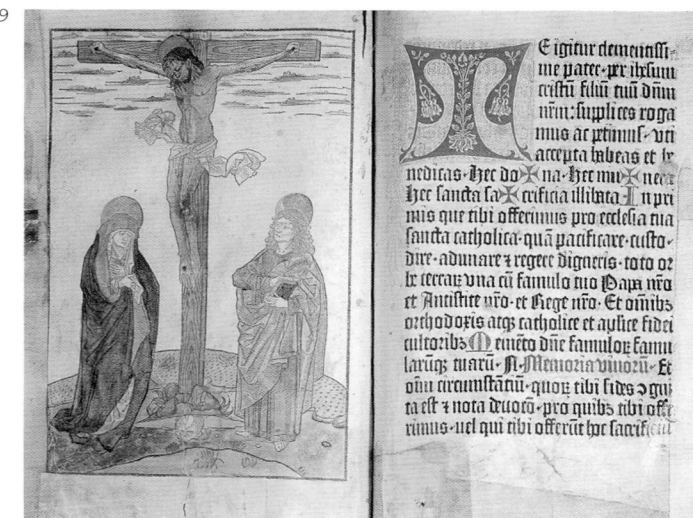

68
Donatus, *Ars minor*, primitive printing (Utrecht? undated).

69
Peter Schöffer (printer), *Vratislaviense Missal* (Breslau), Mainz, 24 July 1483.

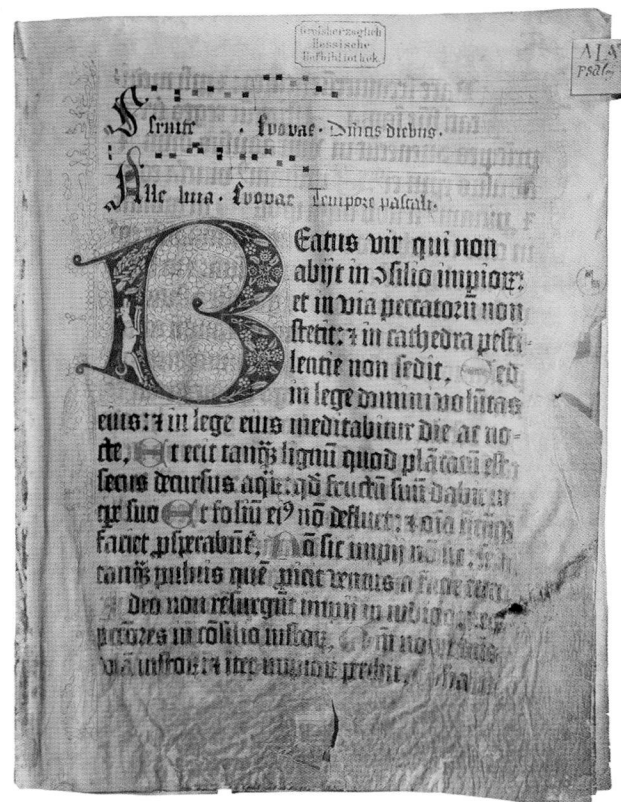

72

![Magnus basilius & poetarum philosophorum legendis libris M. Maronū brenmngarīū(quo fa bricis ataliſcz intertinctus. Stelic]

70
Mainz Psalter, Johannes Fust and Peter Schöffer's workshop, Mainz, 14 August 1457. Three-color printing, two-color initial; letters in the running text approximately ½ in. (1 cm) high.

71
Peter Schöffer, *Corpus iuris civilis. Codex Iustinianus*, Mainz, 1475.

72
Specimen of the type for Johannes Fust and Peter Schöffer's *Psalter*, from their workshop, Mainz, 1457. The character presents forms distinct from the then prevalent Gothic script, marking the onset of a different type of legibility.

75 percent of publications in the early years of printing. The font, just as with the one used in the *Catholicon*, shifted somewhat away from the Gothic, heralding the onset of Roman type. Through the work of Gutenberg, Fust, and Schöffer (soon followed by their peers), typography was from the outset a process in ongoing development. The practice itself, however, remained the preserve of a handful of insiders, who kept it a closely guarded secret—just as the Chinese before them had with respect to paper manufacture. Letterpress, however, could remain limited to a coterie for only a short space of time.

As early as the end of 1450, Mainz was no longer the only focus. New editions of the Bible came off presses in Strasbourg and Bamberg, perhaps even before 1460. Very soon other towns in Germany became active in printing and publishing. The surrounds of Mainz and the Rhineland country were then to be the earliest centers of development for the new technique. These were followed by other workshops that sprung up here and there, thus increasing the geographical range of printing.

In 1462, the town of Mainz was beset by major social, religious, and cultural conflicts (including the so-called War of the Bishops), which were to spark widespread civil disturbances. The positions of the rivaling sides were brought to public attention through printed handbills and broadsides that numbered among the very first printed items of a political nature. Disorientated or chased out by these events, most of the artisans working in the few printworks in Mainz fled the city. Taking with them their expertise, and probably some materials too, these proto-compositors set up new workshops in other German towns, as well as in Italy and France.

One of Peter Schöffer's former collaborators settled in Italy in about 1465. Then, between this date and 1470, typeset printing was implanted successively in Cologne, Rome, Basel, Venice, Nuremberg, and Paris (the most outstanding figures being Anton Koberger in Nuremberg, Johann Amerbach and Johann Froben in Basel, Ulrich Zell in Cologne, and

73
Colophon, page from a history of the Franks, Johann Schöffer's workshop (the grandson of Peter Schöffer), Mainz, 1515.

Johann Mentelin in Strasbourg). In the course of the following decade, the technique made its way to the Netherlands, Spain, Poland, Belgium, and England. In the space of a few years, the practice thus spread all over Europe. By 1480, more than one hundred cities had been recorded as sites for printing concerns. In Mainz itself, by the first half of the sixteenth century, the succession of Peter Schöffer was being ensured by his sons and grandsons. A carefully kept secret in the 1450s, letterpress had, by the final decades of the fifteenth century, been propagated through much of the West.

Stakes and challenges of a new technique

Incunabula represent the starting point of an entirely new activity with far-reaching consequences. Initially a technical, material, and economic affair, the invention of movable-type printing would make its presence felt above all by distributing far and wide articles that rendered the texts they contained (such as scholarly works, literature, information, advertisements, popular prints, etc.) more accessible. Upstream, the mushrooming of the universities and the gradual retreat of illiteracy in the thirteenth and fourteenth centuries constituted conditions favorable both to the uptake of the technique and to the reception of the diverse media it spawned. By way of hawkers (a major vehicle in Germany, for example), printed materials could permeate into different sectors of the population. Further factors also contributed to the diffusion of the book, such as export, practiced by the larger publishers, and the presence of printed products at European fairs (in Frankfurt, Lyon, etc.).

The advent of the typeset book (and its offspring, the periodical) opened up new possibilities for the spread of knowledge and transformed relationships to the text. The long months required for a copyist to write out a text in bookhand and the costs this implied had restricted literary attainments and written culture generally to a narrow and privileged circle. Recourse to xylographic block-books, scarcely less onerous to manufacture, had also remained relatively limited. The development of incunabula occasioned a significant drop in the price of books. As an indication of this, one estimate has suggested that "an unbound copy [reference is made to an incunabulum of 1493] represented the value of 24 ducks or

74

75

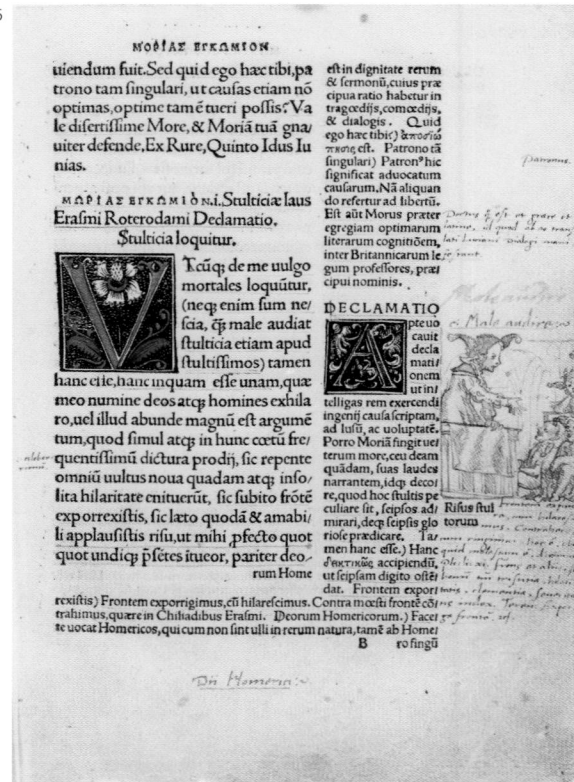

74
Anton Koberger (printer), page from Boethius' *De consolatione philosophiae*, bilingual work in German and Latin, Nuremberg, 24 July 1473.

75
Johann Froben (printer), page from *The Praise of Folly* by Erasmus, Basel, 1515 edition. Erasmus's text in the left-hand column, commentary in smaller type in the right-hand column, and introductory drawing by Holbein in the margin.

76

"Le Colporteur" ("the Hawker"), from the *Cris de Paris*, anonymous collection of eighteen stencil-colored woodcuts dating to the sixteenth century.

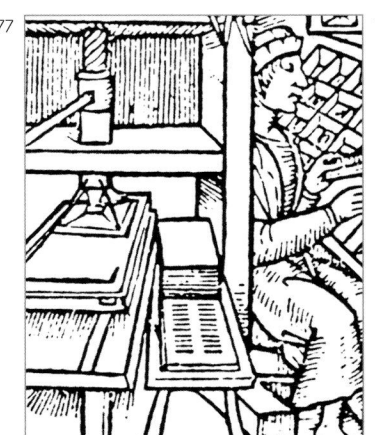

77

On the left of the picture: printing press for typographical composition using movable type. On the right: compositor, c. 1500.

78

Print-shop for manual composition in the Leipzig Akademie für Graphische Künste und Buchgewerbe, 1910.

20 kilos of pork, while a bound copy was valued at six buckets of wine."[47] At one time confined to small groups, the written word could now reach out to the population at large through a capacity for reproduction specific to typesetting. In addition, this process entailed a measure of standardization in production, so limiting the suppressions and disparities that so plagued hand copying. In spite of the separation of the reproductive processes relating to the text from those of the image, the latter, in the wake of the unique position it had enjoyed in the manuscript, remained a significant component of the typeset book.

Around 1500, as the book was hardly leaving the era of the incunabulum, the number of printed texts could already be counted in the millions. More than thirty to forty thousand different publications had already seen the light of day, with a total of ten to fifteen million volumes printed in movable type. During the sixteenth century, print-runs, too, were to increase, doubling, if not more. Correlatively, print revealed its latent power; sensing this, Mainz churchmen had already begun censorship measures. The influence of the written word was supremely illustrated during the Reformation, when the distribution and mass production of printed matter facilitated access to religious texts, fostering new challenges to the Catholic Church. Among other subjects, incunabula dealt with religion, scholasticism, science, education, erudition, Classical scholarship, literature, and more vernacular writing.

The future of printing is bound up with the durability of the techniques devised in Gutenberg's workshop. Already in the fifteenth century, the processes and mechanics had been perfected to the point that they were to undergo little change over more than three centuries. The same presses, the same tools, the same gestures (though under threat today) endured through the ages. It was only in the nineteenth century that printing and composition methods were to alter profoundly as a consequence of the Industrial Revolution and by dint of the development of entirely novel techniques. If the press industry was then to discover the rotary printing press, the basic principles behind the machine were, however, much as before. Advanced equipment has meant that manual composition no longer features in high-volume production, falling into disuse several decades ago. It should be borne in mind, however, that the present-day computer keyboard, a replica of that on a typewriter (as well as that on a Linotype or Monotype), still possesses many of the characteristics of the job-case as it already existed in the fifteenth century: flat, horizontal format, ergonomic shape adapted for easy handling (occasionally, as in the past, tilted), separation of upper- and lowercase, division into modules in which each unit is allotted a particular sign (the key stroke mirroring extraction from the type-box), and so on.

Gutenberg symbolizes the transition between the persistence of medieval heritage and the take-up of modern equipment. If his contribution and that of his entourage were of undeniable importance, the precise fallout is hard to gauge. Some have hailed Gutenberg as the inventor of movable type and the printing press, others limit his role to the development of techniques he had learnt elsewhere, and seek to emphasize parallels and links with paths explored previously in Europe. Similarly, appraisals of his impact range from acknowledgment of his preeminence on the material front to an appreciation of an extraordinary aesthetic creation for which technical aspects had primarily constituted a springboard. In all events, it is a matter of record that Gutenberg managed to combine a certain number of processes, improving them in his workshop with exceptional results. It is possible that he spent about fifteen years rendering the manufacturing process operational and shepherding the first viable products through the press. The longevity of his materials, to which printers will be beholden for more than three hundred years, testifies to the technical repercussions of his realizations.

The Renaissance—fifteenth and sixteenth centuries

79
Geographical map based on gorges reproduced in a work published in 1517–18. Engraving, 8 × 16 in. (20 × 40.3 cm).

The penetration of printing by way of movable type is one of the discoveries, inventions, and upheavals that signaled the end of the Middle Ages and Europe's entrance into the modern era. A few decades after the development of typography in Mainz, Europeans were to journey to distant lands and begin the long march to colonization—Christopher Columbus reached the New World in 1492, Vasco da Gama discovered a sea route to the Indies in 1497, and Fernando Magellan became the first to sail around the world in 1519. These explorations were to transform Western conceptions of the world at the end of the fifteenth century.

Encounters with new lands were accompanied by profound soul-searching that found a parallel in heliocentricism—the theory according to which the Earth does not constitute the center of the universe and which attracted the Church's singular displeasure. Thus were perceptions of the world turned upside-down. In addition, the close of the Middle Ages was marked by wholesale shifts in the structure of global power, including the collapse of the Byzantine Empire in 1453. The medieval empires of Christendom were replaced by the piecemeal constitution of European nations and states. At the same time, Europe was making great strides in technology. These were events that transformed the face of the world and raised the curtain on the Classical age.

The Renaissance inaugurated a period in which the practice of typography played a massive and integral role. Renaissance thought in the cultural, technical, scientific, and artistic fields strove to revive Greco-Latin culture and return to the values of Humanism. The universities underwent notable developments, while, as culture and the written word left the dominion of the Church, a middle class was formed. Man was now recognized as an individual and became the measure of all things. The status of the craftsman evolved towards that of the artist and in the pictorial field generally, secular themes were being added to religious subjects. Aesthetics developed on new foundations, which incorporated mathematical logic and perspectival representation.

Directions in print and graphics
The Reformation and the spread of printing

Ever more widespread, printing was one of the prime movers of the era. Its influence and extraordinary potential are fully exemplified in the Reformation. The reach of the socioreligious challenges of the time are rooted in the propagation of Protestant ideas. As a new media and means of distribution, materials printed in mobile type proved exceptionally effective. Texts by Reformers appeared and circulated in Europe in phenomenal quantities that can be counted in the millions. As early as 1518, Martin Luther's writings were brought out in copies of hundreds of thousands. It is estimated that from then until 1520 more than three hundred thousand copies of Luther's writings were sold. In 1517, he had launched the Protestant movement with the ninety-five theses on the virtues of indulgences (whose sale he denounced) addressed to the Archbishop of Mainz and perhaps actually stuck on the doors to Wittenberg Castle. In 1520, he

80
First edition of Luther's Bible translated into German, Wittenberg, 1534. Title page.

81
Handwritten religious bill on parchment (authorizing the *choriers* [corresponding to minor canons] to seek alms), Saint-Flour (France), 1454. It may be the oldest known French illustrated bill.

82
Printer's bill, Johann Mentel (or Mentels?), c. 1469.

83
Holbein (attributed to Ambrosius and/or Hans Holbein the Younger), sign outside a school master's, possibly commissioned by Oswald Myconius, Basel, 1516. Fir, 22 × 26 in. (55.5 × 65.7 cm).

84
Peter Schöffer, earliest catalog of nineteen typographic-printed books offered for sale (an advertisement for his own bookshop), Mainz, c. 1470.

85
Illustrated bill for a hatter's, block-print, France, fifteenth century.

86
Shop-sign, Rome, 1584.

publicly burned the Papal Bull condemning his *Theses*. Adding to what was to be a sizable written corpus, slightly later he began work on a translation of the Bible into the German language. Brandishing the full might of the printed word, Luther denounced the cult of the image; in his eyes iconolatry is but an obstacle to the unmediated worship of God.

The Reformation also testifies to the strong bonds between religion on the one side and the written word and iconography on the other—a relationship that had already been hand in glove in the Middle Ages, when the book was chiefly the preserve of the clergy. Text and image thus found themselves plunged once again into the heart of conflicts that soon showed the true power and relevance of the new technique. "Printing played a considerable role in the diffusion of Lutheran ideas. The Reformation was the first religious movement to fully benefit from it. Luther himself described printing as 'the greatest and the most extreme act of divine Grace by which the influence of the Gospel is propagated.' Censors were simply submerged in the flood of lampoons: between 1516 and 1524 print-runs multiplied by nine; the number of booksellers in Germany soared from one hundred and fifty in 1518 to nine hundred and ninety in 1524, turning out more than one million items of which at least a third comprised writings by Luther. It was thus that the Reformer stamped his mark on the European mind. Up to about 1550, he remained the most read author."[48]

Buoyed along by this tide of global change, in which of course it participated, printing spread quickly. By the end of the fifteenth century, the technique had established itself in practically every country in central and Western Europe and, by about 1500, there were more than one thousand presses in Europe, scattered over some two hundred cities. Hive of production and intellectual hotbed in one, the printshop represents simultaneously the space where the book takes its material form and its place of publication. If Germany should be considered the birthplace of the first successful developments in letterpress, other countries were soon making their own contributions to the technique, introducing specialties and discovering innovations. Humanist printers active in Italy gave exceptional impetus to the book and to creativity in typography even prior to 1500, before France in its turn made its own distinctive impact during the first half of the sixteenth century.

The printed bill

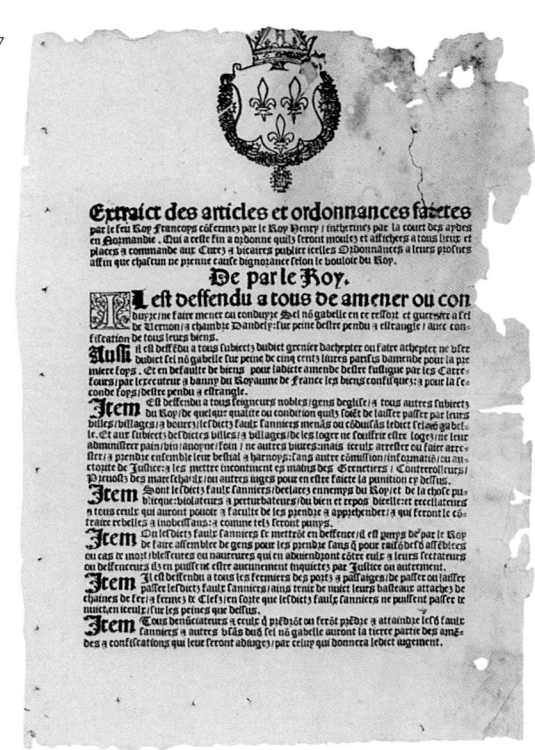

87

87
One of the oldest surviving French royal *placards*, c. 1550 (regulating the *gabelle* [salt excise] under Henry II).

Ever since the technique of typesetting had been developed in the mid-fifteenth century, the book had represented a significant proportion of printed matter, a situation that endured until the eighteenth century. By the end of the fifteenth century and on throughout the following decades, however, other media were also leaving presses. The beginnings of letterpress also benefited the mass production of leaflets, pamphlets, lampoons,[49] and broadsheets, which had previously been in the form of handwritten sheets. "Posters" were also printed, though few of these have survived to the modern era. If some of these bills certainly continued to be produced by xylography, typographical broadsheets of the time resembled a larger page from a book. However, as movable type had dissociated the processes of impression of text and image, a broadsheet or bill could often be composed of words alone. Occasionally, though, woodcut illustrations might be combined with type. Dating to 1454, one of the earliest known (perhaps the oldest) French illustrated bills, handwritten, is exactly contemporary with the advent of typography in Mainz. It was there, in about 1470, that Peter Schöffer issued the catalog of his print-shop in the form of a bill—thus producing, with typographical material, the very first catalog listing printed books for sale in his own store.

Movable-type printing was introduced to England by William Caxton. After studying in Germany, in the Netherlands, and in Belgium, he initially set up a workshop in Bruges, where in the middle of the 1470s he produced one of the first books printed in English. Caxton returned to England in 1476, establishing the first typesetting print-works within the precincts of Westminster Abbey. The first broadsheet and the first illustrated book printed by this process in Great Britain are ascribed to him, dating from 1477. Following William Caxton, a certain number of typographers and printers set up shop in England from Western Europe, a phenomenon that continued until the beginning of the sixteenth century. As further evidence of the migration inherent in the beginnings of typography and the phase of its first expansion, itinerant printers from Germanic countries had been active in Paris since 1470.

By the sixteenth century, many printed bills were state orders enshrining legal edicts. In France, other *placards*, in all probability fewer in number, proclaimed open criticism of government or religion. In 1534, the Affaire des placards (in the course of which bills venting Protestant opposition to the practices of the Catholic Church were stuck up in Paris, in other cities, and perhaps even onto the king's bedroom door) spurred the powers that be into taking action curtailing the freedom of bill-posting and reinforcing controls over the book. Francis I reacted by persecuting the Protestants, accused of heresy. Printers, publishers, and compositors, like Antoine Augereau and Étienne Dolet, were condemned to the stake, while others fled into exile. The poster and the printed word, however, quickly put their special strengths of reproducibility and ease of distribution to good effect.

In France a system of royal privilege (or charter) was soon imposed on each new publication. The printed word was thus made to serve the supreme authority, just as it had echoed to the voices of the discontent (in particular concerning matters of religion). The French king undertook a whole raft of measures that subjected jobbing-printing and bill-posting in Paris to the scrutiny of the regime, and anyone caught contravening these measures risked the death penalty. In 1561, Francis I's grandson, Charles IX, furthered this repressive policy, proclaiming that "all printers, peddlers, and vendors of defamatory placards will be punished, the first time with the whip, the second with their lives."[50] Censorship also turned the screw on printing in Great Britain, where tough controls and restrictions had long been in force.

Gothic and Roman type

If the poster is a powerful vehicle of persuasion, the book is a mighty material agent for the diffusion of thought. The very form of the book, even in its details, has been the object of significant, suggestive, symbolic choices. For instance, as regards characters, an important distinction arose between the use of Gothic and Roman type for page-setting. A considerable number of religious and official texts marry a Gothic style to often angular, linear, and massive forms. The rigorous structure underpinning certain Gothic alphabets conferred an imposing appearance on such writings. Other texts, neither sacred nor liturgical, embraced Roman styles inspired by Humanist scripts that themselves sprung from the Caroline. A brief excursion back into history confirms that a hierarchy between writings had already existed in antiquity. For example, Egyptian hieroglyphics might be reserved for monumental texts, such as official inscriptions and epitaphs, while hieratic script was employed for administrative writings, legal and commercial documents, and finally demotic script met regular, everyday needs. With the appearance of typeset printing, Gothic and Roman characters quickly coalesced into the two main families of type. In Germanic countries, Gothic type was to remain widely used for several centuries, in certain areas until the twentieth century. Although centuries old, it was a form that never ceased evolving, however. Roman type was also employed in the Germanic domain, if in varying proportions according to epoch and region (the cultivated elite of Germany had recourse to it, particularly in the eighteenth and nineteenth centuries). Apart from in Germanic lands, Roman coexisted with blackletter for a relatively brief length of time, before rapidly becoming the type of reference.

Born in the Classical age and enjoying links with the Renaissance spirit, Roman type branched out into a whole new category of forms resulting from the Roman capital, Humanistic scripts, and Caroline minuscule. Be they Gothic or Roman, the very first typographical characters were designed from preexisting models bequeathed or inspired by handwriting and correspond to the transposition of bookhands and lettering over to technical processes and into new materials. Over time, typographical forms shook off their derivation from manuscript bookhands, adopting more strictly calibrated forms with precise contours and distancing themselves from shapes arising from the movement of the writing hand. In a script written by hand, each letter remains, by definition, unique, with each occurrence of the same sign necessarily entailing variations. With movable type, each character adheres to a fixed form.

In the Renaissance, the repertoire of common characters was supplemented and modified by new signs. From this point of view, a certain number of enrichments were already to be found in the Middle Ages; it should be noted that the use of Arabic numerals had been introduced around the twelfth century and that medieval punctuation already included the full point, comma, colon, question mark, and signs for paragraphs, chapter ends, cross-references, and so on. Printed punctuation incorporated new practices and signs, widening the use of the exclamation mark, colon, parenthesis, and apostrophe. Systems of punctuation covering ten or so signs at least can already be identified in the first incunabula books. Interior punctuation (rarely deployed in the Middle Ages) became more frequent, accompanying the increasing number of visual textual divisions—sentences, phrase divisions, paragraphs, subparagraphs, etc., developments that could equally be applied to details of letter design. Movable type served as an understudy for handwritten script, which, for economic or other reasons, it might occasionally supplant. With incunabula, if bookhands were being ousted by typography, illuminations, decorations, and coloring remained at least in part manual operations to be carried out after impression.

47

The handwritten book survived well into the sixteenth century, thought it became rarer. However, typography did not put paid to the art of script and fostered instead a veritable revival that exceeded the ambit of the book. To an extent, the calligrapher took up where the scribe and copyist left off, and forms of script were developed or given a new lease of life, as testified by Cancellaresca. There again, families of letters can be distinguished depending on the nature of the texts in which they appear. Thanks to the publication of the first handwriting primers, various models for writing were soon taken up. For example, Giovanbattista Palatino's handbook, published in 1540 (and reprinted several times until the 1580s), enjoyed notable success. Similar phenomena took place in Italy, England, and Spain, where in particular the quill of Juan de Yciar (whose writing handbook was widely hailed) elevated the art of penmanship to new heights.

The emergence of Roman type

Gutenberg's life is shrouded in mystery, uncertainty, and inaccuracy. "Fewer than forty documents contemporary with his life bear the name of Gutenberg."[51] It appears that his researches lasted between 1435 and approximately 1450. It is during this period that his workshop began producing printed materials, creating for the purpose one of the very first typographical characters—Donatus and Kalendar, dubbed "DK-type."

Between the printing of the 42-line Bible (about 1452–55) and the fall of Mainz in 1462, the earliest printed works concentrated primarily on religious material (constituting approximately three-quarters of the output). Such incunabula provide evidence of the form in which movable type initially appeared and its subsequent transitions. Already, certain engraved character-sets betray the waning influence of historic Gothic and the transition towards Roman (Italian calligraphers and Humanistic printers will soon play a major role promoting the uptake of Roman type). As early as the 1450s, Gutenberg, Fust, and Schöffer created characters that presented alteration with respect to the medieval Gothic form. When Gothic is maintained, it is sometimes joined by designs inspired by Caroline and Humanistic. This resulted in rounder, lighter-looking letters that slowly abandon the density and specific mass of Textura. In Fust and Schöffer's workshop, these new types were used to print the *Durandi Rationale Divinorum Officiorum* (1459) and the Second Mainz Bible (or 48-line Bible, 1462). In addition they appear in the *Catholicon* (1460, perhaps printed by Gutenberg), including a fair proportion of uppercase letters that are no longer Gothic in form but prefigure Roman capitals.

Thus, letterforms were already evolving during the very first decade in which movable type had become a fully established activity. The new characters stressed and consolidated forms that gave rise to many alphabets still used today in large numbers. It may be that the passage in the mid-fifteenth century from the gesture of handwriting to letters drawn and engraved in isolation facilitated or fostered this transition. The first printers, however, by and large stuck by blackletter styles, Textura and Rotunda (Round Gothic). Johann Sensenschmidt's Textura and Erhard Ratdolt's Rotunda are characterized by what is at first glance a remarkable design. In a further sign of rejuvenation, Fraktur letters became the official form in Germany. Breaking with the rectilinear look of Textura, Fraktura is rounder and remained a reference for publishing and the press in Germanic lands until the twentieth century.

As printing was well and truly taking off, German art, too, was entering a particularly fecund phase, with paintings and engravings by Dürer, Grünewald, Holbein, Baldung Grien, Cranach, and so on. In 1525, one of the most outstanding talents in the German artistic Renaissance, Albrecht Dürer, published a work presenting his own form of Gothic lettering based on a system of geometric elements. In the field of the image, engraving played a significant role in the visual arts. The illustrated areas of incunabula were still pulled from woodcuts, with the foremost artists contributing to a practice particularly prevalent in German lands. Albrecht Pfister, a printer in Bamberg, was among the first, in about 1460, to

90

90
First great polyglot edition of the Bible by Cardinal Ximénès at Alcalá, 1514. Page corresponding to the beginning of Genesis.

bring out illustrated books. He printed a text composed in movable type with a woodcut image in a single pass. If Germany was a late entrant in the Renaissance in the fifteenth century, exchanges with Italy, where the High Renaissance was already in full swing, clearly benefited German artists who made visits there—just as the arrival of Italian artists in Germany brought Humanism.

Italy—typography's second homeland

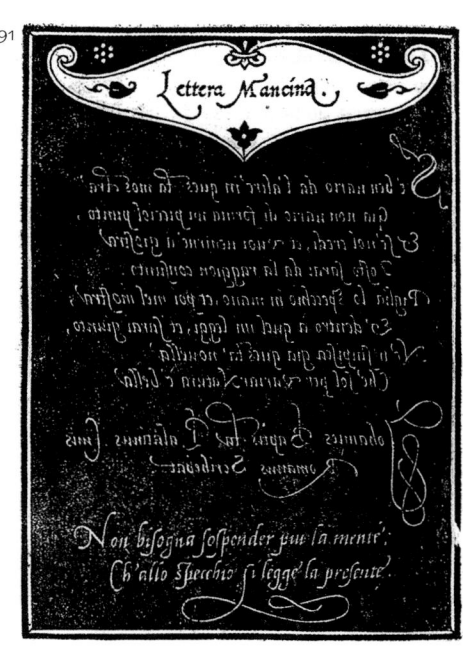

91
Giovanbattista Palatino, writing-book, Rome, 1553 (1st ed. 1540). Plate showing the "Lettera Mancina": Cancellaresca typeface, written right to left.

Germany, birthplace of the fledgling achievements of the typographical technique in the West in the mid-fifteenth century, soon found itself sharing the limelight with neighboring lands. In Italy, new perspectives were opening up in the field of the printed book, with corresponding creativity in typeface design. There, as elsewhere, news of the novel process of reproduction spread initially in the wake of the fall of Mainz in 1462. Italy proved fertile ground for developments in typography. The Renaissance arts of the Quattrocento were sweeping all before them and artistic exchanges with Germany were singularly active, in particular in Venice. In Rome and Florence, too, the intensity of this artistic and intellectual ferment was extremely favorable to the reception of the letterpress technique. Desirous of republishing the Classical literature of Greece and Rome, Humanists proved instinctively receptive to the new practice. Against this backdrop, typography made important advances. Through its overall structure, as well as through the adoption of Roman type, the form of the book was coming into clearer focus. At the same time, image-making benefited from reciprocal influences between Venetian and German artists, who exchanged iconographical and figurative themes.

With regard to the history of the creation of typefaces, the passage from the fifteenth to the sixteenth century corresponds to a watershed. If the editions of Gutenberg, Fust, and Schöffer already employed archaic forms of Roman characters from the late 1450s,[52] a visible transition from Gothic script to Roman letterforms occurs in Italy very soon after 1465. Some of these alphabets are known by the name, "Venetian characters," the Serenissima being at the time a hub for letterpress printing. Like the original equipment and printing processes, these new types proceeded to last for centuries, without falling into disuse, although, over time, they did undergo gradual changes in form. Between 1500 and 1800, the three principal phases were split into Old Roman (encompassing what the Anglo-American domain calls Old Style), Transitional Roman, and Modern Roman. If these umbrella categories are still accepted as the publishing standard and a reference in terms of legibility, they are perceived perhaps very differently today than in former times. Users have become so habituated to them that it is hard to imagine the effects these new alphabets had in the fifteenth century.

Both the book and the letter evolved a great deal in Italy after 1465. If Venice constituted the center of the flowering of Italian typography, other significant poles included Florence, Milan, and Bologna. These unique developments shone brightly for almost half a century, during which exchange, travel, and transmission played key roles. Before the Italian Aldus Manutius came to the fore, the earliest printers to establish themselves in Italy hailed from Germany, such as Konrad Sweynheym and Arnold Pannartz, the brothers Johann and Wendelin von Speyer, and Erhard Ratdolt. The Frenchman Nicolas Jenson, for his part, probably passed by Mainz before settling in Italy. Furthermore, if he in his turn encouraged several of his countrymen to join him there, interchange between the two countries increased, as demonstrated by the Le Rouge family, who became highly active in many book trades by 1470, setting up in Venice and Paris, as well as in other towns in Italy and France.

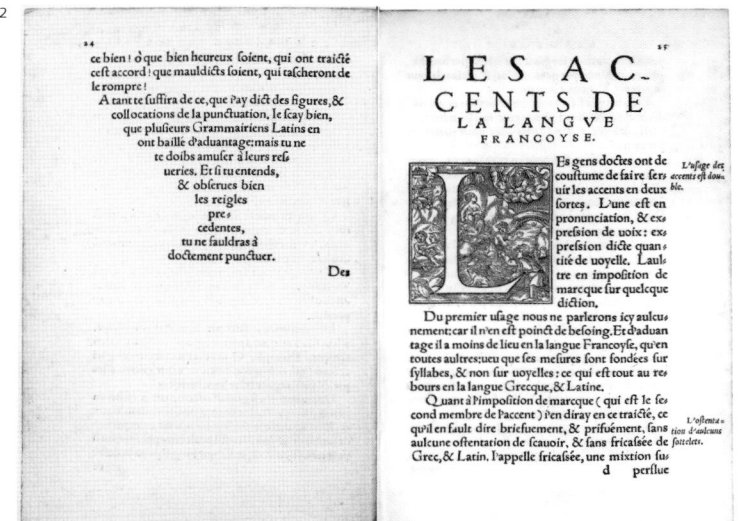

92
Double page with a large ornamental letter from Étienne Dolet's treatise on translation, *La Manière de bien traduire d'une langue en aultre*, Lyon, 1540.

The first printers active in Italy came mainly from Germany and set up shop in the surroundings of Rome. These included Konrad Sweynheym (who had worked for Peter Schöffer in Mainz) and Arnold Pannartz, who together founded a print-works at Subiaco a little before 1465. It was there that the first known Italian books were printed and where, around 1465, one of the earliest (possibly the very first) Italian types appeared; this might also be the first Roman alphabet created as such, incorporating Roman capitals. Starting out from Humanistic script as the chief model, it still conserves traces of blackletter forms. One of the tomes set in this alphabet was a *Lactanctius*, followed a little later by a text by Cicero that deploys another alphabet by Sweynheim and Pannartz. This design testifies to the quest for a new form and contributed to the genesis of a new family of printed letters. In 1468, these two printers settled in Rome—at the very time Roman type seemed poised to supplant Gothic.

93 **raſ arteſ ingenio predıtaſ peroptaſ :el arteſ. preſertım quatuor ultımaſ qua uocant . que plerunꝗ magno ſplend**

93
Type by Konrad Sweynheym and Arnold Pannartz, Subiaco (near Rome), 1467.
The letters clearly present transitional forms.

While Konrad Sweynheym and Arnold Pannartz were pioneers, the book and typography were on the point of undergoing an unprecedented flowering in Venice. Printing was enriched by new elements that compounded burgeoning activity in type design. Nicolas Jenson endowed the new Roman type with a remarkable form. Through his efforts, the letters acquired greater smoothness, and his contribution remains admirable for the exceptional design of both his characters and his page layouts. An engraver (generally presented as Master of the Mint at Tours in France), Nicolas Jenson is supposed to have been sent to Mainz on the order of King Charles VII in 1458. His mission was to learn the movable-type process and to bring back knowledge of it to his own country with the idea of setting up presses there. As is the case with a certain amount of data surrounding Gutenberg, veracity of these facts is not universally endorsed.[53] If Jenson might well have worked at one time for Gutenberg, the death of Charles VII clearly made him lose sight of his mission and, departing from Mainz in 1462, he traveled through Germany before setting off for Italy. Working initially in Venice for Johann von Speyer, he succeeded him in 1470, the year of the latter's death. In the same year, the earliest character by Nicolas Jenson was used in composing a book known, from its author's name, as the *Eusebius*. Esteemed as much for his technical prowess as for the creative aspect of his production, Jenson printed more than one hundred and fifty books in the space of ten years. Through his succeeding publications, he refined the early state of Roman type, bequeathing his name to a typeface. This was probably the first Roman alphabet of appreciable uniformity and harmony, and is particularly agreeable to read. Consummately polished, Jenson's letter designs and page settings became a benchmark for several decades afterwards; today, Jenson type is one of the classics of typography and remains in use. In Venice, contemporaries of Jenson were bringing other innovations in bookwork. Moving away from merely replicating the manuscript, their publications resembled more and more books as the term is now understood. Already in the Italian typography of this period, Roman was getting the upper hand over blackletter, consolidating the growing tendency of this type to be selected for printed books.

94 **poſſem dicere. Porro cū duæ ſint cōſuetudines quæ uirtuti ſubīcidunt:alia qdem quid quodꝗ entiū ſit īſpicit:alia ue ro quid uocetur:atꝗ in hunc modū de rōali philoſophiæ p te diſſerunt. Enimuero moralé philoſophiæ pté ī ſubiectos**

94
Roman type by Nicolas Jenson, Venice, 1475.

In these works distinctive features regarding composition and page-setting quickly emerged. In 1476, Erhard Ratdolt, a German printer and publisher from Augsburg, settled in Venice, where he created one of the earliest known title pages to mention the title of the work, the name of the printer, and the place and date of publication. Previously it had not been regular practice for handwritten and printed books to include a page for the title or for information concerning the production of a work. Ratdolt is also credited with having refined and disseminated the impression of decorative initials, confirming the divorce of the printed book from calligraphy and handwritten interventions generally. Most probably, in about 1470, he was also a pioneer in four-color printing, using a woodcut board for each hue.

95
Page from Plutarch's *Lives of Famous Men* printed in Venice by Nicolas Jenson, 1478. Roman characters. Illumination by Girolamo da Cremona. Jenson called upon the finest miniaturists when issuing Classical texts. The ornamental letter Q shows the author seated before his desk.

If German know-how certainly made inroads in Italy, affiliations and transmissions also played a central role. Like Erhard Ratdolt, André D'Asola made several original innovations and contributions regarding book matter.[54] On the death of Nicolas Jenson, D'Asola took over the famous typographer's printshop. It was probably D'Asola, for instance, who started placing advertisements in books and he was also among the first to employ pagination. A successor to Jenson, D'Asola (known as "Torresani" and by the name, "Andrea Torresano") was the father-in-law of Aldus Manutius[55] (the most famous Venetian printer of the era), with whom he entered into partnership.

The work of Aldus Manutius

Like a number of his peers, Aldus Manutius combined the activities of printer, typographer, publisher, and Humanist. One of the more remarkable aspects of his career relates to the reissue and printing of monuments of Greco-Latin literature. His print-works, baptized the Aldine Presses, embraced some major initiatives that contributed greatly to the ongoing transformations of the book. History ascribes to Aldus Manutius the development of works printed in smaller formats, which were made after 1501 due to a concern with economy, and which he described himself as "little books of handy size."[56] The size of some earlier incunabula and manuscripts imposed high manufacturing costs. In opting to decrease type size and make the text less cluttered, the Venetian printer reduced the size of the book to a scale more in keeping with the hand. For that purpose, he produced the first Italic type designed and engraved in about 1499 by Griffo (Francesco da Bologna). At the same time, Aldus Manutius published the work considered to be his masterpiece, the *Hypnerotomachia Poliphili* (1499), in which the association of text and woodcut illustration results in gloriously harmonious effects.

Previously, Griffo had already created another type used by Aldus Manutius in the printing of a work by Cardinal Bembo (the alphabet from which the type known today as Bembo arose). This character, drawn c. 1495, numbers among one of the first fonts of the Elzevir type.[57] The Italic version of these letters was used for impression after 1501. Inspired by cursive hands, it allows for significant savings in space. The characters are slightly inclined, and are above all narrower than those of Roman.[58] Their oblique shape quickly became a ready alternative to the upright form, serving moreover to hierarchize and differentiate within the text. With the development of Italic type, the smaller-sized book flourished, especially in the publication of poetry. The first Italics maintained the upright capital form, conferring on them a certain cachet and proving, as in ancient times, that the interlock between upper- and lowercase is far from self-evident. As the forms of the initial stage of Roman became more characteristic, following Griffo's pioneering efforts, Italic, too, continued to evolve, as demonstrated in the version employed by Antonio Blado in about 1540, inspired by calligraphy by Ludovico degli Arrighi. Covering both type and the book, Aldus Manutius's contribution has made him a figure of great note. The Aldine editions were pursued by his descendants, and after his death in 1515, he was succeeded by his son and then his grandson,

DE FALSA SAPIENTIA.

se, suaq; confirmet: nec ulli alteri sapere concedit; ne se
desipere fateatur. sed sicut alias tollit ; sic ipsa quoq; ab
alijs tollitur omnibus . Nihilo minus enim philosophi
sunt , qui eam stultitiæ acusant . Quancunq; lauda-
ueris, uer amq; dixeris;à philosophis uituperatur,ut sal
sa.Credemus ne igitur uni sese suamq; doctrinam lau-
danti; an multis unius alterius ignorantiam culpan-
tibus?Rectius ergo sit necesse est,quod plurim sentiunt,

explicabo ; non tanq̃ recenseatur . Igitur;cum illum multa in umbra sedentem
comperissem ; ita initium interpellandi
eum feci. PETRVS BEMBVS FILI
VS . Diu quidem páter hic sedes:& certe
ripa hæc uirens; quam populi tuae istæ
densissimae inumbrant; & fluuius alit ;ali
quanto frigidior est fortasse,q̃ sit satis .
BERNARDVS BEMBVS PATER.
Ego uero fili nuspiam esse libentius soleo;
q̃ in hac cum ripae, tum arborum , tum
etiam fluminis amoenitate:neq; est,quod
uereare,nequid nobis frigus hoc noceat,
præsertim in tanto aestatis ardore: Sed
fecisti tu quidem pérbene;qui me ab iis
cogitationibus reuocasti;quas & libentis-
sime semper abiicio , cum in Nonianum
uenitur;et núc quidem nobis nescio quo
pacto furtim irrepserant non modo non
uocantibus, sed etiam inuitis .
BEMBVS FILIVS . Derep. sci
licet cogitabas aliquid , aut certe de trium

ensuring that the Aldine achievement would continue well into the sixteenth century. Aldus Manutius himself had inherited his materials from his father-in-law, André D'Asola, Jenson's successor: one of those prestigious handovers that are clearly a key phenomenon of the golden age of printing and the book in Italy.

Structure of the book, construction of the letter

In Italy, then, at the turn of the sixteenth century, printers were making fundamental contributions to typography, by perfecting and distributing small-sized printed books, in consolidating the birth of the Roman type, in creating Italic, and in instituting the title page, and so on. This last, rather ornamental and close-set in its initial phase, with woodcut art framing essential information about the publication, subsequently grew less busy.

At the same time, independently of typographical concerns directly impinging on the art of the book, in several countries parallel researches into the letter were being taken up, which found a ready echo in the history of graphic design and writing. Capital letters in particular underwent rationalization. Redrawn along geometrical lines in the Renaissance spirit, the letters were to an extent redefined. It was a tendency foreshadowed in the work of Felice Feliciano, epigraphist and a friend of Andrea Mantegna. According to Albert Kapr, "the first geometrical construction of Roman capital lettering was produced by Felice Feliciano, the Veronese art collector and art historian in 1463."[59] His forms precede other investigations that are occasionally based on them, including those appearing in the famous treatise by Luca Pacioli, *De Divina proportione* (Venice, 1509). In the wake of these far-reaching proposals, many scribes, penmen, and artists in Italy came up with various solutions for the construction of capital letters.

This geometrizing drive with respect to uppercase letters was felt in other nations. In Germany in 1525, Albrecht Dürer published his researches in *Instruction in Measurement with the Compass and Rules of Lines* (*The Art of Measurement*), in which he supplied plans for the application of geometry to architecture, ornament, and other fields, including typography. He pursued leads for a new structure for Roman type that had already been explored in Italy by Feliciano and Luca Pacioli, and it is possible that Dürer's concerns might

96
Griffo (Francesco da Bologna), engraving with Italic letterforms for Aldus Manutius, Italy, c. 1500.

97
Aldus Manutius, text of a page from Pietro Bembo's *Ætna*, Venice, 1495.

98
Erhard Ratdolt (printer), first page of the first edition of Euclid's *Geometry*, Venice, 1482. Believed to be the first illustrated science book and one of the first printed works to include geometric diagrams.

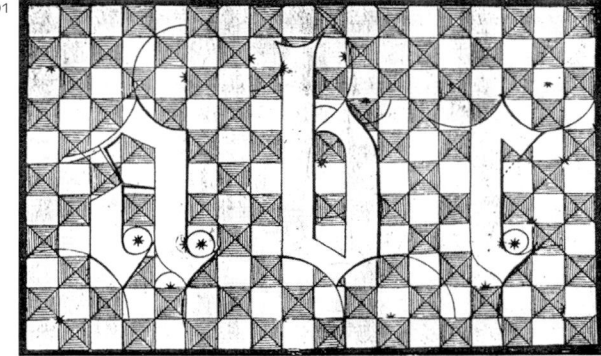

have originated in his voyage to Rome (a common practice among German artists). In accordance with an analogous principle, he created from scratch a geometrical decomposition with horizontal ruling of blackletter (on the Textura model).

A few years after the publication of Dürer's work, the geometric approach to the capital surfaced in France, becoming tangible in *Champ Fleury, ou l'Art et Science de la proportion des lettres* by Geofroy Tory, published in Paris in 1529. Such geometrical concerns consolidated the growing distance from handwritten forms and the search for a measurable, standardized construction dissociated from the manual act. If the proportions of the letters remain related to eye and hand, the outline begins to bears the stamp of a pre-mechanical, constructive logic.

Perhaps, within the impulse to redefine that overran Italy, Germany, and France (and which has been revived countless times since), what was taking shape was a desire to institute a universal system of measurement. Over the centuries, the attempt to create letters with definable or calculable forms, bolstered if necessary by a geometric order, has been a recurrent phenomenon, remaining particularly prevalent today.[60] Moreover, this quest for proportion and measurement split into various divergent paths, a fact that aroused many objections (voiced in various periods and by individuals of every stripe) and even violent rejection—in particular by those for whom writing should always proceed from adroitness of hand.[61]

France and Antwerp

"Therefore accept that almost divine art, which Germany invented, of artificial writing": thus reads the colophon of the very first book printed in France (the *Epistolae* of Gasparino Barzizza, 1470). After Germany and Italy, France soon carved out its own place in the history of the book, typography, and type design, particularly during the first half of the sixteenth century. Thanks to the successes already met with in Germany and Italy, developments, improvements, and new departures were now in the offing in France, too. The work of the Frenchman Nicolas Jenson in Venice had besides provided an early demonstration of this in the 1470s. The evolution of typography and the book in his homeland benefited a great deal from the interest shown it by Francis I. By the same token, printing and printers were now encountering controls, oversight, censorship, and even draconian repression. As a scholar-prince, Francis I had visited Italy, and the French Renaissance only truly began to take wing on his accession in 1515. During his reign, several measures were taken with the aim of monitoring and gathering together every book printed in his kingdom. Taking on the moniker, "Father of Letters," in 1537, Francis I demanded that a copy of each publication be sent to his royal library. In addition and during the same period, the king commissioned a special type from court printer Robert Estienne, who was to cut the famous royal types by Claude Garamond. Besides those of Garamond and Estienne, other great names in typography, contemporaries or sometimes precursors, were to distinguish themselves, such as the Paris-based Geofroy Tory. The French capital was already one of the top cities in the publishing world, while the second typographical center, Lyon (where printing dated back to 1473), was also making significant strides, in particular with the work of Jean de Tournes. In the space of a few years, other workshops sprung up in various towns, in southern France at Albi in 1475, and Toulouse in 1476. By the mid-sixteenth century, movable type had made its way to many other French cities, such as Rouen and Troyes.

99
Construction of the letter R. Left: Felice Feliciano (epigraphist from Verona), beginning of the 1460s. Right: Luca Pacioli, Venice, 1509.

100
Albrecht Dürer, construction of Gothic lettering, Germany, 1525.

101
Construction of Gothic minuscules, beginning of the seventeenth century.

In Antwerp, Christophe Plantin (of French origin) emerged in his turn as one of the major figures of the era. Already, printing was entering a phase of high-volume production, a phenomenon to which, by the number of its presses, workmen, and publications, Plantin's workshop bears generous testimony. In France, printer-publishers (booksellers) were then Humanist scholars who, as in Italy, contributed to the divulgence of the classics of antiquity. In parallel, developments in education and improved literacy levels increased demand for printed matter, not least chapbooks, religious pictures, and handbills.

In 1469–70, the vice chancellors of the University of Paris had convened three German printers—Ulrich Gering, Michael Friburger, and Martin Crantz—and charged them to set up the first printworks in France, at the Sorbonne. By 1470, the press was up and running, and issuing the first book to be printed in Paris, Gasparino Barzizza's aforementioned *Epistolae*[62] (the work, in Latin, had a circulation of a hundred copies). The text is printed in Roman type, like the one in use in Italy, and similar characters, at a still fledgling stage, were already on the way to replacing blackletter. By the middle of the 1470s, there appeared in Paris one of the very first works in the French language, *L'Aiguillon de l'Amour divin*, printed by Pierre le Caron, soon to be followed by *Les Grandes Chroniques de France*, published by Pasquier Bonhomme in 1476–77, a date by which a press in Venice had published a work that numbers among the very first printed dictionaries (German–Italian). Engraving seems to have made an appearance in the French printed book a few years subsequently, in 1481.

The work of Geofroy Tory

Among all the printer-scholars in sixteenth-century France, Geofroy Tory stands out, his efforts having a major impact on the development of the book. Venturing on several occasions to Italy where he undertook his studies, Geofroy Tory settled in Paris as a printer. A peerless exponent of his art, he was also a recognized intellectual and taught at the University of Paris. His activity was wide-ranging and his culture extensive: a philosopher, scholar, translator of Greco-Latin texts, bookseller, and type-founder, he even displayed a notable talent for illustration. By 1530, his competence was such that he was appointed "printer to the king," Francis I. Geofroy Tory continued to steer the art of the book away from the Gothic form, as much in page layout as in choice of types.

Like Estienne and a number of his peers, Tory abandoned blackletter for Roman in religious texts (a significant proportion of publishing at the time). Tory was not satisfied with adhering to existing models and sought novel ways of creating letterforms, proposing new departures in the field of type design. In his famous work *Champ Fleury*, published in 1529, he expounded a project for geometrizing capitals, whose proportions he thus redefined. As we have seen, research along similar lines had already seen the light of day in regions nearby, *inter alia* by Pacioli in Italy and Dürer in Germany. At the end of *Champ Fleury*, Geofroy Tory explains his conception of the letter thus: "It should be noted that letters are so noble and so divine that they should never be misshapen, mutilated, nor altered from their own figure. Because, as I have said [...], they resemble the human body."[63] Seeking to reduce the proportions of the human form to a geometrical construct, he based his work on a square divided into ten parts, horizontally and vertically, into which he inscribed, in addition to the human body and face, letterforms. His capital letters (except for uppercase M and Q) were thus inserted within this square space, a phenomenon towards which more than a millennium previously the *capitalis quadrata* had already been tending. He explained his intentions in the following manner: "the letters are so well proportioned naturally that, in the likeness of the human body, [they] are composed of limbs, that is to say, of numbers of points and lines consisting in equal partition [*consistant en esgalle partition*, i.e., divided equally]."[64] If Geofroy Tory thus brought variations to the letterform, many imperfections subsist (in our eyes) in his approach at the level of typographical detail. For example, among other instances, the space between the words is highly irregular and the employment of the capitals hardly

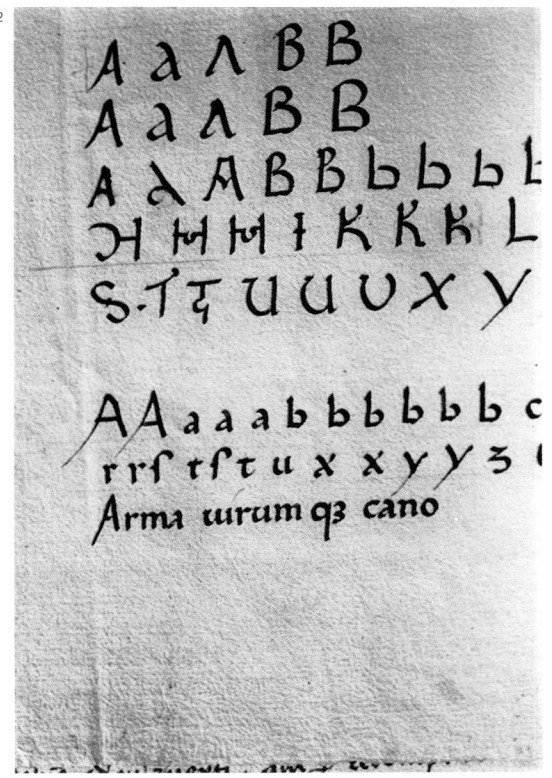

102
Jean Heynlin (German prior and vice-chancellor of the Sorbonne), lettering exercises, c. 1470. "Probably a model devised while the presses of the Sorbonne were in the process of being set up."

103
Page of the first book published in Paris, the *Epistolae* (Letters) of Gasparin de Bergame (Gasparino Barzizza), presses of the Sorbonne, 1470.

104
First Roman alphabet by typographers of the Sorbonne employed by the first letterpress printworks to be established in France, Paris, 1470.

105
Last page of the first book published in Paris, Gasparino Barzizza's *Epistolae*, 1470. Colophon in verse supplying the names of the three Sorbonne printers.

106
Pierre César and Jean Stoll's workshop (of German origin, they were pupils of the earliest typographers at the Sorbonne), type from the beginning of the second Parisian printshop, 1474. Note the original forms of the capitals.

107

108

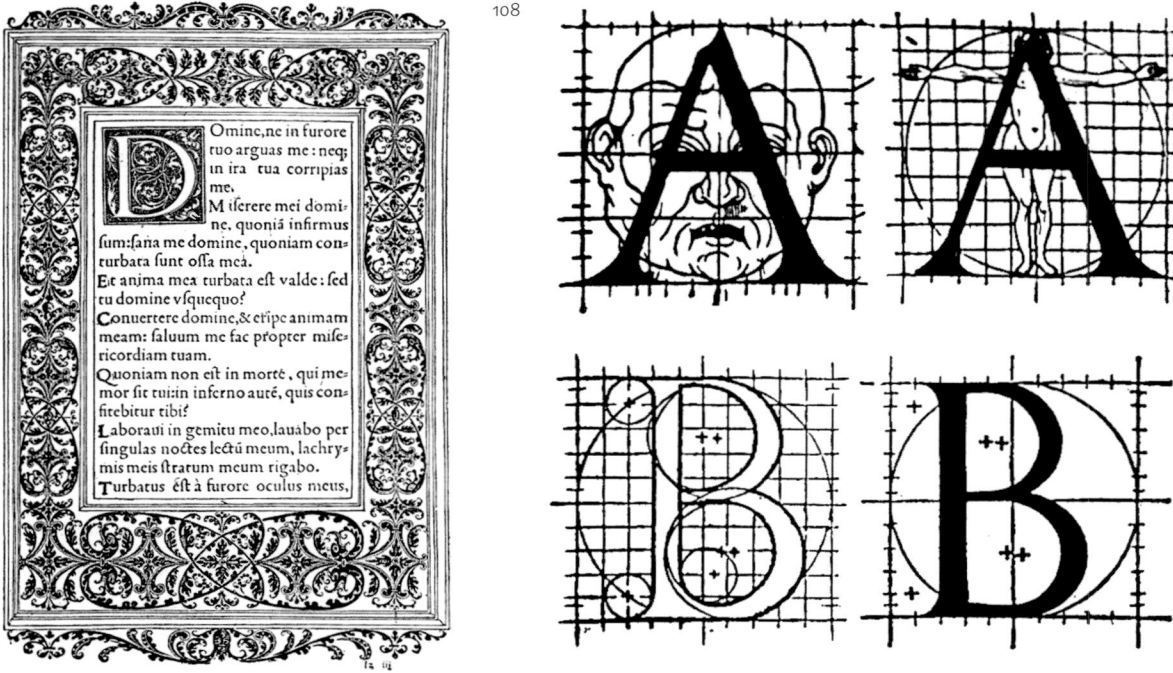

systematic.[65] But Tory was not yet disposed to ponder these aspects of "microtypography,"[66] and in the order of things these questions can surely be considered secondary. Tory also expended his energies establishing rules governing French spelling, pronunciation, and punctuation. It was through his usage that the employment of the apostrophe and the cedilla (i.e., "ç") became uniform. The designs of his Roman font, which were to serve as a model for centuries to come, confirm his role as an initiator and pioneer.

Claude Garamond, Guillaume Le Bé, and the Estienne dynasty

Claude Garamond, born probably some time between 1480 and 1501 (the current state of knowledge does not allow his date of birth to be pinpointed any more accurately),[67] extended Geofroy Tory's efforts. Posterity has conserved his name more diligently, and he still enjoys great renown in the field of typography. In spite of his fame, elements of his biography remain extremely obscure (as is the case with Gutenberg), and these uncertainties impinged on questions of attribution. During his training and afterwards, he is supposed to have come into contact with figures such as Geofroy Tory, Antoine Augereau, and Simon de Colines.[68] Just as in Italy or Germany, apprenticeship with a master remained a preeminent means of transmitting typographical expertise.

Claude Garamond boasts one of the most august names in the history of Renaissance typography. Known above all for his contribution to the field of type design and manufacture, he mastered every aspect of production. In his own foundry, he not only drew designs, but cut, cast, and sold the type himself. Like Jenson in the previous century, Garamond did much to further the shift of letterforms towards the Roman, the historically decisive and durable form. Apart from types—undoubtedly the lion's share of his career—from 1545, he is also noted as a publisher, though his activity in this field was probably of lesser import.

The first Garamond type was being used in 1530, or at a date close to this. The character that bears his name was developed between 1530 and 1540 on behalf of Robert Estienne. As the basis for this enterprise, Garamond had probably studied the Romans and Italics of Aldus Manutius, Griffo, and Geofroy Tory, and perhaps other models, too, such as Jenson's. By pruning them of their medieval atavisms, Garamond modified the demeanor of the letters. Distancing his work from the irregularities inherent in manuscript (and therefore from the special charm that can surround it), he created in France a Roman font that can be considered

& iuftitia, & fanctificatio & redemptio : vt quemadmodum fcriptum eft : qui gloriatur in Domino glorietur. (.:,-?'!') 1234567890. ¶ Æ A B C D E F G H I K L M N O P Qu R S T V X Y Z. á é í ó ú ñ ꝑ ꝑ ꝑ q̃ q̃ q̃ q́ a e n m t abcdefghiklmnopqrſstvuxyzz & ꝰ. ɋ ſt ſſ ſſi fi ſl ſl ſſiffiffl ſb j t̃ r̃ ; à è ì ò ù á é í ó ú â ê î ô û

109

Letterform of the Garamond "r," contemporary version by ITC (International Typeface Corporation).

110

Type by Claude Garamond, *romain parangon*, France, c. 1530–44.

111

Italic *gros-romain* by Claude Garamond.

Lire et Escrire.

Lettre Italique.

a. b. c. d. e. f. g. h. i. lz. l. m. n. o.
p. q. r. ſ. s. t. v. v. u. x. y. z.

Capitales.

A. B. C. D. E. F. G. H. I. K. L.
M. N. O. P. Q. R. S. T. V.
X. Y. Z.

Lettre Romaine.

a. b. c. d. e. f. g. h. i. k. l. m. n. o.
p. q. r. ſ. s. t. v. u. x. y. z.

Capitales.

A. B. C. D. E. F. G. H. I. K. L. M.
N. O. P. Q. R. S. T. V. X. Y. Z.

Ceux ceulx grandement , qui prononcent
boy, coy, ꝛoy, effe, ꝛoy, aché, ec.

Voyelles.

a. e. i. o. u.

---

one of the first, if not the very first, to present such a consummate degree of refinement and harmony. The letters present finer terminations than was the norm and their overall design makes for particularly comfortable reading. In Francis Thibaudeau's eloquent terms, "the purification of form is obvious and one can plainly declare that here, for the first time, with this engraving, writing turns into typography."[69]

Another famous type cut by Garamond was the *grecs du roi*. This also resulted from an order commissioned by Robert Estienne in 1540–41. Francis I wanted an alphabet "to use

112
Fragment of a page from a work published in 1585 by the Compagnie du Grand Navire (an association of booksellers and printers), France.

to print books in Greek to put in our libraries."[70] This character set would be used by Estienne, Parisian printer at court, and earned Garamond the title of "cutter of the king's [type] characters." The French Imprimerie Nationale in Paris houses the entire set of royal punches from which the *grecs du roi* were cast; their heritage value is such that in 1946 they were listed as a historic monument. The *grecs du roi* share the same aura as Garamond's Roman types, which had enjoyed immediate and probably unparalleled success. If many printers purchased the fonts the moment they came out, Garamond was also counterfeited and plagiarized. By the end of the sixteenth century, the type seems to have been used in Germany, Italy, Switzerland, England, the Netherlands, and Spain. The value of Garamond type reaches down to the present-day; it is regarded as a major sixteenth-century type and as a masterpiece in itself, beautiful, superbly readable, timeless.

Claude Garamond died in 1561. The majority of the typographical material from his foundry (punches, dies, type, etc.) was bought up by Christophe Plantin and Guillaume Le Bé. Trained by Garamond, and traveling to Italy like many of his contemporaries, the latter is sometimes presented as his successor. Guillaume Le Bé improved the types used by Robert Estienne and worked among other things on Arabic and Hebrew alphabets. For Christophe Plantin, he engraved a type whose capital foreshadows a later stage of Roman: "The majority of lowercase punches are a repetition, with very few variants, of Claude Garamond's type forms. The handling of the capitals, on the contrary, with the decided fattening-out of the main lines, evinces the almost complete application of the horizontal serif lines adopted partly by Grandjean and standardized by Didot."[71] Le Bé's foundry was then among the most important in Europe and right up to the beginning of the eighteenth century it was headed by his descendants, the celebrated typographer Pierre-Simon Fournier being the son of the last director of the Parisian firm. Although rather neglected, this typographer of the second half of the sixteenth century contributed significantly to type design (as Francis Thibaudeau remarked), at a time when Roman letterforms were already heralding Transitional type forms.

Whereas Claude Garamond is chiefly known as a creator of type, the famed Estienne dynasty distinguished itself in the various allied fields constitutive of printing and publishing. Within this great Humanist family, history recalls above all the work of Robert Estienne—"printer to the king," like Geofroy Tory, and himself son of the printer, Henri I Estienne. It is he who, at Francis I's request, ordered and purchased the Garamond and the *grecs du roi*. He was thus the first to employ types by Claude Garamond—before many other printers and typographers took up the cause. In accordance with the aesthetic and functional dimensions of these alphabets (regularity and simplification, refinement of design, optimization of legibility), Robert Estienne opted for restrained compositions, very different from the abundantly decorative and illustrative trends of the time. His son Henri II together with other descendants pursued his investigations, developing the art of the book *en famille*. In about 1550, Robert Estienne went into exile in Geneva to escape the persecution of the Protestants.

Lyon and Antwerp as centers of printing

With the prestige of royal commissions gilded by the presence of personalities such as Geofroy Tory, Claude Garamond, and Robert Estienne, Paris was the initial focus of printing and typography in France. Soon after the establishment of printworks in Paris, however, French typographical expertise rapidly sprouted in other cities, not only in France, but sometimes also abroad. Several printers, publishers, and type designers of high reputation exercised their craft

113
Jean de Tournes (printer), book of poetry in
italic, *Suyte de la Marguerite des marguerites des
princesses* (Marguerite de Navarre), Lyon, 1557.
Italic by Robert Granjon. Vignette (woodcut)
by Bernard Solomon.

in Lyon. Lyon was particularly known for its popular and illustrated editions.
Above all posterity records the names of Robert Granjon for type design
(drawing, engraving, and casting) and Jean de Tournes for publishing (letterpress
printing and bookselling).

Starting in the mid-sixteenth century, the work of Christophe Plantin soon
made an exceptional impact. Of French origin, Plantin had settled in Antwerp in
1549. At once commercial hub and hive of intellectual activity, Antwerp was at
that time a dynamic city and one of the largest in the world, where ideas were
exchanged freely. The growth of printing also fostered the spread of the
Reformation. Christophe Plantin set up what was a highly productive printshop in
Antwerp in the 1550s, with subsidiaries established in Paris and Leyden.[72] More
than twenty presses were active in Antwerp printers (perhaps even double that at
the period of most intense activity), probably requiring the collaboration of from
one hundred to one hundred and fifty craftsmen. The impact of Plantin's work is
often associated with the launch of book manufacture and printing on an
industrial scale, and he was indeed the head of one of the most significant
printworks of the time (some authorities cite it as the largest).

However, around 1500 (that is to say a half a century before Plantin's
establishment), the German printer Anton Koberger had already headed up a
workshop of comparable scale, equipped with probably more than twenty presses
and employing a hundred artisans. Based at Nuremberg, Koberger's printworks
was in regular contact with outlying countries and had already opened several
branches (in Venice, Vienna, Krakow, and Paris). Among the one thousand five
hundred to two thousand publications brought out by Plantin, the most often
quoted is his celebrated *Biblia Poliglotta* (produced around 1570), an eight-
volume Bible in five languages. At a very early stage, Plantin introduced into his
books images reproduced on copper engravings. His output is as remarkable for its quality as
for its outstanding range. His work won him widespread recognition and he was named
printer to King Philip II of Spain.[73]

Founded in the mid-sixteenth century, Plantin's concern stayed in business for more than
two hundred years. His first successor, Jan Moretus, had married his daughter, Marie, heiress
to the printworks (her descendants would be related to Rubens). By dint of this long
genealogy, the workshop remained active until about 1870. In 1876–77, the workshop of
Christophe Plantin and his successors was converted into a museum (the Plantin Moretus
Museum still exists in Antwerp).

The heavy hand of censorship

If the propagation of French printing during the first half of the sixteenth century owed
something to royal decree, the controls exerted by the authorities put an end to this golden
age. The weight of politico-religious censorship is generally accepted as the cause of a
substantial decline in French printing. With hardly a foothold in Italy and Spain, the
Reformation was simply extirpated in France. There, as early as 1521, control over and
censorship of the printed text had been strengthened by Francis I. Sales were regulated, certain
publications were prohibited, and undesirable books could be consigned to the flames in
public book-burnings; on occasion, even printers perished in the same way. Recalcitrant
publishers, booksellers, printers, typographers, and authors risked prison, sometimes even
death. Many Protestant printers and publishers were forced to choose exile to others lands.
Pursued during the Counter-Reformation, they left to settle in other cities, with Geneva as
one of the principal destinations. There, in the middle of the sixteenth century, Calvin founded
a forum for Protestant ideas whence they spread throughout Europe. The city of Geneva also
represented one of the main distribution centers for printed materials peddling Reformist

114
Book-burning, illustration from the *Liber Chronicarum* of Hartmann Schedel, woodcut, 1493.

dogma and it was from there that many of these writings reached France. In Geneva as in certain other cities, Reformation-minded publishers could continue their activities without the risk of merciless persecution. Several bookselling dynasties were to leave France at this juncture. Robert Estienne for one settled in Geneva in the mid-sixteenth century and his heirs continued working in the city for three centuries, doing much to catapult it to among the first rank of publishing centers.

Like the Estiennes, the descendents of the famous Lyon printer Jean de Tournes long boasted an illustrious name in Geneva. His descendants went into exile in 1585, again to escape religious persecution, and the workshop remained in business there for nearly two hundred years, until 1780. A few years prior to Robert Estienne's departure for Geneva, the printer and publisher Étienne Dolet was pursued by the Inquisition and condemned to death for atheism and heresy. A staunch defender of religious freedom, Dolet published or possessed Lutheran and Calvinist texts. In 1546, he was burned alive on the square of Place Maubert in Paris, together with his books (his publications had already been destroyed by fire two years previously in an auto-da-fé on the square in front of Notre-Dame), charged with "blasphemies and sedition and exhibiting proscribed and condemned books."[74]

In 1534, Antoine Augereau, printer and typographer, had suffered the same fate. These events, a dramatic phase in the history of both printing and publishing in France, testify to the violence inherent in censorship. The severity of persecution in France had a devastating impact on the art of the book, only a few short years after its heyday.

The first century of letterpress printing

As illustrated by the descendants of Peter Schöffer, Aldus Manutius, Estienne, Jean de Tournes, and Christophe Plantin, the role of transmission and association was paramount in the perpetuation and aura of the printing trades during the Renaissance. Prestigious, fruitful, these affiliations were in keeping with the origins of letterpress. The direct descendants of Peter Schöffer, who had married the daughter of Johannes Fust, kept working in the arts of printing until at least 1555 (Fust's son moreover ascribed the actual invention of letterpress printing to his father). In Italy, Nicolas Jenson's equipment passed to his apprentice, André D'Asola (Torresani), the father-in-law of Aldus Manutius, who was to inherit it in his turn. For his part, the publisher, printer, and engraver Simon de Colines was to marry Henri Estienne's widow. In Antwerp, meanwhile, Jan Moretus succeeded to Christophe Plantin whose second daughter, heir to the printworks, he married (Plantin's two other daughters also married printers). Hence, the constitution and development of publishing houses, print-works, and typography relied partly on the family and on matrimonial interests.

Similar types of professional and patrimonial transmission furthered the dissemination of expertise, all the more so since the publishing, printing, bookselling, and typographical trades were then interdependent. Publishing and manufacture remained closely enmeshed practices, just as design and realization were still interwoven.

In parallel with the transmission of know-how, printing and typography were gradually being enriched by new factors and objectives. In the space of a few decades, the creation of a genuine industrial and cultural publishing practice had begun to add to technical mastery and the preoccupation with productivity. Over time, the form of the printed book discovered its autonomy and specificity. Affecting the various components of graphic design (composition, illustration, color, characters, etc.), the interior was being reorganized, along lines that tend to make it appear less cluttered. Justification was introduced, together with centralized balance, running heads, colophons, pagination, visual cues to textual divisions, new-found punctuation marks, signs uncoupled one from the other, and so on. The pages at the beginning and end of the book lent themselves to a host of effects for the eye: the triangular arrangement of the text on the title page (known as a pendant or *cul-de-lampe*), cruciform colophons, heart-shaped texts, or others set in the shape of cups, etc. As in figured verse, writing here revels in its iconic dimension.

The image shared in the transformations affecting the inside of the book. Playing an exceptional role in manuscript work, from the start the image had remained a valued component of the typeset book. "The percentage of illustrated books is considerable: approximately one-third of all incunabula."[75] If in the past illustrations had been printed from woodcuts, the sixteenth century witnessed the spread of copper engraving. During the next century, copper was to replace wood as a means of printing images, and engraving would prove extremely beneficial, for example, in the production of scientific texts. In the sixteenth century, the woodcut tended to be employed to illustrate less exalted publications, while copper engraving was associated with those intended for the cultured elite. From the end of the fifteenth century, with the introduction of movable type, the general aspect of the book tends to become less massive, with the quest for legibility and clarity heralding significant developments. These transformations affect letterform as much as composition and page-setting as a whole. In fact, the advent of technology reconfigured the text—its distribution in space and its inner hierarchy and mobile-type composition amounted to a genuine break with the thousand-year-old practice of the copyist. It was to take several decades, sometimes several centuries, for sentences, paragraphs, chapters, and the other visual demarcations recognized today to become fully established in bookwork. These separations resort to all kinds of graphic devices, from punctuation to the leaving of non-printed spaces. As regards color, incunabulum leaves were mainly confined to black and white. Except for full-scale decorations and manual illuminations, or for complementary impressions in color, typography was to be largely wedded to the monochrome for several centuries.

Upstream of page-setting, other factors relating directly to the text also modified the sixteenth-century book, from its type to its language. In many places, the arrival of the printed book was followed by the adoption of Roman type, replacing Gothic. It was a character polished in Italy and France in the half a century from the 1470s to the 1530s, as demonstrated by the work of Nicolas Jenson, Geofroy Tory, and Claude Garamond. In the course of the sixteenth century, the Roman form began to dominate in a significant proportion of European publishing.

At the same time, another phenomenon of prime importance was transforming writing in the sixteenth century. The Latin language, employed less and less since the thirteenth century, was retreating before the Romance languages. In 1539 in France, Francis I promulgated the ordinance of Villers-Cotterêts that imposed the replacement of Latin by French in notarial and legal instruments: these writings were henceforth to appear "in the French mother tongue and not otherwise."[76] This phenomenon recurred over broad swathes of Europe, with Latin being progressively abandoned about the middle of the century, ousted by vernaculars. Over time, books were commonly to be printed in English, German, and French.

By the turn of the seventeenth century, however, Western typography had emerged from the first great chapter in its history. Meanwhile, it had already traveled round the world, with the first printworks on the American continent being established probably in 1535 by Giovanni Paoli, followed by another in Mexico City in 1539, then Moscow in 1553, India in 1556, Japan in 1590, North America in 1639, and Iran in 1640.[77]

As the Renaissance drew to a close, the onset of the seventeenth century seems to mark a lull in the typographical field compared to the previous era. The seventeenth century, however, was to witness a number of offshoots that were to become significant for later developments: modifications of and experiments on Roman type, the formation of a written and historical culture relating to the printing trades, distribution of periodicals, and so on.

The passage from the seventeenth to the eighteenth centuries

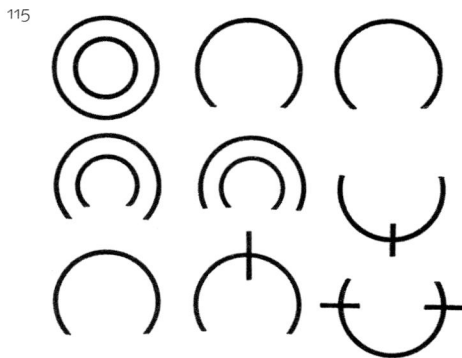

115
Marks for various qualities of herrings, Hamburg, 1702.

116
Pottery manufactory mark, Tervueren, c. 1720.

The close of the Renaissance thus marked the onset of a new era. The political and social climate of the seventeenth century was extremely turbulent, with Europe the scene of large-scale religious and political wars. Monarchical absolutism based on divine right was widely institutionalized and control over the printed word remained very firm. The organization of training and the trades generally was changing and academic systems were imposed upon the guild system. For the history of typography, the seventeenth century is sometimes presented as a fallow period, with few outstanding formal innovations emerging. Certain major dynasties of printers, publishers, and type-founders established in the seventeenth century were still operative, but in France among the more than two hundred thousand Protestants who fled religious persecution were many of the country's printers. They set up workshops in Germany, Switzerland, the Netherlands, and England. Through the intermediary of such networks, publications in French arrived back in France, including a significant proportion of periodicals.

Print practices and printed media

In the realm of printing, after the relative calm of the seventeenth century, the turn of the following century heralded transformations and radical changes. The historian Robin Kinross sees this era as an essential chapter in the history of typography, which, according to him, was on the brink of attaining modernity in the full sense.[78] First all, this was due to the process of printing becoming far less secretive than it had been, at least partially, since Gutenberg. Because demarcations grew up between production (preparation in the workshop, fabrication, printing proper) and publishing activities (publication and planning), this era has been seen as signaling "the beginnings of a separation between 'printing' and 'typography.'"[79]

Generally considered less dazzling than that of the Renaissance, seventeenth-century typographical practice did nonetheless undergo expansion in various areas, as regards media, for example. Broadly, with respect to the book, "at the end of the sixteenth century, forms [...] are limited to a fixed number of types. The priority of the visual element in the constitution of the book was no longer fully experienced and was being hidebound by shopfloor conventions. Over the following decades, the typeset title page gives rise to other pointers. Little by little, the title becomes codified, the name of the author is isolated, the use of type styles and sizes is arranged hierarchically according to the importance of the information it provides; divisions between lines and wording coincide. Immediately informative, unsurprisingly symmetrical— the title page, almost identical to that of today, imposes its restrictive logic."[80] Beyond the book, typography expanded increasingly into other territories, in particular through the propagation of less bulky printed materials, such as handbills. If the seventeenth century saw the advent of paper money in the West, in several countries the periodical (news sheets, canards, gazettes, sporadically issued broadsheets, etc.) began to take root, gaining a still greater hold as the century progressed.

Since the invention of movable type, newspapers and topical or informative media of all kinds had sprung up in diverse forms, including almanacs. In France, the *Kalendrier des bergers*, published from 1491 onwards, is hailed as "the ancestor of the periodical."[81]

117
Upper section of a page from *La Gazette* (French periodical founded in 1631 by Théophraste Renaudot), September 1632. Top: woodcut with one of the earliest specimens of "white lettering."

118
Flier for a hatter's, Great Britain, eighteenth century.

In Venice, gazettes began appearing from the mid-sixteenth century. (Their name derives from a currency, since they sold for a *gazzetta*.) These current affairs publications were distributed in the form of broadsheets or booklets sold by hawkers or other street vendors. Apart from secular woodcuts, they form part of the earliest generation of printed media to reach out to the population at large.

Relating to political or religious events, the first significant development of the press (news periodicals) dates back to the beginning of the seventeenth century when it germinated to the west and north of Europe in urban centers where printworks were already well established. From 1609 on, the earliest intelligencers and journals were probably printed in this manner, in Augsburg, Frankfurt, Antwerp, the Netherlands, France, and England. In 1631 Théophraste Renaudot's celebrated *Gazette* was founded, which "can be regarded as the first French periodical."[82] Renaudot, a physician, had traveled to the Netherlands to gain knowledge of developments in printing. The royal privilege for the *Gazette* authorized him to print "the news, records [*gazettes*], and accounts of all that occurred and occurs as much within as without the kingdom."[83] "Founded [...] with the support of Richelieu, until the fall of the ancien régime it remained the official organ of the monarchy and maintained its privilege over current affairs until the revolution. This monopoly bestowed on it great authority both in France and abroad."[84] Renaudot's weekly initially contained four pages composed over a single column of a format measuring 9 × 6 in. (23 x 15 cm; roughly equivalent to the A5 format used in the UK).

At this period, the *Gazette* as well as other media were on the brink of incorporating the characteristics newspapers still possess today, such as leading articles, supplements, and press advertisements (probably limited to the form of the insert "small ad" until around 1800).

If, in particular for the press, the outlets were multiplying, evidencing a changing typographical landscape (as attested by contemporary depictions of hawkers), another phenomenon was simultaneously occurring that was to be of prime importance for printers. From the end of the seventeenth century, there began to be published handbooks directly relevant to the printing profession in which practical information was pooled.[85] In this manner, typographers, typesetters, and printers could share their know-how beyond word of mouth and hands-on experience. These publications could publicize new findings, from the history of the technology to explanations of methods and material aspects. As an example, Martin Dominique Fertel recommended a number of principles of typographical composition in *La Science pratique de l'imprimerie* (1723), covering detailed questions, such as the title-page: "The main words in a title should be in the largest characters appearing on the page. A pair of long main lines should seldom appear [...]. The words that must be in smaller characters are usually, *la, de le* [...] except where they are joined in the same line to a main word [...]. It has seemed to several workmen bereft of taste that the biggest character on the first page is always most agreeable to the eye."[87] Through such publications, printing and typographical practices gradually became publicly known. It had taken only a few years for the technique of movable type once operational to propagate throughout the West, but ostensibly much longer for it to be constituted into a body of knowledge, transmissible through its own medium—the typeset book.

The Roman character: towards a transition

From the seventeenth century on, the design of Roman type adopted a different form. These alphabets, sometimes qualified as "Baroque," sprung up in the Netherlands, France, and England. In typography, the Baroque spirit only truly expressed itself in decorative forms, in entitling, fancy lettering, initials, and ornaments.

A B C D E F F G
G H I J K L M N
O P Q Qu R S T T
U V W X Y Z
a b c d d e f g h h i j
k l l m n o p q r s t u
v w x y z ſ fb ſt &

119
Union Pearl type, Italic, Grover Foundry, Great Britain, c. 1690. One of the oldest known decorated typographical characters (the matrices survive). "It was not until late in the seventeenth century that the concept of embellishing the initial in the normal roman letter was investigated by typefounders in cast metal types." (Lawson)

With typography remaining largely subsidiary to reading, Roman type was rooted partly in a seventeenth-century classicism that extolled measure, rationality, and decorum. Earlier Renaissance types (designated variously as, *inter alia*, Venetian, Old Style, and Old Roman) constituted the first major categories of Roman. Relatively slowly over time, modifications in letter shape permit the denomination of a second major category, Transitional Roman (it should be noted that these large classes can allow subdivisions).

The seventeenth century experienced several modifications in this respect, which to our eyes may seem slow and understated: the difference between thick and thin strokes tended to become accentuated, construction is directed increasingly towards the vertical, the serifs are more attenuated and slender. The letterforms, increasingly contrasted compared to earlier forms, seem at once more compact and more fluent. These formal adaptations remain palpable during the following century, notably in the work of John Baskerville and Pierre-Simon Fournier (and, *a fortiori*, in their wake). In spite of these progressive modifications, the alphabets remain under a single umbrella category, as described in 1723 by Martin Dominique Fertel who "speaks only about the nineteen usual sizes of a single type which, since it could only be Roman, he does not even name."[87]

The Netherlands and France

Type conceived in the Netherlands numbers among the first to contain the signs of a variation (except for work around the *romain du roi* in France, in particular in respect of Philippe Grandjean's intervention on the project). In the eighteenth century, England and France took up the cause, whereas for a long time Germany was to maintain its practice of the Gothic form. In the Netherlands, several preeminent type designers arose in the seventeenth century, such as Christoffel van Dijck (1601–1669), Anton Janson (1620–1687, who settled in Germany), and the Hungarian Miklós Kis (1650–1702, some of whose fonts were to become known under the name Janson Antiqua). Some of their types are composed of generous forms, and are letters famous for their quality. According to whether they are in upright or italicized versions, the termination can form a point, a rounded apex or a broad, elongated curve with echoes of calligraphy. Some of these alphabets herald forms that, in the next century, typography will make its own, reflecting accentuated contrasts between main lines (stems) and hairlines and with pronounced, very fine serifs. This is a tendency exemplified in the characters of Didot and Bodoni.

As with character design, the fields of printing and publishing were particularly active in the Netherlands. The political and religious environment was conducive, and many a French printer driven out by persecutions or fleeing censorship had already found refuge there in the sixteenth century. In 1648, the Netherlands (then called the United Provinces) became free of Spanish dominion and won political independence and religious freedom. Ten years previously, in 1637, the very first edition of René Descartes' *Discourse on Method* had been printed there (the philosopher was at the time resident in the Netherlands). This spirit of tolerance was compounded by a flourishing artistic scene. The Netherlands enjoyed a significant position in the printing and book sectors, taking over the position that had been occupied by France at the end of the Renaissance.

Following the explosion of the sixteenth century, character design in seventeenth-century France seems to have become a more low-key affair, except for creations such as those by Jean Jannon (1580–1658) and the new alphabet ordered by Louis XIV, the *romain du roi* (devised in the 1690s). Jean Jannon, who trained in the Parisian workshop of Robert Estienne, showed his first fonts in specimens in 1621. His types, known as "of the University," whose conception betrays links with contemporary Dutch forms, have left an enduring name in history. If, a short time afterwards, his characters were indeed

Afcendonica Romeyn.
Quod quifque in ano eft, fci
unt. Sciunt Id qui in Aurum
Rex reginæ dixerit : Sciunt
quod Juno; Neque & futura
in Æ ABCDEFGHIKLMN
OPRSTVWXUYΣ ffl ffl *
([§†?✠℮ ABCDEFGHIKLMNO

120
Christoffel van Dijck, Roman, specimen, 1681.

SZENT

DAVID

KIRALYNAK

és

PROFETANAK

SZAZ ÖTVEN

SOLTARI

A' FRANCZIAI Nótáknak és Verseknek módjokra
MAGYAR Versekre fordíttatak és rendeltetek.
Szentzi MOLNAR ALBERT
által.

Mellyek most ujjolag kinyomtattattak

M. TOTFALUSI

KIS MIKLOS

által.

AMSTELODAMBAN.

MDCLXXXVI. esztendőben.

Miklós Kis, title page, second half of the
seventeenth century.

acquired and employed by the Imprimerie Royale (Royal Printing Works), the information surrounding this event appears inconsistent. The foreword to a volume treating of the royal punches, *Le Cabinet des poinçons de l'Imprimerie nationale* (1963), proclaims baldly that "Jannon sold to Sébastien Cramoisy [the first director of the Imprimerie Royale] the matrices used at the Imprimerie Royale jointly with those already in use." For his part, the historian of typography Alexander Lawson reports that Jannon "suffered the misfortune of having his type-founding materials confiscated by the king's forces at the instigation of Cardinal Richelieu. His punches and matrices were later placed under the care of the Imprimerie Royale [...]. The first use of these Jannon types was in the 1642 production of the cardinal's memoirs."[88]

Jean Jannon's types furthermore betray such a close correspondence to Renaissance characters that they were apparently exhibited under the name of Garamond at the 1900 Paris World's Fair. If production in the seventeenth century derives primarily from a prolongation of Renaissance creations, the transformations of Roman became clearer and increasingly marked as the next century wore on. In the Netherlands, several creators distinguished themselves in the field of letterform design, including the German Johann Michael Fleischmann (1701–1768) and Jacques François Rosart (1714–1774), both engravers for the famous Enschedé en Zonen printing foundry and works.[89] Fleischmann designed several dozen Roman alphabets (recognized for their quality and comprising some distinctive features, such as narrow forms and pronounced serifs), as well as Gothics and characters of calligraphic inspiration.

The work of Jacques François Rosart, who regularly issued specimens of characters, was also of prime significance, with many designs including, among others, scripts, decorative letterforms resembling those of his French contemporary, Pierre-Simon Fournier, ornaments, and musical notation. In 1769, a press advertisement appeared in *La Gazette* in the Netherlands promoting one of his recent creations, one of the first promotional documents of this nature in printed lettering. Creations by both Johann Michael Fleischmann (whose Roman anticipates Neoclassical forms) and Jacques François Rosart were to constitute a fund of inspiration for their immediate followers (for Giambattista Bodoni, in particular).

The role of the British: William Caslon and John Baskerville

In the eighteenth century England and France took up the typography and publishing torch from the Netherlands. Distinguished pioneers in Britain include most notably William Caslon (1692–1766) and John Baskerville (1706–1775), who both sought inspiration from Dutch seventeenth-century types to which British printers were regularly to have recourse. Censorship, which had turned its attention to printing since the very start in England (where, in the seventeenth century, repression had been as severe as in France), was loosening its grip. It was this changing situation that fostered the enterprise and printing business of William Caslon, who set up his own foundry in the mid-1720s. He had already engraved his character (called Caslon) in about 1720, a famous specimen of which he was to issue in 1734. Still an offshoot of Old Style forms, Caslon nevertheless contains Transition features. The clear-cut distinction between hairline and stem, together with fine, elongated serifs, confers precision, clarity, and generosity on the type; the slope of the Italic is particularly marked. With the rapid expansion of his alphabet, William Caslon acquired an international reputation and his type, having made inroads in England, crossed the Atlantic to the American colonies where it was used in the printing of the United States Declaration of Independence (July 4, 1776), as well as the Constitution (1787).

Much in demand in the eighteenth century, by the beginning of the next century Caslon had been abandoned. Repackaged as Caslon Old Face, it experienced an upswing of interest in the twentieth century, however, and has become a historical stalwart. In the trade one can

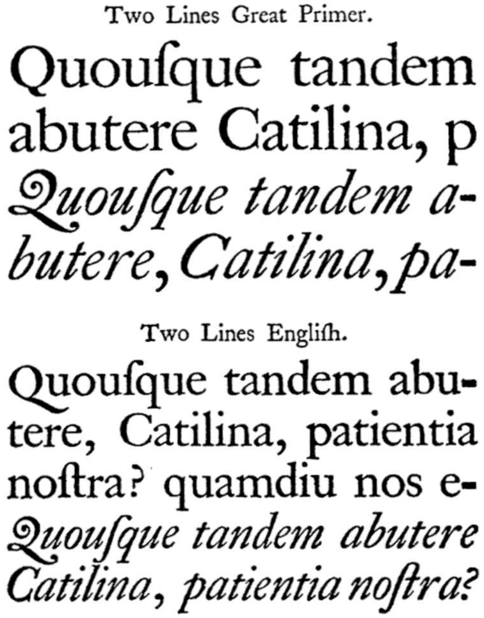

Two Lines Great Primer.

Quouſque tandem
abutere Catilina, p
Quouſque tandem a-
butere, Catilina, pa-

Two Lines Engliſh.

Quouſque tandem abu-
tere, Catilina, patientia
noſtra? quamdiu nos e-
Quouſque tandem abutere
Catilina, patientia noſtra?

CASLON
abcdefghijklmn
opqrsßstuvwxyz
ABCDEFGHIJKLM
NOPQRSTUVWXYZ
1234567890

122
Extract from a type specimen by William Caslon
& Sons, Great Britain, 1763.

123
Caslon type, designed by William Caslon I
(1692–1766), Great Britain, 1720s. (Version
presented by J. Müller-Brockmann in *Grid
Systems*).

even still meet with the phrase, "when in doubt, set in Caslon." William Caslon was prolific, designing fonts for the Arabic, Greek, and Hebrew alphabets, as well as for Latin. The size of his company is proof positive of a successful career. An influential figure, he set himself at the head of a dynasty that continued in business from generation to generation. In 1816, one of his direct descendants, William Caslon IV, was to print a letter design often cited as the first printed sans serif character.

In about 1757, that is to say, a generation after William Caslon I, John Baskerville developed a type of his own. Baskerville has the reputation of being the more innovative of the pair. An unrepentant perfectionist, Baskerville spent more than five years refining his alphabet. His fonts constitute a true Transitional Roman (an intermediate form between the Old Roman and the Modern, or Neoclassical, Roman), moving away from the typically Renaissance form to herald the later stage of the Roman. Certain of Caslon's tendencies are further emphasized. Particularly refined, the signs are more extended, as the letters A and E show, and the serifs are subtler.

By jettisoning weight, the letters become lighter and crisper. If Baskerville is hailed today for its legibility and harmony, it did not, unlike Caslon, meet with immediate success. Indeed it garnered sharp criticism (though it will not be the only type to do that) in Great Britain as well as in the United States, with one critic considering it too "sparkling," and another seeing it as a "means of blinding all the readers of the Nation [the United States] owing to the thin and narrow strokes of the letters."[90]. On the positive side, John Baskerville boasted enthusiastic support from Benjamin Franklin.[91]

Around 1800, the type began to be received more favorably (it had already inspired other alphabets), just as interest in Caslon was waning. Typeface design seems to be the most visible component of the career of John Baskerville, who had started out as a writing master in Birmingham. In addition to this, he also investigated other aspects of letterpress, including printing materials. In order to convey the refinement and crispness of his types, he set up his own foundry-printing works in 1750, assembled what amounted to a production line, concocted a formula for a tacky, high quality ink (a secret he guarded jealously), made improvements to the presses, and even, after years of experimentation, elaborated a process for making a paper blessed with an exceptionally smooth surface.

Historically, John Baskerville (whose team included punch-cutter John Handy) was responsible for three major innovations. As mentioned above, his type is, first and foremost,

BASKERVILLE
abcdefghijklmn
opqrsßtuvwxyz
ABCDEFGHIJKLM
NOPQRSTUVWXYZ
1234567890

124

SPECIMEN

By *JOHN BASKERVILLE of Birmingham.*

I Am indebted to you for two Letters dated from Corcyra. You congratulate me in one of them on the Account you have Received, that I ftill preferve my former Authority in the *if to mean well to the Intereft of my Country and to approve that meaning to every Friend of its Liberties, may be confider'd as maintaining my Authority; the Account you have heard is certainly true. But if it confifts in render-*

125

124
Baskerville type, designed by John Baskerville (1706–1775), Great Britain, c. 1757. (Version presented by J. Müller-Brockmann in *Grid Systems*).

125
John Baskerville, Roman and Italic types, specimens, Birmingham, 1757.

126
Diderot and d'Alembert's *Encyclopédie*, "Art de l'écriture," plate XII. ("Concerning the drawing quill. The drawing quill is so called as it is used to make capital letters, or majuscules, and the lines known as 'gifts.' This quill was used for ruling at the beginning of the last century [...]").

126

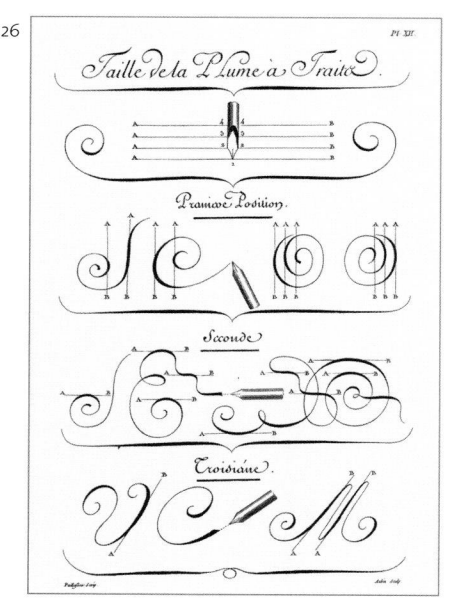

considered by many to be the first Transitional Roman. Then, by splitting the work of typeface design from that of the punch-engraver, he accelerated the demarcation of labor. And, finally, he overhauled the entire range of equipment and materials for typographical printing. If he paid special interest to techniques, in accordance with the finesse of his characters, it is this dual front (that others had essayed before him) that perhaps represents his core achievement. A few years after Baskerville's death, Beaumarchais acquired his types and employed them to print texts by Voltaire. Baskerville's punches are preserved at the University of Cambridge (Cambridge University Press), where, in 1758, he had been appointed printer.

Print and the written word in France

In France, after what was arguably a prolonged lull, creativity in typography and book art again began to pick up. Absolutism and censorship had proved a considerable burden to printing in the seventeenth century. Printing, like the right to post bills, was subjected to control and required official authorization from the court. In 1653, a governmental decree stipulated that "it is forbidden for any printer to print posters or memoranda without permission and for any person to post them under pain of death [sic]."[92] In addition, the Grand Siècle also saw the establishment of academies, which set about imposing their authority. The French Academy in 1634–35 was followed by the Academy of Painting and Sculpture in 1648 (founded by Mazarin), which was instrumental in forging the official *bon goût*, and the Royal Academy of Sciences in 1666.

The *romain du roi*

In 1640, Richelieu set up the Imprimerie Royale within the precincts of the Louvre. Attracted by the quality of Dutch publications, the cardinal brought over from the Netherlands "four press-men and four compositors"[93] in order to train the first team in charge of the Imprimerie Royale, following in the footsteps of the University of Paris, which, nearly two centuries previously, had invited the first printers from Germany.

The vested interest of the powers that be in printing continued to promote creation and production. Just as the *grecs du roi* had been designed by Claude Garamond at the request of Francis I, a "new typography illustrating the reign of Louis XIV" was created, "the typography of Louis XIV or the *Romain du Roi*",[94] also called Grandjean from the name of the man who developed it. This type was to be the exclusive preserve of the Imprimerie Royale. Launched at the very beginning of the 1690s, the type design was a vast project that was subcontracted to the Academy of Sciences. A committee of all the talents, set up to shepherd the project through, devoted itself to a meticulous study of extant characters,

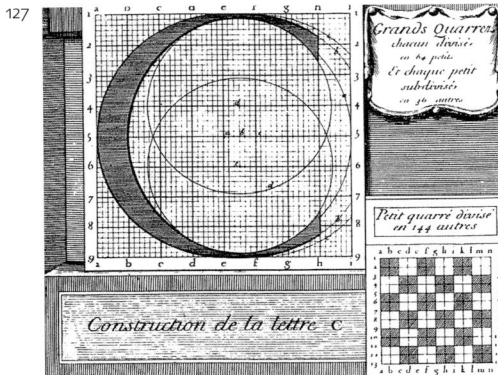

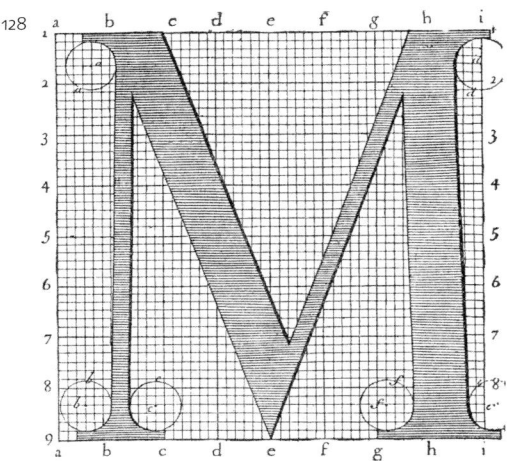

127
Construction grid for capitals for the *romain du roi* (Jaugeon method), France, 1692. Type designed for the Imprimerie Royale in the reign of Louis XIV.

128
Construction of the letter M according to the Jaugeon method. Side of the square divided into eight sections then subdivided into six, forming a grid of 2,304 squares. France.

establishing a system of measurement and a construction grid as the basis for determining the shape of the letters. The composition of the alphabet and the engraving of the punch were entrusted to Philippe Grandjean in 1693. The *romain du roi* is distinguished above all by rational construction and the quest for parameters and calculated solutions, and is a perfect reflection of the attitudes of an era concerned with reason, critiques, and science.

Grandjean takes as its starting point the structure initially established by the committee heading the project: a square grid divided into sixty-four square boxes, themselves subdivided into thirty-six smaller squares (division on one side into eight, followed by subdivision into six—thus in total a screen of more than two thousand micro-squares. For the Italic version, the grid is transformed into a parallelogram so that the verticals of the upright form align with the degree of slope selected. The stems of the *romain du roi* are broader than usual and the hairlines slimmer, their respective thickness attaining a ratio from approximately 1:5 in preliminary drafts (noticeably more contrasted than, for example, in Jenson or Garamond). In the upright version, as compared to earlier Romans, the axis of the letters is rectified and tends towards the vertical (before, characters presented inclined axes, particularly visible in the rounder letterforms). The terminations, tapering almost to nothing, appear more regular and are clearly distinguished from the body of the letter. Constructed from a base assembled with precision (an extreme of the kind), the face tends towards a structural, rationalized logic. If the effect of this standardization is to iron out particularities and irregularities, the alphabet nonetheless possesses a telltale marker: a small horizontal feature added to the natural shape of the lowercase "l" about halfway up. If this detail might be explained by a desire to distinguish royal alphabets from others, it was in fact "the upper horizontal serifs [...] that forced Grandjean to distinguish the lower case 'l' from the capital 'I' by a secant. This tiny addition became the distinguishing feature of types from the State Company."[95] Developed and improved by Grandjean, the *romain du roi* is among the first to display so visibly a Transitional Style. Foreshadowing a renewal in Old Style, it precedes later states of the Roman character (evident, in another fashion, in Baskerville's achievements).

In its time the *romain du roi* served as a spur to the production of other letterforms. If the project was already in embryonic form by the end of the seventeenth century, its completion was a long-term affair and it took half a century to engrave the twenty-one font sizes of the *romain du roi*. On the death of Philippe Grandjean in 1714, a one-time apprentice of his, Jean Alexandre, took over, and it was only a nephew of the latter, Louis-René Luce, who completed the mammoth task in 1745. An "exclusive" alphabet (only the king's print-works could employ it), the *romain du roi* remained the only type used at the Imprimerie Royale until the beginning of the nineteenth century (1811). A mainstay of typographical history, Grandjean undoubtedly draws part of its aura from its regal cachet.

Pierre-Simon Fournier

Following the creation of the *romain du roi*, it is the work of Pierre-Simon Fournier (1712–1768) that occupies the predominant place in eigtheenth-century France. If he severely criticized the approach of the committee initially appointed to oversee the royal type, he nonetheless appreciated Grandjean's contribution to the final commission.

Fournier was heir to a line reaching back indirectly to Garamond, as he was the son of Jean-Claude Fournier, the last director of the great foundry of the Le Bés in Paris, established in the mid-sixteenth century by Guillaume Le Bé (a concern with links to Claude Garamond, Robert Estienne, and Christophe Plantin). Eighteenth century to the core, Fournier's work embodies Classical elegance and Baroque tendencies. It testifies, in its coupling of rational perspective to decorative fantasy, to typography's versatility. Fournier's career covers roughly one hundred and fifty alphabets, drawn by his own hand, for which he would have cut some sixty thousand punches. Fournier is also the author of several textbooks packed with practical and technical data concerning type and typography.

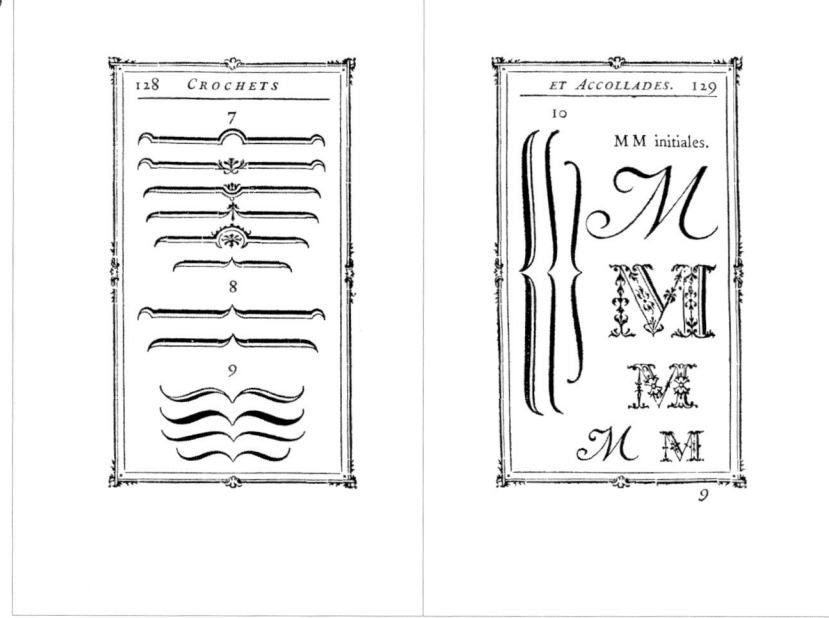

129
Double page from the second volume of
Pierre-Simon Fournier's *Manuel typographique*,
Paris, 1766.

In 1737, aged twenty-five, he brought out his first work, entitled *Table des proportions qu'il faut observer entre les caractères*. The publication was one of the studies from which sprung the typographical system of measuring letter size whose unit is the "point." For this purpose, he based his work on the (old) inch (an ancient measurement roughly equivalent to 2.7 cm, representing a twelfth of the *pied de roi*— the "king's foot"), further subdivided into seventy-two points (12 × 6). This graduated scale enabled him to precisely fix the number of points corresponding to various faces. At the time, in foundries as in printworks, old names were employed to refer to type size, but, as indications of approximate size (that could vary up to a half point), they could not give precise measurements. In this *Table des proportions*, for example, the common designations are replaced by numbers indicating the corresponding type set: 4 points for Perle, 6 for Nompareille, 12 for Cicéro, 44 for Gros-Canon, 96 for Grosse-Nompareille, etc.

At the end of the 1730s, Pierre-Simon Fournier established his own foundry and quickly became one of the leading figures in typography. He created and manufactured his types himself, from letterform design to punch-cutting, and his foundry was probably one of the very few to remain in the hands of a sole trader. To attain his ends, Fournier made a close study of the historical models. In 1742, he published his *Modèles de caractères de l'imprimerie* (though he was not able to print it as type-founders were not authorized to put works through the press). The work contains another important first: "One should also notice that the first suggestion of a 'family' of types comes in his work [as] three variants [...] for a 'cicero' type were shown in the *Modèles*"[96] (the idea of families of type was to catch on in the course of the twentieth century). Plentiful and exceptionally varied, Fournier's typographical legacy covers Roman characters (upright and italic versions), a number of decorative letters, ornamental motifs, innovations in the field of musical notation (on the basis of the "round note" or semibreve), and various categories of special signs (for the Zodiac, planets, phases of the moon, algebra, geometrical figures, etc.).

His Roman forms part of the Transitional Style, one particularity being that of aligning the ascenders with the summit of the capitals so as to obtain "greater uniformity."[97] Fournier's numerous fancy alphabets boast intriguing diversity in their decorative elements and provide important insight into the potential of the ornamental letter. Certain of these letters merely trace a second line running round the outline, while others are clad in floral forms of a Rococo style. Created in their hundreds and readily combinable, his decorative patterns amount to typographical translations of the engraved decorations that were so much in vogue at the time. According to Francis Thibaudeau, he "well deserves [...] to be hailed as the one who introduced into Typography the white, colored, or ornamental letter in its since adopted technical designation of fancy letter [*lettre de fantaisie*]."[98] Fournier's explorations correspond besides to the imminent development of letters of this kind that foundries were to take up more widely from the second half of the eighteenth century. Equally crucial were the writings with which Fournier accompanied his typographical designs and output, even publishing studies for "fonts for printing music." From 1764–66, he issued a further two volumes of his famous *Manuel typographique*, "useful for men of letters and for those practicing in various aspects of the Art of Printing," in which he expounded on how he manufactured his types, displayed his superb collections, and appended a list of European foundries. This publication was joined by other works specifically on the art and practice of typography, thus further consolidating it into an object of knowledge, a corpus that could be shared between all those in the trade. Fournier's writings had immediate repercussions. After studying his types, Giambattista Bodoni for one acknowledged him as a major precursor. Following in the footsteps of Philippe Grandjean, the work of Pierre-Simon Fournier evokes and represents above all type design.

If this sector occupied an important place in the field of typography, many other aspects of graphic creation, of print as a whole, and of the presence of lettering, signage, and notification in the public realms also found expression in France. Over time, this kind of production became increasingly diverse. As typefaces multiplied, so publicity and advertisements, for example, invaded posters and the press. Jobbing-work and printed ephemera, from labels to announcements to fliers, experienced an unprecedented boom. A creative environment, which had up to that point, due to its dependence on the continuity of the Roman character, remained largely stable and apparently unruffled, now exploded into a huge variety of practices and forms.

1728: a story of Paris street signs

Many phenomena exist—long since neglected, forgotten, subsidiary, sidelined, vernacular, or anonymous— that might easily furnish material for a very different history of visual communication and writing. This is demonstrated in the following account of events relating directly to changes in urban signage in the eighteenth century as reported in a text of the nineteenth. We are here a thousand miles away from the fame and royal cachet of a Grandjean, turning instead to how things were on the ground. This phenomenon concerns one of the most widespread occurrences of the written word in the public arena: street signs and house numbers. The text detailed the reactions caused in Paris by an official decision to have them changed.

> "In effect, streets were, one might say, only issued with their birth certificates roundabout 1728, when René Hérault, lieutenant-general of the police, who not only busied himself numbering the houses, but also putting the names of streets on a surer footing. He it was who, in this year, started putting up sheet-metal plates at the entrance and the exit of every street inscribed with what appears to have been their conventionally accepted name. These designations were painted in large black letters on sheets of tinplate cut to the same size and nailed up at the street corner [...]. As for the numbers, they were painted above the doors of the houses, white on a blue- or red-colored ground [...]. Before long it transpired that the sheet-metal plates bearing the street names were becoming particularly accident-prone. In some places, the population of the district, dissatisfied with the fact that preference had been given to one name over another seemingly more to their liking, ripped down the plaques or scratched out the names. Elsewhere, the owner of the house to which, without his consent, a name-plate had been affixed, contrived its disappearance under the pretext of some repair or other, or else of rubbing down and whitewashing the house. The lieutenant-general of police thought it his duty to intervene, and so, on July 30, 1729, he issued an edict forbidding damage to plates placed at the two ends of each street and enjoining owners of houses where such plates had been attached to erect in their stead and place sizeable stone tablets in hard limestone with the names of the streets carved into them."[99]

Typography and literature

To return to printed matter, modes of typographical expression broadened or reconfigured in the course of the seventeenth and eighteenth centuries cover at once modifications to the Roman type, the development of fancy alphabets, the increasing use of certain media, and the aesthetics applied to the interior of the book, as well as other factors.

This era also witnessed a Europe-wide revival in illustrative writing (a genre that had originated at least in the fourth to third centuries BCE). Rabelais's famous "Dive Bouteille," for instance occurs at the end of his *Cinquiesme Livre* in 1565. The Baroque rejuvenation of the *calligramme* (a term that became widely known following the publication in 1918 of a

130
François Rabelais, "La Dive Bouteille," *Le Cinquiesme Livre*, France, 1565.

collection of poems of the same name by Guillaume Apollinaire) recalls the Renaissance practice consisting in placing texts in figurative, pictured, or geometric shapes at the beginning or end of a work. Many sixteenth- and seventeenth-century authors wrote picture poetry, in particular in Germany in the latter century with writers like Martin Opitz and Georg-Philipp Harsdörffer. A proportion of these picture-writings were composed by poets with a taste for imagery and for the iconic dimension of the text.

If the art of illustrated verse and the picture-poem tended to recede from the literary landscape of the eighteenth century (except for researches such as those of Charles-François Panard, and, later, of Pierre Capelle), contemporary writers did undertake new experiments on page layout and typesetting. In Great Britain, Laurence Sterne (1713–1768) played with typography in the landmark English novel *The Life and Opinions of Tristram Shandy, Gentleman*, published as a series of nine books from 1759–67, the first volume of which was an immediate bestseller. Laurence Sterne is one of those writers who express through their work an eloquent interest in the very shape of a text—in this case, an entire novel. He placed great store by punctuation, which he grouped, connected, and arranged into powerful visual effects, with sequences of asterisks or long dashes scattered about the novel in a surprising manner. By contrast, non-printed areas acquire an active role. Certain pages are left blank, others are entirely covered with black ink. The novel is stuffed with typographical oddities. Some sentences, for example, peter out into a succession of broadly spaced asterisks running to several lines, which imparts a visual rhythm to the text. In other sections, the unconventional use of capitals or italic unsettles our reading practices and perceptions.

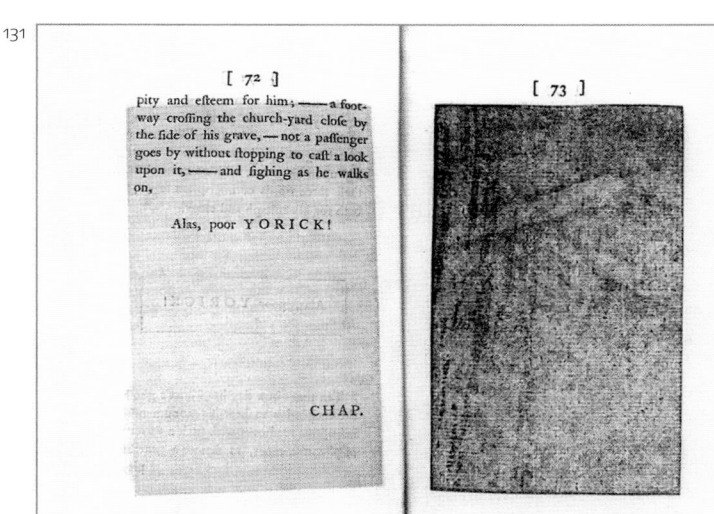

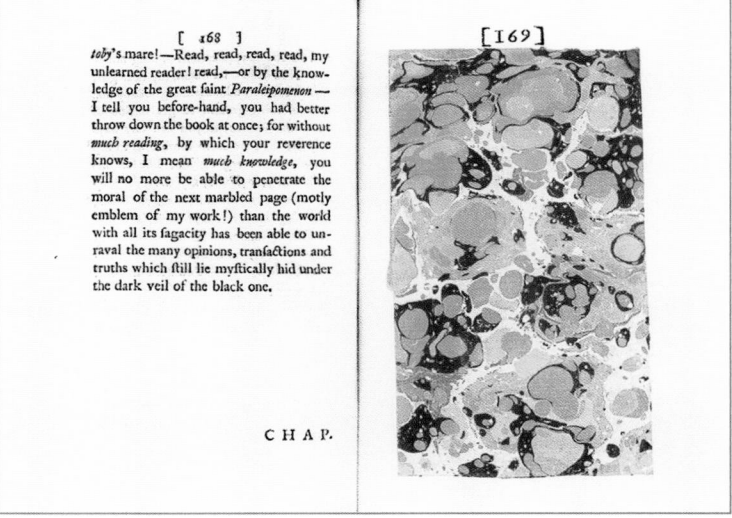

131
Laurence Sterne, two spreads from *The Life and Opinions of Tristram Shandy, Gentleman*, Great Britain, 1759 and 1767.

Sterne's composition is an outstanding experiment in incorporating typography into literature in a full-length text where the flow of typographic color familiar to readers makes way for a dynamic visual space. In this pioneering endeavor, the text is presented as something to be both read and looked at, following the idea Sterne himself had of reading: "The truest respect which you can pay to the reader's understanding, is to [...] leave him something to imagine [...]."[100] The novelist-typographer expresses a concern that was to characterize much literary and artistic modernism, in particular with the avant-garde.

A contemporary of Sterne's, Restif de la Bretonne (1734–1806) also indulged in unusual textual experimentation. At the same time author, publisher, and printer of his writings, he devised typographical games as he was putting the text through the press. In *Le Paysan perverti* published in 1775, he plays with typefaces, with styles (Roman and Italic), and with capital and minuscule letters, varying them depending on the importance or nature of the subject matter. His interest in meaningful typography lasted several decades. Poet Gérard de

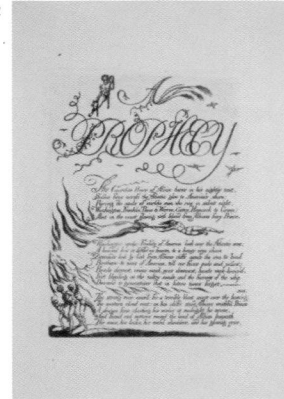

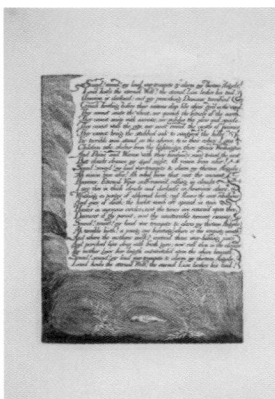
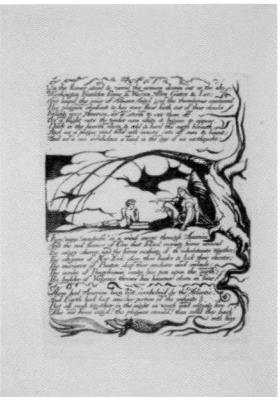

132

132
William Blake, five pages from the illustrated book *America a Prophecy,* published in 1793. Etching.

133
Coqueley de Chaussepierre (1711–1791), double page from his prose-poem-cum-play *The Virtuous Rake* (*Le Roué vertueux, poëme en prose en quatre chants, propre à faire, en cas de besoin, un Drame à jouer deux fois par semaine*), Lausanne, 1770.

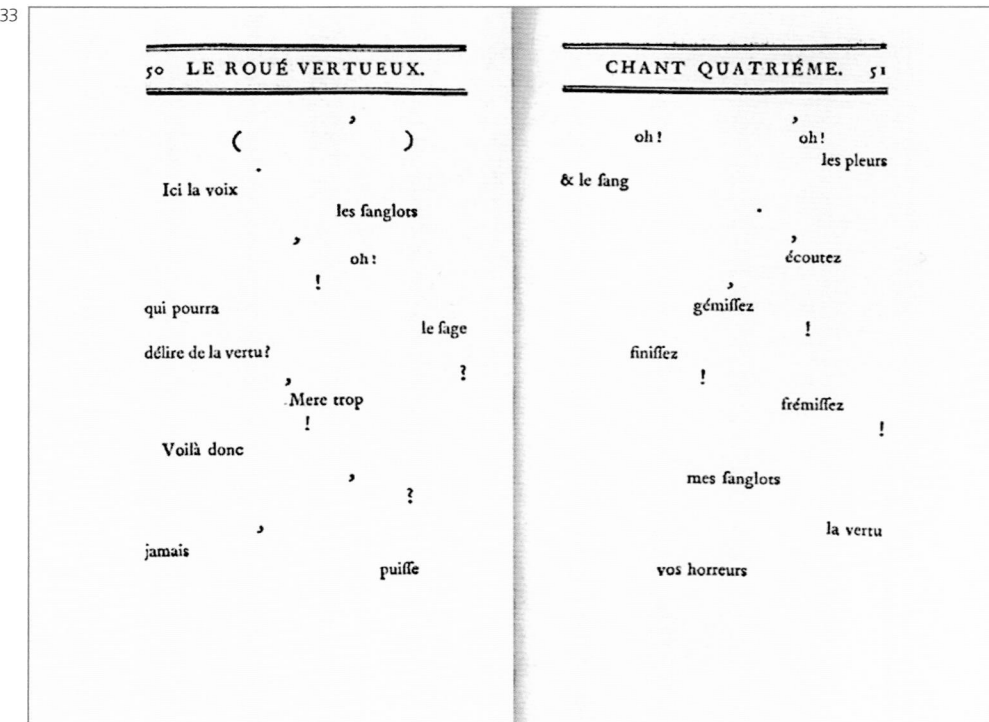

133

Nerval described his work thus: "His system was to employ in one and the same volume types of various sizes that he varied according to the supposed import of the given sentence. Cicero was for passion, for places of powerful effect, the gaillarde for simple narrative or moral observations, [while] small Roman could compact into a tiny space a thousand wearisome but indispensable details [...]. In the middle of words, he might employ either capitals or letters of smaller size."[101]

Numerous explorations in the publishing field were to appear during the second half of the eighteenth century. Around 1790, the English poet, painter, and engraver William Blake contrived unusual associations between text and image. In making his books, he developed a special process, simultaneously engraving poems and illustrations, colored in watercolor after printing. In this manner he brought out several works, including *Songs of Innocence* and *Songs of Experience* (1789 and 1794).

Creations in the last decades of the century, such as the very different approaches of William Blake, Laurence Sterne, Restif de la Bretonne, or Coqueley de Chaussepierre, forged new bonds between the written word and typography, image and layout. Similar

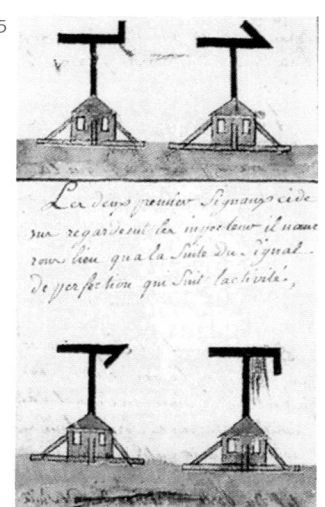

135

experiments—literary, artistic, or hybrid in nature, according to the case (and often linked to type design)—would be taken up in the literature of the nineteenth century and increasingly thereafter. These literary games with image and writing continued the exciting visual adventures undertaken a thousand years earlier by medieval book masters and two thousand years before by the authors, poets, and artists of antiquity.

A turning-point

The turn of the eighteenth century witnessed many experiments and transformations that touched various aspects of typographical creation and graphic production: visual experiments undertaken by writers, the Transitional phase in type design (a determining factor for the overall appearance of the printed word), diversification of the media and fonts employed, increased exposure (in particular in the form of advertisements, announcements, posters, and fliers), the development of a written culture relating to practical life, the growth of the volume of printed materials and their readership, and so on. In effect, the sheer quantity of printed matter snowballed—as variations in the printed page had in its early days.

Print-runs and different media proliferated in Germany and France, while Italy, too, was highly productive. Great Britain played an important role and, like the Netherlands, was a major exporter. In the seventeenth and eighteenth centuries, the Netherlands, France, and England excelled moreover in the field of typographical design, which became a rapidly advancing field. Fournier and Baskerville were now joined by Didot and Bodoni (and thereafter William Caslon IV, Vincent Figgins, etc.) signaling a fresh spurt of creativity. If, with each successive period, typography tended to overlap with the major classifications in art (Classicism, Baroque, Rococo, Neoclassicism, Romanticism, etc.), in the eighteenth century, more signs of its singularity began to heave into view. Made possible by the Industrial Revolution, and furthered by the tumultuous events in France, a new era was in the offing, characterized by the progressive evolution of eighteenth-century ideas in tandem with a philosophical approach that would esteem creativity as an eminently human faculty.

134
First code used in the Chappe brothers' aerial telegraph, letters of the alphabet and other signs encoded as thirty-six signals, France.

135
Aerial telegraph by the Chappe brothers, end of the eighteenth century. The signals emitted by a set of three movable struts placed on turrets are reproduced from station to station. Manuscript by Claude Chappe, signals for the optical telegraph, France, 1794.

136
Fraktur initial by Paulus Franck, from *Schatzkammer allerhand Versalien*, 1601.

137
Mosaic binding, eighteenth century.

136

137

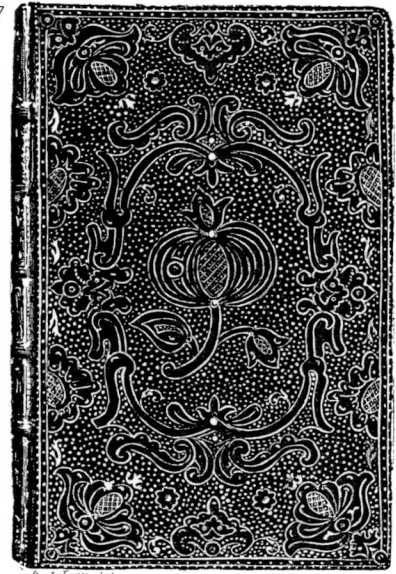

The Neoclassical period

Turbulence in the final decades of the eighteenth century

In Europe, the second half of the eighteenth century announced the coming of profound changes. Worldviews and deep-rooted beliefs were mutating in response to the ideas of the Enlightenment and to the undermining of monarchical absolutism. Beginning at the end of the previous century, the critical and questioning period of the Age of Reason was one of intense intellectual activity.

A different dynamic was now underway in the fields of knowledge, philosophy, technology, and art. As aesthetics was coming into its own as a discipline, so artistic practice was entering the Neoclassical phase, with important effects on typography and typeface design. A pressing need for understanding and knowledge was felt, combined with the development of huge encyclopedic overviews (the first volume of Diderot and D'Alembert's *Encyclopédie* appears in 1751). In parallel with the Classical rationalism of the seventeenth century, reason affirmed its position regarding dogma and blind belief. In the following century, critical thought reviewed rationalism and questioned once again the faculties of knowledge and ethics. Experiment, feeling, sensibility, and observation were emphasized.

In parallel with movements in thought and the arts, the foundations were being laid down for economic transformations. In England, the onset of the Industrial Revolution foreshadowed a shift from an agrarian, rural, and artisan society to an urban and mechanized world that would produce material goods en masse. The steam engine, developed by the Scottish engineer James Watt from 1769 and manufactured since 1776, represented a fundamental leap forward for industry. From now on mechanical processes were able to replace human and/or animal power. This new power source was the occasion of enormous changes, including in the print sector. In the field of communications, Chappe's 1793 telegraph became a means of transmitting messages over impressive distances based on optical telecommunication; a dispatch could now be sent hundreds of miles in a few hours by means of mobile signals encoded with the letters of the alphabet and positioned on turrets visible from a long way

These upheavals rocked every aspect of society and daily life—industrial, technical, political, etc. In France, the revolution resulted in a tidal wave that destabilized the European monarchical system. The sociopolitical undertow from these events was immediately felt in the fields of typography, printing, and the book. Censorship and control, having held back printing developments in France, for instance, were partially lifted during the revolution, only to be reimposed a little later, in particular by Napoleon in 1800. In 1789, the Declaration of the Rights of Man and of the Citizen proclaimed the freedom of the press, though it comprised a measure of restriction. Article 11 was directly concerned with the right to print: "The free communication of ideas and opinions is one of the most precious of the rights of man. Every citizen may, accordingly, speak, write, and print with freedom, but shall be responsible for such abuses of this freedom according to the precepts of the law" In the United States, freedom of the press had been officially enshrined more than ten years before. In a context of rapid change and relaxing controls, of remarkable developments in production and communication, the printing and publishing trades flourished all the more.

In tandem with the book, many other categories of printed matter arose, both ephemeral and more permanent. Newspapers, pamphlets, booklets, lampoons, and advertisements appeared in vast quantities, to which should be added trademarks, trade-cards, labels, etc. Wholly new types of printed material came into being; for instance during the French Revolution *assignats* were produced—financial documents that were turned out in their millions in the Didot workshops. The demand for print was such that night-work became essential in an effort to increase productivity.

Further expansion in media

Chief among the (typo)graphical supports in the course of development at the end of the eighteenth century were the press and advertising, both of which would experience massive expansion during the following century. Before 1800, the press in the West had already made great strides. In France, for example, readership had soared since the seventeenth century. If, before the revolution, the number of newspapers could be counted on the fingers of one hand, in the space of a single decade they shot up from a few dozen to a matter of hundreds. In 1777, the first French daily had appeared, *Le Journal de Paris,* which was later to become one of the most famous news organs. In the United States, dailies were set up in the 1780s in both Philadelphia and New York. Such publications carried a great deal of advertising and announcements in comparison to the space set aside for articles and news. In England in 1785, the creation of the *Times* (under a different name at the time[102]) served as a fillip to the press in Europe since it was one of the very first daily "broadsheet" or serious newspapers; as an indication of its success, its print-run went up from five thousand in 1815 to fifty thousand in 1854, before reaching half a million in 1995.

As for advertising, quite apart from on posters, it too spread through the press, as well as by the time-honored means of shop-signs and manufacturers' marks. A specialist in store advertising in the nineteenth century compared the posters of the time to "real shop-signs possessing the appearance of a gouache or watercolor."[103] If the wholesale distribution of the illustrated color poster is essentially a nineteenth-century phenomenon, the eighteenth-century cityscape, at least in certain urban centers, already found space for shop-signs and other powerful visual cues. The same author considers these as the ancestor of the poster proper and the hoarding, referring to "the gigantic proportions of the old shop-signs of eighteenth-century Paris, when one could see outside a vintner's a huge bottle like the one Rabelais put into Gargantua's hand, or outside a shoemaker's an enormous boot such as an ogre in a fairy tale might have sported."[104] At this time, advertising obviously did not appear in the same guise as today, but still visual communication was effected through forms as different as the classified small ad and shopfront signs of imposing dimensions.

If the advertising bill might have been already up and running in Great Britain and the United States, the revolution in France spurred significant developments in the political poster. Composed of text, it was quite unlike its commercial counterpart. In 1791, new regulations concerning bill-posting instituted the creation of sites specially reserved for official edicts. The latter were printed exclusively in black ink on a white ground, while posters for private individuals had to be printed on colored paper, or at least bisect the white background with a band of color. The growth and diversification of these supports corresponded to growing eclecticism in typography and lettering. Type design and layouts spawned some unusual creations, which nevertheless chimed in with the prevailing atmosphere of rationalization. Under Neoclassicism, typography could revel in elegance, sobriety, grandeur... and standardization.

138
Fairground handbill for the Dalmatine Menagerie, Berlin, 1750.

139
Anonymous, poster advertising fold-up umbrellas and parasols, France, eighteenth century.

The alphabet, meanwhile, developed a third historical form of the Roman character: Modern Roman. There, the distinction from bookhand is reinforced still further, replaced by a rational and calculated construction that again reduces the role played by gesture and the hand. Henceforth, the differences between handwritten lettering and typeface were to become ever greater. (Some tendencies in nineteenth- and twentieth-century typography would often draw on the potential of this division, occasionally seeking to combine the two registers).

Modern Roman and typographical practice
France and the Didot family

France played a significant role in the formation of the Neoclassical type style, in particular through the contribution of the famous Didot dynasty. The new style spread quickly to nearby countries, most visibly to Italy. Nearly a century lies between the preliminary drafts for Grandjean (*romain du roi* or Louis XIV type) and Didot. Between the two, in France, apart from the work of Pierre-Simon Fournier and Louis-René Luce, creativity seemed to have ebbed slightly compared to past achievements. Luce finished engraving the type for the *romain du roi* in 1745, though the character had been outlined more than half a century previously. In 1771, he published his *Essai d'une nouvelle typographie ornée de vignettes, fleurons, trophées, filets, cadres et cartels, inventés, dessinés et exécutés par L. Luce, graveur du Roi, pour son Imprimerie royale* ("An essay in a new typography, decorated with vignettes, florets, trophies, rules, frames, and panels, invented, drawn, and executed by L. Luce, engraver to the King, for his Royal Printing Works.")

In the space of about thirty years, Luce was to engrave some six thousand punches in his leisure time, including Roman, Italic, title characters, vignettes, decorations, ornamental letters, etc. His Roman is characterized by its narrowness, a singularity that compares with Fournier, who also created a relatively narrow (or condensed) alphabet. Luce's type presents a variant of Transitional very close to Modern Roman, a form that was then on the horizon. The transformation of Roman is marked by some readily identifiable stages (three are often recognized), reflecting gradual modifications through intermediate forms (even the passage of Gothic to Roman a long time previously had traversed transitional and demonstrably hybrid forms).

The Didots were another of those feverishly active and influential dynasties that seem to have been typical of the publishing and printing trades to which they so lastingly contributed. Engravers and type-founders, paper manufacturers and typographers, printers and booksellers, bibliophiles and literati, the Didots remained in business for more than two centuries (one was even elected member to the Académie des Inscriptions et Belles-Lettres at the end of the nineteenth century), and their endeavors combined innovations on the technical, aesthetic, and practical levels.[105] Over the generations, the Didot family includes the names of Francois, François-Ambroise, Pierre-François, Henri, Léger, Pierre, Firmin, Jules, Ambroise, and Hyacinthe. The founder of the dynasty is generally considered to be François Didot, apprentice at a printer-bookseller's at the end of the seventeenth century and a registered bookseller by 1713. The family's vocation, however, dates from even before him, seemingly back to a certain Marie-Anne Didot, "bookseller in Paris," in 1698.

The contribution of the Didots to books, typography, and printing is widely recognized for its breadth and diversity, in particular with regard to their eponymous new type, which updates the forms of the Roman prefigured in Grandjean and Baskerville. If some authorities date Didot from the years 1750,[106] the letters acquired their characteristic forms between 1775 and 1790. One of the versions was by Louis Vafflard,[107] a very experienced cutter working to instructions given by François-Ambroise Didot. In 1784, the type attained its most highly finished form in the hands of François-Ambroise's son, Firmin Didot.

Up to about 1830, Didot type split into many variants designed by other members of the family (it was in addition the subject of special, decorated assortments). Didot is a particularly good illustration of how the name of a commonly used character may correspond not to a single form but to various states, *a fortiori* since the term "Didot" was employed to designate characters of a similar kind. Extrapolating recent developments in type design, the 1784 alphabet presents geometrical tendencies, pure and uncluttered, that enhance the qualities of Transitional Roman. The letters are built to a vertical axis, the hairlines are thin and of exemplary finesse, while the stems are markedly thicker, and the serifs (triangular in the past) become finely bracketed. Blessed with a certain grandeur, the shapes of the letters are obtained from a form of design related to construction. Up until about 1830, a new generation of Didots reinforced still further the distinction between thick and thin strokes, refining and purifying the font. The neat polish of the detail reflects formal changes that are not unconnected to technical questions (John Baskerville had already produced a vellum paper specially adapted to his delicate characters). Furthermore, at this time the quest for neatness was being encouraged by the possibilities offered by copper-engraving, by which extremely fine lines could be obtained.

If the font constituted one of the more visible aspects of their work, the Didots contributed to printing in other ways, too. In the context of their efforts to improve the effectiveness of the print process as well as the quality of their product, François-Ambroise played a crucial role. It was he who succeeded in manufacturing a vellum paper inspired by English and Dutch techniques that could be compared in quality to that attained by Baskerville (the extreme delicacy of the Didot hairlines necessitating a very smooth surface). To optimize print-runs, François-Ambroise also overhauled press design—a certain number of components of which were still made out of wood—by using copper platens, iron beds, etc., and brought in the single-pass press. His other innovations include the Didot point—the system of measurement also studied by Fournier—dating to around 1780. Also called the "typographical point," the Didot point remained the unit of type measurement usually employed in Europe, whereas Anglo-American countries utilize the Pica point.[108] The Didot point is calculated from the length of the "king's foot," a fixed unit of French measurement divided into six; the Didot point is at present equivalent to 0.3759 mm. The progressive adoption of this system advanced the standardization of typography and did much to reduce disparities in measurement. Both the Didot and the Pica points have remained international systems of measurement.

Other contributions by the Didots to typography include the development of stereotypy, a money-saving process consisting in molding an entire made-up page of text set in movable type in the same block of lead. Publications in stereotypy constitute an important turning-point in the manufacturing processes both of the book and the periodical. In the 1810s, the Didot plant acquired metal presses, allowing for greater regularity in print quality. After obtaining mechanical and steam-driven presses, the family further benefited from the growth of industrialization in setting up a continuous paper-making machine in the workshop. Certain members of the Didot family were in addition significant figures in the Imprimerie Royale (or Imprimerie Impériale). Pierre was printer to the imperial court in 1812, and then printer to the king, while Firmin was made head of the foundry for the imperial printers in 1811. Jules, too, was printer to the king, a title that Ambroise Firmin-Didot would be the last to hold in 1829.

In about 1810, Napoleon I decided to endow the imperial printers (formerly the Imprimerie Royale) with a type of its own. This was to be the *romain de l'empereur*, intended to replace the Grandjean designed under Louis XIV. Firmin Didot was appointed in charge of the project and created the so-called Didot *millimétrique*, whose point is based on the metric system; the actual alphabet, however, was forged from type he had drawn previously. Because Firmin left such a significant body of work, his descendants chose to couple his first name to their patronymic as a tribute, their surname becoming Firmin-Didot. Prolonging the family tradition, one of his sons, Ambroise Firmin-Didot, was a leading figure in nineteenth-century bibliophily.

ABCDEFGHI
JKLMNOPQR
STUVWXYZ
abcdefghijklmn
opqrstuvwxyz
äöü .,;:!?
1234567890

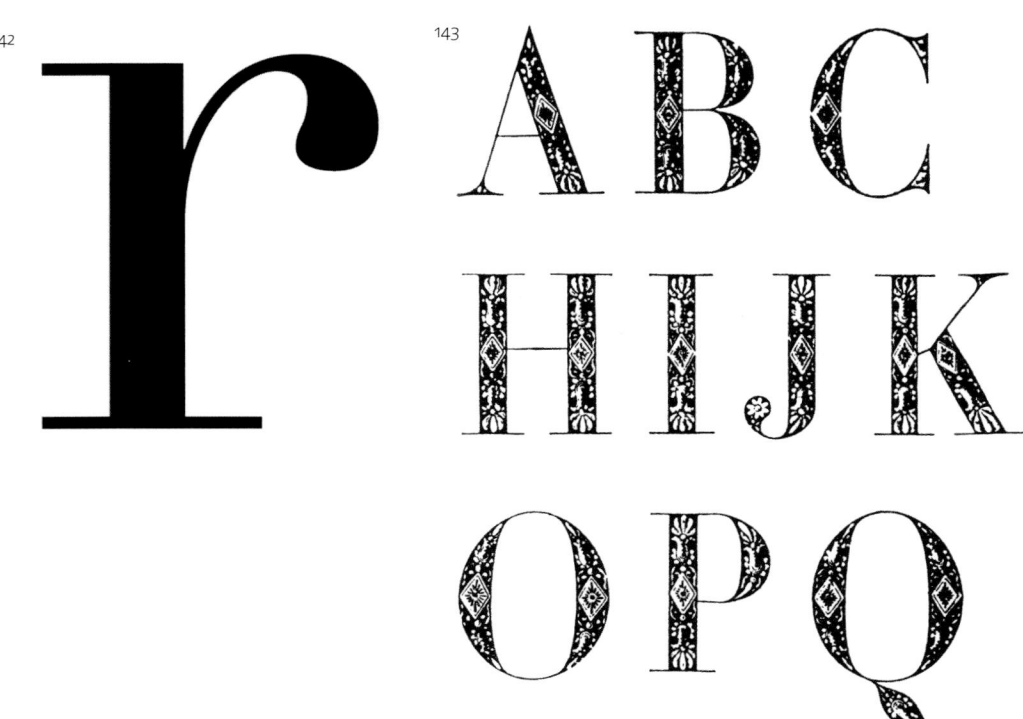

141
Didot type, France.

142
Form of the Didot "r," contemporary digital Linotype.

143
Decorated Didot, Enschedé en Zonen, c. 1820.

Still employed today, Didot's characters are an acknowledged classic. Like other alphabets or types that drastically altered hallowed forms, the reactions they aroused ranged wildly. If some appreciated the alphabet's grandeur—perhaps verging on austerity—others saw its excessive rigor as posing problems for readers, and indeed opinions remain divided. If the printer Sobry rails against "destructive ultra-perfection,"[110] an article of 1862 lauds characters so perfect "that to try to surpass them in terms both of elegance and harmony would be proof of foolhardiness."[110] For his part, in 1905, Émile Javal expressed the gravest reservations: "We do not believe that Didot was particularly inspired in adopting such excessively fine hairlines and we think that this innovation [...] has already been supported for too long by fashion and will very shortly have to disappear."[111] More moderately, the historian Albert Kapr esteems that "Didot types seem intellectual, sober, and cold, but when looked at more closely turn out to be witty and delightful."[112]

Such unfavorable judgments did nothing to prevent Didot meeting with rapid success in European printing. It was introduced in Germany by the end of the eighteenth century where it became a widespread type, a position it was to hold for nearly a century, during which it was widely imitated. Diversifying its enterprise, at the beginning of the 1930s, for instance, the house of Didot brought out *La Route Paris Méditerranée*, reproducing photographs by Germaine Krull and André Kertész, among others.

Giambattista Bodoni's types

The career of the Italian typographer Giambattista Bodoni (1740–1813) forms part of the immediate aftermath of that of the Didots. The typeface that bears his name represents one of his great contributions to typography. Bodoni drew and engraved the type in Parma in about 1787 (Firmin Didot had also fixed the form of Didot in about 1780 or shortly afterwards). Their creations are regarded as two of the first great models for Modern Roman. In spite of some areas of disagreement, the Didots never hid their admiration of Bodoni: "Although we did have a minor contretemps [...] we have, however, always given him his due."[113]

While still very young, Giambattista Bodoni learned the rudiments of the trade from his father, a typographer-printer, assisting him on the shop floor. Aged eighteen, he was engaged as a typesetter in one of greatest printworks of the time, the Stamperia di Propaganda Fide, which is attached to the Vatican. There, he saw his first works through the press and specialized in composing collections in Oriental languages. A few years later, so as to complete his training, he planned to leave for England on the tracks of Baskerville. Although health problems obliged him to abandon his travel ideas, he was soon to enjoy an enviable reputation. In 1768, when not yet thirty years old, Duke Ferdinand of Parma appointed him director of the newly inaugurated Stamperia Reale (Royal Printing Works).

Bodoni's books testify to exceptional professional artistry. The *Epithalamia exoticis linguis reddita* (1775), composed in twenty-five Asian and African languages, is regarded as a masterpiece. Composing and printing books, he also authored various writings and publications concerning typography.[114] Bodoni established his foundry in Parma, where he designed his own type. The integrated process from drawing the letter to the font constituted an essential aspect of his approach. To refine his knowledge still further, he studied types by Pierre-Simon Fournier, whom he admired, John Baskerville, and Johann Michael Fleischmann.

Bodoni type displays the basic characteristics of Didot: reinforced contrast between stem and hairline, slender and horizontal serifs, a powerful vertical impetus. The extenders are ample and the forms expressive of great regularity. Precise and harmonious, overall Bodoni type confirms a change that coincided with new means in production. Giambattista Bodoni observed that attentive study of lettering makes it possible to pinpoint recurring forms. "Anyone examining the letters of any language with care [...] will find one can compose them with a small number of identical parts which are built up differently."[115] By smoothing out repetitive forms in the construction of his alphabet, he achieved admirable regularity. On the other hand, he was of the opinion that it was best to accentuate those characteristics that differentiate certain letters in order to ensure legibility. He gives four criteria that to his eyes determine the beauty of the characters: "The first is regularity [...] variety without dissonance, equality and symmetry without confusion. In the second place come clarity and polish [...]. The third condition is good taste, which chooses the most agreeable forms [...]. Grace is the fourth and final necessity for perfecting the beauty of a type." Relying on his experience and insight, Bodoni explains how it is that, "little by little, literature and philosophy direct the taste of those who study them towards simplicity and sobriety, to the point that the beauty they like best will be one unembellished by hackneyed ornaments."[116] The complete typographer, Bodoni recommended elegant sobriety in book composition as well as for typefaces.

Over time, Bodoni's star shone still brighter. In 1782, when scarcely more than forty years old, he was named "typographer to the chamber" of King Charles III of Spain. Soon afterwards, he set up his own printworks in Parma, and, in the same decade, began issuing his famous *Manuale tipografico*. If the first edition, by his own hand, was issued in 1788, the posthumous, two-volume edition completed by his widow in 1818, a kind of specimen catalog of types representing half a century's work, provides a more thorough exposition of his oeuvre. Containing more than six hundred plates for alphabets (Latin, Greek, Hebrew, etc.), ornaments and vignettes, Jan Tschichold praised it as a "monument of the typographical art."[117]

Although Bodoni always put quality before quantity, he nonetheless drew hundreds of alphabets and the corresponding punches amount to tens of thousands. Among them history has allotted a special place to the upright (roman) version of the Bodoni type. The perfect reflection of the spirit of its time, not long after it came out Bodoni spread widely throughout European printing, meeting a success comparable to that of Didot.

Neoclassical types

Historically, Didot type symbolizes the advent of a new family known as Modern (or Neoclassical) Roman (also known as Didone in the Vox classification of 1952). The name Didot has become a generic designating a vast range of types exhibiting similar features. This category is seen as the third stage of Roman type, after the Old Roman of the Renaissance and

145

145
Comparison between Didot and Bodoni:
Didot digital Linotype (left), and Bodoni
digital version Berthold (right).

146
Comparison between two versions of
Bodoni: Berthold version (top), and Bauer
version (bottom).

147
Bodoni type, Roman for titling,
Giambattista Bodoni (1740–1813), from his
Manuale tipografico, Parma, 1818.

148
Bodoni type, Roman for titling,
Giambattista Bodoni, from his *Manuale
tipografico*, Parma, 1818.

149
Bodoni type, Cancelleresco typeface,
Giambattista Bodoni, from his *Manuale
tipografico*, Parma, 1818.

146

kntw

kntw

147

148

149

the Transitional Roman of the seventeenth and eighteenth centuries, though it may on occasion be considered as the fourth when, for instance, Venetian incunabulum type is treated as a separate form preceding the onset of the three divisions. The formal specificities of Didot and Bodoni (verticality, contrast, construction, slenderness of serifs and hairlines) were to have important repercussions on lettering due to these types' immediate triumph and uptake.

Bell in England and Walbaum in Germany number among the best-known variants of Modern Roman. Bell, a book type designed for the foundry of John Bell, was cut in 1788 by Richard Austin. Walbaum, devised around 1800, was the work of Justus Erich Walbaum, a draftsman, engraver, and type-founder, who at one time had served as an apprentice pastry-cook and grocer. Inspired by Didone type, Walbaum's alphabet was very popular at the time. Similar to Didot and Bodoni, Bell and Walbaum reflect the Neoclassical style, though they are demonstrations of a different strand; Bell, for example, reemploys certain elements of Old Roman, such as triangular terminations. Didot, Bodoni, Bell, and Walbaum type are thus particularly representative of the last great form of Roman.

The changes affecting Roman since the century of Gutenberg had been relatively uneventful. In the eyes of contemporary visual culture, between the Venetian characters of the fifteenth century and the Didones engraved exactly three hundred years later, lettering design had altered at a snail's pace. Over this timescale, alphabets were honed with variations that accentuated contrasts within one and the same sign and refined terminations (from the triangular serif to a slim horizontal), the inclined axis inherited from the pen being answered by a constructive approach reliant on verticality and horizontality. In the course of this process, the letter embraced geometrization, standardization, and rationalization, differentiating itself from bookhand (i.e. local irregularities and idiosyncrasies, strange spellings, fanciful forms, etc.). "As a result of social and technological changes at the end of the eighteenth century, greater changes in letter form occurred within a period of a few decades than had occurred in the course of the previous centuries."[118]

The onset of the nineteenth century: a change of pace

Until the eighteenth century, type-making practices, typographical design, and graphical forms were characterized by comparative continuity. During the nineteenth and twentieth centuries, however, visual communication transformed to such an extent that it is now no easy task (unless one has recourse to testimonies from the time) to imagine how exactly forms were perceived in former times. If various approaches and trends become gradually more identifiable (being, in certain cases, the cause of conflicts of interest or differences of opinion), they rarely seem prey to uprooting or interruption. The successive episodes in Roman type nonetheless occasioned much historical debate (parts of which remain topical) and a measure of upheaval in what was a centuries-long tradition. Grandjean, Baskerville, and Didot each in turn met with admiration or disapproval—the latter response seeming particularly prevalent in the phase known as Transitional. As an example, Pierre-Simon Fournier, raising a question that will remain burning in the twentieth century, reacted vehemently to the principles on which the conception of the *romain du roi* was based, taking issue with the geometric construction of the type: "How is it that minds have so narrowed and taste so retreated as to hobble genius with such bewildering and piecemeal rules? Does one need so many squares to form an O, which is round, and so many circles to form other letters which are square? [...] Genius knows neither ruler nor compass, save for the geometric parts."[119] Fournier's early response to this crucial issue was that drawing by hand and visual sensitivity should prevail over a modular, geometrical, tool-oriented construction that was liable to transform the logic subtending the production of (typo)graphical forms.

For practically three centuries—apart from in certain registers (such as ornamentation)— typography's course in the Classical age had been almost accident-free, but, after characteristically gradual modifications, this tranquil period came to a close during the

150

150

Manuscript, collection of treatises on grammar, Turkey, eighteenth century. Text inscribed within rectangular frames and surrounded by glosses occupying the double-page spread in an original manner.

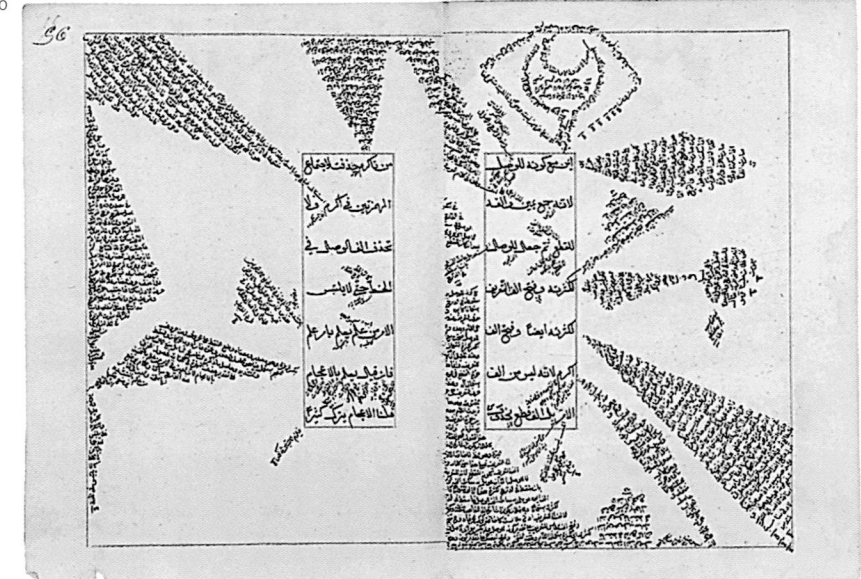

eighteenth century. The nineteenth century would break new ground and brand-new ideas would appear that would turn their back on the burden of tradition and the power of the academy. The origins of these unprecedented initiatives are to be sought in the underlying economic, technological, and aesthetic situation. Gathering pace over time, artistic trends and currents would reflect an uncertain, fluctuating world. Pictorial practices would undergo profound transmutations in style, approach, and subject matter. Like painting, typography and graphic design would progress at an accelerated rate, buoyed along by innovation and novelty, and moving away from reproduction and models. The technical advances brought about by galloping industrialization would play a key role, and fresh possibilities would flow from the technique of lithography and from the mechanization of printing, papermaking, and photography. Whereas the techniques devised by Gutenberg had stayed the course well, the nineteenth century altered the game totally.

For example, wooden press components were gradually replaced by metal equivalents and entirely metal presses were first designed around 1800 by Stanhope and Walker. Daily output could thus be increased tenfold compared to the old methods—and still more with Friedrich Koenig's power-driven press and the replacement of manpower by steam in the 1810s. Koenig mechanized the entire process, doing everything "that heretofore had been done by hand— taking up the ink, spreading it, and applying it to the type, in fact everything save inserting and removing the paper."[120] Thanks to these new tools, the age-old quantitative constraints meant nothing and productivity in printing soared phenomenally.

The introduction of industrial production methods was thus instrumental in both the background changes and the breakneck speed of the period. For Henri Focillon, "Stephenson's [steam engine] is the most expressive and most dramatic image of the new order, but industrial forms of production had been born before its dizzying trajectory."[121]

Notes

1 Paul Needham, "Johannes Gutenberg et l'invention de l'imprimerie en Europe," *Les Trois Révolutions du livre* (exh. cat., Musée des Arts et Métiers/Imprimerie nationale: Paris, 2002), 181.

2 Anne-Marie Christin, *L'Image écrite ou la Déraison graphique* (Paris: Flammarion, 2001), 11 (1st ed. 1995). See also the rest of the text that deals with the iconic origin and the visible aspect of the sign, writing, the alphabet, and typography.

3 See for example, A.-M. Christin, op. cit., 12, 18, et passim.

4 See for example, *Naissance de l'écriture* (exh. cat., Ministère de la Culture/RMN, Paris, 1982), 17.

5 The expression is Roland Barthes' in "Variations sur l'écriture," in *Le Plaisir du texte* (Paris: Seuil, 2000), 38. "Anthropology would suggest [that] in the caves pre-graphical figures were organized in a radial manner [...]; it can be appreciated that these symbolic arrays must have functioned in coordination with an oral context. So the entire syntagmatic relationship between the oral and the written is already posited. We tend to think of this relationship in the form of an imbalance: sometimes it is the image, we think, that merely illustrates the word, and at others the contrary is the case and the word as it were serves as just a caption to the image. It would surely be more correct to say [...] that the bond between image (or its continuation, writing) and the word is statutory, and that through these two languages, the body is distributed equally."

6 *Naissance de l'écriture*, op. cit., 48.

7 *La Naissance des écritures. Du cunéiforme à l'alphabet* (Paris: Seuil, 1994), 15 (a French translation).

8 Although commonplace, the description of Chinese writing as "ideographic" (or "pictographic") is debatable and these terms might be considered misleading. Among others, the portmanteau expression "morphemo-syllabic" has been proposed, together with "monosyllabic logograms."

9 Logogram and phonogram: graphical signs respectively representing a word and a sound (indicative of the pronunciation in the second case).

10 Joaquín Galarza, "Une écriture haute en couleur," *Le Courrier de l'Unesco*, April 1995, 18.

11 For a long time, the alphabetic phase of writing was perceived and/or qualified as "progress," a perspective now controversial, notably in the perspective of (re)valorizing other writing systems and of analyzing the loss that the alphabet may represent. On the question of "alphabeto-centrism" (a term borrowed from Barthes), see for example, David R. Olson, "Les croyances concernant l'écrit [...] Le système alphabétique d'écriture est supérieur techniquement," in *L'Univers de l'écrit*, and A.-M. Christin, "Mirages de l'alphabet," in *L'Image écrite ou la Déraison graphique*, op. cit.

12 Phoenicia corresponds to a coastal region of the Near East covering part of what are now the nations of Israel, Lebanon, and Syria.

13 Called "continuous script" [*scriptio continua*].

14 "Controverse que présente Platon dans le *Phèdre*," as transcribed by C. Ehm, *L'ABCdaire de tous les savoirs du monde* (Paris: Flammarion, 1996), 70.

15 *La Naissance des écritures. Du cunéiforme à l'alphabet*, op. cit., 20.

16 Simmias probably lived around the island of Rhodes.

17 "Unlike with Greco-Latin Antiquity, where the concept of creativity was absent and where the very idea of a creation was hardly conceivable, thirteenth-century philosophers and theologians turned their thoughts to the notion of the origin, the beginning, the first principle of all things. But, in a theological perspective, there was no question of attributing genuine creativity to humankind, still less of conceding him the power of artistic creation. The idea of artistic creation itself was eschewed as it was the sole privilege of God," M. Jimenez, *Qu'est-ce que l'esthétique?* (Paris: Gallimard, 1997), 34.

18 The codex appeared at the very beginning of the Common Era, coexisting together with the ancient scroll (*volumen*) until the fifth century, and then with the medieval scroll (*rotulus*) during the Middle Ages. Unrolling vertically, the medieval scroll may have fostered a page layout along a single column.

19 Parchment is supposed to have been invented in Pergamon (current Turkey) in the second century BCE to compensate for a shortage of papyrus. It is manufactured from the skin of ram, goat, sheep, or ewe. The finest parchments, made from the skin of still-born calves, are called vellum. By extension, vellum also designates a very fine, white paper.

20 In Nina Catach (recapping findings in earlier studies), *La Ponctuation. Histoire et système* (Paris: PUF, Que sais-je? no. 2818, 1996), 25 (reprint).

21 Ibid.

22 The rustic capital (*capitalis rustica*), known among Romans in the first century CE, presents the form of a rather rapid cursive handwriting. Inscribed with brush and quill, sometimes slightly inclined, the *rustica* is narrower than the *quadrata* and appears more spontaneous. The *capitalis monumentalis* is another, contemporary Roman script. As for the *quadrata* capital, occasionally dated to the beginnings of the Common Era but probably from the fourth to fifth centuries, it was used to inscribe texts, titles, and initials for several centuries.

23 Initially king of the Franks, Charlemagne became Emperor of the West in 800. The territories he conquered during his reign extended his empire to central Europe.

24 The "double" alphabet (the use in parallel of capital and small letters) was called into question in the 1920s by certain avant-garde artists. The propositions of their alphabets however remained on the drawing-board, probably because, from the outset, capitals, like minuscules, have kept their characteristic symbolic or pragmatic functions. There remains the possibility, however, that the idea of a unique alphabet will resurface some time in the future and that the simplification it represents will one day meet with a purpose.

25 In *La Ponctuation. Histoire et système*, op. cit., 21.

26 Ibid.

27 "It should be realized that 'visual' reading only is a recent phenomenon. If at various periods it has not been nonexistent [...] it has been sufficiently rare to be noted as something exceptional [...], and this situation, quite unlike ours, has lasted, in normal reading, until the modern era. In the Middle Ages, in general, reading was for someone else, or as if one was dictating or reading for someone else" (ibid., 16).

28 On the variety of Gothic lettering, their history and their later development see: A. Kapr, *Fraktur* (Mainz: Hermann Schmidt, 1993); P. Shaw, "The Calligraphic Tradition in Blackletter Type," Scripsit, vol. 22, nos. 1 and 2, Washington, summer 1999; P. Bain and P. Shaw (eds.), *Blackletter. Type and National Identity* (New York: The Cooper Union for the Advancement of Science and Art, 1998); two works, including an exhibition catalog).

29 *L'Aventure des écritures. La page* (Paris: Bibliothèque nationale de France, Cahiers pédagogiques, 1999), 13. See too, regarding the history and emergence of scripts in the wide sense, three exhibition catalogs, *L'Aventure des écritures. Naissances* (1997), *L'Aventure des écritures. Matières et formes* (1998), *L'Aventure des écritures. La page* (1999) (all Bibliothèque nationale de France).

30 These expressions are respectively in Charles Higounet, *L'Écriture*, (Paris: PUF, Que sais-je ?, 2003), 107 (1st ed. 1955) and Marius Audin, *Le Livre. Son architecture, sa technique* (Forcalquier: Robert Morel, 1969), 7 (reprint).

31 Olivier Lavoisy, "Invention du papier en Chine," *Encyclopædia Universalis*.

32 Wang Zhen, printer active between 1290 and 1333.

33 Wood entered the composition of paper in large quantities in the nineteenth century to compensate for a shortage of rag.

34 An incunabulum is a printed work dating from the earliest phase of printing before 1500.

Etymologically it refers to the Latin *incunabula* – "cradle," "beginning," "origin."

35 Jean Toulet, "Livre," *Encyclopaedia Universalis* (Paris, 1995, 929) (Corpus, 13). Some of the information used here derives from this study cosigned by Henri-Jean Martin and Jean Toulet.

36 Guy Bechtel, *Gutenberg* (Paris: Fayard, 1992), 505.

37 Extract from a text published in the Netherlands in 1588. Quoted by A. Kapr, *Johann Gutenberg* (Aldershot: Scolar Press, 1996), 100.

38 "*Ars artificialiter scribendi*," in the words of a formula of the 1440s borrowed from Procope Waldfoghel; the "act of writing artificially" formed in Latin in text from the 1440s; expression quoted by G. Bechtel, op. cit., 308.

39 The Donatus is an abridged version of the Latin grammar of Ælius Donatus, a famous fourth-century grammarian.

40 Henri-Jean Martin, "Gutenberg," in *Encyclopædia Universalis*.

41 The Golden Canon was reconstituted by, among others, Jan Tschichold in the middle of the twentieth century. He rehearsed the principles of composition and the proportions characteristic of the beauty of the medieval manuscript. Studies by Rául Rosarivo have demonstrated that Gutenberg's Bible derives its structure from such a canon.

42 Original format of the copy of the B42 conserved in Burgos is 16 × 12 in. (40 × 29.2 cm) that is to say, approximately equivalent to the UK's present-day A3 format.

43 With the first incunabula, handwritten initials and other elements were added to the printed text. Thereafter, a basic outline of the initial was incorporated into the printing to facilitate the calligrapher-illuminator's task. Occasionally, medieval manuscripts implemented the same process, the initials being obtained by rubbing or stamping a printing form engraved in relief.

44 Color printing became operative with the Psalter—probably for the first time successfully. Tests had been made already on B42, where some headings were printed in red with a second pull in the press.

45 The colophon comprises a few lines of text at the end of the work containing various pieces of essential information on the conception and realization of the book (title, author, scribe or typographer, bookseller, place, and date of printing).

46 B. Blasselle, *Histoire du livre* (Paris: Gallimard-Découvertes, 1997), 51.

47 Stephan Füssel, *Die Welt im Buch* (Mainz: Gutenberg-Gesellschaft, 1996), 46.

48 Bernard Vogler, "Réforme," *Encyclopædia Universalis* (Corpus 19), (Paris, 1995), 669.

49 A lampoon is a relatively brief text characterized by a satirical or scurrilous tone.

50 Quoted by L. Gervereau, *La Propagande par l'affiche* (Paris: Syros-Alternatives, 1991), 11.

51 G. Bechtel, op. cit., 13.

52 Certain of these characters have been explicitly designated as Gothico-Roman.

53 Regarding these uncertainties, and as an example of historical interconnections (particularly significant with respect to the diffusion of graphic design and typography), see, A. Kapr, *Johann Gutenberg*, op. cit., 253, and more particularly, G. Bechtel, op. cit., 18–19. Pierre-Simon Fournier, for his part, relates in his *Manuel typographique* (1766) that Jenson "was sent from Mainz by order of Louis XI to try to learn with Schöffer the new art by which Books were made". See too, n. 67.

54 The basic literature on typography rarely expands on the contributions of Erhard Ratdolt and André D'Asola, although they were clearly important figures for the beginnings of printing.

55 Aldus Manutius, born in 1449 or 1450 (that is at the very moment Gutenberg's printshop was on the brink of entering into operation) and dying in 1515, is also known as Aldo Manuzio and Aldo Manuzzi.

56 Quoted by M. Audin, op. cit., 33. These small-size printed books are however very unlike the current concept of the "pocket-book" that arose between the nineteenth and the middle of the twentieth century and which made a vast range of texts accessible to a wide readership (high print-runs and low costs).

57 The Elzévir (or Elzévier) family made their mark in the Netherlands with a major publishing and printing business in the sixteenth and seventeenth centuries. The name "elzevir" is commonly employed as a name for one of the early stages of Roman (triangular-shaped serifs and low contrast between stem and hairline), to which Garamond and Bembo belong.

58 The various meanings of the term "Roman" can lead to confusion. If the word indicates the form of the character that succeeded Gothic script (blackletter, broken-script), it also means (in) "normal" font, in opposition to "Italic."

59 Albert Kapr, *The Art of Lettering* (tr. I. Kimber, Munich: Saur, 1983), 89.

60 The preliminary drafts for the Futura character by Paul Renner were to constitute one of the foremost expressions of the geometrization of fonts in the mid-1920s.

61 Some examples of similar objections taken from various contexts: Pierre-Simon Fournier (eighteenth century), concerning the *romain du roi*: "Does one need then so many squares to form an 'O,' which is round, and so many circles to form other letters which are square? [...] The genius knows neither rulers nor compass, except for geometrical parts" (see note 119) László Moholy-Nagy (1923): "The letters of the alphabet can never be forced in a preestablished form; for example, the square" (see note 9, chapter 3). Claude Mediavilla: "Geometrical construction and the rationalization of forms using ruler and compass aroused something of a fad during the Renaissance. This 'constructivist' vogue [...] has resulted in certain foreseeable errors. In point of fact, the men of the sixteenth century had a rather poor grasp of the idea behind the ancient Roman *lapicida*. Their desiccating attempt at geometrization was not however without consequences on contemporary graphics; we suffer from these misunderstandings which have, unfortunately, acquired, due to their venerability, a certain force of law and truth," *Calligraphie* (Paris: Imprimerie nationale, 1993), 100.

62 *Epistolae*, by Gasparino Barzizza.

63 In *Champ Fleury* (Geneva: Slatkine Reprints, 1973), f. LXXIX; 1st ed. G. Tory and G. de Gourmont (Paris, 1529).

64 Cited by R. Peignot, "L'esprit des lettres" (*De plomb, d'encre et de lumière*, Paris: Imprimerie nationale, 1982), 101.

65 The irregularities presented by Tory's typographical oeuvre are described by F. Thibaudeau, *La Lettre d'imprimerie*, vol. 1 (Paris: Bureau de l'édition, 1921), 183–184.

66 Though in former use, the term "microtypography" was utilized by Jost Hochuli in a lecture in 1982. For him, this term indicates "the details of the typography" and "deals with type, letter spacing, word composition and their spacing along the line, and the line space in the column." Contrariwise, macrotypography "determines the format, dimension, and arrangement of the columns of text and illustrations, the distribution of the titles and the pacing of captions."

67 It should be noted that the date of birth of Garamond, surely the best known of the type-engravers of French Renaissance, ranges from between 1480 and 1499, and even 1501. It seems that only professional sources systematically report these uncertainties as to date. Garamond was born around 1480, according to Albert Kapr, around 1490, according to Max Caflisch, and around 1500, according to Alexander Lawson. The Larousse and Robert dictionaries, the *Encyclopaedia Universalis*, and *La Civilisation de l'écriture* give his birth as 1499.

68 Antoine Augereau was a French printer and punch engraver. Associated with the Affaire des Placards, he was condemned to

death at the stake on Place Maubert in Paris in 1534 (as Étienne Dolet was to be). Simon de Colines (1480–1546) was simultaneously a renowned publisher, printer, bookseller, engraver, and type-founder. He also printed many works decorated by Tory. Having married Henri I Estienne's widow, he also collaborated with his son-in-law, Robert Estienne.

69 F. Thibaudeau, op. cit., 16.

70 "*[P]our servir à imprimer livres en grec pour mectre en noz librayries*"; quoted by J. Paillard, *Claude Garamont* (La Courneuve: OFMI-Garamont, 1969), 20.

71 F. Thibaudeau, op. cit., 224.

72 Located in the Netherlands, from the eighteenth century onwards, the town of Leyden was to become a world center of printing. The Elzévirs had already made it their home in the sixteenth century.

73 Antwerp at the time belonged to Spain.

74 H.-J. Martin and R. Chartier (gen. eds.), *Histoire de l'édition française*, vol. 1 (Paris: Promodis, 1982), 264.

75 J. Toulet, art. cit., 929.

76 Cited by H. Walter, *L'Aventure des langues en Occident*, Paris: Laffont, 1994, 244.

77 After Stephan Füssel (1999).

78 In his essay *Modern Typography* (London: Hyphen Press, 2004), Robin Kinross develops the idea that (printed) typography is modern by nature and by definition. As he sees it, this modernity is truly expressed from around 1700 on. He thus dissociates his ideas from those of other historians who assimilate typographical modernity to a shorter period and to a narrowed perspective, reducing it sometimes to twentieth-century modernism alone, beginning in the nineteenth century, or among the European avant-gardes of the early twentieth century.

79 R. Kinross, ibid., 22.

80 J. Toulet, art. cit., 933.

81 Jacques Wolkensinger, *L'Histoire à la une* (Paris: Gallimard—Découvertes, 1989), 23.

82 P. Albert (ed.) La *France, les États-Unis et leurs presses. 1632–1976* (Paris: Centre Georges Pompidou, 1977), 22.

83 J. Wolkensinger, op. cit., 25.

84 "In 1762, it adopted the title of *Gazette de France* that it kept until it folded in 1915. As with many of the earliest European news periodicals, it long remained devoted solely to presenting news items [...] *Le Journal de Paris*, the first French daily, was born on July 1, 1777. The *Gazette*'s privilege prevented it from dealing with political matters and its contents are often disappointing in the narrowness of its coverage," *La France, les États-Unis et leurs presses*, op. cit., 22 and 56.

85 The interest of this new kind of publications is described by Robin Kinross in his book *Modern Typography* (op cit., chapter II). In particular he quotes (pp. 23 and 32) the *Mechanick Exercises* of Joseph Moxon (1683) and *La Science pratique de l'imprimerie* by Martin Dominique Fertel (1723).

86 Cited by F. Thibaudeau, op. cit., 269–270.

87 Fernand Baudin, quoted by J. Laliberté, *Formes typographiques. Historique, anatomie, classification* (Quebec: Les Presses de l'Université Laval, 2004), 7. Leaving aside blackletter Gothic, still in use in some countries.

88 Alexander Lawson, *Anatomy of a Typeface* (London: Hamish Hamilton, 1990), 136–137.

89 The Enschedé en Zonen printing works, located at Haarlem in the Netherlands, was founded in 1703 by Izaac Enschedé. The workshop was extended by a foundry in 1743. The firm acquired international fame for its dedication to quality and for the fact that the direct descendants of Izaac Enschedé continued the business until 1991.

90 Quoted by A. Haley in the magazine *U&lc*, vol. 11, no. 4, February 1985, 15.

91 American politician, author, and inventor, Benjamin Franklin was very interested in typography. The brother of a printer, he set up his own printing works in Philadelphia in 1730.

92 Cited by L. Gervereau, op. cit., 16.

93 F. Thibaudeau, op. cit., 240.

94 *Le Cabinet des poinçons de l'Imprimerie nationale* (Paris: Imprimerie nationale, 1963), 3rd ed.

95 *Les Caractères de l'Imprimerie nationale* (Paris: Imprimerie nationale, 1990), 64.

96 R. Kinross, op. cit., 28.

97 Pierre-Simon Fournier, cited by A. Kapr, *The Art of Lettering*, op. cit., 150.

98 F. Thibaudeau, op. cit., 294.

99 Édouard Fournier, *Histoire des enseignes de Paris* (Paris: E. Dentu, 1884), 67–68. "Several of these plaques are preserved today at the Musée Carnavalet [in Paris]. [...] Forty years ago, one could still see, on many street corners in Paris, the old name engraved on a piece of hard limestone embedded into the wall of the first house on the street, because, since the street had had its name inscribed on the stone, [...] nobody had thought of changing this official name, however bizarre, strange, and incomprehensible it might be [...]. How many old streets owed their name to signs which [...] had remained in the same place for two or three centuries!" (p. 68). See the continuation of the text (that summarizes an eighteenth-century study) concerning streets in Paris, a good number of which still exist, that owe their name to signs, such as surnames, pictures, rebuses, puns, word plays, low-relief, etc.

100 D. Grant (ed.) *Sterne* (London: Rupert Hart-Davis, 1950), 109 (*Tristram Shandy*, II, xi).

101 Quoted by M. Butor, *Essais sur le roman* (Paris: Gallimard, 1992), 128.

102 The newspaper, a broadsheet initially entitled the *Daily Universal Register* was founded in 1785 by John Walter. It was renamed the *Times* in 1788.

103 É. Fournier, op. cit., 443.

104 Ibid., 442.

105 See A. Jammes, *Les Didot. Trois siècles de typographie et de bibliophilie* (exh. cat., Paris: Bibliothèque Historique de la Ville de Paris/Musée de l'Imprimerie de Lyon, 1998).

106 Many works devoted to the history of typography seem to trace back the first Didot types to specimens dating from 1775 or 1784, while others indicate still more remote dates. According to Francis Thibaudeau, they date from 1757; Georges Jean though opts for 1755, making the earliest Didots

contemporary of Baskerville (1757), though without yet the full panoply of characteristics that was to make them such a success. (F. Thibaudeau, op. cit.; G. Jean, *L'Écriture mémoire des hommes* (Paris: Gallimard, 1987).

107 The spelling of his name varies depending on the source—Louis Vafflard, Pierre-Louis Waflard, Pierre-Louis Wafflard.

108 The Pica point, an Anglo-American typographical measurement, entered general use at the end of the nineteenth century and corresponds to a unit of 0.351 mm or 0.0148057 in.

109 Cited by R. Kinross, op. cit., 32.

110 Quoted by M. Audin, op. cit., 78.

111 Ibid.

112 A. Kapr, *The Art of Lettering*, op. cit., 178. Designer and typographer, Albert Kapr (1918–1995) is also the author of a number of reference books on typography and scripts (notably *Johann Gutenberg* and *Schriftkunst* [*The Art of Lettering*]).

113 Quoted by A. de Margerie, *J. B. Bodoni* (Paris: Jacques Damase, 1985), 41.

114 His volume, *Saggio tipografico di fregi e maiuscoli* was published in 1771.

115 Giambattista Bodoni, cited by A. Kapr, *The Art of Lettering*, op. cit., 178.

116 Quoted by A. de Margerie, op. cit., 50–51 and 56.

117 Jan Tschichold, *Livre et typographie* (Paris: Allia, 1994), 31 (French translation).

118 A. Kapr, *The Art of Lettering*, op. cit., 178.

119 Cited by F. Thibaudeau, op. cit., 264. Fournier took against the initial construction of the *romain du roi* as devised by the first commission in charge of the project (this was not Grandjean's final design). See n. 61.

120 Friedrich Koenig, quoted by G. Martin, "Imprimerie," *Encyclopædia Universalis* (Paris, 1995), 1026 (Corpus 11).

121 Henri Focillon, *La Peinture aux* XIXe *et* XXe *siècles* (H. Laurens, 1928), 2.

Decisive changes

*"In the course of the nineteenth century, the image began by stirring and then burst into life;
and man discovered the art of sound reproduction whose effects will reverberate long and hard.
Faced with this competitor, the written word initially reacted by sustaining its power for renewal
with posters with aggressive typefaces and crude and provocative illustrations."*[1]

Henri-Jean Martin

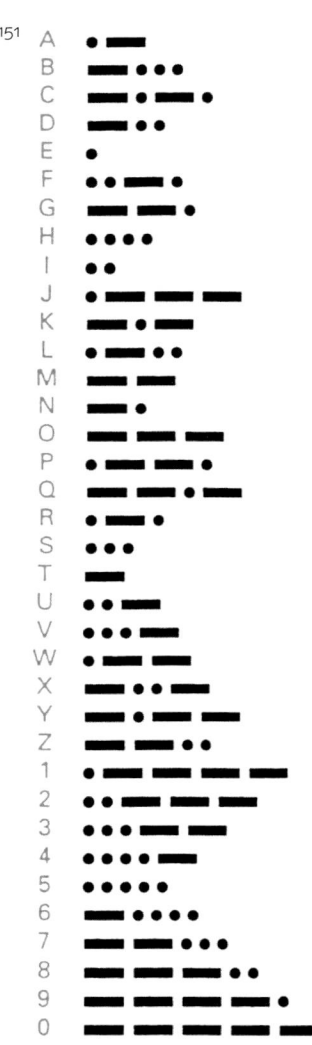

151

151
Samuel Morse: alphabet coded
as a sequence of dots and dashes
for the United States electric telegraph.
Code developed in 1838.

Like other crafts, for a long time printing and typography remained wedded to their cottage-industry beginnings. If this marriage had already proved somewhat uncomfortable in the eighteenth century, the nineteenth century and its avatars, with their attendant upheavals, were to transform radically the course of developments. In the space of a few decades, enormous economic, political, and social changes were to have their effect on all the practices and forms of visual expression. The chief factors powering these transformations had evolved as much out of the Industrial Revolution as from the turbulent sociopolitical backdrop generally. Europe witnessed wars, riots, and pitched battles arising from class conflict, while the constitution of new nation-states continued apace. Through the speed of urbanization and the onrush of technology, a new urban culture sprung up, one that transformed lifestyles in the West forever.

Throughout the nineteenth century, living spaces and buildings embraced new approaches to architecture, while the invention of new means of transport (tram, railroad, bicycle, car, subway) had an impact on the relationship of man to his environment. In the field of communications, the invention of the telegraph (and later, for instance, of the telephone) meant the more rapid transmission of information, consequently increasing shipping and transport speeds and reconfiguring the whole notion of time. The Industrial Revolution had direct and significant repercussions on the printing sector and on the numerous media dependent on its processes of reproduction—and this well before the situation shifted again with the new potential of photography. These ongoing changes made for exceptional transformations, deep-seated and durable, on the social front. Economic and social ructions churned the urban landscape and upended patterns of everyday life. Ideas and culture were prey to profound philosophical and artistic questioning.

Each in his own way, Marx, Nietzsche, and Freud devised a new understanding of the functioning of society and of what it means to be human, unpicking existing mechanisms and delving deep into the hidden face of what had always been unspoken. Rather than proposing explanations en bloc, their thought and that of others tended to be directed towards overarching questions, while the insights of sciences such as sociology and psychology made it possible to change the way human behavior and other factors could be viewed.

This change in the air also profoundly altered artistic practices. By the middle of the nineteenth century, the grip of Church and State had weakened still further, thereby furthering the emergence of modern art. Whereas hitherto the power to create was a privilege enjoyed by divine power alone, now humankind, too, was permitted to seize the reins. Emboldened by their new-found status as true creators, artists joined forces in movements and turned the academic system that had prevailed since the seventeenth century upside-down. Mimesis receded before other modes of representation, with more room granted to the expression of subjectivity, of sensations, of inner feelings. Hegel, in locating the crucial break that was about to take place, proclaimed that artists had arrived "at the end of Romantic art" and "on the threshold of modern art."[2] After 1820, novel and ever more exigent artistic trends emerged one after the other to take the floor: Romanticism, Realism, Naturalism, Impressionism, Symbolism, and so on.

Graphic design and typography

The upheavals of the nineteenth century and of the periods shortly before and after naturally had a direct and visible influence on developments in graphics and typography, which now found themselves in a changeable and responsive climate, one in which they soon found active parts to play. On a technical level, in the space of about a century, these trades had morphed from still semi-artisanal practices into a genuine industry, while the demarcation of labor between design and manufacture phases was becoming ever more clear-cut. With developments in mechanization, graphic design seemed above all to evolve in response to the fallout from technology. With the mechanical manufacture of paper, the automation of printing, the invention of lithography, and the mechanization of composition, the print landscape was almost unrecognizable. To these transformations were added new possibilities for image-making introduced by chromolithography and photography. Teeming with pictures, print media could occupy an increasingly dominant place in everyday life, while parallel improvements in literacy ensured a ready reading market.

Apart from the book, print media mushroomed like never before. If formerly the book had enjoyed an unassailable position, the nineteenth century saw the spectacular rise of rival forms of typography and graphic communication (not the least of which were the billboard and the popular illustrated press) that brought into the public forum a burgeoning mass of print. In parallel with the intimate relationship between the book and its reader, the community nature of the ever-expanding print environment was being reinforced. The nineteenth century hailed the consecration of advertising, of the periodical, illustration, and popular literature, while books of popular science and other forms of knowledge were sold in untold quantities. Advertising, dividing its attention between the billboard and the press, was consequently to constitute one of the most widespread graphic forms. Massed ranks of hoardings arrived in every major city in Europe as in the United States. Advertising was born from mass production, and the abiding issue was how to make supply square with demand. By the end of the nineteenth century, with the lifting of censorship and other forms of prohibition that had encumbered the press and bill-posting alike, graphic media could now play a full part in everyday existence without hindrance.

The increased levels of literacy fostered a new situation that coincided with significant innovations in the domain of graphics. It is true that the typography of this era has been the subject of severe criticism, with some analysts accusing it of sacrificing quality to quantity over a period they judge as overlong; this is the case, for instance, with a proportion of graphic material and advertising from the Victorian era, in which visual overkill seems to have constituted a concerted strategy. Although such reactions are justified with respect to certain aspects of the printed production of the nineteenth century, it should not blind one to the rewards lurking in much superior graphic and typographical material of the time. In the space of a few decades, several innovations were introduced that paved the way for a rebirth in graphic innovation that was to be brilliantly confirmed during the first third of the twentieth century.

Inventions and technologies

Technological developments, since they have a direct impact on everyday practices, compounded the effects of social, political, economic, cultural, and artistic factors on graphic design and typography in the nineteenth century. The rate of technological advance and invention speeded up as never before. It was a phenomenon that accelerated over the decades, with the second half of the century witnessing the ascent of the modern industrial complex. The generalized uptake of mechanization transformed many sectors that had relied up to that point on craftsmanship and the productive logic of small-scale industry. Steam power (and later electricity) was quickly supplanting power supplied by animals and men. The rhythm of life and of the economy was reshaped by means of transportation that ushered in an utterly

152

152
French reading-book, *Nouvel Alphabet de l'enfance*, Metz, 1867. 5 ¹⁄₂ × 3 ¹⁄₂ in. (14 × 9 cm). Above, the letter for the lesson is reproduced in upper- and lowercase and in various types.

new relationship between man and speed. In 1814, the English engineer George Stephenson designed a locomotive capable of drawing several coaches and devised the principle of steam traction on rails. In a breathtakingly short space of time, thousands of miles of railroad were to be laid, permitting speeds of up to thirty miles per hour. While other inventions of the time (such as the electric bulb in 1879) were having a decisive impact on the human environment, the second part of the nineteenth century climaxed with an authentic revolution in transport.

Information transmission constituted another sector in flux. Communication cables were laid, and telephone poles erected, which, added to railroad construction, were assembled into national and international networks. Information could now be transmitted over distances without the need to physically move humans or animals.

In 1837–38, the process was simplified by means of the electric telegraph[3] employing the code of Samuel Morse, a transmission of binary digits in the form of dots and dashes. Later, sound transmission by means of the telephone (Alexander Graham Bell, 1876) and reproduction by gramophone (Thomas Edison, 1877) added a further dimension to telecommunications. As regards the mail, the invention of the postage stamp[4] (England, 1840) greatly increased its marketability, as did the postcard[5] (Austro-Hungary, 1869). The exchange of signs over distances brought into being a new transnational space of information and communication, which in turn called for the massive deployment of graphics and typography.

Technological progress in printing and typography had immediate influence on graphics, in particular through the invention of new techniques of impression, reproduction, and composition. Lithography facilitated the mass production of images: with the introduction of color, the process was behind the unprecedented expansion of the chromolithographic poster that soon became omnipresent (as indeed it still is) in the urban landscape. Then photoengraving made possible the reproduction in print of photographic images. The successful development of methods of mechanical composition considerably accelerated a practice that had been extremely labor intensive. A century after the embryonic phase of print mechanization (metal and steam-powered presses), the appearance of offset in about 1900 brought radical modifications in terms of print costs and speeds. In the wake of these various inventions, the sheer volume of printed matter increased enormously during the nineteenth century. Compounding the impact of technology and economic factors, the shifting artistic landscape joined forces with graphic design to usher in far-reaching changes in visual perception as well as in the creative arts.

These modifications are exemplified by the ongoing evolution of architecture: developments in metallurgy, by allowing combinations of iron, reinforced concrete, and glass, raised the thorny question of function, and certain architects, in reshaping the role of ornament or else forsaking it altogether, regarded structure as the essential dynamic. This novel approach is encapsulated in the famous saying of Louis Sullivan, the central figure in the Chicago School, "form ever follows function." In 1898 Sullivan stated: "I should say that it would be greatly for our aesthetic good if we should refrain entirely from the use of ornament for a period of years, in order that our thought might concentrate acutely upon the production of buildings well formed and comely in the nude."[6] The idea that the beautiful has to be redefined with respect of the useful was reaffirmed, and the art of building on a large scale was entirely rethought in the light of functionalism (a tendency that was to have a notable impact on graphic and typographical experimentation in the early decades of the twentieth century). Through a combination of technical developments, artistic mutations, and economic demands, the nineteenth century witnessed the arrival of graphic material as a popular idiom, while the media of visual communication morphed into articles of mass consumption. As with a number of other (typo)graphical products, the soaring development of the press and publishing now reached the masses.

153

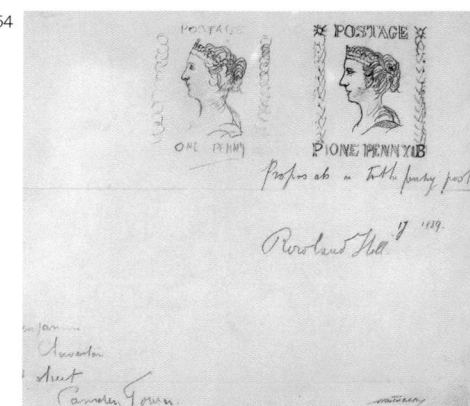

154

153
The first postage stamp in the world, the Penny Black, with the profile of Queen Victoria, officially introduced for postal use in Great Britain on May 6, 1840.

154
Original drawing for the Penny Black stamp, Sir Rowland Hill, Great Britain, 1839.

Lithography, a new freedom

The invention of lithography represents a quantum leap in visual communication and is a significant factor in the distribution of printed material. Previously, the printing of type and pictures was obtained by means of engraving, a time-honored but laborious and costly process. Furthermore, cutting the type punch and engraving the illustrations comprised two distinct phases. Nevertheless, images engraved on wood were sometimes incorporated into the typographical form, making it possible to print text and pictures simultaneously. Copper-engraving, finer than its counterpart on wood, needed to be printed on special presses, and was once again separate from the text matter. With lithography, words and images can readily appear on one and the same support (although variants exist printed with a combination of lithograph image and letterpress). Although certain labor-intensive techniques such as xylography had earlier allowed this, these two elements of graphic idiom could henceforth be feasibly reduced to a unified process leading from design to printing. As a reproductive technique, lithography constitutes a wholly novel procedure, offering pride of place to drawing and to gesture.

Lithography was invented between 1796 and 1798 in Bavaria by Aloys Senefelder. He came across the process by chance: scribbling a list of clothes for the laundry on a stone, he realized that what he had written could be printed off. Following a few tests, he developed a lithographic technique that consists in writing or drawing on the flat surface of a stone using a greasy substance (such as chalk or ink). Bavarian limestone, porous and with a very fine grain, happens to be particularly well suited to this process. After inscription, the stone is moistened with water; as the fat repulses the water, the ink only takes in the greasy areas. Thus prepared, the printing surface simply has to be run through the press.[7] Lithography offers three special advantages for graphics: technical simplification, the possibility of integrating text and image, and the potential for large-scale, serial printing. Still a craft, lithography lies at the crossroads of earlier techniques of reproduction and fully industrialized printing processes. As it calls for a combination of technical know-how and artistry, in generally a skilled craftsman is required to transfer the design to the stone. The process also allows far more nuances of the same hue to be reproduced than in other forms of print-making. Chromolithography developed in conjunction with the rise of lithography: each color has its own stone, and impressions are obtained by superposition, obviously calling for pinpoint registration. For creative artists, the new process with its breakthrough in the use of color instigated a medium with a wholly new look, permitting a vast palette with unusual mixtures.

Developed in 1837, chromolithography kick-started the era of the modern poster, allowing eye-catching, colorful, and high-keyed images to be easily reproduced on a large scale. Lithography spawned many other media and types of illustration, such as illustrations in books and magazines, in calendars, and on labels of every kind. In parallel, lithography was a printing process tailor-made for the reproduction of works of art, in particular oil paintings; there again, its use led to the popularization of the image concerned. Throughout the nineteenth century, the process repeatedly demonstrated its ability to reproduce texts and images in large formats and in massive numbers, thereby confirming its capacity for mass-distribution and its democratizing potential.

The papermaking and newspaper industries

Just at the time when lithography was being invented and on the point of becoming a new means of reproduction, profound transformations were taking place in traditional printing too. Two outstanding developments occurred between 1796 and 1798. The first was the use of metal in place of wood in the manufacture of the presses. Output could increase significantly: in 1797, the earliest entirely metal presses attained runs of more than three thousand sheets a day. Such levels of productivity represented a tenfold increase over the Gutenberg hand-press, estimated at three hundred to one thousand five hundred sheets a day. In 1814, the first steam

155

155
The first French postage stamp, issued on January 1, 1849, representing the goddess Ceres. By Jacques-Jean Barre, chief engraver at the Mint.

156
Charles Motte, *Pleut-il? Ou les surprises*
(Is it Raining? or, the Surprises),
early nineteenth century. Print.

157
Roger Fenton, Photograph of London, c. 1850.

158
Watermark "C HARRIS 1846," English mechanical
laid paper (the paper used by Victor Hugo for
the manuscript of *Les Travailleurs de la mer*).

press[8] was used in London to print the *Times*. With production levels of one thousand sheets per hour, newspapers could now strike out for even larger readerships; back-to-back printing also greatly augmented the profitability of the process.

The second development was in paper manufacture. Like printing, the manufacture of paper was vastly affected by the growth of mechanization. In 1798, Louis-Nicolas Robert designed "a papermaking machine" capable of manufacturing rolls of web a dozen meters in length. Robert was promptly employed by Didot Saint-Léger, a member of the famous printing family, who purchased his invention from him (others joined in the manufacture and the marketing of these machines, and the shenanigans surrounding this enterprise finished up in the courts). The first fully operational machine was manufactured in England in 1803, through the intermediary of the Briton John Gamble, brother-in-law of Didot Saint-Léger who had gained access to Louis-Nicolas Robert's plans. If England thus became the first country to possess a real papermaking industry, mechanical production processes for paper were quickly propagated throughout the West.

Paper manufacture was to undergo another transformation, this time brought on by shortages in its raw material. Since its introduction in Europe in the twelfth century and even before, paper had been manufactured principally from rag. In the nineteenth century, responding to the sudden dearth of worn fabric, it was mixed with wood chip and soon, around 1880, wood pulp was being used on its own (before our era, the earliest Chinese paper was manufactured from vegetable fiber such as hemp, mulberry bark, and bamboo). Paper became a less expensive and therefore more common material, the use of wood allowing it to be made in greater quantities. Other major changes awaited processes of reproduction and letterpress printing: the mechanization of composition, up and running towards the end of the nineteenth century, and the arrival of photoengraving (around 1850), which facilitates the reproduction of photographic images. Initially, these inventions seem generally to have impinged solely upon the technical aspects of printing and typography. Thus, photography was to be used initially for reproducing pictures before becoming an integral component of graphic language.

Photography: "writing" and "light"

More even than lithography, photography afforded vast opportunities in the field of the visual arts. Images of reality—objects, spaces, the environment generally—could now be caught on the wing, captured, and preserved. Though it was officially announced only in Paris in 1839, the invention of photography was a far earlier affair, and is ascribed to Joseph-Nicéphore Niépce. A printer-lithographer by trade, his initial intention had been to find a method of

159
Joseph-Nicéphore Niépce (1765–1833), *Point de vue du Gras*, France, 1826 or 1827. Process engraving on tin plate sensitized with bitumen, 6 ¹/₂ × 8 in. (16.6 × 20.2 cm). This is one of the very first known photographic documents, a replica of the original reproduction dating to 1952. View taken by Niépce from a window in his country house in the village of Saint-Loup-de-Varennes. A handwritten inscription on the back of the plate notes: "*The first results obtained Spontaneously by the action of the light. By Monsieur Niepce De Chalon sur Saône* [sic]." The plate, rediscovered in 1952, is extremely difficult to reproduce because of its low visibility and very weak contrasts.

160
William Henry Fox Talbot, *The Haystack*, extract from *The Pencil of Nature* (London, 1844–46), the first volume to be illustrated with photographs, glued.

161
William Henry Fox Talbot (1800–1877), photogenic drawing, Great Britain, c. 1839. Talbot began experimenting with "photogenic drawing" in 1834, improving the process about 1839–40.

162
Louis-Émile Durandelle, construction of the Comptoir d'Escompte, Paris; beneath the glass canopy, 1881.

automating engraving reproduction; starting in the mid-1810s, he experimented with reactions for various photosensitive surfaces. Ten years later, Niépce managed, at the end of what was probably a very prolonged exposure time, to fix on a tin plate the view from a window in his country house. Dating from 1826 or 1827, Niépce's landscape *Point de vue du Gras* was one of the first known photographic documents.[9] Subsequent photographic experiments further widened the potential of the new process. Louis-Jacques-Mandé Daguerre improved the invention by fixing images on iodized-silver copperplate. Samuel Morse (the inventor of the electric telegraph and the Morse code), who was among the first to see daguerreotypes, confessed himself mightily impressed by their fineness of detail, writing at the time that no painting or engraving could hope to compete with it.[10] A contemporary of Daguerre's, the Briton William Henry Fox Talbot explored the possibilities of paper, obtaining the first negatives, allowing positive photographs to be produced in unlimited quantities (known as the calotype process, 1839). Fox Talbot also carried out "photogenic drawings" (the technique had been trialed previously), forerunners of the famous photogrammes of Man Ray, László Moholy-Nagy, and Christian Schad in the 1920s. For this, Fox Talbot placed an object on a sheet of paper covered with silver salts and exposed it to sunlight, resulting in an image-print of the subject showing light on a dark ground. Fox Talbot was also the author of the first book of photographs, *The Pencil of Nature* (1844–46), which was tipped-in with photographs of portraits, architectural monuments, sculptures, and even engravings.

As lithography was entering its initial developmental phase, photography remained relatively underdeveloped, and the reproduction of images was most often obtained by a form of engraving. Before photoengraving made mass reproduction of photographs technically possible in the 1870s, illustrators had to make do with working directly from photographs (a practice that was in addition fairly widespread among painters, including Degas, Courbet, Ingres, and Delacroix). When printing techniques were developed that ensured repeated reproducibility, photography could be printed at least well as wood-engraving, and at lower cost, with enhanced precision, and with an appreciable saving in time. Thus photography, so conducive to the recording of visible reality, had major knock-on effects on engraving, painting, and drawing.

Another invention made the medium more favorable to public use: in the 1880s, George Eastman developed a small, handheld camera. Photography promptly became "every person's art form," and the amateur photographer was born. Armed with these advances, photography was poised to conquer the hallowed pages of the press. Hitherto, newspapers and magazines, had, to a greater or lesser extent, remained dependent on engraving for original artwork as much as for reproduction.

The new form of photoengraving allowed the newspaper industry to scale up from craft to fully mechanized output. By transferring the image through a screen onto the photographic surface, the new process facilitated the reproducibility of photographs, the origin of a massive increase in the daily "consumption" of images (still today, the phenomenon is one of relentless growth, on paper as on screen).

In 1895, the invention of the cinematograph brought yet another dimension to photography: the rapid and seamless sequencing of fixed images to achieve an illusion of motion. Graphics, already challenged by photography, now encountered the power of cinema (which, however, was to offer it in turn a new whole platform). The moving image fostered motion, greater dynamism, and a search for tension even within the frame of the unmoving image—paths energetically explored for instance by the Futurists in their graphic output.

New developments in printing

In the second half of the nineteenth century, printing technologies underwent a further series of fundamental transformations. The regime of mechanization, which had previously affected both the press and papermaking, now accelerated with the introduction of the rotary press and the automation of type composition. Each technical improvement improved productivity, often resulting in considerable savings in time.

The rotary press, in which flatbed printing is replaced by mechanically inked rotating cylinders, was invented in the United States in the 1840s. After an exploratory few years, the new machine could deliver up to twenty thousand recto-verso printed sheets an hour. The unprecedented efficacy of the rotary press heralded an exponential rise in print mass, the production speeds obtainable marking a watershed for printing, typography, print-runs, the printed image, and the history of visual expression alike. Due to huge increases in print-runs, newspapers, books, and magazines were made increasingly accessible.

Yet another technological advance further cut the time taken to prepare material for printing. Type composition had hitherto remained a manual process, with the characters being placed on galley one by one, just as they had been for four centuries. Even for the most adroit craftsmen, the composition of lengthy texts (books and newspapers) represented a titanic task. From the 1820s, the search was underway for a means of automating typographical composition and mechanizing type-founding; the objective was to save time and shave manufacturing delays to the minimum (symptomatically the era also witnessed the first typewriters, cumbersome machines that nonetheless burgeoned into the more user-friendly models of the twentieth century).

163
Jean Andrieu, *Désastres de la guerre*. Pont d'Argenteuil, photograph registered for copyright in Paris in 1871.

164
Smeeton and Blanchard, *Pont d'Argenteuil*. View from the Gennevilliers embankment, after the photograph of Monsieur Andrieu, engraving published in *L'Illustration*, July 15, 1871, France.

Linotype (the name is a contraction of the expression "line of types") was the first machine to successfully combine casting and composition. Invented in the United States by Ottmar Mergenthaler (an American of German origin and a watchmaker by trade), after further development it came into service in 1886. The entirely automated composition of text is realized by means of typing on a machine whose keys select and align the selected matrices (the positive form of the letters required). Whenever a line of text is complete, hot metal is automatically cast into the matrices; after the metal hardens, the type-bar obtained is ready for impression and the matrices return to their starting position. The Linotype machine, by multiplying the speed of composition virtually by ten, also represented an exceptional gain in productivity, allowing workmen to set from six to nine thousand characters an hour, whereas,

in optimum conditions, the manual method could attain a maximum of no more than some one thousand five hundred. Initially devised to speed up the printing of newspapers, the invention was partially financed by a New York press conglomerate. In 1886, the *New York Tribune* became the first newspaper to be composed on a Linotype machine. At the same time, another machine similarly intended to automate composition was in the pipeline: the Monotype, invented by an American, Tolbert Lanston, and patented in 1887. As its name implies, Monotype composes and casts the type in units. It consists of two distinct machines. The first, on which the text is inputted on a keyboard, encodes the output on a strip of punched paper tape. This strip is then introduced into a second machine, which decodes it, casting the types automatically one by one. If the print quality of Monotype was superior to that obtained with Linotype, the greater efficiency of the latter ensured that it was the technique of choice for upwards of seventy years, especially for ephemeral reading matter and publications in which print quality was not the paramount criterion (newspapers, mass-market paperbacks, promotional materials, etc.). Linotype and Monotype machines began to come on stream at the end of the nineteenth century; the latter indeed was even being used in some areas in mass production from the very start of the 1890s. These two inventions, created on American soil, soon triumphed in Western Europe, being taken up widely by the beginning of the twentieth century.

Together with other machines, inspired by or complementary to them (such as Ludlow and Intertype), these techniques brought the industrialization of printing to a head. Such technical developments accelerated the growth in printed matter and provided quantities of reading that were made available to an increasingly literate and educated population among which literacy was no longer exceptional. Henceforth, every print operation, from inputting the text to the delivery of the final printed page, was to become a mechanized process. By accentuating labor demarcation, these new mechanisms for typesetting were simultaneously driving a wedge between the typesetter-inputter and the typographer or printer.

Designed to increase profits and productivity, transformations in the mechanics of composition and impression primarily affected the technical, manufacturing aspects, while questions of conception, design, and form tended to take a backseat. Artwork was essentially limited to the busy profusion of Victorian fantasy, and an unsatisfactory balance had to be struck between a highly evolved technology and a plethoric graphic environment. By the end of the nineteenth century, several figures and movements were reacting against this precarious situation. William Morris and the Arts and Crafts movement were to adopt a position based on rejecting mechanization, calling for a return to traditions of craftsmanship and medieval values. Such ideas were capable of producing articles of great quality in visual and material terms, utterly divorced from the sphere of mass production, since handicraft and the close work it demanded was expensive and limited production to small quantities. Yet galloping mechanization also generated the opposite attitude among some creative artists, who

165
Linotype machine, Model 8, the United States.

embraced its technical advances unreservedly. However, this latter reaction was to be on the whole a later phenomenon, except for original contributions by sometimes isolated figures. If new graphic forms loomed on the horizon in the final decades of the nineteenth century, the search for a fusion between design and industry was only to bear fruit during the following century in the context of groundbreaking movements or schools, when the Werkbund, Russian Productivism, and the Bauhaus strove to imagine new artistic forms adapted to the mechanized environment.

Type and typography: a creative surge

Throughout the nineteenth century, the rise of technology and the development of communications propelled the visual energizing of type design and graphics towards profusion and exuberance. If this eclecticism spawned some noteworthy innovations (in particular at the beginning and the end of the century), it was also fed by historical references. In this intermingling of genres and styles, type attained enormous diversity and fell prey to some curious hybridizations. Newspapers, magazines, advertisements, catalogs, and other printed periodicals and ephemera were adorned with a bewildering variety of typographies that redrew the boundaries of visual perception.

Traditional typefaces, conceived for the benign pleasures of private reading, were not enough for the visual appetites of these new media; their refined forms, crafted and honed over the centuries, no longer corresponded to the overwhelming need for immediate impact. As industry developed, type design was characterized chiefly by quantity, as well as by novel formal solutions intended to meet pressing new demands. The continuous development and improvement of earlier material, such as had been the custom since the fifteenth century, began to be overtaken by a new wave, and it would seem that, henceforth, the predominant factors became innovation and visual novelty, together with a given typeface's capacity to catch the eye and its attendant commercial repercussions. Not only was the book no longer the medium par excellence, it was no more addressed solely to a cultivated elite; entering the public arena, it found itself assailed by other forms of written culture, such as the popular press.

Nineteenth-century type design stemmed from a number of landmark styles. The first two decades of the century introduced a succession of trailblazing innovations: the creation of alphabets in bold, and of types without serifs (both forms that subsequently became universal), as well as the invention of the Egyptian face with its slab serifs. Then, from the 1820s on, type entered a lengthy phase of visual competition during which decorative and ornamental aspects prevailed (Louis John Pouchée's engraved alphabets exemplify this stage). As the century wore on, the letter was subject to a host of graphic fantasies, until, at the end of the century, a need for clarification and improvements in quality was felt.

British innovations

At the beginning of the nineteenth century, Great Britain, which had already distinguished itself in the previous century with the work of Caslon and Baskerville, occupied a central role in typographical design. London was one of the first true metropolises and England's industrial might made it a leading European power. The resurgence in type design proved strongest where the Industrial Revolution flourished. In the space of only about fifteen years, several whole new categories of type came into being, in a foretaste of the feverish rate of change that was soon to affect the sector. Every one of these innovations represents an important step forward.

Robert Thorne, decorative-type manufacturer and the owner of a foundry in London, was among the first to make his mark. In about 1803, pursuing research by his master Thomas Cotterell, he designed a bold type, Bold Roman (or Fat Face). Thorne based his work on a Didot-type letter, fattening out the main strokes until they were roughly ten times thicker than the hairlines. Widely distributed, Robert Thorne's alphabet fathered a multitude of descendants. In France, similar characters were to appear around 1810, the boldest versions being dubbed "Norman." In England as in France these new alphabets were used especially for poster lettering as their sturdy appearance was ideally suited to attracting the passer-by. From the 1840s on, Bold Roman became hugely successful and split into innumerable fancy versions that became widely available. Meanwhile, on similar principles, British foundries were devising an extremely bold version of Gothic type. The second major (re)creation of the era is owed to William Caslon IV, whose great-grandfather of the same name had been a renowned figure in the first third of the previous century and creator of the by now classic typeface. In 1816, William Caslon IV signed the catalog of his foundry with some words printed in (capital) block letters. According to the typography historian Alexander Lawson, "this 28 point type, produced in capitals only, was the first sans serif to be purveyed as a printing type." The distant heir of stone inscriptions more than two thousand years old, this category of type continued to appear in British lettering for several decades thereafter. For the time, the suppression of letter terminations was certainly a daring move. As the serif had formed such an integral part of the letter, be it drawn, engraved, or printed, since Gutenberg, William Caslon IV's initially unpopular type was at the beginning something of a laughing-stock. What is more, these terminations constituted one of the principal distinguishing signs of the threefold evolution of Roman type (Old Face, Transition, and Modern). To early nineteenth-century eyes, sans serif type seemed nothing short of anomalous, and its apparently truncated, cropped form was resented by some as an amputation. Much derided at its inception, sans serif type was eventually to achieve the success that it has enduringly enjoyed throughout the twentieth century.

The ball started rolling in about 1830 when certain foundries created a lowercase variant of the type, proposing a condensed version (sans serif having, up to that point, been used chiefly on eye-catching platforms such as billboards and advertisements). The term "sans serif" itself was not used until 1832, when it was coined by the Englishman Vincent Figgins for one of his typefaces. It took a further twenty or so years for sans serif type to come into its own, but by the end of the century it featured in the majority of European and American foundry catalogs and consequently attained widespread use. Types without serifs can be regarded as one of the most audacious typographical innovations of the early nineteenth century. More than an alternative in thickness or in the shape of a serif, more than a modification, refinement, or honing, sans serif laid the foundations for a total transformation of the form and construction of the type alphabet. By harking back to a long-forgotten aspect of lettering, it unveils its elementary structure, a circumstance that has made sans serif particularly amenable to the far-reaching typographical experiments of the twentieth century.

Contemporary with the researches of William Caslon IV, another great typographical creation came to the fore in or around 1815. Vincent Figgins, a type designer and creator of a foundry in London, drew the first models of capitals known as "Egyptian," characterized by thick, rectangular serifs and by a reduction in the distinction between main lines and hairlines.[11] Egyptian, like Bold Roman, was a roaring success, spreading during the 1830s and 1840s to France, Germany, and the United States, to the point that it partially supplanted Didot characters, and appeared in innumerable alternatives—light, shadow, condensed, etc. Vincent Figgins also created many fanciful alphabets, including a shadow face in 1815. Like William Caslon IV's sans serif and Robert Thorne's Fat Face, Vincent Figgins's Egyptian testifies to a need for renewal and contributed engagingly to the ensuing diversification of typefaces.

Born at a time when England stood at the vanguard of the typographical scene, these three types, each in its own manner, expressed an underlying drive for root-and-branch change and signaled a decisive shift to industrialization. Crucially, they were also the cause and forerunners of a new appetite for the visual, coinciding, for instance, with the discovery of the principle of extraction of contours from the study of visual phenomena and the perceptual effects of optical illusions.

166

CANON ITALIC OPEN.

CUMBERLAND.

CANON ORNAMENTED.

TYPOGRAPHY.

TWO LINES ENGLISH EGYPTIAN.

W CASLON JUNR   LETTERFOUNDER

TWO LINES ENGLISH OPEN.

SALISBURY SQUARE.

167   TWO LINES PICA, ANTIQUE.

ABCDEFGHIJKLMNOPQR STUVWXYZ&,:;.- £1234567890

168

venezianischer Porträtmalerei

169

A B C D
E F G H
I J K L M
N O P Q
R S T U V
W X Y Z
a b c d e f
g h i j k l
m n o p
q r s t u v
w x y z

170

A B C D
E F G H
I J K L
M N O P
Q R S T
U V W
X Y Z

171
Tuscan typefaces, nineteenth century. The top two lines show two variants of a typeface characterized by ornamentation of the outlines. The characters of the bottom line widen out to finish in serifs that are both solid and elegant.

172
Ornamental capitals by Gustav Schelter, Leipzig, 1847.

173
Blackletter, William Caslon IV, London, 1821.

174
Decorated alphabets engraved on boxwood, from a unique collection, Louis John Pouchée's workshop (type-founder in 1810s and 1820s), London, c. 1820.

175
Victorian alphabet, Heather Lightface.

176
Vincent Figgins, 1835.

171

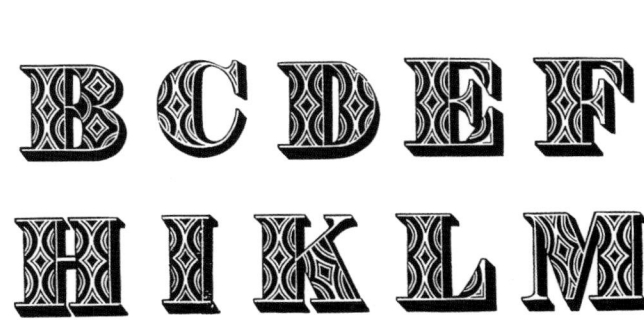

172

BALDUEN.
BERN & GADO
BREMEN
CHARLES.
BENKO DORUS
CHEMNITZ
KANTON
MENGE ALBUM
WILHELMSBAD
NIEDERLAGE

173
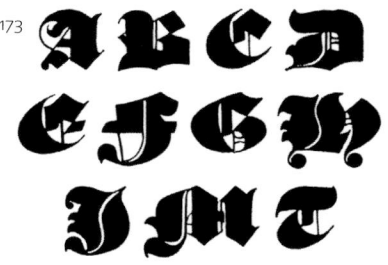

174

175

176

Eclecticism and exuberance

In the 1830s and 1840s, Victorian graphic design spread throughout the West. It was a period of abundance, richness, and diversification, combined on occasion with a degree of ponderousness. From now on, the preponderant factors were to be decoration and imagination, a far remove from the striving for essential form characteristic of a William Caslon IV. A plethora of letterforms arose and alphabets appeared in a dizzying array of ornamental variants. For foundries, the sale of type constituted a profitable business. As against the innovations of the early part of the century, these new alphabets displayed elaborate or outlandishly contrived shapes. This is the case for those types known as "Tuscan" and "Italian" (or "English-Italian"), which also originated in Great Britain—alphabets intended less to enhance legibility than to amuse the eye.

England also saw the birth of the first Clarendon in about 1844–45. The earliest model, designed by Robert Besley with assistance from the engraver Benjamin Fox, came from the

177

Fann Street Foundry in London. The character was based at the same time on bold and Egyptian types, whose serifs it softens. At the outset, Clarendon's function was to highlight sections of text, a role previously ascribed to italic. Clearly no fancy type, it combines easy reading with a certain visual impact, an amalgamation of strength and readability. In 1850, Robert Besley expatiated on the merit of his designs: "while they are distinct and striking, they possess a graceful outline, avoiding on the one hand, the clumsy inelegance of Antique or Egyptian Characters, and on the other, the appearance of an ordinary Roman letter thickened by long use."[12] The alphabet was quickly taken up and the name Clarendon is used to designate the entire family spawned by this initial model.

From the 1830s to the 1880s, many fancy alphabets carved in wood were created in Europe and probably still more in the United States. Thanks to their large size, they greatly increased the impact of the captions then invading advertisements. Starting in the mid-nineteenth century, they appear as the predominant element in posters, a role they were to keep until challenged by the lithograph in about 1870. Technical developments encouraged still further formal freedom in typefaces and in the visual pleasure they could procure. One of these, lithography, brought with it a metamorphosis in type. Unshackled from lead, wood, and even engraving, lettering could be written as flowingly as drawing. This liberty of line, if it favored fanciful designs, also afforded marvelous delicacy. With lithography, one could go beyond creating alphabetical sets for the printing case and invent letterforms for special, ever-changing, and, in general, temporary compositions.

177
Anonymous poster, Payn & McNaughton,
United States, 1847.

Loud, decorative characters were an invasive species in the typographical landscape of the nineteenth century. First arising around 1840, they continued to hold their own throughout Victoria's reign and even beyond.[13] Myriad forms of Victorian period typography were ornamental and colorful; they could be treated in perspective or distorted, stretched, dismembered, or overloaded to the point of being unrecognizable. Yet these extravagances were counterbalanced, particularly in the 1860s, by a studied return to historical models. In England, in about the middle of the century, Caslon was the subject of the one of the best known of these typographical rehabilitations. Meanwhile, in Germany, France, and the United States, other long-lost types were resurrected. Though utterly distinct from Victorian typography per se, these benchmark typefaces were nevertheless also dragooned into its voracious eclecticism.

Typography was thus passing though a prolonged period during which the prevailing vogue was for novel mixtures of genres and styles motivated by a single and single-minded desire: to amaze. The raison d'être of all this versatility, abundance, and sheer variety, was then not to pursue the idea of form in the classical sense, but to remain one step ahead in an environment of visual saturation. The impact of the image served to sell the product, to attract, to convince. Commercial factors were also at stake; for several decades, visual competitiveness had generated a huge market for enticing typefaces, which were jumbled together to produce the maximum effect. Many printed documents from the period, ephemera in particular, seem to vie with one another in imaginativeness, though such an approach also spilled over into bookwork. Production parameters, too, served as a spur to increases in quantity and decoration, rather than to the exploitation of the non-printed space.

Victorian poster design tended to place the text at the center of the composition, covering the entire surface. The popular vertical poster-format was dominated by numerous lines of text. In these kinds of compositions it was quite common for typeface or style to change every single line. Bold forms and fancy alphabets thus took center stage and traditional unities in type selection were cavalierly abandoned. The all-important factor was to stand out in the madding crowd.

Symptomatic of a new age, this phenomenon, which appears to have been one of the many consequences of the Industrial Revolution, initially showed its true colors in Great Britain before extending to Europe and the United States. Until the 1860s, before photography was employed in printing, the forms of printed matter that did not feature engraving were often exclusively typographical. The arrival of chromolithography increased the possibilities available, facilitating overlay and blends of hues. The very look of graphic design was changing, as pictures, rather than type, increasingly filled posters and the press. In the United States as much as in France, satirical illustrations and drawings were used widely during the period, their popularity evolving in lockstep with their ease of reproduction.

Towards the end of the Victorian era, after several decades of intense diversification and visual abundance, graphics eventually returned to the question of equipoise. History has generally ascribed a certain lack of taste, even mediocrity, to this turbulent period. The period did, however, witness more than just formal busyness, with numerous creations combining a strongly decorative tendency with a preoccupation with formal excellence. These, then, should be regarded as the first faltering steps towards a new era that will be ushered in by the potential of recent technologies as much as by the onset of genuine mass communications. The Victorian explosion of forms should also be acknowledged as paving the way for the conquest of an unprecedented freedom, which, no longer burdened by the lessons of the past, could focus on forging expressions capable of conveying a sense of renewal.

From this point of view, nineteenth-century typography as a whole could be said to have both inflected its trajectory towards autonomization and to have reinvigorated the visual potential of its own individuality.

New perspectives in typography

After opening with creations that have since become iconic, the nineteenth century saw the propagation of a highly eclectic typography. Traditionally, it had been a labor-intensive craft that was the preserve of a close circle of initiates. Victorian design permeated typography with a dazzling variety of forms that put paid to the rigor and meticulousness of an earlier era. This pervasive movement, however, had by the end of the century given rise to a reaction embodied by several figures and tendencies intent on reviving the values of craftsmanship and participating in the new artistic currents.

The career of William Morris at the Kelmscott Press (1891–98), for instance, revived medieval and Renaissance practices that ran counter to the developments of technology and to their social repercussions. At the same time, Art Nouveau was swelling into an international movement in which typography was to play a noteworthy and wholly unprecedented role. As we have seen, at the same time, by the last decade of the nineteenth century, the use of sans serif type was consolidated, and new alphabets were being designed as much for the press as for bookwork. The prevalent Roman type—or Gothic in Germanic lands—was now joined by the sans serif and Egyptian alphabets, both evolving in the 1810s. The availability of types in

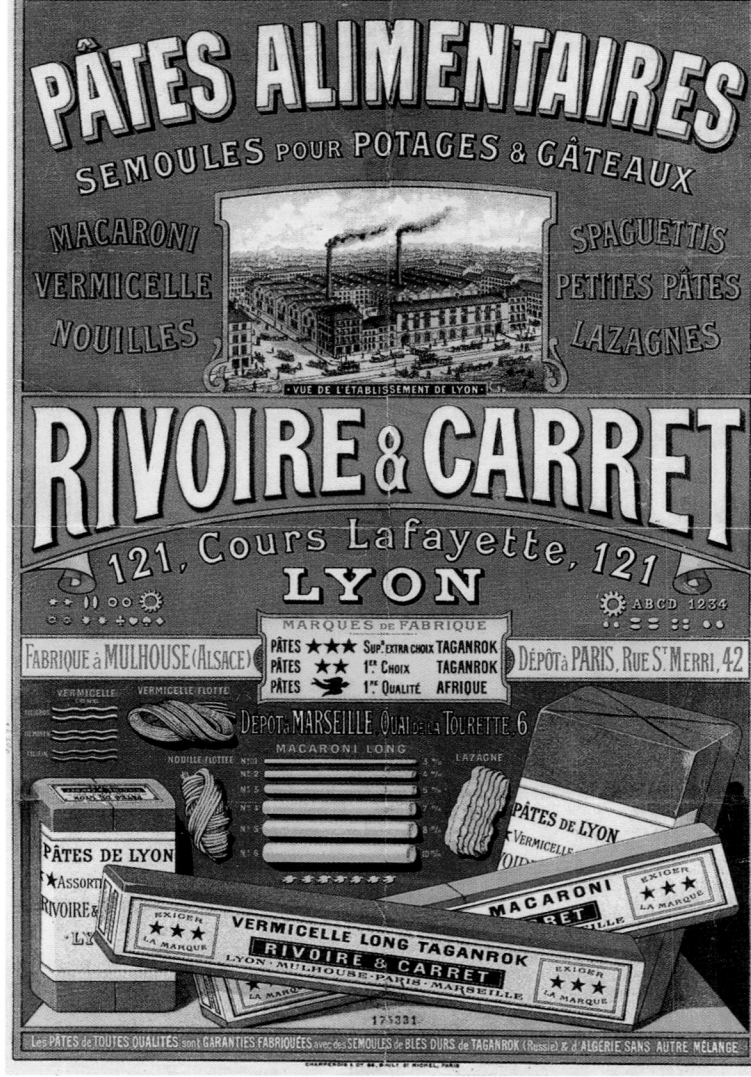

178
Anonymous flyposter, *Encre japonaise, Antoine,* Paris, 1869. 10 1/2 × 7 in. (27 × 18 cm).

179
Anonymous poster, *Pâtes Rivoire et Carret,* France, 1889.

several variants became common currency towards the end of the century, with the result that whole families of alphabets, in various degrees of boldness and/or different sizes, emerged, adding to the impressive expansion in fancy types.

The panorama opened up by such a plethora of forms altered the way typographical creation was regarded and afforded fresh impetus to the methods used in exploring the specificity of its functioning and organization. For example, in the 1890s, one of the first exercises in type classification was undertaken by Morris Fuller Benton.[14] Typography became the subject of revitalized interest, with attention being redirected to the phenomena of legibility and to ocular activity during reading. The earliest experiments on legibility, however, date to the end of the eighteenth century and are ascribed to Jean Anisson. His study, consisting of a comparison between Garamond and Didot, concluded that Garamond was superior for more distant reading. During the nineteenth century, other analyses cast light on the fundamental phenomena of the reading process and the eye movements involved in visual perception. It turned out that the reader's perception of a text arises from complex and unexpected operations: "the reader guesses rather than reads, [...] half a word, sometimes a quarter of a word is sufficient for him to guess it in its entirety, [...] the near totality of readers read only the upper part of a line, [...] during reading, eye movement occurs in jerks. The reader divides the line into a certain number of sectors of approximately ten letters."[15] Taken together, these ideas widened typography's scope of impact and brought into dramatic relief the nature of the challenges arising from the compression of the mechanics of reception. Telltale indicators of the changes underway, the issue of type legibility and the study of the reading process, like the search for type classification, also contributed to fresh insights into typographical creation.

The press and publishing as mass media

180

By the mid-nineteenth century, the industrialization of printing was having decisive knock-on effects on popular culture. The press and published books reached the masses in ever-diminishing timeframes and in ever-growing quantities. At the beginning of the century, the spectacular rise of publishing was kindled most especially by the market for the popular novel, to which were added home encyclopedias, in response to the era's insatiable thirst for knowledge. In this field, too, the image could turn its powers of attraction and persuasion—qualities particularly prized for book covers, for instance—to good effect.

Several factors contributed to the mounting popularity of the press: the expansion of printing generally, developments in the postal service, and the partial lifting of censorship. With manufacturing costs falling precipitously, selling prices could accordingly be lowered. Up until then, the press had been the preserve of a well-off and educated social strata. Having raised itself to the rank of "Fourth Estate",[16] the press, as it evolved into a genuine mass media, acquired an increasingly significant role. For the first time, as magazines, newspapers, and periodicals proposed analysis and commentary on the social and political situation, the population at large had access to reasonably priced sources of information treating topical issues. Splitting its coverage into various thematic headings—history, geography, the sciences, etc.—the press began to uncover great swathes of human knowledge, growing into an opinion-forming and instructive media. The rise of the press contributed actively to the spread of education, and further benefits were to accrue following the growth in the pocketbook in the mid-twentieth century. If the rise of the press seems

180
Journal de Paris, number 343, December 9, 1783.
Le Journal de Paris was the first French daily,
founded in 1777.

exponential, major developments had already been underway since the eighteenth century. In France, one of the very first daily newspapers appeared in 1777. *Le Journal de Paris* comprised four book-sized pages and was a great success, surviving until 1840. Its print-run had reached twelve thousand by 1790, by which time there were already more than five hundred newspapers and periodicals in France. After 1848, the French working classes could indulge their fondness for the medium with *La Presse*, a popular daily set up by Émile de Girardin in 1836, presenting the new face of newspaper publishing.

In the United States, new low-cost newspapers were dubbed the "penny press," and relied for financing on income from advertising. For economic reasons, typography remained small and dense. In the 1840s and 1850s, the first crop of weekly new magazines sprung up: *The Illustrated London News* (London, 1842), *Die Illustrierte Zeitung* (Leipzig, 1843), *L'Illustration* (Paris, 1843), *Illustrated Newspaper* and *Harper's Weekly* (the United States, 1850s and 1857). In Great Britain and in France, coffee houses and "reading rooms" placed a wide range of daily publications and other periodicals at the disposal of the public.

The image in the press

In the 1830s, the press and publishing began to exhibit growing familiarity with illustration—now easier to reproduce thanks to the countless technical developments that had come on stream. In the space of one or two decades, a number of illustrated periodicals

aimed at broader and increasingly targeted readerships (including women and children) were established. Since 1830, periodic publications placed their emphasis on content and productivity over graphic and typographical appearance. Care over form and layout, significant but not imperative, was to become a preoccupation only at a later stage. On the other hand, illustration was already making headway and in newspapers became the subject of close attention, with illustrators and caricaturists experimenting in what soon became a popular idiom of a wholly novel kind. Caricature was principally a French and British phenomenon that, by engaging with political realities, was reveled in by satirical organs especially.

The illustrated press was to attain its apogee in the final decades of the nineteenth century. Besides woodcut and wood-engraving, lithography and photogravure made still greater use of novel techniques of creating and reproducing images. Pictures were henceforth to find a place of choice in magazines, a phenomenon that contributed greatly to the growing success of the press.

In the United States, the Civil War prevented the publication of many magazines between 1861 and 1865. The conflict, however, as the subject of groundbreaking illustrated reports, was one of the very first to be fully documented by the illustrated press. However, as photographs were not yet reproducible on a large scale, engravers preserved their documentary value by taking them as a starting-point for a painstaking transference into their own medium. After the end of the Civil War and with just a few years of interruption, by the 1870s the American press had quickly returned to its former volumes.

In France by the end of the century, circumstances were rosy both for the poster and the illustrated press. Contrary to a widely held belief that sees it as prohibitive (because of the omnipresent sign "Défense d'afficher" — "No Flyposting"), in fact the celebrated French law of July 29, 1881, enshrined the freedom of publishing, of the press, and of bill-posting. The very first article of the law amends earlier edicts in stipulating that in principle "printing and bookselling are free." Article 5 meanwhile states that "any newspaper or periodical can be published, without preliminary authorization and without providing a guarantee." A year after the lifting of censorship, there numbered some nearly four thousand newspapers in France. In 1886, *Le Petit Journal* (created in 1863) — which, only a few years after being set up was being produced on a special press turning out some twenty thousand units an hour — reached the symbolic threshold of a million copies, a figure representing the highest print-run of any newspaper in the world at the time.

Around 1880, other factors were conspiring to increase the popularity of newspapers and magazines, especially economic parameters that continued to drive down costs. Over the decades, newspaper advertising expanded beyond the confines of the "small ad" and became increasingly significant for financing publications in which it was more and more visible.

181
The rotary presses developed for printing the daily *Le Petit Journal*, France, print, 1868. Journal was set up in 1863, with a run of four hundred thousand copies in 1869, rising to a million by around 1890.

182
Advertising poster for *Le Petit Journal*, France, c. 1909.

Manufacturing costs were also squeezed by the use of rotary presses,[17] and by the recourse to mechanized composition. At the same time, advances in photoengraving, which made reproducing documents in half-tone possible, marked a turning-point in the history of graphics: even in the press, the image was no longer to be confined to engraving or lithography. Since such processes made it possible to reproduce all kinds of illustrations, paintings as much as photographs, it represents a crucial historical landmark. From the 1890s on, magazines such as *Harper's* and the *Berliner Illustrierte Zeitung* featured photographs in their pages. Less expensive than engraving or illustration, photography also helped to hold down costs.

Print, reading, and the elimination of illiteracy

At the end of the nineteenth century, to adjust the balance between the visual dimension and financial or economic and technological factors, explorations were being undertaken that would signal a step-change in graphic and typographical design for the press. The 1890s testified to a growing interest in typographical form that had a parallel in the interest in the reproducibility of the photographic image. In this context, the artistic changes afoot at the end of the century proved highly influential. Some extremely recherché artistic reviews appeared in the ambit of Art Nouveau and its ancillary tendencies: *The Studio* (England, 1893), *Jugend* (Germany, 1896), *La Revue blanche* (France). *The Poster* and *Harper's*, meanwhile, furnished a wholly new kind of outlet. Devoted to art and culture, these reviews were the brainchildren of graphic designers and artists of reputation, and some benefited from innovative and meticulously crafted layouts. Hitherto, great artists had always provided illustrations for the popular press, but the composition, page-setting, and visual appearance seldom seemed to be of prime concern. Typography was frequently called upon, however, and orders were tendered to type designers for alphabets specifically intended for use by the press. For example, Century, conceived in 1894 by Theodore Low de Vinne and Linn Boyd Benton for *Century Magazine*, presents a far narrower form than the average, with reduced contrast, and yet it remains eminently readable. Its compactness also made it possible to reduce the space occupied by the text. In newspapers, just as in posters, it seems that a careful and systematic approach to typography came later than care over the image, which appears to have overshadowed questions such as reading and the arrangement of text. Universal access to the press took precedence over graphic considerations, which seemed little more than matters of comfort and added value compared to other, more pressing imperatives.

The advent of the newspaper as a mass medium constituted an event that was part of a policy of lowering illiteracy levels and improving educational provision. In Western Europe by the end of the nineteenth century, literacy seems to have percolated down to practically every layer of the population; henceforth, access to help in reading and writing was provided to the great majority of adults. By about 1900 in Great Britain and France the literacy rate had attained roughly 90 percent. Insofar as the greater part of the population could now engage with text, written culture henceforth impinged on an ever-swelling number of individuals. Improved literacy made relevant to a larger proportion of the population the concept of text as well as typography, as the latter gradually ventured beyond the confines of its hallowed preserve and became more accessible, entering new arenas and finding itself confronted with new challenges.

Typography became the business of, if not everyone, then of a far greater number than heretofore. This new direction was confirmed at the turn of the twentieth century and was consolidated over succeeding decades. Seen in this perspective, the literacy drive that took place in the second half of the nineteenth century has to be regarded as an exceptional event with vast repercussions, and probably a necessary precondition for the seismic shift now about to affect every aspect of printing.

A revival in the arts and graphics

183
Victor Hugo, drawing, project for the mantelpiece in the dining room at Hauteville House, Guernsey. Throughout the house, the Delft tiles are arranged into the initials "V" and "H".

184
Victor Hugo, drawing for the fireplace in the dining room of Hauteville House. Dining room inaugurated in 1857, with wall decoration in Delft tiling surmounted by an overmantel in the shape of a double "H."

If nineteenth-century society endured profound changes—economic, political, industrial and cultural—the arts were similarly embarking on new paths. From the very start of the century, there are signs that artistic attitudes were shifting and that they were beginning to challenge traditional pictorial codes and customs, and question the concept of what was acceptable. Following the relaxing of political and religious tutelage, art could allot a greater role to the subjectivity of its protagonists and to individual expression; academic respect for the subject was no longer paramount. The importance of the individual and of sensibility, so ardently defended by the Enlightenment during the previous century, continued with Romanticism, which exalted imagination, personality, and intuition. Turner's paintings, which project feelings in a novel way, are among the most eloquent testimonies of this pictorial vein. Pure conformity with the visible began to recede before the translation of a personal vision.

The divorce from tradition was brought to a head in realist and naturalist painting. By choosing to bring into their works scenes from everyday life and to turn away in general from religious subjects, painters such as Courbet outraged the bourgeoisie, while a picture like Manet's *Olympia* could occasion a full-blown scandal. In 1874, the debut exhibition of the Impressionists—a term coined in derision—met with total rejection. Monet for his part confessed he was "enamored of the sunbeam and the reflection."[18] Delving further into what became a new pictorial viewpoint and confirming the autonomy of painting, the Impressionists forsook perspectival representation and close detailing alike. If in composition and unity of viewpoint they still respected the template of traditional painting, they conceived of style and facture very differently. Ever more radical art movements stormed into the breach, further distancing themselves from mimesis. With Cézanne, Symbolism, the Nabis, and Art Nouveau, a clear distinction is drawn between the subject and the picture; the capacity of expressive power intrinsic to the image is now free to be explored. The subject is tackled as if it were inflected by the imagination, through intuition and feeling, through states of mind, emotions, dreams—and angst.

The development of modern art was paralleled by the rupture of traditional literary models. Roland Barthes dates this break to the middle of the nineteenth century, explaining that, after centuries of "transparency" and "unity," literature burgeoned into modernity when it fissured into a "plurality of writings." "Writing is [...] the morality of form, the choice of that social area within which the writer elects to situate the nature of his language."[19] Barthes thus pinpoints the shift from tradition to modernity to when classic continuity tipped over into modernist multiplicity. This analysis of literary evolution also throws light on the transformations that affected graphic design and typography (which are after all made up of written forms), and the mutations they underwent seem comparable.

Graphics and typography, then, launched themselves as if by right into the turbulent seas of art's new condition in the nineteenth century. Embracing these new ideas, they reacted to, or catalyzed, formal developments. A metamorphosis was well and truly underway. Like their counterparts in literature, their exponents undertook experiments in the diversification of writing and distanced themselves from the concept of continuity. Emboldened by these artistic sorties, they exalt the freedom of the typographic phrase, exploring uncharted territories of the visual and generating original images. This new category of images sent shockwaves through the world of graphic design and beyond, through certain key artistic conceptions that would later be picked up by avant-garde artists of the early twentieth century.

To gauge its full measure, however, it was going to be necessary to slough off the "traditional schema [according to which] art creates and the applied arts, including advertising, only follow." Toulouse-Lautrec was one of these radical innovators: "Never before in the field of painting or of the graphic arts had such large surfaces of pure color ever been seen [...]. Not before [...] Matisse's great canvases of around 1910 does one see paintings with colored surfaces of comparable dimensions."[20]

This stage in graphic design first dawned on posters in the final third of the nineteenth century—a conception that emerged particularly in works by painters or graphic artists. Henceforth, the limelight was to be occupied by the transitory, by dynamic forms, by shimmering colors. On occasion even, a work's impact and allure can be accentuated by the feeling that is incomplete. In times when relationships to time and space were in flux, the advertising hoarding was poised to usher in a new mode of perception.

Arts and Crafts and the Private Press movement

Well before the vogue for Art Nouveau, however, a highly individual artistic movement took shape in 1850s England: Arts and Crafts. Industrialization had by then already made deep inroads into British society, as demonstrated in 1851 by London's Crystal Palace, a glass and steel construction that earned vocal disapproval from John Ruskin and was erected for the Universal Exhibition. Founded on social conviction, the Arts and Crafts movement aimed to counter Victorian aesthetics and sought alternatives to mechanical manufacture. Industrialization, they declared, had driven a wedge between artist and craftsman, throwing discredit upon the "minor" arts, which had become totally divorced from "art proper." Partisans of the Arts and Crafts movement were of the opinion that the machine cannot impart artistic value to the things it makes and moreover deprives craftsmen of their livelihood and their expertise. In their view, labor organized in this fashion condemns the workman to a role subsidiary to the machine.

Mechanization had already been the subject of stormy debate well before it was condemned by the Arts and Crafts movement; in 1830, for example, the employees at a Parisian printworks smashed the mechanized presses that had so vastly increased output. In a similar vein, social reformers such as John Ruskin and his disciple William Morris were determined to restore human dignity to the manufacture of everyday goods. Ruskin pursued a mordant critique of a society turned upside down by what he saw as unsustainable modes of labor demarcation; for him, the key was to revive craftsmanship in every form of applied art, from everyday articles to constructions with a practical use or a decorative function. For this purpose, handiwork was seen as the only means of production capable of guaranteeing artistic quality and the survival of good taste. The practice of craft was viewed as conducive to social welfare, since, as well as satisfying consumer demand, it led to the blossoming of the craftsman-manufacturer. The Arts and Crafts movement sought to advance social and political ideals expressed through its aesthetic statements and the means of manufacturing its products.

At the head of the Arts and Crafts movement, William Morris embarked on a multifaceted career combining architecture, decorative arts, design, drawing, painting, and writing. As a social reformer, his wish was to fuse art and life. The other members of the movement were from various walks of life, including artists, architects, draftsmen, craftsmen, writers, and philosophers. Morris quickly opted to move away from painting to devote himself to the applied and decorative arts. Grounding his enterprise in medieval practices and aesthetics, he also strove to advance fine art and craftsmanship in tandem. In 1861, with a number of Pre-Raphaelite artists, he founded Morris, Marshall, Faulkner, and Co.,[21] the commercial success of which ensured him prosperity. Describing itself as "fine art workmen in painting, carving, furniture and metals,"[22] the society was set up to produce decorative objects and furniture in a

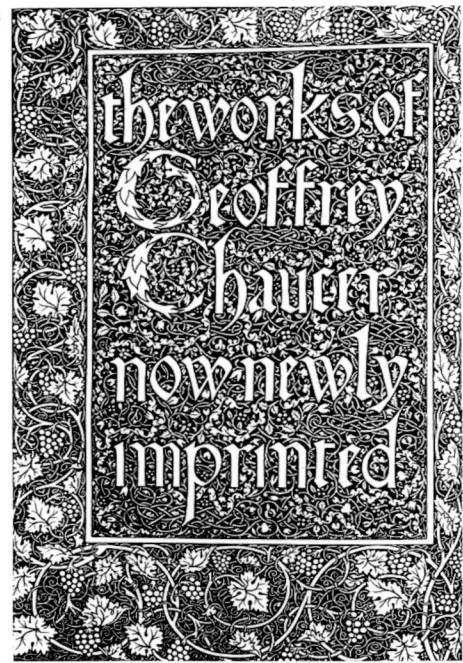

185
William Morris, pages from *The Works of Geoffrey Chaucer*, printed at Kelmscott Press in 1896, illustrated with wood-engravings by Edward Burne-Jones, Great Britain (leaves located at the beginning and about the middle of the volume). The text of this work, considered Morris's masterpiece, is set in Chaucer type, for which Morris was inspired in particular by a Gothic type by Peter Schöffer, used in 1462.

craft context. The output of the Arts and Crafts movement thus stemmed from a wide range of métiers and practices in the decorative and applied arts. Frequent recourse to decorative items (furniture, crockery, tapestries, wallpaper, stained-glass, etc.) was on the stylistic level accompanied by a diversification in forms that could be elaborately ornate, or else more rustic, more directly Gothic-inspired, or again pared down, simplified, and geometrical. This last tendency, accentuated over time, was characteristic of some of the furniture output of Morris and Co.

In 1891, succeeding his interest in decorative furnishings and homeware, William Morris turned his attention to the fine book and founded a print-shop, the Kelmscott Press. There again, his prime concerns were excellence in book design, improving type quality, care over page layout, and incomparable craftsmanship. He based his book designs on those venerable models he most admired and took inspiration from calligraphy, illuminated manuscripts, and incunabula, resorting to Gothic or early Roman typefaces.

During the few years of its existence (1891–98), the Kelmscott Press published more than fifty titles, each printed in one, two or three hundred copies. The two endeavors considered his masterpieces both appeared in 1896: *The Works of Geoffrey Chaucer*, illustrated with wood-engravings by Edward Burne-Jones, and *The Canterbury Tales*. Each volume from the workshop was painstakingly produced, as much in its design as in its realization. Moreover, Morris strove to return to the processes used in the early days of printing and brought over from Germany inks of the highest quality, and employed handmade rag paper. Each book emerges as a harmonious ensemble, every element of which has been painstakingly put together: the relationship between text, image, and surface decoration; page layout; proportion; typeface and initials; binding and quality of materials, etc. In pages that are a delight to the eye, each treated in the fashion of a richly decorated tapestry, the ornaments, engravings, initials, and text of *The Works of Geoffrey Chaucer* interlock to the point of covering the entire surface of the paper. The modernist designs developed in the Kelmscott Press, however, offered a counterbalance to its attachment to the past. For example, the visual unit of the book was not the single page but the double-page spread. Similarly innovative designs were undertaken by Stéphane Mallarmé in France and had a notable influence on twentieth-century avant-garde artists. In accordance with the spirit of the Arts and Crafts movement, all the ingredients employed in the book were to be produced by hand and by the gestures of the craftsman.

The smallest typographical unit, too, had to satisfy the ideals of what was soon a famous publishing house. Advised and often swayed by the renowned printer, Emery Walker, William Morris successively created three typefaces: Golden, in 1890, followed by Troy and Chaucer in 1892 and 1893 (cut by Edward Prince). These alphabets were based on medieval and early Renaissance forms: Golden was inspired by Nicolas Jenson's Roman, Troy was derived from Gothic models, while Chaucer was a variation of Troy in a smaller size. Each of these alphabets reflects nostalgia for manuscript letterforms. If they diverge from modernity in terms of their visual impact, they are evidence of the extraordinary attention paid to the tiniest detail, which together collaborate to create an overarching unity of design. Partaking in what was a mounting concern, William Morris also applied himself to microtypographical questions, rethinking the role of space in the text, tackling questions such as leading, kerning, and word spacing. Of the opinion that space must be reduced to a minimum, Morris recommended to "avoid undue white between the letters," stipulating "the lateral space should be [...] no more than is necessary to distinguish clearly the division into words and [...] should be as nearly equal as possible," and, finally, "the whites between lines should not be excessive."[24] The magnificence and sumptuousness of the works of the Kelmscott Press offer copious testimony to these ideals.

Among the protagonists of the Arts and Crafts movement, William Morris played a principal role. Closer inspection of his oeuvre, however, reveals a certain ambivalence. In the creative field, in spite of his defense of a neo-medieval, archaizing aesthetic, Morris emerges as a

186
Arthur Mackmurdo, title page for *Wren's City Churches*, Great Britain, 1883.

pioneer of design in his drive for quality as much as in his determination to find a place for art in life. The social ideals he espoused, though, struggled to find an outlet. Rare and costly, editions issued by the Kelmscott Press—like so many medieval manuscripts—could in general only be addressed to a cultivated, bibliophile elite.

Ranged behind the dominant figure of William Morris, the Arts and Crafts movement incorporated numerous groupings of craftsmen, such as the Century Guild and Art Workers' Guild. Arthur Mackmurdo occupied an iconic place within the Century Guild, of which he was one of the founders. He is generally seen as a precursor of Art Nouveau, as his curvilinear graphics, his lettering, floral motifs, and illustrations testify. Other renowned artists, such as the controversial figure of Aubrey Beardsley (closer to Art Nouveau proper) and Walter Crane, also put their weight behind the Arts and Crafts movement. Against the backdrop of renewed interest in the book, Crane holds a special place through his pioneering efforts in the field of the children's book. Popularizing this type of publishing, he produced magnificent illustrations and graphics; this departure represented a new phase in the history of publishing, one whose importance can be gauged in terms of the educational function of the book.

One of the major offshoots of the Arts and Crafts exhibition unveiled in London in 1888 was the Private Press movement, which, taking its cue from Arts and Crafts, promulgated a demanding and fresh approach to printing and the book. The guiding principle was to restore aesthetic, formal, artistic, and material qualities to print, free of undue focus on profit. Private presses sprung up all over Britain, in particular the Ashendene Press (St. John Hornby, 1894), the Vale Press (Charles Ricketts, 1896), and the Doves Press (Emery Walker and T. J. Cobden-Sanderson, 1900). In seeking to forge a new aesthetic, certain printworks, such as the Doves Press, turned away from medieval inspiration, promoting unfussy designs closer to the modern spirit.

If the movement was British in origin, in the 1890s, the influence of Arts and Crafts and of English art generally soon crossed the Atlantic to propagate in the United States. The American arm of the Private Press movement was illustrated by several celebrated typographers: Bruce Rogers, Frederic William Goudy, and Daniel Berkeley Updike (Riverside Press and Merrymount Press). Many American guilds and printworks soon joined the movement, perpetuating its traditionalist tendencies. Beside Updike, Goudy, and Rogers, other great names in typography emerged, such as William Addison Dwiggins, Bertram Goodhue, and Thomas Maitland Cleland. The majority of these used Morris's work as their model and thus enshrined his legacy. Daniel Berkeley Updike gained his fame as a printer, while Frederic William Goudy made his mark as a type designer. Both wrote several important textbooks on the history of typography and typefaces. Bruce Rogers and William Addison Dwiggins also contributed to the field of type design. The graphic designer William Bradley, another key figure in the United States, applied himself at the same time to the Arts and Crafts movement and to Art Nouveau. Like their British counterparts, some American designers began in the commercial field before moving away to reconsider book or type design. Their work formed the basis for a (typo)graphical culture specific to the United States, a practice that hitherto had remained, to a greater or lesser extent, under European influence.

After England and the United States, the Arts and Crafts movement made its way to the European continent during the second half of the nineteenth century. This and the Private Press movement were soon flourishing in Germany, Belgium, Holland, and elsewhere. Belgium developed a particular strand of the current in which Henry Van de Velde, then at the onset of his career, was the foremost exponent. In the Netherlands, the work of the architect Petrus Josephus Hubertus Cuypers testifies to an identical drive to return to traditional craft and past values, as well as to embrace industrialization and seek new paths.

Artists and craftsmen alike had to reposition themselves with respect to industrialization, a now inescapable facet of culture. Since it turned its back on the consequences of the Industrial

Revolution en bloc, the Arts and Crafts movement soon hit the buffers of its self-inflicted constraints. The heirs to the movement, eager to reap the benefits of mass production—or at the very least convinced of the necessity to do so—opted instead to embrace mechanization. Although the ideals of the movement were then only partially realized, the convictions of William Morris and his contemporaries did raise awareness of the importance of artistic value and herald the rebirth of design as an aspect of the applied arts. In addition, the philosophies of John Ruskin and William Morris inaugurated a new conception of art and culture. Henceforth, both these entities were to be directed at the people, rather than a privileged class—an ideal that was to become entrenched in twentieth-century cultural and artistic life. If, in about 1900, the desire to fuse art, craftsmanship, and life had already proved a key objective for artists, subsequent practitioners were to replace handicraft with industry.

The new poster

By placing the bulk of their emphasis on quality, practitioners of Arts and Crafts turned their attention to durable artifacts, such as books and furniture. More transitory products, like the poster, seem to have remained in the background, although some figures in the Private Press movement did turn their hand to the medium. It was only with Art Nouveau, together with its parallel currents and experiments in the 1890s, that the poster was given real impetus; within the space of a few years, the visual impact of advertising artwork was to find itself utterly transformed.

The "poster" had existed for millennia, at least in an archaic form. In antiquity, as in the Middle Ages, it had, of course, been handwritten or painted. With the invention of reproductive techniques, however, by the fifteenth century it was already being printed. At the start, it was more often purely typographical in nature (small one-color bills, royal *placards*, official edicts), or else confined uniquely to the image (shopfront signs for traders and craftsmen, for example). Forms bearing the text and the image could be interlocked and printed together, but the techniques employed (hot-metal movable type and woodcut) remained two juxtaposed means, distinct and disparate.

In the sixteenth and seventeenth centuries, in France in particular, regulation proved onerous, blocking the development of the poster and ensuring that it remained primarily a text medium until the seventeenth century. As we have seen, the poster at this time was intended above all to be read; its principal function was to inform and visual impact was not paramount. Moreover, the cost of engraving meant that the artistically inclined poster would always remain exceptional, while the size of a given advertisement would be limited by its being printed from woodcuts. In the eighteenth century, the appearance of these posters began to change; images became more frequent and color started to feature more often. At this juncture, the creation and reproduction of the image still had to rely on engraving. But the role of the poster was to evolve, running parallel with the rise in the use of advertising, which, by about 1800, had already transformed the urban environment. Many advertisements were devoted to the world of leisure: the circus, the zoo, and every other kind of entertainment. Posters were also marshaled to promote new books and, more generally, in Europe as in the United States, to advertise newspapers, plays, travel, and exhibitions, as well as all manner of goods and services.

In the United States by about 1850, the poster acquired a new weapon: built up from more than one woodcut, it could now attain some six and a half to thirteen feet along each side. These billboards often publicized shows such as the circus, theater, rodeo, etc. At the same time, another original approach to the poster was being developed by Jean-Alexis Rouchon, a wallpaper manufacturer in France. In 1844 he devised an "application of wallpaper impression to color printing for posters."[25] Employing draftsmen for the visual component, he created posters containing large areas of flat, high-keyed tints thanks to the superimposed impression of woodcuts. His posters, too, attained sizes of approximately $6^{1}/_{2} \times 10$ ft. $(2 \times 3$ m$)$.[26]

By round about the middle of the nineteenth century, the metamorphosis of the poster was being aided by plummeting costs, larger formats, and increased print-runs, with lithography becoming the favorite medium. In the 1860s, improvements in lithographic presses made it possible to produce pullings numbering several thousand copies. In France, the very first lithographic poster, produced for a book, dates to 1836. As lithography was also a means of artistic creation, it was thus naturally an open invitation to new departures in creating artwork. It also made it possible to design text and illustration in one and the same act, using the same tools that allowed colors to be blended and mixed at will.

Early forays into the chromolithographic poster have often been viewed as bereft of artistic merit. Such a judgment cannot, however, be applied to the unique contributions of those painters and graphic artists who endeavored to explore the creative and expressive potential afforded by the new process. By showing precocious interest in lithography as a means of widening the scope of their work, these artists endowed it with a specific artistic value. In France, this phenomenon is particularly visible in the oeuvre of Honoré Daumier, Paul Gavarni, and Denis Marie Auguste Raffet.

It was besides in the France of the 1860s and 1870s that the art of the poster took a new and crucial turn. The trend was announced in the work of Jules Chéret, whose posters stand at the crossroads of developments in painting, drawing, and graphics. Established in Paris in 1866, Chéret would set up his own printworks there. An earlier stay in Great Britain had enabled him to train with some of the foremost chromolithographic printers of the era[27] and he had already noted some of the very large American color posters printed from woodcuts. Chéret's oeuvre comprised a voluminous output of advertising lithographs.

Other European artists helped to forge the so-called "artistic" poster. Some of their creations became and remain famous, such as Édouard Manet's *Les Chats*, a rare example by that artist, designed in 1868 to illustrate a novel. Another example is the only poster by Fred Walker in 1871, promoting a play, *The Woman in White*, since regarded as the origin of quality advertising in Great Britain. Fred Walker explained his approach in the following, strangely prophetic, manner: "I am bent on doing all I can with a first attempt at what I consider might develop into a most important branch of art."[28] In the posters by Manet and Walker, the artwork covers practically the entire surface. The text, likewise in monochrome, surrounds the image in a sort of frame that remains quite separate from it.

The 1890s witnessed the flowering of the art poster, and this on an international scale. Artists working in Paris, a good number of whom came from abroad, played a key role, and the phenomenon was to coalesce around Art Nouveau, then at its fullest expansion. While the poster was affirming its artistic pretensions, it also took on what are now considered to be its intrinsic persuasive, even titillating, qualities. Its erstwhile informative function became blurred and made way for graphics that were evocative, suggestive, bewildering, or seductive.

187
Joseph W. Morse, poster, *Five Celebrated Clowns*, New York, 1856. Color poster printed from woodcuts, 8 ft. 6 in. × 11 ft. 3 1/2 in. (262 × 344 cm).

188
Édouard Manet, illustration on a poster for *Champfleury–Les Chats*, lithograph, France, 1868.

189

The advent of Art Nouveau marks a decisive turn in graphic practice. Resolutely future-orientated, this umbrella movement was uniquely equipped to shake off the shackles of history. Hitherto, each successive current had been linked to a preceding style and often preserved visible avatars of earlier forms. This had been the case for the typographical classicism of the sixteenth, seventeenth and eighteenth centuries, and in the nineteenth century it had remained true of Arts and Crafts, with its nostalgia for things medieval, and then of the progressive revival of classic typefaces. The audacious formal rethink behind the creation of letterforms in the 1810s (with sans serifs and the first Egyptian faces) thus found an echo at the end of the century in the changes and originality that drove Art Nouveau.

The style sprung up in the 1880s and 1890s, reaching its apogee at the 1900 Paris Exhibition, and lasting well into World War I. International in scale, Art Nouveau crisscrossed Europe, arising in France, England, Germany, Belgium, the Netherlands, Austria, Italy, and Spain, and soon gained ground in the United States. The name given to the movement varied depending on the country concerned—here underlining its modernity, there its youth, its innovative energy, or independence: Modern Style in England, Art Nouveau or Style Moderne in France, Jugendstil (Youth Style) in Germany, Sezessionstil (Secession style) in Austria, Nieuwe Kunst (New Art) in the Netherlands, and Modernista in Spain.

The movement sought to join art with industry. All over the Western world, the proponents of Art Nouveau determined to embrace the industrial age and to adapt to the principle of series manufacture, all the while advocating the reintroduction of stylized natural elements. This was the impressive aesthetic transformation they inaugurated. It was an era in which the design of forms for the environment had been laboring against a tide of mechanization and industrialization. Like the Arts and Crafts movement, Art Nouveau focused particularly on the decorative and applied arts, and strove to reconcile the "major" and "minor" arts: the creation of artifacts and fabrics, architecture, and furniture-making number among the principal sectors concerned. In the graphic design field, innovative ideas concentrated especially on posters, reviews, books, and typeface design. The new style, abundantly represented in the urban fabric and already international in ambit, soon became genuinely popular. Its success proved a boon to the poster, as commercial advertising underwent phenomenal expansion between 1880 and 1900.

Amusing and familiar, advertisements were by now admired by the public and even sought after by collectors. To fulfill demand, specialized stores were set up selling reproductions of posters (of the type the general public continues to purchase more than a century later) and the vogue was such that by the end of the century the French had coined the term "affichomanie" ("poster-mania").[29] Above and beyond its commercial pulling power, the poster was being transformed into an art object that was given house room, advancing the aspiration of Art Nouveau to espouse popular art forms as well as to embrace industry and trade. Jules Chéret—as we have seen, a pioneering figure in the "new poster"—was even awarded the Légion d'honneur for the "creation of a new artistic branch by finding room for art in paintings for commerce and industry." Empowered by the interest it aroused, advertising could now reinforce its impact and allure, and become a key medium in mass visual communication.

In France, the *affichistes* (poster artists)—Toulouse-Lautrec being the foremost among them—played a crucial role in this transformation. In Great Britain, Belgium, Germany, and Austria, their contemporaries were scarcely less active but came to the forefront after 1900, when they busied themselves grafting some of the future offshoots of Art Nouveau. The dissemination of Art Nouveau and of other, parallel currents owes much to the countless

189
Georges Lemmen, cover for Octave Maus's review, *L'Art moderne*, 1894.

190
Hector Guimard, project for the cover of the *Revue d'art*, France, 1899. India ink, pencil, and watercolor on tracing paper, 16 × 10 1/2 in. (40 × 26.5 cm).

191
Hector Guimard, poster for the exhibition *Salon du Figaro, Le Castel Béranger*, France, 1899–1900. Lithograph, 35 × 49 in. (89 × 125 cm).

192
Postcard *Le Style Guimard. Le métropolitain. Station des Champs-Élysées* (at the time, the rue Marbeuf station), published in 1903. A rare photograph showing the original way the entrance signs were hung.

195

193
Victor Prouvé, with the assistance of Camille Martin for the enamelwork and René Wiener for the binding, boards for *Salammbô*, École de Nancy, 1893. 16 1/2 × 13 in. (42 × 33 cm).

194
Hector Guimard, plan for the "model B" entryway for the Paris Métro, main elevation, drawing signed but undated, c. 1900.

195
Anonymous, sign for a coffee-house, bronze, 1900.

exhibitions and reviews that promoted them. In France, from the end of 1880 and in particular during the following decade, the movement hosted a vast number of events. These new exhibitions seemed to mushroom everywhere: in 1890, in New York; in 1894, in London and Milan; in 1895, in Boston, New York and Chicago; in 1896, in Brussels, Dresden, Vienna, and Barcelona; and in 1897, in Moscow and Oslo. Reviews, too, were published in these cities, ready to diffuse the new spirit, disseminating ideas, and reproducing the fashionable posters of the time. Some of these periodicals became particularly famous, like *The Studio* in England, *La Revue blanche* in France, and *Pan*, *Die Woche*, and *Jugend* in Germany. Besides the reviews, books of a new type appeared entirely dedicated to the poster, like *Les Affiches illustrées* by Ernest Maindron, published in 1886. Collectors, gallery-owners, and entrepreneurs also played a significant role in the promotion of Art Nouveau, including Siegfried (known as Samuel) Bing in Paris—whose gallery, opened in 1895 and named Art Nouveau (borrowing from an earlier title), was to give a name to the movement—and Louis Comfort Tiffany[30] in New York. In many places, fin-de-siècle posters were to trumpet the wonders of leisure and entertainment products as well as pleasure generally. From these images, there emanated a devil-may-care atmosphere, awash with illusory promises. When human figures did appear, the color advertisement appeared at once intriguing and immediately familiar. Whatever the actual object of the advertisement might be, it was frequently associated with a figure, generally a woman. (Today, the use of human figures is a commonplace, almost hackneyed, element in an advertising vocabulary in which the female body predominates.) Art Nouveau was also fond of other motifs, such as delicate flowers and plants, or graceful animals, and the representation of woman in conjunction with these flora proved an enduring theme. Art Nouveau graphics rely on strong stylization and curvilinearity, though this varies considerably according to country. In France and Belgium, undulating forms, curve and counter-curve, and the arabesque predominate. In Germany, Austria, and England, decorative features run to simpler, more geometric forms that seem to prefigure the energetic avant-garde of the 1910s and 1920s. Sometimes derived from vegetal or animal forms, in certain cases the motifs verge on the abstract, as in some examples of German Jugendstil. Generally, the decorative aspect—be it sober or complex—remains uppermost, and line plays a critical role in the graphic design language.

Following in the footsteps of the Impressionists in their disregard for convention, these painters-cum-poster artists liberated line, surface, color, and lettering simultaneously. Realistic figuration lost ground before schematization, symbolization, stylization, and allusion. The poster took up this movement of emancipation, moving away from rigidity of representation and espousing new, dynamic, and enticing forms. A formal vocabulary came into being; since both sprung from lithography, text and image no longer arose from distinct techniques, but could be designed and perceived as a single unit. Lettering, uncoupled from its dependence on the typographical character, could reconnect with natural handwritten forms—although it often made way for the image or the illustration that continued to comprise the central element in the great mass of posters.

The extremely diverse artistic tendencies that inspired Art Nouveau included Arts and Crafts (without the rejection of industry), Symbolism, Romanticism, and many other manifestations of pictorial modernity. The historic sources of Art Nouveau could range from the Gothic, Renaissance, and Baroque, to Oriental and Celtic arts. The Japanese print also represented a significant source of inspiration for Art Nouveau. These prints had been widely introduced into Europe during the second half of the nineteenth century, especially through the intermediary of the Universal Exhibitions in London in 1862, Paris in 1867, and Vienna in 1873. The art of the Japanese woodcut quickly made a strong impression on European artists of every stripe. In addition to the sheer quality of their impression, these prints freighted a number of characteristics and expressive forms that Western practitioners proceeded to make their own: mastery of surface values, asymmetry, flat tints, the special role allotted to line and

196
Utagawa Kunisama, Japanese color print, 1796.

197
Stamping of a vegetal composition (banana leaf, with rose or prunus), China, Qing Dynasty, engraving c. 1856. Leaf stamp, early twentieth century, 5 1/4 × 9 1/2 in. (31.3 × 24 cm). Plate engraved after a painting by Ding Wenwei (painter, calligrapher, poet).

198
Paul Signac, *Application du cercle chromatique de M. Ch. Henry*, chromolithographic work based on the principles of Neo-Impressionism. Printed on the back of a program for *Le Théâtre Libre*, 6 × 7 in. (15.5 × 18 cm).

contour, ringed silhouettes, and so on. Quite distinct from the shading, modeling, and illusionist perspective of the West, the linear treatment and blocks of color used in Japanese woodcuts allow subtle suggestions of depth and volume. Hugely stimulated by this kind of palette, Art Nouveau was to branch out into diverse graphic idioms that resist pigeonholing into one, wholly circumscribed style.

The variety of its influences and the intersecting genres it covered have succeeded in blurring the boundaries of Art Nouveau—a problematic that recurs with subsequent tendencies. Moreover, since some of its major figures also swam in other waters, they cannot be categorized solely and uniquely as protagonists of Art Nouveau. Artists and designers assimilated to the style, bolstered by the ongoing changes in the plastic arts, were to fashion a wholly original visual world, within which the poster conveys a novel aesthetic.

Far from limiting itself to purely aesthetic concerns, the movement pursued precise goals: to turn advertising into an art form, to endeavor to forge a new balance between art and technology, to integrate art into the environment, and to contrive a form of art adapted to the industrial age. As it unfolded, Art Nouveau transfigured graphics—with, first and foremost, the poster, which, in 1898, was described as merely the "mobile, transitory image demanded by an era in the thrall of vulgarization and eager for change."[31]

The birth of the art poster in France

In the final decades of the nineteenth century, the swelling tide of posters was transforming the visual environment of the city . Their graphics were generous, immediate, high spirited. Paris, one of the very first cities to see its walls inundated with hordes of posters, played host to several talents of the time, not least Chéret, Toulouse-Lautrec, Mucha, and Steinlen.

The French law of July 29, 1881 meant that posters could be affixed more or less anywhere and advertising became omnipresent. From the start, the construction of the Parisian subway envisaged sites specially reserved for posters.

This developing art form was thus presented with a new way of reaching out to the pedestrian, outside as well as inside public spaces. Independently of these advertising objectives, the poster also signaled the popularization of two-dimensional art forms generally. Success was meteoric: lithographs signed Chéret and Toulouse-Lautrec were torn down at night, stolen by poster-mad connoisseurs. To satisfy this enthusiasm, certain printers specialized in reproducing posters, whose dimensions were, for practical reasons, often reduced. Significantly, these reproductions sometimes remove the text and preserve solely the image; in reproduction, a poster, once the advertising "hook" had been expunged, acquired something of the aura of a picture or an icon.

Jules Chéret, initiator of the revival

The invention of the "modern poster" is unanimously ascribed to Jules Chéret. "No artist has won the affection of the general public as unerringly as M. Jules Chéret,"[32] said Ernest Maindron, one of the earliest historians of the form, in 1896. Chéret's creations beguiled not only the man in the street, but artists such as Monet, Degas, and Rodin as well. Chéret's activities with respect to the poster originated in his admiration for painting; he had discovered Watteau, Fragonard, and Rubens at the Louvre, Turner and Constable in London, and Tiepolo in Venice (Chéret's later career was devoted primarily to painting). Son of a typographer, Chéret was born in Paris in 1836, and started work aged thirteen as an apprentice lithographer, learning the secrets of draftsmanship. He then left for London for several years where, as we have seen, he acquired his consummate mastery of the techniques of lithograph.

His earliest posters date back to 1858. In 1866, he settled in Paris, where his works quickly brought him success, though his graphic idiom was not yet fully developed. At this time, his artwork remained cluttered and somewhat lackluster, and it was twenty or so years before he had forged his inimitable style. Over time, his images acquired greater impact, with

compositions dominated by one central element. Such a unified focus constitutes a significant development in graphic creation, in particular for printed materials that have to be absorbed in the blink of an eye. Chéret's colors became more lively, in a bright range of yellows, reds, blues, greens, and oranges; the mottled grounds set off the shaded gradations. The black outline drawn around the element became less emphatic, and was sometimes replaced by blue.

Exceptionally prolific, Chéret seems to have been the first to try his hand at chromolithography in this manner. At the end of the 1880s, as his style was maturing, he had already designed a thousand or so posters. The orders he received were most often for the promotion of shows such as cabarets or dances, or consumer products. In celebrating the pleasures of life, his work thus pays tribute to the "comforts" of industrialized society. Chéret's solution, which was to become a leitmotiv, consisted in placing in the scene a young female figure known as "Chérette." If this kind of personification appeared original for the time, it quickly became a recurrent formula. As regards text, it was Chéret himself who determined the overall composition of his posters, though it was unlikely that he actually drew the lettering; that was probably handed over to Madaré. If the image occupies the majority of the poster surface, the text espouses the same fluid, supple, and dynamic style.

Chéret's oeuvre foretold of an impressive aesthetic revival, without, however, amounting to a break with the prevailing graphic codes such as others will cause later. His graphic language imposes keen, ample, and spontaneous lines that evoke movement and lightness. His figures, depicted in dynamic poses, boast an instantaneity that verges on the photographic. Chéret's work, while not wholly bereft of complexity, is a significant move away from the overloaded graphic language that dominated his century. Once he had developed his style, Chéret offered the same gamut of responses to diverse commissions; become a portmanteau figure, his Chérette serves wine, invites one to a concert, smokes a cigarette, etc. In this fairyland (a sphere of visual communication at once in and outside reality), the depiction of woman—ever young, arousing, graceful—was predominant. Already, the artifice of commercial advertising is plain to see: it reflects an idealized world that borrows from reality only what it sees as optimistic, enjoyable—and, of course, marketable.

199
Jules Chéret, poster for *Folies-Bergère. La Loïe Fuller*, France, 1893, 3 ft. 7in. × 2 ft. 8 in. (110 × 82 cm). Poster issued in four different sets of colorings on dark grounds (yellow and purple, blue and yellow, green and orange, green and orangey-red).

Toulouse-Lautrec

Henri de Toulouse-Lautrec was born in 1864, just as Chéret was starting out on his career. If he was indeed influenced by his predecessor, he proved an independent spirit: his was a far from sanitized or perfect world, quite possibly due to the fact that his life was wracked by suffering and tribulations. His turbulent adolescence seriously and durably compromised his health, affecting his motor functions. Settling in Montmartre, he haunted its dance-halls, theaters, and *café-concerts*; his was a riotous, nocturnal existence given over to alcohol, which wreaked havoc with his health. He died aged only thirty-six in 1901 (Chéret, thirty years his senior, survived him by a further thirty years).

Infirm and sorely tested by life, Toulouse-Lautrec depicted the world in powerful, raw scenes, devoid of window-dressing. Far from the idealized and ethereal atmosphere of Chéret, Toulouse-Latrec chose to dramatize his subjects, and, abandoning a central figure like Chérette, his posters often convey an uncomfortable asymmetry or a tension-filled equilibrium. He emphasizes deformities and imperfections almost to the point of caricature (for this reason, the famous singer Yvette Guilbert preferred Steinlen, whereas the dancer Jane Avril ascribed her celebrity to the artist). In energetic, daring compositions, Toulouse-Lautrec painted or drew the sordid side of life, translating humanity as he found it, complete with its

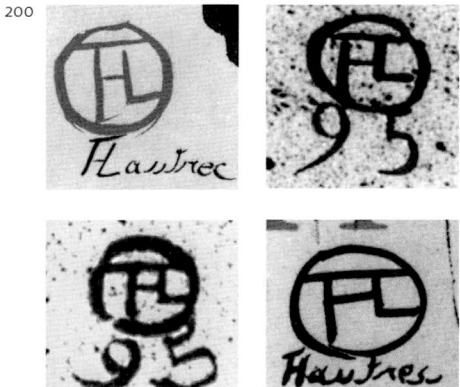

200
Henri de Toulouse-Lautrec, monograms with date or signature, 1893, 1895, 1895, 1896.

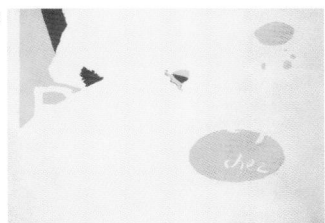

201
Henri de Toulouse-Lautrec, study for
the poster *Reine de joie*. Charcoal, 5 ft × 3 ft. 5
in. (152 × 105 cm).

202
Trial impressions of Toulouse-Lautrec's
chromolithographic poster, *Reine de joie*.
Successively: low red and yellow trial; high black
with inverted overprint of high red and yellow
trial; high yellow, red, and black trial.
27 × 35 in. (68 × 89.5 cm).

203
Henri de Toulouse-Lautrec, poster for
the publication of the book *Reine de joie* by
Victor Joze, 1892. Chromolithograph,
4 ft. 10 $^1/_2$ × 3 ft. 3 in. (148.5 × 99.5 cm).

miseries and its alcoholism. His color range was appreciably different from Chéret's too,
sometimes more limited, understated, with yellow, green, orange, and gray predominating,
encircled by a razor-sharp black outline or dotted with touches of red. In places, raw paint
spatters the surface of the artwork. As regards lettering, this was often in the artist's own hand
and appears simultaneously as an accompaniment and adjunct to the image.

Unlike Chéret, whose activity as a poster artist led to an abundant output in print,
Toulouse-Lautrec was known essentially as a painter and a draftsman (talents for which he
was admired by both the Fauves and the Expressionists), whose posters encapsulate the
overlap between art and publicity. He was to design no more than about thirty posters, all
chromolithographs, except for the very last, since his lithographic output developed in the
main outside the domain of the poster. In 1890, Toulouse-Lautrec received a commission for a
debut series of posters for a cabaret, the famous Moulin-Rouge. The others he was to execute
over the space of a decade, until his death in 1901. The poster *Divan japonais* (1893)
represents one of his strongest and most synthetic compositions. Although relatively few in
number, his creations fulfill a crucial role in the genesis of the modern poster and still rank
among the most famous examples of the genre. Chéret can certainly be regarded as a pioneer
in his exploration of the genre, but Toulouse-Lautrec affirms its maturity as an art form. His
compact, cyncial vision, undeviating and corrosive, confers unparalleled energy and power on
his works. As regards the image, Toulouse-Lautrec's graphic idiom appears personal and
independent, wholly distinct from that of Art Nouveau.

The Nabis

Formed in 1888, the group of artists known as the Nabis included most notably Paul Sérusier,
Pierre Bonnard, Maurice Denis, and Édouard Vuillard. Like Toulouse-Lautrec, the Nabis
showed a keen interest in Japanese prints and in recent developments in the visual arts.
Among them, Maurice Denis and Pierre Bonnard signed a small number of posters; as for

204
Édouard Vuillard, poster, *Cyclistes prenez Becane* (liqueur), 1890.

205
Pierre Bonnard, poster for *La Revue blanche*, 1894. Chromolithograph.

Édouard Vuillard, he designed just one, though relatively well known, for an aperitif called Becane. In all probability, Toulouse-Lautrec's own interest in poster art had been whetted on seeing an example by Bonnard entitled *France-Champagne*. The Japanese print was a strong influence on poster design at this time: the graphic treatment, with flat tints and lines, as well as the symbolic rather than mimetic form, aided the quest for a condensed and meaningful language. Although comparatively few in number, posters by the Nabis nonetheless possess a very particular artistic value. Perhaps the Nabis were attracted to the medium—a support affixed to walls and characterized by multiple printings—because of the possibility it offered of being able, if temporarily, to escape from the artistic hothouse of Salon and studio. The intention was to create ephemeral works for a broader public outside the normal coteries. The Nabis did not attempt to devise or refine a specific style, and did not in fact pursue a precise concept of the poster, as many graphic designers were to later on.

For the time being, however, advertising was not specifically a task for graphic designers. Valorized above all as a plastic form, it was reinvented by the efforts of painters, so it is hardly surprising that the image often remained preeminent. However, certain explorations did reflect a strong textual presence that could, for example, occupy up to half the surface—as in Vuillard's *Becane* posters (dominating the whole composition, the wording is the first element to strike the eye) and Bonnard's *France-Champagne*. Perhaps these creations can be seen as embryonic versions of the avant-garde typographic poster.

Foreign *affichistes* in Paris: Grasset, Steinlen, and Mucha

French artists were not alone in adding a touch of distinction to the mass of posters in Paris at the end of the nineteenth century, as the city attracted a number of European artists to the hub of the art scene. Among these, Eugène Grasset and Théophile Alexandre Steinlen from Switzerland settled in Paris in 1871 and 1881, while the Czech painter and poster artist Alphonse Mucha established himself in the city in 1887.

Eugène Grasset not only produced posters and illustrations, but also textile and type designs. His works, falling within the general ambit of Art Nouveau, testify to a quest for contemporary forms, though lose little of the prevailing taste for medieval art, Japanese prints, and the Pre-Raphaelites. Like Chéret, he made great use of the image of woman in posters advertising a wide range of products, including bicycles and ink. Having studied architecture in Zurich, Grasset's style is patently less loose and more tightly structured than his contemporary Chéret's. A heavy, dark-toned outline separates flat tints in restrained color schemes. His rather static compositions rely on a detailed finish and an elaborate backdrop, a far remove from the impression of incompleteness that bestows such dynamism on Chéret's work.

Another famous poster artist and illustrator of Swiss origin, Théophile Alexandre Steinlen settled in Toulouse-Lautrec's Montmartre, where he met many of the great writers of the time (including Verlaine, Zola, and Maupassant). Steinlen was possessed of strong social convictions; converted to socialism, he dreamed of a better world in which inequalities would be reduced and the downtrodden lifted up. He portrayed the lives of a sometimes wretched populace in drawings he published regularly in satirical reviews. His posters for social or political causes naturally defend similar positions. Like the posters he was to design during World War I, these are expressive transcriptions of daily life. Freed from the concerns of advertising, his drawing is more rigorous, enhanced by an understated range of colors. Steinlen's graphic oeuvre visibly has a political axe to grind, endowing it with a documentary quality (a similar dimension is present in some of Toulouse-Lautrec's work). Steinlen thus had no urge to reflect an idealized or inaccessible world, preferring the kinds of scenes with which

206
Alphonse Mucha, cover and inside page
from *Ilsée, princesse de Tripoli* (by Robert
de Flers), Paris: L'Édition d'art, 1897.
The whole work was designed by Mucha,
who decorated each page. Printed in
252 copies, 9 1/2 × 12 in. (24.2 × 30.1 cm).

207
Théophile Alexandre Steinlen, poster,
Tournée du Chat noir, France, 1896.

208
Alphonse Mucha, poster for Job cigarette
papers, 1898. Chromolithograph printed
in Paris, 3 ft. 3 in. × 4 ft. 10 1/2 in.
(101 × 149.2 cm). One of the two posters
designed by Mucha for Job, whose initials
are used as a motif for the composition's
background.

209
Alphonse Mucha, poster, *Gismonda. Sarah
Bernhardt*, Théâtre de la Renaissance,
1894. Chromolithograph printed in Paris,
2 ft. 5 in. × 7 ft. 1 in. (74.2 × 216 cm).

the man in the street can readily identify. His advertising material seems at odds with his socially engaged works: for foodstuffs, for example, he used images of girls and cats. Peaceful and serene, these images are imbued with the prevailing *japonisme*.

In a quite different idiom, Alphonse Mucha has more in common with the strand represented by Chéret and Grasset. In 1894, a fortunate combination of circumstances led to his creating a poster for the great actress Sarah Bernhardt. This clamorous debut signaled the beginnings of his fame since, enchanted with the result, the star was to make him her poster artist "by appointment" for several years. Mucha, too, constructs many of his posters around a prominent and highly decorative female figure. If the women he represents possess a somewhat dynamic allure, his graphics and the manner in which the space is filled confer a certain static quality. His surfaces are ringed by substantial outlines, in the manner of cloisonné. His women resemble creatures in a dream, wearing ample robes and twiddling their interminable locks; looking almost goddess-like, they reflect the influence of Byzantine art as much as Rococo and Pre-Raphaelite styles. His expressive register combines the characteristics of Art Nouveau with a personal facture that became known as the *style Mucha*.

In France, Chéret, Toulouse-Lautrec, Grasset, Steinlen, and Mucha number among the most important late nineteenth-century poster artists. Many others, less known because less individual (or simply overshadowed), played a similarly active part in the poster renaissance. Abel Faivre, Adolphe Willette, and Jules Alexandre Grün, for instance, worked out of Montmartre, like Toulouse-Lautrec and Steinlen. The influence of the main talents can also be sensed in the work of Paul Berthon, Emmanuel Orazi, and Georges de Feure. Others, too, have earned a place in history, such as Pal, Eugène Ogé, O'Galop, and Lucien Métivet. Because the poster maintained an immediate bond with drawing and painting, its creators also include many of the great draftsmen and caricaturists, as is the case with Leonetto Cappiello, recognized in France as one of the major poster artists of the beginning of the twentieth century.

Supremely active in the genesis of the art of the poster, by the end of the nineteenth century Paris abounded in artists and draftsmen alive to the temptations of advertising. Its heyday, however, began to come to an end around 1900; France's role was on the wane and many other countries filled the breach, such as Great Britain, Austria, Germany, Switzerland, the Netherlands, and the United States.

Graphic art continued developing in more industrialized nations with relatively well-educated populations. In about 1900, a new graphic language emerged in Scotland and in Germanic countries resolutely turned towards constructive, abstract, and geometric forms.

Great Britain
Aubrey Beardsley, Walter Crane, Dudley Hardy, and John Hassall

In spite of a career cut tragically short—he died in 1897, aged only twenty-five— Aubrey Beardsley, like Toulouse-Lautrec, became a leading figure of his time. As early as 1891, Edward Burne-Jones was encouraging him to develop his artistic talent. Regarded as one of the earliest exponents of British Art Nouveau, Beardsley created an original oeuvre, which was characterized in particular by illustration, including several posters, and which was to be the object of severe criticism. His drawings for the epic *La Morte d'Arthur* in 1892–93 (text by Thomas Malory printed for the first time by William Caxton at the end of the fifteenth century) and Oscar Wilde's *Salome* in 1894 were two of his most memorable successes. Part of his work was published by the art and literary review *The Yellow Book*, which he co-founded and for which he was art director, until he was dismissed in 1895 following Wilde's infamous trial.

His idiosyncratic idiom is redolent as much of Japanese art and ancient Greek vases as of Arts and Crafts, the Decadent spirit, or paintings by Whistler and Mantegna. Uniform tints and contrasts are the principal elements in a graphic style dominated by delicacy of line, accentuated surfaces, minor distortions, unusual compositions, and abbreviated backdrops. Great black or colored masses are counterbalanced by delicate, precise, and sometimes

210
Aubrey Beardsley, erotic ornamental letter (among his very last creations), Great Britain, c. 1896.

211
Aubrey Beardsley, preparatory drawing for the cover of Oscar Wilde's *Salome*, Great Britain, 1894.

intricate lines. In his drawings, Beardsley delves into a state of mind, a feeling, an aspect of human behavior. Vice is not absent, becoming more and more explicit in erotic drawings whose aim is perhaps less to shock than to undermine conventions and taboos. Beardsley's daring, though, created a scandal and he was the target of more than one sarcastic remark, as his not especially flattering nickname "Weirdsley Daubery" testifies. Although subject to vehement criticism, the originality and modernity of Beardsley's language nonetheless exerted a great influence in England and the United States.

Beardsley's British contemporaries included some notable graphic designers and poster artists. Walter Crane, known initially for his illustrations and through his adherence to the Arts and Crafts movement, pursued a career with a significant teaching component, becoming director of the Royal College of Art of London in 1896. In addition, Crane established firm links with the German Jugendstil and the Vienna Secession. Beardsley himself found a significant source of inspiration in the work of the elder artist.

In around 1895, the art of the poster was being tackled in England by a number of other talents. One of them, Dudley Hardy, was a pioneer of the color poster. While a student in Paris, he had been much impressed by Chéret. Some of Hardy's posters present the uniform ground typical of the era. The image—often a figure, as in Chéret—emerges from this ground in which nothing else competes for the attention of the eye. The dynamism of his compositions is enhanced by lettering of an original style. The systematic use of a contour line round each surface testifies to the assimilation and persistence of Japanese influences. One of his posters, *The Yellow Girl*, gave rise to the following telling comment: "The effect was startling and no advertisement had ever achieved its purpose more simply or completely."[33]

Like Dudley Hardy, John Hassall studied in Continental Europe (at Antwerp and Paris), coming to the fore in the 1890s. His posters were of a commercial as well as cultural nature. Dudley Hardy and John Hassall both created a style associating uniform swathes of bright color with a strong outline forming the basis of the design. Thanks to the very different contributions of Aubrey Beardsley, Walter Crane, Dudley Hardy, and John Hassall, the British were significant in developing the artistic cachet of the poster.

The Glasgow School

In Scotland, the Glasgow School served as a bridgehead for ongoing modernization. Known also as the "Glasgow Four" or simply "The Four," the Glasgow School included four artists: Charles Rennie Mackintosh, Herbert MacNair, and their wives, the sisters Margaret and Frances MacDonald. The group formed at the beginning of the 1890s and their collaboration lasted until 1906. Convinced of the ideas of the Arts and Crafts movement and paying tribute to Art Nouveau, the Glasgow Four sought to refashion the forms of architecture, design, furniture, textile, and graphics. An architect, Charles Rennie Mackintosh was the linchpin of the group. Hermann Muthesius,[34] at the very beginning of the century, already characterized him as a pioneer: "If one desired to draw up the list of the creative geniuses of modern architecture, Charles Rennie Mackintosh's name would have to appear among the first.[35]

The style forged by the Glasgow Four stands at the crossroads between two dominant trends: the decorative and vegetal aspect of Art Nouveau and the birth of a rationalized design associated with simplified, geometric forms. As in the work of the Beggarstaffs, the designs are flat and the third dimension attenuated. By marrying freehand curves and geometry, the Four created an individual idiom. Line prevails over the whole composition: curvilinear forms are accompanied by hatching, by grids of squares, or stylized roses; simplicity and decoration thus attain a subtle balance. The Glasgow School's quest was for an ideal design, with roles assigned to dream and poetry. If their oeuvre can be partially assimilated into Art Nouveau, it clearly had little in common with the French strand of the tendency. In what is an advance for the time, the Four invented simplified, well-tempered forms, forerunners to some extent of the kind of functional design that arose at the turn of the century. And in point of fact, in 1897,

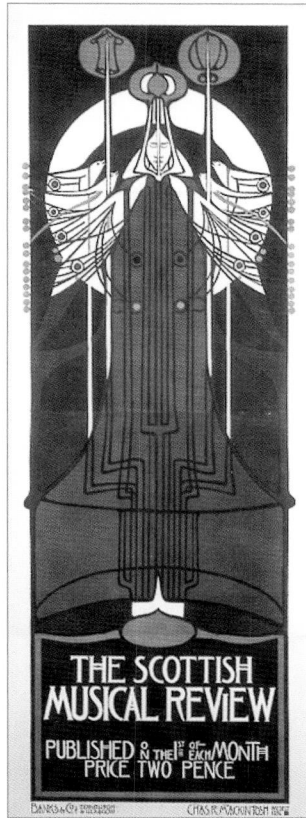

212
Charles Rennie Mackintosh, poster,
The Scottish Musical Review, Scotland, 1896.

213
Charles Rennie Mackintosh, wall-clock
designed for the Glasgow School of Art, c. 1900.

the Vienna Secession drew significant inspiration from their work. By the turn of the century the group's Europe-wide reputation was being enhanced by a series of exhibitions staged in Liège, London, Paris, Vienna, and Turin.

Belgium

In Belgium, as in Great Britain, fin-de-siècle graphic art oscillated between an elaborate Art Nouveau with its attendant female, and a design style teetering over into abstraction, geometry, and schematization. Brussels was at the time one of the forcing-grounds of Art Nouveau, in the same league as London, Glasgow, Paris, and Munich. Artists were active as much in the poster as in architecture, which, in Belgium, was enjoying a particularly fertile period, the chief talents being Victor Horta and Henry Van de Velde. Heralding future designs, their works tended to jettison superfluous ornament in favor of structures that are at the same time organic and functional. The same tendency surfaced in the Belgian poster, which seems less prettified than in France, though it falls short of the more sober and rectilinear approach of the Glasgow School.

Around the 1890s, two groups of artists formed in Brussels: the group of Les xx (Les Vingt) and La Libre Esthétique. The greatest *affichistes* of the era were very much involved, such as Privat Livemont, Henri Meunier, and Fernand Toussaint, who were all to discover Chéret's works and absorb the influence of Parisian trends. Thanks to the active support of patrons, a seedbed of young artists elevated the poster to the rank of a fine art. Privat Livemont, one of the best-known poster artists of his generation, was to attain international fame. Trained in Paris, he opened his own studio in Belgium in 1890. His graphic style shares Mucha's strongly outlined and sinuous decoration, with the same symbolic use of female figures. His lines, however, appear more tense and his treatment less illustrative. Privat Livemont even varies the thickness of his black contours as frequently in drawings as in ornaments and lettering, a feature that confers a distinctive quality on his poster art. In spite of the fame he enjoyed during his lifetime, Privat Livemont is not now regarded as a creative force or as one of the main precursors of graphic art in Belgium.

Henry Van de Velde

Henry Van de Velde, on the other hand, has always occupied center stage. Like that of the Glasgow School, his career throws a bridge between Art Nouveau and the onset of geometrical design with its cleaner lines.

Van de Velde is one of those protean creators who excelled in several disciplines: architecture, design, theory, and so on. He started studying painting, only to abandon it in 1894 (a key date in the development of Belgian art) to devote himself to the applied arts, thus following a trajectory previously taken by William Morris. It was indeed the Englishman's design philosophy that served as a guiding light to the ideas of Van de Velde—to the point that he was chosen by the grand duke of Saxon-Weimar in Germany as an "artistic advisor appointed to raise the aesthetic level of production in every handicraft and industry in the land."[36]

Above and beyond Art Nouveau, Van de Velde's oeuvre spanned other artistic movements in Germany. In 1907, he was among the founder members of the Werkbund (from *Werk*, "work," and *Bund*, "alliance, union"). Playing a crucial role in the fresh approach to teaching methods being explored at the time, the following year, in 1908, Van de Velde was officially named director of the Weimar School of Arts and Crafts, which he was to head until 1915 and which was to constitute in part the basis for the Bauhaus in 1919. If he initially rooted himself in the Arts and Crafts movement and the painting of the Pont-Aven School, he was soon voicing more personal objectives: to create for all, to embrace mechanization, to combine art with industry, and to further identical ideals in architecture and in design. With these precepts in mind, he upheld the demand for quality inherited from the Arts and Crafts movement, while transforming decoration by way of an elegant functionalism that reined in

214

214
Henry Van de Velde, graphic for *Tropon* foods, c. 1898.

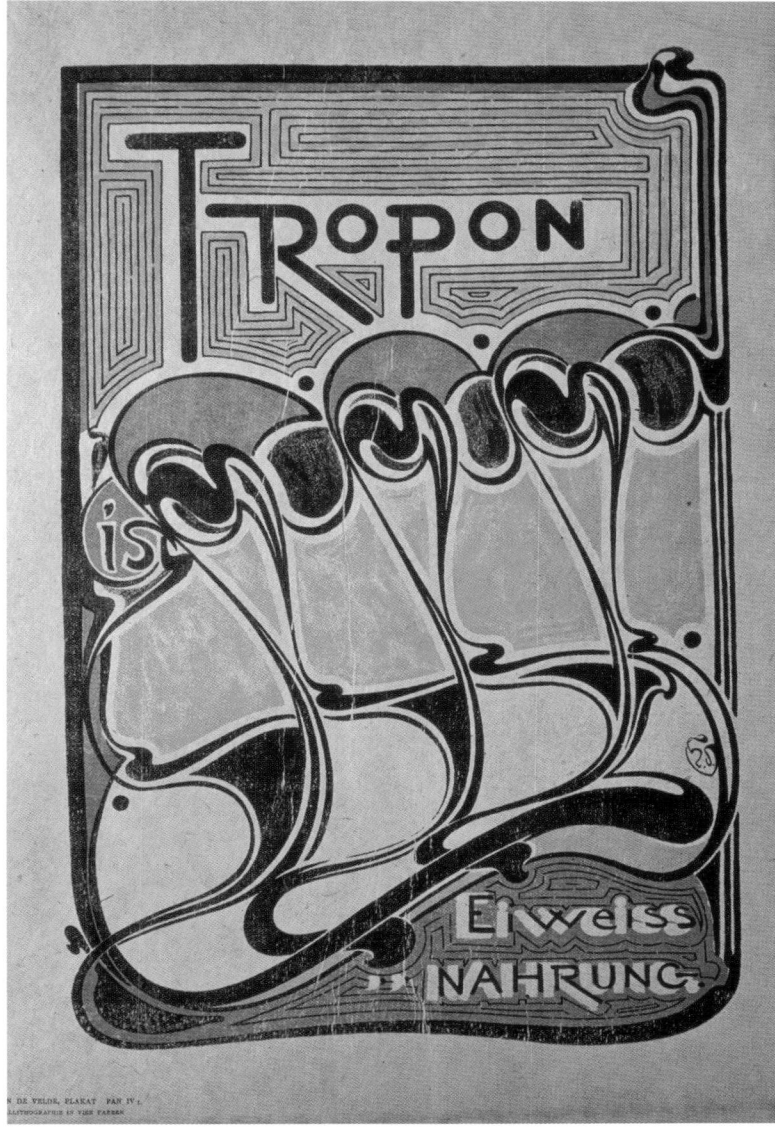

215

215
Henry Van de Velde, poster, *Tropon*
(food product containing egg white, produced
by the Tropon factory at Cologne-Mülheim),
1897 or 1898.

ornament. Pursuing this vein, in 1895 Victor Horta announces a new departure in Art Nouveau: "Let's give up the flower and the leaf, let's keep the stalk."[37] Henry Van de Velde's graphic corpus covers the design of books as well as ephemeral media. In 1897, an exhibition of his work in Dresden earned him several commissions from the publishing, advertising, and public relations industries.

In Belgium as in Germany, the informed eye of a number of industrial magnates and retailers was to constitute a necessary precondition for the further development and production of graphics. Following an exhibition of his work, Van de Velde was awarded an account by the Tropon factories, manufacturers of a foodstuff based on egg white. The brief was to design a logo, the product's packaging, and a promotional poster. Van de Velde's solution was an astonishing visual—a daringly modern project that has gone down in history. The chromolithographic poster features an abstract design repeating the same, arabesque-based motif (which might be interpreted as alluding to the separation of egg white from yolk). Reveling in abstraction and in the pleasure of color, Van de Velde embarked on a decisive stage for the development of modern graphics; if skill is applied, commercial demands can be satisfied by sheer ornament to create artwork that is at once absorbing and charming.

For the lettering, Van de Velde dared to employ a virtually geometric, sans serif typeface. In order to imagine the effect of such a poster in 1898—right in the middle of Art Nouveau and against the backdrop of the continued prevalence of Victorian graphic styles—one has to forget the intervening graphic designs of the twentieth century (a similar effort is called for to contextualize the Beggarstaffs' *Cinderella* poster of 1895). In the Tropon poster, any trace of the past, of tradition, of classicism, of academism is erased; like the furniture of Charles Rennie Mackintosh, it represents a seismic shift in the field of design. New forms are built up, turned resolutely towards the future. Like few creations of its time, the Tropon poster belongs to a repertoire of imagery that seems able to cross time without ageing.

The Netherlands

In the Netherlands, the revival in graphics began shortly before 1900. This may seem a tardy date for a country that, in the twentieth century, has regularly distinguished itself on the international scene by the quality of its graphics as much as by its typography (and of course, further back in history, this geographical region and its vicinity boasted a remarkable tradition in printing and typography, with illustrious names such as Plantin and Elzevir as early as the sixteenth century). By the end of the nineteenth century, however, the "Victorian" style was still widespread in the Netherlands, as in so many other countries, and, moreover, in terms of format, fin-de-siècle Dutch posters tended to be rather modest. The most influential Dutch poster artists were often painters and architects, such as Jan Toorop, Johan Thorn Prikker, Hendrik Berlage, Jan van Caspel, and Roland Holst. Some, such as Toorop or Thorn Prikker, were evidently members of the Art Nouveau (or Nieuwe Kunst) movement; others remained wedded to Symbolism, while others again treated the poster more pictorially or handled it in a more obviously "craft" style.

216
Jan Toorop, poster, *Delftsche Slaolie* (salad oil),
Netherlands, 1895.

Jan Toorop's poster for *Delftsche Slaolie* is probably one of the most famous achievements in the development of the Dutch art poster. Conceived in 1895 to advertise an edible oil, it shows two women, one of whom is preparing a salad; throughout the poster there weaves a curvilinear mesh, creating an enveloping atmosphere (a style reminiscent of American psychedelic posters of the 1960s). By and large, Dutch graphic art around 1900 is so diverse that it cannot be reduced to any one current and this variety gives little hint as to the markedly constructivist and experimental dimension that engulfed the Dutch avant-gardes from the 1910s on.

Advances in American graphic style

American poster artists at this time often resorted to European models. Since the mid-nineteenth century, the poster had obtained a visible presence in the United States, where it was of large size, awash with artwork, and, after the introduction of the chromolithograph, showed itself splendidly colorful. Although of exemplary quality in terms of technique, these posters seemed to have little room for aesthetic concerns. As Charles Cochran, a friend of Aubrey Beardsley, vouchsafed after his first visit to New York in 1891: "The huge theatrical posters, though beautifully printed, were utterly lacking in taste as regards design and colour."[38]

Towards the end of the nineteenth century, however, the poster in the United States was acquiring new visual qualities. Around 1890, both the art poster and European Art Nouveau were making inroads into the United States, and posters by Mucha and Chéret were already available. Initially, the influences came from France and England. European endeavors awakened keen interest on the other side of the Atlantic, so much so that the American press began to place orders for them, an intercontinental exchange that mounted in the 1920s and 1930s. Since 1889, for example, Eugène Grasset had been commissioned to design posters and covers for magazines, in particular for *Harper's Bazaar* and *Harper's Magazine*. *The Chap Book* reproduced works by Aubrey Beardsley and Toulouse-Lautrec, while magazines specializing in the poster displayed European examples in their columns. Often nourished by these influences, several American graphic designers came to the fore after 1890. Initially, their posters adhered closely to the European vein, although a specifically American genre gradually arose as the years passed. These graphic pioneers included Edward Penfield, Will Bradley, and Louis Rhead; they all often received orders from publishers and press conglomerates. Vastly popular, newspapers and magazines reached massive circulations in the United States, where literacy rates were high and which enabled American graphic design eventually to forge a character of its own.

Each number of a magazine, for instance, had to be adorned with a different cover; once created, this would be enlarged into a promotional poster, a practice that has since become entrenched. Contrariwise, many British periodicals kept the same cover over successive numbers. If the press played a key role in the development of an American graphic style, the cause was also served by the plethora of posters and advertisements. As in Europe, the passion for the poster took over the cities of the United States soon after 1890. One of the very first American books specifically devoted to the form, *The Modern Poster*, was to come out in 1895.

Edward Penfield, Will Bradley, and Louis Rhead

An adherent of the Art Nouveau style, Edward Penfield was one of the most distinguished American graphic designers of the era, whose efforts to forge a genuinely American style testify to obvious artistic concerns and are regarded in some quarters as epoch-making. From 1893 on, he worked for the monthly magazine *Harper's*, designing a promotional poster for each number. The visuals resulting from this commission were a predominant influence on the fledgling art poster in America. Drawing inspiration from British works, French posters

217
Edward Penfield, *Harper's*, February, 1897.

218
Will Bradley, drawing for *The Inland Printer*,
United States.

219
Will Bradley, cover for *The Bookman* (New York),
1900.

220
Will Bradley, *The Chap-Book*, poster or book
cover, United States, 1894–95.

221
George Frederick Scotson-Clark, poster
for *The New York Recorder*, United States, 1895.

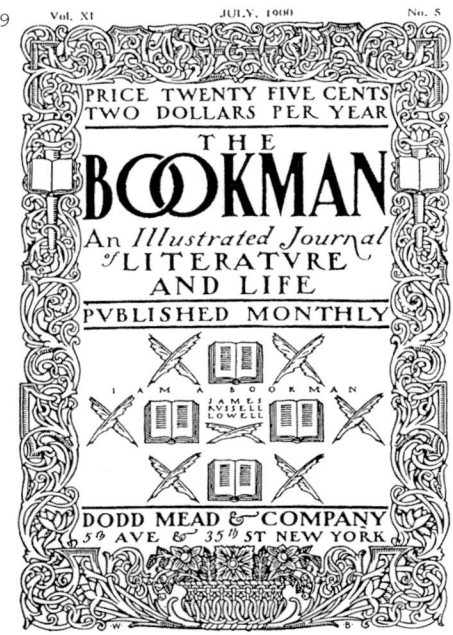

(Steinlen, Toulouse-Lautrec, and Bonnard), and Japanese prints, Penfield also showed an interest in the graphic legacy of Egyptian antiquity that he could see for himself in the collections of New York's Metropolitan Museum. For six years, Penfield remained the sole originator of posters for *Harper's,* in which he often featured well-heeled readers perusing or carrying the journal. In the space of a few short months, his style acquired a specific character that parted with realism to introduce a more synthetic approach in which outlines, uniform blocks, and warm colors predominate. The use of space is generous and the point of view sometimes unusual, while the overall impact is reinforced by the suppression of details and background. The compositions conferred an important role on the lettering, which is integrated into the image. Quite apart from his career at *Harper's,* Penfield was to obtain many other orders for posters, which are as emblematic of the revival of graphics as they are representative of his own oeuvre.

Will Bradley was another key player in the formation of American Art Nouveau. His expertise extended from poster to type design, via magazine covers, book design, and illustration. From modest stock, Will Bradley was self-taught in the trade. His initial interests covered the Arts and Crafts movement, the craft industry, American typography, the work of Aubrey Beardsley, and Japanese art. Whereas Penfield derived at least part of his inspiration from the French poster, Bradley was more influenced by British examples. With a career beginning in the mid-1880s, his style gelled during the following decade to reach full maturation in about 1894. From this time, he designed a series of posters and covers for magazines in an Art Nouveau style, working for, among others, the reviews and magazines *The Inland Printer, The Chap Book,* and *Harper's Bazaar*. His compositions combine asymmetry, contrast, decoration, and undulating forms. Bradley set up his own print-works in 1894 based on the model of William Morris's Kelmscott Press founded three years before; as a publisher in 1896 in Boston, Bradley brought out his own literary and arts review, *Bradley: His Book*. From 1896–98, several high-quality volumes came off his presses, since rechristened the Wayside Press (the printshop was bought out in 1898 by the University Press at Cambridge, Massachusetts). With an interest in the at once sober and robust style of colonial graphics, Will Bradley's idiom at the time veered towards the chap-book style. The versatility of his activities led him to take on an advisory role for the American Type Founders Company (ATF) and to acquire renown as art director on several magazines. As an initiator, Bradley's oeuvre had considerable impact on American graphics and was widely imitated. He and Penfield were instrumental in developing a specifically American graphic style, both manifestly susceptible to European influences and yet bearing its own very personal stamp.

Like Edward Penfield and Will Bradley, Louis Rhead was a central contributor to American Art Nouveau and all three figures feature among the principal graphic designers of the end of the nineteenth century in the United States. Of British origin, Louis Rhead spent the bulk of his career on the other side of the Atlantic. Like his contemporaries, he brought out many books and magazine covers, while his earliest poster, dating to 1889, is a further example of the continuing reconfiguration of visual vocabularies. Close to the medieval colorism of Eugène Grasset at the beginning of the 1890s, Rhead's creations were to evolve towards a more personal language. Other American poster artists and graphic designers emerged at the same time as Rhead, Bradley, and Penfield, each, in various degrees, making their mark in history, such as Maxfield Parrish, Will Carqueville, Ethel Reed, George Frederick Scotson-Clark, and Frank Hazenplug.

Creating posters in which an authentic concern with form combines with commercial demands, together they laid the foundations for a new visual world. American advertising took wing and discovered its own special voice. Contrary to some European designers and poster artists (William Morris, Théophile Alexandre Steinlen, etc.), this new graphic idiom did not seem particularly focused on social ideals, but, more pragmatically, sought to please the viewer. Symptomatically, it was round about this time that marketing and market research first appeared in business practice.

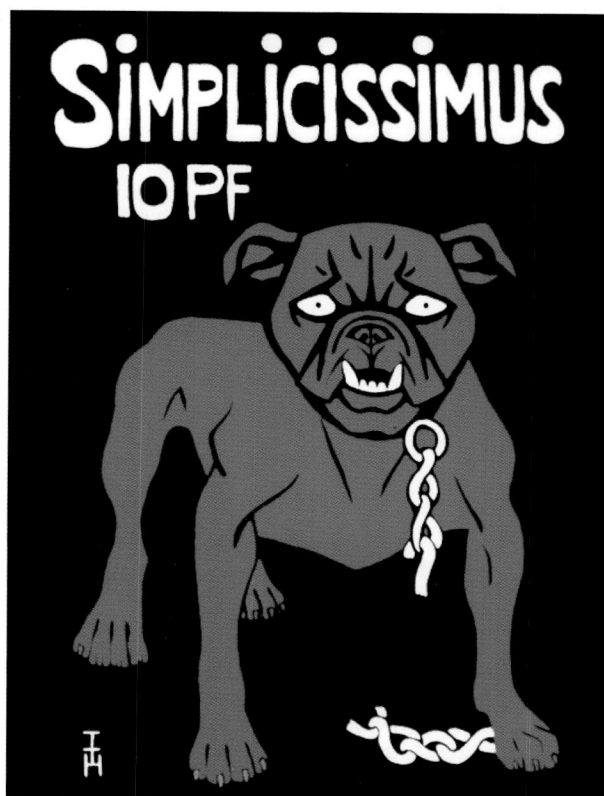

222

222
Thomas Theodor Heine, graphic illustration
for the poster and cover for the satirical review
Simplicissimus, Germany, 1897.

Jugendstil in Germany

Fanning through France, England, Belgium, and the United States, Art Nouveau also began to make its way in Germany. There, as in Scotland and Austria, the movement acquired some distinctive characteristics. Jugendstil[39] explored linear, geometrically orientated, and sometimes less decorative forms, a route similarly explored by the Glasgow School. Thomas Mann described the movement as "an ingenuous cult of line, decoration, form, and sensuality.[40] Rather different from the French pictorial, illustrative , and sometimes florid approach, the German version of Art Nouveau went in for more abstract, symbolic, and concise forms. The new Jugendstil quickly gained ground, adapting itself to a great range of artistic fields, from fine to applied arts, as well as handicrafts. This reshaping affected painting, tapestry, design, interior design, and architecture, while also feeding into the fields of graphics and typography.

Until the last years of the nineteenth century, the German poster, molded by historical references, seems to have made little artistic progress (the posters of Franz von Stuck, for example, are at once traditional yet distinct from the sometimes ponderous graphics of the time). The beginnings of Jugendstil graphics betray the influence of both English and French Art Nouveau, developments that reinforced the autonomy of a graphic domain that was partially dissociating itself from pictorial practice proper. The role of typography was also evolving, and, no longer content to play second fiddle, it was determined to venture beyond the confines of the image to take on a more central role.

In 1896, two events in the German graphic sphere confirmed this revival: one was the publication of a poster, *Die alte Stadt*, by Otto Fischer, promoting an "exhibition of the arts and crafts trades in Saxony." Quite unlike the overblown busyness of conventional advertising, Otto Fischer's use of the medium was eminently unusual. Using a fresh, bright palette, his simplified graphic style exploited flat tints and contours, a clear distinction between the planes, and a textual hierarchy that proved at once uncomplicated and effective. The launch of the art weekly *Jugend* in Munich was the other significant event of 1896, as the magazine spawned the very term "Jugendstil." Like *Pan* (a cultural review founded in Berlin in 1895) and *Simplicissimus* (a satirical periodical set up in Munich, again in 1896), *Jugend* soon gained tens of thousands of subscribers and so peddled the new style to a wider public. Thanks to such periodicals, as well as to the gradual emergence of a genuine poster art, the year 1896 marks the true onset of Jugendstil, a movement that was to thrive for over a decade.

Apart from Munich, the current soon engulfed Berlin, Darmstadt, and Weimar. Berlin and Munich were the two main hubs of German poster art, remaining so even after the demise of Jugendstil. The German vein of Art Nouveau owed much to the work of Peter Behrens, Henry Van de Velde, Otto Eckmann, Thomas Theodore Heine, and Hermann Obrist; other, less known, graphic designers were just as active, such as Bruno Paul and Fritz Rehm and many collaborated on magazines associated with Jugendstil. In the work of Peter Behrens and Henry Van de Velde (who were then working respectively in Darmstadt and Weimar), Jugendstil constituted a transitory stage, a stepping-stone to the modernism of the next century. The impact of Jugendstil is visible in diverse aspects of visual expression, most particularly in the poster, magazine, illustrated book, typography, and type generally.

These new voices in German poster art were greatly advanced by the interest shown in their work by lithographer-printers. Naturally, posters often publicized cultural events such as exhibitions, new books, and so on, but they also promoted consumer products and businesses. The posters and magazine covers of Thomas Theodore Heine, art director at *Simplicissimus*, rank among the most unusual. With his unwavering political and social convictions, he chose an allusive critical idiom, overtly political posters being prohibited in Germany up to World

War I. Thomas Theodore Heine's style, compact but powerful, is redolent of the Beggarstaffs, or of certain aspects of Japanese prints, combined with the pointedness of American or French poster artists. Its visual impact arises from simple compositions based on blocks of color and smooth outlines. Like Heine, many Jugendstil graphic artists transposed Art Nouveau into a more abstract and structural register—a far cry from floral ornaments, idealized women, and pictorial lettering—where it is the strength of line and color that is paramount.

In the poster as elsewhere, Jugendstil influenced type design, too. Otto Eckmann and Peter Behrens, for example, created typefaces for the Klingspor foundry. Conceived in 1900 or a little before, Eckmann-Schrift probably represents one of the very first Art Nouveau typefaces. It is an alphabet that bears the name of its creator—like Behrens-Schrift, which dates to 1901–07—and is in line with the same tendency.

Jugendstil came into its own at the turn of the century. By this time, however, although the movement had arisen there, in France Art Nouveau was already on the wane. The early twentieth-century French poster (except for Cappiello and a handful of other talents) did not constitute a genuine school, while Jugendstil, on the other hand, was instrumental in beginning a revival in the German poster that was to continue unabated until at least the 1930s.

The Vienna Secession

As in Germany, the new art made inroads into Austria during the closing years of the nineteenth century. There, too, forms tended to be geometrical, less illustrative, and at times simplified, although at others elaborate and complex. Functionalism was progressively taking shape, with the tone being set by architects as early as the 1880s. The Viennese architect Otto Wagner glimpsed "a new birth of artistic creation."[41] This phenomenon concerned all the visual arts, as well as architecture and the applied arts, embracing graphics, furniture, design (toys, tableware, jewelry, etc.), and interior architecture: whatever the object treated, however, its decoration seemed increasingly geometrical in spirit. Around 1900, this concentration of geometrical and abstract motifs coalesced into a genuine Austrian style.

Passing through a period of intense creativity, Vienna was, however, plagued by profound sociopolitical traumas: the Austro-Hungarian Empire had lost part of Germany and Italy, and the Habsburgs were in free fall, with Empress Elisabeth the victim of an assassination in 1898. In spite of this, artistic and cultural life was rich and varied, with unparalleled experiments in the intellectual, musical, and artistic spheres and new conceptions of man and art in the air. Franz Wickhoff and Aloïs Riegl made their mark with a fresh approach to art history; Freud, exploring the realm of the unconscious, adumbrated a new perspective on human behavior and forged the psychoanalytical method; and composer Arnold Schoenberg was already writing early works that prefigured the atonal and dodecaphonic systems of music to come.

Inevitably, against this particularly vibrant backdrop, major artistic shifts were soon afoot. The year 1897 saw a landmark: the foundation of the Vienna Secession—the Vereinigung bildender Künstler Österreichs (the Association of Austrian Visual Artists)—chaired by Gustav Klimt and including among its ranks personalities as influential as Koloman Moser, Alfred Roller, and the architects Josef Hoffmann and Joseph Maria Olbrich. Extrapolating from reforms already undertaken by the Arts and Crafts movement and continued by the Glasgow School and Henry Van de Velde, the movement set itself up against officialdom and rejected "bourgeois" art studded with historical references and pseudo-Baroque personifications. In point of fact, and well before the Secessionist movement, Viennese design had already been the subject of remarkable experiments from about 1870, when the Thonet brothers' company began retailing an inexpensive but high-quality range of furniture, including chairs in clean-cut, simplified forms. Based on the technique of bentwood, Thonet pieces sold well beyond the borders of Austria, pulling off the much-vaunted trick of combining art with craft, and attaining high production yields (as attested by the meteoric success of Chair No. 14, dating to 1859, and manufactured in the tens of millions).

223

223
Page from the catalog for the firm of the Thonet brothers, Vienna, after 1873.

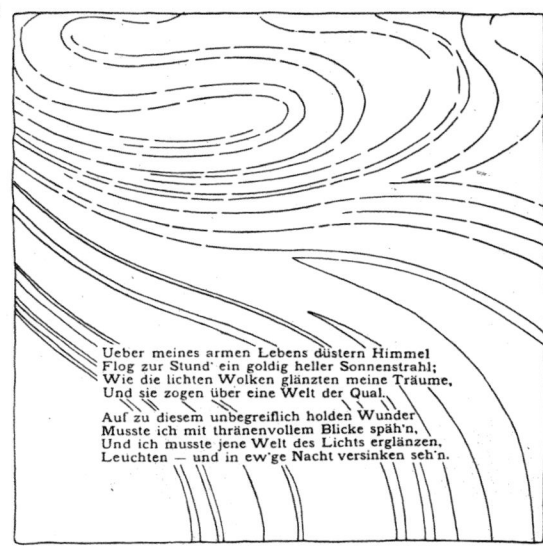

In 1898, the Secession set up its own review, *Ver sacrum* (Sacred Spring). The publication's avowed objective was to promote the group's ideas and publicize its members. It enunciated its key tenets in the very first number: "We make no distinction between 'grand art' and 'minor art,' between art for the rich and art for the poor. Art belongs to all."[42] The cover of the launch issue represents a tree whose roots have burst through the tub in which it is planted: a symbolic image of future growth, dynamism, and the jettisoning of time-worn constraints. In their turn, the Secessionists elevated the applied, decorative, and industrial arts to the level of painting and sculpture. Their ambition was to design objects that would improve daily existence, to attain their social ideals, to break with the elitism of the access to art, to educate the eye of the masses, and to free their work from shackles of the academy.

The protagonists of the Secession often defined themselves as industrialists or manufacturers. Striving to create an art that would be their own, at the same time autonomous yet receptive to contemporary European ideas, they did not disavow tradition, but sought, through their works, to offer a different viewpoint. From the very start, Secession style was torn between classical handling and experimentation. The style wedded decorative forms and geometric elements, only discovering its true path when it threw its lot in with abstraction and geometry. In the graphics of Koloman Moser and Alfred Roller, for instance, the repetition of motifs and the semigeometrical, semicurvilinear stylization of the lettering are accompanied by sacrifices in terms of legibility that are counterbalanced, however, by an attractively original idiom. The image is often composed of an assemblage of simple forms (circles, rectangles, triangles, checkerboards, reticulations) and relatively sober schematic elements (wavelets, stars, eyes, arrows), often reiterated until they cover the entire surface. Roller, Koloman Moser, and Joseph Maria Olbrich were at the forefront of the association's graphic wing, and designed books, posters, postcards, covers, and page layouts for *Ver sacrum*, as well as stamps. Josef Hoffmann and Otto Wagner, more celebrated as designers and architects, were also active on the graphic front; Secessionist artists often displayed protean talents. In the world of forms, there thus came into being a current that surged through typography, graphics, object design,

227
Koloman Moser, poster, *Thirteenth Exhibition of the Vienna Secession*, 1902. Chromolithograph, 5 ft. 10 in. × 2 ft. (177.2 × 59.7 cm).

furniture, textiles, interior decoration, and architecture. In addition to coherence and harmony, this output was typified by elegance, artistry, and refinement.

A vigorous institution, the Secession soon made contact with foreign artists, organizing regular exhibitions, where, in addition to its own works, it would show contemporary art from Western Europe. Through these, the Viennese public came to discover artists as varied as Auguste Rodin, Pierre Puvis de Chavannes, Eugène Grasset, Charles Rennie Mackintosh and his wife Margaret MacDonald, Henry Van de Velde, and Ferdinand Hodler. The poster for the first Secession exhibition, however, designed by Klimt in 1898, signaled a departure from the graphic idiom that was to characterize the movement; the image appears illustrative and narrative, nearer to allegory and symbol. Certain elements in this poster prefigure new departures: the vast, almost square non-printed surface occupies the central position, an asymmetrical layout that offsets the chief visual component over to the right side, while the text below, divided by a fillet, fits into a rectangle like the image in the upper portion, thereby playing an essential role in structuring the unit.

Later posters for the Secession exhibitions of 1902 and 1903 by Koloman Moser and Alfred Roller attest to a graphic style that has made the transition into the new century, in search of an unusual, unconventional, and yet by the same token sturdily constructed visual world. Here, the lettering may occupy up to half the surface area of the poster, and may even become a graphic element in its own right, an element to look at rather than to read, to the point of jettisoning legibility in an effort to ensure impact and originality. One and the same graphic *parti pris* fuses abstract lettering, image, and pattern into a single, astonishing harmony. Koloman Moser—a still more influential figure since he taught at the Kunstgewerbeschule (School of Applied Art) in Vienna—appears to have been chiefly responsible for developing this graphic language in which arrangements of squares and the contrast between black and white predominate. His furniture, like his graphic decoration, is assembled from geometrizing forms, with every other type of ornamentation kept on a tight rein.

The expressions of the open mindset of Viennese modernity were fuelled by abstraction, linearity, geometry, and rigor, as well as the pleasure afforded by decorative forms. Once again, graphic art was diverging from illustration and painting and gelling into an autonomous artistic praxis. More than any other movement, it is perhaps the Vienna Secession that throws the bridge between the Art Nouveau style and the avant-garde graphics of the future. Heralding a clean break, it is lively, sometimes functional, observant of its own codes, and with its own formal repertories. Secessionist creation reached European audiences generally when its output was unveiled at the Paris Universal Exhibition of 1900. After the dynamic freedom sought by practitioners of Art Nouveau, artists and designers adopted other artistic languages, partially throwing off tradition, without ever completely rejecting it. New forms of expression were germinating that would transform the world of graphics and invest decorative and applied arts with new values. The era around 1900, therefore, is a transitional period, with Vienna at the heart of a groundswell that was intrinsically interdisciplinary.

The Secession, however, never attained its ideal of "art for all" due to a lack of funding from industry and of stumbling-blocks encountered in breaking with the marketplace; rather like the sumptuous publications of the Kelmscott Press, Secessionist pieces were bound to remain the preserve of an elite. What is more, the group was not exempt from polemic and serious internal strife. The idea of molding the arts into a "total work of art" met with caustic criticism from personalities such as Adolf Loos and Karl Kraus, bringing about the resignation of several members of the association.

Practices in flux

The Vienna Secession was just one of the many currents that, by the end of the nineteenth century, were to transform the conception of design, graphics, and typography in the West. In the space of between twenty and thirty years, graphic style evolved from the pictorial

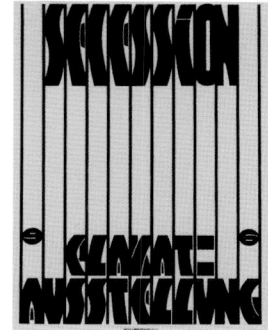

228
Ernst Eck, poster for
an exhibition of posters
by the Vienna Secession, 1912.
3 ft. 1 in. × 2 ft. ³/₄ in.
(95 × 63 cm).

229
Franz Wacik, poster for
an exhibition of posters by
the Vienna Secession, 1912.
3 ft. 1 in. × 2 ft. ³/₄ in.
(95 × 63 cm).

tendencies of a Chéret to a more self-governing practice. The upshot was a new conception of visual creation that aimed to be unexpected or original, to marshal the power of abstraction and color, focused on expressiveness, impact, simplification of line, surface effects, contrast, and so on. The protagonists behind this change in direction had come from very diverse points of departure: some could be said to be card-carrying members of Art Nouveau, while others were only on the fringes of the movement, and others still worked outside any identifiable current. Art Nouveau appears like a catalyst, an essential stimulus to the ongoing changes, one that was exceptional because of its international sweep and also because it affected so many different art forms. Artists and designers thus began to cast a fresh eye over other artifacts. The purpose was to revalorize applied art and crafts, and to urge both the functional and decorative aspects of art towards industrial production, with the aim of benefiting a larger public. This objective, however, was sooner said than attained. It demanded not only that elements in the backdrop to daily life be designed or adapted to new times, but also that they be convertible to inexpensive and easy-to-distribute mass production. From this point of view, the poster was something of an exception: its presence did indeed "benefit" a wider audience, even when it was the work of a great artist.

With design things are rather different. Its early twentieth-century innovations had little bearing on the public at large and this situation lingers on today. Often the fruit of a narrow creative remit, articles by designers of the first rank remain in general inaccessible to the market as a whole—a phenomenon that is further entrenched by the fact that they tend to be sold out of specialized stores and their appreciation calls for a measure of initiation.

As a style, Art Nouveau centers on the question of decoration in design. If it eschews ascetic functionalism, it cannot for all that be reduced to a mere decorative adjunct. Responding to a certain approach to comfort, well being, and pleasure, decoration has to couple utility with charm and elegance—that is, it has to combine functions of different species. If curves and arabesques are there to delight the eye, they also contribute to contemporary living spaces and engage with a search for expressive forms that reflect modern existence. At the turn of the twentieth century, the issue of form and its relationship to function was becoming a central concern for designers and contributed significantly to developments in graphics. Creators were having second thoughts, and began to embrace industry and take on board its means of production; it was no longer worth fighting the machine—it was better to adapt to it. A similar attitude motivated the quest for functional, more rational forms.

After the decorative profusion of the Victorian era and the vogue for flowery, undulating Art Nouveau, the search for efficiency and the uptake of mechanization led to crisper graphics—more compact, more concise, brisker. Impact no longer relied on charm or refinement alone—but rather on concentration and attractive force. Architects, too, turned to questions of utility and function. In 1896, Louis Sullivan came up with his famous formula: "form [...] follows function." Otto Wagner defined the "functional style" as the "style of the future," while Henry Van de Velde, the Chicago School (including Frank Lloyd Wright), and many other architects in the West shared similar conceptions.

Within the applied arts, the poster was one of the supports most receptive to these epoch-making upheavals. Yet despite the widespread presence of the art poster throughout much of Europe and the United States, in Spain, Italy, and Scandinavia, the poster seems to have taken a backseat, in spite of notable figures such as Alexandro de Riquer and Ramon Casas in Spain, Marcello Dudovich, Adolfo Hohenstein, and Leopoldo Metlicovitz in Italy, and Hans Tegner and Albert Engström in Scandinavia. If Art Nouveau developed in so many places, though, it was not an especially long-lasting bloom; by the first years of the twentieth century, it had given way to decorative overkill and was heavily plagiarized. Yet it gradually overlapped with other styles, spawning a new generation of transitory forms and paving the way to an industrial approach. A corner was turned on the road to modernity. The ideals that were to lead to De Stijl, to Constructivism, and to the Bauhaus were, if unsteadily, already current.

Affirmations of modernity

Typographical experiments in the book

After 1900, as Art Nouveau was beginning to wane, the graphic landscape was already showing symptoms of a new direction. If the art poster, as it had come to the fore in the final decades of the nineteenth century, represented a major field of development in the field of visual expression, there occurred in tandem another phenomenon that was to strongly influence the evolution of the poster, especially typography. Away from the clamorous ritual of advertising, writers and typographers had been experimenting with new approaches to book design, paving the way for a rethink of page and text layout. Traditionally rather conservative in spirit, nonetheless book design had already proved to be of interest for both the Arts and Crafts and the Private Press movements, as illustrated by William Morris's printed output. Prior to these endeavors, other writers strived to convey literary content through more openly visible forms: as we have seen, in the eighteenth century, Laurence Sterne and Restif de Bretonne experimented with typography and layout. Several centuries before that, Rabelais had toyed with texts verging on the image in an original scripto-visual amalgam whose sources date back, at the very least, to the picture writings of antiquity. Ornaments such as the vignette and *cul-de-lampe* or pendant had also always flourished within the ambit of the book.

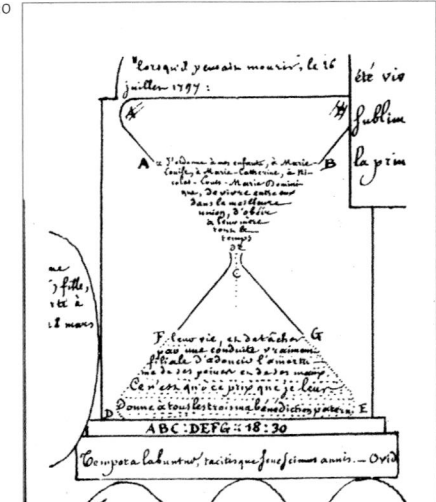

230
Nicolas Cirier, composition in the shape of an hour glass from *L'Apprenti administrateur. Pamphlet pittoresque (!) littérario-typographico-bureaucratique* [. . .] [sic] (The Apprentice Administrator. Picturesque Litterario-Typographico-Bureaucratic Lampoon), Paris, 1840.

In the nineteenth century, other famous authors turned their attention to changing the internal appearance of the book and discovered inventive roles for typesetting. Lewis Carroll and Stéphane Mallarmé, for instance, thought of the page, or double page, as a space open to any kind of composition. In laying out the text dynamically, or in drawing attention to its presence, they ignored the norms of page-setting—the traditional page "template" with its divisions and time-honored distribution into margin and text column, its centering—and short-circuited the perceptive reflexes it stimulates. Similar typographical explorations were relatively frequent throughout the century, as testified by the experiments of author Charles Nodier and artist James McNeill Whistler. Such researches exceeded the framework of the book, encroaching onto other (typo)graphic surfaces, such as the *calligramme*; by mid-century, they are also to be found in the satirical press, ever fertile ground for typographical amusements.

The year 1830 saw the appearance of a highly unusual work: Charles Nodier's *Histoire du roi de Bohême et de ses sept châteaux*, with Romantic illustrations by graphic artist Tony Johannot. Integrating text and image to an astonishing degree, the book also boasts some surprising typography (reminiscent of Sterne's *Tristram Shandy*). There appear *calligrammes*, games with typefaces and capital letters, extended words, truncated lines, spaces deliberately left unprinted, and onomatopoeias—all as diverting to look at as to read. This reorganization of the page is seconded by a text that can be called, at the very least, a non sequitur, where the customary fluidity of an unfolding narrative text is replaced by unforeseen and surprising effects.

Several decades after Charles Nodier, Lewis Carroll continued these typographical adventures in *Alice in Wonderland*. For example, the poem "The Mouse's Tale" follows an undulating route in the course of which the chain of type gets narrower and narrower, so that, as it is read down the page, the "tail" peters out to nothing. For Lewis Carroll, as for Charles

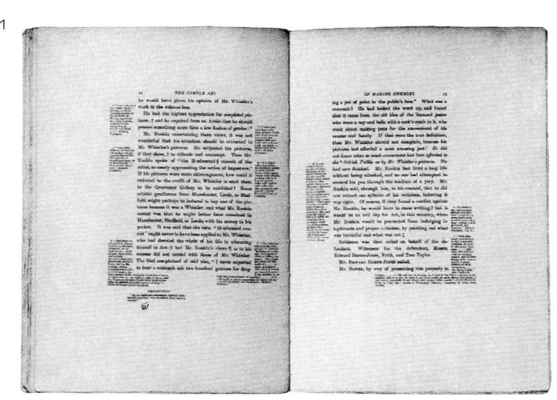

231
James McNeill Whistler, double page from *The Gentle Art of Making Enemies*, London and Edinburgh, 1890.

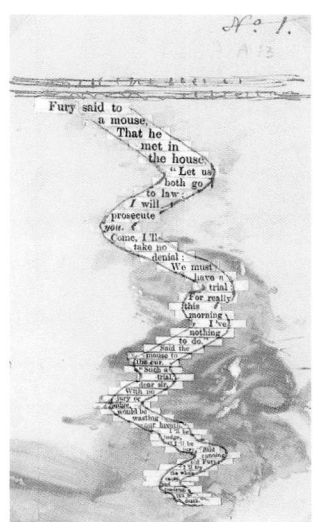

234

AND A LONG TALE. 37

so that her idea of the tale was something like
this :——"Fury said to
a mouse, That
he met
in the
house,
'Let us
both go
to law:
I will
prosecute
you.——
Come, I'll
take no
denial ;
We must
have a
trial :
For
really
this
morning
I've
nothing
to do.
Said the
mouse to
the cur,
'Such a
trial,
dear sir,
With no
jury or
judge,
would be
wasting
our breath.'
'I'll be
judge,
I'll be
jury,'
Said
cunning
old Fury :
'I'll try
the whole
cause
and
condemn
you
to
death.'"

232
Lewis Carroll, handwritten version of
"The Mouse's Tale," from the manuscript book,
Alice Underground, c. 1864.

233
Lewis Carroll, collage, final form of
"The Mouse's Tale."

234
Lewis Carroll, first printed version of
"The Mouse's Tale," as it appeared in *Alice
in Wonderland*, published in 1866.

Nodier, the aim was to stimulate perception of the text through new forms, to arouse visual curiosity through the configuration of the lines, the words, and even of the letters.

The poet Stéphane Mallarmé's desire to act on the visual dimension of the text was similar and has earned him a preeminent place in the history of typography. If his experiments relate more closely to literary and poetic modernism, it was the overlap between the arts that was instrumental in their creation. Mallarmé was much preoccupied by questions of typographical form and space, and it was only after twenty or more years of research that his text, *Un Coup de dés jamais n'abolira le hasard* (A throw of the dice never will abolish chance), saw the light of day. Printed in the international review *Cosmopolis*, the first publication of this famous piece dates to May 1897 (later editions of the poem, at the beginning and the end of the twentieth century, transcribe the author's stipulations more adequately). The extremely unusual page-setting of *Un Coup de dés* is designed to unfetter textual space—over the sequence of pages, Mallarmé unfurls a single sentence that, after the first printing, did away with punctuation altogether. The poet disposes the words and groups of words in a variable manner over the surface of the paper, introducing unexpected blank spaces and shifts, and playing with variations in type size. The only remnants of usual text composition are horizontality and a fragmented concatenation, "the whole without innovation, save for a space left in reading."[43]

Fellow poet Paul Valéry provides valuable insight: "It seemed to me that I saw, for the first time, the figure for a thought placed in our space... Here, truly, extension spoke, dreamed, gave birth to temporal forms. Waiting, doubt, concentration were become visible entities. My sight was confronted by silences which as it were took on physical form [...] There was murmuring, insinuations, thunder for the eyes, a spiritual storm borne up from page to page [...] I felt [...] gripped by its innovative appearance [...] Finally, he has tried [...] to elevate a page to the potency of a starry sky!"[44]

Even before *Un Coup de dés*, Mallarmé had been already turned his hand to a dizzyingly ambitious literary project that remained unfinished at his death. "What? It's difficult to say: a book, quite simply, in many volumes, a book which would be a book, constructed and premeditated, and not a collection of chance inspirations, however marvelous they might be... I will go further, I will say: the Book—persuaded as I am that, at bottom, there is only one."[45] For this project, Mallarmé was to introduce diagrams into the body of the text corresponding to the number of pages, print-run, selling-price, and so on. With *Le Livre*, he was thus attempting to devise a "work entirely liberated from its author, from the objects of the world." "[It is] slavery, routine, and lies to read starting with page 1 of the book, then on to page 2, and so on.[46]

Fulfilling a determinant historical role, Mallarmé's researches furthered the quest for an express typographical spatiality that would make the most of visible resources with an unexpected selection of typefaces and unevenness in kerning. In *Un Coup de dés*, this is added to a scheme of differentiating lines of text by alternating roman and italic, upper- and lowercase, and by the interplay between balance and asymmetry, and contrasts in size—all features that were major aspects of graphic modernism. Dying in 1898, Mallarmé never saw an edition of *Un Coup de dés* that took his intentions into account more scrupulously than that issued by *Cosmopolis*—for instance the version in the N.R.F. in 1914 (with the aid of his son-in-law and of André Gide) and more especially the Ronat-Papp edition of 1980.[47]

For his part, André Gide also concerned himself with the typographical aspect of the text, such as page layout, use of punctuation, the distribution of capital letters and italics, the employment of leading, issues of space, choice of formats, etc. His *Nourritures terrestres* appeared in May 1897, at the same time as *Un Coup de dés*, and indeed the two writers were unstinting in their praise for each other's work.[48].

At the end of the nineteenth century, another artist undertook experiments in reshaping the book: inspired by the endeavors of his close colleague Mallarmé, James McNeill Whistler designed asymmetrical layouts for a number of books. Whistler's designs also emphasize unexpected shifts, highlighting the non-printed space and imparting dynamic thrust to the setting of the text. Thus, during a century that experienced massive upscaling in the volume of print, authors, artists, and printers—from Nodier to Whistler via Carroll, Gide, Mallarmé and many others besides—subjected the book to typographical experiments that rejuvenated its visual potential. Artistic and literary practices conspired to redraw the appearance of a support that in the past had generally remained faithful to an enshrined classicism. A graphic space, a vein in book design, grew up that welcomed every sort of formal experiment. Thus, above and beyond activities directly related to printing and allied trades, creative typographies could now germinate in an author's writings as published, as well as in his drafts (where all kinds of divisions, unconventional organizations, and tangles of text had always appeared), from the letter to typographical color, by way of the word, word groups, and the line. The first decades of the twentieth century confirmed this vogue, with avant-garde movements keen to tackle the book form, in children's literature, plays, novels, collections of poetry, and so on.

The Wiener Werkstätte

At the turn of the century, several other impulses to graphic creation arose that threw into stark relief the return to bookwork (with the iconic example of Mallarmé's experiments of 1897 in mind) and the renewed impetus in poster design. The Wiener Werkstätte (Vienna Workshop) was one such impulse. Founded by Josef Hoffmann, Koloman Moser, and the industrial patron Fritz Waerndorfer, and inaugurated in the Austrian capital in 1903, the Wiener Werkstätte was soon joined by many artists and designers. Receptive to the groundswell of change around them, the members of the group reverted to craft traditions, all the while aiming at modernity by way of multidisciplinary creativity and wide-ranging interests. In their 1905 program, Josef Hoffmann and Koloman Moser defined their objectives and the means they envisaged: "We want [...] to create simple utensils. We start from function; the primary condition will be practical value [...]. Every time it is feasible, we allow for ornamentation, but without foisting it on ourselves."[49] Affiliations with William Morris and the Arts and Crafts movement are clearly established, although the protagonists of the Wiener Werkstätte did not look back to medieval and Renaissance art, but forward to what it was to become. As heirs to the Vienna Secession, the members of the Wiener Werkstätte created a seamless blend of geometric partition and decorative artistry. Their forms embrace the charm and delicacy of ornament, while simultaneously making strides on the road to functionalism. Be it in furniture, architecture, or graphic design, their designs tended to be directed towards geometry (the square, in particular) and an expanded range of contrasts. Smaller articles, jewelry, and wallpaper readily found place for decorative motifs. Convinced of the need to federate the arts, the members of the Wiener Werkstätte worked on a vast range of objects and materials, among them bookbinding, glassmaking, and textiles.

The Palais Stoclet[50] in Brussels testifies to a single thread running through the various forms of creation: if the buildings are the work of Josef Hoffmann, the interior décor too reflects a unitary conception of exceptional coherence. The artists and artisans who worked there brought a harmony and completeness to its construction that is palpable in the smallest details.

Eager to make their mark on the daily environment in the broad sense, the members of the Wiener Werkstätte began to turn their attention to the field of visual communication. They produced posters, postcards, and invitations, created business identities, monograms, and programs for the theater. The Wiener Werkstätte logo, probably designed by Koloman Moser,

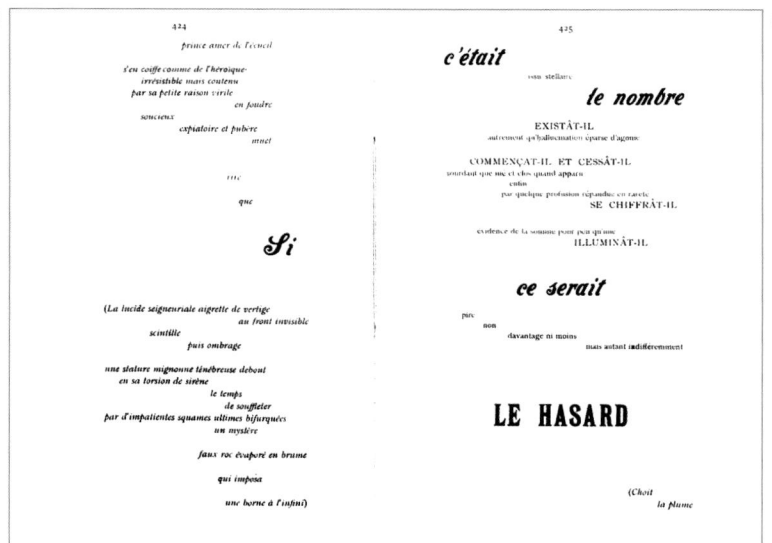

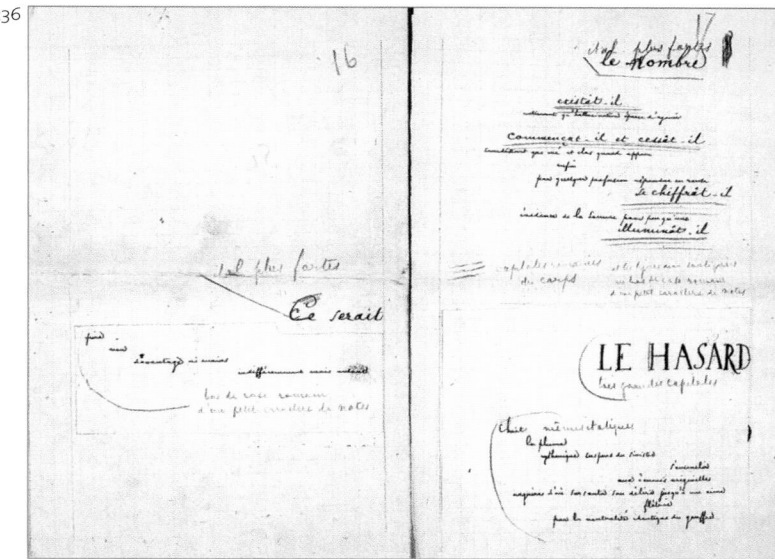

235
Stéphane Mallarmé, *Un Coup de dés jamais n'abolira le hasard*, (A throw of the dice never will abolish chance) double page from the first edition in the periodical *Cosmopolis*, no. 17, London, 1897.

236
Stéphane Mallarmé, *Un Coup de dés jamais n'abolira le hasard*, autographed manuscript on a book of graph paper.

237
Stéphane Mallarmé, *Un Coup de dés jamais n'abolira le hasard*, cover, Paris: N.R.F., 1914.

238
Stéphane Mallarmé, *Un Coup de dés jamais n'abolira le hasard*, double-page spread, 1914.

239
Stéphane Mallarmé, untitled manuscript sheet (together with a transcription), undated, for his long-term project, *Le Livre*. "The manuscript is, in the main, an outline of the structure of the *Book* and conditions the *Book* needs to fulfill in order to exist." (From Scherer, p. 125).

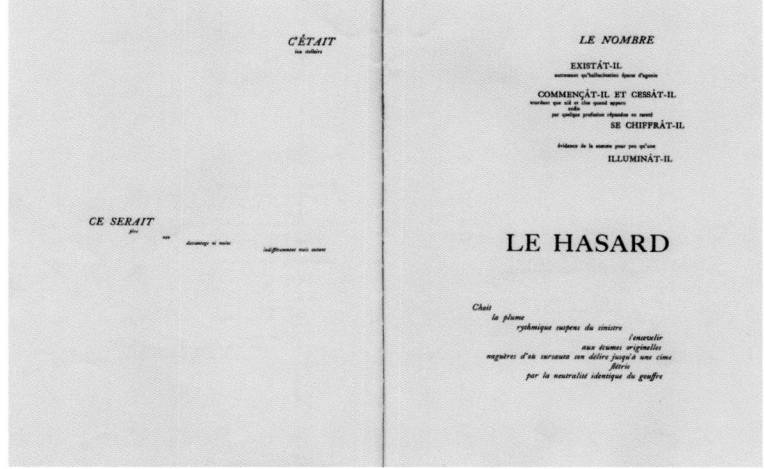

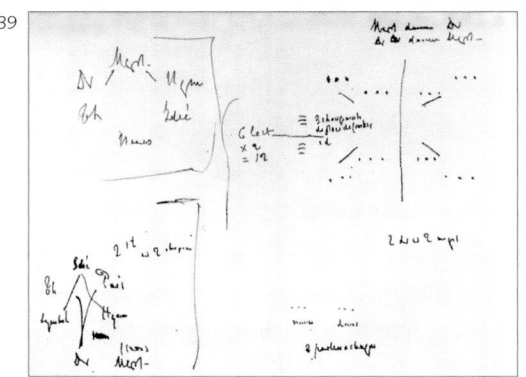

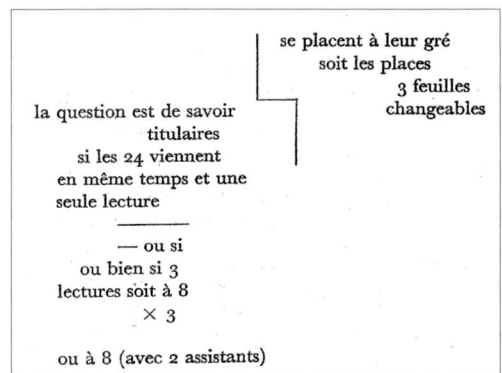

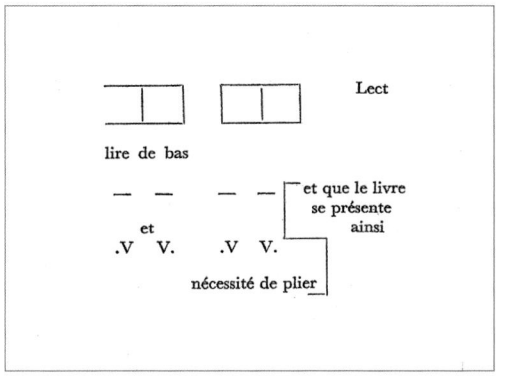

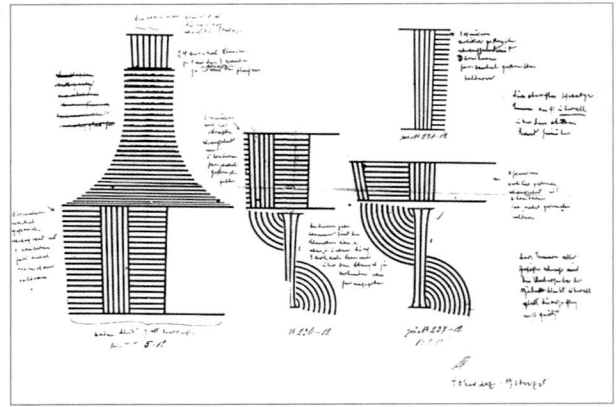

240
Josef Hoffmann, plan for a coffeepot, Austria, c. 1925–28. Pencil and black lead on squared paper.

241
Josef Hoffmann, set of glasses with carafe with designs, 1910–11 (translucent glass, small diamond-dust balls, and bronzite decoration).

242
Ditha Moser, playing card, Wiener Werkstätte, c. 1905.

243
Ugo Zovetti, printed fabric for a work-coat, Wiener Werkstätte, c. 1914.

represents two W's of different designs, embedded one into the other inside a square. Simple, original, and distinctive, this mark was reproduced on all the workshop's administrative and promotional documents: business cards, invoices, envelopes, posters, packing paper, and so on. It could well be one of the very first examples of a visual identity to be applied to all material emanating from a single organization. Following this logo, the members of the workshop were identified by various monograms in which two, or sometimes three initials were intertwined. Some of these, highly graphic and synthetic, were inscribed within a circle on a principle similar to that of Toulouse-Lautrec.

If there is a Wiener Werkstätte tenor in graphic design, the techniques of communication it adopted cannot be reduced to a single style—as is manifestly demonstrated by the series of approximately one thousand postcards brought out between 1907 and 1913 by more than fifty artists, including Gustav Klimt and Egon Schiele. Moreover, certain typographical works, as well as other forms of printed matter, were the work of multitalented artist-designers rather than of specialized professionals.

At this time, the future of the Wiener Werkstätte was threatened by severe financial difficulties. Fritz Waerndorfer, the group's backer, was threatened by bankruptcy and emigrated to the United States. The workshop nevertheless managed to restructure itself and continued in business until the 1930s. Once again, however, it fell prey to a downturn, which, this time, proved insurmountable. Like William Morris, the members of the Vienna Workshop aspired to integrate art into the forms and objects of everyday living patterns, although once again their meticulously crafted creations were bound, to some extent, to remain destined for the wealthy or for enlightened connoisseurs.

The Beggarstaffs

At the turn of the century, England also enjoyed rejuvenating experiments in the area of graphic creation. Contemporary with the Glasgow School, a new artistic partnership that went by the name of the Beggarstaffs nurtured an individual and original conception of the graphic. The pseudonym was adopted by painters and brothers-in-law William Nicholson and James Pryde when they began working in tandem in 1894. Their joint career, although brief and not especially well known, introduced an innovative style. Studying painting in Paris, they held Toulouse-Lautrec in very high regard: "One man we admire, and that is Toulouse Lautrec. He is one of the few artists who understand what a poster is and should be."[51]

Finding the name on a bag stamped "Beggarstaffs Brothers" in a stable, they quickly dropped the "Brothers" and went on to sign creations that appear out of the ordinary—indeed astonishing—for the time, and which often met with incomprehension on the part of their patrons, to the extent that some were rejected. The misfortunes that beset the firm forced the Beggarstaffs to throw up the enterprise in 1900; it had lasted only six years, during which time the cooperation had realized a total of a dozen posters. Their admiration for Toulouse-Lautrec was accompanied, naturally enough, by a keen interest in Japanese prints, and their

244
The Beggarstaffs (William Nicholson and James Pryde), *Cinderella* poster, Great Britain, 1895.

characteristic style, at once dense and understated, imparts an impression of space and immense simplicity. Patently, the Beggarstaffs' had hit on an unusual idiom for the time.

Their graphic style relies on the technique of collage (one that would be fully explored in the avant-garde art of the 1910s, in Cubism, Dada, and photomontage): sometimes, the forms, cut out in colored paper, combine in compositions made of uniform tints. Consolidating their search for a form of expression that would be at once simple and immediate, the Beggarstaffs tend not to outline these broad areas of color. When lines do appear, they stand alone and are used to draw a particular element in the composition, the only color they outline being that of the support. The impact of the silhouetted tints and colorful contrasts is intensified by a restricted palette. The lettering, far from being subordinated, finds its role integrated into that of the artwork, acquiring a status that redefines the interconnections between text and image. The poster for *Cinderella*, created in 1895, is characteristic of the Beggarstaffs' style, and is likely to have appeared surprising to their contemporaries. Others among their handful of posters are designs for *Don Quixote* and *Hamlet*, but also for *Rowntree's Cocoa*. Thanks to their broad swathes of color, their compositions seems to breathe freely, an effect reinforced by the presence of unprinted surfaces. The use of empty space, an essential factor in the changes that were to affect visual expression at the end of the nineteenth century, and scarcely discernible in so many Victorian graphics, here makes a welcome comeback.

The Beggarstaffs' originality did not greatly further their career, nor attain anything like commercial success. Few were receptive to their work, yet their practice highlights the ongoing search for a strong, effective, and autonomous design with a tendency to economy. Their graphic style is symptomatic of the gradual shift towards an atypical aesthetic designed for immediacy and effectiveness that is wholly distinct from pictorial practices. Over one hundred years old, their *Cinderella* poster seems to have passed through the intervening decades unscathed; there is nothing old-fashioned about a design that, even today, makes an eye-catching statement.

A revival in German graphics

Like Austria, after 1900 Germany became a major driving force in the transformed graphic landscape. On the shoulders of Jugendstil, tendencies intent on innovation gradually developed. After a rather slow start, industrialization accelerated considerably in the first decade of the twentieth century, making Germany a fertile ground for the orientation of art toward industry. As designers and draftsmen sought genres unencumbered by stylistic roots in the past, among all forms of (typo)graphic creation, the poster benefited especially from this

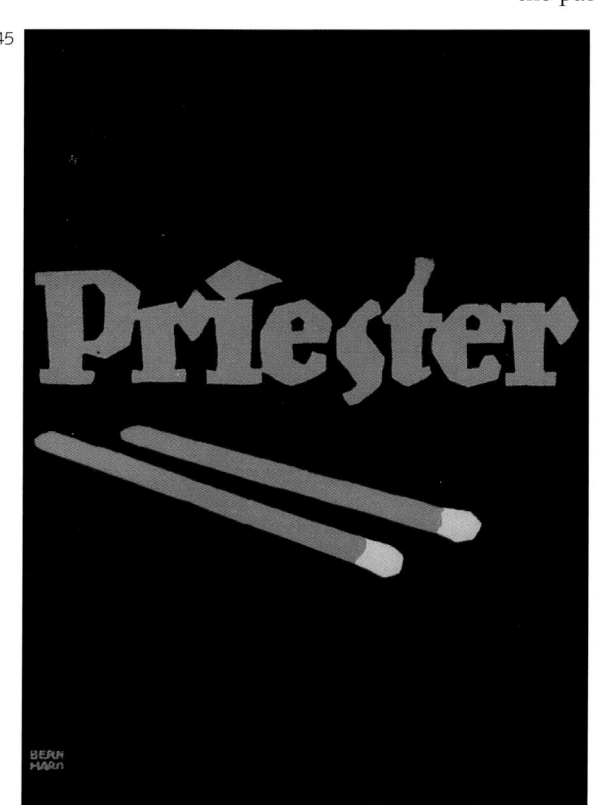

245
Lucian Bernhard, *Priester* (matches) poster, Germany, c. 1905. Historic example of the *Sachplakat*.

dynamic climate. Some designers, convinced of the need for a radical rethink in terms of standardization and efficiency, eliminated all ornament and embellishment, preserving a single, monolithic dimension, or else focusing on a handful of telling details. If their aesthetic presents affinities with the Wiener Werkstätte, German creators were interested as much in craft as in industry and made limited recourse to pattern and decoration.

The poster's role among forms of creation in a thriving print sector was crucial. Publishing and the art of the book were entering a fecund period that was to endure for at least another thirty years. This transformation of the book was aided by typographers, printers, and publishers of brilliant reputation (such as Fritz Helmut Ehmcke, Emil Rudolf Weiss, and Paul Renner). Type design and the paperback book experienced change and expansion. In a geographical zone where the use of blackletter type had been synonymous with printing since its genesis, some publishers were now opting for Roman typefaces.

Much preoccupied with the typographical aspect of his texts, the poet Stefan George went as far as setting his writings in sans serif type. For some of his creations, Peter Behrens took the same path, although, in early twentieth-century Germany, this was still not a common choice. The high-water mark of the German poster, between 1900 and 1914, led to the creation of surprising works. Berlin (the city of business and commerce) and Munich were two hives of artistic activity, as much for Jugendstil as for the other graphic tendencies then emerging. A considerable number of illustrious artists worked in these cities, with Lucian Bernhard and Ludwig Hohlwein, in Berlin and Munich respectively, among the most representative poster artists in Germany at the time. Ernest Growald, managing director of the lithographic print works Hollerbaum & Schmidt in Berlin, played a notable role. Alert to the imminent transformations of graphic language, he engaged several Berlin poster artists; creatives, artists, patrons, and manufacturers were thus able to meet under the roof of a single print firm. Consolidated by initiatives of this nature, a new type of poster arose in Germany and soon gained ground. Known as *Plakatstil* (literally "poster style"), the current thrived until the beginning of the 1930s. If it was novel in terms of graphic impact, the German poster often seemed to limit itself to modest formats, as in the Netherlands.

Lucian Bernhard and Ludwig Hohlwein

In Berlin, Lucian Bernhard was devising a striking type of poster, both concentrated and concise in appearance. Essentially self-educated, in 1905 Bernhard took part in a contest for a

246

246
Ludwig Hohlwein, *Ernemann Cameras*,
Germany, c. 1912. Curved enameled plate,
23 $^1/_2$ × 15 $^3/_4$ in. (60 × 40 cm).

poster advertising matches by a firm called Priester. Starting out by arranging the product around an ashtray, a cigar, and other objects and figures, he reconsidered his original plan, gradually eliminating more and more elements until only two matches survived, alone, seemingly gigantic, against a dark, plain ground. The highly diagrammatic twins are indicated simply by two areas of unmodulated color: two sloping, thick red lines that terminate to the right in blobs of yellow. Bernhard merely adds the trade name *Priester* in extra bold lettering, so proportioned that it traverses the entire width of the poster. Initially rejected by the jury appointed to judge the competition, Bernhard's entry eventually emerged triumphant.[52] The prizewinner soon struck out as a poster artist, working for the printers Hollerbaum & Schmidt.

By only a handful of posters, among them one for Priester matches, Bernhard made a notable contribution to the growth of the *Sachplakat* (literally "poster-object"), which in Bernhard's hands often reduced text and image to its barest essentials. These posters show a highly abbreviated, stylized representation of the article to be advertised accompanied merely by the trade name. Informative in nature and immediate in impact, the text is presented in bold or extra bold, increasing the density still more when set other than in Gothic. Schematization results in a formal reduction to a few areas of flat tint, often over a bright uniform ground in a restricted palette. Their immediateness and condensation (which might be seen as harking back to the centuries-old lineage of the shop-sign) give these dazzling compositions an imposing presence.

According to similar principles and as in his poster for Priester's, for Stiller shoes Bernhard drew a single piece of footwear, close-up, and surmounted by the maker's name. For Steinway & Sons' pianos, he chose an abbreviated representation of the instrument, once again accompanied by the trade name. Lucian Bernhard was particularly prolific and created hundreds of posters. Some, dating from World War I and later than his work for Priester and Stiller, are entirely typographical and clearly demonstrate his interest in text elements. He lavished equal care on size, position, and letterform—all well adapted to the demands of advertising effectiveness. His choice of lettering was to prove an inspiration to a number of type designers, while for his part, from the 1910s on, he began to create alphabets of his own. Settling in New York the following decade, Lucian Bernhard continued to design types, in particular for the American Type Founders Company, completing around thirty alphabets or more. Through his recourse to the *Sachplakat*, Bernhard created a unique range of posters. His influence was quickly felt, for example on the graphic designers Julius Gipkens and Hans Rudi Erdt who crossed his path in the Hollerbaum & Schmidt printshop, and who adhered to the *Sachplakat* principle. This printer-shop thus became a productive crucible where poster artists and graphic designers could poll their ideas: Julius Klinger, Ernst Deutsch, and Jo Steiner—renowned talents from Vienna from the end of the nineteenth century—were also to work there.

Like Lucian Bernhard in Berlin, Ludwig Hohlwein played a major role in graphics in Munich, where the other driving forces included Emil Preetorius and Olaf Gulbransson. An architect by training, Hohlwein turned to graphics in 1906, beginning his career at roughly the same time as Bernhard. Again like the latter, he started out as a poster artist, developing a largely autodidactic practice initially influenced by the Beggarstaffs. Similarly productive, he acquired a measure of fame in graphic design milieus and among important patrons. Like Bernhard, Hohlwein made a notable contribution to the art of the poster and is one of the twentieth- century's most reputed artists in the domain, with a number of pieces remaining instantly recognizable.

His visual material often contains objects or figures reflecting patterns of contemporary middle-class life. If the compositions adopt the use of schematically treated flat areas of color combined with the presence of a plain, sober, and understated ground, the content is not limited to the schematic forms of the *Sachplakat*. Following the example of Bernhard, Hohlwein visibly paid particular attention to typography, using serif typefaces and the more current Gothic forms, as well as alphabets without serifs. The texts of his posters sometimes appear in an eminently readable bold type over a few lines grouped into a square. The dominating element, the image, is lodged at the heart of the composition, preserving the eminently narrative and illustrative dimension of the poster (a dimension toned down in Bernhard's work), while the draftsmanship finds room for geometric elements. On discreet and dark-toned grounds, Hohlwein emphasizes the most significant elements with flat tints of unmixed color. In an original and individual fashion, certain features in the foreground are also configured by use of color. Producing an increased impression of flatness, as well as reinforcing the effect of formal stylization and the flatness of the color blocks, this bestows a graphic quality and power on his posters. Over time, Ludwig Hohlwein won fame and fortune, and his creations began to serve needs other than product promotion, such as propaganda and ideology. During World War I, he turned his expertise to making billboards for the war effort, while in the interwar period, his acknowledged talent as a graphic designer led him to accept commissions from the Nazi regime.

By the beginning of the century, through personalities as influential as Lucian Bernhard, Ludwig Hohlwein, and other graphic designers, the art of the poster enjoyed great exposure in Germany. Bearing new forms, the production of German poster artists, in spite of partial overlap with the work of the Beggarstaffs, can surely be said to resemble no other. In some German artwork, all trace of the pictorial and decorative past of the poster has been erased; a new idiom arises that preserves only the plastic quality and artistic value of its sources of inspiration. In addition it should be stressed that, as with a considerable number of turn-of-the-century poster work, the *Sachplakat* and *Plakatstil* were tailor-made to forge a partnership with the worlds of commerce and industry, an association that had far-reaching repercussions on the history of graphics.

The Werkbund and Peter Behrens

In addition to the years 1905 and 1906, the dates the careers of Lucian Bernhard and Ludwig Hohlwein began, 1907 was another key date for the development of applied art in Germany, as it witnessed the foundation of the Werkbund (from *Werk*, "work" and *Bund*, "alliance, union"), an association gathering together designers, architects, craftsmen, industrialists, and publishers. By the turn of the twentieth century, Germany, like the United States, had attained the rank of global industrial power (a role previously the preserve of Great Britain), a situation that would prove particularly favorable to the association's ambitions. As a forum for experiment and reflection, the group confessed to the strong influence of the Arts and Crafts movement, and it also betrayed a number of features in common with the Wiener Werkstätte, although there are significant dissimilarities, too. One of the founder members of the Werkbund, Hermann Muthesius, advocated pursuing the search for objectivity to its logical conclusions and eschewing all forms of decoration. In fact, Muthesius was sent by the Prussian government to study the thriving art scene in Great Britain for several years as an aesthetic "spy."

On his return, many reforming artists obtained key positions in German art schools. One notable difference between the Germans and the English was that the former did not promote the rejection of mechanization. Through their aim to "improve the design and quality of German products,"[53] the Werkbund saw their mission to reconcile art and industry, without abandoning craft, and to articulate the applied and fine arts. The title of the movement's 1914 exhibition, *Applied arts—industry, trade, architecture*, amounts to a significant statement of the direction and aspirations of the Werkbund. If the association adhered to specific objectives though, it was soon split by internecine conflict: Hermann Muthesius preached standardized

247
Logotypes for AEG (General Electricity
Company), Germany, from c. 1896–1914.
From top to bottom: Franz Schwechten,
c. 1896 (column 1), Peter Behrens, 1908 and
1914 (column 2).

248
Peter Behrens, turbine factory for AEG,
Germany, 1909.

and mechanized mass production, a notion that met with firm opposition from Henry Van de Velde. The latter's opinion was that the artist's contribution ought to reflect the well-being of that individual, his personality, and talent. Similar divergences arose when the designers came to tackle the basic problem of how to situate their activities within the context of industrialization, mechanization, and large-scale production. Calling into question traditional practices and conventional formal solutions, they refocused their concern on the needs arising from mechanical/serial production, an attitude that was to have considerable ramifications. Another question was to determine exactly to what extent the designer should see himself as an artist and how to make clear the respective assets of function and decoration. Theirs then was a point of view that throws light on many aspects of twentieth-century graphics.

One of the foremost figures in the Werkbund was Peter Behrens. With his nomination in 1907 as art consultant to the firm AEG (the general electric company), this multitalented designer found himself confronted with a mission that was exceptional for its time. Electricity was a relatively recent energy source and AEG was an extremely active player in the sector. A major industrial force on the international stage, AEG headed up any number of German companies and employed around seventy thousand people worldwide. Its chief executives, Emil and Walter Rathenau, placed great emphasis on design quality and turned to the professionalism and competence of Peter Behrens to develop and harmonize the company's product line from top to bottom—including visual communication.

From buildings to lettering, the project covered the design of factories and of workers' housing estates, object design (lamps, kettles, teapots, and so on), and graphic design, as well as stores and trade-show stands. In the graphic field, Behrens devised a visual identity (logo and graphic charter), and created a house typeface, as well as company stationery, catalogs, and posters. The result was a corporate style intended to appear on every entity produced by the company (printed matter, consumer articles, constructions), thus maximizing exposure. Behrens was to head up this vast project of global design, its prime objectives being an artistic coherence and a unifying conception in the service of a focused marketing strategy. In response to the sheer size of the brief, Behrens opted for a punchy, simplified design adapted to the needs of industry. He came up with several versions of the logo made up of the three letters A, E, and G inscribed in geometric forms. A comparison with the logo designed by Otto Eckmann for AEG in 1900 (in an Art Nouveau vein) demonstrates that a new industrial design vocabulary was in the offing, showing Behrens moving away from Art Nouveau and towards functionalism. Preeminently representative of the Werkbund's position, his output marked a watershed in the development of modernism, in common with that of other contemporary figures whose researches also aimed to integrate recent means of production. Behrens's work was among the very first experiments of this kind on such a scale; a similar move to cooperation between designers and industrialists surfaced almost simultaneously in the Olivetti company (in 1908) and expresses the same drive to quality and coherence in the development of forms (articles, identity, architecture, posters, etc.).

The collaboration between Peter Behrens and the AEG company came to an end in 1913 and he subsequently focused increasingly on architecture. In addition to his work for AEG, his contributions to typography included a typeface made for the Klingspor foundry. His typefaces include Behrens-Schrift (1901–07), Behrens-Antiqua (1907–09, a face initially tabled for the AEG company) and Behrens-Mediaeval (1914). Like so many of his contemporaries and more than one creative talent from a later generation, Behrens made his mark through artistic versatility and an aptitude for multidisciplinary approaches. After his training as a painter, at the end of the nineteenth century Behrens had elected to move away from the pictorial to turn to architecture, design, graphics, and typography. In Vienna too, as we have seen, the need was felt to unite artistic practices in order to build a consensus of the arts.

The poster in Switzerland

If a revival in visual expression came to the fore at the end of the nineteenth century in Austria, in Germany, and elsewhere, Switzerland was a slightly later entrant onto the shifting stage of Western graphics. Eager to join the fray, however, Swiss artists such as Grasset and Steinlen had settled in Paris. In Switzerland itself, however, until about 1900 many posters still bore the imprints of the classic approach. As in other countries, the more resolutely contemporary forms of the poster were created by painters. Ferdinand Hodler had begun to change his visual statements of this kind by about 1890, choosing formal stylization and pure colors. This tendency took root among a definable group of graphic designers in the first decade of the twentieth century, as shown, for instance, by Robert Hardmeyer's poster for the Waschanstalt laundry, sometimes considered one of the earliest—if not the first —in the new, bold graphic style. Arrived at in 1904 or slightly later, the composition shows a highly stylized rendition of a cockerel. Flat tints, schematization, and bright colors predominate; the text—brief, sturdy and without serifs—prioritizes legibility. Such a work evinces a relationship with German *Sachplakat*, the Swiss version of which will harbor realistic leanings. In Switzerland, the field of poster art numbers several representatives of prime importance, such as the painters Emil Cardinaux and Burkhard Mangold, who participated in the renewed interest in the medium between 1905 and 1910. As in Germany, the role of printers, in particular that of Wolfensberger, was once again key. The revival quickly gained in focus and, by around 1910, the Swiss art poster movement had gathered ground. A new generation of creatives came into the limelight, including Otto Baumberger (born in 1889) and Otto Morach (born in 1887). Although ostensibly a late starter compared with neighboring countries, the graphic landscape in Switzerland cleared the ground for practices that, as with the Netherlands, were to play a starring role in the work of the avant-garde, and in particular during the second third of the century.

249
Robert (Emil?) Hardmeyer, *Waschanstalt* (Zurich laundry), Switzerland, after 1904. Curved enameled plate, 16 1/2 in × 12 in. (42 × 30 cm).

250
Robert (Emil?) Hardmeyer, *Waschanstalt* poster (Zurich laundry), Switzerland, 1904 or a later date. Chromolithograph, 4 ft. 2 in. × 2 ft. 11 1/2 in. (127.8 × 90.5 cm).

Leonetto Cappiello

As we have seen, the breathtaking creative drive that gripped Paris for twenty or more years was extinguished after 190 it appears that few poster artists managed to take up the flame of their illustrious predecessors from the turn of the century until the 1920s, at which point a new generation of great artists entered the scene. The figure of Leonetto Cappiello stands out against this unpromising backdrop, a personality with little in common with contemporaries such as Jean-Louis Forain, Pal, or Sem. A draftsman and caricaturist of Italian extraction, Cappiello settled in Paris at the end of the 1890s. His exceptionally popular poster style evolved over time, gradually jettisoning all but the most essential compositional elements. It seems that for Cappiello graphic power resided first and foremost in line, in the conciseness of the stroke: "A line, alone, can convey grandeur, nobility, sensuality; it offers the synthesis of every sensation, it is the concentration of all knowledge; it is line one must seek, giving secondary importance to color and details."[54] Progressively, Cappiello strove to synthesize his graphics around a central element, a focus shared by the German *Sachplakat* in which a poster's artwork zeroes in on a schematic representation of the object advertised, accompanied by just the trade name. Frequently, Leonetto Cappiello was to employ allegory, associating the object of the advertisement with a character, a face, or an animal. Breaking with the hackneyed use of female figures (a scheme exemplified in the work of Jules Chéret), he let loose a motley crew of expressive figures. Conscious of the magnetic power they could exert, Cappiello seeks to astonish and surprise with posters. Acting as representatives of the product, his seemingly animate creatures constituted an effective means of drumming both visual and message into the minds of passers-by. The poster artist pursued "a precise and clear idea," melding synthetic expression and dynamic handling, and combining simplicity and immediacy with his own personal stamp. Although Cappiello allotted prime importance to line in his compositions, the often bright colors are responsible for much of their attractiveness. The text block is often relegated to a space at the base of the poster. In order to accentuate the impact of the central element, Cappiello readily resorts to complementary or contrasting colors, and many of his posters obtain their effects from a marked contrast between elements in the foreground (image and text) and the color of the background. It is also likely that Cappiello was among the first poster artists to grant such a preponderant role to black, especially in all-over backgrounds.

Leonetto Cappiello's highly modern oeuvre is characterized by strong originality. He designed in the region of three thousand posters—an exceptional number, comparable to the output of Chéret. Cappiello's style is clearly distinct from tendencies in German and Austrian poster art. His corpus could be seen as a foretaste of the French poster of the 1920s and 1930s, (a style which was prefigured in the final decades of the nineteenth century). In France, the generation of poster artists that succeeded Cappiello admits to owing him a great deal, as shown in the following resounding tribute signed by Cassandre, Loupot, Carlu, and Jean Colin: "It is surely a victory to put all others in the shade, to manage, as you have done, to become for an entire generation, *the* Poster [*l'Affiche*], you alone—the Poster with a capital 'P.' Not that we are forgetting of course, the great men who came before you, Toulouse-Lautrec and Chéret, 'for us, you have been living proof that one can, without fear of going down in the world, produce completely, utterly artistic work using the billboard as gallery.' Moreover, Cappiello, while we're about it, we have to concede that all of us, more or less, started out 'doing Cappiellos.'"[55]

251

251
Leonetto Cappiello, poster, *Cinzano*, Paris, 1910. Chromolithograph, 10 ft. 4 3/4 in. × 6 ft. 6 3/4 in. (317 × 200 cm), three sheets (note the use of a black ground).

252 In der Schrift ist der Geist alles; die Form kommt erst danach. Erst wer beides besitzt, kann sich den alten Meistern vergleichen.

WANG SENG-K'IEN

253 ABCDEFGHIJKLMNO
PQRSTUVWXYZÆŒØ
1234567890
abcdefghijklmnopqrstuv

254 Akzidenz-Grotesk
Akzidenz-Grotesk
Akzidenz-Grotesk
Akzidenz-Grotesk
Akzidenz-Grotesk

255 ABCDEFGHIJKLMNOP
QRSTUVWXYZ abcdef
ghijklmnopqrstuvwxyz
.,-;:"!?   1234567890

ABCDEFGHIJKLMN
OPQRSTUVWXYZ
abcdefghijklmnopq
rstuvwxyz
.,-;:   1234567890

252
Altgrotesk demi-bold, Haas foundry, Münchenstein (Switzerland), 1880.

253
Clarendon type. The first typeface of this kind was designed by Robert Besley and cut by Benjamin Fox in about 1844–45, within the ambit of the Fann Street Foundry, London.

254
Akzidenz-Grotesk, *Berthold types* catalog, Berlin, 1988. Alternatives: light, plain, demi-bold, bold, extra-bold; dating respectively to 1902, 1898, 1909, 1909, and 1968.

255
Franklin Gothic, Morris Fuller Benton, United States. The design of Franklin Gothic, published by the American Type Founders Company (ATF) in 1905, was begun in 1902.

Typeface design

If the medium of the poster filled a key role in the field of visual expression in many countries (before as well as after 1900), type design, too, was gearing up in terms of production and distribution. Three new families of alphabets had already appeared at the beginning of the nineteenth century: bold Roman, sans serif and Egyptian (slab serif). Following these historical innovations, succeeding decades experienced the growth of Victorian types, combinable in abundance and favorable to open forms and effects of magnification.

At this juncture, however, a number of creations appeared that were at odds with this tendency. Clarendon is one example, an alphabet that appeared in London in 1845, ascribed to Robert Besley. Used above all for titles and other brief texts in bold, Clarendon afforded first-rate legibility combined with a solid form. The letters, faithful to the spirit of time, were in general rather four-square, and their broad serifs underline their affiliation with Egyptian brought out about thirty years previously. If offerings like Clarendon came into their own around mid-century, the 1890s witnessed the onset of a further revival in type design. Designers and craftsmen now rethought the question of letter design, seeking something totally distinct from the vitality and exuberance characteristic of many typefaces and letterforms of the time, and aspiring to return to traditional artistry and to raise the basic quality of typography. Side by side with this appeal to historical sources, type design continued to extend its range. Thus, in the wake of Art Nouveau, and under the umbrella of its propensity for abundance and generosity, certain alphabets began to indulge in the interplay between curve and counter-curve. Often bearing vegetal ornaments, some of these types are distinguished by marked stylization in letterform or curvilinear swashes punctuated by curved or fluid embellishments. Among the best-known alphabets of this movement one should include Grasset (1900), Auriol (1901), and Behrens-Schrift (1901–07), all three bearing the name of their designers.

Contemporary with Art Nouveau, other variants of type were born, reflecting various registers and expressing the search of forms in keeping with the spirit, and demands, of the time. The onward march of sans serif, less preoccupied by adornments and ornament than by a limited set of variations around a basic form, went on apace. Although the historical model

Cheltenham Oldstyle
Cheltenham Wide
Cheltenham Medium
Cheltenham Bold
Cheltenham Bold Condensed
Cheltenham Bold Extra Condensed
Cheltenham Bold Outline
Cheltenham Oldstyle Condensed
Cheltenham Italic
Cheltenham Medium Italic
Cheltenham Bold Italic
Cheltenham Bold Condensed Italic
CHELTENHAM BOLD EXTRA CONDENSED TITLE
Cheltenham Bold Extended
Cheltenham Extrabold
Cheltenham Inline
Inline Extra Condensed
Inline Extended
Cheltenham Medium Expanded
Cheltenham Medium Condensed
Chelt Extrabold Shaded
Cheltenham Bold Italic Shaded
Cheltenham Bold Shaded

THE CHELTENHAM FONT
❡ It is in characters not differing in any material item from these (the designer trusts) that this new font will be cut.

THE CHELTENHAM TYPE
Quaint enough will be this type lacking exactly what chiefly gives the Italic, its qualities of dash & zip; i.e. the kerns. J.

A HAPPY FACE IS A FACE THAT GIVES JOY, AND THE CHELTENHAM—*SO APT, SO FITTING*—IS THIS KIND

IT is undoubtedly the *most popular type face* that has been brought out in recent years. Judging by the *satisfaction* with which it was received the design was a most *fortunate* one, and it came at an opportune time measured by the demand which immediately sprang up. Scarcely had the *American Type Founders Company* finished the *fourteen sizes* in the *Cheltenham Oldstyle series* when requests came for an *Italic series* to go with it. The present series of *Cheltenham Italic* was the result. Its introduction met with an *immediate success*, and orders came in from the largest publishers and job printing offices, until now it is hardly possible to pick up a publication of any merit without a showing of the complete series of both the *Cheltenham Oldstyle* and the *Cheltenham Italic* being prominently displayed therein. A still further demand necessitated designing the other Cheltenhams shown on following pages. In fact, many among the most prominent advertisers in the country have *requested* that this face be the one used to *display their matter* as it so fittingly challenges the eye of the reading public. The distinguished character of the *Cheltenham family* is so pronounced that the first glance reveals a design of decidedly unusual character that shows *qualities never before attained* in any other type face. *It is in a class by itself.* In cutting the other *Cheltenhams* to complement the *Cheltenham Oldstyle* the same lines that gave distinction to the first series were followed, and all have been as satisfactory as the original one. The *Cheltenham* family has been the type sensation of the year, and their necessity in every properly equipped printing plant is quite apparent

Cheltenham Oldstyle and Cheltenham Italic in combination

256
Series of variations on Cheltenham, c. 1918.

257
Bertram Goodhue (American architect), original outlines for Cheltenham, United States, 1900. The first specimen of this type for bookwork dates to 1903.

258
A characteristic ATF advertisement promoting Cheltenham, 1906.

of William Caslon IV, dating back to 1816, was issued fully decades before the type family it spawned entered regular use, by around 1900 letters of this sort were being widely distributed. One of the more representative alphabets bearing the stamp of this new vogue, Akzidenz Grotesk, made its appearance in the collections of the German foundry Berthold, in 1898. This sans serif alphabet, of rather regular appearance, is employed primarily in titles and advertising. Akzidenz Grotesk was taken up in the United States and in Great Britain, where it was renamed "Standard." This new designation captures the all-purpose talents of the typeface, its sober and functional appearance, as well as its relative neutrality. As if to confirm its key role in the genesis of sans serif, Akzidenz Grotesk went on to inspire, in a more or less direct fashion, the creation of many alphabets, such as Franklin Gothic and Helvetica, published in 1905 and 1957; moreover, in the course of the second third of the twentieth century, several graphic designers close to the International Style, among them Anton Stankowski, adopted it as their favorite type. The use of Akzidenz Grotesk remained high throughout succeeding decades, placing it among the great alphabets of the nineteenth century.

In around 1900, the attraction of sans serif type was enhanced by the ambient diversity of letters generally, since Art Nouveau typography lingered long into the early years of the twentieth century. In Germany, type designers, imbued with considerable calligraphic artistry, were now also creating alphabets in this style, in addition to Roman and Gothic typefaces (the use of blackletter having remained prevalent in Germanic lands since the fifteenth century). In this respect, Rudolf Koch's output is particularly impressive, as his work covered Gothic, calligraphy-inspired letterforms, sans serif alphabets (Neuland and Kabel, in 1923 and 1927 respectively), and even fancy geometric sans serifs (Zeppelin, 1929).

Pushing further in the direction of modernity, type designers from many other countries focused their concerns on quality. As in Germany, creation in the United States was especially fertile, and production hit new highs. The 1890s saw the rise of Bruce Rogers, a figure who is considered to be one of the very first independent typographer-type designers. In 1892, the confederation of several foundries within the American Type Founders Company (ATF) constituted a significant event in the arena of American typography. The company secured

259
Factory making wooden type, Lucerne, Switzerland (undated document, c. 1900?).

260
Advertisement for Odol, c. 1900.

261
Title page of *La Lettre d'imprimerie* by Francis Thibaudeau, published in Paris in 1921, set in Auriol by the Peignot & Cie foundry after a dummy provided by Thibaudeau.

the collaboration of several graphic designers and typographers of the first rank, such as Will Bradley, Frederic Goudy, Linn Boyd Benton, and his son Morris Fuller Benton, as well as the German poster artist Lucian Bernhard (the great representative of *Sachplakat* in the 1900s).

In 1896, Bertram Goodhue created Cheltenham, another American typeface—like Theodore Low de Vinne and Linn Boyd Benton's Century typeface—intended for everyday reading. Created to optimize legibility (elongated ascenders, truncated descenders), the alphabet enjoyed wide usage, from titles to posters. In 1902, Morris Fuller Benton drew and began cutting Franklin Gothic for the ATF. This sans serif type, available in numerous variants, is still widely available today. These creations offer confirmation of the noteworthy expansion of the sans serifs group, with the ATF catalog featuring some fifty models by the beginning of the century. Many typefaces designed around 1900 speak of the need to adapt to the industrial world, to take account of productivity, and to integrate into the urban visual environment. Like other alphabets of its time, Franklin Gothic was a homogeneous unit and preserves certain forms of the Roman (like the letter G). Morris Fuller Benton created other well-known sans serifs, such as Alternate Gothic and News Gothic, respectively in 1903 and 1908 (his typeface legacy is by all accounts considerable).

The imperatives of quality, legibility and ease of reading, as well as profitability were given added urgency by the accelerating lifestyles of the nineteenth century. Advancing step by step with graphics, by the turn of the twentieth century the design of alphabets seems to be entering a new chapter. Eclecticism reigned; each type of alphabet is accepted on its own terms, from restoration of historical models in Roman to sans serifs and Egyptian categories, via all kinds of fanciful creations and innumerable variants in letterform. Typography, its history ransacked, was stormed by a plethora of tendencies—from the spread of the sans serif to the flowering of Art Nouveau. After centuries of classicism and several decades in the Victorian mode, type design entered a phase of measure and openness: already, typographers had to know how to juggle savoir-faire, harmony, diversity, innovation, and imagination (or eccentricity), symbolized by the variations of one and the same alphabet in multiple forms—a much-prized exercise at the time.

The nineteenth century: a stormy crossing

From type design to poster composition and many facets of graphic production, vast areas of visual expression were either transfigured or came into being in the course of the nineteenth century. These upheavals stemmed to some extent from the wholesale changes affecting societies in varying degrees of industrialization. While creators sought to regain control over the process as a whole, transformations in the means of production accentuated the gap between the design and manufacturing phases. Other developments, such as improved schooling and the gradual elimination of illiteracy, combined with other factors to contribute to the uptake of the supports of graphics and typography by new mass media (some posters were distributed internationally), and to the development and creation of a commercial art.

The reorganization of modes of production and reception were seconded by new approaches to representation and perception stemming from the artistic explorations of the nineteenth century. This new-found receptivity to multiple and diversified practices was a development quite unlike any in earlier centuries and opened up telling perspectives, for graphics generally as well as for typography.

In 1893, sensing the far-reaching consequences of this transmutation, John Grand-Carteret exclaimed: "Today marks the triumph of the document and one can affirm that the twentieth century will see the onset of a major revolution whose seeds we can already discern: graphic language, the Image, going hand in hand with literary language, Writing."[56] The following year, in 1894, Octave Uzanne published his article "The End of Books" in a New York magazine: "It was about two years ago that the question of the end of books was exercising groups of booksellers, artists, men of science and learning one memorable evening [...] Printing, in my opinion, is threatened by death by the various devices for registering sound that have yet to be invented (and the progress of electricity and modern mechanism reinforces this opinion)—Gutenberg's invention is fated sooner or later to fall into desuetude as a means of current interpretation of our mental products [...] Printing is very easy to replace by phonography. [...] I believe that [...] the printed book is about to disappear."

NOTES

1 H.-J. Martin, *La Naissance du livre moderne* (France: Cercle de la Librairie, 2000), 475.

2 Quoted by M. Jimenez, *Qu'est-ce que l'esthétique?* (Paris: Gallimard, 1997), 198. Georg Wilhelm Friedrich Hegel (1770–1831), German philosopher whose thought has been ceaselessly reinterpreted, and who confronted "the crisis affecting the thought of the Enlightenment and philosophical idealism" (*Encyclopédie Bordas*). Concerned as much with philosophy as with law, history, and religion, he is in particular the author of a voluminous aesthetic theory which is "undoubtedly the first work, in the history of Western culture, to combine a reflection on artistic activity in its relations with the historical process of man in general, a definition of the concept of beauty in its diverse manifestations and a general history of Art." (F. Châtelet).

3 "Telegraph": from the Greek *tele*, "far off," and *graphein*, "to write."

4 The very first postage stamp in the world, the Penny Black, was illustrated with the profile of Queen Victoria. Switzerland and Brazil created their first stamps in 1843, the United States in 1847, and France in 1849. Its invention of the postage stamp means that Great Britain is the only country never to indicate the name of the country of issue on its stamps.

5 Initially a purely textual media, the postcard gained its illustrative component in about 1870 and experienced runaway success, and in Germany, for instance, nearly fifty thousand cards were sold following the debut issue. The very first illustrated postcard is dated 1869 (from the Austro-Hungarian Empire). In the following years, postcards began appearing in many nations in Western Europe and in the United States (Germany, Belgium and Luxembourg in 1870; Switzerland, the Netherlands, and Denmark in 1871; Sweden, Norway, and Russia in 1872; France, Spain, and the United States in 1873; Italy in 1874). The postcard propagated rapidly throughout the world (Greece, Turkey, Argentina, Egypt, Brazil, and so on).

6 *Ornament in Architecture*, as quoted in R. Twombly and N. G. Menocal, *The Poetry of Architecture* (New York: W. W. Norton 2000), 267.

7 As with silkscreen printing, lithography is a planar printing method. The two other categories of prints are impression in relief (woodcut and linocut) and intaglio (copperplate, etching, etc.).

8 The invention of the steam press, in which Friedrich Koenig was instrumental, followed hard on the heels of developments in entirely metal presses (Charles Stanhope, end of the eighteenth century). First employed in Great Britain to print the *Times* newspaper in 1814, the steam press allows a run of some eight hundred to one thousand sheets an hour (figures which were soon to increase five-fold).

9 The photographic image of the countryside of Saint-Loup-de-Varennes *Point de vue du Gras* is scarcely visible today and does not actually present the contrast one sees in reproductions. Niépce probably took the landscape out of his window for purely practical reasons, without an aesthetic forethought and with no specific concept of framing. The print was unearthed in London in 1952. See on this subject: H. Gernsheim, "La première photographie au monde," *Études photographiques*, no. 3, November 1997, Société française de photographie, Paris (1st ed.: "The 150th Anniversary of photography," *History of Photography*, no. 1, January 1977).

10 Cited by M. Frizot, *Histoire de voir*, vol. 1 (Paris: Photopoche, 1989), 12.

11 It seems commonly held that characters with slab (rectangular) serifs were baptized "Egyptian" because of the passion for Egypt that had caught on during Napoleon's campaigns in the country. It is equally possible that this designation is not unconnected with the arrival of the first collections of Egyptian art in the British Museum in 1834.

12 Quoted by A. Lawson, *Anatomy of a Typeface* (London: Hamish Hamilton, 1990), 315.

13 Victoria was queen of Great Britain from 1837 to 1901. Her name is often used in referring to a period that covers the last two thirds of the nineteenth century and has also come to be employed in the field of visual expression. In the West, graphics, typography, and the type of the time, when designated as Victorian, refer to the characteristics of abundance, imaginativeness, exuberance and/or over-elaboration.

14 Morris Fuller Benton ranks among one of the major type designers for the American Type Founders Company (ATF), a company set up in 1892, which embraced a number of American foundries. After 1900, the ATF occupies a predominant role in the manufacture and distribution of type. Morris Fuller Benton designed more than two hundred fonts for this foundry, including Franklin Gothic (1905–12; designed in 1902) and News Gothic (1908).

15 Quoted by P. Duplan and R. Jauneau, *Maquette et mise en page* (Paris: L'Usine nouvelle, 1982), 12–13. These explanations of the reading process derive from studies undertaken by Leclerc in 1843 and by the ophthalmologist Émile Javal in 1905.

16 The press was baptized the "Fourth Estate" (i.e. power in the land) in 1787 by the British politician and author Edmund Burke.

17 Rotary presses are continuous presses whose mechanism is based on a set of rotating cylinders.

18 Quoted by M. Pleynet, *Les Modernes et la Tradition* (Paris: Gallimard, 1990), 82.

19 R. Barthes, *Writing Degree Zero*, in S. Sontag (ed.) *The Barthes Reader* (London: Cape, 1982), 36.

20 J.-H. Martin, "Art et publicité," *Art & publicité 1890–1990* (exh. cat., Paris: Centre Georges Pompidou, 1990), 16–17.

21 The firm was renamed Morris and Co. in 1875.

22 Cited in *D Graphic Design Sourcebook* (Little, Brown, 1987).

23 Vat (handmade) paper was widely used in Europe until the end of the eighteenth century. It is manufactured by hand, sheet by sheet, out of rope hemp and linen rag.

24 Quoted by R. McLean, *Typographers on Type* (London: Lund Humphries, 1995), 5.

25 Quoted by L. Gervereau, *La Propagande par l'affiche* (Paris: Syros-Alternatives, 1991), 40.

26 Sizes of 108 × 88 in and 112 × 56 in.

27 A trip to Great Britain was a common choice among lithographers from the Continent, eager to acquire the most up-to-date expertise on the matter. At that time, Owen Jones and Charles Knight numbered among the best British printers.

28 Fred Walker, quoted by A. M. Fern, *Word and Image* (New York: Museum of Modern Art, 1968), 12.

29 The French term "*affichomanie*" testifies to the intensity of the vogue for posters in the 1890s. The word is supposed to have been forged around the end of the nineteenth century by Octave Uzanne, author, critic, and bibliophile particularly concerned for the future of the book.

30 Painter and interior decorator, Louis Comfort Tiffany was art director of the Tiffany firm.

31 In the original preface to vol. 3, 1897, in R. Marx, *Les Maîtres de l'affiche, 1896–1900* (Paris: Chêne, 1978), 14. Roger Marx was administrator of the École des Beaux-Arts, before becoming inspector general of the provincial museums in 1889. In his art criticism, he supported the role of the so-called "minor" arts with respect to the "major" ones. His interest in decorative and applied art naturally led him to the poster and he was among the first to envisage a museum entirely devoted to the new art form.

32 Quoted by B. Hillier, *Posters* (London: Weidenfeld & Nicolson, 1969), 49.

33 A. E. Johnson, quoted by B. Hillier, ibid., 98.

34 Hermann Muthesius founded the German Werkbund in 1907. Architect and interior decorator, he undertook the customary journey to Britain, returning filled with admiration for the Arts and Crafts

movement and architectural modernity generally. Bolstered by these influences and following his analyses of what was happening in England, in the Werkbund Muthesius sought to conjoin the demands of industrial production to quality design.

35 Quoted by A. M. Porciatti, "Mackintosh et la critique," in G. Laganà (gen. ed.), *Charles Rennie Mackintosh* (Milan: Electa Moniteur, 1990), 35.

36 Quoted by P. Cabanne, *L'Art du vingtième siècle* (Paris: Aimery-Somogy, 1982), 31.

37 Quoted by J. Prouvé, *Pionniers du XXᵉ siècle. Guimard, Horta, Van de Velde* (Paris: Musée des Arts Décoratifs, 1971), 6.

38 Charles Cochran (1898), quoted by B. Hillier, op. cit., 135.

39 The German term Jugendstil is forged from *Jugend*, "youth," and *Stil*, "style."

40 Quoted in the glossary to J. Clair (gen. ed.), *Vienne 1880–1938*, (exh. cat., Paris: Centre Georges Pompidou, 1986), 756.

41 Quoted by B. Hillier, op. cit., 202.

42 Quoted by F. Werner, *Koloman Moser* (Pierre Mardaga, Belgium, n. d.), 9.

43 Preface to S. Mallarmé, *Un Coup de dés jamais n'abolira le hasard* (Paris: Gallimard, 1998).

44 P. Valéry, "Le coup de dés, lettre au directeur des Marges ;" the text appeared in 1920 in the journal *Les Marges* (now in *Œuvres*, vol.1 [Paris: Gallimard, 1980], 624–626); partially quoted by A.-M. Christin, "De l'espace typographique [...]," A. Zali (gen. ed.), *L'Aventure des écritures. La page* (Paris: Bibliothèque nationale de France, 1999), 195.

45 Quoted by J. Scherer, *Le "Livre" de Mallarmé* (Paris: Gallimard, 1957), xv.

46 J. Scherer, ibid., 23–24.

47 On the particularities of the various editions of *Le Coup de dés* and their degree of conformity with Mallarmé's original intentions, see Jean-Claude Lebensztejn's study "Note relative au Coup de dés," in *Critique. Revue générale des publications françaises et étrangères*, no. 397–398, June–July 1980, 633–659.

48 On typographical aspects in *Les Nourritures terrestres*, see D. Steel, "Les Nourritures terrestres: ponctuation, typographie et mise en page," in D. H. Walker and C. S. Brosman (eds.), *Retour aux* Nourritures terrestres (Amsterdam and Atlanta: Rodopi, 1997), 141–154, (acts of the Sheffield symposium), March 1997.

49 Quoted in *Vienne 1880–1938*, op. cit., 284.

50 The Palais Stoclet in Brussels is a significant work in the history of architecture and the decorative arts. The construction, interior installation, and the decoration of the palace were undertaken between 1905 and 1911 by a number of collaborators on the Wiener Werkstätte in what is a union of the arts symptomatic of the Zeitgeist.

51 Quoted by B. Hillier, op. cit., 115.

52 The circumstances surrounding Lucian Bernhard's participation in this competition (the unfolding of his project together with the jury's reaction) are explored by Philip B. Meggs in *A History of Graphic Design* (New York: Wiley & Sons, 1998).

53 Quoted in *Graphic Design Sourcebook*, op. cit.

54 Leonetto Cappiello (1912), quoted by C. Frèches-Thory, in *Cappiello* (Paris: Réunion des musées nationaux, 1981), 15.

55 Quoted by R. Bargiel-Harry, ibid., 112.

56 Quoted by R. Bachollet, *John Grand-Carteret* (Cahiers de l'Alpe, 1990), 11. French author John Grand-Carteret (1850–1927) studied the history of manners in terms of imagery and representation, with particular attention to the social role and importance of the image.

57 O. Uzanne, "The End of Books," *Scribner's Magazine*, no. 2, vol. 16 (New York, 1894), 221, 224, 230. "It was about two years ago that the question of the end of books was agitated in groups of booksellers, artists, men of science and learning on a memorable evening [...] printing [...] in my opinion is threatened by death by the various devices for registering sound that have yet to be invented. I do not believe (and the progress of electricity and modern mechanism forbids me to believe) that Gutenberg's invention can do otherwise than sooner or later fall into desuetude as a means of current interpretation of our mental products [...printing] is very easy to replace by phonography, which is only in its initial stage [...] the printed book is about to disappear."

**Part 3
Contents**

The first third of the twentieth century

The avant-garde floodtide

"Since around 1910, throughout the world, young artists [...] have sought the best way of expressing themselves, to solve the problems that painting, sculpture, writing, and musical composition placed before them. They do not aim at art, but at sincere expression. Intuitively, they turned back to the basic concepts underpinning their means of expression: the painter to color, the sculptor to volume, the architect to space, the composer to sonority, the writer to the word. Their work has made it possible to rediscover emotional and sensory sources which had been lost."[1]

László Moholy-Nagy

A society in constant flux

The turn of the twentieth century was fruitful terrain for many artistic and graphic practices. More and more, pictorial and plastic experiments tended to leave well-trodden paths, defying mimesis and making audacious, risk-taking statements, providing evidence of increasing radicalization. Caught in the spotlight of change, all over Europe design and architecture embarked on a quest for transformative and evolutive solutions. With the British Arts and Crafts movement, the Glasgow School, the Wiener Werkstätte, and the German Werkbund, elements of modernity began to emerge. Creators were increasingly exposed to the presuppositions and consequences of industrial production. The step-change to a techno-industrial civilization was accompanied by a snowballing phenomenon of urbanization. In this period of hell-for-leather industrialization—if unequally operative depending on the countries concerned—migration from rural areas fundamentally transformed civilizations (as an indication, the rate of urbanization to the eastern United States shot up from 15 percent in 1850 to 40 percent in 1900, to exceed 55 percent by 1930).

If the nineteenth century had been the theater of major upheaval, by around 1900 deeply transmuting processes—social, political, cultural, artistic, and so on—were underway. The harnessing of electricity and unprecedented developments in transport transformed humankind's relation to the environment, while the recording of movement by the cinematograph urged art to ask new questions. In the fields of the social and political sciences, forms of conception, analysis, comprehension, and perception were being invented, reinvented, or developed—Marxism, psychoanalysis, phenomenology, linguistics, etc.—which were to feed back into the whole outlook of the twentieth century.

Faith in reason, progress, and science, too, was wavering. Freud, in exploring the unconscious, prepared the way for ideas that would reject superficial accounts and build into a parallel, dual reality. Thus analyzed, the understanding of human behavior was entirely rethought with respect to psychic activities that welled up from profound, unspoken mechanisms. At the same time, lifestyles and the whole social landscape were in upheaval; the face of the urban environment was soon to be unrecognizable. Speed itself seemed to impart a new pace to life, sharing in a seamless current of change that constantly sought to attract passersby to pictures, readers to texts, and listeners to sounds. Visual communication intensified, industrial development bringing with it the rise of commercial advertising. With the development of the radio (the telephone having been developed by Alexander Graham Bell in the mid-1870s in the United States), sound was to discover its own platform. As the new century dawned, these factors were compounded by other phenomena that left their mark on the era, totally rescheduling the human environment.

The arts, graphics, and typography

This shifting context proved highly favorable to the development of attitudes that took their distance from, if they did not always actually break with, preexistent systems. Avant-garde culture in literature, the arts, and in the intellectual field generally, quickly sloughed off the forms, codes, values, and languages of the past. Sometimes utopian, many incipient

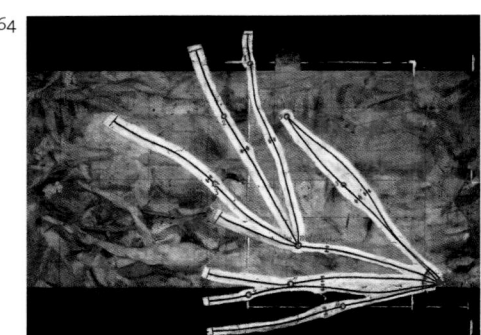

264

264
Marcel Duchamp, *Réseaux de stoppages étalon* (Network of Stoppages), 1914. Oil and pencil on canvas, 5 ft. × 6 ft. 6 ¹/₂ in. (148.9 × 197.7 cm).

movements defined themselves with respect to the social and environmental transformations underway, as well as to notions of the contemporary to which they hoped to contribute. The search for freedom, radicalism or protest were soon at work, in cahoots with the move to the abstract, such as Marcel Duchamp's iconoclasm, Dadaist subversion, and other disruptive questionings and innovative researches into expression. Codes, it seemed, were there to be transgressed, entrenched forms were there to be transcended; novel perspectives opened up and revolutionary ambitions were fueled. An unparalleled phase of artistic emancipation and activity was in the offing.

The phenomena of renewal gathered pace, and art movements sprang up at breakneck speed. A swarm of "isms" jockeyed for position: Fauvism, Expressionism, Cubism, Futurism, "Abstractivism",[2] Vorticism, Dadaism, Suprematism, Constructivism, Productivism, Neoplasticism, etc.; all movements in which the letter and the graphic image took on a salient role. This thirst for a reenergized expressiveness was felt in many European nations, with Milan, Moscow, Munich, and Paris some of the busiest hotbeds for avant-garde activity. The plentiful circulation of ideas and experiments electrified the transnational dimension of the phenomenon. Information on the contemporary art scene was disseminated ever more widely by manifestoes, exhibitions, journeys, conferences, posters, performances, and publications. At stake, however, were not just issues of form—the question of the social and political function of art was also addressed. The position of the arts in society was to be ascertained by various yardsticks—by its practical value (as emerges in the interest aroused by functionalism), or else by its impact as protest. The destruction of an idea of art stigmatized as "bourgeois" surfaced as one of the period's most urgent goals. Freed from religious and political shackles, breaking with perennial tradition, art now strove to turn to the people and to exist in new forms. In its haste, avant-gardism was not exempt from self-referentiality.

The movements that followed on were adventurous, impetuous, even caustic and provocative. In 1900 Rodin first exhibited *Walking Man*—a figure in locomotion bereft of head and arms. Picasso, for his part, caused a scandal with *Les Demoiselles d'Avignon* in 1907. The years that followed transformed what was believed possible in art and reinvented artistic processes. These researches impinged on many areas of the creative arts: painting, sculpture, architecture, graphics, typography, music, literature, and so on.

In the first decade of the century, in 1905, two movements set the tone for what was afoot in the visual arts: Fauvism, in France, and Expressionism, in Germany. In Fauvism, color was invested with new power; bright and applied pure, it communicated emotion, strength, passion. The movement created a furor, with "Fauve" ("wild animal") initially a derisive term (just as Cubism was to be). In Germany, Expressionism set up disturbing or troubling ideas in vibrant pictures galvanized by a strident or angst-ridden expressive power. The artistic heat was soon to be turned up further; by about 1907, Cubism could be seen germinating in canvases by Braque and Picasso.

Pictorial statements increasingly abandoned the traditional aim of subject recognition. The handling of paint, customarily subordinated to the object represented, attained fresh power, dynamism, and autonomy. Continuing along a trail that had begun in the nineteenth century, artistic investigation now tackled problems of light, color, form, scale, and space head-on. Other materials and processes challenged the hegemony of paint. Braque introduced lettering into his pictures at the beginning of 1910; Picasso went further in 1912 with scraps of newsprint and commercial materials such as labels. Together, they explored sampling, appropriation and collage, artistic processes that have since remained an inexhaustible and highly fruitful source for graphic practice.

265

266

265
Pablo Picasso, *Landscape with Posters*, summer 1912. Oil on canvas, 19 × 24 in. (48 × 61 cm).

266
Gino Severini, *Nord-Sud*, 1912. Oil on canvas, 19 1/4 × 25 in. (49 × 64 cm).

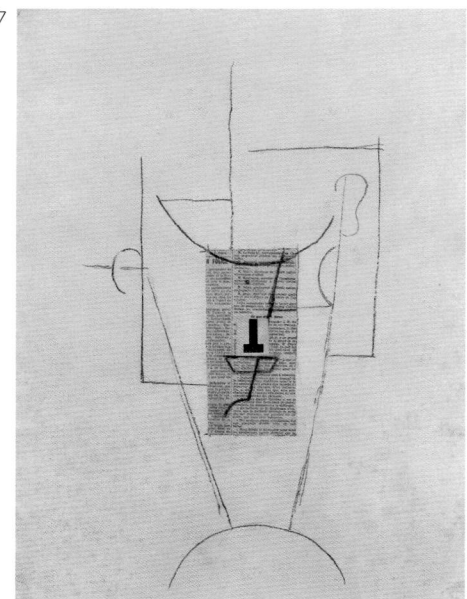

267
Pablo Picasso, *Head of a Man*, 1912. Lead pencil and glued papers on paper, 24 ³/₄ × 18 ¹/₂ in. (63 × 47 cm).

268
Carl Otto Czeschka (1878–1960, member of the Wiener Werkstätte), composition for a poetical text, 1905.

In the prewar period, the art scene was in a state of effervescence. The very beginning of the 1910s resounded with the rumblings of Italian Futurism and the deployment of the abstract, opening up a plastic space explored by many painters, including Kandinsky (*With the Black Arc, Improvisations, The First Abstract Watercolor*), Kupka (*The First Step, Disks of Newton, The Vertical Planes*), Delaunay (*Disk, Electric Prisms*), Picabia (*Caoutchouc, Udnie, Abstract Composition*), the Rayonists, Larionov and Goncharova (*Sunny Day, Composition*), Mondrian (*Picture No. 1, Tree A*), Balla (*Iridescent Compenetration*), and lastly Malevich (the motif of the square), who gave the green light to Suprematism—a form of art that had probably been thought up as early as 1913. "Suprematism distills all painting into a black square on a white canvas."[3] The same year, Duchamp carried out the eminently iconoclastic artistic gesture of the first readymade.

As at the end of the nineteenth century, parallelisms arose between evolutions in art and (typo)graphic developments. The visual arts appropriated the letter, the written word, typography, the printed image, photography, the processes of advertising, and so on. In the creations of Futurists, Cubists, and Dadaists, graphic space is liberated, implodes. Composition freed itself from the traditional frame, generating unexpected arrangements and requiring a wholly new perceptive state. As proclaimed loud and clear by Marinetti, the "typographical revolution" was playing an active part in the constitution of what was an original graphic idiom.

Visual expression was now finding new outlets. If the nineteenth century had witnessed the relentless rise of the poster, the press, jobbing-work, and typefaces through the industrialization of production (before this, it was the book that had been the preeminent sector for the printed word), the onset of the twentieth century witnessed a diversification in media that was handled differently by the various protagonists in progressive art. Leaflets, handbills, manifestos, and other printed protests, or poems to declaim, read and/or look at, *calligrammes*, "words in freedom," multiple collages, prints—tirelessly, "the avant-gardes played with words, forms, and ideas",[4] affirming the interdisciplinarity and interconnection of the arts.

Artists indulged in a multiplicity of activities: writing, praxis, theory, painting, sculpture, and design. Confirming a tendency that had been rekindled at the end of the nineteenth century, applied art and the fine arts could now interact in new ways. The fields of graphics and typography opened up in a quite exceptional manner; a wind of change swept away everything and anything to do with classicism, tradition, or playing safe. Graphic creations went in for impact, dynamism, contrast, asymmetry, tension, fragmentation, and non-linearity, as well as other optical effects. Together these means were channeled into novel, sometimes explosively energetic visual statements. Jettisoning their secondary role and all subordination to readability, texts and other forms of message were becoming objects to be looked at in their own right. Neither was formal arrangement indifferent: until now, text and image had most often taken on recognizable, codified, even hackneyed forms. Henceforth they might be disrupted and recomposed in atypical ways, appearing in a wholly new light and upsetting accepted perceptive codes, by encouraging viewers to examine, understand, and decipher differently.

The tonality of Expressionism

German Expressionism appeared in 1905 as a contemporary of Fauvism. The movement, possessed of sometimes poignant expressiveness, left an enduring mark on the first decades of the century.

A first group gathered in Dresden was called Die Brücke (the Bridge), in which Karl Schmidt-Rottluff, Emil Nolde, Ernst Ludwig Kirchner, and Erich Heckel took active part. Severing all links with Impressionism and academism alike, they sought to exteriorize and visualize human tension, expressing the anguished or hostile face of the environment. As if in parallel with the chromatic violence of the Fauves, their handling was both turbulent and disturbing. The movement spilled over from the pictorial into the cinematographic field, and made an impact on architecture, illustration, and the poster, as well as on book and periodical

269
Hans Poelzig (?), poster for the film, *Der Golem.
Wie er in die Welt kam.* (Paul Wegener),
Germany, 1919–20. Chromolithograph,
4 ft. 7 in. × 2 ft. 11 ³/₄ in. (140 × 91 cm).

270
Ernst Ludwig Kirchner, poster for the exhibition,
KG Brücke, Germany, 1910.

271
Vojtech Preissig (Czech artist, typographer, and
teacher, 1873–1944), typeface eschewing the use
of curves, c. 1914.

272
Ernst Ludwig Kirchner, list of the members
and supporters of the group Die Brücke in 1909,
Germany, 1909. Woodcut, 6 ³/₄ × 4 in.
(17.2 × 10.6 cm).

publishing. In each artistic form it explored, the Expressionist vision was imbued with profound originality. In the graphic arts, the favorite techniques were woodcut, linocut, and lithography, often in limited editions. By dint of its inherent materiality, the woodcut exacerbated the expressive power of line, bringing out the contrast between black and white. The sheer power of discontinuous, wavering lines generated images with edgy, powerful forms. Words and lettering, often carved into the wood itself with scant concern for prettiness or grace, appear distinctive and rough-hewn—angular, distended, deformed, raw, and unyielding.

The intensity of the image in another favorite Expressionist genre, cinema, owes much to light and shadow. In the graphic and typographical field, meanwhile, the search for contrast and tension is expressed through the disposition of black and white, and through a mode of handling that presents a direct challenge to the viewer by its use of formal distortion and the deployment of almost electric color schemes. These working methods generated some extraordinary images; dominated by dissonance, they seem harnessed to the depths of the soul, allowing the figure and the human to be expressed completely.

In 1911, the movement expanded further with the foundation of Der Blaue Reiter (the Blue Rider) by Wassily Kandinsky and Franz Marc in Munich: "the choice of form [...] is determined by inner necessity."[5] The movement consolidated the prevailing drive of artists to make their work as individual as possible. For Franz Marc, art can mitigate "the tricks played on our senses by our transitory life."[6] With Der Blaue Reiter, although it was coupled to sociopolitical convictions whose flames were fanned by World War I, Expressionism became less strident. In reaction to such profound mutations, art could do little but voice its torment and inner turmoil. Soon, confronted by a world at war, expressions of revolt and distress became ever more urgent, and art ever more *engagé*. In searing posters, Käthe Kollwitz transmitted a vision of society that, shortly after the war, placed its hope in humanism. Like her, many artists turned to socialism, and sociopolitical questions continued to haunt facets of Expressionism. Persuaded they could contribute to the constitution of a better and more humane society, many artists of the time embraced utopian ideals.

157

Italian Futurism explodes onto the scene

As the polar opposite of Expressionism, Futurism was sounding its own alarm call. Its watchword was the unconditional acceptance of industrialization and mechanization, and the movement coalesced around concepts such as movement, dynamics, energy, and violence. Futurism was kick-started by the publication of Filippo Tommaso Marinetti's *The Futurist Manifesto*, a virulent text issued on February 20, 1909, on the front page of the French daily, *Le Figaro*.[7] For Marinetti—writer, poet, lampoonist, and rabble-rouser—Paris seemed to be the ideal echo chamber in which to broadcast this most astonishing of artistic movements. The avowed goal of his radical position was the destruction of the looming shadows of the past— that is, the wholesale rejection of academism, aesthetic tradition, good taste, and bourgeois attitudes. His kind of activism called for the physical annihilation of traditional cultural forums, such as museums and libraries. Trenchant forms and polemic violence accompanied ideals that from the very start had extremist leanings. In his 1909 proclamation, Marinetti states his desire "to sing the love of danger." "There is no beauty elsewhere than in struggle. No masterpieces which don't have an aggressive component [...]. We want to glorify war [...] the destructive acts of the anarchist, beautiful Ideas that kill, and contempt for woman."[8] By the same token, Marinetti expressed a fervent admiration for strength, for the powers that be, for revolt, audacity, risk, speed and instantaneity, technology, mechanization, the industrial city and the megalopolis. Futurism's statement was one of revolution and polemic; its radicalism was later to rally to the fascist cause.

These aspirations were attended by an influential exploration of spectacular, powerful, innovative forms. Desirous of making a tabula rasa of a past they considered superannuated and unfairly restricted to a coterie, the Futurists fanned the cultural agitprop flames in an effort to clear the ground for a new world order, embracing for the cause industrially marked aspects of modernity, such as mechanization, acceleration, relentless dynamism, and so on. "To the conception of the imperishable and the immortal in art, we oppose that of becoming, the perishable [...] and the ephemeral," Marinetti declared.[9]

If the movement initially focused on writing and literature, it quickly extended over many fields of visual art, adopting diverse forms of expression for its aims (painting, sculpture, architecture, cinema, fashion, typography, and graphics), the whole interwoven with sociopolitical agendas and sometimes corrosive ideas. In their turn, the Futurists strove to abolish the distinction between "major" and "minor" arts. Other figures flocked to join the movement, congregating around the central figure of Marinetti, including the painters Carlo Carrà, Giacomo Balla, and Gino Severini, as well as the painter and sculptor, Umberto Boccioni.

Their ideas were in the main diffused through propaganda, advertisements, and other mass-media forms of communication. The Futurists handed out leaflets, mounted soapboxes, threw pamphlets from airplanes, towers, or speeding cars, organized processions and firework displays, took advertising space in newspapers, pasted eye-catching posters on walls, and held Futurist "soirées"—raucous shows-cum-performances in the course of which fights often broke out. Among the innumerable spheres of activity Futurism made its own, graphics, typography, and writing occupied pride of place. Appearing in diverse guises, the text and the word lay at the heart of every Futurist enterprise. Marinetti, having announced the adoption of "free verse" in poetry, soon ushered in his *"parole in libertà"* — "words in freedom."

The Futurists pored over every aspect of the written word, their pieces becoming ever more daring and original. Practiced *inter alia* by Boccioni, Cangiullo, Carrà, Marinetti, and Soffici, *parole in libertà* upended compositional order, replacing it with eye-catching textual dynamics. The language chain is often stripped bare, ousted by chaotic, juddering, and in certain cases plethoric congeries of signs. A new (typo)graphic register emerges, dependent on surprising and disturbing effects. Ardengo Soffici—painter, writer, and an important figure in the movement—declared, "the letter, on its own, in itself, in its abstract form as an ancient

273
Filippo Tommaso Marinetti,
Manifeste du futurisme, part of
the front page of *Le Figaro* dated
February 20, 1909, France.

274
Filippo Tommaso Marinetti, *Mots
en liberté (Premier record)*, 1914.
India ink on paper,
13 3/4 × 10 1/2 in. (35 × 26.5 cm).

275
Enamel plaque by Filippo
Tommaso Marinetti.

276
Filippo Tommaso Marinetti, *Mots
en liberté. Vive la France, Mots
en liberté. Duel, Propulseur,
Bombardement aérien*, 1914–15 and
1915–16? Ink and collage on paper,
12 × 12 3/4 in. (31 × 32.5 cm),
ink on paper, ink on letter paper,
ink on paper, all 8 1/2 × 10 3/4 in.
(21.5 × 27.5 cm).

273
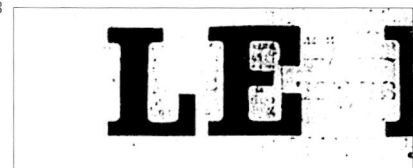

274
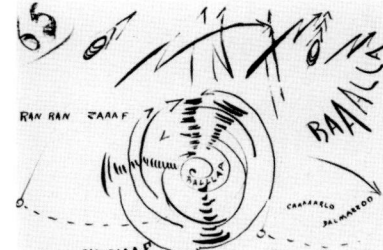

275

276

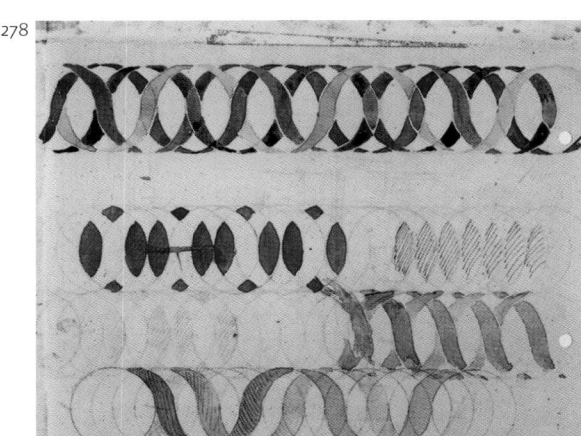

277
Giacomo Balla, manifesto for an exhibition at
the Galleria Angelelli, Rome, 1915. Watercolor
on paper, 3 ft. 1 in. × 2 ft. 1 1/2 in. (94 × 65 cm).

278
Giacomo Balla, *Iridescent Compenetration*,
study, 1912–13. Watercolor on paper, 7 × 8 1/2 in.
(18 × 22 cm).

ideographic sign, possesses emotional power."[10] If they rather turned their backs on the traditional book, Futurists embraced many other textual supports—boards illustrated with *parole in libertà* as well as other graphic compositions, poems, leaflets, posters, postcards, and letterforms intended for the architectural space.

The very form of words took on a visible, eloquently expressive power, sometimes rumbustious, dissonant, or discordant. Letters might be hand-drawn or set typographically— or else both, in tandem. The usual course of language, punctuation, and syntax were ignored in favor of a pictorial dimension of the text that privileged visual appeal. In 1912 and 1913 Marinetti composed the first book entirely printed in *parole in libertà* with the onomatopoeic title, *Zang tumb tumb*. In a further manifesto of 1913, the firebrand of Futurism proclaimed he would kindle "a typographical revolution aimed especially against the idiotic and nauseous idea of a book with its outmoded verse, its handmade *faux* sixteenth-century paper, and adorned with galleons, with Minervas, Apollos, grand initials, and swashes—with mythological vegetables, missal ribbons, epigraphs, and Roman numerals. A book must be a Futurist expression of our Futurist beliefs. Better still: my revolution is directed against what is dubbed the typographical harmony of the page, which runs contrary to the ebb and flow of style as it unfolds across the sheet. We will thus employ, on the same page, if need be, three or four differently colored inks and twenty different typefaces. For example: italics for a series of similar and rapid sensations, bold for violent onomatopoeias, etc. A new, typographically pictorial conception of the page."[11]

Pursued with great hue and cry, the Futurist "typographical revolution" proved a tonic for graphics, in particular through "*tipografia in libertà*." Their ambitions should doubtless be situated in the context of contemporary visual culture and perceptions, keeping in mind adjacent phenomena such as the striking use of close-up in the movies. The attraction of what is on occasion virtually volcanic typography derives to an extent from the fact that here text also functions as image and is endowed with a visual dimension that outranks its role for reading or decipherment. Meaningful names were often bestowed on these pieces, such as "written painting" or "picture-poems."[12] Lively and full of vigor, and designed for optimum impact and maximum disorientation, these compositions conflate different typefaces and forms of writing and deploy a whole gamut of type weights, as well as montage and collage.

The acts of liberation undertaken by the Futurists contributed greatly to the redrawn graphic equation. One of its major figures was the multitalented artist Fortunato Depero. Writer, painter, sculptor, interior decorator, and graphic designer, he worked in the fields of theater, music, fashion, and installation, and was immensely active in the applied arts. Depero discovered Futurism in about 1913, leading to the creation of an "*onomalingua*" in 1916—a "universal language in which tradition has no purpose," imbued with incoherence and "derived from onomatopoeia, *bruitism*, the brutality of Futurist words in freedom."[13] In 1919, he founded the Casa d'Arte Futurista, devoting himself to, among a host of other activities, furniture, decoration, graphics, and advertising, by which he was fascinated. As he said himself, "the art of the future will be a branch of advertising [...] for example, Pirelli [...] produced millions of tires to give the world speed, and increase it—isn't that a poem? a drama? a picture? a formidable structure of the utmost poetry?"[14] Forsaking a tendency in Futurism to disarticulation, Depero's graphics tended to be arranged in an orderly manner, and he created a personal panoply of forms, some of which are discernible at the level of typographical detail. His graphic oeuvre concerned the publishing sector, as well as the promotion of products such as the aperitif Campari and San Pellegrino. An active campaigner for the unity of the arts, in about 1923 Depero started employing the concept of "*architettura tipografica*," designing several exhibition stands and pavilions where the letter is marshaled as a structural component rather than merely as an adjunct stuck onto the façade. In 1927, he published his celebrated "bolted book," *Depero futurista*—an object much admired by Kurt Schwitters. The piece, which presented pieces from his studio (including advertising), is

279
Farfa (pseudonym of Vittorio Osvaldo Tommasini), poster, *Apéritif Pinocchio Anselmo*, Italy, 1928. Oil on canvas, 5 ft. x 3 ft. 2 ¹/₂ in. (142 x 98 cm).

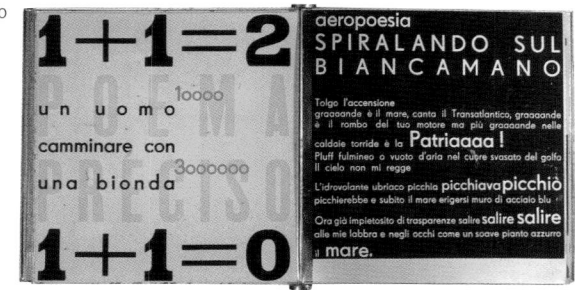

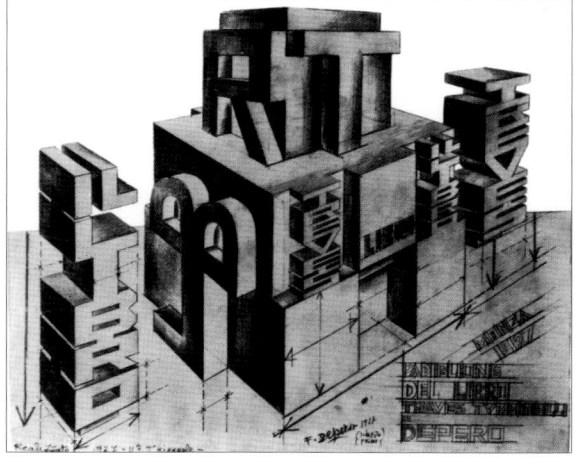

composed of some eighty plates enclosed in two cardboard covers, the whole fixed together by a pair of bolts. By the end of the 1920s, Depero had lived successively in Paris and New York and designed a number of review covers, including for *Vanity Fair* and *Vogue*; this side of his work reveals parallels with Art Deco. Depero was one of a number of avant-garde graphic designers who found an outlet for their talents in American magazines. Besides Depero, many others contributed to the scope and popularization of Futurism. "Depero was one figure among many who contributed to the scope and popularization of Futurism."

The movement constitutes a mine of creative (typo)graphic forms. Letters, together with the manner in which they are linked and distributed in space, had seldom reached such heights before, although the fundamental reshaping of perception undertaken by the pioneers of Cubism also played a determinant role. Nourished by this novel approach, the Futurists produced vast quantities of compositions that treat text as raw material, to the point that their work was followed up in subsequent graphic developments. The movement's policy of dynamic expansion soon saw it developing in or forging connections with places outside Italy—in particular in the shape of Cubo-Futurism, Vorticism, and Stridentism. Futurism caused direct or indirect repercussions in many countries, such as Russia, Great Britain, Czechoslovakia, Poland, Spain, and the United States. In addition, many of the means explored by Futurism were to be taken up by Dada, such as new types of poetry, agitprop, provocation, the (it should be said, radically different) use of advertising media, and so on.

161

Although it was at its loudest between 1909 and 1914, Futurism continued after World War I into the 1920s and 1930s, by then partly won over by extremist ideas. By dint of the initial violence of its positions (that were, perhaps, part and parcel of its invasive attitude to space and its artistic ferocity), the status of Futurism is a thorny question. Behind its fascinating formal and creative rejuvenation, many of its postures were rooted in a dictatorial regime or derive from ideologies of a similar stripe. The Futurists preached intervention as soon as World War I began, and, fired by nationalism and patriotism, many of their number (including Marinetti) decided to join with Mussolini. Certain graphic designers were thus drawn to collaborate with the fascist regime, harnessing their activism to the cause of totalitarian propaganda.

Russian Futurism

Although the Italian influence is manifest and immediate, the Russian version of Futurism differed in important aspects. The poet-artist, Ilya Zdanevich, had probably been in correspondence with Marinetti from 1911, and the following year he read out one of Marinetti's proclamations. In 1914, Marinetti came to Moscow in person to give lectures, meeting with resounding success. Russian artists and writers, however, quickly gave their own twist to the movement. In 1912 there appeared *A Slap in the Face of Public Taste*, a virulent manifesto that marked the movement's launch. If the Russians were to borrow from the vitality and revolutionary attitudes of the Italians, they rejected their political positions and their seditionary nationalism alike. Russian Futurism proper was short-lived, lasting from approximately 1912 to 1916.

Although they turned their backs on the czarist cultural heritage, the Russians did not advocate total dismissal of the past. Above all they retained the means of action and aesthetics of the movement's Italian incarnation. Through exhibitions, reviews, travel, and communication, painters and poets had already become familiar with other strands of the European avant-garde. Russian art was undergoing significant homegrown developments too: Rayonism was already underway and Suprematism was precipitating out of the works of Malevich. One of the more outstanding facets of Russian Futurism resides in the associations it forged between painting and literature (poetry, in particular). The movement thereafter extended even to the theater and the cinema, and also to more theoretical domains. Vladimir Mayakovsky, David Burliuk, Iliazd (Ilya Zdanevich), Alexei Kruchenykh, Kasimir Malevich, Olga Rozanova, and Velimir Khlebnikov number among the principal figures who all sought to add their contribution to the ongoing climate of artistic change. The influence of Cubism led some of them to adumbrate what they called "Cubo-Futurism."

In their turn and in their own manner, the Russian Futurists formed part of a vast swell of artistic rejuvenation that expressed itself through new conjugations of materials, forms, and colors. Manifesting a close interest in typography, lettering, composition, and page-setting, visual artists and poets would often work hand in glove on a publication. Unlike their Italian counterparts, they did not seek to celebrate mechanization with works in metal or industrial materials; they initially preferred relatively simple, low-cost craft processes: stencilling, recycled wallpaper, handwritten lettering, etc., up to and including potato printing. Several started work on what they dubbed "Zaum" (often explained as "transrational" language), since "the artist is free to express himself not only in common language but also in [a] personal language"[15] distinguished from others by the fact that its components possess no definable meaning. This utopian project consisted in forging a poetic form of expression that would do without usual linguistic meanings and conserve only words, syllables, and signs, in fragments, splinters, and shards. Several writers were instrumental in formulating Zaum, including Kruchenykh, Khlebnikov, and Iliazd, who evolved a unique linguistic practice offering an original amalgam of signs for the eye and the interpretative and imaginative faculties, in place of standard codes of significance. Each developed his own individual

286

286
Iliazd (Ilya Zdanevich), cover for *Ledentu le phare* (Ledentu as Beacon), work composed in Zaum, Paris, 1923.

287
Iliazd (Ilya Zdanevich), cover for *Mylliork* by Alexei Kruchenykh, Russia, 1919.

288

289

290

Natalia Goncharova, poem, "Mirskontsa"
(World Upside Down) by Velimir Khlebnikov
and Alexei Kruchenykh, 1912. Collages for the
covers by Goncharova, 7 $^1/_2$ in. × 5 in.
(19 × 13.2 cm).

289
Alexei Kruchenykh, 1921. Found printed paper
(left) and pencil (right), 7 × 5 in. (17.6 × 13.2 cm).

290
Vassily Kamensky, *Naked Among the Clad* by
Vassily Kamensky and Andrei Kravtsov, 1914.
Letterpress on painted papers, 7 $^3/_4$ × 7 $^1/_2$ in.
(19.5 × 18.7 cm).

dimension of Zaum. Khlebnikov offered clarification of its raison d'être: "We want the word to courageously follow painting."[16] For his part, Iliazd, author of a sophisticated version of transrational language, reflected that "each sound […] reflects the world of the emotion […] it] is this key that leads to the understanding of the system that governs the cosmos."[17] In 1923, he brought out an epoch-making work entirely made up of Zaum, a stage drama entitled *Ledentu le phare* (Ledentu as Beacon). In it, Iliazd presented fifty-three "typographic pictures"[18] in which each character is evoked by a particular selection of letters and phonetic elements. By that time, the poet was living in Paris, having arrived in 1921 there to settle definitively. Although published with a preface by one-time Dada poet and critic Georges Ribemont-Dessaignes, the little interest it aroused among his Parisian peers was frankly disparaging (the same chilly reception had greeted the Italian Futurists' debut exhibition in Paris in 1912).

This kind of research joined a long line of experiments in visual writing, though Iliazd was quick to claim precedence with respect to later creations, even accusing Lettrist poetry of out-and-out plagiarism: "The year 1946 in Paris was marked by the appearance of Isidore Isou. […] Isou passed off his imitations of the phonetic poets of the 1920s and of Zaum poetry as the discovery of a new form of poetry he baptized 'Lettrist.'"[19]

291
Cover of *Blast* review, "War Number," London, n°. 2, July 1915. Designed and edited by Wyndham Lewis.

292
Edward Wadsworth (British painter and participant in Vorticism, 1889–1949), Vorticist alphabet, 1919.

Vorticism in Britain

British Vorticism had much in common with both Italian and Russian Futurism (Marinetti had indeed traveled to London a number of times at the beginning of the 1910s). Painter Wyndham Lewis and poet Ezra Pound were the principal figures in a movement that the former had launched in 1912, and which was named Vorticism by the latter in 1914. "The vortex," declared Pound, "is the point of maximum energy."[20] From the start, the movement was vocal in its advocacy of dynamism, rhythm, energy, and the machine. These are of course recurrent features of Futurism, although, as in Russia, Vorticist practices were distinct from those of the Italians. If writers and artists of the British avant-garde had been exposed to Italian Futurism in 1912 at an exhibition in London, analytical Cubism represented another significant influence. Vorticism, like the Italian wing, indulged in a range of activities, turning its hand to the visual arts—including painting and typography—and dance. Desirous of making a "tabula rasa of the years 1837 to 1900,"[21] (i.e., Victorian culture), these artists aspired to breathe new life into the forms and colors of abstraction, "as abstract as music."[22] Opposed to the unfocused and disorderly state of Futurist agitation, if equally enamored of independence, they forged their own graphic and pictorial repertoires. "[…] Vorticist style can be characterized by the use of elements which are well defined by straight lines or geometrical arcs, and of forms with snipped contours making up almost abstract compositions […] the use of movement can only be understood in relation to the machine aesthetic."[23]

The Vorticists did not forget typography—as seen, for instance, in two numbers of their review *Blast* that appeared in 1914 and 1915 with Wyndham Lewis as editor-in-chief. Vibrant, open, and unconventional, the review's layout was set in a powerful style, combining lettering in wood with sans serif alphabets and a marked taste for capital letters. To that they added strong colors, mixtures of fonts and weights, the use of geometrical motifs, and unusual page compositions. The Vorticists thus brought their own particular angle to the profound urge for innovation in the field of typography that was already visible in Italy, Russia, and Germany.

At the outbreak of World War I, the movement dispersed as many of its members set off for the Front, and, although Vorticisim lasted until about 1920, it petered out relatively quickly. Less known than some other trends, Vorticism cannot be considered a major movement, though certain influences can be detected here and there among the European avant-garde, in particular in England itself, as well as in Russia.

Suprematism: new horizons

Slightly later than the Russian and British versions of Futurism, Suprematism came to the fore in Russia between 1913 and 1915. Suprematism was in essence pictorial, and emerged from the paintings of Kasimir Malevich (also its theorist), who gave the movement its name in 1915. The launch of Suprematism is generally accepted to coincide with Malevich's *Black Square on a White Ground,* a canvas famously exhibited in 1915, probably conceived in 1913, and carried out in 1914 or 1915.[24] A few years later, in 1918, Malevich painted the equally notorious *White Square on a White Ground*. These two major works amount to a drastic distillation of the means of pictorial expression, composition, form, and color (close, *mutatis mutandis*, to the language of typography that canonically distributes preexistent black forms over a white ground). Using a similar economy of means, Suprematist painters explored a restricted repertoire. For forms, they restricted themselves to the square, rectangle, circle, triangle, and cross; for colors: red, black, and white, later supplemented by yellow, green, blue, and brown. A pictorial minimalism that does not seek to conceal its graphic nature, Suprematism is the painting of "pure feeling."[25] Malevich himself stated: "[The] most important thing is that it makes use of the void."[26] The artist explored an original optical approach centered on the notion of movement, dynamic sensation, and the presence of diagonals or sloping lines. Suspended on canvas, these geometric forms create highly original spaces. Malevich's graphic and typographical output also partakes of this Suprematist register: in geometric abstraction, the space is marked— punctuated—by asymmetric elements ready to tip over or set up tensions; all directions that were to be followed in the genesis of *Elementare Typographie* and New Typography.

By the end of the 1910s, Russia had embarked on the Bolshevik Revolution that led to the constitution of the USSR. In 1919, Malevich declared that Suprematism was dead; in its wake, Constructivism took shape. In this guise, Suprematist aesthetics penetrated deeply into fields of applied art as varied as posters, publishing, design, furniture, etc. In Russia, the period around 1920 was characterized by pronounced artistic politicization and engagement, to the point that certain practitioners decided to reject painting and dedicate their art to the service of the community so as to create a utilitarian art.

Experiments in lettering and writing in France

France's position within the avant-garde hothouse was distinguished by an absence of the virulence and revolutionary fervor that characterized many approaches to graphics and typography in other countries. Still, the Parisian avant-garde, if it was bereft of some of the zeal of the Futurists that had spilled over into Russia and Britain, was nonetheless the theater for diverse experiments in lettering and typography. As early as 1913, Guillaume Apollinaire and Sonia Delaunay explored the visual and expressive dimension of word and text. In 1916, at a time when the Zurich Dada was in full swing, Pierre Albert-Birot was also embarking on a reconsideration of typographical composition.

Among those who integrated a graphic component into their literary productions, a good number were either practicing painters, or had an interest in that art form. In this regard, the recent introduction of print and lettering

293

294

293
Kasimir Malevich, project on the cover for the cycle of lectures by Nikolai Punin, 1920. Gouache, India ink, and pencil on cardboard, 8 ³/₄ × 5 ¹/₂ in. (22.5 × 14 cm).

294
Kasimir Malevich, cover, *First Cycle of Lectures by Nikolai Punin* (a work intended for teachers of drawing), 1920. Chromolithograph, 8 ¹/₂ × 5 ¹/₂ in. (21.4 × 14 cm).

295
Kasimir Malevich, poster for the film *Doctor Mabuse*, 1922–27. Oil on canvas, 3 ft. 5 ³/₄ in. × 2 ft. 3 ³/₄ in. (106 × 70.6 cm).

296
Kasimir Malevich, *Lady at the Advertising Column*, 1914. Oil and collage on canvas, 30 × 25 in. (71 × 64 cm).

295

296

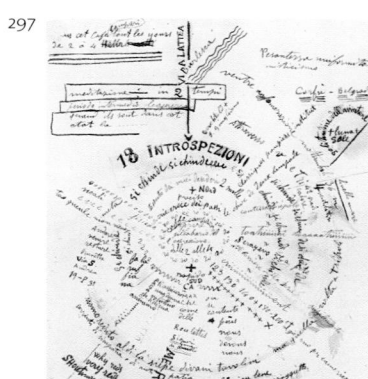

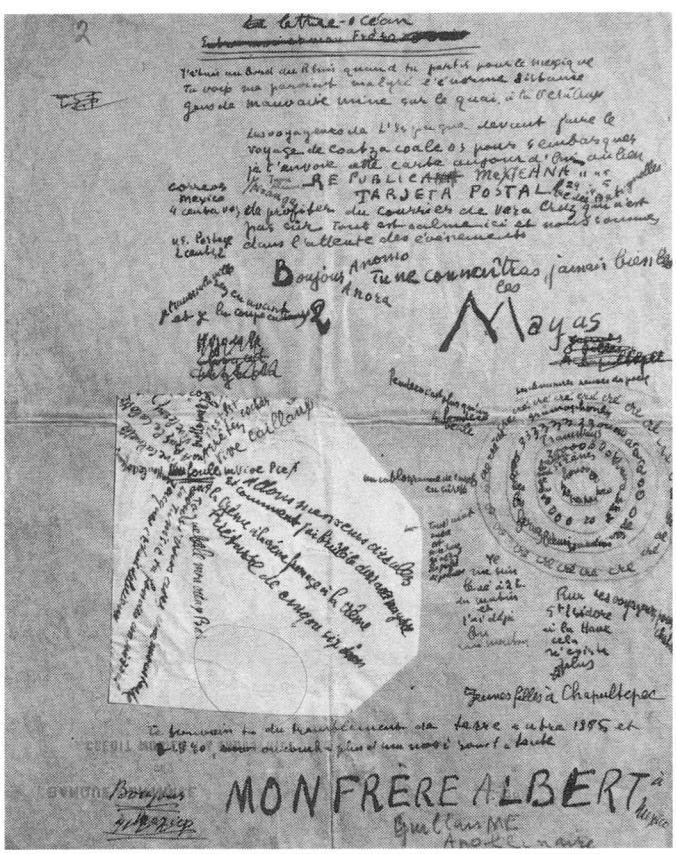

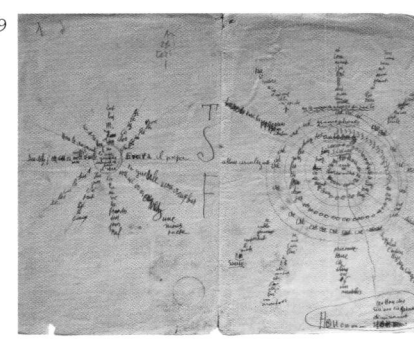

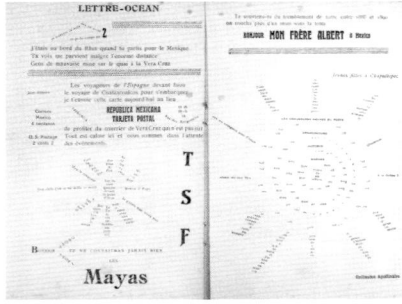

297
Carlo Carrà, *13 Introspections*, 1914. Ink, pencil, and collage on paper, 10 1/2 × 8 in. (26.5 × 21 cm).

298
Guillaume Apollinaire, *Lettre-océan*, preparatory manuscript.

299
Guillaume Apollinaire, *Lettre-océan*, first "lyrical ideogram." Above: *Lettre-océan*, preparatory manuscript. Below: *Lettre-océan*, first *calligramme* published June 1914 in *Les Soirées de Paris*, no. 25.

300
Marius de Zayas, "Femme!", page from the review *291*, no. 9, November 1915.

into Cubism probably constituted a major source of attraction and a determining influence. Pierre Albert-Birot publicized these Cubist researches, reproducing them in his review *Sic* ("sounds, ideas, colors, forms"). Apollinaire was enthusiastic in his praise (he had met Picasso as early as 1904), noting that "Picasso and Braque introduce into their works art lettering from shop-signs and other pieces of writing because, in a modern city, inscriptions, store-signs, and advertisements play an all-important artistic role."[27] Other painters also demonstrated considerable interest in lettering. Sonia Delaunay and Fernand Léger, for instance, would readily incorporate words or fragments of writing into their compositions.

As elsewhere, writers betrayed their concern with typography by intervening in the page-setting of their own texts. Apollinaire began his researches into "*poèmes figurés*" in 1913 or shortly before. The group was published in 1918, in the posthumous collection entitled *Calligrammes: Poems of Peace and War*. If the majority of the poems, in verse, can be read in the customary manner, others are composed more unexpectedly: words are laid out vertically; a whole page radiates or explodes; elsewhere, the page-setting is illustrative of an object or a creature. One of the best known of these poems is "Il pleut" ("It's raining"): the letters follow one beneath the other, forming sloping lines like driving rain. Of course, Apollinaire is here reworking the age-old tradition of picture verse, but he invests it with a new dimension: "Pushed to this point, these bold typographical artifices benefit from a visual lyricism almost unheard-of before our era. These devices could be advanced further to achieve a synthesis of the arts and music, painting, and literature."[28]. Some of Apollinaire's *calligrammes* were to appear in the review *Soirées de Paris* in July 1914—that is to say, practically at the same time as the first edition of Mallarmé's famous *Un Coup de dés*.[29] The same year, with the outbreak of war, Apollinaire also joined up in the French Army, resulting in a delay of a few years before the first edition of his *Calligrammes* collection. Although he remained on the margins of Futurism, he knew the members well enough and entered into correspondence with

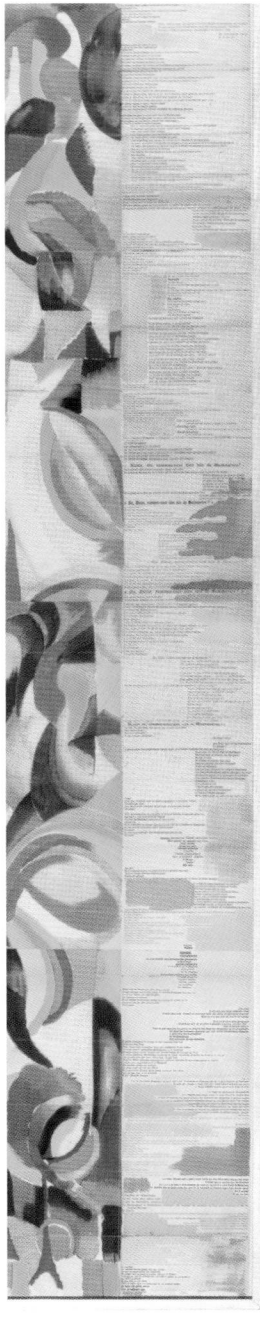

Marinetti; the Italian review *Lacerba* even published one of his poems (Apollinaire, however, entertained misgivings about Futurism). Intending his *calligrammes* to be "an idealization of 'free-versist' [*vers-libriste*] poetry,"[30] Apollinaire, in keeping with the spirit of his time, declared: "And I too am a painter."[31]

Sonia Delaunay's work was initially concerned with pictorial and plastic space. From 1911, she showed an interest in the applied arts, making textiles, various articles, and stage sets. In 1913 and 1914, her production began to include creations that overlap with the field of visual communication: writing paper, posters, book covers, page-settings, free compositions, and so on. The elements of her graphic repertoire include lettering and circular forms, treated in rhythmical compositions of color and contrast. Essentially exploratory in nature, her work for posters, such as *Dubonnet* and *Chocolat*, remained on the drawing-board. Following processes that may be compared, in part at least, to those of the German *Sachplakat*, Sonia Delaunay arranges the letters of the trademark or the product for which the poster is intended (a word in relatively large dimensions, accompanied on occasion by some schematic artwork) in a profusion of bright hues. She thus managed to attain great appeal with a relatively restricted range of elements, playing with form and color to create graphics that are a pleasure to the eye. Sonia Delaunay was to embark on any number of graphic and/or typographic projects. She produced "illustrations" for Blaise Cendrars's text, *La Prose du transsibérien et de la petite Jehanne de France*, based on abstract forms and figures in a geometrizing vein. Dating to 1913, the work reflects immense originality. Known as the "First Simultaneous Book" (that is, intended to be read and looked at "simultaneously"), it does not have the usual book shape, but opens up vertically like a medieval scroll. Aided by Sonia Delaunay, Blaise Cendrars himself undertook the typesetting. She explains their ideas: "The letters for the printing were our choice and employ different typefaces and sizes; this was really revolutionary for the time."[32] Variety in typeface aimed to "express the emotion, speed, slowness, motion, [and] depth [...] of the poem."[33] Sonia Delaunay's sense for the graphic, be it applied to books or posters, remains closely related to her visual art and bears the imprint of geometric abstraction, then on the brink of breaking into the mainstream.

301
Sonia Delaunay and Blaise Cendrars, *La Prose du Transsibérien et de la petite Jehanne de France*, text by Blaise Cendrars, "First Simultaneous Book," watercolor and printed text (extract), Paris, 1913. 6 ft. 5 1/3 in. × 14 in. (199 × 36 cm).

302
Sonia Delaunay, project for the Dubonnet poster, 1914. Glued papers on cardboard, 12 3/4 × 18 1/3 in. (32.5 × 46.5 cm).

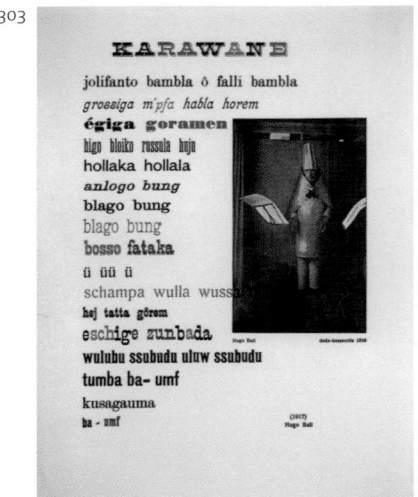

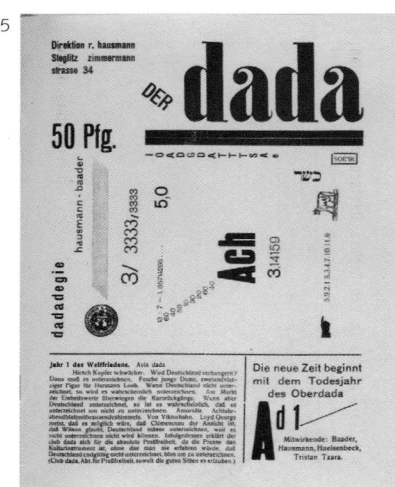

303
Hugo Ball, poem "Karawane," 1917. Set next to a photograph of Hugo Ball in his costume at the Cabaret Voltaire, Zurich, 1916.

304
Tract *Dada soulève tout*, joint text, Paris, 1921.

305
Cover for the review *Der Dada*. Germany, 1919.

Besides Sonia Delaunay, Guillaume Apollinaire, and Blaise Cendrars, many other artists and writers in France turned their talents to typographical experimentation. As in Italy, Russia, and Britain, these researches tended to overlap with literature or with the visual, decorative, and applied arts, flowing into Futurism or, after 1916, intersecting with Dada. Thus, the *calligrammes* of Francis Picabia share in the turbulent attitudes of *mot-librisme*. Another painter-poet, Pierre Albert-Birot, swam in the European avant-garde current; as a writer, he penned *calligrammes* and other letter games, such as *Poèmes à hurler et à danser* (Poems to bellow and dance to). His review *Sic*, founded in 1916, welcomed both Cubism and Futurism. Establishing links with Dadaism, Pierre Albert-Birot explained that "the initials of the words *Sons, Idées, Couleurs*, say, in Latin, yes [that is "*sic*"] to life, and offer defiance, in midst of war, to the powers of death and despair."[34]

Through art, as well as through literature, and often through both, (typo)graphic creation found a number of expressive outlets in the French avant-garde around the middle of the 1910s. Owing to its very disparity, however, this research cannot be identified as a movement nor encapsulated in an "-ism" (unlike, for instance, Futurism, *mot-librisme* [*parole in libertà*], Cubo-Futurism, or Vorticism). They were composite phenomena that absorbed the work of writers, artists, and sculptors, but stood apart from the direct violence paraded by the Futurists and the revolutionary proclamations, tub-thumping, and squabbling of other movements.

Dada: revolt and derision

One movement intent on brandishing the avant-garde flame good and high emerged right in the middle of the war. To start with, Dada's alarm calls were against the state of society and the tragedy of the war, excoriations of "bourgeois" culture and all its values. The year 1916 was a terrible one: the conflict, although practically a stalemate, left an unimaginable toll of death and injury. Resistant to any attempt at rational explanation, Dada, in Tristan Tzara's eyes, represents "a state of mind [...] useless like everything else in life."[35] He went on to proclaim: "Dada means nothing." The Dadaists recoiled from academism and all forms of institution, from theory, and from assimilation to any specific style. Unsettling at the very least, the movement was grounded in contradiction, derision, self-mockery, and humor; in the ridiculous, the strange, and the unpredictability of the absurd; in the bewildering power of negation, in anger, outrageousness, and nonsense. The whole was condensed into formulas, such as "yes = no."

The movement was launched in Zurich by several artists and writers who had sought refuge in Switzerland during the war. In February 1916, the poet Hugo Ball, with his partner Emmy Hennings, both immigrants to the city from Germany, opened the Cabaret Voltaire. There, art, literature, and linguistic performance were to be harnessed in new ways, inspired by the radical experiments of Futurism, including their public readings. The Dada team included Richard Huelsenbeck (also from Germany), Jean Arp (from France), and Tristan Tzara and Marcel Janco (both from Romania). Events were staged in 1916 and 1917: exhibitions were organized, Hugo Ball offered lectures on Kandinsky, and the Cabaret Voltaire presented works by Marinetti, Apollinaire, and Cendrars. Here, as elsewhere, constant cultural interchange played a part in a dazzlingly dynamic environment.

The desire to hybridize the arts, or at least to harness them together, thus found a new expressive outlet. Against a backdrop of barracking and subversion, through Dada printing and graphics entered into still closer relations with writing, poetry, and periodicals, as well as with the sounds of reading. The crucial issue was to break linguistic habits and hijack meaning through completely original interconnections or associations between letters, words, syllables, and signs; resulting in strings of incongruous utterances such as "*rendre prendre entre rendre rendre prendre prendre / endran drandre / iuuuuuuuupht / là où oiseau nuit 1000 chante sur le grillage.*"[36] Responding to the catastrophe of the war, artists expressed themselves through fragments, chance, and processes like collage and montage. Taken as a

whole, these ingredients, already tried out by Cubism and Futurism, transfigured graphic and typographical vocabularies. Dada, however, presents an uneven attitude to graphic media, with leaflets, pamphlets, handbills, texts and collages taking up the lion's share, with rather fewer posters. Hugo Ball pulled the fabric of language apart to create phonetic poems made up of aural or visual rhythms. The review *Dada* featured extremely diverse page-settings and composition. The movement's struggle, then, was against anything and everything that functioned as a system, appealing instead to the imagination and opening up new horizons.

Away from Zurich, Dadaism appeared simultaneously in New York. Francis Picabia and Man Ray were among the main figures on that side of the Atlantic, together with Duchamp, whose first *objets trouvés* date to 1913 and 1914. In Europe, Dada made inroads into many nations, in particular Germany (Berlin, Cologne, and later in Hanover with Kurt Schwitters) and France (Tristan Tzara made his entrance into Paris in 1919). In Berlin, the movement morphed into a committed activity and Dadaists plunged into the political free-for-all. There the group coalesced in 1917, and included Raoul Hausmann, John Heartfield, Otto Dix, and Hannah Höch, among others. Germany at that time was being torn apart: the defeat in the war was followed by the abdication of Wilhelm II, the proclamation of the Weimar Republic, and the repression of the Spartakist rising in 1919.[37] In gaining a political wing, Berlin Dada found itself rallying with anarchism or communism; in 1918, John Heartfield and George Grosz adhered to the German Communist Party (KPD), for which they actively campaigned.

Berlin proved a focus for intense activity in photomontage. Highly rated, this new graphic outlet was taken up with equal vigor by the Constructivists. If the invention of photomontage is sometimes ascribed explicitly to Berlin Dada at the end of World War I, the process was also essayed in Russia at the end of the 1910s, and, in addition, had been practiced around the mid-nineteenth century and employed at the beginning of the twentieth century in postcards. The Dadaists however, did invest photomontage with a new visual power and significance, with the process forming part of the overarching contemporary trend for recycling objects and materials.

In Zurich, Dadaists produced collages with paper or scraps of cloth; in Berlin, they would combine fragments of photographs and printed texts. By 1918, Raoul Hausmann, Hannah Höch, and John Heartfield were all practicing photomontage. Their unexpected juxtapositions of images and meanings set up a new semiotic space through which they could express sociopolitical engagement in the form of diatribe, provocation, or denunciation. In the work of the Berlin Dadas photography was to become an almost routine process, second to other distinctive genres of the movement such as photomontage, collage, and appropriation. Messages and expressions could now be propelled into being by the evocative power of the image, with the collages of John Heartfield numbering among the most searing and hard-hitting examples. Indifferent to formal appearance (and still less with anything like an aesthetic dimension), Heartfield aimed to collapse meaning into provocative statements. Tapping straight into reality, his works were reproduced in large numbers in German periodicals.

Dadaist typographical and linguistic experiments were as unparalleled as their approach to photography. In deconstructed page-settings, type and characters mix; the text buckles or advances in serried ranks. If the Futurists sought to deflate the text and the letter, Dada accelerated the linguistic steamroller still more. Humorously or noisily, derisively or nonsensically, Dadaists employed language in fragments and off-cuts, as a reconstituted collage. Dada writing raises eyebrows, turns things inside-out, poses awkward questions: "This summer, elephants will be wearing moustaches—and you"; "make way for the Dada that kills"; "down [with] words"; "Helen telephones better"; "the wind favorable to blue feathers."[38]

306
Hannah Höch, *Von Oben* (From Above), photomontage, 1920.

307
Raoul Hausmann, ABCD (portrait of the artist), 1923–24. Collage and India ink on paper, 16 × 11 in. (40.4 × 28.2 cm).

In Hanover, Kurt Schwitters's protean career exhaustively explored the intersection between typography, writing, poetry, graphics, and art. Although allied to the Dada current, the (typo)graphic oeuvre of this unclassifiable artist was to reach its acme in the 1920s and 1930s. At the beginning of the 1920s, Dada was receding before new artistic tendencies. Some took on its inheritance, such as Surrealism and Neue Sachlichkeit (meaning "New Objectivity," a term in currency from 1923). By means of Verism, for instance, George Grosz avows having "attempted to convince this world that it is ugly, sick, and hypocritical."[39] If Dada certainly galvanized the situation, the nonsense, negation, and contradictions it preached verged on self-destruction, and, like other avant-garde currents, its lifespan was necessarily limited by its capacity for renewal.

Like Futurism, the eruption of Dada had a significant and durable impact on the graphic firmament. Its experimentation with collage, photomontage, and textual disarticulation opened up new routes for graphics and typography, and echoes of Dada continue to reverberate through the artistic sphere.

308
Johannes Baader, *Gutenberggedenkblatt* (Homage to Gutenberg), 1920. Collage, 13 3/4 × 18 1/2 in. (35 × 46.5 cm).

The 1910s: a turbulent avant-garde

Dada's fading star heralded the close of a particularly energetic phase for the avant-garde. From Cubism to Dada, artistic currents tended to be innovative, radical, nonconformist, virulent, and even shocking or violent. After World War I, militant and provoking attitudes were replaced by calmer, more measured practices. The issues of man and his environment or the sociopolitical context remained on the agenda but were tackled very differently. Revolutionary or rebellious movements, with their close ties to painting and literature, also contributed to a revival in the applied arts, which, in the 1920s and 1930s, were to turn increasingly to concepts such as functionalism, rationalism, and Constructivism. The avant-garde enthusiasm of the 1910s brought with it a wholly new dynamic, forging utopian ideals and affording fresh impetus to the union of the arts. Already at work, function-orientated control and a search for effectiveness were being actively pursued as the war drew to a close: movements such as De Stijl, Constructivism, and the Bauhaus appear as consolidated and more organized forms of earlier endeavors. In addition to Italy, Russia, France, and Germany, other Western countries were contributing to the ongoing (typo)graphic renaissance, including England and the United States, formerly predisposed to traditional approaches. In one telling sign of the times, the 1913 Armory Show in New York proved to be a truly groundbreaking exhibition of modern art. New initiatives appeared over the horizon in the fields of graphics, typographical design, and the creation of typefaces. The year 1914 brought the foundation in the United States of an organization dedicated to graphics—the American Institute of Graphic Arts (AIGA).

Since the turn of the century, magazine illustration had been dominated by a popular genre, an essential component of the success of many periodicals that preceded the emergence of graphics in more contemporary styles. If British practices remained strongly anchored in tradition, they were gradually being overtaken by more up-to-date styles influenced by Vorticism and other forms of expression. Some pioneering achievements heralded this change loud and clear. Signage in the London Underground, for instance, was subjected to a significant graphic and typographical rethink. From the end of the 1910s, the transport network obtained a special alphabet of its own (a considerable number of avant-garde typefaces in the same vein are in fact later, dating from the 1920s or beginning of the 1930s). For the purpose, calligrapher Edward Johnston conceived a sans serifs face, called Underground Railway Sans, or just plain Underground.[40] The typeface, for the system's exclusive use, was ordered in the mid-1910s by Frank Pick, at the time the subway's sales manager. The design of the type had been completed by Johnston in 1916 and was cut in 1918. The letters of the alphabet, created from simple geometrical forms, are unvaried in stroke thickness. In what was by all accounts a trailblazing move, the calligrapher had come up with a new type, the "geometric sans serif," which became very much in vogue in interwar researches (Johnston's letterform has remained in use on the London Underground, slightly altered and now called New Johnston). Johnston also redesigned the company's visual identity at the end of the 1910s. Thanks to the personality of Frank Pick, who commissioned Johnston and was in charge of London Transport's communication and promotion departments, typefaces, posters, and corporate styling created for this account have acquired a worthy place in the pantheon of British commercial styling. Many of these orders for transport signage were specially created by graphic designers and typographers in what proved to be an exceptional case of collaboration between professionals and industrialists (or public services). Like many other pioneering experiments begun in the first decades of the twentieth century, it has echoes of Peter Behrens's earlier endeavors for the AEG company, or, later, in the design identities sought by the Olivetti company or the Dutch post office.

In many respects, the avant-garde of the time was exceptionally rich and complex. It combined a utopian dimension with an acute awareness of everyday realities. Expressionism had let out a howl of anguish at the human condition, while Cubism took up the most humdrum materials and reassembled them; Futurism banged the drum for the industrial age, while Dada banged the table in outrage. If graphics and typography found a place in each of these movements, their practices could not be said to be part of design proper, being rather symptoms of an eagerness to forge new artistic and literary forms. The idealism of Art Nouveau and the historicism of the Arts and Crafts movement were but a distant memory. In a sudden crescendo, art was uprooting its aesthetic values and references. Artists and writers of the 1910s threw themselves into high-flown experiments with the word, the voice, and sound; on screams, slogans, manifestos, fragments, and photography; on the broken image, on assembly, disassembly, and reassembly. The dust stirred up by this maelstrom of the imagination, this tornado of meaning and perception, settled to reveal unexpected perspectives—sculptural, visual, textual, auditory and perceptive—which constituted, to a certain extent, fertile ground for both typography and graphics.

309
Anonymous, range of enamel plaques for Odol mouthwash, Germany, c. 1920. Relief plaques, 19 $^3/_4$ × 12 in. (50 × 30 cm).

310
Lucian Bernhard, enamel plaque for Manoli cigarettes, Germany, c. 1910. Curved plate, 23 $^1/_2$ × 29 $^1/_2$ in. (60 × 75 cm).

311
Anonymous, enamel plaque for Odol mouthwash, Germany, c. 1910. Curved plate, 7 $^3/_4$ × 15 $^1/_2$ in. (19.5 × 39.5 cm).

309

311

310

World War I

The poster as propaganda weapon

The war years transformed the geography of the artistic and cultural landscape, curtailing or redirecting developments in the avant-garde. The bloodletting echoed the violence of Futurist attitudes as expressed in 1909 by Marinetti in his first manifesto: "We want to glorify war—the only hygiene for the world—militarism, patriotism [...] our heart [...] is fed by fire, hatred, and speed." Not one to mince words, Marinetti identified art and literature with a cry of rage: "We wish to exalt outbursts of aggression [...], the slap and the punch [...]. Because art can be nothing but violence, cruelty, and injustice."[41] As war broke out, the world waded into a bloodbath, the result of defensive nationalisms, of the protection of state borders and colonies. As the forces of the industrial complex were marshaled in the unfolding destruction, the voices of humanism were drowned out. The population had only a dim perception of the terrible scale of the conflict since it was, partially at least, deliberately hidden from their eyes. In their desire to sway the masses, the leaders of the countries involved were quick to appreciate the propaganda power of the poster. During the period 1914–18, commercial advertising thus necessarily took a backseat to political and war posters. These constituted a powerful tool in the battle to convince the people of the justice of the cause and to urge them on in the war effort both at the Front and back home.

Praising courage and heroism, or else appealing to the safety of the family or fatherland, these posters were sometimes insidious, other times baldly imperative: "Your country needs you," "On les aura!" ("We'll get'em!" or "Up and at'em!"), "Fate tutti il vostro dovere" ("Do your duty to the full"), "Souscrivez!" ("Subscribe!"), "I Want You...," or simply "Go!" A highly effective propaganda tool, the poster was also a useful lever for applying pressure. By means of accusatorial, finger-pointing slogans, those harboring misgivings about the war effort could be cast as treacherous shirkers or dishonest cowards: "Be honest with yourself." "Be certain that your so-called reason is not a selfish excuse." "Enlist today." "Daddy, what did *you* do in the Great War?" and others besides.

Governments in the nations at war set up propaganda units or entrusted the task to specialized organizations, sometimes calling upon reputable poster artists and illustrators, such as Ludwig Hohlwein and Lucian Bernhard in Germany, Théophile Alexandre Steinlen in France, or James Montgomery Flagg in the United States. Depending on the country, the war poster took on a very different face, reflecting each land's expertise and attitudes. German artists, for example, capitalized on recent developments in advertising, in particular in channeling the impact of the *Sachplakat*. In Great Britain and the United States, popular press illustration (in the ascendancy since the turn of the century) from now on served more belligerent ends. In addition, the use of the poster altered as the conflict wore on.

Some early war posters featured solely text—just like the political or administrative bills issued over the centuries by monarchies and governments in the West. Soon, however, the powers that be grasped the potential impact of pictures in the public space. Written appeals were now seconded by billboards, which derived their power from an image that, taken in at a glance, communicated directly, making its point and remaining etched in the public memory—be it unconsciously. The image's ability to persuade and convince was soon being requisitioned by every side in the ordeal. No matter that the dead, wounded, and POWs could henceforth be

312
Jules Abel Faivre, government loan poster,
On les aura! 2ᵉ emprunt de la défense nationale.
Souscrivez (Up and at 'em! 2nd National Defense
Loan. Subscribe Now!), Paris, 1916.

313
Achille Mauzan, poster, *Fate tutti il vostro dovere*
(Do Your Duty to the Full) created for Credito
italiano, Milan, 1917. Chromolithograph.

314
Alfred Leete, recruitment poster, *Join Your
Country's Army*, Great Britain, c. 1915.
Shows Lord Kitchener, minister of war.
Artwork used previously in 1914 on the cover
of a periodical with a different title.

counted in hundreds of thousands, poster artwork was careful not to mirror the appalling cost of the conflagration. At the beginning of World War I, posters turned a blind eye to the pain and suffering, drawing a discreet veil over the dramatic reality of battle. Pictures of the period preferred to accumulate positive images that were vigorous and heartening. The human figure became omnipresent, sometimes in the form of one or two individuals, at others with a raised fist or a pair of boots standing in for humanity as whole.

If graphic style differed from country to country, the language of the poster seemed to forge a rhetoric answering a specific need. The power of photography and photomontage had hitherto been relatively under-exploited, mostly for technical reasons, and the war poster reverted to illustration or limited itself to the written word. Historians have tended to stress the aesthetic poverty of printed materials during the war (weakness in drawing, want of plastic qualities, etc.), but this observation cannot be said to hold good for the entire visual production of the time and many surprising counterexamples can be quoted. Sometimes manifestly unrelated to the formal daring of the avant-garde, war iconography tended to address itself to the masses, to the population at large in the countryside and in the factories. Its crucial aim was to use pictures, symbols, and slogans to persuade, to win over minds, to lead the way, to hammer the point home. On the surface offering social cohesion or models for citizenship, these posters in fact vehicled exhortations or injunctions. Their main function is not to inform, nor to clarify events, still less to pacify; their aim, employing skills and tricks acquired in advertising, was to control the way people behave in time of war. In pleading their case, they deployed an entire raft of themes (some of which were to find favor with the dictatorships of the interwar period): patriotism, nationalism, work, the family, the soil, hearth and home, and the figure of the military man, as both father and hero.

A second genre pleaded for funds or belt-tightening, calling attention to the increasing demand for working women (to replace men in the fields and factories), as well as launching charity campaigns and appeals for moral support, etc. The poster was also used as a recruiting aid in lands where military conscription was not at first on the statute book—Great Britain, and then in the United States in 1917, for example. "Your country needs you," Lord Kitchener, then minister for war, appealed on a famous British poster by Alfred Leete. "I want *you* for the US Army," bawled Uncle Sam (as drawn by James Montgomery Flagg), wagging his finger at the passerby.

Germany

Graphically speaking, the German poster features some particularly interesting examples. Whereas France had passed through a golden age of advertising during the final decades of the nineteenth century, the period leading from 1900 to the outbreak of war seems to have been particularly fertile in Germany, and the art of the poster had already reached a distinguished level. Poster artists who had been productive since the beginning of the century now put their shoulder behind the war effort, such as Lucian Bernhard, Ludwig Hohlwein, Julius Gipkens, and Hans Rudi Erdt. After 1914, this still relatively recent medium shifted its emphasis from cultural promotion or commercial advertising towards propaganda. One of the more significant poster artists of the 1914–18 period was Ludwig Hohlwein, already an important prewar figure who was also to pursue his career during the rise of Nazism. Graphic styles explored in Germany since the turn of the twentieth century now found themselves transferring to the war poster: flat blocks of color, contrast, care in lettering, close links between text and image, concision, an aesthetic dimension, etc. The culture of the poster—a German constant—consolidated and fed into wartime graphics, benefiting from a preexisting sensitivity on behalf of the public to such material. Moreover, during the conflict, magazines and exhibitions reproduced and publicized posters issued by the enemy; German posters thus entered a kind of competition that contributed further to their uptake.

315

315
Berliner Illustrirte Zeitung, front page from n°. 16, April 16, 1916.

Great Britain

Wartime graphics in England exploited many of the themes common elsewhere: male heroism, female dignity and courage, family values, the might and unity of the Allies, charity appeals, accusations of fence-sitting, condemnation of enemy atrocities, and so on. Since conscription was not yet instituted in Great Britain (the introduction of obligatory service dates from 1916), garnering volunteers became an urgent matter; recruiting posters and other printed matter hence became an essential component of general mobilization. A particularly effective tactic was to reproduce visuals in various formats and in several color schemes. Before being turned into a poster, in 1914, Leete's famous Lord Kitchener composition had been used as a magazine cover. The portrayal of the minister is one of the most famous British posters of World War I. To fully appreciate its impact one has to imagine what such an image represented at the time; illustrated posters printed in color were a rather recent phenomenon and the masses were less attuned to the propaganda potential of visual messages. What could be more striking for the collective consciousness than the face and outstretched hand of the minister for war in person, asking for the help of each able-bodied man? Such an image combines the effectiveness of the *Sachplakat* (making its point in a direct and concise way), the properties of a montage, and the communicational potency of chromatic realism. The composition is arranged so that, together with the slogan, the model's face and hand encapsulate the essence of the message, hammered home through a powerful deployment of the demonstrative function of the poster itself in the shape of a symbolically charged personification. The oversized word "You" is perceived before all the other eye-catching and imperative terms. An icon of the early use of persuasive power in wartime, this poster does not employ hints and nudges to attract volunteers; it orders you to do so, as it is already couched in the terms of an order.

Much artwork partakes of a similar category of message. Some forms use women and children: images of worthy housewives inciting their husbands to enlist, or, in a scene set after the war, youngsters innocently asking their father what his role was during the conflict. Among the main figures in British poster art during wartime, Frank Brangwyn and Gerald Spencer Pryse designed recruiting posters. Brangwyn's graphics, in which drawing plays an essential role, exude a serious atmosphere, rather like Steinlen's offerings in France. Following the example of many other graphic designers and illustrators, including John Hassall, Brangwyn was an official war artist and worked for the Parliamentary Recruiting Committee.

Here, as in other countries, services specializing in propaganda relied on the potential of the poster, collaborating actively with poster artists. The demands and nature of propaganda were fulfilled by huge print-runs (these will be equally impressive, if not more so, during World War II). By the end of 1915 it is likely that between two and three million posters had already been issued in Britain. As elsewhere, the searing reality was often masked from view, and the actual progress of the engagements and their repercussions on the ground were swept under the carpet. Courage and heroism were of course much in evidence, combined with compelling, even imperative injunctions to join up. Divorced from the horror of the Front, posters exhorted men to sign on the dotted line. In step with the poster, the press, too, sifted the news and overlooked the hardships of the battlefield.

In Britain, war imagery seemed to emphasize the psychological or civic dimension, highlighting the duties incumbent upon the men (or, failing this, denouncing their cowardice), the resignation of the womenfolk, and their joint responsibility to the children—or else stressing the necessity for the war and hence for its untold violence.

France

The themes exploited in the poster in France overlap with those in other countries: family, motherland, courage, national symbols, etc. The contribution of talented draftsmen, who had been active before the war, produced (as in Germany, although along different lines) powerful

316

316
Théophile Alexandre Steinlen, poster for a day in support of the infantryman, *Journée du poilu organisée par le parlement*, France, 1915.

175

317
Maurice Neumont, poster, *On ne passe pas!*
(No-one gets past!) *1914–1918*, France, 1918.
Chromolithograph.

318
Jules Abel Faivre, government loan poster,
3ᵉ emprunt de la défense nationale.
Crédit Lyonnais. Souscrivez, France, 1917.
Chromolithograph.

319
Marcel Falter, government loan poster, *Emprunt
national. Société générale. Pour le suprême effort*,
France, 1918. Chromolithograph.

320
Jean Droit, government loan poster, *Souscrivez
au 3ᵉ emprunt de la défense nationale*, France,
1917.

321
B. Chavannaz, national loan poster,
Emprunt national, France, 1918.

imagery of high quality. This is the case with posters designed by Théophile Alexandre Steinlen and Jean-Louis Forain.

At the beginning of the century Steinlen had already made himself a witness to his time, forging a personal style with documentary leanings. At the same time draftsman, lithographer, poster artist, and painter, during the war Steinlen developed an expressiveness of gesture, portraying new situations; his posters are often reproductions of thorough pencil sketches. Besides draftsmen already recognized for their artistry, an upcoming generation of *affichistes* were emerging into the limelight, such as Jules Abel Faivre, Francisque Poulbot, and Fouqueray. A well-known poster by Jules Abel Faivre of 1916, exhorting passersby to subscribe to a loan, shows a valiant, robust-looking soldier, exclaiming: "*On les aura*". His right hand is on his rifle, his left is held high in the air, stretched out diagonally across the entire poster; his expression is both optimistic and trustworthy. If such a visual seems to some extent unconcerned with avant-garde graphic idioms, it is no less effective and hard-hitting for that—surely one of the mainsprings of its appeal. Minutely delineated, Faivre's poster is based on a partially narrative and realist style that speaks directly to a mass audience accustomed over the decades to such illustrations in the popular press. The thrilling vision dangled in front of passersby here is once again strong and positive—a far cry from the true horror of war. Many miles from posters of this kind, in October 1915, Henri Barbusse noted that "everything had been turned over, full of rot and debris. It feels like a cataclysm [...]. The stench of a mass grave. One walks on shrapnel, on broken weapons, with, everywhere, live shells, tattered pieces of equipment, dubious-looking heaps of clothing clogged in brownish mud. A few corpses. One really fresh."[42]

The United States

322

THAT LIBERTY SHALL NOT PERISH FROM THE EARTH BUY LIBERTY BONDS
FOURTH   LIBERTY   LOAN

322
Joseph Pennell, poster, *That Liberty Shall Not Perish from the Earth*, United States, 1918. Lithograph.

Drawing and illustration played an equally essential role in the American war poster. If the nation entered the conflict comparatively late, in 1917, the government quickly set up structures responsible for getting its point across. The Division of Pictorial Publicity was established (an organization that paid particular attention to the aesthetic value of posters), as well as the Division of Advertising and the Committee on Public Information, also created in 1917. A governmental propaganda-orientated body, the mission of this last was to channel public opinion by organizing exhibitions and lectures, preparing broadcasts, issuing posters, and so on. The goal was to win round a population that until then had proven less than wholehearted in its support of the nation's entry into the war. The government did its best to commandeer the persuasive power of imagery, employing techniques related to various advertising devices. To inculcate its message as broadly as possible, the government's propaganda services printed huge volumes of material, purchasing industrial quantities of space. Print-runs for posters reached stratospheric levels, from ten thousand to a million copies. Some posters seemed destined for blanket coverage, such as the famous depiction of Uncle Sam by James Montgomery Flagg. It represents an alternative of Alfred Leete's equally famous British poster. The drawing is livelier in the American version, however, and the figure appears less stiff, less overbearing, and more expressive, while the text—"I want you..."—appears as a strap-line beneath the image. The star-spangled hat—another graphic embellishment—also symbolizes the nation and focuses the message on the idea of recruitment. This poster was printed in an extraordinary five million copies.

American propaganda services set great store by the quality of the image. Many posters, however, were content to rehash or hark back to preexisting material. In addition to James Montgomery Flagg, among the principal poster artists active in the United States were Charles Dana Gibson (a renowned press illustrator who was brought in to oversee the Division of Pictorial Publicity), Howard Chandler Christy (another press and book illustrator), Joseph Pennell (who had been well known from the 1880s), Maxfield Parrish, Fred Spear, and Fred G. Cooper. This last, also a type designer, based many of his posters around text, although he would also choose powerful images redolent of German posters.

In its major themes, American war graphics resorted to the kind of incentives already prevalent in Europe: recruitment drives (conscription had not yet been introduced), appeals to women to take on voluntary work, loan appeals in support of the war effort, etc. Sometimes the American tone seems more incisive, more direct, sharper-edged. One peremptory harangue hit home: "We fight, you give." According to American poster artist and illustrator Charles Buckles Falls, a picture on a wall has to have something aggressive about it: "a poster should be for the eye what a shouted demand is to the ear."[43]

In time of war: the poster in new garb

Each in its manner and according to specific means of organization and strategies, the various countries involved in the war developed propaganda of their own that was to exist as a necessary and permanent communication channel linking the authorities with the masses. If the themes deployed drew on a common repertoire, the images they gave rise to were far from identical. Italian posters, for example, are sometimes described as visually impoverished and graphically weak. In countries distant from the battlefront, such as Australia, the reality of the conflict was not concealed to the same extent, and cruelty and horror made an appearance on posters.

In Russia, the revolutions of 1917 saw war imagery ousted by political sloganeering. The support of many avant-garde artists for the Bolshevik Revolution occasioned a huge upswing in graphic production of great quality (posters, newspapers, books, and printed matter generally), often in a pre-Constructivist vein. Switzerland and the Netherlands, neutral during the war, were two important havens for the avant-garde during the conflict; it was in Zurich that the Dada movement came into being in 1916, while the Netherlands saw the development of Mondrian's Neoplasticism, as well as the De Stijl movement after 1917.

For the countries engaged in the conflict, the years 1916 and 1917 accentuated the crisis. The disastrous stalemate seemed ready to drag on without end. In Great Britain, Italy, and France, protest erupted in strikes and civil unrest. In reaction, the propaganda only hardened. World War I sapped Europe's vitals, leaving the countries involved bloodless and practically in ruins. Overall, the death toll ran to nearly twenty million—almost as many in the civil population as among the armies—not counting the millions maimed. Such realities scarcely surface on the posters, produced and manipulated to perform a different task. With relatively little competition from other media of comparable appeal and impact, it was the poster that played the crucial role in the years 1914–18. As a support, in 1914–18 the poster offered many advantages, being relatively inexpensive and permitting the dissemination of powerful messages. Moreover, drawing enabled the artist to produce a complete graphic composition from scratch: the artist is not forced to represent, or even to refer to, reality, and is far from obliged to inform. And if avant-garde tendencies had been to an extent on hold during the war, immediately afterwards avant-garde energies were once again being channeled into trends and schools. Traumatized by the drama of the war, art regained its vitality, reactivated, and endeavored to set itself up on a different footing with respect to reality. The applied arts became more abstract in their language, paving the way to Functionalism. Detaching themselves from aesthetic idealism, and turning their backs on violent Futurist utopias, artists and creators tried to make themselves useful, to reengage with life. At the same time, incipient currents in painting, such as Neue Sachlichkeit and Surrealism, were on the brink of opening up fresh perspectives for art.

323
Anonymous, poster, *Buy United States War Savings Stamps*, United States, 1918. Lithograph.

324
Arthur S. Mole and John D. Thomas, *The Human US Shield: 30,000 Officers and Men at Camp Custer*, Battle Creek, Michigan, 1918. Silver halide print, 12 ³/₄ × 10 ¹/₄ in. (32.5 × 26.2 cm).

325
James Montgomery Flagg, *Boys and Girls! You Can Help Your Uncle Sam Win the War. Save your Quarters. Buy War Savings Stamps*, United States (undated). Chromolithograph,
2 ft. 5 ¹/₂ in. × 3 ft. 6 ¹/₄ in. (75 × 105 cm).

326
Anonymous, poster, *Finish the Job. Subscribe to the "Victory" Liberty Loan*, 1918. Chromolithograph.

327
Anonymous, print, *We Own War Savings Stamps*, United States, c. 1918. Lithograph.

Continuation and reconstruction in the avant-garde

By the end of World War I, several European countries found themselves on the critical list. The morale of the population was at a low ebb, the economy on its knees, and social protest was brewing. New political regimes were soon in place. On the artistic and cultural levels, the avant-gardes of the first two decades of the twentieth century continued defying earlier tendencies in an openly challenging frenzy of daring, surprising, dissenting, and/or subversive innovations. This period of avant-garde activity was prolonged by currents that aspired to participate in reconstruction (on the social, political, economic, and cultural fronts) or to subject society to critical scrutiny.

The turbulent events of the end of the 1910s led many artists and designers to orientate their efforts towards developing a new and better society. In the immediate postwar period, an entire section of the avant-garde was intent on reconstruction, moving away as much from Futurist extremism as Dada raillery. The burning issue was how to revive the failing environment and improve daily life.

By and large, this new direction, motivated in the main by the effects of the war and the resultant crises, embraced industrial machinery and techniques, and plastic artists and visualizers began to ponder over such questions as utility, function, clarity, effectiveness, and communication. Preoccupied by the sociopolitical situation, some threw off completely the aims of "art for art's sake" and set about making their art useful. Increasingly, artists and intellectuals, often highly politicized, consigned so-called "bourgeois" ideals to the scrap heap.

This reconfiguration of artistic practice valorized art's social component, such as *la forme utile* (useful form) and functionalism. In architecture, as in other branches of the decorative and applied arts, functionalism came to the fore around 1920. Louis Sullivan's famous edict formulated in 1896—"form [...] follows function"—was to be followed to the letter between the wars. In a quest for contemporary solutions in step with reality, novel visual languages were framed around concepts such as structure and limpidity. The aesthetics resulting from this attitude tended to privilege formal simplification. Ornament and decoration, already decried in the prewar period, were now regarded as obsolete. The genesis of form was closely bound to the importance accorded to function—or rather to the manner of conceiving and defining function. It was an approach that had been foretold already in certain works by the Chicago School, the Wiener Werkstätte, and the German Werkbund. Gaining ground increasingly in the 1920s, this was a tendency that affected the visual and plastic arts, architecture, graphics, typography, design, and furniture-making. In Russia, the Constructivists posed the question of the role of art in society. In Germany, the concept of functionalism underwent significant developments in the 1920s, as attested by the Bauhaus's change in direction.

Europe-wide communication between artists was just as rich: links between Moscow and Berlin developed apace and relations also accelerated between Germany and the Netherlands. Periodicals such as *Blok, Dada, Der Sturm, De Stijl, Die Aktion, Het Overzicht, i 10, Lef, L'Esprit nouveau, Ma, Mécano, Merz,* and *391,* and so on, purveyed information, and diffused new ideas and works from city to city in durable form. These movements left their mark on graphics and typography, impregnating them with the ideals they vehicled. One of the guiding principles of this graphic renaissance led to conciseness and concentration that increased the effectiveness of message transmission, thereby gaining, according to need, impact or legibility. Typography played its part in these researches and advanced on new foundations. The incorporation of photography into the graphic realm, in conjunction with processes of montage and collage, unseated the primacy of drawing and led to far-reaching developments.

The crucial steps seem to have been taken in central and Eastern Europe, in Russia in particular, and at the geographical crossroads that was Germany. Other countries, including the Netherlands, Switzerland, Czechoslovakia, and Poland, also witnessed significant levels of activity. Creatives contributed fruitfully to this renewal of (typo)graphic idiom, following in the wake of artistic and literary experiments. Insights of earlier avant-garde movements were to be soft-pedaled or reworked. Numerous, often multitalented designers and artists played a decisive role: Alexander Rodchenko, El Lissitzky, László Moholy-Nagy, Herbert Bayer, Kurt Schwitters, Jan Tschichold, Theo Van Doesburg, Piet Zwart, Karel Teige, and Henryk Berlewi, as well as others. In the graphic field, many of their explorations coalesced into a phenomenon dubbed the "Neue Typographie."[44]

The Russian dynamic: Constructivism

Even before the end of World War I, the Russian contribution to the avant-garde revival had been outstanding. Under the wing of the Russian Revolution, forerunners of Constructivism drew their sources from Suprematism. From 1917 to the end of the 1920s, the tendency crept into many of the visual arts, particularly the applied arts. Vladimir Tatlin and Alexander

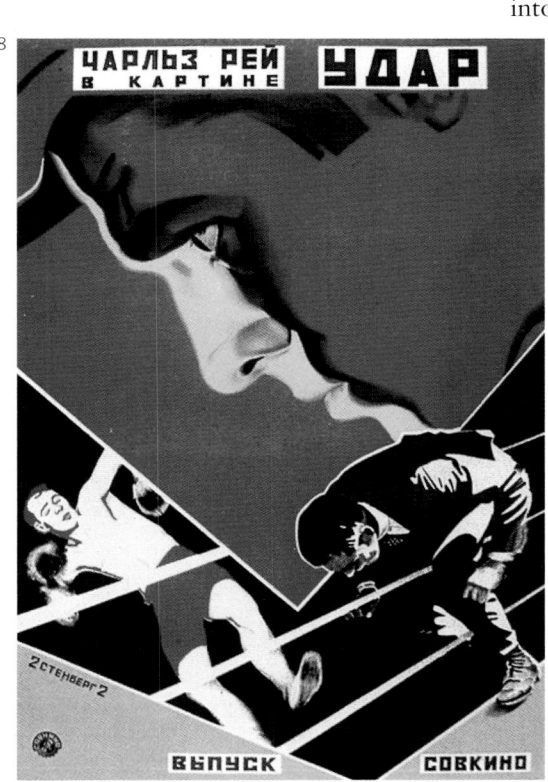

328

Rodchenko were among the principal representatives of Constructivism, to which other great names adhered, such as El Lissitzky, Gustav Klutsis, Liubov Popova, Varvara Stepanova (Rodchenko's partner) and Alexei Gan. In the first half of the 1910s, Russian protagonists had already started or joined several avant-garde currents, in particular Futurism, Cubo-Futurism, Rayonism, and Suprematism. Artists and poets thus discovered new outlets for their talents, from which some astonishing and original graphic and typographical projects emerged.

Functionalism, which made inroads simultaneously in Western Europe, also found a place in Russia, taking on a special form. In Constructivism, defined, to some extent, by sociopolitical ideals, art was to link up with the utopian plan of reframing society. A number of Russian intellectuals and artists had been overtaken by revolutionary zeal, and together with, and in the service of, the Bolshevik Revolution, their avowed aim was social change. Some adhered without further ado to the urge to transform the environment and table new political agendas. In a society in flux, the stake was to rebuild it while taking into account the consequences of industrialization. Consequently, machines, factories, production plants, and technologies were to be used to lever in transformations in practical existence. "We have no need of a mausoleum for art in which to worship dead works, but of living factories of the human spirit: in the streets, in the trams, in the factories, in the workshops and the workers' homes,"[45] declared Vladimir Mayakovsky in 1918 in a tone Marinetti would have endorsed. In 1922, Alexei Gan clarified the way the movement was heading: "The time of the social and the rational is upon us [...]. Everything must be thought through technically and functionally."[46]

Opposed to "art for art's sake" and promoting instead a utilitarian art, the principal partisans of Constructivism eschewed all aesthetic and formal ideals and all religious and philosophical subordination. Like a number of movements before them (such as the Wiener Werkstätte), Russian Constructivists programmed an art for the people, and dreamed of making society just and egalitarian. This ideal seemed on the brink of becoming a reality as a new government came to power. A substantial Constructivist wing rushed to the aid of the state propaganda machine. Rather than developing along aesthetic lines, its beginnings were marked by enthusiastic political commitment, as well as a belief in technology and functionalism.

328
Georgii and Vladimir Stenberg, poster for the film *Scrap Iron* (Charles Ray, United States, 1921), Soviet Union, 1926. Chromolithograph, 3 ft. 6 ¼ in. × 2 ft. 4 ¼ in. (105 × 72 cm).

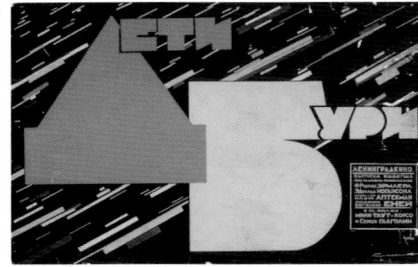

329
Mikhail Wechsler, poster for the film *Children of the Storm*, Soviet Union, 1926.
2 ft. 3 ¹/₂ in. × 3 ft. 5 ³/₄ in. (70 × 106 cm).

330
Anonymous, poster for the film *The Symphony of the Donbass* (Dziga Vertov), Soviet Union, 1931. Chromolithograph, 24 ³/₄ × 34 ¹/₄ in. (63 × 87 cm).

331
Georgii and Vladimir Stenberg, poster for the film *The General* (Buster Keaton, United States, 1926), Soviet Union, 1929. Chromolithograph, 3 ft. 6 ¹/₂ in. × 2 ft. 6 in. (108 × 71 cm).

Not all subscribed to these new, sometimes radical, orientations. A scission occurred in 1921, between partisans of productivism and a utilitarian conception on the one hand (such as Vladimir Tatlin), and certain painters and artists on the other, like Malevich, Kandinsky, and the brothers Naum Gabo and Antoine Pevsner, who were intent on safeguarding the autonomy and spiritual dimension of art. El Lissitzky took up a midway position, while the advocates of utilitarian art formed a school in which productivism, dedicated to the realization of utilitarian articles, made a stand. Against the backdrop of a worsening economic situation, artists believed that, by lining up in the service of the community, they might develop solutions that would end mass poverty. Forging new formal perspectives, Constructivism and the tendencies associated with it explored any number of fields in the creative and visual arts: architecture, set design, industrial design, furniture, fashion, painting, cinema, photography, and so on. Many media from the busy sectors of graphics and typography participated in and were altered by these trends, in particular, posters (for books, films, etc.), publishing (including children's books), periodicals (covers and page-layout), and visual poetry. Essential to the rejuvenation of graphics, Constructivism took a decisive step by its individual use of photomontage, hugely extending its range of uses.

Graphics and typography

Sorely lacking in materials, Russian artists were not always able to attain their objectives. Their three-dimensional creations were not inevitably followed by industrial production—far from it. Many projects for newspaper and bookselling kiosks, for example, remained only models. On the other hand, the graphic arts and visual expression underwent phenomenal developments. In the service of the new Communist Bolshevik State, media proliferated, constituting an ideal propaganda weapon for the ruling ideology in the battle for hearts and minds. Within this framework, around 1920, graphics, typography, and photography sparked sometimes spectacular changes on the formal level. If Cubism, Futurism, and Dadaism had already shaken up the art world, Constructivism in its turn ushered in a vocabulary and a

332
Vladimir Mayakovsky, Rosta Window, extract from a series of posters on current events in politics, economics, and military life, 1920.

333
Varvara Stepanova, Alexander Rodchenko in a clown's costume, 1924. One of a series of projects for geometrically designed costumes created for a book evening given at the Academy of Social Education.

grammar capable of being formed into highly innovative compositions strongly inspired by the rigor and concision of Suprematism. The palette of Alexander Rodchenko and El Lissitzky, for example, frequently combines black and red (in the past a feature of both ancient manuscripts and incunabula), guaranteeing impact and contrast.

Among the various supports involved, the poster was one of the more predominant and had made great strides by the turn of the 1920s and in following years. In 1924, an exhibition was organized in Moscow entitled *Six Years of Posters*. In addition to the use of color, a raft of initiatives led to a revolution in visual practice that, in the poster, combined the introduction of photography, ample recourse to geometry and to the diagonal, dynamic juxtapositions, and the exploration of divers montage processes. Many posters were produced to promote state publications, including films and books (with slogans such as "books underpin the construction of socialism"). Rodchenko, the brothers Georgii and Vladimir Stenberg, Varvara Stepanova, and Vladimir Mayakovsky were particularly active in these fields. The Stenberg brothers created a process of their own, often basing designs on photographs or photograms projected onto a wall using an apparatus developed for this specific purpose. Propaganda for the state industries, too, was in full cry. Print-runs for a poster could reach twenty thousand.

Numerous visual materials explored the power of photomontage, while others stuck to drawing—such as the "Rosta Windows," a series of illustrations created specifically to appeal to the illiterate. The Rosta agency, a state body with the responsibility for communicating current events, was briefed to transmit its message as a sequence of separate, visually arresting images. Vast numbers of these posters were turned out between 1919 and 1922; one hypothesis is that they were plastered over storefronts to conceal the empty shelves inside.

Quite apart from posters, Constructivists designed a number of books, jackets, covers, and page layouts for reviews (*Lef*, *Novy Lef*, *The USSR in Construction*, etc.). Moreover the magazine *Lef* published an article on photomontage in 1924. Sharing the growing interest in the procedure in the 1920s, Alexander Rodchenko, Gustav Klutsis, and Nikolai Prusakov employed it frequently. Like photography, typography played an essential role in Constructivist graphics, as manifest in works by Rodchenko, El Lissitzky, Liubov Popova, Alexei Gan, and Solomon Telingater. For his part, El Lissitzky placed the accent on the optical dimension of the printed text, explaining that "words [...] are not perceived by hearing, but sight [...]. Ideas have to be inculcated using the letters of the alphabet."[47]

If Constructivist typographies and graphics often make their point by powerful and original visuals, this is probably due to the fact that they were made by artists from more than one discipline rather than by specialists in typography. Their research centered on textual form, often characterized as uncluttered and clean-lined, that embraced many experiments— dynamic, new, astonishing or playful, sometimes simple, at other times complex. The vitality and energy of the expression seems often to override legibility. If Russian Constructivism offers a graphic vocabulary that is unique (and, in addition, immediately recognizable by the presence of Cyrillic), it affords many points in common with Western European graphics, in particular German and Dutch.

Schools and contacts; collaborations and repercussions

In the aftermath of the war, exchanges between avant-garde artists remained intense throughout Europe, a phenomenon exemplified by the Berlin–Moscow axis. In 1922, the *Erste russische Kunstausstellung* (First Exhibition of Russian Art) was held in Berlin. A year earlier, El Lissitzky had left his homeland for Germany, meeting Walter Gropius, László Moholy-Nagy, and Theo Van Doesburg in Berlin. In a series of dynamic interactions, he spread Constructivist ideas in Germany, visited the Bauhaus, and collaborated with Kurt Schwitters in Hanover and with Jean Arp in Switzerland. Regarded as a key and influential figure in the forum of interchange between Russia and Western and central Europe, El Lissitzky also established links with the other side of the Atlantic. He contributed to a host of reviews in

334
Anonymous, poster, *The Camera in the Service
of Socialist Edification*, 1931. Chromolithograph,
printed photomechanically, 30 × 21 in.
(71 × 54 cm).

different countries—*Merz* (Germany), *Ma* (Hungary, then Austria), *De Stijl* (the Netherlands), and *Broom* (the United States), among them. Seeping through what was a vast network of interchange, in the 1920s the Constructivist impulse made its way into most of central Europe, crossing many nations—Czechoslovakia, Poland, the Netherlands, Germany, and Switzerland. In Russia, designers and artists were being trained again. Schools of art and teaching programs were reorganized, often on Constructivist or productivist footings. Vhutemas, the High Arts and Technical Workshops, founded by Lenin, opened in Moscow at the end of the war. This establishment, presenting some links with the Bauhaus, embraced industrial design and functionalism; Kandinsky, Tatlin, Rodchenko, and El Lissitzky all taught there. Marc Chagall, for his part, took over the direction of the Fine Arts School in Vitebsk (currently in Belarus) in 1919, offering posts there to Kasimir Malevich and El Lissitzky. In 1920 in Moscow, Inkhuk, the Institute of Artistic Culture, was set up with a program devised by Kandinsky. The following year, Inkhuk—now joined by Rodchenko—abandoned its visual arts program and turned to design and its applications. The plethora of schools and other organizations in synergy with the new artistic practices did much to widen the scope and range of Constructivism and productivism.

Numerous collaborations sprung up between artists, designers, and poets, stimulated by the spirit of collective labor. El Lissitzky busied himself with his famous *Dlja golosa* (For the Voice), a book with origins in a text by Vladimir Mayakovsky, published in 1923 and composed entirely of experimental typefaces. The same year, the Mayakovsky–Rodchenko tandem founded the "advertising constructors" bureau, with the first overseeing the editorial side and the second the visual. The partnership resulted in a mass of graphic media, often intended to bolster the government's ideology. Rodchenko's artistic position, like that of Tatlin, was totally dedicated to the regime, and to industrialization and the onward march of technology. A man of many parts, Rodchenko concerned himself with painting, sculpture, architecture, photography, graphics, typography, design, and the cinema. Committed to creating photographic expressions of maximum impact, he observed that "for now, the most interesting shots [in photography] are those taken downwards, upwards, or obliquely."[48] Wholly intent on the utility dimension of his art, Rodchenko abandoned painting to devote his time exclusively to the applied arts.

Another major exponent of photomontage, El Lissitzky also left a sizable and multifaceted oeuvre, including in the graphic domain. The *Proun*s—his own invention—took his pictorial-graphic researches into the realm of multidirectional space. In 1925, with Jean Arp, he published *The Isms of Art*—a work whose typographical design he ensured—in which we are informed that "Constructivism proves that limits between [...] an art object and technological invention cannot be determined."[49] Constructivism dreamed of a world where industrial production would help to respond to the question of social inequality, where mass poverty would be eradicated by recourse to machines, and where the artist would jettison "art for art's sake," and place all artistic practices in the service of the revolution. The onset of Constructivism accompanied Lenin's assumption of the reins of power, and his death in 1924 dealt a blow to the propagation of the avant-garde. With the introduction of Stalinism, a school of propagandist realism gradually ousted all other artistic currents. Towards the end of the 1920s, El Lissitzky, Rodchenko, and Gustav Klutsis were some of the great propaganda artists who had closed ranks with Stalin's regime. By the beginning of the following decade, socialist realism had been established as a new artistic credo. In 1931, a decree by the party central committee covered, among other items, "poster production." The following year, this same committee set up the Union of Soviet Painters, controlled by the party, the only officially sanctioned art organization.

Henceforth, artistic life in the Soviet Union was to conform to the ideology in place and to

335
Gustav Klutsis, poster, *Fifth Plan for Work*, Soviet Union, 1930.

336
Gustav Klutsis and Salomon Telingater, Soviet Union, 1931. 11 × 8 ¼ in. (28.2 × 21.2 cm).

the aesthetics of pure propaganda. The Stalin personality cult invaded posters and was endlessly rehashed on every vehicle of visual expression. As abstract art and Constructivism were no longer welcome in state propaganda, graphic designers and others creatives retrenched to media less public than the billboard. Artists lived under constant threat of repression: Kasimir Malevich was imprisoned, tortured, then released in 1930, the year Vladimir Mayakovsky committed suicide. Alexei Gan and Klutsis, arrested at the end of the 1930s, were interned in labor camps where they were to perish in 1942 and 1944 respectively. If, by the beginning of the 1930s, annihilation loomed for Constructivism in the Soviet Union, the German avant-garde was soon to be confronted by a scarcely less enviable fate; with the advent of nazism, artists and intellectuals had to choose between escape or inner exile—or carry the flag for the regime.

Developments in Constructivism in Europe

During the 1910s, pre-Constructivist artistic forms were already discernible, as the movement spread towards the West, from Poland to the Netherlands, passing by Hungary, Czechoslovakia, Yugoslavia, and Germany. By dint of its strength and scope, the movement promptly left an imprint on the European avant-garde in the first half of the 1920s. Depending on the nations concerned, the movement adopted different forms and names, directly influencing contemporary movements and schools, such as De Stijl and the Bauhaus. Constructivism laid the stress on functional, rational, and effective design. In Germany in 1923, for example, the first Bauhaus (once so close to Expressionism and handicraft, and imbued with a certain mysticism) redefined itself as a meeting-place for the arts and industry, in particular under the influence of El Lissitzky and László Moholy-Nagy. Transnational exchange, collaborations, personal encounters, and reviews are once more some of the many factors behind the steady progress of Constructivism, supported by personalities such as El Lissitzky. By the very beginning of the 1920s, in a lecture given in Warsaw, El Lissitzky offered a description of the Russian current; the effect on the Polish avant-garde was instantaneous. In 1921 and 1922, he was in Berlin where he organized the First Exhibition of Russian Art and met Moholy-Nagy and Van Doesburg for what proved a profitable exchange of views. From that point, El Lissitzky's influence on the Bauhaus became increasingly visible. Moholy-Nagy, for his part, came from Hungary, passing through Vienna before settling in Germany. Lajos Kassák, the central protagonist in Hungarian activism, also stayed in Berlin in 1922, and attended the exhibition of Russian art. Such comings and goings furthered active interconnections and osmoses within the avant-garde that soon consolidated into genuine networks.

Czechoslovakia

Czechoslovakia was hit by the Constructivist wave at the very start of the 1920s. The political situation at the time was highly charged. In 1918, the Czech and Slovak people split off from the Austro-Hungarian Empire, joining to form an independent state, with Tomas Garrigue Masaryk being elected president of the new Republic of Czechoslovakia. The avant-garde quickly found this part of Europe a significant forum for expression. Karel Teige and then Ladislav Sutnar were among the busiest figures on the artistic scene. According to Sutnar, "For Czechoslovakia after 1918, the republic's democratic freedom was a stimulating reality that produced a climate of optimism."[50] In the fledgling Czechoslovakia, Teige and Sutnar were actively involved in regenerating typography.

In 1920, the pioneering Teige co-founded with a group of artists and writers the organization Devetsil (Nine Forces). The previous year, he had already started writing for many of the country's cultural reviews. A painter, writer, poet, and theorist, he also left a significant graphic legacy. Teige had thoroughly studied and assimilated many of the avant-garde currents of the 1910s (Italian, Swiss, German, Russian, and so on). Introducing Constructivism into Czechoslovakia, he also published many texts reflecting his conception of

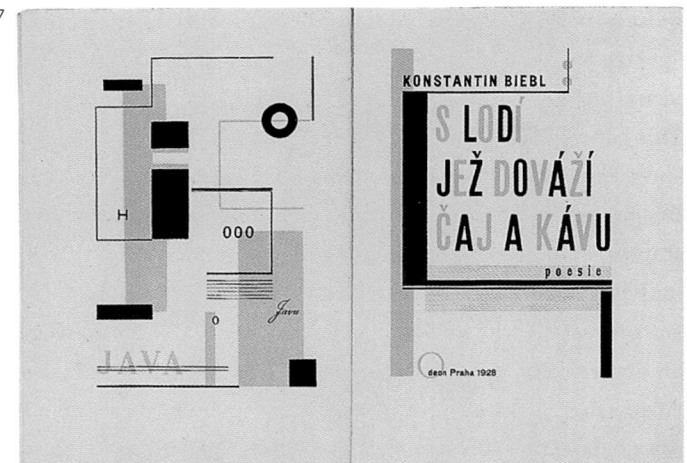

Státní grafická škola v Praze 1932-1933

337
Karel Teige, frontispiece and title page for the book of poetry, *S lodí, jez dovází caj a kávu*, (With the Boat that Brings Tea and Coffee) (Konstantin Biebl), Prague, 1928.

338
Ladislav Sutnar, cover of the review *Zijeme* (We are Alive), Czechoslovakia, 1931. Review published by Druzstevní Práce.

339
Ladislav Sutnar, cover for the 1932–33 annual report of the National School of Graphic Art, Prague, 1933.

340
Karel Teige, letter "M," composition for the book of poems by Vítezslav Nezval, *Abeceda*, Prague, 1926. Montage of photographs of the Constructivist dancer, Milca Mayerová, and fragmentary designs for geometrical letterforms. Photographs by Karel Paspa. 9 × 12 in. (23 × 30 cm).

art and typography. In 1922, he made the case for "Constructivist thought": "Geometrical rigor, functional organization, economy of means, and quality of construction are not only technical demands, but aesthetic ones too."[51] In its advocacy of Constructivism, Teige's oeuvre gives free rein to montage, typography, and photography. In 1927 (that is to say, a year before the publication of Jan Tschichold's *Neue Typographie*), he issued a text entitled "Modern Typography" in which he underscored the need for formal innovation, for detachment from the past, and the role of structure and construction. His own graphic practice ranged widely from phototypographic experiments and visual poems to page-settings for avant-garde Czech reviews, such as *ReD*, and truly exceptional book covers. By the end of the 1920s, by which time Teige was enjoying a certain renown in Europe, he gave a series of lectures at the Dessau Bauhaus.

Like Karel Teige, Ladislav Sutnar came to the forefront of the Czech art world in the beginning of the 1920s; both artists belong to the same generation, born respectively in 1900 and 1897. Sutnar completed his painting and graphic studies at the National School of Graphic Art in Prague in 1923, beginning to teach there in the same year and advancing to director in 1932. In Sutnar's eyes, "ideas for a new functional design appeared [in Czechoslovakia] around 1922. This new concept materialized initially in architecture, then in typography, product design, and exhibition design."[52] Like Teige and so many others, Sutnar promoted the idea that contemporary artistic practice has to slough off its traditional legacy. His approach was that art can no longer be confined to local or national preoccupations and must be constantly receptive to influences from abroad. Won over to Constructivism, the Bauhaus and the embryonic New Typography, Sutnar adopted a functionalist perspective. His graphic oeuvre, at the same time refined and powerful, is particularly concerned with typography, photography, montage, and interior and exterior space. He sought to make simple, effective, dynamic compositions, making abundant use of sans serif type. Sutnar designed numerous book covers as art director for the great Prague publishing house Druzstevní Práce from 1929 to 1939. Like Teige, he too produced the layout for several reviews, including *Zijeme* (We are Alive). Sutnar's graphics incorporate the ideals of the New Typography, particularly in the publishing field. In this work can be seen the same combination of sans serif and photography, the same role allotted to the nonprinted surface, photomontage, asymmetrical compositions, structures created by grids, and so on. After 1939, his career was to be based in the United States, where he was appointed to design the Czechoslovak pavilion for the Universal Exhibition in New York. Sutnar was never to return to Europe. In 1938, the territories of Czechoslovakia were annexed to the German Reich. In March 1939, as Sutnar found himself in New York, Nazi armies marched into Prague. Sutnar pursued an active career in the United States until the mid-1970s. Remaining close to avant-garde publishing and expression, he was to design in particular catalogs for industry in which informative clarity dominates, as well as visual identities and graphic liveries for many firms.

As evidence of his breadth of thought and his influence, Ladislav Sutnar, like Karel Teige, was the author of a number of significant texts on design and graphics. Teige and Sutnar can be considered the two figureheads of the Czech avant-garde. It should be remembered that an earlier generation in the same region had boasted Alphonse Mucha (born in Moravia), who had enjoyed fame in Paris in the final years of the nineteenth century before he settled back in Bohemia in 1910. Besides Karel Teige and Ladislav Sutnar, the 1920s saw a number of Czech graphic designers and poster artists join the avant-garde, an artistic activity that was to last nearly two decades, from the very beginning of the 1920s (after the creation of the Czechoslovakian Republic following the demise of the Austro-Hungarian Empire) to 1939, the year the German army entered Prague. There again, developments in graphic design appear by and large concomitant on the geopolitical scene.

Poland

341
Henryk Berlewi, construction *Mechano-Faktura*, 1924. Gouache on paper.

Polish graphic designers also made their mark on Constructivism at the beginning of the 1920s thanks to regular contact with neighboring lands. El Lissitzky, in Berlin by the end of 1921, delivered several lectures in Warsaw, increasing the awareness of Russian Constructivism among Polish progressives. His influence on Henryk Berlewi was instantaneous. The latter, having trained as a painter in Antwerp and Paris, had practiced design and begun to publish his thoughts on art. Berlewi was one of several figures to make a major contribution to the revival of the Polish (typo)graphic landscape. His career was manifestly orientated towards Constructivism, and unfolded in Germany between 1921 and 1923, in particular in Berlin and Hanover. At that time he laid down his theory of "Mechano-Faktura" ("mechanical reproduction") that sought to valorize formal simplification and the two-dimensional aspect of graphics. Berlewi, too, advocated the idea that "art must break definitively [...] with the excessively sensitive, hysterical, romantic, and individualist aesthetics of the past. It must create a new plastic language, accessible to all, in keeping with the rhythm of life today."[53] Berlewi invented sans serif compositions combining playfulness and rigor, and powerfully inflected by an array of geometrical elements often limited to black, red, and white. Back from Berlin in 1924, in Warsaw Berlewi co-founded the advertising agency Reklama-Mechano with the Futurist poets Aleksander Wat and Stanley Brucz. Like their Czechoslovakian peers, they began adapting the new graphics to commercial and product promotion material, as one of Berlewi's avowed objectives was to publicize and promulgate the new artistic forms by making such graphics familiar.

Other significant figures, such as Wladyslaw Strzeminski, Tadeusz Gronowski, and Mieczyslaw Szczuka also actively contributed to the recalibration of Polish graphics. Born in Russia, Strzeminski was particularly active in the fields of graphics and typography. As a member of an artistic association in Vitebsk, he had already worked with Malevich. In 1924, in Warsaw, he co-founded the Blok group, which synthesized various avant-garde influences (Cubism, Suprematism, and Constructivism).

At the time, artistic groupings proliferated in Poland, as elsewhere, being established and sometimes dissolving in rapid succession. The group published the review *Blok* in which Mieczyslaw Szczuka and Henryk Stazevski participated. Strzeminski also joined the groups Praesens, a.r. (in Lódz), and Abstraction-Création. Far from the hard-edged and rigorous vein of Constructivism, his approach to typography reflects a liberated insouciance. His best-known works include book covers and the minimalist Komunikat alphabet (1930–32), which evinces a manifest interest in the question of the limits of reading, legibility, recognition, and visibility in a typeface. Playing a significant role in the ongoing international exchanges, it was Strzeminski who invited Malevich to Poland in 1927 for an exhibition of the latter's work. Strzeminski based his own teaching methodology on the Bauhaus approach.

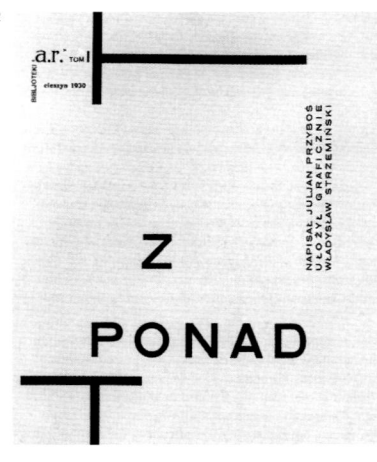

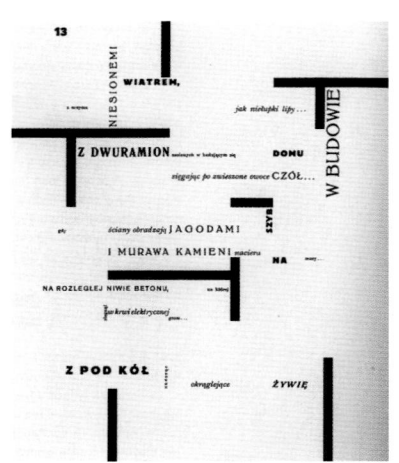

a b c d e f g h i j k l ł m

n o p q r s t u w y z

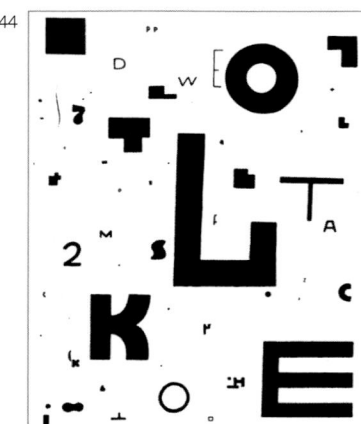

342
Wladyslaw Strzeminski, inside pages and cover of the collection of poems, *Z Ponad* (Above) by Julian Przybos, Poland, 1930.

343
Wladyslaw Strzeminski, *Komunikat* alphabet, Poland, c. 1930–32.

344
Wladyslaw Strzeminski, typographic composition, Poland, 1924 or 1925.

If Henryk Berlewi and Wladyslaw Strzeminski shared affinities for typography alone, other graphic designers, such as Mieczyslaw Szczuka, incorporated photography and montages in their compositions. Tadeusz Gronowski, for instance, is regarded as one of the chief forerunners of the modern poster in Poland. Strongly influenced by trips to France, he was of the opinion that "the art of the poster will tend [from now on] to formal simplification and the concise presentation of the subject and turn its attention to details."[54] Through the work and action of figures such as Berlewi, Strzeminski, Szczuka, and Gronowski, Polish graphic design was totally transformed and diversified. The geographical situation of the country, between Germany and the Soviet Union, probably made it an ideal space for the crosscurrents and convergence of the avant-garde. Although the 1920s were marked by the advent of Constructivism, other forms of plastic receptivity (inherited from Cubism, Futurism, Expressionism, or Dada) also made their presence felt. While some artists appealed to universal forms, Constructivism in central Europe in fact took on a distinctive face depending on the country to which it spread.

Hungary

Like Poland and Czechoslovakia, Hungary discovered Constructivism early on. There, too, artistic practices were closely related to the political landscape. Traumatized by World War I, in 1918 the country was the stage for a middle-class revolution. The next year, Socialist revolutionaries seized power and the Republic of the Councils was proclaimed. Its chief, Béla Kun, set up a dictatorship of the proletariat, a regime that was to end in failure. A few months later, the Romanians seized Budapest and counter-revolutionary forces marched into the city.

A reactionary government was established in 1920, with the result that Hungary forfeited two-thirds of its territory. Meanwhile, in 1924, the Communist Party managed to undergo a reform of its own. Fleeing this turbulence, sociopolitical or otherwise, some Hungarian artists settled in nearby lands, often heading north and west. László Moholy-Nagy chose exile in Vienna in 1919, before settling in Berlin. In 1920, Lajos Kassák also left for Vienna, establishing himself in Berlin in 1922 before returning to Budapest in 1926.

In Hungary itself, since 1915, artists and intellectuals had been joining the revolutionary cause and adopting communist ideologies. Artists and intellectuals participated significantly in Hungarian activism. The spokesman for the national avant-garde, Lajos Kassák, was a major figure of the era. In 1915, he founded the Budapest review *A Tett* (Action), the spearhead of Hungarian Activism. The following year, he established the collective "Ma" ("Today"), formed of artists very close to the social movements, together with a review of the same name. The periodical was outlawed in 1919 (as *A Tett* had been during World War I), although it restarted publication in Vienna in 1920. Significant work in typography appeared in Hungary in reviews and other visual media. By the beginning of the 1920s, the sources of influence, which initially included tendencies of the 1910s such as Expressionism, Futurism, Dadaism, and so on, were being increasingly channeled into a Constructivist syntax. In spite of the repression, artists managed to find expressive outlets. And although Lajos Kassák and László Moholy-Nagy were clearly the principal figures of the time, other, lesser-known artists also took part in the Hungarian graphic revival, such as Sándor Bortnyik, Mihály Biró, and the painter Robert Berény, all of whom were important poster artists. Many creatives enjoyed exceptional careers abroad, like Vilmos Huszár (installed in the Netherlands since 1905 and highly active in De Stijl), Marcel Breuer (who left to study at the Bauhaus in 1920, becoming professor there), and photographer André Kertész (who settled in Paris in 1925).

Hungarian Constructivism forged close links with the revolutionary utopias born in the 1910s. The majority of artists adhering to the movement were close to the Communist Party and defended its social ideals with vigor. By and large, art without a political aim was not countenanced, as it was supposed to contribute to the creation of the new world by actively furthering social change. From its creation in Russia in the wake of the 1917 revolutions, Constructivism made a stand in a number of countries. Prevalent throughout central Europe, the movement also made its mark in the Netherlands, where, as in Germany, it intersected with other avant-garde tendencies, for example with New Typography, and among graphic designers, typographers, and plasticians, such as Piet Zwart, Paul Schuitema, Jan Tschichold, Max Burchartz, László Moholy-Nagy, and others.

The Dutch avant-garde
The De Stijl movement

Taking no active part in World War I, the Netherlands enjoyed an economic boom in the interwar period, thus escaping the profound sociopolitical upheaval that affected many other European countries. If the social commitment of Dutch artists did not seem to be accompanied by the revolutionary zeal encountered in other lands, the period 1914–18 witnessed an upswing in creativity in the Netherlands under the influence of neighboring avant-gardes and in response to a home-grown urge for transformation. De Stijl and Neoplasticism represent the two pillars of the Dutch avant-garde, heralding a transitional phase that by the onset of the 1920s was reaching a climax.

The Netherlands, traversed by various artistic influences (Cubism, Futurism, and Dadaism), sought to develop exchanges with Constructivism, the Bauhaus, and other figures in Germany. In the field of architecture, Hendrik Petrus Berlage transmitted many of the ideas of Frank Lloyd Wright following a trip to the United States in 1911.

The radical movement De Stijl (the Style), was formed in 1916 (the year that saw the eruption of Dada in Switzerland), and consolidated the following year. Centered on the

345

345
Lajos Kassák, *Zajos* (Noisy), 1920. Collage and ink on paper, 5 3/4 in. × 4 1/6 in. (14.8 × 10.7 cm).

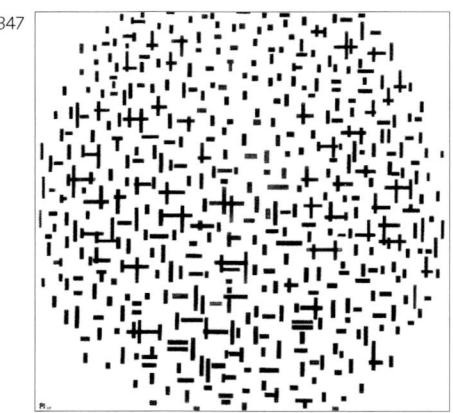

346
Piet Mondrian, *Composition Trees 1*, 1912.
Oil on canvas, 32 × 24 ¹/₂ in. (81 × 62 cm).

347
Piet Mondrian, *Composition in Line*, 1916–17. Oil on canvas, 3 ft. 6 ¹/₂ in × 3 ft. 6 ¹/₂ in. (108 × 108 cm).

348
Jacobus Johannes Pieter Oud, project for coloring the frontage of the De Unie café, Rotterdam, 1924. Executed in 1925, destroyed 1940, reconstructed on a new site in 1985.

unifying figure of Theo Van Doesburg, the group branched out into several artistic fields. In October 1917 in Leiden close to The Hague, the group launched a journal, *De Stijl*. It was to include contributions from Piet Mondrian, who was to strongly influence the direction of De Stijl. Mondrian had been in Paris from 1911 to 1914, where he discovered Cubism. In his search for a purified geometric abstraction, by the end of the 1910s Mondrian had created Neoplasticism, adumbrating its doctrine in 1920. Its principles are based on simplicity and rigor: horizontal and vertical black lines of variable thickness delimit uniform areas of color in blue, yellow, red, gray, white, or black. It was these elements that constituted De Stijl's initial plastic and graphic vocabulary. Confirming directions that can be discerned elsewhere, De Stijl's interests ranged equally over the fine and applied arts, concerning itself, *inter alia*, with a broad sweep of the visual arts, including painting, sculpture, architecture, interior decoration, furniture, typography, graphics, and textiles. In addition to the figures of Theo Van Doesburg and Piet Mondrian, the movement attracted the architects Jan Wils and Jacobus Johannes Pieter Oud, furniture-maker and architect Gerrit Rietveld, painter Bart Van der Leck, Belgian painter and sculptor Georges Vantongerloo, Hungarian artist Vilmos Huszár, poet Anthony Kok, and even Italian Futurist Gino Severini.

De Stijl was exacting as to the choices and principles it adopted, and its calculated approach was founded on a limited range of forms. In the tenth number of its review, in 1921, Raoul Hausmann, Jean Arp, László Moholy-Nagy, and Ivan Puni (also known as Jean Pougny) voiced their adhesion to the movement in concise terms: "We are fighting for an elementarist art [...]. We demand the abolition of styles so as to establish the Style!"[55] The movement's partisans banished all recourse to emotion and imagination, relying uniquely on methodological coherence. In 1923, Theo Van Doesburg and the architect Cornelis Van Eesteren appealed for "a new plastic unity [...] founded on the knowledge of primary and universal elements of expression." In their eyes, "this harmony is founded on the awareness of contrast, [...] dissonance, etc. [...] The multiplicity of contrasts sets up enormous tensions which, by reciprocal suppression, result in balance and repose. It is this equilibrium of tensions that forms the quintessence of the new constructive unity." This declaration reveals the proximity of De Stijl's adherents to what was to emerge as the New Typography. Highlighting the radical break on which their position was based, they held that "personal taste, including an admiration for machines [...] is unimportant in realizing a unity between art and life. Mechanization in art is an illusion like all the others (Naturalism, Futurism, Cubism, Purism, etc.)." The following year, 1924, Van Doesburg and Van Eesteren declared that they had "examined architecture as the plastic unity of all the arts [...]. We have scrutinized the bilateral relationships between measure, proportion, space, time, and material [...]. The era of destruction is completely over. A new age is dawning: the great age of construction."[56]

The best-known achievements of the movement include the Blue and Red Chair and the Schröder House (1918–23 and 1924) by Gerrit Rietveld, and the cover for the first number of the review *De Stijl*, whose main illustration is by Huszár (the lettering above is sometimes also ascribed to the same artist). Whereas Mondrian had eschewed the curve completely, in their compositions other members of De Stijl (such as Van Doesburg) went beyond the rectangle and reinstated the diagonal, or else took the liberty of using non-primary colors. The organizer of the movement, Theo Van Doesburg, was at once a theorist, painter, sculptor, designer, architect, typographer, and poet. Breaking free of the trammels of Neoplasticism, he now proclaimed "the introduction of inclined surfaces, of dissonant surfaces, in opposition to gravity and to static, architectonic structures."[57] It was the enterprising Van Doesburg who had published the movement's review, assisting in its layout. The typesetting he selected for his poetry also demonstrates a precocious interest in typography. It may have been in 1919 that he designed an experimental geometrical alphabet composed of capital letters organized around the basic form of a square and built up from a set of orthogonal bars.

Traveling to Belgium, France, Germany, and Italy, Van Doesburg did much to propagate

ABCDEFGHIJKLM NOPQRSTUVWXYZ

De Stijl's ideas abroad. He established links with members of the Bauhaus, visiting the school, and settling in Weimar in 1921. If he never obtained a teaching post at the Bauhaus, his presence in Germany nevertheless made a strong impact on its students as well as on other artists, for example through the "De Stijl course" timetabled at the beginning of 1922. Van Doesburg also worked with Kurt Schwitters, in particular on projects for periodicals and books in which typography occupied a key role. Impressed by Dada, he brought Schwitters to the Netherlands. He even tried his hand at Dada, composing strange poems signed with the pseudonym "I. K. Bonset," and, having met Raoul Hausmann, he founded the review *Mécano*. Maintaining and cultivating his contacts, Van Doesburg took part in a Constructivist congress in Weimar in 1922 where he joined El Lissitzky, László Moholy-Nagy, Tristan Tzara, and Jean Arp among others. The central figure in the movement, Van Doesburg met an untimely death in 1931 at the age of only forty-seven. The *De Stijl* review ceased publication and the movement gradually evaporated. Conserving much of its teaching, however, artists and designers now sought more personal approaches. In the mid-1920s, while De Stijl was at its high-water mark and loosening the strictures of its initial tenets, Dutch graphics witnessed the confirmation of new talents: Piet Zwart, Paul Schuitema, Hendrik Nicolaas Werkman, Gerald Kiljan, Cesar Domela (then in Berlin), followed by Henny Cahn (born in 1908), Dick Elffers, and Wim Brusse (born 1910).

Piet Zwart, Paul Schuitema, and Hendrik Nicolaas Werkman

The exemplary graphic designer Piet Zwart was born in 1885. An architect by training and trade he also worked as a designer, practicing successively with Jan Wils and Hendrik Petrus Berlage, two renowned architects strongly influenced by Frank Lloyd Wright. Zwart also experienced the aftereffects of the Wiener Werkstätte and echoes of Dadaism, as well as benefiting from the energy of De Stijl. Around 1920, several opportunities came up that enabled him to exercise his talent for graphics and typography. In about 1917, he designed letterheads for the architect Jan Wils, and, in 1921, he embarked on typographical composition proper while working for the Lagafabriek company based in The Hague. In the meantime, he had established contacts with the figureheads of Neoplasticism and De Stijl, including Mondrian, Van Doesburg, and Rietveldand had met other major names in the avant-garde of the 1920s, such as Schwitters and El Lissitzky.

In 1923, Zwart started a noted collaboration with Nederlandsche Kabelfabriek (NKF), a company manufacturing electric cables sited at Delft. Producing literally hundreds of press advertisements and promotional documents, Zwart was to work at NKF for nearly ten years. Initially, he was responsible for the conception of advertisements for the trade press. Afforded considerable leeway in this role, Zwart nonetheless eschewed daring or unusual typographical compositions. In 1926, he received an account to design a catalog for NKF (to be realized in collaboration with a professional photographer) that is regarded as one of his most accomplished achievements and is a stalwart of histories of graphic design. In what was an original approach, Piet Zwart began to associate photography and montage in typographical production. Distinct from the principles of De Stijl, he employed the circle as well as the rectangle and other geometrical abstract forms, often in conjunction with sans serif type. Zwart, like other Dutch designers of the interwar period and since, offered a graphic design service to public bodies, working throughout the 1930s for the post and telecommunications

349
Theo Van Doesburg, project for the floor decoration in the ground-floor entrance, stairway, and corridors in the De Vonk holiday home, Noordwijkerhout, 1918. Gouache and collage on gray cardboard, 3 ft. 2 1/2 in. × 29 in. (98 × 73.5 cm).

350
Theo Van Doesburg, unique alphabet composed of uppercase letters, typeform based on a squared-up grid subdivided into five, probably 1919. Photograph, 1 1/4 × 6 3/4 in. (3.5 × 17 cm). The original design for this typeface is no longer extant, only a photograph surviving. Van Doesburg used it regularly from 1919 on, with other artists employing it from the beginning of the 1920s.

351
Theo Van Doesburg, project for a cover designed for a competition for the periodical *Klei* (Clay), the organ of the brick and roof-tile manufacturers' confederation, 1919–20 (the project was passed over). Pencil, gouache, ink, and collage on transparent paper, 31 1/2 × 22 1/2 in. (80 × 57 cm).

companies on projects for stamps, promotional publications, and exhibition stands. In 1931, he was invited to give several lectures at the Dessau Bauhaus. The following year, he was dismissed from his post as a teacher at the academy of Rotterdam due to his political opinions. Ten years later, in 1942 and 1943, he was to be interned by the Nazis.

Paul Schuitema (1897–1973) presents a number of points in common with Piet Zwart: he, too, was employed in the commercial sector and collaborated with the public administration services, making a significant contribution to the advent of Dutch graphic design. He also shared Zwart's interest in photography and montage, participating actively in the development of the New Typography. Fulfilling a pedagogical role and firmly committed to socialism, like Piet Zwart, Paul Schuitema felt the influence of Dada and De Stijl, while preserving a measure of autonomy. In about 1925, he turned from painting, in which he trained initially, to devote himself to design and graphics, consequently working for industry as well as for public bodies, including, again, the post and telecommunications services. As with Zwart's collaboration with the NKF, Schuitema's work for the Van Berkel company lasted for several years and proved exceptionally fruitful. The company was an international business retailing weights and rendering materials for the butchery trades. Van Berkel's styling remit covered visual identity, writing paper, promotional documents, and designs for stands and exhibitions. Schuitema responded to this order with a graphically limited vocabulary of sans serif type and restricted palette (predominantly red, black, and gray).

In 1926, he discovered an interest in photography, a technique he was to teach himself two years later. In his work for Van Berkel, Schuitema was to make ample use of photos, often in overprint, superposing monochrome images in combination with typographical elements. The visuals created for Van Berkel were influenced by the fledgling phototypographic technique, which confers an unusual feel on the designs. Like his contemporary Zwart, in the second half of the 1920s Schuitema experimented with photography with a typographical inventiveness that helped to build the Dutch version of New Typography. Both then enjoyed a significant career that took in public services as well as commercial and industrial graphic portfolios, platforms sometimes woefully bereft of creativity. Symptomatic of their international awareness and reputation, Schuitema and Zwart became the first two foreign members of the Ring Neuer Werbegestalter (New Advertising Designers' Society), or NWG, a group of graphic designers working in advertising, founded in Germany in 1928 under the presidency of Kurt Schwitters.

For his part, Hendrik Nicolaas Werkman (born in 1882) was a unique figure in Dutch graphics between the wars. Belonging to the generation preceding that of Zwart and Schuitema, he had begun his career in 1900. Remote from dominant styles and tendencies, Werkman's oeuvre is that of an idiosyncratic, almost marginal loner, and focused on experimental typography. Living in the north of the Netherlands, at Groningen, he opened a printing plant in 1908. Though it increased in size over the years, material difficulties forced Werkman to cease trading in 1923. He then set up another, more modest workshop, bringing out a review, *The Next Call*, ten numbers of which appeared between 1923 and 1926. In these publications, and other projects, Werkman could give free rein to his typographical researches, forging a uniquely individual style with a strong experimental slant. Working in the main with the typographical material of his own printshop (including wooden letters), his were lively and original compositions in which type is assembled and superimposed with panache. There is nothing programmatic or systematic about Werkman; instead he shows tangible pleasure in form and an inquisitive imagination that presents affinities with the tone of Dada: disjointed forms, unexpected effects, and great boldness in composition. A solitary genius, Werkman remained the sole contributor to *The Next Call*, a periodical he wrote, designed, set, printed, and even distributed, initially only within the artistic milieu of Groningen before spreading it to other cities in which the European avant-garde flame burned.

Werkman's promising career came to a tragic end in World War II. German troops invaded

352
Piet Zwart, project for the carpet in the lounge in the Villa De Arendshoeve, Voorburg, 1921. Gouache and collage on cardboard, 12 3/4 × 18 in. (32.5 × 46 cm).

353
Piet Zwart, double-page spread from the catalog for the electric cable manufacturers NKF (Nederlandsche Kabelfabriek), Delft, 1933.

354
Piet Zwart, extract from a catalog for the Trio printworks, The Hague, 1929.

355
Piet Zwart, photographic cover for the *De Komische film* (Constant Van Wessem), 1931. Letterpress, 8 3/4 × 7 in. (22 × 17.5 cm).

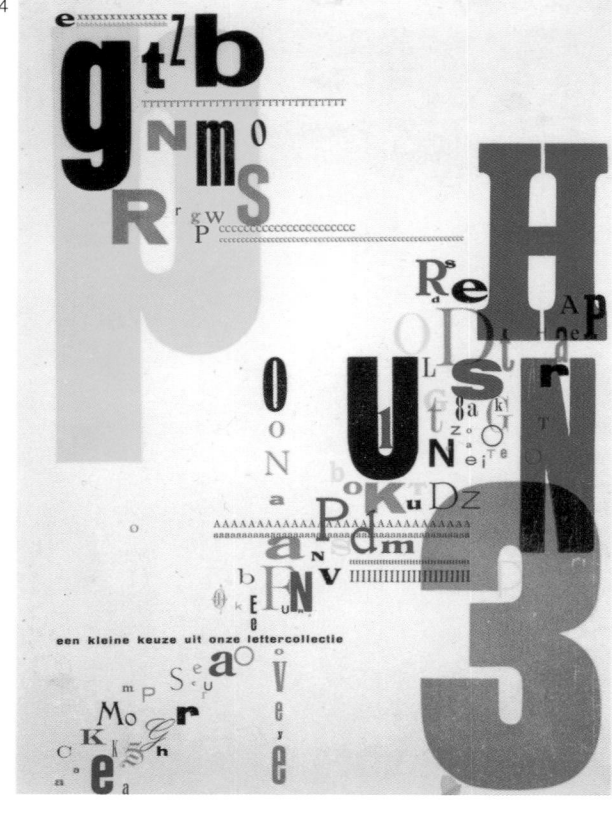

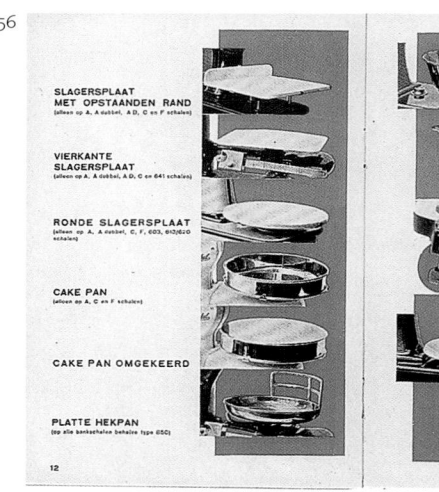

356
Paul Schuitema, double page from the promotional document, *Toledo Berkel Snelwegers* for weighing equipment made by the firm of Van Berkel, Rotterdam, 1927.

357
Hendrik Nicolaas Werkman, *Composition with the Letter X*, Netherlands, 1927–28 (?). Hand-press, 18 × 11 3/4 in. (45.8 × 29.7 cm).

358
Hendrik Nicolaas Werkman, cover for the review, *The Next Call*, no. 1, Groningen, 1923.

359
Anton Kurvers, poster, *Tentoonstelling* for an exhibition on urban planning, Netherlands, 1923. Chromolithograph, 3 ft. 3 in. × 31 in. (100 × 79 cm).

360
Jacob Jongert, enamel plaque, *Van Nelle's Tabak*, Netherlands, around the middle or end of the 1920s. Flat plate, 3 ft. 2 ¹/₂ in. × 19 in. (98 × 48 cm).

his country in May 1940 and occupied it until 1945. Engaged in the Resistance, Werkman used his experience as a printer to issue clandestine texts supporting human rights. On March 15, 1945, shortly before the Netherlands was freed from the yoke of the Reich, the Nazis arrested him and seized illicit publications they dubbed "Surrealist trash." Werkman was executed by firing squad on April 10 in the middle of a forest. Only a few days later in Groningen, the work that had been confiscated disappeared in a fire sparked during the liberation of the city.

The diversity of Dutch graphic design

In addition to witnessing the emergence of figures like Piet Zwart, Paul Schuitema, or Hendrik Nicolaas Werkman, Dutch (typo)graphic practice in the interwar period thrived and diversified, as testified, for example, by the revival of the poster and the return of some to traditional practices. A further example of this diversity is provided by the review *Wendingen*. Founded in 1918 by the architect Hendricus Theodorus Wijdeveld, who also had a hand in the visual design, the art periodical *Wendingen* was a surprising and rather stylized publication. More than one hundred numbers of the review were to come off the presses. Often complex, the form of the review was structured by a tight-knit skein of capital letters and fillets, accentuating a strongly constructed space. At the end of the 1910s, Wijdeveld—under the influence of architect Mathieu Lauweriks, whose typographical work based on orthogonal and geometrical lines was scarcely less unusual—designed a set of highly original typographical posters based on similar graphic ideas. The poster in the Netherlands then entered a phase of wholesale transformation and *Wendingen* tracked it closely, highlighting the role of German *Sachplakat* in its development. In 1917, a polemic flared up between the idealist poster artist Richard Roland Holst and Albert Hahn. The former advocated a decorative, refined line, whereas the latter opted to design posters like "a shout" by the "use of strongly contrasting colors and simple shapes, since these make a more immediate appeal."[58]

The creations of Jan Sluyters, another significant poster artist of the time, are marked by an individual and stylish freedom of line. With his love of drawing and sinuous curves, Sluyters was radically at odds with De Stijl, although the effects he sought were scarcely less novel. The majority of the creators of the 1920s constituted a second generation of poster artists; the medium's revival in the Netherlands dated back to the last years of the nineteenth century, with Jan Toorop, Theo Molkenboer, Johan Thorn Prikker, and C. A. Lion Cachet. On other fronts, Dutch interwar typography testifies to a pronounced inclination to traditional values, with Jean François van Royen, Sjoerd Hendrik de Roos, and Jan Van Krimpen as main advocates of this tendency, the latter two specializing essentially in book work and type design. Van Royen was to work for the postal and telecommunications service for nearly forty years, and oversaw its graphic styling. In charge of corporate identity for the Dutch mail, Van Royen commissioned typographers and designers of reputation (such as Piet Zwart, in 1928). Stamp design was a particularly strong sector in the Netherlands in the 1920s and 1930s, Sjoerd Hendrik de Roos, for his part, composed a great number of alphabets from 1909 to 1947, working from 1907 to 1942 for the Lettergieterij Amsterdam. Jan Van Krimpen was a prolific creator of Roman type in the classic vein, designed from the 1920s to the 1940s. From 1925 to his death in 1958, he served as both advisor and type designer for the famous Enschedé en Zonen printworks.[59] From the mid-1910s to the end of the 1930s, Dutch typography and graphics boast a number of productive creators.

Graphic experiments at this time were extremely diverse in nature, spanning the experiments of De Stijl, through significant contributions to New Typography

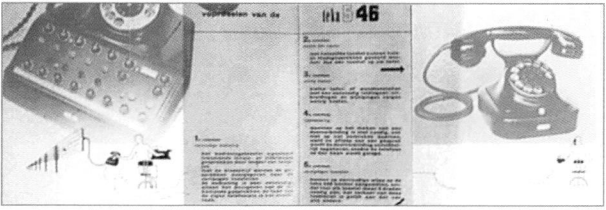

361
Henny Cahn, brochure, *Teka-Rijkshuistelefonen*, for the post and telecommunications company, The Hague, 1938.

and innovative approaches to various media (posters, stamps, etc.), to works imbued with an enduring respect for tradition. The rigor of De Stijl was overlaid with Dadaist energy and the spirit of Constructivism, as well as with an acute receptivity to previous achievements in the avant-garde. The bonds woven with nearby countries, with Germany in particular, played a crucial role in the graphic environment. As in Germany, moreover, Dutch artists were active in various cities, a distribution that favored autonomy in working style and diversity of expression. One of the outstanding aspects of Dutch graphics resides in De Stijl's role in creating typography whose effective compositions combine a sense of space and contrast with simple characters, photography, and montage. All in all, the Netherlands at this time, like the Soviet Union and Germany, constituted an especially fertile and productive graphic scene.

Germany at the heart of the European avant-garde

Like Russia, Poland, Czechoslovakia, and the Netherlands, Germany was an active force in reenergizing European art after World War I. Against a background of the ongoing search for artistic roots, graphics and typography—just like architecture, painting, and design—were to be tirelessly questioned, revised, and adapted. Creation in the visual communication field proceeded from interferences and interaction with other areas of art, as many participants in the typographical renaissance had initially worked in other artistic disciplines. Graphic and typographical creation had not yet been established as autonomous disciplines (except with respect to a significant proportion of the profession of type design); it remained associated with adjacent branches of design, in addition to being nourished by contacts with contemporary painting and arts.

If artistic activity in postwar Germany burgeoned, the political, social, and economic situation was particularly fraught. Defeated in war, the country had to relinquish part of its territory. The latter stages of the decade saw the brutal defeat of the Spartakist rising, and the abdication of Kaiser Wilhelm II followed by the establishment of a republic. Germany had become a unified state relatively late, in 1871. By the end of the nineteenth century it had been transformed from an agrarian society to one undergoing rapid industrialization, attaining the rank of major industrial power by the beginning of the twentieth century, with its economy booming right up to 1914. The postwar period witnessed a succession of workers' insurrections, galloping inflation, and the rise of ideological extremism. In such a context, many artists showed a deep concern for social and political questions.

The two great intellectual and artistic centers were then Berlin and Weimar. Berlin attracted some figures from the foreign avant-garde, such as Kasimir Malevich, El Lissitzky, Alexander Rodchenko, László Moholy-Nagy, and Theo Van Doesburg. Some were to settle in the city, while others stayed only temporarily. And although avant-garde movements such as Constructivism, Expressionism, and Dada were alive and well in Germany, around 1920 other tendencies begun to spring up, like the November Group and New Objectivity, which reinvented figuration to reflect a dysfunctioning social universe. Henceforth, art would regard itself as committed and, buoyed up by sociopolitical ideals that strove for equity and pragmatism, in sync with its time. Artistic life in postwar Germany was intense, finding expression in painting, architecture, photography, cinema, and the theater. Equally active, the ever-transforming fields of graphics and typography were as much the subject of visual experiment as of public (i.e., institutional, municipal, and industrial) commissions.

The vigorous state of graphic design in Germany is demonstrated by the particularly creative period stretching from the end of the war to the beginning of the 1930s. Against this effervescent background, several currents, phenomena, and personalities came to the fore: the New Typography (created by the work and thought of many European creators prior to being formulated by the specifically professional contribution of Jan Tschichold); the experiments at the Bauhaus; and the singular enterprise of Kurt Schwitters, as well as a large number of figures active in various cities in the country—László Moholy-Nagy, El Lissitzky, Herbert Bayer, Walter Dexel, Willi Baumeister, Cesar Domela, Max Burchartz, and many others besides.

The New Typography

Especially representative of a direction taken by graphics in the interwar period, the New Typography emerged around 1920. Initially eschewing practical applications, its ideas were clarified, detailed, theorized, presented, and illustrated in a number of publications (i.e., essays, articles, books, and special numbers of periodicals). Tschichold, Schwitters, Moholy-Nagy, and El Lissitzky were among those who attempted to articulate the New Typography and its variations. Author of several works on the subject and its chief spokesman, Jan Tschichold published a text entitled *Die neue Typographie* in 1928. If the title is sometimes regarded as the origin of the expression "New Typography" (and the work probably did encourage a wider acceptance of the term), five years previously László Moholy-Nagy had signed an essay of the same title ("Die neue Typographie"), published in 1923 in the book *Staatliches Bauhaus Weimar*. In it, Moholy-Nagy defends the notion that "typography is an instrument of communication" and that "the form of this communication must be as clear and effective as possible." Such functional demands, however, did not lead him to adopt a dogmatic position—far from it: "The very nature and goal of any printed material supposes the greatest freedom in its arrangement of lines—not exclusively the horizontal—as well as in the choice of typefaces, weights, geometrical forms, colors, etc. The flexibility, variety, and vitality of the materials for the composition impose on us a new typographical language which should be subjected solely to the rightness of the expression desired and the effect produced."[60]

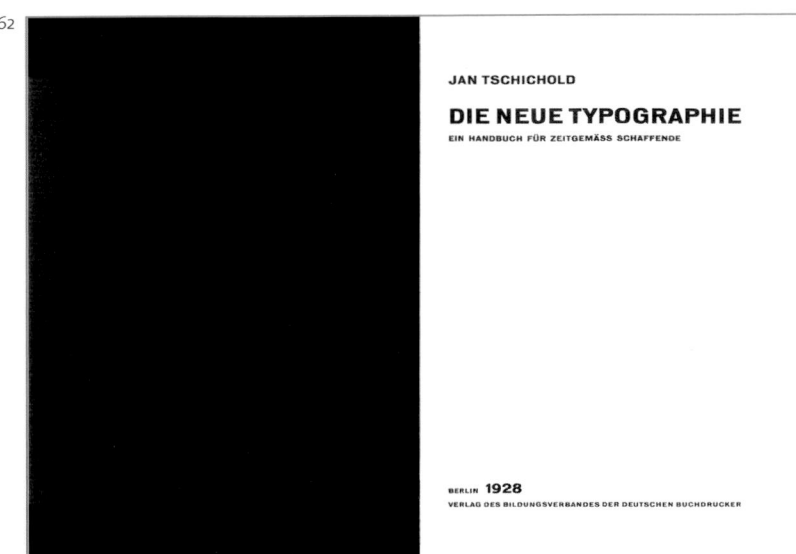

362

362
Jan Tschichold (author and designer),
double-page spread showing title page
of his *Die neue Typographie*, Berlin, 1928.

The emergence of a new typography that wanted to be simple, serviceable, and balanced was confirmed in central Europe sometime around 1923. In a way, the Futurist "typographical revolution" was simply continuing down its path, if now redirected with a new concern with function. Though reflecting a certain diversity, little by little New Typography acquired its telltale characteristics: asymmetry of composition, sans serif type, predilection for the lowercase, use of photography, dynamic use of the diagonal, presence of geometrical and elementary forms, search for contrast, hierarchization of typefaces and weights, use of primary colors, absence of traditional decorative elements, and use of the grid. (The Swiss graphic designer Theo Ballmer, for example, made extensive use of grids—the remote descendants of medieval ruling and ancient systems for imparting structure on script). Typographers were intent on rethinking topics such as impact, adequacy, space, and function, in order to adapt their trade further to mechanization and to industrial means of production. El Lissitzky called for "economy of expression." In their advertising agency, Max Burchartz and Johannes Canis strove for "maximum functionality." Moholy-Nagy regarded "clarity, concision, and precision" as essentials.[61] Several theorists in Germany tackled the question of how advertising is perceived; in sync with the spirit of the New Typography, one of them declared that "to any perceptive act [...] accomplished in a clear awareness of contrast there is a corresponding amplification in effect."[62]

For many artists, the New Typography was the subject of concrete applications (promotional posters, documents, visual identities, etc.). The poster was a major beneficiary of typographical conceptions that brought impact and sparkle to the medium. El Lissitzky, Schwitters, and Burchartz all took part in this new departure, while at the same time the graphic repertoire

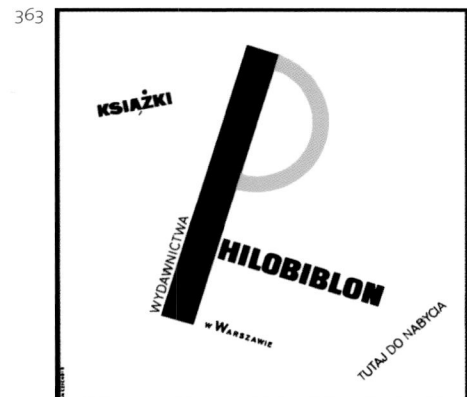

363

364

363
Jan Tschichold, small typographic poster for the Warsaw publisher Philobiblon, 1924. Signed Jan Czichold. Black and gold on a white ground with a black border. 13 3/4 × 13 3/4 in. (35 × 35 cm).

364
Jan Tschichold, typographic creation for the title of the Polish periodical, *Tambour*, 1924.

spread throughout Europe—in the Netherlands, the Soviet Union, and Poland. The blossoming of the New Typography probably owes a great deal to the receptivity of the avant-garde at the beginning of the twentieth century and to its transnational dimension, as well as to the technical and artistic advances of previous decades. In the long run, the protagonists of the 1920s are the descendants of the Arts and Crafts movement, the Glasgow School, and turn-of-the-century *affichistes* (famous or less known); of the Wiener Werkstätte, of the *Sachplakat*, and the Werkbund; of Cubism, abstraction, Futurism, and Dada. In spite of manifest differences in working practices, a bridge half a century old links William Morris to Jan Tschichold.

Jan Tschichold, theoretical typographer

Jan Tschichold was born in 1902 in Leipzig and died in 1974. He acquired a taste for script while still very young through his father, a letter- and sign-painter, and at just twelve years old, he made a lengthy and instructive visit to the World Exhibition of the Book in Leipzig, where he lapped up information that was to stand him in good stead. His education allowed him to benefit from teaching dispensed in various schools; he learnt penmanship and lettering, and discovered a passion for the arts of the book. In the school at Grimma, he discovered works by supreme calligraphers such as Rudolf von Larisch and Edward Johnston. He pursued his studies at the Academy of Graphic Art and through the book trade at Leipzig, where he consolidated a knowledge of writing culture, through, among other things, the meticulous study of Italian Renaissance calligraphy. This training period led him to register at the Kunstgewerbeschule (School of Applied Art) in Dresden. His at once complete and specialized training afforded him a solid footing in letter design and penmanship. From this point of view, Tschichold is an exceptional figure among the representatives of the typographical revival of the 1920s, most of who tended to be multitalented painters, creators, and/or architects rather than trained typographers.

He had barely graduated from the school of Leipzig, when, in 1921, he was called upon to teach lettering design there. His professional career started at the same time with the design of hand-drawn advertisements. In 1923, when only twenty-one years old, Tschichold traveled to Weimar to visit the landmark Bauhaus exhibition. For him, this was a voyage of discovery that represented a genuine revelation. The Bauhaus was at the time radically changing direction and becoming increasingly receptive to De Stijl and to Russian Constructivism. Making his way through the exhibition, Tschichold would have encountered work by the greatest figures in the Bauhaus, such as the painters Johannes Itten, Lyonel Feininger, and Wassily Kandinsky, the architect Walter Gropius, and the polymath artists Josef Albers, Oskar Schlemmer, and László Moholy-Nagy, among others. His knowledge, which had been anchored in a mastery of the skills inherited from a rich tradition, was thus now allied to a growing admiration for the modernity he could see about him. His 1924 poster for the Warsaw publishing house Philobiblon testifies to the influence of Constructivism and heralds his own particular brand of typography. Eventually the author of more than fifty books and one hundred articles, Tschichold quickly became one of the most active foci of the development of typography.

In 1925, he published "Elementare Typographie" (Elemental Typography) in a special number of the review *Typographische Mitteilungen*. With a print-run (according to Tschichold in 1930) of nearly thirty thousand, the repercussions of this little booklet were felt in many quarters. In it Tschichold presented work by Schwitters, Moholy-Nagy, El Lissitzky, Bayer, Baumberger, Mart Stam, and his own hand. The aim was to show and disseminate Constructivist ideals and contemporary typographical creations. In addition to his writings, the publication also incorporated texts by El Lissitzky on advertising ("Die Reklame") and by Moholy-Nagy on "Typophoto." Although he had only recently come across these avant-garde tendencies, Tschichold expressed his unconditional support for an innovative and reform-orientated graphics. He described his theory of elemental typography in ten points. In his eyes, "the purpose of any piece of typography is communication [...] The communication must

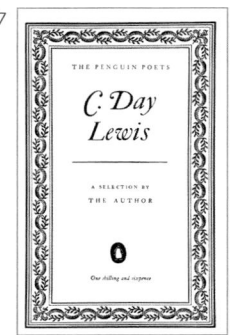

366

367

368
für den noien menfen eksistirt nur
das glaihgeviht tsvifen natur unt
gaist· tsu jedem tsaitpunkt der

365
Jan Tschichold, poster for the film, *Napoleon*,
1927. Shown at the Munich picture-house,
the Phoebus-Palast. 3 ft. 10 ³/₄ in. × 33 in.
(118.5 × 84 cm).

366
Jan Tschichold, cover for the book, *Mensch
unterm Hammer* (Men under the Hammer)
by Josef Lehnard, Leipzig, 1931.

367
Jan Tschichold, cover for the collection, *The
Penguin Poets* (Penguin Books), 1949. Printed
black and green on light-green paper.

368
Jan Tschichold, project for a unique alphabet,
research into a new form of writing,
phonetic version, 1929. Study: 1926–29.

appear in the briefest, simplest, most urgent form [...] The elemental letterform is the sans serif
in all variations: light, medium, bold, condensed, expanded," although he went on to concede
that for "the setting of continuous text [Roman] still [...] has the advantage of better legibility
over many sans serifs." Tschichold recommends the use of contrast, of hierarchization of forms,
of rules and fillets "as internal means of organization," of the DIN standard for formats
(Deutsche Industrie Norm, as for example, in the present-day A4 or US letter format for writing
stock) and of lowercase, "the writing of tomorrow." (Kurt Schwitters for one was to express
dissent at the exclusive promotion of lowercase preached simultaneously by Tschichold and by
Bayer at the Bauhaus in 1925). There was one further significant point: "Photography has to be
included among the elementary means of the new typography." He prudently concludes this
1925 text with the observation that "elemental typography is not something final or
absolute,"[63] recommending tolerance and expressing a willingness to evolve that later events
were to bear out.

In about 1922–23, Jan Tschichold met and befriended László Moholy-Nagy, who
introduced him to the Suprematists and the Russian Constructivists, including El Lissitzky, as
well as to several members of the Bauhaus. Tschichold was thus able to widen his circle and
form new connections—with Kasimir Malevich, Alexander Rodchenko, Piet Mondrian, Theo
Van Doesburg, Kurt Schwitters, Wladyslaw Strzeminski, Henryk Stazewski, Jean Arp, Sophie
Taeuber-Arp, Piet Zwart, John Heartfield, and Man Ray, among others. These relations
afforded him a bird's-eye view of the diverse nature of the most up-to-date practices. The desire
to diffuse what seemed to him relevant and cutting-edge ideas led to the publication in 1928 in
Berlin of Tschichold's key work, *Die neue Typographie*. In it he summarizes and describes the
characteristic aspects of a new approach that would privilege more than ever the search for
rational and uncomplicated solutions. The illustrations in the book were borrowed from many
artistic movements (Expressionism, Cubism, Futurism, abstraction, Suprematism, and
Constructivism) and from creations in the field of typographical design, with contributions by
Vladimir Tatlin, El Lissitzky, Lajos Kassák, Theo Van Doesburg, Piet Zwart, Kurt Schwitters,
Willi Baumeister, Walter Dexel, Herbert Bayer, Man Ray, etc. *Die neue Typographie* was
presented in the form of a reference book for printing professionals (typesetters, printers, and
typographers), but the bulk of print material produced at the time remained quite separate
from avant-garde concerns, and was rooted in centuries-old conventions. (It should be noted
that Gothic lettering had remained in everyday use in Germany since the Middle Ages). A
partisan of radical transformation, Tschichold attempted to clarify the fundamental parameters

that act on the field of visual communication and typography in the public arena.

By the end of 1920, Tschichold could apply his new typographical schemas in commissions. In particular, he created an important series of film posters for a Munich movie-house, the Phoebus-Palast, combining photography and two-color lithography for which he drew the lettering himself. Around 1930, he turned his hand to creating new varieties of typeface, experiments that spawned a project for a universal alphabet (in 1929; geometric in tendency, without differentiation between upper- and lowercase letters and including a phonetic alternative), Transito (1931), and a Gothic alphabet for which only roughs remain. In addition to his practice and theoretical writings, Tschichold had been teaching typography and penmanship at the Meisterschule für Deutschlands Buchdrucker (School of German Master Printers) in Munich from 1926, invited to the post by Paul Renner (the creator of Futura), who was director of the school at the time. As the 1930s continued, Tschichold's career entered choppy waters. Early in 1933, as the Nazis took power, he was arrested and imprisoned for several weeks, learning in jail that henceforth he would be forbidden to teach. In the 1930s and subsequently, Tschichold went back on his earlier convictions, reevaluating his passion and fascination for the avant-garde and reintegrating into his conception of typography the penchant for history-based expertise he had inherited from his youth.

The Bauhaus, between craftsmanship and industry

Given the dynamism of Germany (typo)graphic creation of the 1920s, the Bauhaus should be regarded as just one phenomenon among others. If the school was just one of many hives of activity with insightful concerns about graphic design, its special characteristic was that it brought together so many excellent teachers in one forum. It thus could raise questions about the interaction between artistic disciplines, openly transmitting to a younger generation an avant-garde orientation that combined production, publication, and pedagogy, fostering the convergence of personalities and more individual approaches in addition to collective outlooks. The Staatliches Bauhaus opened its doors in 1919, during a period of significant sociopolitical upheaval that saw the abdication of the emperor and the proclamation of the Weimar Republic. This, however, did nothing to prevent the development of the school's progressive education programs. The Bauhaus, the result of the fusion of two Weimar art schools (the School of Visual Art and the technical school, previously directed by Henry Van de Velde and transformed into a military hospital during the war) thus stood on solid foundations.

On the recommendation of Van de Velde, Walter Gropius was appointed director. Son and nephew of architects, he became assistant to Peter Behrens and already enjoyed a certain fame thanks to works such as the Fagus factory at Alfeld (dating to 1910). The opening of the Bauhaus was proclaimed by a founding manifesto published in the press that identified the school as a "cathedral of socialism" (the government of the region, Thuringen, was then Socialist), the cathedral embodying an imposing model of the ideal of collective ardor on which its many artistic practices collaborated. This utopian ideal was another example of the ongoing quest for a synthesis of the arts based on solidarity and unification. At this time, one aim of the school was the union of fine art and crafts. The sources of influence on the first Bauhaus were many and varied: in addition to the key concept of "construction"[64] (as incorporated from architectural terminology), the school's starting points included the Arts and Crafts movement, Expressionism, the Werkbund, De Stijl, and abstraction, although in addition its teachers borrowed from the medieval concept of the relationship between master and apprentice. Such hybrid inspirations nurtured the work of the school's members in various areas, giving rise to a range of works that belie the monolithic label, "Bauhaus style." Just as Jan Tschichold (outside the Bauhaus) stressed that "there is nothing final and absolute" in the typography of the period, so Johannes Itten wrote that "the essential slips through formulas."[65]

369

370

369
Karl-Peter Röhl, lithograph announcing the inauguration of the Bauhaus, March 1919.

370
Johannes Itten, *Composition*, 1922.

371
Anny Wottitz, wood and parchment binding for
Chorus Mysticus, the Bauhaus, bookbinding
studio, 1923.

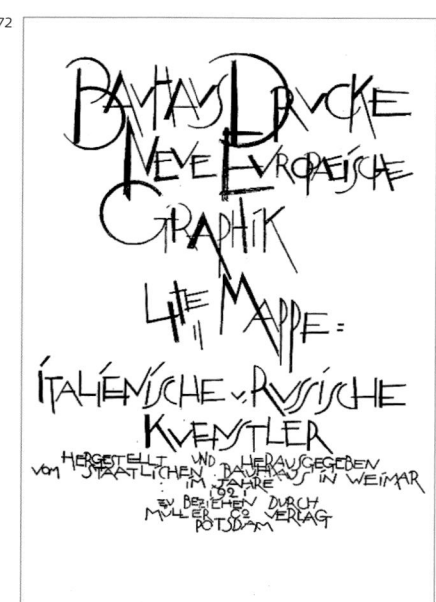

372
Lyonel Feininger, title page, *Italienische und
Russische Künstler* (Italian and Russian Artists)
part of the New European Graphics series,
issued by the Weimar Bauhaus, 1921.

Among the earliest masters at the Bauhaus were Kandinsky, Feininger, Itten, and Klee. The syllabus proposed weaving, pottery, bookbinding, set decoration, and metalwork, as well as other subjects. For the first two or three years of its existence, typography and graphics do not seem to have figured explicitly on the Bauhaus program. However, there exist documents such as invitation cards and graphic materials relating to school life, as well as to the visual identity of the body as a whole. The beginnings of the Bauhaus as established in Weimar were broadly based on craft practices. The basic course provided a pedagogic framework that encouraged students to acquire the fundamentals as a necessary preliminary to the conception of projects. The school's objective was not to promote one style over another, but rather to make it possible for each student to develop his or her personality through a conception of design couched in terms of function and environment. Part of the research undertaken was directed towards the social function of art; the artist-craftsman-creator-designer-manufacturer was called upon to reconsider his role in the social fabric and how he might contribute to improving living conditions.

The first Weimar Bauhaus possessed an art printworks directed by Lyonel Feininger that was centered on engraving techniques. Questions of typography and graphic design were to be tackled a few years later as a result of the significant changes the establishment underwent in 1922 and 1923. Certain members of the school felt the enduring influence of Theo Van Doesburg, then present in Weimar. An eminent figure in De Stijl, he gave courses promulgating his artistic theories that were attended by a number of students of the Bauhaus, although he was never to obtain a post as professor in the school (Vilmos Huszár was openly critical of the work of the first Bauhaus, which he qualified as "Expressionist marmalade.")[66] After De Stijl, in 1923, came the impact of Constructivism in the shape of Moholy-Nagy, who arrived to replace Itten. The same year, the Bauhaus organized a sizable exhibition of its output in response to a demand from the regional parliament of Thuringen (on which the city of Weimar depended) that the school justify its existence. Although Germany was passing through an acute economic slump, the exhibition (featuring in particular everyday objects, such as furniture, fabrics, and so on) proved a runaway success. Switching from the initial aim of combining art and craft, the Bauhaus was to change tack substantially, and a new motto was proclaimed: "art and technology: a new unity."

Since 1922, Walter Gropius had been struggling to set up a limited liability company to distribute Bauhaus products with the hope of turning a profit. Many objects designed at the school reached the production stage and, indeed, some particularly successful examples are still being manufactured (such as the lamp by Wilhelm Wagenfeld and Karl Jucker). In spite of the dissent within the teaching body arising from the school's new direction (as demonstrated in the positions of Klee and Kandinsky), the new objective was adopted, and work at the school was henceforth to be directed towards use, function, production, and technology. The emphasis was to be on art in the service of the recently industrialized society, a realignment that is probably explained by the deepening economic crisis.

If the revival of the school was greeted with enthusiasm, its future was regularly under threat. In 1923, the Socialists lost power in Thuringen and the government that succeeded it forced the Bauhaus to close its doors. The school then headed for Dessau, a city located in the last province still in Socialist hands. Faithful to his motto, Gropius designed a building of glass and reinforced concrete to house the new establishment. The Dessau Bauhaus was drastically reorganized and was to include a printshop and an advertising studio. Between 1923 and 1925 the practice of typography and graphics was well and truly settled in a school now offering courses such as advertising (a field in which some of the painters on the staff had already become involved). From then on, the graphic output of the Bauhaus was to become some of its best-known work. Its formal repertoire focused on geometry and concerted simplification. Primary colors—together with black, white, and gray—were frequently used, a palette that embodies perhaps the ultimate rejection of the styles of the last century.

László Moholy-Nagy, Herbert Bayer, and Joost Schmidt

László Moholy-Nagy (born in 1895) seems to have been the first of the teachers at the Bauhaus to embark on a concerted approach to graphic and typographical design emerging from avant-garde practices. He participated actively in the school's publications, designing, for example, the book (1923), in which he published his text, "The New Typography." In it, he announced that "the intervention of photography in the poster brings with it [...] a notable change. To be instantaneously effective, the poster must take every element into account [...] the two new possibilities for the poster are, 1. photography, which henceforth affords us the most striking and extensive narrative resources, 2. a marked contrast with that typography that marshals an incalculable range of possible variations by an astonishing combination of letterings."[67]

A key figure in the genesis of New Typography, Moholy-Nagy also held that typography must attain "clarity" and "legibility." Within the Bauhaus, he brought his passion for the avant-garde, his immense interest in typographical material, his knowledge of Constructivism (through the crucial influence of El Lissitzky), as well as an exceptional gift for photography and photomontage. In 1925, in an article entitled "Contemporary Typography," he recalled the importance of the concepts of contrast (in the elements) and tension (in space). His conception of *typophoto* was a development of the recent combination of the two media: "photography is highly effective when used as typographic material."[68] Moholy-Nagy also shared the emergent vocabulary of the New Typography: sans serif characters, unusual dynamics, asymmetrical balance, the presence of geometric elements and rules, etc. The graphic designs he created for the Bauhaus would have seemed novel to contemporary eyes: in designing, for instance, the visual identity for the school's publishing arm, he chose to combine a circle, a square, and a triangle—typical of the graphic orientations of the era—while covers for books published by the Bauhaus were adorned with original amalgams of typography and photography. In Moholy-Nagy's hands, typographical material became the object of the interplay between light, depth, transparency, and substance (the relation between typography and light, hardly a frequent concern, has returned to the forefront—if from a wholly different perspective—in designs for computer screen and monitor).

Herbert Bayer was another of the most active representatives of Bauhaus graphics. Like any number of his more enterprising contemporaries in the fields of graphics and typography, he was a multidisciplinary artist, at the same time painter, sculptor, exhibition designer, and, later on, photographer. Born in Upper Austria in 1900, Bayer was a former pupil of the school; from 1925 he was on the staff, heading up the printing workshop. In 1923, while he was still a student in the Bauhaus, he designed the bills that the bank of Thuringen brought out to compensate for spiraling inflation. Their design is unusual for this type of printed matter, and the banknotes are among the earliest concrete realizations of the New Typography, through which Herbert Bayer pursued the search for effectiveness and simplification, then uppermost in the minds of many designers. Bayer was to be instrumental in consolidating the use of sans serif type (which the printshop in Dessau possessed in many sizes), the predilection for lowercase letters (even recommending their exclusive use), the potential of contrast, and construction using orthogonal rules. Following the example of many of his contemporaries, he tried out new compositions associating photography, typography, abstraction, and asymmetry in combinations where red and black are frequently employed (as in the Soviet Union), together with primary colors. In his search for immediacy, clarity, and all-embracing solutions, graphic forms were to be subjected to standardization, and such normalization even affected formats.

This focus on lowercase, as against capital letters, had been in the wind since 1925. At the bottom of the Bauhaus stationery a little saying appeared, intended to promote this typographical viewpoint: "we write everything in lowercase, as this saves us time, why two alphabets for only one word [...]? why write in capital letters when one does not speak in capital letters?" In the same period, in 1925–26, Bayer designed the Universal typeface. According to the avant-garde logic of always starting afresh, Bayer aimed to eradicate every

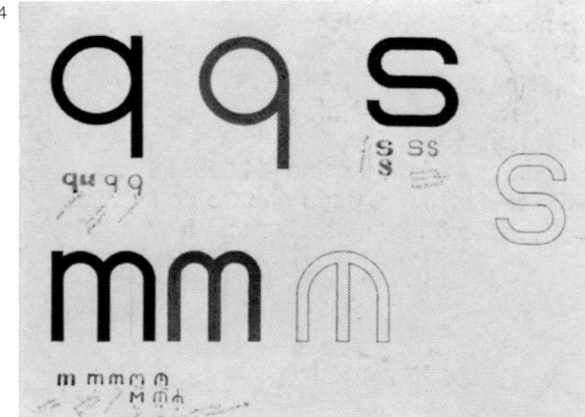

373
Herbert Bayer, Universal, 1925—26. Unique
alphabet comprised solely of lowercase letters.

374
Herbert Bayer, study for Universal, 1925.

375
Herbert Bayer, project for a wall decoration in
the Weimar Bauhaus stairway, painting
executed for the school's exhibition in 1923.

376
Herbert Bayer, project for a kiosk selling and
advertising "P" cigarettes (illuminated sign with
a smoking cigarette), 1924. 25 × 14 in.
(64 × 36 cm).

377
Herbert Bayer, invitation for the final festivities
at the Weimar Bauhaus, 28 and 29 March, 1925.

378
Herbert Bayer, *The World of Letters*, watercolor,
1928–29.

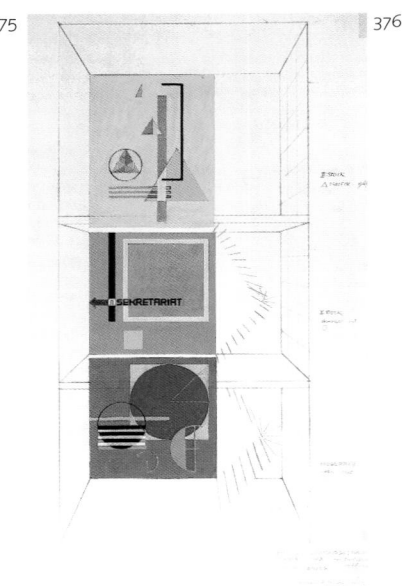

379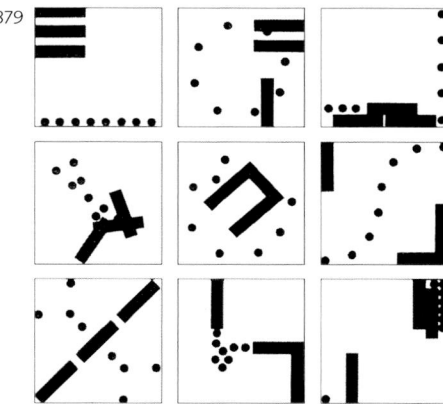

379
Joost Schmidt's teaching methods at the
Bauhaus. Work presented by a student, 1930.
Subject: "Three equal rectangles + eight points."

380
Joost Schmidt, promotional document for
Bauhaus wallpapers, c. 1930.

trace of history, and created an alphabet that was geometric, simplified, and perfectly representative of his ideals. Many of the letters were formed on the base of a circle or half-circle and were designed in lowercase only. The type was developed in several alternatives (bold, condensed, etc.). The very name of the face speaks volumes as to its objectives (the Univers family, which does not have direct links with Universal, was to be designed thirty years later). Like other creators in the domain, Bayer sought to come up with a typeface of a wholly novel kind, whose form would be unlike any earlier style. Proceeding from a position comparable to Futura—a contemporary creation—Universal was never commercialized, however, meaning that every time it was used it had to be drawn afresh.

Herbert Bayer dealt with the school's printed output (publications, posters, etc.), in addition to setting up a curriculum for the students. He also won outside orders (such as catalogs for companies), working directly with industry just as other sectors in the school did. Retrospectively, he explained that the Bauhaus represented "an invaluable heritage of timeless principles as applied to the creative process." "We are not to impose aesthetics on the things we use, to the structures we live in [...] purpose and form must be seen as one."[69] With Bayer, the industrial, functional, and economic dimension of Bauhaus graphic design found its confirmation. He was also interested in the application of graphics and typography to built and public spaces, in particular kiosks and exhibition stands (some members of Futurism and De Stijl displayed similar concerns that served as an opportunity to combine lettering and architecture). In 1928, he left the Bauhaus to settle in Berlin (Gropius and Moholy-Nagy were to leave the same year). There, he directed the major advertising agency, Dorland (in which several Bauhaus students were to find jobs), and turned to photography. Bayer and his team were to handle some sizable industry portfolios. In the opinion of the agency's founder, "Bayer's advertising style [...] exploded the box of traditional advertising design [...]. His Bauhaus- and Surrealism-influenced projects aroused great curiosity."[70]

Joost Schmidt (born in 1893) succeeded Herbert Bayer at the Bauhaus. In the meantime, the workshop had been renamed the "advertising studio" (Walter Peterhans was to direct the photography section from 1929). Another alumnus, Joost Schmidt, designed one of the posters for the famous Bauhaus exhibition at Weimar in 1923. If his convictions led him to try new typographical forms, Schmidt permitted himself more eclectic choices, rather different from the predilections of his predecessor. He desired, for instance, to preserve typeface variety, a notion that earned him the support of Moholy-Nagy in 1923. Even more than before, the Bauhaus advertising studio found itself responding to extramural orders, from accounts in advertising to exhibition hosting. Like Bayer, Schmidt was also conscious of the interest of typography in the wider world, devoting part of his course to spatial, three-dimensional representations of the letter. As regards advertising, he was of the opinion that graphic design must clarify the message, and not translate into commercially eye-catching graphics an ostensibly objective content.

Bauhaus graphic design

László Moholy-Nagy, Herbert Bayer, and Joost Schmidt were the three main teachers at the Bauhaus in the field of visual communication (for lettering design, Mies van der Rohe, the school's last principal, was to turn to the painter Hanns Taddäus Hoyer, Schmidt's successor). If each, in accord with his convictions, developed his own personal approach, all three nevertheless number among the partisans of a radically new typography, such as it was being formed at that time in Germany as in certain neighboring countries. From the very start of the 1920s, this emerging current benefited from the cross-fertilization between Constructivism and De Stijl. A few years later, consolidating these recent directions, the New Typography was formulated, making concrete the urge for synthesis, for simplification, and for the incorporation of typography into a lateral understanding of the arts.

If a substantial proportion of Bauhaus graphic design is couched in a repertoire of

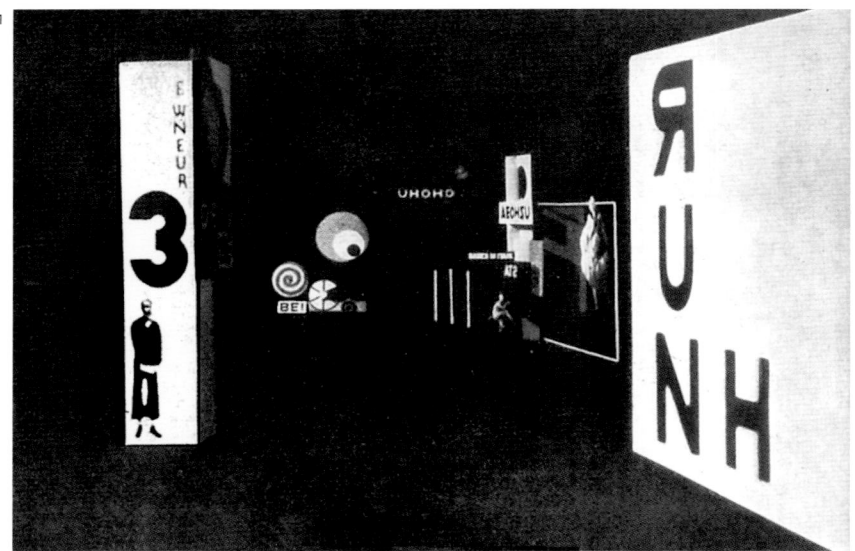

381
Bauhaus, "studio for plastic experimentation,"
Heinz Loew and Franz Ehrlich (students),
project for illuminated advertising (public
square, street, shop-window, theater), 1928.
In the review, *Bauhaus* no. 4, 1928.

identifiable forms, this cannot be extended to all of the establishment's output. Desirous of "avoiding all rigidity," the school's leading figures were from the start opposed to any notion of "style." Instead, the school's (typo)graphic creations betray a measure of diversity. This is proved, for instance, by a lithograph advertisement by Karl-Peter Röhl for the inauguration of the school in March 1919; the school's Expressionist beginnings; Lyonel Feininger's printed oeuvre; certain pieces from the binding workshop; the timetable designed with a brush by Lothar Schreyer for the six-month period covering winter 1921–22; the lettering for various visual poems; a number of compositions by Johannes Itten; certain experimental domains (based on collaging, assembling, distorting, and superimposing newsprint and photography); Joost Schmidt's "misshapen" three-dimensional lettering; the original use of the typewriter for textile motifs; and the related lines of research pursued around phototypography. From a pedagogical point of view, and including graphics and typography, one of the Bauhaus's essential contributions resides in the introduction of a fundamental course (experimentation on materials, textures, and colors, and the focus on elementary components) that could be extended along similar lines. Another significant aspect was the school's multidisciplinary approach, whose objective was to adapt to modern industrial means of production and introduce artistically created forms into daily living patterns.

Enforced closure

If the Bauhaus had traversed a wonderfully fertile period at the end of the 1920s, from the very start of the 1930s, the school was once again prey to serious difficulties. The architect Mies van der Rohe took over the direction of the establishment in 1930. The following year, the school entered a critical phase from which there was to be no escape. Students were divided between pro-nationalists and anti-Nazis, while the National-Socialist party won local elections in Dessau in 1931. In 1932, the town council elected to close the Bauhaus. On July 8, the local press pointed out the school for public vilification: "The disappearance of this so-called higher school of formal design will remove from German soil one of the most representative embodiments of the tendency to a Judeo-Marxist art. May its complete demolition shortly follow [...] where this dishonorable glass palace stands [...]."[71] Expelled, in 1932 the Bauhaus made off to Berlin. Soon after, the Dessau building designed by Walter Gropius was to be ransacked (the glass smashed, the rooms plundered, and furniture, materials, and documents thrown out of the windows). At the beginning of 1933, after Hitler gained power, Nazi police obtained a search warrant, sealing off the school and the farm, alleging that it was a hotbed of communism. Rumor had it that certain members of the Bauhaus had escaped abroad. After several meetings between Mies van der Rohe and the Nazi authorities, the school closed its doors forever in July 1933. To the Nazis, the school was "one of the main havens for the Judeo-Marxist conception of art, so far removed from art that it can be only regarded as a pathological condition."[72]

This brutally enforced closure meant that the Bauhaus was to have lasted exactly as long as the Weimar Republic (1919–33). More than one thousand two hundred students had passed through the school, contributing greatly to the development and diffusion of the avant-garde spirit. During its comparatively brief existence, the Bauhaus was often at odds with the contemporary political climate and assailed by financial problems. On two occasions, the establishment had had to up-sticks and find another location. If the events of 1933 ended with its permanent closure, its objectives lived on in the men and women who made them their own and in the plans realized at the school. As Ludwig Mies van der Rohe's celebrated definition put it, "the Bauhaus was not an institution with a well-defined program, it was an idea [...]. Only an idea can produce such effects."[73] And it is true that the Bauhaus experiment, itself the result of the cross-fertilization of countless influences, was to spawn innumerable descendants. In Germany, several art schools were inspired directly to integrate graphic design into their curriculum as early as the 1920s. Beyond the frontiers of Germany, the Bauhaus met with significant resonance in Europe, before being felt in, among other places, the United States and Japan. From 1933, many figures from the school, including Gropius, Moholy-Nagy, Albers, Breuer, and Bayer, fled in exile across the Atlantic. In this fresh context, one that proved favorable to the reception of European avant-garde applied art, they pursued on American soil the research they had initiated in Germany and elsewhere, as much in the field of architecture as in various sectors of design. Pedagogic experiments also continued, and the hope that the Bauhaus would enjoy an aftermath in the United States was soon realized. In 1937, Moholy-Nagy decided to found the New Bauhaus in Chicago, where he managed to attract several former Bauhäusler. Overhauled in 1939, the establishment, reminiscent of its predecessor in the obstacles it encountered to its progress, soon changed its name —and the Bauhaus was finally consigned to history. If the significance of the Bauhaus remains difficult to gauge with precision, it is nonetheless considerable. Its vast heritage is probably due to the fact that its practices, steeped in issues of use and function, were based on ideals of simplification, accessibility, and a universal, communicable language. This quest for a utopia (a universalist claim to harness artistic forms for daily life, the very concept of unambiguous communication) built through concrete, tangible, and pragmatic demands is, of course, a sign of openhandedness that is tinged with paradox.

Germany in the 1920s: a creative forcing-ground

After the conclusion of World War I until 1933, Germany proved the theater of significant developments in graphics and typography. There, many originators contributed actively to the impetus given to visual communication—specialists, multifaceted artists, members of the Bauhaus, creators originating in Eastern Europe, and so on. Among the principal actors of this dynamic scene were Jan Tschichold, László Moholy-Nagy, and Herbert Bayer, the influential Constructivist El Lissitzky, Kurt Schwitters, Raoul Hausmann, and John Heartfield (who collaborated with the extreme leftwing press), Ludwig Hohlwein (active since the beginning of the century), and many other artists and/or graphic designers. Such a proportion of creative minds proved to the great benefit of graphics and typography, with some practitioners making their name in the more specialist field of type design—some as draftsman-calligraphers, others as artists or designer-manufacturers.

The role of associations

As was the case elsewhere, and as the avant-gardes of the 1910s had already demonstrated, periodicals and other publications bolstered progressive movements in the Weimar Republic actively and consistently. Exhibitions also played a role in mediating with the public. What is more, associations and groups forged between graphic designers allowed convergent or complementary practices to crystallize or gain in coherence. The Werkbund, founded in 1907, continued its activities until the beginning of the 1930s; as an association, it provided a benchmark for artists, sculptors, and originators of all kinds eager to rethink their activities with respect to the new socioeconomic realities. Founded in Berlin in 1919, the Bund deutscher Gebrauchsgraphiker (Union of German Graphic Designers) was established as a confederation of artists, designers, and graphic designers engaged in the avant-garde. The Ring Neuer Werbegestalter [74] (Circle of New Graphic Designers in Advertising) or NWG was one of the most significant associations in the area around 1930. Founded on the outskirts of Frankfurt in 1928 on the instigation of Kurt Schwitters and architect Robert Michel, from the

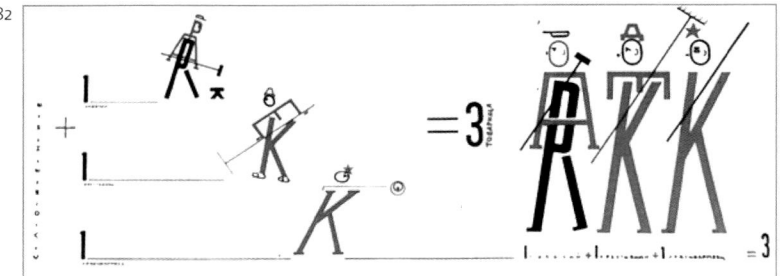
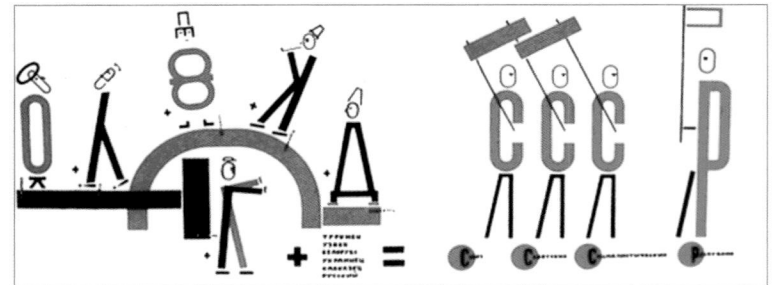

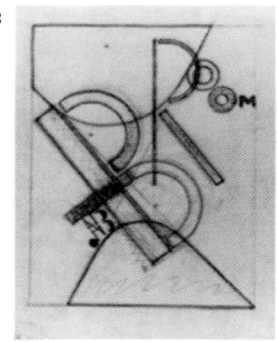
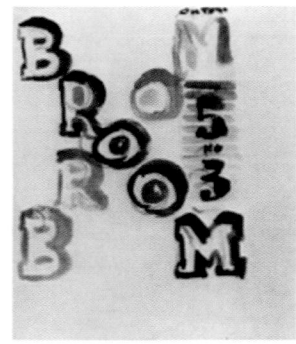

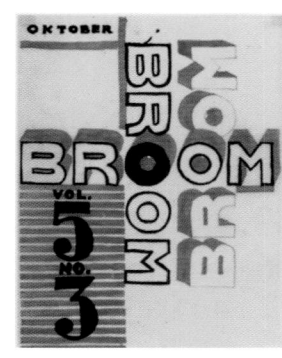

382
El Lissitzky, *The Four Operations*, compositions based on typographical elements, 1929.

383
El Lissitzky, five sketches for the cover of the American review, *Broom*, 1922. Left: pencil on paper and watercolor on paper, pencil on graph paper. Right (in color): ink and watercolor on paper.

384
El Lissitzky, cover for the American review, *Broom*, February 1923. Approx. 11 × 8 ³/₄ in. (28 × 22 cm).

start the NWG attracted a number of figures active in Germany. Chaired by Kurt Schwitters, it was formed initially of Jan Tschichold, Georg Trump, Robert Michel, Friedrich Vordemberge-Gildewart, Walter Dexel, Cesar Domela, Willi Baumeister, and Max Burchartz, who were followed by Hans Leistikow, Werner Gräff, and then Piet Zwart and Paul Schuitema from the Netherlands. Other graphic designers of repute, both German and foreign, joined the NWG's activities, including John Heartfield, Herbert Bayer, the Czech Karel Teige, the Hungarian Lajos Kassák, and Theo Van Doesburg, Johannes Molzahn, Otto Baumberger, and the Frenchman Cassandre. The NWG organized exhibitions on contemporary graphics, presenting, for example, the work of the Czechs Sutnar and Teige. These itinerant exhibitions were shown abroad (e.g., in Switzerland and the Netherlands) as well as in Germany.

The NWG embraced the cause of avant-garde conceptions in typography and graphic design, in which the New Typography occupied an undeniably key place. Such an association—as a place practitioners could meet and share ideas and convictions—became the focus for cultural diffusion. Like the members of the Werkbund (in particular Peter Behrens), those of the NWG tended to regard the various facets of design as a unit. Little by little, the concept of inclusive design and of global communication gained ground—be it for business, the administrations, or any other institution.

El Lissitzky, László Moholy-Nagy, and Kurt Schwitters

The dynamic landscape of 1920s Germany was receptive to experiments in nearby countries, as attested by the strong influence of El Lissitzky and Moholy-Nagy on graphic design.

The Russian artist El Lissitzky stayed intermittently in Germany before living in Switzerland from 1921 to 1925. Before World War I, he had studied architecture at Darmstadt. In 1919, Marc Chagall invited him to teach at the School of Fine Arts at Vitebsk, where he met Kasimir Malevich. Subsequently El Lissitzky became involved in Vhutemas in Moscow. In addition to architecture and teaching, El Lissitzky practiced painting, graphic design, typography, and photography. In 1919–20, he began to create his famous *Proun*s, conceived as "switching stations between painting and architecture."[75] Already an influential representative of Constructivism, in 1921 he left for Berlin, where he greatly increased awareness of the movement. As the era was conducive to interchange, he also encountered several other highly active proponents of the avant-garde, thus familiarizing himself with Dada, flirting with De Stijl, and visiting the Bauhaus. He became acquainted, in particular, with Theo Van Doesburg and Kurt Schwitters. Lettering was to play an increasing role in the work of El Lissitzky. His position was that typography must strive above all for visual effectiveness: it is an "active, articulated structure," which "reflects the dynamics of spoken language."[76] In 1923, he outlined his concept of typography in the article "Topography of Typography," which appeared in the review *Merz*. There, he stressed the visual and expressive role of textual composition. As he saw it, type should favor "optics over phonetics." Reversing the usual concept of graphic design in publishing, he considered that "the organization of the space of the book [...] ought to correspond to the tensions and pressures of its contents." His 1923 text also states that: "The vast domain of print [...] must be superseded [by the] electro-library" (a surprisingly intuitive notion that has much in common with Octave Uzanne's predictions at the end of the nineteenth century, quoted above). Inclined to practical experimentation, El Lissitzky set about applying the ideas he defended and publicized. In the book *Dlja golosa* (For the Voice), he set poems by Vladimir Mayakovsky using typographical material from which he drew an expressive power, one that confers a sense of the iconic on the text. Following this experiment, he was to abandon the traditional arrangement of words in consecutive sequence. These experiments were continued in *A Story of Two Squares*, an album conceived in 1920 and appearing in 1922 and intended to awaken the curiosity of children. It tells of the adventures of two squares, red and black (sometimes presented as symbolizing Bolshevism and Suprematism). The text invites readers to play: "Take a piece of paper—fold it; some sticks—color them in; some bits of wood—get

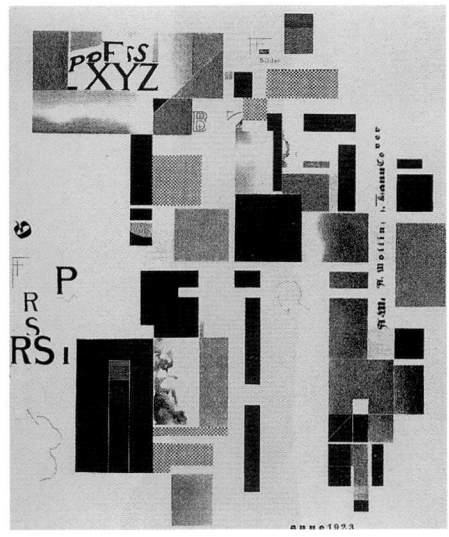

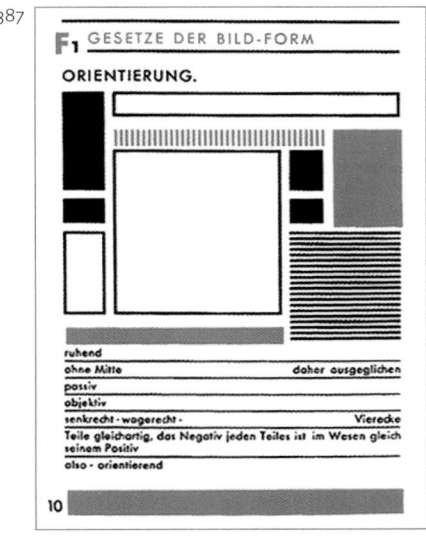

385
Kurt Schwitters, *(Aschooff Ellen)*, 1922. Collage, 9 1/2 × 7 in. (24.3 × 18.3 cm).

386
Kurt Schwitters, *Merz 3. Merz Mappe*, Hanover, 1923. Lithograph, 22 × 17 1/2 in. (56 × 44.2 cm).

387
Kurt Schwitters, inside page of the brochure, *Die neue Gestaltung in der Typographie*, 1930.

building." In addition, El Lissitzky produced some astonishing covers for the American cultural review *Broom*. He also designed promotional media, in particular for the Pelikan company,[78] for which in 1924 he composed an advertisement incorporating a photograph (according to Tschichold, El Lissitzky was the first to use a photogram in advertising). Consequently, photography was to join typography in El Lissitzky's graphic work.

The Hungarian László Moholy-Nagy was, like El Lissitzky, to have considerable influence on German graphic design. He became involved in the arts after having abandoned his law studies. Shortly after the war, following the overthrow of the Republic of the Councils in Hungary, he went into exile at the end of 1919, initially to Vienna. He was finally to settle in Berlin in 1920 where, like so many others, he encountered several avant-garde figures then in the heat of the action, such as Schwitters, Van Doesburg, Jean Arp, and El Lissitzky, whose works were to mark his own profoundly. An exhibition of his work, as early as 1920 in Berlin,

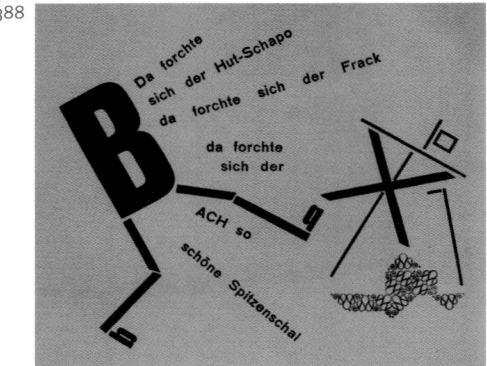

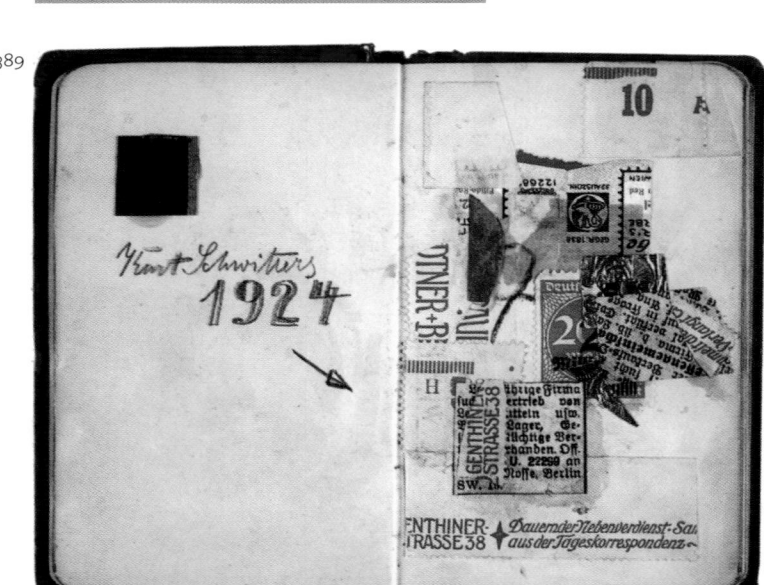

made his approach better known. His artistic and professional practice combined painting, sculpture, graphics, photography, cinema, and publications. In 1923, Walter Gropius invited him to teach at the Bauhaus, where he directed the preliminary course, replacing Johannes Itten, and where he became involved in the printshop. Herbert Bayer and Joost Schmidt, future teachers of graphic design, were among his pupils. Singularly active within the school, Moholy-Nagy had arrived at a moment of significant change; the Bauhaus was being redefined, accentuating the integration of technology into artistic fields. Keen on photography, Moholy-Nagy was to adhere fully to the school's new direction. Through teaching and professional practice alike, he made significant contributions to graphic design, combining an interest in the revival of typography with an experimental approach to photographic media. In 1923, in his article "The New Typography" (published by Bauhaus), he laid down some of his ideas on the matter, pleading above all for "absolute clarity in all typographical work."[79] The Bauhaus book series, which he commissioned and whose basic visual design he oversaw, testifies to his graphic vision—abstract, constructed, dynamic, spatial, neither conventional nor ponderous. In conjoining typography, photography, and abstraction, Moholy-Nagy's graphics were sometimes close to Bauhaus aesthetics, though elsewhere they could be highly personal. In 1925, Moholy-Nagy clarified his concept of *typophoto*: "The use of photography has cleared the way for a typography capable of introducing new dimensions [...]. Light is a new artistic medium, like color in painting or sound in music."[80] His graphic designs thus edged towards a new expression integrating depth and shadow, the indistinct and light, resulting in an original visualization and spatialization. Moholy-Nagy turned the typographical object of the alphabet into a photographic object, as against "the rigidity of current typographical practice." Anxious that the spirit of the time should breathe through his compositions, the theorist appealed to "the simultaneity of sensory perceptions" and "the pace of present-day life."[81]

In addition to graphic design, Moholy-Nagy worked in many creative fields. He came up with the pithy and still pertinent formula that many designers strive to make their own: "design is not a profession; it's an attitude,"[82] with the implication that designing for everyday environments is more a question of possessing an alert and open frame of mind than of subscribing blindly to a preexisting corpus of knowledge.

Whereas with El Lissitzky or Moholy-Nagy the affiliation with Constructivism is manifest, the creations of Kurt Schwitters (1887–48) are far more heterogeneous. Another major figure of the time, the work he developed might be called, at the very least, unclassifiable. Aware of the Arts and Crafts movement and the Werkbund, he responded to and engaged with many avant-garde practices, borrowing from Cubist collage, taking part in Dada (through which coursed a more expansive form of Futurism), and rubbing shoulders with Constructivists. A plural artist, Schwitters worked in all media, combining painting, collage, sculpture, assemblage, architecture, set design, performance, music, poetry, typography, graphics, advertising, and publishing. At the beginning of his career, he characterized himself as apolitical. In 1918 Schwitters met Dadaists Raoul Hausmann and Jean Arp and took part in some events. However, his encounter with El Lissitzky and Theo Van Doesburg in 1922 channeled his interests in the direction of Constructivism, Neoplasticism, and De Stijl. The complementarity of these influences, Dadaism and Constructivism in particular, determines the originality of an oeuvre that is capricious and humorous, exceptionally diverse, but always coherent. In 1923, Schwitters shifted decisively towards Constructivist art; it was the same year the Bauhaus left off its Expressionist and handicraft beginnings and moved to construction and technology (in particular under the influence of Van Doesburg and Moholy-

388
Kurt Schwitters, Käte Steinitz, Theo Van Doesburg, inside page of *Die Scheuche. Märchen, Merz*, no. 14/15, 1925.

389
Collage signed Kurt Schwitters in Nina Kandinsky's notebook, 1924. 4 × 2 ¹⁄₂ in. (10.4 × 6.5 cm).

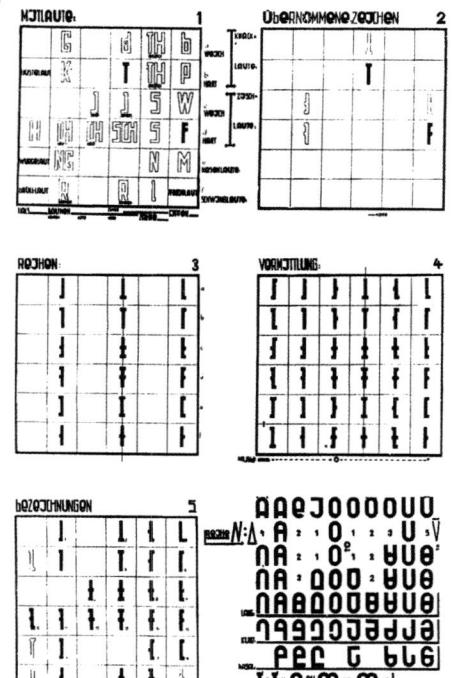

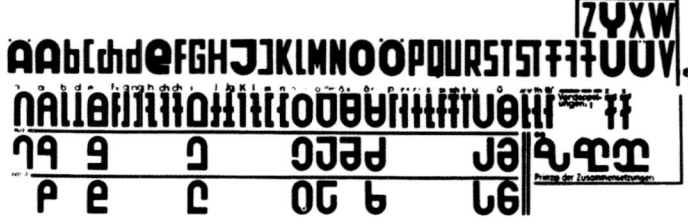

390
Kurt Schwitters, *Neue plastische Systemschrift*,
project for a "new systematic plastic form of
writing," studies accompanied by versions
of "E" and "F," 1927.

Nagy). Communicating intensely with his contemporaries, in 1926 Schwitters became sporadically involved in the Bauhaus.

In 1919, Schwitters had given a name to his protean art: "Merz," the "second syllable of the word 'Kommerz' [...] cut out and glued, from an advertisement for the Kommerz- und Privatbank."[83] Subsequently, cut-and-pasted printed matter was often to feature in his work. At the same time, at the beginning of the 1920s, he began trying his hand at advertising, graphic design, and typography. In 1923, he launched the review *Merz*, which he continued to bring out until 1932. From the year of its first publication, the review served as a forum for the promotion and diffusion of new voices in graphic design. With Van Doesburg, Schwitters designed a small poster for a "Petite soirée dada" (1922–23) where the information is piled up into a dance-like visual chaos not unlike some Futurist compositions. In the same period, he worked out a philosophy of graphic design, embracing ideals such as impact, simplification, and construction. As a graphic designer and author, he contributed forcefully to the development and definition of New Typography. According to his own statements, he took up advertising graphics as a response to his straitened circumstance (undoubtedly related to the economic crisis): "A man has to survive. So once again I looked around for the next best job. This time it was advertising and typographical design in general."[84]

In 1925 in Hanover, Kurt Schwitters set up the Merz Werbezentrale advertising agency,[85] which dealt particularly with portfolios from industry and business (clients would include Pelikan and Bahlsen among others). As Schwitters saw it, "good advertising is cheap, practical, clear, and concise, employs modern methods, and possesses a strong form."[86] From this point of view, he was at one with the partisans of reform and modernization in graphic design, such as El Lissitzky, Max Burchartz, and Walter Dexel. Schwitters was to become one of the principal actors and promoters of New Typography. In 1924, in Number 11 of his journal *Merz* entitled "Typoreklame," (Typo-advertising) he published his "Theses on Typography," ten in number, in which he presented a synthesis of his vision of new typography. In a preamble to the main text, he expounded one of the central tenets of progressive modernity: "As regards typography, one can lay down an infinite number of laws. The fundamental principle: never do as others have done before you."[87] His (typo)graphic creations well reflect this effort to divorce the past. His best-known work in the area covers advertisements and the logo for the Pelikan company, as well as books for children. After 1929, he was head of printed communication for Hanover City Council (responsible for visual identity, graphic media in the public transport system and at cultural venues, and so on).

From the beginning of the 1920s, Schwitters had been introducing fragments of printed matter into his collages. If text plays a role in his collages, often in a fragmentary form, Schwitters was equally concerned with typographical detail, with units such as letters, and with their design. In 1927, he devised a program for a Neue plastische Systemschrift (new plastic systematic writing): "Thoroughly optophonetic [...it] demands that the complete image of the written word correspond to the complete sonority of the language." Following this logic, Schwitters investigated the absence of correspondence between the form of a letter and its sound. Thus, "there exists a great resemblance between E and F and a great difference between E and O. Yet, on the level of sound, E and O are more closely related than E and F."[88] In his alphabetical system, Schwitters distinguished the form of the consonants (narrow, thin, and angular) from those of the vowels (round, wider, and bold). The last version of his writing system constitutes an alphabetical set whose signs are no longer recognizable at all, unless one is told of the code. A readable version of this alphabet featured on two typographical posters in 1927 (one advertising a concert at the Frankfurt Opera House). Schwitters's work strongly marked the history of graphic design and typography. Lettering

and graphic meaning also occupied a significant place in Merz—"this new process whose principle lies in using every material."[89] Without forfeiting anything of his originality, Schwitters thus contributed to the collective rethink of graphic design in which Dutch, Russian, German, Polish, Hungarian, and Czech minds were also exercised.

As for a number of the protagonists of the time, the 1930s was to affect the course of Schwitters's career in unforeseen ways. In 1937, Schwitters's Merz appeared in the Nazi exhibition of Degenerate Art in Munich, and he fled into exile to Norway. In more than one respect, his multiform oeuvre is representative of the rich vein opened up in the field of the typography by dint of the close relationship between plastic experiment and creativity in graphic design.

The plural nature of graphic design in Germany

Interwar Germany boasted an enviable range of talent. Quite apart from Schwitters, Moholy-Nagy, and El Lissitzky, there were other distinguished and influential graphic designers of comparable mastery. The impact and resonance of the revival to which all contributed derives partly from the fact they worked in different cities in Germany (sometimes moving from one to the other), which thus each became veritable seedbeds of creativity. Experiments in graphic design and typography were undertaken in Berlin (Domela, Bayer), Frankfurt (Leistikow, Renner), Leipzig (Tschichold), Munich (Tschichold, Trump, Renner), Stuttgart (Baumeister), Hanover (Schwitters and, sporadically, El Lissitzky), Bochum (Burchartz, Canis), Essen, Jena (Dexel) and in schools at Dessau (Moholy-Nagy, Albers, Bayer, Schmidt), Magdeburg (Dexel, Molzahn), and Breslau/Wroclaw (Molzahn). To this is added the international dimension of the phenomenon, due to the cosmopolitanism of the members of the NWG as well as visits or the permanent residence of significant figures from abroad. Other names emerged, such as Karl-Peter Röhl and Werner Gräff (two former members of the Bauhaus), and Anton Stankowski (who worked with Burchartz and Canis).

Through their practice, researches, writings, convictions, and teaching, the many graphic designers active in the Germany of the 1920s made a personal contribution to reshaping graphic design. In 1924 in Bochum, Max Burchartz and Johannes Canis set up an agency, Werbe-Bau. Burchartz, a colleague of El Lissitzky and Schwitters, had also come into contact with the first Bauhaus. The Werbe-Bau's remit was to reinvent the forms of industrial design and cultural communication. Like them, Walter Dexel and Willi Baumeister, sharing in the views of the New Typography (without, however, giving up the use of capital letters), explored optical contrast and asymmetric dynamics. In 1927, Walter Dexel published his article "Was ist neue

391
Anonymous, enamel plaque for the Hamburg newspaper, *Echo*, Germany, c. 1930.
Flat plate, 3 ft. 2 ½ in. × 19 in. (98 × 48 cm).

392
Studio Foto ringl + pit (Ellen Auerbach and Grete Stern), advertisement for Petrole Hahn shampoo, photograph, Germany, 1931.

Typographie?" printed in Gothic type in the *Frankfurter Zeitung*. There he affirmed that "our paramount objective is rapid and optimum legibility." Regarding typography as a specific service, and not as personal artistic expression, he continued: "Our public is no more interested in our experiments than in our tastes or artistic values [...]. It is not art's business to write that Tartempion cigarettes cost five pfennings or that Bergner is playing at the theater tomorrow [...]. The visual message has to be clear, neutral, concise, and stick to the essentials."[90] Just as firmly attached to the concept of effective mediation (of a social and informative nature), Karl-Peter Röhl and Werner Gräff both explored systems of signage as an aid to orientation and circulation in public places. At the crossroads of functional and universal forms, this sector of graphic design is above all concerned with its collective and public dimension, in which it is a question of situating the information within the group and

393
Walter Dexel, illuminated sign for a hotel in Jena, 1925 (reproduced in *De Stijl*).

394
Heinrich Mittag, enamel plaque for *Leibniz-Keks* biscuits, Germany, c. 1920. Curved plate, 13 × 19 3/4 in. (33 × 50 cm).

395
Julius Klinger, poster *Tabu* (cigarette paper supposed to reduce nicotine absorption), 1919.

social space. Such projects overlap with certain aspects of New Typography, in particular its preoccupation with utility, its search for norms and standards, and what it saw as its widening brief.

Since 1925, the philosopher and logician Otto Neurath in Vienna had been outlining a "method of statistical visualization" for which he had pooled a range of numerical data so as to tackle the intractable "question of an international language." In 1935, Neurath was to rename his system "Isotype" (International System of Typographic Picture Education). It so happened that around the same time, Henry C. Beck developed the first geometric diagram for the map of the London Underground. Each of these projects (the Isotype, public signage, the "diagrammatic" map) stems from visual solutions to which the New Typography and contemporary currents brought concrete and innovative elements.

Typeface design: a surge in experimentation

In Germany where graphic designers, typographers, designers, and painters were to rethink letterforms in response to future-orientated ideas, the vitality of typographical creation also found expression in the field of type design. Typeface design thus aimed for simplification, geometrization, and standardization, tinged, for some, with universalizing tendencies. At the turn of the twentieth century, sans serif type had already made unprecedented progress in the commercial sphere throughout the Western world. In the Europe of the 1910s, typeface development seems to have become a more sporadic affair: here and there letterforms and alphabets sprang up, intended as much for the poster as for descriptive or other applications in architectural space. Three years after Edward Johnston's Underground type, in about 1919, Theo Van Doesburg developed a typeface in keeping with the aesthetics of De Stijl, composed of capital letters inscribed within a square format (with the exception of the "I"). Despite Germany's continued use of Gothic lettering since the Middle Ages, from the middle of the 1920s several visual artists strove to create letterforms within the framework of their artistic practice. A certain number of experimental types thus appeared in the multifaceted corpus of creators such as Albers or Bayer, who had trained in architecture or painting.

While avant-garde typographical creation reflected various convergences, it also brought about dissension (as it had done in previous centuries). Even if this criticism remained under the surface, it was far from negligible. In his 1923 article "The New Typography," Moholy-Nagy states that "legibility can in no case be subordinated to an *a priori* aesthetic" and reflects that, in fact, "letters of the alphabet can never be forced into a preestablished form; for example, a square."[91] Moholy-Nagy is probably referring here to the lettering conceived by members of De Stijl. In the same way, Bauhaus typography did not carry all before it, and was widely criticized even by other members of the avant-garde, such as Walter Dexel, for instance. And although

396

Rudolf Koch, Kabel, Germany, 1927.

396

ABCDEFGHIJKLMNOPQRSTUVWXYZ

abcdefghijklmnopqrstuvwxyz

(&$1234567890¢£.,:;'"''--·-—.˙%/!?[]«»)

after 1925 several members of the Bauhaus advocated the exclusive use of lowercase, with the aim of disposing of the dual nature of the alphabet, few graphic designers outside the school seem actually to have followed this directive (although later it did take root in graphic design). Kurt Schwitters, Max Burchartz, Johannes Canis, Willi Baumeister, and Walter Dexel used capital letters as well as small, some tending even to privilege capitals on media such as posters. Max Bill, on the other hand, was to remain marked by the allure of lowercase lettering after his stint at the Bauhaus, as his typography was long to attest.

Only a handful of the experimental typefaces from the period (such as Futura, Kabel, and Erbar) were ever actually manufactured and widely distributed. Futura was designed by Paul Renner, a typographer and type designer who had initially trained in architecture and painting (he was in addition the director of the Meisterschule für Deutschlands Buchdrucker [School of German Master Printers] in Munich, where Tschichold was invited to teach at his request). The first sketches for Futura were completed in 1925. The alphabet is constructed along strongly geometrical lines and certain letters were endowed with highly original shapes (the "a," "g," and "r" for example). With a view to manufacturing Futura, the Bauer foundry (based in Frankfurt) asked Paul Renner to modify its design so that the pronounced characteristics of certain letters were toned down and closer to more usual forms, concessions that ensured Futura enjoyed a long life. The first version was completed in 1927, and in subsequent years was cut in bold and Italic alternatives. Since then, the face has remained in daily usage. Less well known but still current, Erbar was an earlier creation than Futura. It was conceived in 1922 by typographer and type designer Jakob Erbar. After Johnston's Underground, Erbar probably represents one of the first typefaces of this new stamp. Then came Kabel, created in 1927 by type designer Rudolf Koch for the Klingspor foundry. Kabel presents geometrizing letterforms (as the designs for "b" and "g" betray) that, just like Futura and Erbar, possess rather long ascenders.

397

Paul Renner, Futura, montage of proofs assembled from engravings of trial letters, Germany, c. 1927. Plates employed for correcting and alerting the letters and other signs.

398

Paul Renner, studies presented as the very earliest examples of Futura, Germany, before 1927 (1924–25?).

397

399

abcdefghijklmnopqrſstuvw
Grönland xyz Spitzbergen
12345 Magdeburg 67890
AABCDEFGHIJKLMMN
NOPQRSTUVVWWXYZ
UNION PHÖNIX OASE

400

The second half of the 1920s saw mounting research and achievement in the field of type design. Lucian Bernhard (a major poster artist at the beginning of the century, and among the inventors of the *Sachplakat*) designed the Bernhard Gothic face, produced in 1929 by the American foundry ATF. It is perhaps from this typeface, which Bernhard drew for his posters, that Block (Berthold, 1908) was derived, a rather imposing sans serif type, very bold and available today in digital format, and moreover highly prized by Roman Cieslewicz.

401

In Germany during the same period, another series of typefaces arose that, in keeping with their experimental approach, moved away from archetypical forms to become essentially research proposals or projects. For the majority, these alphabets did not reach the stage of industrial production nor wide distribution (at least in their time), and were primarily limited to the handpress. These reflect above all a thoroughgoing determination to simplify, standardize, and universalize forms, such as with Herbert Bayer's Universal alphabet, for the Bauhaus, whose ambition is clear enough from its appellation.[92] Josef Albers, also under the auspices of the Bauhaus in the mid-1920s, was to develop the Stencil alphabet for use on posters. Its letterforms are also composed from a restricted range of geometrical forms (mainly the square, quadrant, semicircle, and triangle), with the construction element appearing in the spaces (generally vertical) separating its components. Contrary to Bayer's Universal and the recommendations of dyed-in-the-wool Bauhäusler, Stencil kept faith with the distinction between lower- and uppercase letters.

Jan Tschichold, for his part, also strove to renew alphabetical form. In 1929, he was working on a project for a universal mixed typeface, a hybrid between capital and small letters in a single alphabet. He, too, had fallen prey to the prevalent taste for geometric figures. Pursuing his ideals further, he designed a phonetic version of a typeface whose purpose was to attain equivalence between graphic sign and sound (Schwitters's "systematic" and "optophonetic" writing, which also proposes the graphic transposition of oral forms, manifests comparable concerns). Tschichold also designed the Transito typeface that entered production in the Netherlands in 1931. Like Albers's Stencil, this combinatory alphabet applied to each letter a visible logic of construction based on simplified elements. Tschichold's typefaces should be measured according to the yardstick of his formative training. He started out with a thorough familiarity with traditional designs (to which he was subsequently to return), but the need for understatement as well as experimentation in typography became seen as both complementary and essential. With Tschichold, as with Albers, Schwitters, or Bayer, the new alphabetical forms conceived in Germany between 1925 and the very beginning of the 1930s accompanied lines of research opened up by New Typography. As they continued to be used, some of the types of the era (including Futura, Kabel, and Gill, created in Britain) reveal the relevance and appeal of the pressing need to overhaul the classic forms of the past.

Graphic design in the 1920s: social ideals and constructive aims

If the 1920s brought upheaval in (typo)graphic forms, this phenomenon was particularly acute in central and Eastern Europe. After the hullabaloo of Futurism and Dada, eyes were now focused on reconstruction, be it in an experimental or rational vein. The headline movements grew up in Russia (and then the Soviet Union), the Netherlands, Germany, Czechoslovakia, Poland, and Hungary. In spite of political turbulence, dire inflation from 1923 onwards, and the crisis of 1929, industry developed apace, followed inevitably by visual communication. As in the Netherlands and elsewhere, a number of graphic designers and artists (Heartfield, Domela, El Lissitzky, Schuitema, and Zwart) can be seen to adhere to a certain number of convergent ideals: hopes for a better world, an ambition to reconcile the "major" to the "minor" arts, and the urge to situate their creations with respect to the community. Although many were filled with a desire to contribute usefully to the development of a new and more just society, graphic designers of the 1920s, through their responses to commercial orders from the industrial world, in fact participated in the expansion of the business society (a phenomenon that was to accelerate and expand in the period after World War II). From this point of view, graphic design and typography are multifaceted practices—at the same time objects of artistic experimentation and in step with consumerism and the economy, envisaged as a means of action in the social domain. In Germany as in Russia (the Soviet Union from 1922), this engagement lies at the heart of the conception of forms for the wider environment. In France or Great Britain, on the other hand, it seems that graphic design tended to be less taken up with sociopolitical concerns.

Throughout central and Eastern Europe in the 1920s (and sometimes even before), graphic practices converged towards constructive tendencies. The considerable uptake of photography and montage into the graphic repertoire, combined with the search for optical synthesis and typographical effectiveness, is the key characteristic of visual communication in the interwar period, a tendency highlighted by the emerging concept of graphic design per se. The first known use of this term dates to 1922 in the writings of the American William Addison Dwiggins, yet another multitalented creator. Graphic design and *typophoto* were to enter into the spirit of the transformation of conventional outlets of the profession, such as the billboard, advertising, typography, and visual communication as a whole. Stress was now laid on an unprecedented dynamism, on conception, on rationalization. At the same time, there evolved a style of design intended for information, centered on concision, smoothness, and immediacy of reading and comprehension. In the broad sense, graphic design was becoming a force to be reckoned with and was poised to turn its inexhaustible sources of invention to good account.

Photography and montage in Germany and Russia

It is a remarkable fact that graphic communication embraced photography and montage as early as the end of the 1910s, in the heyday of the avant-garde. Political troubles were more than a background to the emergence of photomontage; in point of fact, they formed the context from which it was born. The enormous popularity encountered by this new means of expression was to continue for several years. It is no easy task, however, to determine exactly when the floodgates opened. It is generally thought that photomontage came into its own towards the end of World War I, that is to say, nearly a century after the invention of

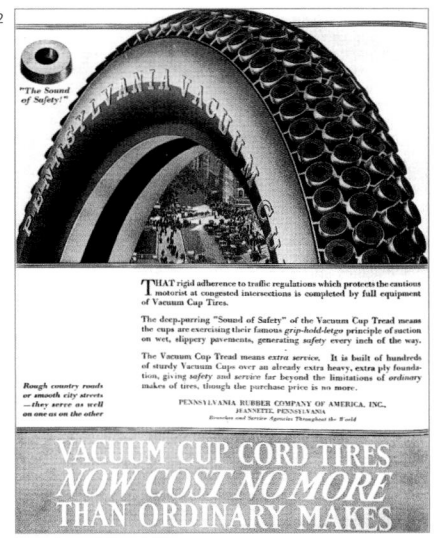

402
Herbert Bayer, press announcement appearing in the American magazine, *Vanity Fair*, September 1922.

403
Gustav Klutsis, postcard, *The physical education of the workers–fulcrum of the Socialist construction*, Moscow, 1928. 6 × 4 ¹/₄ in. (15 × 10.8 cm).

photography. (History dates the practice of amateur photomontage to around 1860, perhaps even before.) Responsibility for the resurgence in avant-garde circles of photomontage—constantly reshaped between 1916 and 1920–22—is often disputed between Dadaists and Constructivists. It seems that the process broke through at more or less the same time in Germany and Russia, with German Dadaists perhaps slightly in the vanguard. According to George Grosz, he and John Heartfield invented the process in 1916. As regards Russia, Gustav Klutsis dates it to 1919–20. In the years following the foundation of the Dada movement, German Dadaists made great use of the process: Raoul Hausmann (to whom certain historians ascribe its paternity) and Hannah Höch adopted it as an essential component of their work. In parallel, Russian Constructivists revealed the expressive power of collage, montage, and photography. Alexander Rodchenko may well have practiced photomontage from 1919 (or from 1922, according to his friend Varvara Stepanova), and Gustav Klutsis (one of its chief exponents) from 1922, and many others followed in their wake, such as Solomon Telingater, Varvara Stepanova, Nikolai Prusakov, Alexei Gan, Semion Semionov, and Sergei Sienkin. Among the Constructivists, just as among a number of Dadaists, from the start photomontage freighted a political and social dimension, exemplified in the anti-Nazi work of John Heartfield. (Heartfield, originally Helmut Herzfeld, had, along with George Grosz, originally Georg Gross, anglicized his name in 1916 in reaction to the injustice suffered by Britain during the war.)

In Raoul Hausmann's words, "the Dadaists [...] were the first to use photographic material to create a new unity that extracted from the chaos of war and revolution a new ideal image comprised of structural elements often contradictory from the thematic or spatial point of view. They realized that their method could marshal substantial propaganda power [...]."[93] German Dada thus discovered the power and appeal of photographic montage, a new instrument in visual expression endowed with a capacity to win over and persuade that derived from processes intrinsic to it (e.g., visual abbreviation, meaningful associations, telescoping, and divergences in scale).

By the end of the 1910s, Germany was racked by political and social upheaval. The Dadaists, in particular in Berlin, expressed their awareness of the impending crises from an early stage. The work of John Heartfield—employing printed materials recuperated or taken from his own collection, as well as photographs ordered by the artist—numbers among the most incisive of all political photomontage. He had been involved in the new process since 1916 or 1918, but in 1929, as the economic crisis worsened and the Nazis drew up the battle-lines, the tone of his work hardened noticeably. Hitler and Nazism became his principal targets, and the German press soon started reproducing his militant photomontages on a massive scale. The ascendant illustrated popular press made the genre its own with AIZ and BIZ (the *Arbeiter Illustrierte Zeitung* and the *Berliner Illustrirte* [sic] *Zeitung*) among the best-known periodicals of the time. Heartfield collaborated regularly on AIZ and in his hands montage and photography became tools in an often acidulous social critique.

Apart from in the press, photomontages were soon being printed on book covers, advertisements, posters, and newspaper small ads. In the 1920s, the process was adopted by several graphic supports. In 1922, Herbert Bayer employed photography and montage in a newspaper advertisement for a make of tire that was reproduced in several American reviews; such conceptions remained daring and novel in advertising graphics, however. In succeeding years, photography and montage gained still more ground, as much on posters as in other types of promotional literature. Photography and montage thus became further weapons in the arsenal of visual communication

In Russia as in Germany, photomontage possessed an eminently political character from its inception. According to Gustav Klutsis, "photomontage is a characteristic aspect of Soviet revolutionary art and its sphere of application extends beyond the USSR. The German Communist press [...] uses methods of photomontage widely in all its publications."[94]

215

Photomontage, in partnership with lettering, bestowed especial impact on the propagandist poster. The hybrid medium was equally in vogue in the commercial sector, such as in book publishing, in the press, and on film posters. Many graphic supports were thus to discover new uses for photography, from which they could derive an entirely fresh visual appeal (with, among other devices, techniques borrowed from cinema, such as the use of close-up and of bleed that suggests elements out-of-shot). With photography and montage, the movie poster, too, entered a golden age in the 1920s in both the Soviet Union and Germany. The adoption of photography (as an image, both readily reproducible and reasonably priced) confirmed faith in the technique and the drive to mass-production, an integral component of the new society.

Varvara Stepanova regarded the photomontage process as a special variant of illustration. As she saw it, "the complexity of the mechanisms and forms of objects in our industrial culture forces the Constructivist artist-producer to leave off the handicraft methods he used in drawing objects and embrace photography. It is in this manner that photomontage was born [...]. The first photomontages were produced in our country by the Constructivist Alexander Rodchenko in 1922 as illustrations to the work of Ivan Axionov, *The Columns of Hercules*."[95]

Graphic design, typography, and photography: unusual cross-fertilizations

The development of the photomontage technique owes a great deal to the conjunction of a number of events in the art world: Cubist collage and démontage; the Russian theory of cinematographic montage; the rise of the cinema (even before World War I in Russia); the effervescent layout of Futurist compositions; the turbulent heterogeneity of Dada collage; the synthetic effectiveness of abstractionism; the search for a new expressive potential for (typo)graphic forms, and so on. In defining his idea of *typophoto* in 1925, László Moholy-Nagy explained himself as follows: "Typography is printed information, visualized thought. Photography is the visual representation of what is optically perceptible. *Typophoto* is the most precise figuration of information."[96] Beyond the definition of a new graphic language, Moholy-Nagy was concerned with the needs of an evolving society, in particular in the urban environment, a place requiring other modes of visual stimulation: "Each era possesses its own optical temper. Ours is determined by the cinema, by neon signs, and by the simultaneity of sensory perceptions. Creativity thus embarked on new and constantly expanding fields, including in the photographic domain. The typography of Gutenberg, which has endured almost to our own day, was driven exclusively by linear dimensions [...]. Hitherto, we held fast to materials and techniques of composition which preserved [...] purity of line, but which prove incapable of conveying the pace of present-day life."[97] The process of photography—rather than photomontage—occupies an essential place in Moholy-Nagy's work where transparencies, enlargements, superpositions, writing with light, amalgams of typography and photography, and effects of soft-focus, shade, and depth conspire as one.

Although far from as ubiquitous in advertising as it has since become, during the interwar period photography already offered artists an effective tool for conveying an impression of objectivity. As Moholy-Nagy explained, in a way, the adoption of an iconic register that rendered an image of reality directly corresponded to the spirit of New Typography. The message, verbal or visual, must be concise and direct, and it should make its point in dynamic fashion. Indeed, the specificity of the German *Sachplakat* of the 1900s can be considered to anticipate the search for objectivity and effectiveness that was revived by the use of photographic images. Steady improvements in means of reproduction meant that by the 1920s photography could be used for posters, a medium that had previously ignored the technique. Chromolithography, the favorite technique for pioneers in the modern poster at the turn of the twentieth century, required *affichistes* to be above all artists or draftsmen (out of about thirty posters designed by Toulouse-Lautrec, it seems that only one is not a lithograph). The image thus

404

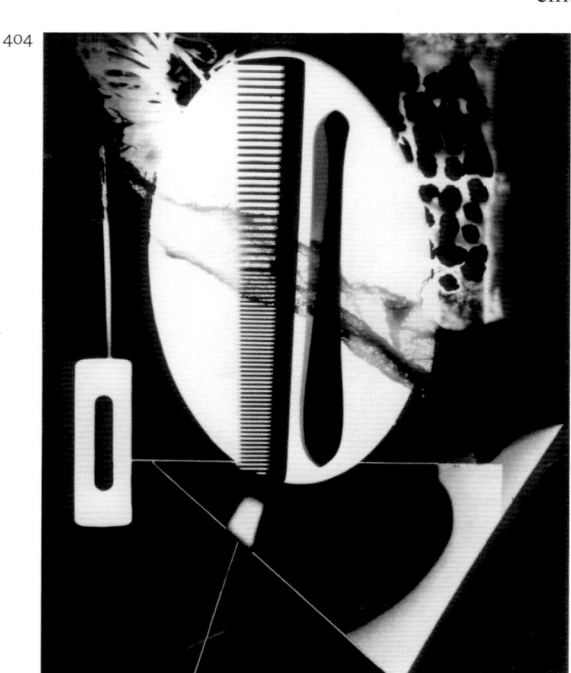

404
Man Ray, *Second rayograph*, 1922. Gelatin-silver print, rayograph, 8 × 6 in. (22.2 × 17.1 cm).

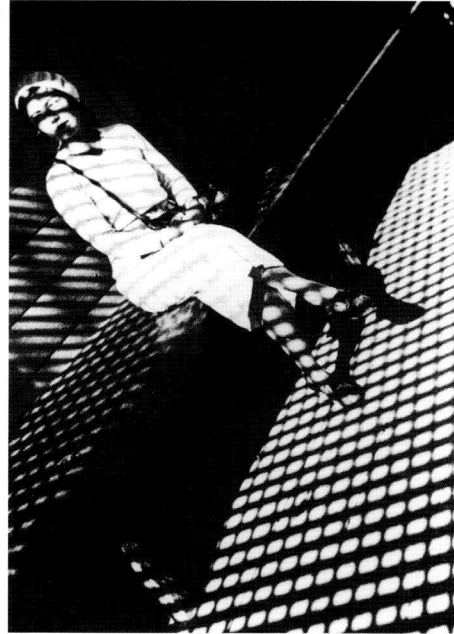

405
Alexander Rodchenko, *Girl with a Leica*, 1934.
12 × 8 in. (30 × 20.3 cm).

406
El Lissitzky, promotional material for Pelikan
inks, 1924. One of the first examples of the use
of a photogram in a printed advertisement
(the very first, according to Jan Tschichold).

407
László Moholy-Nagy, untitled photogram
(moulinet and lampshade fixings), Berlin, 1929.
15 $^1/_2$ × 12 in. (39.7 × 30.3 cm).

played the central role in the poster, with lettering confined to the remaining usable space.
With the introduction of photography, however, the poster no longer had to resort to drawing in
the same manner, so that graphic form gradually took on a fresh significance. In Germany, the
Soviet Union, the Netherlands, and Switzerland, cutting-edge graphic designers were quick to
adopt the photo. In France, on the other hand, chromolithography, drawing, and painting
remained dominant in the work of the principal graphic designers and poster artists of the
interwar period (Cassandre, Charles Loupot, Jean Carlu, and Paul Colin). In their hands,
however, drawing took on a new expressive dimension, thanks among other factors to the
concepts of montage and assemblage. Charles Loupot's poster for Twining Teas (1930),
dominated by a gigantic capital T, is a prime illustration of the evolution of attitudes to the
poster, above and beyond the nature of the technique employed. In Germany, the protagonists of
the New Typography regarded photography as a competitor poised to oust hand-drawn
illustration. Aided by the pervasive enthusiasm for mechanization, industrialization, and mass
production, for many the photographic image soon gained the upper hand. One has to make an
effort of imagination to measure the full impact of the irruption of photography on large-scale
graphic media.

Photomontage, a means of expression quite distinct from that of painting, shares certain
characteristics with the Cubist vision, such as fragmentation, *découpage*, decomposition-
recombination, collage, and so on. According to Gustav Klutsis, "there are in photography

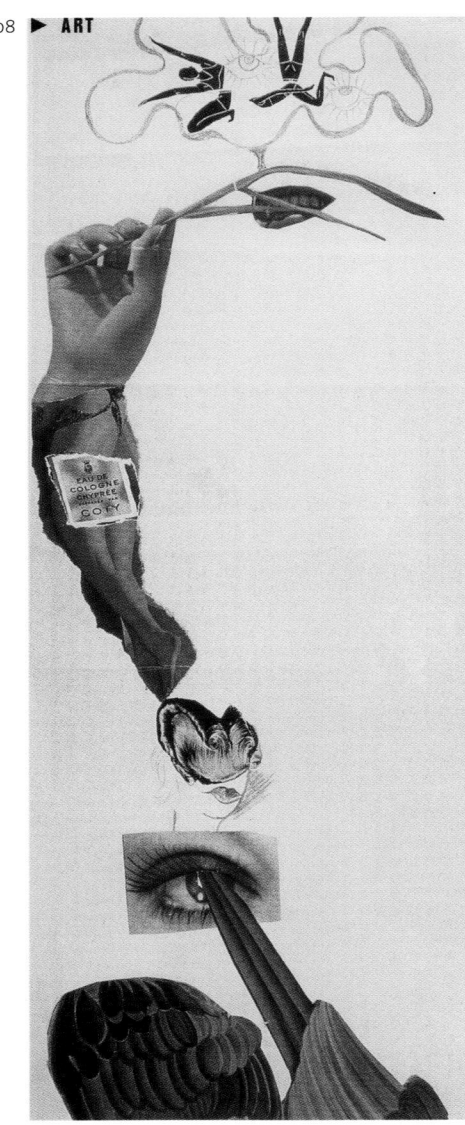

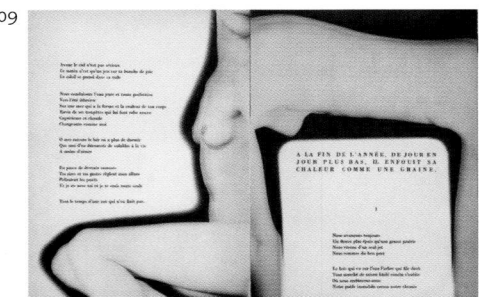

408
Jean Arp, Oscar Dominguez, Marcel Jean, and
Sophie Taeuber-Arp, *Cadavre exquis* (Exquisite
Corpse), 1937. Torn printed photographs, pencil
on paper folded and unfolded, 24 1/4 × 9 in.
(61.6 × 23.6 cm).

409
Paul Éluard and Man Ray, *Facile* (Easy), Paris,
1935. 7 × 9 1/2 in. (18.2 × 24.4 cm).

possibilities for montage which have nothing to do with the composition of a picture."[98] As photography partially replaced drawing, a new relationship between text and image sprang up that transfigured graphic form generally. If Gutenberg's discovery had, for a time, driven a wedge between the written word and the image, chromolithography allowed lettering and drawing to flow from the same tool (although the gestures employed might well be rather different). Through this encounter with photography, typography attained a new status that occasioned adjustments in the respective roles played by the picture and writing. Less liable to serve as an ancillary element, typography increasingly occupied a central position, and an offshoot of the typographical poster arose that can be seen as an extension of the age-old practice of the typeset handbill. In the unique work of László Moholy-Nagy, text and photography sometimes fuse into a single entity: the written word appears as photograph, while photography explores its own modes of writing. The "light writing" of the photogram indeed reflects a visual correspondence with the typographical writing of graphic design. A fervent partisan of modern techniques, Moholy-Nagy was actively in favor of photography even outside the confines of his own oeuvre. In 1925, the publishing arm of the Bauhaus issued his book *Malerei, Fotographie, Film*. In 1929 in Stuttgart, he organized a groundbreaking exhibition entitled *Film und Foto*.

During the second half of the 1920s, Jan Tschichold produced his theory of New Typography and clarified the new role now incumbent upon photography. In 1925, in the "Elemental Typography" issue of *Typographische Mitteilungen* he was to expound this new conception of typography in ten points. The fourth point defends the idea that, "In the present visually attuned world, the exact image—photography—also belongs to the elemental means of typography." Conscious he was sailing into uncharted waters, however, Tschichold progressed cautiously, as demonstrated by the tenth and final point: "Elemental designing is [...] not absolute or conclusive. Elements change through discoveries that create new means of typographical designing—photography, for example—therefore the concept of elemental designing will change continually."[99]. Such remarks—at least in their intentions—run counter to the tendency to reduce research in the 1920s (and more largely from the interwar period to the 1960s) to a monolithic modernism inclined to dogmatism and intransigence. For graphic artists and visualizers, the choice of typography and montage initially sprang from their fresh appeal and from their propensity to operate with different categories of images. For them, the issue was to make an impact through images torn from reality, to recompose a combination of iconic fragments so as to extract meanings and impressions (as John Heartfield does in his powerful, politically charged photomontages). In the minds of many graphic designers of the period, photography often corresponded to an ideal of objectivity, transparency, and equivalence, a far cry from the misleading exploitation of the medium as in the retouched photographs representing political figures (widespread during the Stalin era, for instance), or in the fakery and flimflam of advertising (such as gigantic objects sanitized of even the tiniest imperfection). It was an ideal that also seemed to chime in with a predilection for the sobriety of sans serif typefaces.

Depending on the countries concerned, the new graphic attitude served many and varied goals. In Germany, it fulfilled the requirements of advertising, business, and the public services, as well as publicizing information of a cultural nature. In Russia and the later Soviet Union, graphic production immediately took on a political, propagandist dimension. In the Netherlands, as in Germany, the New Typography found a focus in advertising and the public sector particularly. Widely used from the 1920s, the introduction of photography and montage into graphics wrought a metamorphosis in its formal aspects, and in this respect it constitutes a crucial phenomenon—as much for the avant-garde as for their heirs.

The 1920s and 1930s in France

The situation of France in the interwar years is unusual. Although it was the cradle of the modern poster at the end of the nineteenth century and was still a magnet for the artistic avant-garde, France appears to stand outside the spurt in graphic creativity that coursed through

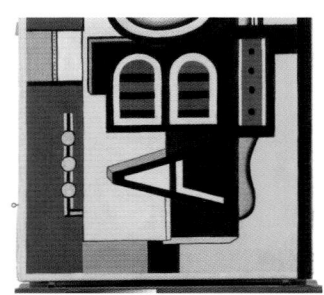

410
Fernand Léger, *The Typographer*, second state, 1919. Oil on canvas, 31 × 25 $^{1}/_{2}$ in. (81 × 65 cm).

411
Fernand Léger, rough for the poster advertising the film, *La Roue* by Abel Gance, 1922. Gouache, 12 × 9 $^{1}/_{2}$ in. (31 × 24.5 cm).

412
Fernand Léger, double page from *La Fin du Monde filmée par l'Ange Notre-Dame* by Blaise Cendrars, Paris, 1919.

413
Fernand Léger, *Still Life ABC*, 1927. Oil on canvas, 25 $^{1}/_{2}$ in × 36 in. (65 × 92 cm).

central and Eastern Europe from the 1910s onwards. On the face of it, (typo)graphic experiments in the Futurist, Dadaist, Constructivist, and Bauhaus vein found little echo in France. The "typographical revolution" and the transfiguration of graphic design were overlaid in France by less root-and-branch efforts at revival. With the exception of a handful of celebrated examples, compared to other countries, graphic design and typography seemed to have been employed for relatively few early twentieth-century experiments in France. From this point of view, it is probably the oeuvre of Leonetto Cappiello that assures the continuity between the pioneers of the chromolithographic poster and graphic artists between the wars. France seemed to keep its distance, passed over by the tide of exchange that ebbed and flowed between the protagonists of the avant-garde elsewhere in Europe, a phenomenon quite probably reinforced by its geographical position (Great Britain also occupied a comparatively less important place in these central European interactions).

Nonetheless, a number of personalities did emerge in France from the first half of the 1920s (that is, at the same time as Moholy-Nagy, El Lissitzky, and Tschichold in nearby lands), above all in the domain of the poster, and often connected or assimilated to the Art Deco movement. Paving the way, several painters and writers had testified to a renewed interest in lettering and graphic design. As we have seen, the word and printed fragment had appeared in the Cubist experiments of Braque and Picasso at the very beginning of the 1910s, while the posters of Sonia Delaunay, some dating back to 1914, feature lettering as essential graphic components. By the same token, Fernand Léger, who also designed posters, incorporated in his compositions fragments of letters and inscriptions; a canvas entitled *The Typographer* dates to 1919. Writers, too, explored visual qualities through the type- and page-setting of their texts, as illustrated by Guillaume Apollinaire's *Calligrammes*, published in 1918. As the poet saw it, mass visual communication and the world of print had transformed contemporary sensibilities, since "catalogs, posters, advertisements of all types, believe me, they contain the poetry of our epoch."[100] In his preface to a later reprint of *Calligrammes*,

Michel Butor explains that "Apollinaire was one of the first to understand in a poetic sense that the appearance of new means of reproduction and transmission, the gramophone, the telephone, the radio and the cinema [...], means of preserving and broadcasting language or history without recourse to the written word, brought with them a cultural revolution that forces us to adopt a new approach to writing, and in particular a questioning attitude to an object hitherto fundamental to our civilization—the book." In France, these kinds of researches seem mainly to have been undertaken by artists and writers, as opposed to the multidisciplinary creators working elsewhere in Europe

Art Deco: an upswing in poster art and publishing activity

Following World War I, Paris remained extremely active artistically, with painters and sculptors congregating in Montparnasse. In the applied arts, the Art Deco movement soon gained in importance, acquiring a receptive audience in the process. Exempt from functionalist researches and Constructivist practice alike, the current was a mix of extremely diverse influences. Art Deco was to engage with the transformations affecting society and shared in its passions for travel, exoticism, variety, luxury, and sport.

The new style soon invaded many sectors of the decorative and applied arts: architecture, interior decoration, furniture, domestic object, fashion, graphic design, and typography (in particular in posters, magazines, and books). Coalescing in Paris in 1925 in the ambit of the International Exhibition of Modern Decorative and Industrial Arts, the movement soon propagated throughout Europe and in the United States. Inspired, broadly speaking, by Cubism, Art Deco is a decorative style whose purpose was to decorate the forms and spaces of daily life. Geometric elements fulfill an important role in the style, but one very different from that opted for in central European graphics; Art Deco could draw as much from floral motifs, Art Nouveau, craftwork, or illustration as from Cubism or geometric decoration. In the graphic field, Art Deco is characterized by the use of blocks of color, line patterns and motifs, warm tones, and limited recourse to photography. The style was soon to be seen all over posters and on book and magazine covers, as well as in typeface design.

Shortly before the mid-1920s, and in parallel with the emergence of Art Deco, the French poster embarked on a revival of its own, patently distinct from the trends already underway in the Netherlands, the Soviet Union, and Germany. It is indeed a unique phenomenon that can scarcely be compared to movements abroad. A new generation of graphic and poster artists appeared, whose production was to continue seamlessly into the 1930s. Several protagonists appeared simultaneously, between 1923 and 1925: Cassandre (born 1901), Charles Loupot (1892), Jean Carlu (1900), and Paul Colin (1892). Of all of these, it is the career of Cassandre that remains incontestably the best known and most celebrated (his seems the only name from the French graphic landscape of the first half of the twentieth century to be etched in the collective memory). Charles Loupot's oeuvre, although neglected, is similarly singular and original, continuing unabated into the postwar era. If all made a contribution to a renewal in the art of the poster, some even transgressed its two-dimensional nature (converging with Fortunato Depero's desire for an advertising medium that would combine, inter alia, sound and space): "Metal hoardings in three dimensions were developed by Carlu [and...] Loupot; Jacno invented the 'speaking' poster."[101] Advertising was then able to invade larger spaces; the 8 × 10 1/2 ft (2.4 × 3.2m) poster format became widespread, and vast graphic surfaces occupied walls, gables, railings, metal panels, and yards of painted canvas.

Others came to the fore in the domain of the poster, graphics, and graphic design in the 1920s and 1930s, including Leonetto Cappiello, Pierre Fix-Masseau (a disciple of Cassandre's), Jean A. Mercier (active from the very start of the 1920s), Paul Iribe, Charles Gesmar (Mistinguett's poster artist by appointment, born at the beginning of the century and dying young in 1928), and Jacques Nathan-Garamond (born in 1910). Raymond Savignac, known above all in the postwar period, was, from 1935, assistant to Cassandre. Alexey

414
Leonetto Cappiello, sketch for a stock cube, *Bouillon Kub*. Ink on paper, 9 1/4 × 6 in. (23.5 × 15 cm).

415
Leonetto Cappiello, poster, *Bouillon Kub*, Paris, 1931. Chromolithograph, 9 ft. 11 in. x 13 ft. 1 1/2 in. (303 x 400 cm, four sheets).

414

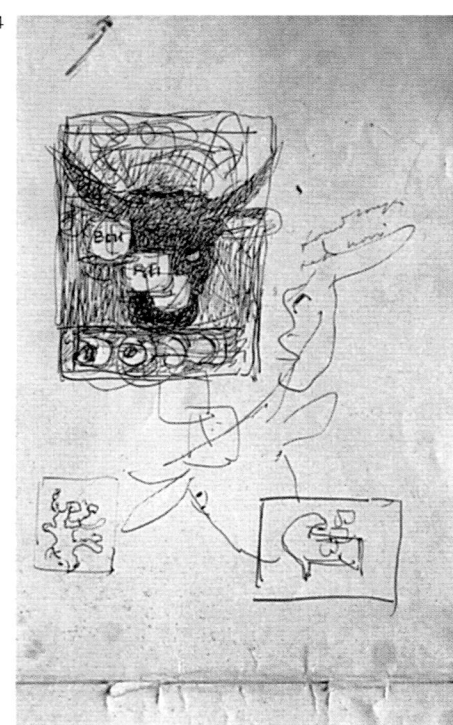

415

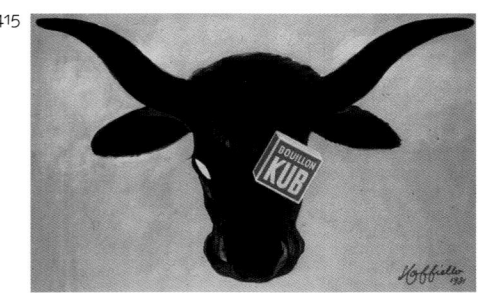

LES QUATRE GRANDES FAMILLES CLASSIQUES			
Le ROMAIN ELZÉVIR A EMPATTEMENT *TRIANGULAIRE* Alphabet minuscule extrait de la *Caroline romane* et adapté à l'empattement des capitales romaines d'inscription par NICOLAS JENSON à la fin XV° siècle.	**Le ROMAIN DIDOT** EMPATTEMENT *A TRAIT FIN HORIZONTAL* Transformation de la minuscule romaine d'après le principe d'empattement innové par GRANDJEAN dans son *romain du roi* et généralisé par F.-A. DIDOT au XVIII° siècle.	**L'ANTIQUE** SANS EMPATTEMENT ⚘ Adoption de la forme romaine de l'alphabet de Nicolas Jenson pour l'ajouté d'une minuscule au type primitif des majuscules phéniciennes.	**L'ÉGYPTIENNE** EMPATTEMENT *RECTANGULAIRE* Adoption de la forme romaine de l'alphabet de NICOLAS JENSON pour l'ajouté d'une minuscule aux majuscules des inscriptions grecques.
Minuscule *Elzévir.*	Minuscule *Didot.*	Minuscule *Antique.*	Minuscule *Égyptienne.*
Sous-Familles : *Les* LATINES	*CLASSIQUE DIDOT*	(1) Dans la constitution de la minuscule on re- trouve toutes les particu- larités d'empattements caractérisant et classi- fiant les capitales. ——	*ÉGYPTIENNE Anglaise*
Empattement triangulaire horizontal adapté à la graisse de corps de l'Égyptienne angl. —— ⚘ *Les* DE VINNE	*Ajouté d'empattements triangulaires, maintien de la finesse des déliés.* —— *Les* HELLÉNIQUES	*REMARQUE.* — Aucun dessin d'alphabet de lettres d'imprimerie ne peut se soustraire à la loi de l'empattement et quel qu'on puisse l'imaginer, il contiendra fatalement dans ses terminaisons de	Arrondissement intérieur des angles d'empatte- ment. **Sous-Famille :** *Les* ITALIENNES
Retour à l'attaque d'empat- tement de l'Elzévir avec reprises horizontales. ——	Montants bi-concaves réa- lisant l'empattement triangulaire. ——	jambages, sa coupe et sa graisse, des éléments- types permettant de le classer à première vue dans l'une des quatre familles classiques ou de leurs sous-familles. ——	Empattements renforcés; traits intérieurs amaigris.

416
Classification of typefaces according to Francis
Thibaudeau: Elzevir, Didot, Antique, Egyptian.
In *La Lettre d'imprimerie*, 1921.

417
Cassandre, cover for the American magazine,
Harper's Bazaar, March 1938.

417

Brodovitch, of Russian origin, fled the revolution of 1917 and made France his temporary home; after 1924, he designed posters for department stores or brands of aperitif, but he is best known for an exceptional contribution to magazine art direction developed during the American part of his career. In the publishing field, the Art Deco outlook on graphic design was made better known through the publication of *Mise en page* by Alfred Tolmer, published in 1931. In 1927, the foundry of Deberny & Peignot set up the trade periodical, *Arts et métiers graphiques*, which publicized work by French graphic designers overseas.

The review also played an energizing role in the sector of typeface design and distribution, following Charles Peignot's initiative to create something new in font design in the 1920s and 1930s. Active collaboration began with Cassandre by the end of the 1920s. Apprised of the success of Futura, the French foundry bought up the rights so as to manufacture its own version, called Europe. In 1921, Francis Thibaudeau—at the time working in the famous foundry—published *La Lettre d'imprimerie* (Printing Typefaces) in two volumes.[102] Thibaudeau's book offers a meticulous study of the evolution of typographical form and page-setting since the Renaissance, and proposes his well-known classification of typefaces established according to the "shape of the serif" (usually called the "Thibaudeau classification" and often heralded as being the first of its kind): "Didot, Antique, Egyptian [and...] Elzevir [...] constitute, in the classification of *La Lettre d'imprimerie*, four perfectly characterized family-types, each possessing their own unarguable elements; and the opportunity arises here to state that they are the only letterforms endowed with such a privilege [...]. In our classification, the foremost derivatives of these four traditional families split into subfamilies that are subdivided in their turn in a certain number of varieties."[103]

Cassandre

Adolphe Jean-Marie Mouron was born in the Ukraine in 1901, and settled with his family in Paris in 1915. Employing the pseudonym "Cassandre," he was to become the best-known poster artist in France in the interwar period. His fame and the enduring appeal of his work (some posters remain familiar to the general public even now), compounded by the often hagiographic treatment of his life-story, surrounds his work with an enviable aura. Filled with admiration for his oeuvre, Paul Rand even went as far as to declare that "after all, our epoch can boast of only one A. M. Cassandre."[104]

Graphic designer, typeface creator, and set decorator, Cassandre's first ambition had been to make his way as a painter. In 1918, at seventeen, he began attending classes at drawing and painting studios—the École des Beaux-Arts, very briefly, then, among others, the Académie Julian and the Académie de la Grande Chaumière. It was, however, as a poster artist that he was to make his breakthrough and earn his livelihood, even if he continued to paint (in particular during World War II). Cassandre's trajectory initially followed that of the majority of the main figures in avant-garde graphics in central and Eastern Europe, who had initially trained in painting or architecture.

From the very start, Cassandre's creations reflect direct links with Cubism—the "key event of the last twenty years."[105] Other avant-garde influences can be detected, however, such as Futurism, Purism, and Surrealism. Cassandre was keen on the cinema, and his compositions benefit from a noteworthy concision in framing. His career also felt the impact of the work of poster artist Leonetto Cappiello (the figure who forms the bridge between the 1890s and 1920s). If the new types of advertising appearing at the end of the nineteenth century constitute one of the foundations of Cassandre's approach, he nevertheless forges a repertoire of imagery that is his alone (for example, the female figure, whose role is so central in the posters of the 1890s, is rare in Cassandre's work). Although he took part in a poster contest in 1919, his work as an *affichiste* proper probably dates to 1921. His first important advertisement comes

418
Cassandre, poster for Au Bûcheron, a Parisian department store specializing in furnishings and interior decoration, 1923. Lithograph, 5 ft. × 13 ft. 1 $^1/_2$ in. (150 × 400 cm).

419
Cassandre, poster for a Parisian department store, *J'achète tout aux Galeries Lafayette*, 1928. Lithograph, 10 ft. 6 in. × 7 ft. 10 $^1/_2$ in. (320 × 240 cm).

420
Cassandre, project for an untitled, unpublished poster; unidentified format and date. Gouache.

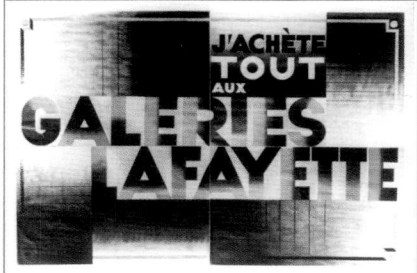

from 1923 and concerned Au Bûcheron (a furniture department store), for which he produced the artwork. This graphic, which earned him the main prize at the 1925 International Exhibition of Modern Decorative and Industrial Arts, nonetheless aroused the wrath of Le Corbusier: "Tumult hits the streets. Le Bûcheron hangs out the bunting on boulevard Saint-Germain [...]. The populace gets it, finds it very funny. This Cubism is, however, far from funny, it is false [...]. A formula pinched then mistreated by a dauber. [...]. When one goes in for 'the modern' like this, there are no depths to which one will not stoop."[106] Hachard (who published his posters from 1924 to 1927), had alerted Cassandre moreover to the risks such boldness carried: "What you're doing won't sell, but it's marvelous advertising."[107]

Cassandre's graphic idiom soon acquired a voice of its own, with posters for the aperitif Pivolo in 1924, for the newspaper *L'Intransigeant* in 1925, and for the locomotives *Nord Express* and *Étoile du Nord* (one of his best-known posters) in 1927. Cassandre first expounded his ideas in 1926, in the review *L'Affiche*. From the outset, he voiced his support for the fledgling media: "More and more, painting is evolving into individual lyricism [...]. The poster, on the other hand, tends towards a collective and practical art, endeavoring to eliminate all characteristics of the artist as an individual [...]; it has to be capable of being reproduced in series of thousands of copies, like a pen or a car, and intended just like them to render services of a material nature and fulfill a commercial function."[108] Cassandre here echoes a point of view very different from those avant-garde currents striving for the union or fusion of the arts. In other aspects, however, he was closer to the prevailing tendencies: the search for impact, appeal, renewal, simplification, and dynamism; the importance of the role of lettering, and so on. Having outlined that his "method is primarily geometrical and monumental," he goes on to explain why the art that interests him most is architecture, as it is centered on "a more schematic concision, [...and] the use of larger surfaces."[109]

Significantly, Cassandre accorded a foreground role to lettering; the word is used advisedly and in preference to "typography," since Cassandre himself drew the texts for his posters (like many of the Russian Constructivists), just as he drew the other figurative and graphic elements, instead of resorting to photography. "Too long ignored and underestimated by our predecessors, lettering surely plays a key role in the poster. It is the great star of the wall since it, and nothing else, has the task of communicating to the public the magic formula that sells. It's important for the poster artist to always start with the text, locating it, as far as possible, in the center of the composition. The design is to be centered on the text and not the converse. [...] In former times, the lettering was placed in position at a later stage, every which way,

421
Cassandre, mock-up of the Heemaf poster
(Dutch lithograph for an electricity company),
1930. Gouache.

422
Cassandre, mock-up of the Van Nelle poster
(Dutch lithograph for a brand of coffee), 1931.
Gouache, 3 ft. 11 in. × 5 ft. 3 in. (120 × 160 cm).

423
Cassandre, project for the poster, *Nord Express*,
unpublished, oil on panel (detail), 1927.

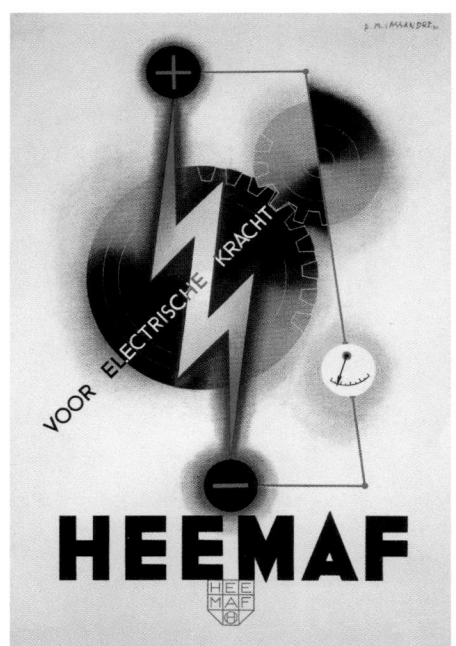

421

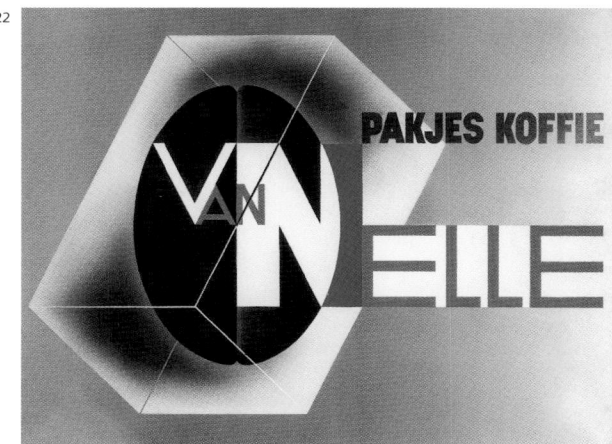

422

423

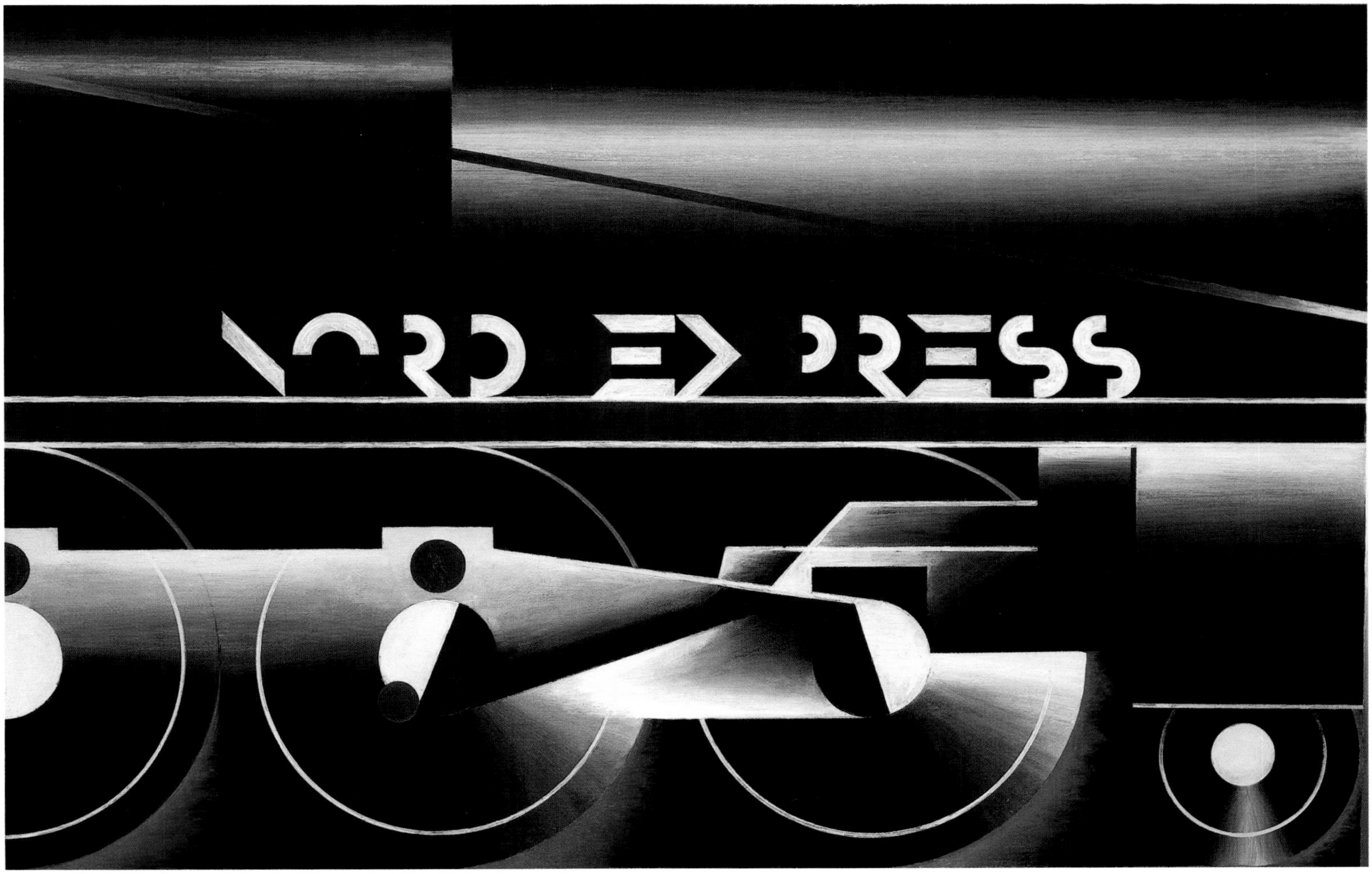

424

424
Cassandre, Bifur typeface, issued by the foundry
of Deberny & Peignot, 1929.

either overlaid, diagonally or transversely, or in some fortuitous corner. This can no longer be countenanced [...]. I am not unaware that the applied sciences have just found against capitals in favor of 'lowercase' as being more readable than the former. But I remain firmly attached to capitals. In my opinion, small letters are simply a manual distortion of monumental lettering, an abbreviation, a cursive degeneration that can be laid at the door of the copyists. My preferences are necessarily guided by an architectural conception of the poster [... and] towards the unadulterated product of square and compass, towards primitive, lapidary lettering, that of the Phoenicians and Romans."[110]

From the end of the 1920s, Cassandre began to venture into new territories as he received orders from abroad, working, for example, for a Dutch publisher (1927–31), for Swiss and Italians (in 1935 and 1936), and for the American magazine *Harper's Bazaar*, for which he was to design a cover every month from 1937 on. In 1933, Cassandre started his teaching career (he was to found a school for graphic design the following year) and, at the request of Louis Jouvet, took up set and stage design. In addition, and above and beyond his work as an *affichiste*, Cassandre was also busy creating some highly unusual typefaces. There then began his close cooperation with the foundry of Deberny & Peignot—the new director of which, Charles Peignot, the artist had met at the International Exhibition of Modern Decorative and Industrial Arts in 1925. From the end of the 1920s and through the 1930s, Cassandre designed three typefaces that were manufactured and marketed by the Parisian foundry: Bifur, Acier, and Peignot. The plans for Bifur, his first font, probably date to 1927; it was issued by the foundry Deberny & Peignot in 1929. According to Cassandre himself, "Bifur is not a decorative typeface" but "advertising type, [...] designed for printing a word, a single word, a poster," for which he "tried simply to endow the word with the iconic power it possessed in times past."[111] These remarks extrapolate thoughts Cassandre had already outlined in a text of 1926 in which he defined the role of lettering in the poster: "A poster is not a picture. It is first of all a word. It's the word that gives the orders, that conditions and drives the advertising agenda [...] only the word possesses the ability to confer unity and meaning onto a poster."[112] Blaise Cendrars, who signed the text for a brochure presenting the Bifur typeface, talks of "words that slam," remarking that "one has to follow the typographical fashion."[113] A reflection of Cassandre's convictions, Bifur features a single alphabet of capital letters that comes in various alternative forms (Bifur and Double Bifur). It is constituted above all by a contingent of original combinations, consisting in a set of minimal forms and optional additive counter-forms. Such a typeface, strongly structured and designed to exploit to the maximum the tension-filled space of the poster, seems not unconnected with the Constructionist drive that at the time was coursing through many central European movements.

After Bifur, Cassandre was to design Acier (Noir and Gris), produced in 1930, and Peignot, designed as early as 1933 or 1934 but brought out in 1937. If Peignot type was intended for

425

425
Cassandre, posters *Dubo, Dubon, Dubonnet*
(triptych for the aperitif Dubonnet), published
1933, non-identical to the initial 1932 design.
Lithograph, 10 ft. 6 in. × 7 ft. 10 1/2 in.
(320 × 240 cm) each.

YVES SAINT LAURENT

setting regular text, it was also capable of fulfilling the needs of "mural typography," being also "engraved on wood for posters, in bold and demi-bold."[114] At the outset available in three weights, Peignot is an original, even strange, face, whose lowercase borrows more extensively than usual from capital forms, in what is a sort of hybrid of the two categories. Certain sources imply that Cassandre initially wanted to create a single type and that he was asked to add a version in capitals to his proposal for marketing reasons (ten years earlier, Paul Renner had had to tone down the more idiosyncratic aspects of the Futura draft to get his typeface published). In lowercase Peignot offers certain analogies—with respect to its intention rather than its form—with the unique alphabets conceived at the end of the 1920s in Germany by Bayer, Schwitters, and Tschichold, although Peignot was issued later and remains in use today. To Cassandre's eternal disappointment, it seems that neither Peignot nor Bifur enjoyed the commercial success hoped for. In the monograph devoted to his father, Henri Mouron recalls that, when Cassandre committed suicide in 1968, there lay "on his desk a letter from a major foundry [...] informing him that [...] it was halting production of his new typeface."[115]

It is above all as a poster artist that Cassandre made his mark in the 1930s, for example, with the famous *Dubo Dubon Dubonnet* series of 1932, made for the eponymous aperitif,[116] or the surprising and colorful image for Nicolas wines of 1935, "after Dransy," that foreshadows future graphic designs based on optical effects. These two posters were published by Alliance Graphique L. C., a small-scale concern founded by Maurice Moyrand in 1930, with both Cassandre and Charles Loupot on its books (its guiding principle was that both graphic designers would work on the same accounts), and which folded in 1935. Under its auspices Cassandre was to realize nearly fifty posters, while Loupot saw only two of his projects published.[117] As was customary, Cassandre employed the process of chromolithography. From the very beginning, he worked with the aid of a draftsman-lithographer, to whom, however, he left little room for maneuver as regards design: "My collaborator is but a docile mechanic. Of course, I leave up to him neither the selection, nor the appearance, nor the placing of the lettering."[118] Faithful to the tradition of the graphic artist-craftsman and unique author of his images, Cassandre was only exceptionally to make recourse to photography. He would compose, build, draw, write, and synthesize graphic designs which are his and his alone, and which convey his convictions. Because he wanted his poster to be "monumental," in form as well as in format ("80 × 120 [cm] is no better than a calling-card," "my architectural conception of the poster," " lapidary lettering, [...] the only one that is genuinely monumental"[119]), Cassandre conjured up new and powerful pieces of artwork.

If his work shows little in common with that produced by poster artists in central and Eastern Europe, and if he does not seem to have pursued similar goals (in particular in terms of social commitment), his work cannot readily be reduced to stylistic formalism or to its decorative dimension alone.[120] His observations show a determination to acquire a new level of effectiveness, by designing posters with a strong mural presence, capable of striking up an immediate relationship with passersby. Contemporary American practitioners (who shared in this viewpoint) showed great interest in his work. Interestingly, Cassandre himself did not always feel the fascination for the poster one might think; in fact his enthusiasm waned and was replaced, in subsequent years, by profound disillusion. In an interview of 1926, he stated that he had harbored "in former times [...] the most extreme disdain for the poster. Since then [...] I've changed a great deal."[122]

Charles Loupot

Another graphic designer to bequeath a significant body of work, Charles Honoré Loupot has always seemed to have been overshadowed, partially by Cassandre and perhaps, also, because he never taught or transmitted his ideas in writing. (His oeuvre is now more accessible thanks to the publication in France in 1998 of a monograph devoted to him.[123] If his collaboration

427

with Cassandre in Alliance Graphique L. C. was scarcely to Loupot's advantage (he was both less monumental and less productive), Cassandre nevertheless acknowledged him as a first-rate colleague: "[…] Loupot, whom I regard as a master […]."[124]

Loupot was to settle in Paris in 1923 (the year Cassandre began to make a name as a poster artist). In the 1910s, he would have witnessed the beginnings of the modern poster in Switzerland, where he had lived for a time. The young Loupot, a great traveler who had lived abroad, had absorbed various cultures. Of Franco-Italian descent, he was born in Nice in 1892. His family settled temporarily in Spain before moving to Lausanne. In 1911, Charles Loupot left home to follow courses at the École des Beaux-Arts in Lyon, studying in particular painting and drawing. It was there, even before World War I, that he tried his hand at the poster, composing one in 1913 for a student dance. On the outbreak of war, Loupot left to fight at the Front, but, wounded, he was discharged and returned to Lausanne in 1915. During the conflict, he composed designs for two war posters. Perfecting his knowledge of lithography (practiced at a very high level technically in Switzerland), he embarked on a career as a poster artist and draftsman.

The first poster to show his emergent artistry as a graphic designer and launch his career was intended for a department store (following the example of Cassandre's poster for Au Bûcheron) and dates from 1916. In Lausanne, where the first part of his career unfolded (1914–23), he designed a number of posters. Faithful to a characteristic common in late nineteenth-century advertising, Loupot allotted the central role to the human figure, generally female, and more rarely men or children. During these first few years, his graphic idiom evolved notably. "[…] Loupot's posters of the years 1916–18 have a multipurpose feel […]. But how could it be otherwise as the artist was allowed no idea as to what his mock-ups were to be used for? […]." Apparently, during this formative period, Loupot worked directly for a printer and without any contact with the client. "The printer […] would get a good price for the drawing on a first-come first-served basis, sometimes […] selling it on to two or even three firms! Among Loupot's Swiss works we discover the same images blithely singing the praise of stores run by L. Nordmann and S. Knopf, or Frères Loeb and Innovation."[125] (Intriguingly, this (re)use of the same visuals in various contexts is redolent of the repeated use of engravings in book illustration at the beginnings of printing, when a single depiction of a city, for instance, might masquerade as that of any number of towns.)

Charles Loupot's designs in Switzerland were of a transitory nature, somewhere between the new poster as inherited from the end of the nineteenth century and more personal, stylized graphics. Attention has tended to concentrate on the French period of his career, which extended from 1923 to the 1950s. Loupot probably traveled to Paris at the behest of Leonetto Cappiello's printer. He arrived just at the moment when Cassandre, Jean Carlu, and Paul Colin were coming up through the ranks. Like them, Loupot gradually arrived at a singular graphic universe that is hard to classify.

His debut posters in Paris immediately stuck out from the crowd: "The presence of these new images in an urban setting, dominated by a rather standardized style of advertising, could hardly pass unnoticed […] the two pieces for Voisin cars, in green and white […]" came as a shock, arousing polarized reactions. "[They] fell like two great stones into the duck-pond of the advertising imagination. They created something of a minor scandal, and then, little by little, a few came to their defense, timid at first, then increasingly vocal—and well deserved to be sure."[126] A "minor scandal" is an understatement: in fact these pieces of artwork for Voisin, announcing a new master in the poster world (like Cassandre's exactly contemporary work for Au Bûcheron, moreover), were met with brickbats. Loupot's work at this time was adopting the form for which he became known in the 1920s. Gradually, he moved away from the pictorial idiom to invent his own graphic system, with Nicolas wines, Peugeot, Monsavon, Valentine paints, and the aperitif Saint-Raphaël numbering among his clients. In his view, "one has continuously to surprise the indolent eye with simple and perfect graphics."[127]

428

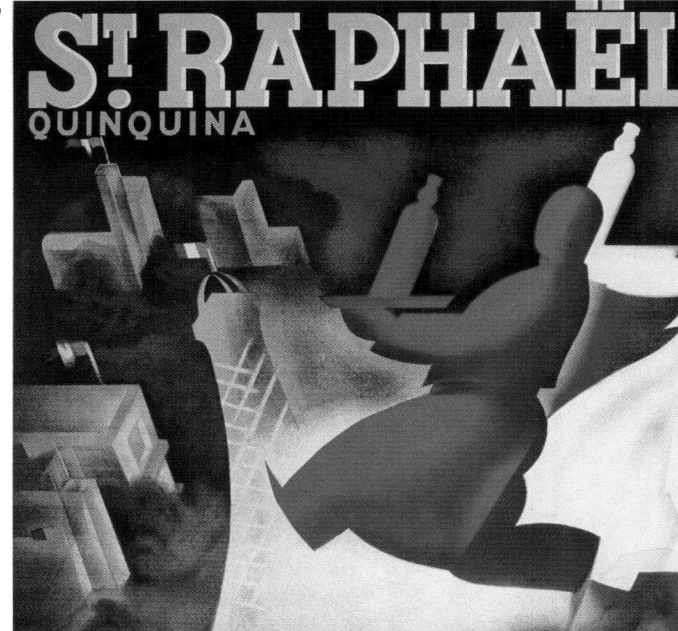

429

430

432

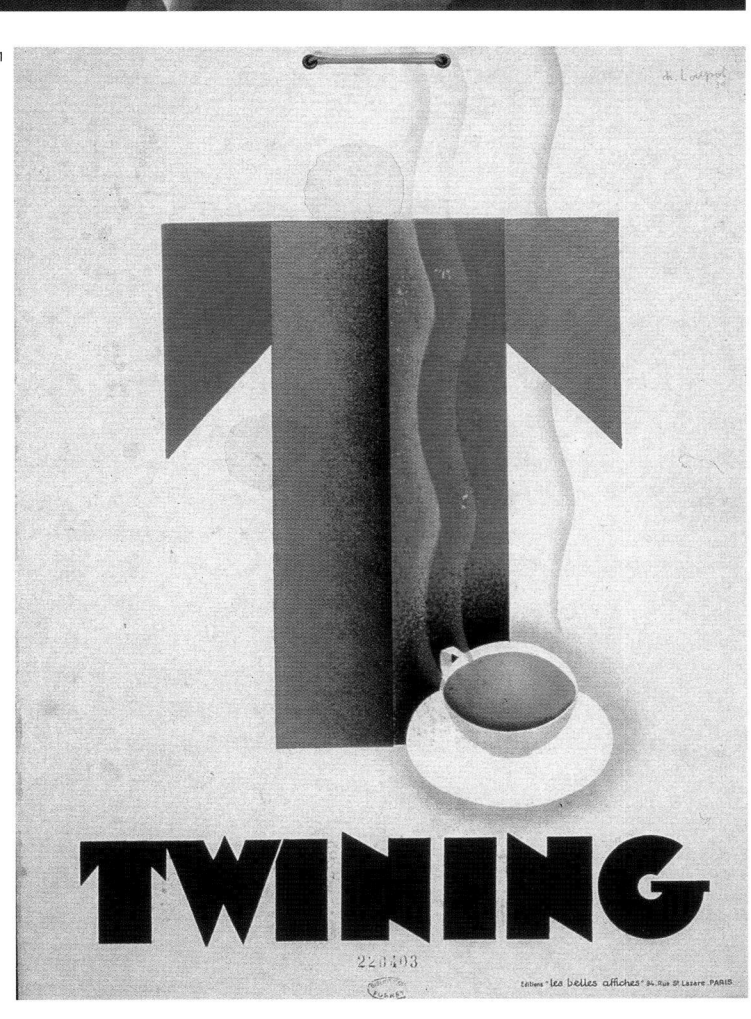

431

428
Poster for Saint-Raphaël predating those of Charles Loupot.

429
One of the first Saint-Raphaël posters by Charles Loupot, 1937. Chromolithograph, 5 ft. 3 1/4 in. × 3 ft. 11 1/2 in. (160.5 × 121 cm).

430
Charles Loupot, advertisement for Saint-Raphaël on street furniture (undated).

431
Charles Loupot, poster for Twining Tea, 1930. Chromolithograph, 5 ft. 3 in. × 3 ft. 11 in. (160 × 120 cm).

432
Charles Loupot's studio, advertisement for Saint-Raphaël, as utilized on the back cover of French magazines for about ten years (mid-twentieth century).

If his brief collaboration with Cassandre within Alliance Graphique L. C. at the beginning of the 1930s was not to his advantage, in the course of the 1920s and 1930s the pertinence and originality of his graphic language affirmed itself. His exceptional poster for Twining's Tea—with its massive capital T—dates to 1930. The essence of the poster is composed of the letter alone, gigantic, asserting an irreducible presence, an amalgamation of letter-word, phonogram, and phonetic notation. The message is reduced to an imagined essence—creative, not preexistent. With such pictures-cum-letters—a near cousin of the researches centered on concepts of objectivity and construction that were being pursued abroad—Loupot shows himself in agreement with the tenets Cassandre espoused, which define the role of the text in the poster as the driving force, primordial and monumental.

Like many contemporary French poster artists, Loupot drew everything: the text and the image, both of which embody a search for harmony that is constantly being reinvigorated. Yet there exist few posters by Loupot where the figures are dominated by the text. Generally, the text appears in the lower part of the composition, arranged around a central vertical axis. Starting from the mid-1920s, Loupot began to modulate his graphic repertoire, juggling in turn pictorial representation and a graphic formal schematization that could verge on the abstract. From this point of view, the most significant part of his oeuvre is his work for the aperitif Saint-Raphaël (a flavored wine), a collaboration that commenced in 1937 and lasted up until about 1960. In addition to the poster and commercial styling, Loupot also realized for this product graphic designs intended to be reproduced on sheet-metal plates, as well as over thousands of wall surfaces of vast size. Prior to Loupot's involvement, the advert for Saint-Raphaël had shown (probably since 1910) the detailed, silhouetted profiles of two waiters in a café. Loupot kept the figures and treated them in various manners, from dreamlike image through to complete schematization. Over time, the initially narrative and pictorial imagery evolved into a set of simplified and geometrical forms, later still divided up and recomposed into graphic designs in perpetual metamorphosis, yet always readily identifiable. In this connection, the managing director of Saint-Raphaël records an anecdote that shows how vibrantly Loupot's designs made their visual impact, without even having to be read: "What can you read over there?" "I don't need to read it—it's Saint-Raphaël."[128]

Thus, Loupot's graphics gradually passed from handed-down forms to abstraction, leading the poster from an illustrative tradition to a new graphic style that was, in addition, quite distinct from other, phototypographic experiments. In disassembling and reassembling abstraction-prone forms, Loupot contributed to the success in the postwar period of a deconstructed, playful vein in graphic expression. During World War II, Loupot's activity as a graphic designer had to mark time so, like Cassandre, he turned to painting. After 1945, his career took off again and its developments once more proved significant. By 1951, he was surrounded by new collaborators and founded his own agency, Les Arcs. At the end of his life, he was still preoccupied with the need to adapt the poster to the constantly changing conditions of its reception: "Nowadays, a poster can no longer be descriptive. It is made to be glimpsed at a hundred and twenty an hour, from a train or car [...]. Abstract painting is perhaps the poster of tomorrow."[129] It has to be noted that—if not in his own works—his wish is far from being realized even today. Loupot asked tough questions of the language of graphic design and created his own personal vision in an important oeuvre that still remains difficult to categorize.

Jean Carlu and Paul Colin

Like his peers Cassandre and Charles Loupot, Jean Carlu was another active figure in the French poster renaissance that started in the mid-1920s. He initially wanted to be an architect, a profession practiced by several members of his family (Jacques Carlu, his elder brother, had a hand in building the Palais de Chaillot in Paris); to that end he studied at the École des

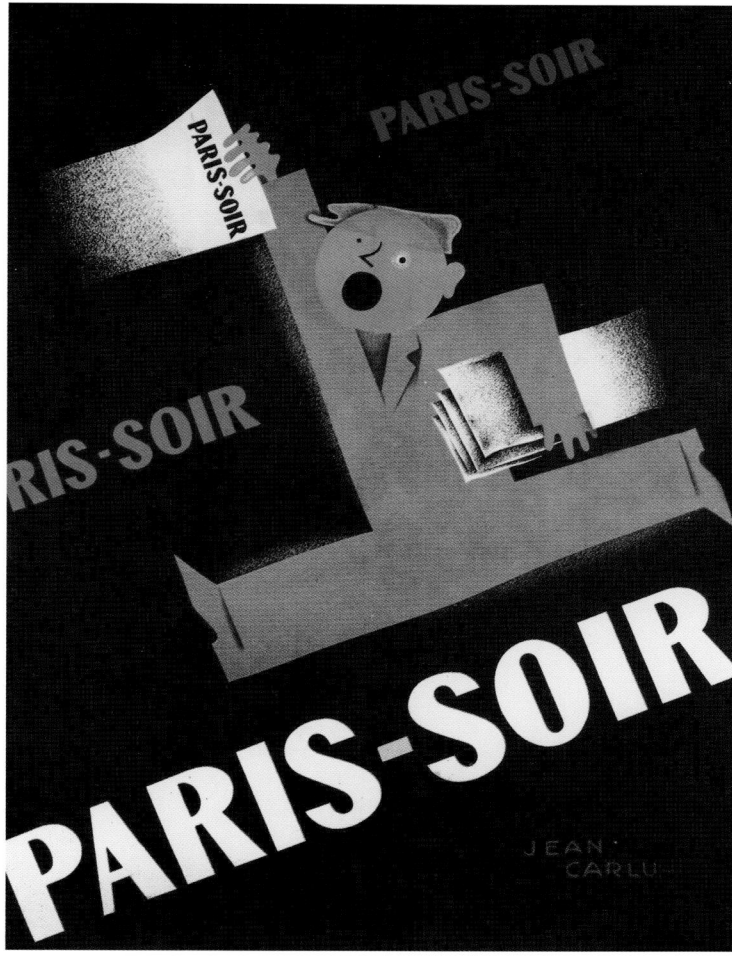

433

433
Jean Carlu, poster, *Paris-Soir*, 1928.
Chromolithograph, 5 ft. 2 in, × 3 ft. 10 ¹/₂ in.
(157.5 × 118 cm). "I used the lettering from *Paris-Soir* to [capture] the idea of a newspaper seller whose cry is heard getting closer and closer in the evening. [...] while respecting the principle so dear to Cappiello and many others: a light-colored patch on a dark ground, a dark-colored patch on a light ground." (Jean Carlu, 1980).

434
Jean Carlu, poster for an exhibition of the Union des Artistes Modernes, Galeries Georges Petit, 1931.

Beaux-Arts in Paris. Having previously expressed an interest in graphic design, in 1918 he entered a poster contest. The day the jury (chaired by Leonetto Cappiello) was to convene, Carlu fell victim to a tram accident in the course of which his right arm was severed.

Greatly influenced by Cubism and by the work of Cappiello, he then embarked on a career as a graphic designer, focusing on advertising and illustration. Like many of his colleagues, he started out painting and drawing compositions for posters, often advertising consumer goods, such as toothpaste, cigarettes, or soap, as well as cultural events or products, such as art museums, theaters, exhibitions, or records. From the end of the 1920s, he was seeking new forms and materials for his advertisements, creating billboards incorporating metal elements in relief (*Disques Odéon*, 1929) and luminous neon signs (*Cuisine électrique*, 1935). Carlu, of the opinion, like so many others, that messages should increase in density and that impact is paramount (probably inspired in this by the ideas of Albert Gleizes), exclaimed that "the poster [...] cannot be satisfied with attracting the eye of a passing pedestrian. It has to strike him in such way that he never forgets it [...]. The poster has to be a closed composition, given rhythm by a simple, geometric system."[130]

A pacifist much concerned with humane and social values, in Paris in 1932 he founded the Office de Propagande Graphique pour la Paix, which was to issue a certain number of his posters in favor of peacemaking and against rearmament. No alluring or carefree image, the poster *Pour le désarmement des nations* (For Multilateral Disarmament), dating to 1932 and published with the assistance of the SDN, is one of his best-known works. Associating a poignant photomontage with geometric but symbolic and powerful graphics, Carlu depicts the panic-stricken face of a woman and a child about to be obliterated by a bomb.[131] More than

Cassandre or Loupot, in whose works the use of photography remains rare, Carlu often made recourse to it in reproducing faces (that of Hitler, in particular), or to enhance the sense of reality and drama.

Like Cassandre, Carlu started to teach in the middle of 1930s at the École Nationale des Arts Décoratifs in Paris, where he offered courses in graphic art from 1935 to 1937. He was then appointed curator of the advertising pavilion for the International Exhibition of 1937. At the end of the 1930s, again like Cassandre, Carlu left to work in the United States. In 1939, he found himself in charge of organizing the French pavilion at the International Exhibition in New York. For Cassandre (working mostly for the press and in advertising), business hardly flourished in the United States. Carlu, on the other hand, was to live there from 1940 to 1953, and, if he is hardly a household name in France, his work was much appreciated on the other side of the Atlantic. During World War II, he produced a great number of posters for the US Office of War Information; one of them, *America's answer! Production*, remains a memorable image. After the war, the French government assigned Carlu to other technical curatorial projects in the United States. Back in France in 1953, he worked for another twenty years or so as a graphic designer in advertising and as an art director. In a career lasting half a century, Carlu designed more than six hundred posters, yet his oeuvre, like that of Loupot, remains little known.[132]

Paul Colin is regarded as another figurehead in French poster design from the mid-1920s to the end of the 1930s. Of all of these artists, he was probably the most productive, with a body of work running, by his own reckoning, to some one thousand five hundred posters (other estimates range between eleven hundred and more than two thousand). His graphic and pictorial repertoire was close to that of his French contemporaries and his posters were often devoted to dance or variety shows, ballets, stage performances generally, and the cinema, being less often concerned, apparently, with commercial goods or everyday or industrially manufactured articles.

Born at Nancy, Paul Colin arrived in Paris in 1913. If he found it difficult to make his way in painting (in which he had trained initially), his poster for *La Revue nègre* in 1925 met with a favorable reception and launched him as an *affichiste*. The same year saw him collaborating at the Théâtre des Champs-Élysées as a graphic and set designer. With his knowledge of painting, like so many of his contemporaries, the graphic design he developed was partially inherited from Cubist ideas. In his compositions the image takes the central role, with the painter's touch remaining palpable, and the artwork focused and unified. Less crucial, the hand-drawn text generally occupies a band at the edge of the poster, often laid along a central axis running the entire width of the surface. In 1926, he opened the Paul Colin School, which he directed and where he promulgated his conception of the poster. (Friedrich Heinrich Kohn Henrion, Herbert Leupin, and Bernard Villemot were among his pupils.) Shut during World War II, the school was to reopen after the conflict, keeping Colin's teaching alive for some forty years. In addition to his activity as a poster artist, Paul Colin practiced painting, drawing, costume design, and decoration, as well as stage and set design. Between 1939 and 1945, he was to produce a number of war posters, like Carlu in the United States, but contrary to Loupot and Cassandre, who moved away from graphic design during this period to devote their time to painting. All four artists remained productive until the 1960s or 1970s.

Graphic design and art

In the 1920s and 1930s in France, many points of contact arose between the poster and pictorial practice. In addition to productions by professional graphic designers, numerous painters also created posters, many of which were intended to promote exhibitions or festivities; this was the case, for instance, with Picasso, Braque, Matisse, Foujita, Chagall, and Goncharova. A new art of the poster that drew inspiration from, among other phenomena, Cubism, appeared in the middle of the 1920s just as the Art Deco movement was blossoming, and which indeed posters of this time tend to resemble. Profiting in this manner from recent artistic experiments, the poster

435
Paul Colin, poster, *Prenez l'R, apéritif supérieur*, 1933.

435

436
Printed wallpaper designed by Jacques-Émile Ruhlmann, 1925.

437
Eileen Gray, "Ivory-ebony" rug, c. 1930.

threw off its allegiance to symbolism and its narrative, illustrative, and idealist dimension, seeking redefinition as a graphic space—containing synthetic forms and color blocks, with a focus on a central element—which attempted to take account of a new perceptual rhythm. It is no easy task to classify the French poster of the interwar period, save by the label "French School." This is all the more acute as various pictorial influences coincided and mingled: Surrealism, Cubism, Purism, and abstraction (with the creation of the group Cercle et Carré and the association Abstraction-Création, and the publication of the manifesto of Concrete art at the very beginning of the 1930s). Constructivism was less pronounced, although personalities from the Bauhaus were asked to present the Werkbund at the Salon des Artistes Décorateurs in 1930 in Paris, where typography was included along with other sectors in design.

The Union des Artistes Modernes (UAM), founded in Paris in 1929, aimed to establish a "truly social art," a harmonic union between the applied arts accessible to all that would rely on "balance, logic, and purity."[133] The association dealt in many forms of artistic and environmental creation; architecture, sculpture, furniture, graphic design, glassmaking, and lighting. Several poster artists joined its members, some at the very beginning of the 1930s, among them Cassandre, Jean Carlu (1931), Charles Loupot (1933), Paul Colin, and Charles Peignot. Certain graphic designers, such as Loupot and Cassandre, set up a firm distinction between the poster and painting. Generally, even when the poster occupied a key place in their careers, they were, either regularly or sporadically, to undertake other activities in parallel (set and stage design, painting, exhibition or costume design, for example). Compared to their Russian, Hungarian, Dutch, or German contemporaries, however, French graphic designers do not seem to have been so involved in the fields of design and architecture, while their pictorial practice remained a sideline. Their creations were quite unlike the new dimension being brought to graphic design in central and Eastern Europe, not least because photography was to find little place in their output. Moreover, the principal French graphic designers of the era do not seem to have written copiously on their subject. Apart from a handful of documents (interviews, specialist articles, reviews, and a scattering of other publications), they left few books or fundamental texts proposing broad analytical or descriptive overviews. Conversely, certain European protagonists wrote abundantly: Tschichold, El Lissitzky, Van Doesburg, Schwitters, or before them Johnston, to quote only a few, actively published articles, books, manifestos, reviews, special numbers, didactic texts, and so on, which closely mirrored the contemporary scene. In the graphic field, the French seem to limit their exchanges with the avant-garde abroad, precisely at the time when ideas and projects circulated intensively elsewhere in Europe. For these reasons, figures in the world of the French poster of the 1920s and 1930s appear marginalized with respect to the weft and weave of artistic movements in other climes.[134]

Great Britain

Even more than France, Great Britain stood apart from the welter of Continental exchange. In the wake of the Arts and Crafts movement, designers, visualizers, and typographers upheld the role of craft and the place of traditional forms in an increasingly industrialized society. If one area of their (typo)graphic practice was intent on preserving and forming part of the historical heritage, several experiments in genuine modernity were also undertaken. Like elsewhere, a succession of nonstandard or original graphic idioms had broken through since the end of the nineteenth century—by way of the Glasgow School in Scotland (around the central figure of Charles Rennie Mackintosh), the Beggarstaffs, Vorticism (in 1912, following Marinetti's several visits to London at the beginning of the decade), or with the new approach to signage in the London Underground (from 1913 onwards). From the 1910s to the 1930s, a number of substantial achievements testify to the activities of the British avant-garde. The fields of typeface design, posters, books, and other printed media sought new forms of communication and came up with a range of visual proposals. The British graphic design scene in the interwar period was thus split between guardians of tradition and progressives.

The domain of letter design, for instance, could boast the very different talents of Stanley Morison, Edward Johnston, and Eric Gill, while Edward McKnight Kauffer, Austin Cooper, Ashley Havinden, and Tom Purvis thrived as poster artists. For his signage project for the London Underground, Frank Pick—an exceptional patron with a genuine concern for written forms—called upon the collaboration of many practitioners, artists as well as professionals. Among the poster artists active in England, many had initially learned painting or plied this trade in parallel. Just as in France, some remained close to drawing and pictorial expression, with less inclination to photography, photomontage, and phototypography.

Commissions and creators:
Frank Pick, Edward Johnston, Edward McKnight Kauffer, and Henry Beck

In Great Britain as elsewhere, the role of patrons and advertisers was an all-important adjunct and context for conditions favorable to the development of graphic design. Numerous firms (including many transport companies) solicited work from poster artists and draftsmen. Following the example of Frank Pick for London Underground, Jack Beddington, advertising director at Shell-Mex, turned to many and varied talents (such as Paul Nash and Edward McKnight Kauffer) for graphics promoting, for example, motor vehicles. Maritime concerns (which were to work with Norman Wilkinson, Austin Cooper, and Dudley Hardy), railroad companies (with Tom Purvis and Frank Brangwyn), and airlines, as well as the Post Office (for which posters were commissioned by Sir Stephen Tallents) also played their part.

Following the relatively recent pioneering experiences of a group of inventive promotional materials for Odol, Henry Van de Velde's work for Tropon, and the cooperation between Peter Behrens and AEG, British graphic designers now found themselves faced with a major commission whose result remains highly visible today in a busy public space. Before the war, London Transport had started to collaborate with designers with the aim of creating a strong, coherent visual identity. The project was instigated by sales manager Frank Pick and included the commission of the now-famous typeface by Edward Johnston for the exclusive use of the London Tube: Underground Railway Sans, completed in 1916 and manufactured in 1918. (Johnston was a noted calligrapher and an acknowledged expert in the history of letterform— as well as the author of *Writing & Illuminating & Lettering*.)

Based on traditional proportions and Renaissance scripts, Underground is one of the most representative forms of geometric sans serif—a character that it surely did a great deal to popularize. Here, Johnston not only demonstrated his mastery of letter design, but he also added a feel for construction, resulting in an ingenious cross between two approaches (whereas the tendency up until now had been to adhere to one and decry the other). For example, a certain number of the capital letters in Underground can be inscribed within a square. One distinguishing feature is that the O (upper- and lowercase) takes on a circular form, thus also fitting into a square, as is also the case with the letters M, Q, and X. Another discreet but readily visible characteristic: the dot surmounting the lowercase letters "i" and "j" also takes the form of a square inclined to 45 degrees and balanced on its tip. The whole alphabet, moreover, benefits from simplified forms, an agreeable roundness, and a comfortable pitch. Serving simultaneously for signage and identification, Underground is a prime example of an innovative typeface commissioned directly by a public utility company for its specific use. Slightly altered in 1979, and renamed New Johnston, the initial alphabet survived the twentieth century and into the twenty-first intact, without the need to replace it. From this point of view, Edward Johnston's solution has had a radically different fate from the Art Nouveau forms chosen in 1900 for the lettering on the shelters of the Paris Métro.

As an addition to the order for the font, Frank Pick turned to other graphic designers for posters, which turned out to be rooted in the Victorian idiom. In 1915, he decided to apply to the American Edward McKnight Kauffer, active in England in the interwar years, as well as to a host of other talents, including Frank Brangwyn, Graham Sutherland, Austin Cooper, Frank Newbould, and Paul Nash. Pick also even occasionally worked with artists such as Man Ray and Moholy-Nagy (who was living in exile in England from 1935). McKnight Kauffer, born in the United States in 1890, had studied painting (as well as lettering) in San Francisco and Chicago, and then, before the outbreak of war, in Paris. In Chicago in 1913, he was to visit the Armory Show, where he became fascinated with the European modern art exhibited, just as Jan Tschichold had been captivated by the Bauhaus exhibition at about the same age. Setting out for Europe, McKnight Kauffer traveled to Germany, France, Italy, and Algeria before settling in London in 1914. Interested in Cubism, he frequented the Vorticists and practiced painting, which he gradually left to start a career as a graphic designer. One of his best-known posters, *Flight*, was used in 1919 as an advertisement by the *Daily Herald* newspaper. According to McKnight Kauffer himself, it represented the first—and indeed only—English Cubist poster.[135] It was during his British period (1914–40, that is, a quarter of a century), that McKnight Kauffer acquired his reputation as a poster artist. From around 1920, he began receiving orders from several companies, including London Underground (for which he composed nearly one hundred and fifty posters), Shell-Mex, and British Petroleum. Between 1927 and 1929, he was to work for the Crawford agency directed by Ashley Havinden (another figure involved in Cubism-inspired advertising artwork). In 1930, McKnight Kauffer was appointed art director for the publishing house of Lund Humphries, and little by little his work gained international recognition. In 1937, the New York Museum of Modern Art devoted a retrospective to him, following its 1936 exhibition, *Posters by Cassandre*. McKnight Kauffer's creations, like those of French poster artists of his time, cannot be pigeonholed, as his graphic language ranges from works in which the central role is allotted to illustration, to complex assemblies of text, drawing, and other imagery.

Meanwhile, Frank Pick found himself gaining more and more responsibility within the company. By 1933, he was managing director of the London Transport company, an umbrella organization absorbing the former Underground Group and incorporating all public transport in the city. Over about thirty years, Pick was to develop for London Transport a distinctive graphic design, including corporate identity, typeface, and a large number of posters. At the beginning of the 1930s, at the initiative of a young industrial draftsman, Henry C. Beck, this portfolio was completed by a new map for the Underground. In 1931, Beck, in an effort to convey and clarify the entire subway network in a rational fashion, chose a radically new solution in map-making, which, if it was less faithful to geography, aided consultation significantly. He decided to replace the inextricable bundle of intersecting rails with a schematic diagram comprising horizontal, vertical, and oblique lines (inclined to 45 degrees). To balance the information available, he proportionally increased the size of the far fuller center of the network. Following encouragement from his immediate colleagues, Henry Beck unveiled his plan in 1931 (the year it was designed) to the publicity department of the company running the subway. The initial response was incomprehension: "The schematic treatment was thought to be too 'revolutionary.' My Underground map was handed back to me and that, it seemed, was to be the end of it."[136] Once again, an unusual form, in spite of its suitability, was received with shock and disbelief before meeting with approbation. A year after this failure, in 1932, Beck tried his luck once again, and was this time successful: the first diagrammatic map of the London Underground was accepted. From the very start, and to conserve the unity of the company's design identity, the proposal made use of Johnston's typeface. Printed for the first time in 1933, this diagrammatic plan seems to have been well received by travelers. Beck continued to tinker with his map up until 1959, making countless corrections and modifications. In spite of subsequent changes to the system, the current state of the plan preserves the principle and the originality of the 1933 diagram. Henry Beck's design proved a pioneering effort in terms of information, cartography, and signage.

438
Edward Johnston, new version of the visual identity of the London Underground commissioned in 1918 by Frank Pick. A revised idea of the corporate identity that had existed since 1908, composed of a blue horizontal bar over a red circle.

439
Man Ray, posters *London Transport—Keeps London Going*, two sheets used especially on London Underground's advertising panels, 1930s.

440
Edward Johnston, Underground Railway Sans, for the exclusive use of the London Underground. Also called Underground, Johnston, Johnston Underground, Railway Type, or Railway.

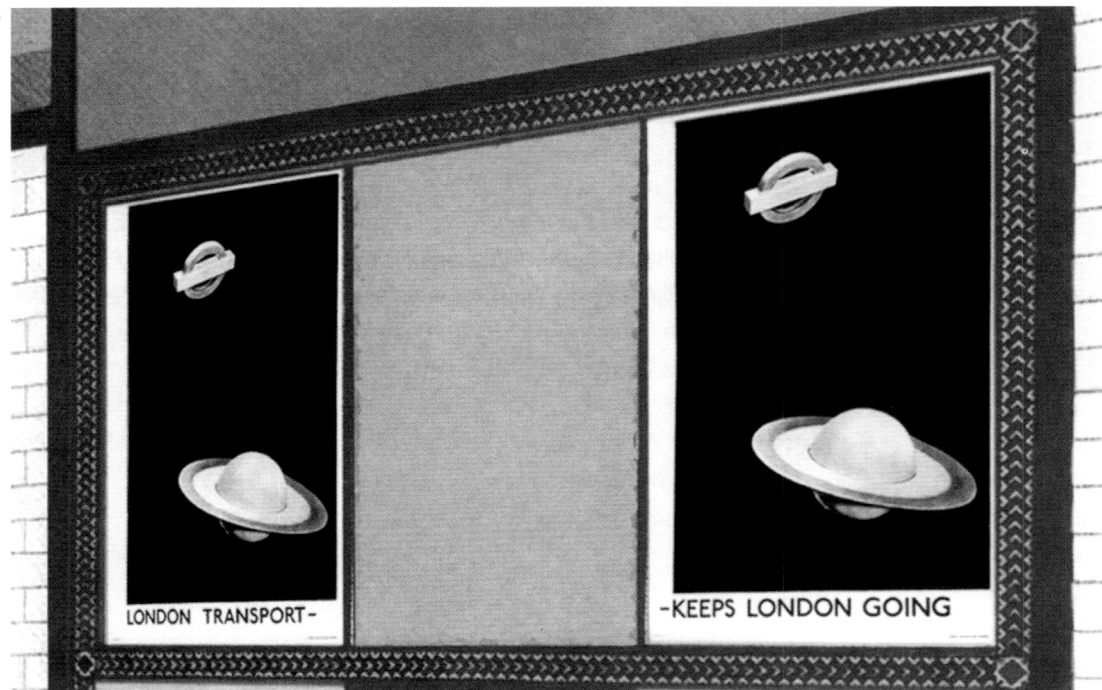

ABCDEFGHIJKLMN
OPQRSTUVWXYZ
abcdefghijklmnopq
rstuvwxyz 123456
7890 (&£.,:;'!?-*"")
ABCDEFGHIJKLMN
OPQRSTUVWXYZ
1234567890

First complete map of the London
Underground, 1908. The irregular design
gives the impression that it is a true
geographical plan.

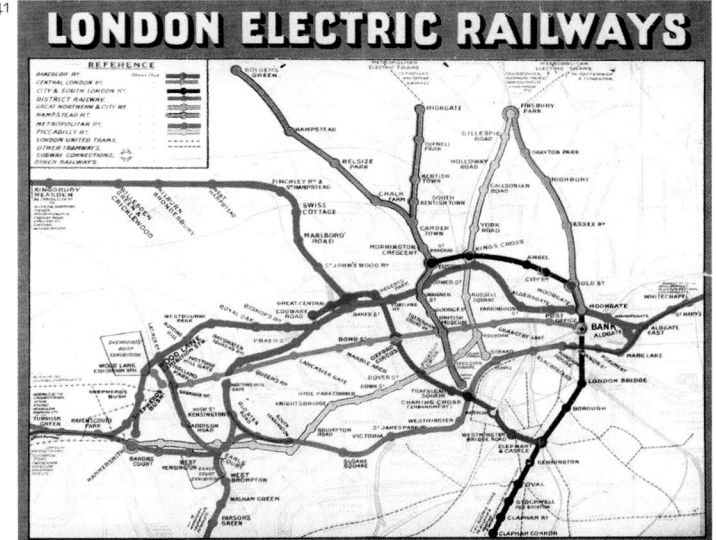

441

442

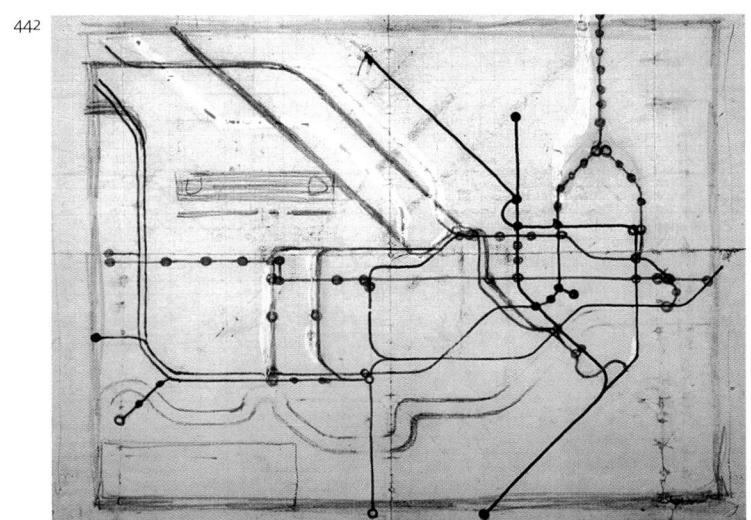

443

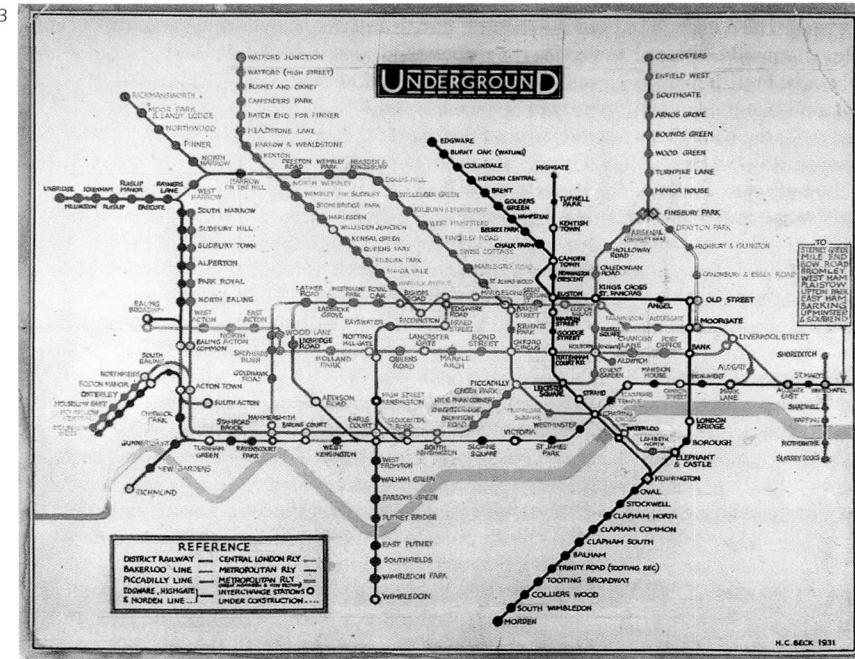

444

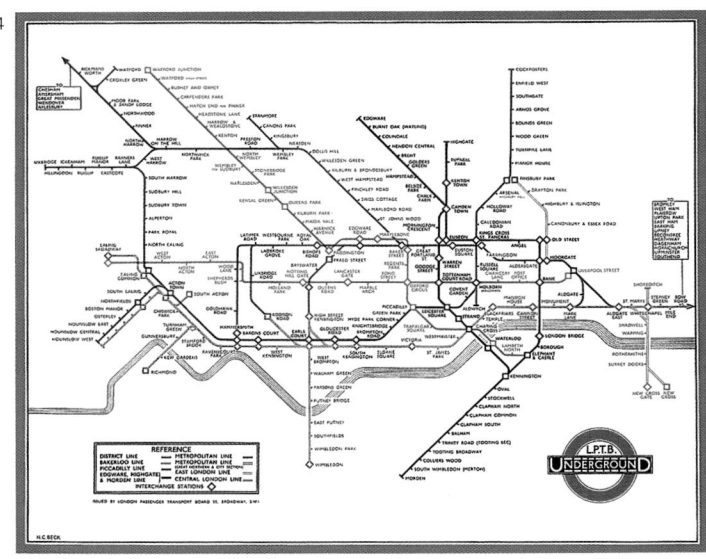

442
Henry Beck, original sketch for the
diagrammatic plan of the London Underground,
c. 1930. The lines representing journeys can
occupy a horizontal or vertical position or one
inclined at an angle of 45 degrees.

443
Henry Beck, diagram as presented to the
Underground's publicity department. Artwork
rejected in 1931, but accepted the following
year.

444
Henry Beck, first poster of the diagrammatic
plan of the London Tube, 1933.

Type, printing, and publishing

In interwar Britain, the fields of typographical printing, the press, and publishing were undergoing a significant change in direction. At the dawn of the twentieth century, after the Arts and Crafts and Private Press movements had already brought about important developments through their reliance on quality and respect for tradition, fundamental reforms in printing began in the 1910s and lasted until shortly after World War II, with the eventual acceptance of industrialization as one of its linchpins.

Such bold departures were heralded in an increased number of insightful publications dedicated to the book and to typography, which advocated a wholly new approach to everything from type manufacture to page-setting. Around the end of 1910, in a process of rehabilitation that embraced typefaces as varied as Bembo, Caslon, Baskerville, Fournier, and Bodoni, landmark models of historical alphabets were adapted to machines such as the Linotype and Monotype. Conscious of henceforth inescapable developments in technology, typographers and printers were confronted with the need to redefine their methods and working practices. A succession of periodical publications and books followed, explicating these ongoing reflections, as evidenced, for instance, in 1913 with the publication of the review *The Imprint* (co-edited by Edward Johnston), on which Stanley Morison collaborated. (According to the typography and Tschichold specialist Ruari McLean in 1970, Morison is one of the two most important personalities of twentieth-century typography, along with the author of *Die neue Typographie*.) Imprisoned during World War I as a conscientious objector, Stanley Morison devoted his long career to the practice and history of typography, publishing more than fifty works devoted to the latter and to printing. The first, *The Craft of Printing*, appeared in 1921. In 1923, he was collaborating on the launch of the review *The Fleuron*, a now famous periodical of traditionalist bent and a million miles away from the Continental avant-garde, published first by Olivier Simon and then by Morison himself. In 1929, his essay "First Principles of Typography" was published initially in the *Encyclopaedia Britannica*, then the following year in the last number of *The Fleuron*.

In addition to writing, Morison was quite as productive in the field of type design and manufacture. He was consultant in typography to the Monotype company from 1923 until his death in 1967, and from 1929 to 1960 he fulfilled the same office for the London *Times* newspaper. Morison had been appointed in 1929 to design a new typeface for the newspaper, and headed the development of the celebrated Times New Roman.[137] Commissioned from the Monotype company by the newspaper, and elaborated by Victor Lardent from an analysis of sixteenth-century Roman and later characters (including Plantin and possibly a model from the beginning of the twentieth century), the font was envisaged initially for the newspaper's exclusive use.

Times was roughed out in 1930, engraved in 1931, and used for the first time by the broadsheet in 1932. A popular font if ever there was one, it has forfeited its exclusive character and has been available to printers generally since 1933. The mission of the *Times*'s new type was to simultaneously save space and attain optimal legibility. Its effectiveness derives from its focus of clearly established formal options: relatively short extenders, reinforced contrast between main and hairline strokes (compared to Renaissance models), termination in slender serifs, and compact overall width. Having met these criteria, and been formulated at the outset for the press, Times New Roman has since acquired the status of a design classic, still widely employed in publishing and now one of the standard digital fonts of choice.

Other talents came to the fore in type conception in Great Britain, The American Bruce Rogers, a creator of several typefaces, made England his residence for a period in the 1910s and at the end of the 1920s. On the avant-garde flank of typography, Eric Gill took up where Johnston left off, in particular with his Gill Sans, although Joanna and Perpetua were also his

445

ABCDEFG HIJKLMNO PQRSTUV WXYZ

abcdefghijkl mnopqrstuv ?æœ&£ 1234567890

445
Eric Gill, Gill Sans medium type, c. 1928–30.

446

447

abcdefghijklmnopqrsß
tuvwxyz
ABCDEFGHIJKLM
NOPQRSTUVWXYZ
1234567890

creations. Born in 1882, by the very beginning of the twentieth century Gill was pupil of, then assistant to, Edward Johnston, after having worked for a few years in an architect's practice. In point of fact, the type that bears his name owes a great deal to Underground. The now legendary Gill Sans was initially composed in 1926 and finalized from 1927 onwards, and was cut by the Monotype company in 1928. Compared to the geometrically colored alphabets of its time, it conveys a far more drawn feel, with all the fluidity of handwriting. In Britain, Gill Sans quickly enjoyed a very favorable reception, and soon became one of the most popular sans serif typefaces, but its success did not spill over onto the Continent nor the United States, where it was long ignored.

Eric Gill's activities also covered publishing (once again, like Johnston and Morison, with whom he was to collaborate). In 1931, he published *An Essay on Typography* (revised 1936), a small-size work set in Joanna and regularly peppered with pilcrows. The text is conspicuous in possessing ragged margins (infrequent in running text at the time), allowing for natural regularity in word spacing and ensuring homogeneous typographical color over the page; the surface looks very different from standard rectangular composition. In the opening lines of his text, Gill proclaims that the conflict inherited from the nineteenth century between partisans of industrialization and defenders of craft is no longer salient for typography, and that from now on it will be incumbent upon its practitioners to try to reconcile the power of industrialism with the human side of handicraft.

Other telling experiments and achievements during the interwar period and beyond were to mark the fields of publishing, typography, and printing in Britain. In 1935, for example, publisher Sir Allen Lane launched the publishing house Penguin Books, with the intention of issuing high-quality, inexpensive paperbacks. Between 1947 and 1949, Jan Tschichold, who had settled temporarily in London, was assigned to rethink the entire Penguin imprint range (to be replaced by Hans Schmoller, who was to work at the firm until 1980). Beatrice Warde was another figure of the time presenting affinities with tradition. She was born in the United States and worked at the beginning of the 1920s for the American Type Founders Company (ATF). Marrying typographer Frederic Warde, she left for England, collaborating in particular on the review *The Fleuron*, before becoming involved in promotion and publishing in the Monotype firm. Except for a few outstanding achievements (including Underground and Gill Sans), British typography of the period fell back on values inherited from tradition, as against those avant-garde experiments determined to do without all semblance of historical form.

Emboldened by the efforts of a handful of trailblazers such as McKnight Kauffer, graphic design ventured into modernism, aided by the uptake of mechanization and the expanding catchment of media outlets. If the concerns of British reviews often seem remote from avant-garde practice, the formation of several associations attests to a will to partake in the changing climate of typography and applied art. The Design and Industries Association, influenced by the example of the German Werkbund, was founded in London in 1915 (Frank Pick was a member), with its main goal to improve design for industrial products. The Society of Typographic Designers (STD)[138] was set up in 1928 on the initiative of a number of typographers and is still active in the field of type design, organizing publications, seminars, and so on. Thus, the panorama of English graphic design during the first decades of the twentieth century appears composite, profitably combining highly diverse practices, although on the whole marginal with respect to the effervescent situation in central Europe. If poster artists, as in France, might try their hand at Cubism, they seemed to have been little influenced by movements and schools like De Stijl, Constructivism, or the Bauhaus. On the other hand, in the realm of typography, a typeface such as Underground presents strong links with the geometrically or Constructionist-tinged alphabets designed overseas.

Graphic design and typography transfigured

448
Bauhaus weaving studios, project for a textile with a pattern designed by Hans-Joachim (Hajo) Rose in 1932 on a typewriter. The textile was made at a later stage.

449
Jan Van Krimpen, Open Lutetia, manufactured by Enschedé en Zonen, Haarlem (Netherlands), 1928. Imre Reiner, Initiales Floride, foundry of Deberny & Peignot, Paris, 1937. Alessandro Butti, Semplicità Ombra font (shadow version of a sans serif alphabet), Nebiolo foundry, Turin, 1930.

In the years between the wars, transformations in graphic design and typography across Europe—in Great Britain, France, Germany, the Netherlands, Italy, the Soviet Union, Czechoslovakia, Poland, and Hungary—accelerated dramatically. Only nations located at the northernmost and southernmost ends of the continent (in particular, the Iberian and Scandinavian peninsulas, except, however, for Sweden where the poster flourished in the 1910s and 1920s) appear relatively untouched by the wave. By and large, the United States, too, was to take up with avant-garde experiments from the 1930s onwards. What had seen the light of day in Europe as the expression of a complete break with tradition, in reaction to social, political, or economic events, was little by little reconstituted and popularized as a wholesale redefinition of the conception and praxis of the applied arts. In spite of the painful aftereffects of World War I, the quest for modernity in art was pursued without stint. Through all the "-isms," and the trends and schools that shadowed them, graphic designers and typographers found themselves presented with a huge variety of registers of expression and a vast panoply of forms, from the simple to the complex, the ascetic to the decorative, the chaotic to the functional. The great strides made in these fields during the first third of the twentieth century are all the more astonishing as, not only were they often the work of multifaceted artists (including many painters and architects) trained in fine art, but these figures frequently had to make do with traditional printing equipment that seems, in retrospect, crude and unwieldy. If graphic design thus increased in plasticity—in particular with the uptake of photography and the influence of abstract and constructed art—or else was buoyed up by a liberating expressivity, simultaneously typography was undergoing a metamorphosis of its own, often radically departing from its classical heritage. In the medium term, the abandonment of the historical legacy of printing entailed an eventual readjustment, a phenomenon illustrated by the telling personal position of Jan Tschichold from the 1930s.

The exact nature of developments in graphic design, however, varied along geographical lines. If the Constructionist and functionalist flank took precedence in the Soviet Union, the Netherlands, Germany, and later on in Switzerland, the practice of drawing and painting tended to remain uppermost in the work of poster artists in Great Britain and France. In Italy, the late Futurism of the 1920s (in 1930, Marinetti was to publish a *Manifesto of Futurist Cuisine*) now unfolded in parallel with Art Deco. Beginning in the 1920s, new approaches to graphic design mushroomed elsewhere in the world. Inspired by Futurism and launched in 1921, Stridentism in Mexico aimed to combine art, literature, and music; the movement was to spawn posters and book and magazine covers, sometimes in the form of woodcuts, imbued with a trenchant and powerful graphic style by the likes of Ramón Alva de la Canal and Leopoldo Méndez. In Asia, graphic design sprung up in Japan where it coalesced around several groups of artists and creatives, such as the Association of Advertising Artists, created in 1926.

In Europe too, by and large, avant-garde advances prospered. If they were forced into the background in the Soviet Union in the early 1930s, and thoroughly stifled in Germany after 1933, progressive voices were to reappear or continue elsewhere, with fresh conviction and already embarking on a new phase. Switzerland, Italy, and the United States were to take up the torch from those countries in which the avant-garde had made its mark in the 1920s. Many protagonists (even if some initially might have worked for the regimes concerned) were to react against the rejection and even extirpation of the creative spark imposed by European dictatorships, and scattered throughout the Western world in the search of a new homeland or simply a haven in which to make a living. The cultures and circumstances they met on their travels, however, were often to consolidate their earlier experiments in graphic design. Concomitantly, the impact of new developments such as the consumer society, mass culture, and the audiovisual domain,[139] were to alter profoundly the trajectories of graphic design and typography.

Notes

1 László Moholy-Nagy, extract from the transcription of a lecture given in 1943 and reprinted in *László Moholy-Nagy* (exh. cat., Musées de Marseille/Réunion des musées nationaux, 1991), 443.

2 Term utilized by Hans Arp and El Lissitzky in *The Isms of Art*, 29 (1st ed. Eugen Rentsch, 1925; reprinted by Lars Müller, Switzerland, 1990).

3 Kasimir Malevich, quoted by H. Arp and El Lissitzky, ibid., ix.

4 J. Clair, "Une modernité sceptique," in J. Clair (gen. ed.), *Vienne 1880–1938* (exh. cat., Paris: Centre Georges Pompidou, 1986), 57.

5 Extract quoted by M. Jimenez, *Qu'est-ce que l'esthétique* (Paris: Gallimard, 1997), 312.

6 Quoted by Cabanne, *L'Avant-Garde au xxe siècle* (Paris: André Balland, 1969), 123.

7 Italian in origin, Marinetti studied in Paris and spoke fluent French. The original version of *First Futurist Manifesto* was written in French.

8 Tommaso Marinetti, "Manifeste du futurisme," in *Le Figaro*, February 20, 1909, 1.

9 Tommaso Marinetti, quoted by G. Lista, *Le Livre futuriste* (n. p.: Panini, 1984), 91.

10 Ardengo Soffici, quoted by G. Lista, ibid., 7.

11 Tommaso Marinetti, *L'Imagination sans fils et les Mots en liberté: manifeste futuriste* (1913); reprinted in B. Blistène and V. Legrand (gen eds.) *Poésure et peintrie*, (exh. cat., Centre de la Vieille Charité/Musées de Marseille/Réunion des musées nationaux, 1993), 494.

12 Expressions recorded by G. Lista, op. cit., 7 and 119.

13 Fortunato Depero, quoted by G. G. Lemaire, *Les Mots en liberté futuristes* (Paris: Jacques Damase, 1986), 25–26.

14 Fortunato Depero, "Le futurisme et l'art publicitaire," ibid., 33.

15 Alexei Krutchunykh, quoted in P. Hulten (gen. ed.) *Futurism and Futurisms* (London: Thames & Hudson, 1986), 496.

16 Velimir Khlebnikov, quoted by O. Djordjadzé (collective), *Iliazd* (Paris: Centre Georges Pompidou, 1978), 12.

17 Iliazd, ibid., 15.

18 Each "typographic picture" corresponds to a page in the book.

19 Iliazd, op. cit., 65.

20 Ezra Pound, quoted in P. Hulten (gen. ed.) *Futurism and Futurisms*, op. cit., 542.

21 A Vorticist tenet as announced in *Blast*; see P. Hulten (gen. ed.), *Futurisme et futurismes*, (Milan: Electa., 1986), 189.

22 Quoted by F. Popper, *Kinetic Art*, (London: Studio Vista, 1968), 53.

23 F. Popper, ibid., 53–45.

24 The motif of the square was in all probability in embryo in 1913, a date subsequently inscribed by Malevich on the back of the most famous version of *Black Square on a White Ground*. Some historians see this as antedating; others are of the opinion that Malevich was in fact according priority to the date of the initial draft and not to its final realization.

25 Quoted by Cabanne, *L'Art du vingtième siècle* (Paris: Aimery Somogy, 1982), 91.

26 Kasimir Malevich, quoted by E. Kovtoun, *Malevitch* (Paris: Flammarion, 1990), 105.

27 Guillaume Apollinaire, "Die moderne Malerei," *Der Sturm*, February 1913; reprinted in a French translation by Mme Ehrengard-Michel in *Chroniques d'art* (Paris: Gallimard, 1960), 273; quoted by D. Abadie, "Sonia Delaunay, à la lettre," *Art & publicité 1890–1990* (exh. cat., Paris: Centre Georges Pompidou, 1990), 348.

28 Apollinaire, 1917, definition of his *Calligrammes*; quoted by J. Peignot, *Du calligramme* (Paris: Chêne, 1978), 3.

29 A first version of *Un Coup de dés* appeared in May 1897 in the international review *Cosmopolis*.

30 Guillaume Apollinaire, quoted by M. Butor in the preface to the collection *Calligrammes* (Paris: Gallimard, 1966), 7, reprint.

31 Guillaume Apollinaire, cited by J. Peignot as an epigraph to *Du calligramme*, 3.

32 Sonia Delaunay, cited by D. Abadie, op. cit., 353–354.

33 Miriam Cendrars, ibid., 346.

34 Pierre Albert-Birot, quoted by J. Peignot, op. cit., 100.

35 Tristan Tzara (1922), cited by A. Bosquet, "Tzara, Dada ou le langage saboté," *Le Monde*, August 9, 1996, 24.

36 Ibid.

37 A socialist and communist movement headed by Karl Liebknecht and Rosa Luxemburg, assassinated during its suppression in 1919.

38 "*Cet été, les éléphants porteront des moustaches, et vous,*" "*place à dada qui tue,*" "*bas les mots,*" "*Hélène téléphone mieux,*" "*le vent favorable a des plumes bleues.*" Dada sayings and "proverbs" (c. 1920), cited by F. Sullerot, "Des mots sur le marché," *Art & publicité*, op. cit., 211–213.

39 George Grosz, quoted by H. Arp and El Lissitzky, op. cit., XI.

40 The Underground Railway Sans typeface is also known as Underground, Johnston, Johnston Underground, Railway Type, and even Railway.

41 Tommaso Marinetti, "Manifeste du futurisme," op. cit.

42 Henri Barbusse, October 14 1915, "Carnet de guerre" in *Le Feu* (Paris: Flammarion, 1965), 440–441.

43 Quoted by E. Metzl, *The Poster*, (New York: Watson-Guptill Publications, 1963), 101.

44 The expression "New Typography" is often ascribed to Jan Tschichold, spokesman of the movement and author of *Die neue Typographie* (Berlin: 1928). It was in fact being used previously, probably from the start of the 1920s. In *Staatliches Bauhaus Weimar* (1923), Moholy-Nagy also published a text entitled "Die neue Typographie," while Walter Dexel wrote "Was ist neue Typographie?", printed in 1927 in the *Frankfurter Zeitung*.

45 Vladimir Mayakovsky, quoted in J.-L. Ferrier (gen. ed.) *L'Aventure de l'art au XXe siècle* (Paris: Chêne/Hachette, 1988), 293.

46 Alexei Gan, ibid., 833.

47 El Lissitzky, quoted by C. Leclanche-Boulé, *Typographies et photomontages constructivistes en URSS* (Papyrus, 1984), 38.

48 Alexander Rodchenko (1928), cited by H. Gassner, "Débats constructivistes […]," *Art & publicité*, op. cit., 288–289.

49 Quoted by H. Arp and El Lissitzky, op. cit., XI.

50 L. Sutnar, *Visual Design in Action* (Hastings House, New York, 1961), c/1.

51 Karel Teige, quoted by R. Baur, *La Nouvelle Typographie* (Actualité des arts plastiques) (Paris: Centre National des Arts Plastiques, 1993), 50.

52 Ladislav Sutnar, op. cit.

53 Henryk Berlewi, quoted by R. Baur, op. cit., 47.

54 Tadeusz Gronowski, cited by A. Weill, *L'Affiche dans le monde* (Paris: Aimery Somogy, 1991), 265.

55 Quoted by K. Passuth, *Moholy-Nagy* (Paris: Flammarion, 1982), 393.

56 Texts cosigned by Theo Van Doesburg and Cornelis Van Eesteren, reprinted in *Theo Van Doesburg 1883–1931* (exh. cat., Kunsthalle Nuremberg and Kunsthalle Basel, 1969), 60–61.

57 Theo Van Doesburg, quoted by Cabanne, *L'Art du vingtième siècle*, op. cit., 837.

58 Quoted by D. Dooijes, *A History of the Dutch Poster 1890–1960* (Amsterdam: Scheltema en Holkema, 1968), 28.

59 Enschedé en Zonen printing works: see n. 89, part 1.

60 László Moholy-Nagy, reprinted by F. Baudin, *L'Effet Gutenberg* (Paris: Cercle de la Librairie, 1994), 447.

61 El Lissitzky, Max Burchartz and Johannes Canis, and László Moholy-Nagy, cited by U. Brüning, "Typographie constructiviste et publicité," *Art & publicité*, op. cit., 292, 293, and 291.

62 W. Moede, ibid., 295.

63 Jan Tschichold, extracts from "Elementare Typographie" (1925), as in R. Kinross, *Modern Typography*, op. cit., 106.

64 The word "Bauhaus" was coined from the terms *Bau*, "construction, building," and *Haus*, "house." So Bauhaus means literally "house of construction."

65 J. Itten (1961), *L'Art de la couleur* (Paris: Dessain et Tolra, 1979), 11.

66 Vilmos Huszár, quoted by M. Droste, *Bauhaus 1919–1933* (Cologne: Taschen, 1994), 54.

67 László Moholy-Nagy, reprinted by F. Baudin, op. cit., 447–448.

68 László Moholy-Nagy, quoted by R. Hollis, *Graphic Design in the 20th Century* (London: Thames & Hudson, 2001), 60.

69 Text by Herbert Bayer (1961), reprinted in B. Meggs, *A History of Graphic Design* (New York: John Wiley & Sons, 1983), 340 (1st ed.).

70 Walter Matthes, quoted by E. Neumann, "De l'enseignement du

Bauhaus au métier de graphiste," *Art & publicité*, op. cit., 318.

71 Quoted by L. Richard, *Encyclopédie du Bauhaus* (Paris: Aimery-Somogy, 1985), 126.

72 Quoted by Ph. Dagen, "Il y a 70 ans. Le bref été du Bauhaus," *Le Monde*, September 19–20, 1993, 2.

73 Quoted by Cabanne, *L'Art du vingtième siècle*, op. cit., 101.

74 The NWG was created in 1928 based on a group formed in 1927—the Gruppe radikaler Reklamegestalter in Deutschland.

75 El Lissitzky, quoted by J.-C. Marcadé, *L'Avant-Garde russe* (Paris: Flammarion, 1995), 450.

76 El Lissitzky, quoted by U. Brüning, op. cit., 296.

77 El Lissitzky, "Topographie de la typographie" (1923); reprinted in *Poésure et peintrie*, op. cit., 504.

78 Pelikan manufactures printing, writing, and stationery products.

79 László Moholy-Nagy, reprinted in F. Baudin, op. cit., 447–448.

80 László Moholy-Nagy, quoted by R. Baur, op. cit., 54.

81 László Moholy-Nagy, reprinted in F. Baudin, op. cit., 448.

82 László Moholy-Nagy (1946), quoted by H. M. Wingler, *The Bauhaus* (Cambridge, Mass./ London: MIT Press, 1986), 202 (1st ed. 1962).

83 Kurt Schwitters, cited by H. Bergius, "Kurt Schwitters [...]," in S. Lemoine (gen. ed.), *Kurt Schwitters*, (exh. cat., Paris: Centre Georges Pompidou/Réunion des musées nationaux, 1994), 38.

84 Kurt Schwitters, quoted by D. Steel, "dada – adad," *Word & Image* (vol. 6, no. 2, 1990), 209.

85 At first named the Werbe-Gestaltung Kurt Schwitters, the Merz Werbezentrale agency was to open a Dresden branch overseen by Margit von Plato.

86 Kurt Schwitters, quoted by S. Lemoine, "Merz, Futura, din et cicéro," *Art & publicité*, op. cit., 244.

87 Kurt Schwitters, "Thesen über Typographie," *Merz (Typoreklame)*, no. 11, 1924; reprinted by S. Lemoine, "Merz, Futura, DIN et cicéro," *Kurt Schwitters*, op. cit., 189.

88 Kurt Schwitters, "Suggestions pour l'élaboration d'une écriture systématique," ibid., 222.

89 Kurt Schwitters, quoted by H. Bergius, op. cit., 38.

90 Walter Dexel, extracts from the article "Was ist neue Typographie?" (1927), quoted by R. Baur, op. cit., 73.

91 László Moholy-Nagy, reprinted by F. Baudin, op. cit., 447.

92 The name of the Univers typeface, designed by Adrian Frutiger and released in 1957, betrays similar ambitions, which its sober form makes all the more realizable.

93 Raoul Hausmann, quoted by J.-M. Palmier, *Avant-garde photographique en Allemagne, 1919–1939* (Paris: Philippe Sers, 1982), 9.

94 Gustav Klutsis, quoted by F. Jobard, "Photomontage politique," *Signes* (no. 13–14, April 1995), 39.

95 Varvara Stepanova (writing in 1928), cited by A. Lavrentiev, *Varvara Stepanova* (Paris: Philippe Sers, 1988), 178.

96 László Moholy-Nagy, reprinted by F. Baudin, op. cit., 448.

97 László Moholy-Nagy, ibid.

98 Gustav Klutsis, quoted by C. Leclanche-Boulé, *Le Constructivisme russe. Typographies et photomontages* (Paris: Flammarion, 1991), 88.

99 Jan Tschichold, as in Kinross, op. cit., 107–108.

100 Guillaume Apollinaire, quoted by A. and I. Livingston, *Graphic Design and Designers* (London: Thames & Hudson, 2003), 17.

101 A. Weill, op. cit., 214.

102 Francis Thibaudeau worked on this historical didactic survey from 1915. He had already worked in 1903 on the publication of the general specimen for the foundry of Georges Peignot et fils.

103 F. Thibaudeau, *La Lettre d'imprimerie* (Paris: Bureau de l'édition, 1921), 422.

104 P. Rand, *A Designer's Art* (New Haven/London: Yale University Press, 1985), 235.

105 Cassandre (extract from an interview published in December 1926), quoted by A. Weill, op. cit., 200.

106 Le Corbusier (1923), cited by H. Mouron, *A. M. Cassandre* (Geneva: Éditions d'Art Albert Skira, 1985), 26. A substantial proportion of the quotations here (infra) concerning Cassandre's career have been taken from this monograph written by Henri Mouron, the artist's son.

107 Hachard, ibid., 10.

108 Cassandre (1926), ibid., 15.

109 Cassandre (1926), ibid., 16 and 22.

110 Cassandre (1926), ibid., 18–20.

111 Cassandre, quoted by J. Peignot, *Typoésie* (Paris: Imprimerie nationale, 1993), 61.

112 Cassandre (1926), quoted by H. Mouron, op. cit., 19.

113 Blaise Cendrars, document reproduced by J. Peignot in *Typoésie*, op. cit., 72–73 and 81.

114 Extracts from Peignot's specimen published in 1937, reproduced by H. Mouron, op. cit., 93.

115 H. Mouron, ibid., 153.

116 His son recalls that Cassandre probably just finished off the then current pun, "Dubon Dubonnet."

117 Loupot probably ceased working with the Alliance Graphique after 1932.

118 Cassandre (1926), quoted by H. Mouron, op. cit., 18.

119 Cassandre, quoted by H. Mouron, ibid., 18 and 20.

120 This conception of certain facets of Cassandre's oeuvre, and of French graphics of the interwar period generally, which views them as symptomatic of stylistic modernism, recurs in a number of works on graphic design.

121 Extract from the introduction to the catalog accompanying the first exhibition of posters by Cassandre in the United States (1936); quoted by H. Mouron, op. cit., 101.

122 Cassandre, quoted by H. Mouron, ibid., 155.

123 C. Zagrodski, *Loupot* (Paris: Le Cherche Midi, coll. L'Art de l'affiche, 1998). Most of the information mentioned here concerning the career of Charles Loupot is drawn from this mono-graph, which "lists and describes all the printed posters by Charles Loupot known to date" (36).

124 Cassandre (1926), quoted by H. Mouron, ibid., 23.

125 C. Zagrodski, ibid., 12.

126 C. Zagrodski, ibid., 16, quoting Roger L. Dupuy, extract from an article published in the review *Vendre*, in 1924.

127 Charles Loupot, quoted by A. Weill, op. cit., 208.

128 Remarks by Max Augier, cited by C. Zagrodski, op. cit., 96.

129 Charles Loupot, quoted by C. Zagrodski, ibid., 33.

130 Jean Carlu, "Réflexions sur l'esthétique de l'affiche," *Arts et métiers graphiques* (no. 7, September 1928), 437–438.

131 This is Hadley Richardson, Hemingway's first wife.

132 The Musée de l'Affiche in Paris devoted a retrospective to Carlu's work in 1980–1981. See *Jean Carlu* (exh. cat., Paris: Musée de l'Affiche, 1980–1981).

133 Extract from the UAM manifestos reproduced by A. Barré-Despond in *Union des artistes modernes* (Paris: Éditions du Regard, 1985), 541 and 546.

134 See on this subject: R. Jubert, "Cassandre. Tschichold. Deux conceptions de la création (typo)graphique européenne des années 1920 et 1930," *Les Cahiers du Musée national d'art moderne*, no. 89, "Design graphique" (Centre Georges Pompidou, Autumn 2004), 24–43.

135 Edward McKnight Kauffer, in A. Weill, op. cit., 224.

136 Henry C. Beck, quoted by K. Garland, *Mr. Beck's Underground Map* (London: Capital Transport, 1994), 17.

137 The face previously used by the *Times* newspaper was called Times Old Roman. Times New Roman also exists in a slightly different form, named Times Roman.

138 The Society of Typographic Designers (STD), initially called the British Typographers Guild, was henceforth to be known as the International Society of Typographic Designers.

139 In the course of the 1920s, radio was to make great strides in the United States as in Europe; the shift from silent film to talkies occurred in 1927; animated film and the cartoon continued their expansion to become extremely popular; the recording and reproduction of sound on magnetic tape was developed in the 1920s and the 1930s; in the United States, television programs were widely broadcast from 1941, and so on. See, for example, the quotations (passim) by Octave Uzanne taken from his article, "The End of Books," by László Moholy-Nagy as to the "optical spirit" of his era, by El Lissitzky in excerpts from his article "Topographie de la typographie," or again by Michel Butor in the preface to Apollinaire's collection, *Calligrammes*.

**Part 4
Contents**

From the rise of totalitarianism to World War II

Totalitarianism: avant-garde exile and survival

The rise of totalitarianism

In the early 1930s, the amazing saga of European avant-garde movements took a dramatic new turn. The economic impact of the stock-market crash of 1929 and the ideological and political consolidation of totalitarian states crushed modern culture. Freedom of thought, creativity, and expression, loudly proclaimed by the avant-gardes and finally won after hard struggle, was steadily driven out by the authoritarianism and constraints imposed by the new regimes. Stalinism, Italian Fascism, and Nazism insisted that artistic production be employed for state propaganda. In the East, Stalin's rise towards absolute mastery of the Soviet Union began in 1924, the year of Lenin's death. In Italy, Benito Mussolini (an active socialist prior to 1914), founded the National Fascist Party in 1921—which he himself described as "reactionary, antiparliamentarian, anti-demoliberal [sic], and anti-socialist."[1] Following Mussolini's march on Rome in 1922, King Victor Emmanuel III asked Il Duce to form a government, and Mussolini consolidated his dictatorship throughout the 1920s by granting himself full powers, establishing a totalitarian-type regime, and allowing only a single party. Fascism proclaimed "everything [to be] in the State, nothing against the State, nothing outside the State."[2]

In Germany, meanwhile, Adolf Hitler came to power somewhat later. In 1919, he had taken charge of a German workers' party, renamed the following year the German Workers' National Socialist Party (NSDAP). Many intellectuals misjudged the content of National-Socialism, at least at the time. After the failure of a putsch in Munich in 1923, Hitler spent part of the following year in prison, where he began to write *Mein Kampf* (My Struggle). Germany then seemed to recover some calm, especially as the crushing defeat of the war faded (along with the losses dictated by the Treaty of Versailles). For a while, Germany's economic growth pushed Nazism to the sidelines, at least until the crash of 1929 began to wreak its terrible effects on the country. In the early 1930s, unemployment, poverty, and steep inflation created a climate that favored the rise of extremists. (By way of example, the number of unemployed in Germany grew from two million to six million between 1929 and 1932.) In 1930, 107 Nazi representatives were elected to the Reichstag. In 1932, Hitler lost the presidential election to the very conservative Marshal Paul von Hindenburg. After an escalating series of governmental crises, Hindenburg appointed Hitler to the post of chancellor on January 30, 1933 (and on Hindenburg's death in 1934, Hitler would succeed him as president). Meanwhile, the NSDAP had emerged as the country's sole party (on the model of the Fascist Party in Italy, which became a single-party state in 1928). The Germany Communist Party was disbanded, labor unions were outlawed, concentration camps were established, and the process of stripping away a cultural identity began. The "new order" quickly came to dominate. The Führer borrowed the concept of antidemocratic totalitarianism and intolerance from Il Duce.

In Germany, as in the Soviet Union and Italy—although varying with specific case and period—the rise of dictatorship led to a shift, a weakening, or an elimination of the artistic work of the previous decades. Nazism, Fascism, and Stalinism imposed their own visual codes in terms of aesthetics and rhetoric, without necessarily rejecting the forms developed by avant-garde practice (as witnessed by similarities in graphic style). Glorious images of the supreme leaders invaded poster art and other supports, accompanied, for example, by brief

244

exhortations to join the party. Although propaganda through imagery (including intensive use of posters) had already been widely employed during World War I, the totalitarian governments of the 1920s and 1930s were able to assess and swiftly exploit this instrument of power. The history of political posters took on a new shading. Authoritarian imagery was developed around subjects, signs, and values typical of the artistic output of the new visual codes. Such images glorified party, nation, family, discipline, and race, not to mention peasants and workers and, of course, the dictator himself; then there were the themes of the powerful male body, the feminine role of good wife-and-mother, and the optimism of youth, and finally the concepts of courage, duty, outstanding exploits, the wearing of uniforms, emblems, and so on. Such imagery was elaborated in diverse formal registers and styles.

Avant-garde phenomena were not thrown out indiscriminately; although they were repressed, some techniques might still contribute to the efficiency of propaganda. Abstraction was generally banned in favor of figurative immediacy, yet it nevertheless continued to survive and was employed in certain media (including posters), as was the technique of photomontage. However, the major trend entailed a return to realistically drawn or painted pictures, as witnessed by the spread of socialist realism in the Soviet Union from the late 1920s onwards, as well as national-socialist realism in Germany. Many posters employed illustrations. Bombast, nineteenth-century academicism, and references to antiquity (notably the Roman Empire) all abounded in imagery tinged with a sense of the past and tradition. It was sometimes heavy-handed, although not always. In various realms of artistic production, some artists were able to satisfy the regime's expressive criteria—in Germany, for example, they included architect Albert Speer (who joined the National-Socialist Party as early as 1931, and was appointed minister of armaments and munitions in 1942), sculptor Arno Breker, film-maker Leni Riefenstahl, and painter Adolf Wissel. The abundant use of ideological, political posters—a key tool of visual propaganda—assumed a crucial role. Hammering the message repeatedly, sometimes to the point of obsession, posters vastly multiplied their powers of persuasion, as proven by the fact that they were sometimes printed in colossal numbers. In addition to the message they conveyed, posters were used as a tool for haranguing crowds, mobilizing large gatherings, and organizing parades and other showy demonstrations.

Whereas the avant-garde's graphic style was typified by its powerful drive for innovation and its transdisciplinarity (combining literature, fine art, decorative art, and the applied arts)—a drive that did not necessarily exclude extremist attitudes— the dictatorships' visual message came across primarily as the raw expression of an organized, calculated system that relied on correct procedures. The people promoting totalitarianism felt that avant-garde artists and intellectuals (much of whose work and ideas would be hard to monitor and control) had to be driven out or eliminated unless they agreed to toe the line. Nazism described modern art as "degenerate"[3] and, among other epithets, "Judeo-Bolshevist." Stalinism considered modern art to be "antinational."[4] In Germany itself, the situation became so unfavorable as cultural repression became so strong, indeed violent, that many advocates of a cultural and artistic avant-garde went into exile. "There were hundreds and thousand of intellectuals, poets and writers who fled the Nazi dictatorship in 1933. In a matter of months, Germany was emptied of its writers, poets, actors, artists, architects, directors, and professors."[5] Many headed for the United States (often New York or California), others for Great Britain or other European countries. Although several members of the Bauhaus were among these persecuted individuals, other Bauhaus figures worked under the National-Socialist regime for a while.

Whichever path they took, many graphic artists and typographers (including some top-rate artists) suffered a rupture in their careers in 1933 and the years immediately afterward. Some of them lost their teaching posts after Hitler was named chancellor of the Third Reich. Right

450

450
Poster in support of the Spanish Republic, *Que haces tu para evitar esto?* (What are you doing to prevent this?), Barcelona, 1937. The photo has been taken, then recomposed, from another poster.

from 1933 Paul Renner was suspended (and would be permanently dismissed in 1934) from his post of director of Munich's Meisterschule für Deutschlands Buchdrucker (School of German Master Printers), and Jan Tschichold lost his teaching job there. John Heartfield, meanwhile, left for Prague in 1933, where he continued to run his publishing house, Malik-Verlag, notably publishing AIZ. In 1937 Kurt Schwitters left for exile in Norway (going on to Great Britain in 1940). Many former Bauhaus teachers headed for the United States between 1933 and 1938: Josef Albers, followed by László Moholy-Nagy, Marcel Breuer, and Walter Gropius (all three of whom went first to England), Ludwig Mies van der Rohe, and Herbert Bayer. Many other European graphic designers would also live or work briefly in the United States during this period, either for political or professional reasons. Between 1934 and 1939 they included, among others, Joseph Binder, Herbert Matter, Gyorgy Kepes, Will Burtin, Ladislav Sutnar, and Leo Lionni. In Europe itself, cultural restrictions began to spread beyond Germany and Italy into occupied countries, triggered by Germany's annexation of Austria and the Sudetenland (Czechoslovakia) in 1938, not to mention the invasions of Poland (1939) and the Netherlands (1940), and the occupation of France. Dictatorships considerably restricted—when they didn't totally halt—the work of graphic artists and typographers. Furthermore, economic depression weighed very heavily on the industrial world on which the graphic design sector partly relied, notably for commercial work. The stock-market crash triggered by American speculation and over-production soon crippled Germany, followed by Italy, France, and England. The phenomenon was so widespread that many graphic designers struggled to stay afloat in the 1930s (and all the more so in the first half of the 1940s, when commercial orders dried up, indeed vanished), whether they remained in their home countries or went abroad. Exile led to a shift in career for all, due to the change in conditions, the problems of immigration, other chance factors, and the specific conjunction. Some people adapted well; others did not (German film-makers, for example, found emigration particularly trying).

451

451
John Heartfield, original art for a photomontage published in Kurt Tucholsky's book, *Deutschland, Deutschland über alles*, 1929 (p. 163).

Despite the extent of repression of the avant-gardes and plans for their extinction, and apart from the way that some governments managed to exploit them, certain aspects of (typo)graphic modernism spurred direct offshoots in Europe itself. Italy and Switzerland, for instance, maintained continuity with the movements of the 1920s. In some places, certain artists and writers put up active resistance to cultural persecution and constraint. In Great Britain, the Artists' International Association (AIA), founded in 1933, became immediately politicized, declaring itself opposed to fascism; its membership included typographer Eric Gill. In Germany itself, John Heartfield elaborated a darkly biting oeuvre and contributed to the illustration of Kurt Tucholsky's book, *Deutschland, Deutschland über alles* (1929), in which Tucholsky delivered a sweeping social criticism of nationalism and militarism.[6] Even prior to 1933, Heartfield had expressed sharp criticism of Hitlerism through his collages and photomontages, massively distributed through the press. Ten years later, the printing of illegal texts would become part of the active Resistance movements in countries at war—printers and typesetters kept presses rolling in secret, at the risk (and sometimes cost) of their lives.

The art system under the Nazis

National-Socialism's censorship of the arts was apparent well before Adolf Hitler acceded to the post of chancellor. *Mein Kampf*, begun in 1924, already called for the government's totalitarian control of artistic and literary output. "This cleansing of our culture must be extended to nearly all fields. Theater, art, literature, cinema, press, posters, and window displays must be cleansed of all manifestations of our rotting world and placed in the service of a moral, political, and cultural idea."[7] Thus a decade before he became chancellor, then president, of the Third Reich, Hitler announced his program of eradicating the avant-garde arts. In *Mein Kampf*, he also expressed the uncompromising radicalism of his opinion of avant-garde culture, claiming that

the art produced during the Weimar Republic was the work of the mentally ill.[8] And indeed, as soon as their power permitted it, the regime's authorities persecuted vast sections of modern art and literature. In 1929, Hitler named Joseph Goebbels as head of propaganda for the NSDAP. At the end of that same year, the party joined a coalition that won parliamentary elections in the German state of Thuringia. Certain Bauhaus figures were already the object of repression, and the works of several artists (including Paul Klee and Wassily Kandinsky) disappeared from Weimar museums. More specifically, when it came to graphic design, the text of *Mein Kampf* identified the potential propaganda power of posters, going so far as to anticipate and prescribe exactly how they should be used. "All effective [posters] must be limited to a very few points and must harp on these slogans until the last member of the public understands what you want him to understand by your slogan. As soon as you sacrifice this slogan and try to be many-sided, the effect... is weakened."[9]

Starting in 1933, what had previously been a policy tested in a specific region of Germany became a strict program of cultural surveillance and censorship. A ministry of information and propaganda, headed by Goebbels, was established in March 1933. The stranglehold extended everywhere—any message originating from without was prohibited. All sources of

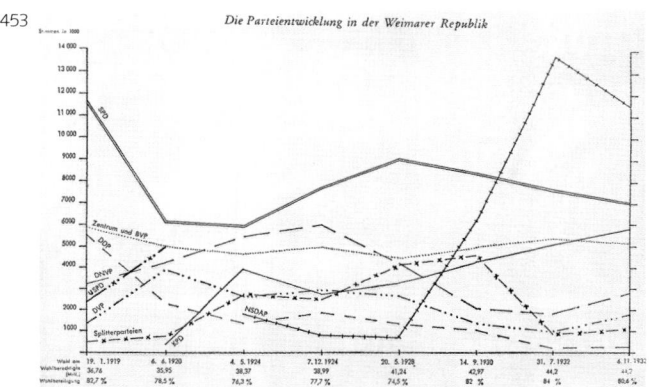
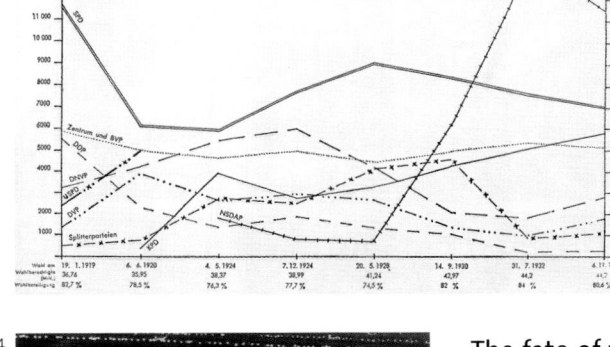

information, media, and means of expression were subjected to monitoring—book publishing, the press, movies, posters, and so on. Intellectuals and teachers were arrested, schools were closed. On May 10, 1933, Goebbels organized a vast book-burning ceremony in front of the Berlin Opera House: twenty thousand novels and scholarly books went up in flames (including the work of Sigmund Freud, Franz Werfel, Thomas Mann, Erich Maria Remarque, and Albert Einstein). Ideas were put to the torch, and with them the productive output of printing and typography, perceived as channels for disseminating ideas that the Nazis sought to destroy.[10] Goebbels swiftly began reorganizing and requisitioning all means of communication and information liable to reach the masses. Soon all the methods, impact, and persuasive powers of graphic design, typography, and printing would be brought to heel.

The fate of the Bauhaus and its artists

The Bauhaus was one of the new regime's first targets. As a laboratory of ideas, a space for utopias, and a temple of artistic exploration, the establishment could hardly survive the advent of Nazism. Already in 1932, the municipal council in Dessau, where the Bauhaus was initially founded, decided to close the school at the urging of the Nazis. The school then reopened as a private institute in a disused telephone factory in Berlin-Steglitz. "The Berlin Bauhaus was nothing but a poorly reproduced copy of Dessau. It henceforth became a much more traditional technical training institute. It resembled a dying person kept artificially alive."[11] In 1933, Mies van der Rohe ordered the removal of a swastika erected in front of the building; on April 11 of that year (just one month before the famous book-burning events in Berlin), the police invaded the premises, alleging it was a site of Communist propaganda. Thirty students were arrested. The next day, the newspapers published misinformation. As far as the Nazis were concerned, the Bauhaus constituted "one of the prime havens of the Judeo-Marxist conception of art, so removed from art that it can only be considered a pathological syndrome."[12] Using a series of highly explicit and foreboding compound adjectives and epithets, they described rationalistic Bauhaus architecture as "degenerate and beJewed,"[13] thereby targeting the social housing policies pursued in Germany since the 1920s. Although Mies van der Rohe entered into negotiations with Nazi leader Alfred Rosenberg, the Bauhaus teachers ultimately met for the last time on July 20, confirming the dissolution of the school. For the third and last time, the Bauhaus closed. Despite many internal problems, the establishment had lived through the fifteen-year Weimar Republic with an unflagging determination to experiment. Such a hub of activity, suddenly brought to a halt, would

452
Benno von Arendt, banner holders on the East–West Berlin Charlottenburg route, 1939.

453
Chart showing the growth and decline of various political parties during the Weimar Republic.

454
Nazi parade at night. During huge nocturnal events, thousands of torches would spell out "Heil Hitler" and form swastikas.

generate offshoots in the form of various ramifications in sundry places, including the United States, where many Bauhaus teachers emigrated. During its temporary existence the school made a major contribution to the development of design in synergy with the other arts, always striving to conceive environmental forms most appropriate to the times in the context of a resolutely open and multidisciplinary atmosphere.

Within the Bauhaus and elsewhere, avant-garde designers, architects, and painters found themselves oppressed by the Nazi regime. In the Bauhaus itself, the teaching staff decided to dissolve the school in July even though the Gestapo had offered to allow it to remain open on condition that Kandinsky and Hilberseimer were replaced by teachers favorable to national-socialism. At other art schools in Germany, many teaching artists lost their jobs (including the representatives of the New Objectivity movement). Many of them were obliged to emigrate, while others professed loyalty to the new regime, either temporarily or permanently. Such was the case of Expressionist painter Emil Nolde and Expressionist writer Gottfried Benn, as well as certain members of the New Objectivity school, including Alexander Kanoldt and Franz Radziwill, both of whom joined the NSDAP only to find themselves later disavowed. Several well-known graphic artists worked for the Reich on an occasional basis, then emigrated

455
Paul Renner, cover of *Kulturbolschewismus?* (an essay by Renner on "Bolshevist culture," published by Eugen Rentsch), Germany, 1932. Printed in red and black, 8 1/2 × 5 3/4 in. (22 × 14.5 cm).

456
Herbert Bayer, double-page spread of a leaflet for the *Deutschland* exhibition in Berlin, organized by the Nazi Party, 1936.

457
Herbert Bayer, poster for the show of *Deutsches Volk Deutsche Arbeit* (German People, German Work), 1934.

458
John Heartfield, original of the photomontage published in *Arbeiter Illustrierte Zeitung* in March 1934 with accompanying text ("The old motto of the 'New' Reich: blood and iron")

shortly afterward (such as Herbert Bayer), whereas others collaborated in a sustained fashion, sometimes over the long term (such as Ludwig Hohlwein). Few artists or creative designers mounted active opposition or resistance to the Nazi regime, clearly due to the scope of repression and the risks involved—John Heartfield, a most singular figure here, decided to leave Germany in 1933. Quitting a totalitarian state, exiled designers did not seem particularly inclined to pursue a politicized oeuvre denouncing the regime in the country they had just abandoned. Reacting to the impact of rupture, they sought first of all to continue their careers in a foreign land. As far as typographers went, however, Jan Tschichold (who emigrated to Switzerland after being imprisoned for several weeks and losing his teaching job) openly railed against National-Socialism. "The creators of the New Typography and related trends were, like myself, firm enemies of Nazism... as such, I and my wife were long placed in 'preventive detention,' that is to say, in prison, at the start of the so-called Third Reich."[14]

Nazi output and "Degenerate Art"

Unable to fulfill the state's requirements, artistic modernism found itself publicly branded as undesirably degenerate. In a matter of months, right from early 1933, the avant-garde was roundly assailed. The Reich's artistic output was unilaterally propagandist and highly directive (just note the intensive use on posters of exclamation marks, with all their rhetorical power); it did not, however, become totally uniform. Initially, Joseph Goebbels and Alfred Rosenberg differed on this issue, the former advocating a certain contemporaneity, the latter demanding a return to the past. Hitler oversaw the production of a certain number of posters and graphic designs for party propaganda, when he didn't actually design them himself, including the typography. (As the main instigator of Nazi hatred of modern art, already apparent in certain passages of *Mein Kampf*, Hitler had twice failed to win admission to the Academy of Fine Arts in Vienna in the first decade of the twentieth century). Hence different registers of graphic design coexisted, ranging from conventionally realistic posters to Ludwig Hohlwein's bold graphics, via highly drawn or illustrated visuals, and even some avant-gardist approaches. In the fields of architecture, painting, and sculpture, it appears that the academic, bombastic registers dominated more markedly, as witnessed by an architectural megalomania that looked towards the Neoclassical, ancient, and Renaissance repertoires. Painting glorified the Führer, heroism, virtue, race, patriotism, the land and farmers, landscape, work, family ties, and so on. Painting espoused a *Heimatstil* (patriotic style) that reflected a series of specific allusions, values, and themes (some of them also found in posters). Once the cultural life of Weimer and its antecedents had been banished, there followed an imposed aestheticizing of artistic output that precluded all creative independence and freedom of expression.

In 1936 Munich hosted an exhibition of *Entartete Kunst* (Degenerate Art), one year prior to

the larger, more famous show of the same name, also held in Munich. The poster advertising the 1936 event, by Hans Vitus Vierthaler, shows every sign of being a caricature of a poster by El Lissitzky (*Beat the Whites with the Red Wedge*, 1919–20).[15] The overall visual layout is comparable, notably the point of a triangle invading the center of a circle, plus angled lines of text accompanying the dynamics of the thrusting point. Such mimicry might stem, directly or indirectly, from the use of a figure of modernism, from a hatred of Bolshevism, or even from Nazism's exploitation of avant-gardist forms (prior to returning to Moscow in 1925, El Lissitzky had spent several years in Germany, where he largely contributed to the dissemination of Constructivism). Vierthaler's visuals assume a special and highly specific role, namely announcing a show of art intended for public condemnation. Munich's 1937 *Entartete Kunst* exhibition featured seven hundred and thirty works. Over one hundred artists associated with modernism (including many leading figures) were thus placed beyond the pale of society. In the realm of graphic design, they included Walter Dexel, El Lissitzky, Max Burchartz, and Johannes Molzahn, alongside the likes of Wassily Kandinsky, Johannes Itten, Oskar Schlemmer, Piet Mondrian, Otto Dix, Paul Klee, and others. Many recent artistic forms were thus officially outlawed, placed before a public invited to view them with contempt. By castigating modernist movements, no doubt starting with Impressionism, Expressionism, and Cubism, the Nazi leadership was rejecting the whole trend of artistic exploration (an exploration that paradoxically served as the basis of the graphic revival on which they themselves relied). In *Mein Kampf*, Hitler had already condemned uncontrollable pictorial modernism. "Anyone to whom this seems strange need only subject the art of the happily Bolshevized states to an examination, and, to his horror, he will be confronted by the morbid excrescences of insane and

459
Hans Vitus Vierthaler, poster for the 1936 *Entartete Kunst* show in Munich. Color lithograph, 3 ft. 11 in. × 2 ft. 11 in. (120 × 84 cm).

460
Poster for the 1937 exhibition of *Entartete Kunst* (Degenerate Art) in Munich. Text set in Wallau, a typeface designed by Rudolf Koch in the late 1920s.

461
View of one room of the 1937 *Entartete Kunst* show with works by Klee and Nolde.

degenerate men, with which, since the turn of the century, we have become familiar under the collective concepts of Cubism and Dadaism, as the official and recognized art of those states."[16] The official catalog of the 1937 *Entartete Kunst* show explained that "Degenerate Art often serves that aspect of Marxist, Bolshevist ideology whose goal is the systematic destruction of what remains of racial awareness."[17] That same year, Goebbels described the condition of artists and their relationship to the party: "German artists today feel freer and more emancipated than ever before.…. Artists of worth have been sincerely convinced by National-Socialism. They are with us, and we are with them."[18] Back in 1933 already, Goebbels had set up the Reich's chamber of culture, which came to control Germany's entire artistic output.

National-Socialist imagery and graphic design

Not all of Germany's leading graphic artists and typographers of the 1920s met with the same fate. Depending on opportunities, circumstances, personal convictions, and readiness to compromise, some of them agreed to work for the regime while others fled or offered visual resistance to the propaganda. Several of them worked for the government for just a brief period in the mid-1930s. One after another, many of them were stripped of their teaching posts: Jan Tschichold and Paul Renner in Munich, Max Burchartz in Essen, and Emil Rudolf Weiss in Berlin (Staatschulen für freie und angewandte Kunst) as early as 1933, Walter Dexel in Magdeburg in 1935, and somewhat later Joost Schmidt, after having cooperated with the regime. Although many leading figures from the Bauhaus emigrated (as did other artists such as Kurt Schwitters), some graphic designers remained in Germany after being dismissed from their teaching posts. Often they were only able to get back into business after 1945, thereby experiencing a long interruption in their still-early careers (some French poster artists experienced the same situation). Apart from several well-known cases, it would seem that relatively few famous graphic artists worked for the Nazi regime; if true, this fact would seem to suggest that most artists' convictions, quest for autonomy, and discovery of new typography and graphic style were ultimately incompatible with the Reich's policies. Herbert Bayer—who had previously been a student and then a teacher at the Bauhaus, and later headed an advertising agency in Berlin—initially worked for several Nazi exhibitions, as did some of his colleagues. He designed, for instance, the catalog for a 1935 show called *Das Wunder des Lebens* (The Miracle of Life), which included a portrait of Hitler, and he also worked on a publication for the *Deutschland* exhibition of 1936, which featured several swastikas. Bayer's work with the new regime did not last, however, and one of his paintings was even included in the Degenerate Art show of 1937—he left for the United States in 1938. According to Paul Renner's biographer, "Bayer later painted out all those elements that made explicit Nazi references" on copies of items relating to the *Deutschland* exhibition in his private collection.[19] Perhaps that is one of the reasons, within a broader phenomenon of willful, collective oversight, for our lack of knowledge about the activities of typographers and graphic designers on behalf of dictatorships and/or war propaganda (probably closely related to their economic need for commissioned work). It is moreover likely that a significant number of Bauhaus alumni worked for the National-Socialist government in the mid-1930s,

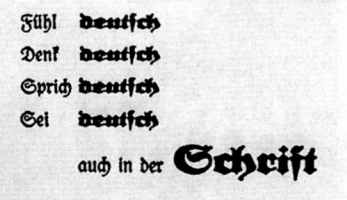

462
Ludwig Hohlwein, poster, *L'Allemagne* (Germany), Munich, 1935.

463
M. Ludwig, *Deutscher, für Dich!*, 1932–33.

464
National-Socialist poster, *Deutsche! gebt dem System die Antwort! wählt Hitler!*, 1932 (?).

465
National-Socialist poster, *Arbeit und Brot durch den Nationalsozialismus*, 1932.

466
Election campaign poster, *Das Volk wählt Liste 1, Nationalsozialisten*, 1932.

467
Slogans on early Third-Reich stickers ("Feel German, Think German, Speak German, Be German even in your choice of script").

468
Anonymous, election poster, portrait of Hitler against black background, 1932–33.

469
Anonymous, *Ja! Führer wir Folgen dir!* (Yes, Führer, we'll follow you!), NSDAP, 1933.

470
Mjölnir (Hans Schweitzer), *Unsere letzte Hoffnung: Hitler* (Hitler, Our Ultimate Hope), 1932.

even though an artist like Heartfield had already produced some of his anti-Nazi collages and photomontages.

Those graphic artists who openly deployed their skills on behalf of the National-Socialist Party worked notably in the realm of posters, a key medium given its powers of persuasion, dissemination, visibility, and propaganda (the very reasons posters had already been used during World War I). Ludwig Hohlwein, Theo Matejko, Mjölnir (the nom-de-plume of Hans Schweitzer),[20] and Wiertz were among the regime's better-known poster artists. Hohlwein, a key figure in the new poster movement prior to World War I, worked steadily for the Third Reich, designing a certain number of posters in this capacity. Mjölnir and Matejko were also among National-Socialism's official designers. Although party posters echoed the values and themes also found in painterly output, they placed special stress on the figure of the Führer and on depictions of the masses. Emanating from the highest spheres of government, posters became a favored method of communication, putting Hitler in direct touch—through his image—with the loyal masses, as well as with casual crowds and passersby. Plastered on walls, these pictures provided visual resonance to what public speeches and orations were offering the ear, and vice versa (Hitler and Goebbels were famously eloquent, for that matter).

As far as Nazi leaders were concerned, art was a tool of propaganda, an instrument of political ideology. Banishing the untamable dimension of modern painting, they looked back to styles associated with Neo-realism, Neo-romanticism, and Classicism (or just plain bombast) to forge a dominant national style. Yet in the realm of the graphic arts, these registers did not encompass all output—far from it. Hohlwein's posters, for instance, blithely featured heroes, mythical figures, athletic bodies, and classical busts even as they retained a visual dynamism and a globalizing graphic composition designed to enhance impact and efficiency, which Hohlwein had acquired from previous experience. As also occurred in Fascist Italy, some designers working for the regime employed techniques of (photo)montage in posters and other media. The Third Reich's exploitation of posters, emblems, and other devices of visual communication contributed vastly to Goebbel's propaganda campaign, designed to have a massive impact on people. "Official propaganda envisaged using 'media' that were new at the time. Thus as early as 1933 Nazi leaders came up with the idea of replacing the photos of athletes and movie stars found in packs of cigarettes by pictures of the armed forces of neighboring countries bristling with weaponry, or by pictures of soldiers of the new German army in the form of young, smiling men with attractive features."[21] All kinds of common, everyday objects were emblazoned with the party emblem, as witnessed, for example, by a cylindrical piggy-bank with a full-length swastika in its Nazi version (a black, clockwise-pointing cross in the middle of a white circle, set against a red ground). Although difficult to assess, the importance of this imagery and its exploitation played a fundamental role in the process of spreading Nazism, simultaneously glorifying, unifying, valorizing, and neutralizing. The idea of strength, power, and mastery suggested by this symbol was aimed at a people sorely tried by economic depression, hence receptive to such symbolism during a particularly difficult period.

The role of typography: Gothic lettering

In the framework of government publications, typography was an issue of special concern and decisions were based on awareness of the impact the form of a text might have on the message. Initially, and up to 1941, Gothic lettering—also known as blackletter typeface—was a primary feature of the regime's graphic style. Gothic lettering had been favored for its specifically German nature at several points in the past, at least since the early nineteenth century and in particular following the Napoleonic wars. Commonly used by German printers ever since it was devised in the Middle Ages, blackletter typeface was also used by certain avant-gardists and opponents of the Nazi regime, both before and after 1933. When looking back at the Weimer Republic today, while it might be tempting to automatically associate sans serif letterforms with progressive or revolutionary trends on the one hand, and Gothic

471
NSDAP poster announcing a Nazi rally in Munich in May 1920.

472
National-Socialist leaflet for local elections in Dessau, October 25, 1931, calling for a halt to expenditure on the Bauhaus and the demolition of the school building.

473
Article on the search (and closure) of the Berlin Bauhaus on April 11, 1933. The title reads "Search of the Steglitz Bauhaus turns up Communist documents" (*Lokal-Anzeiger*, Berlin, April 12, 1933).

lettering with traditional or conservative tendencies on the other, the actual practices of the 1920s and 1930s invalidate this assumption. Many texts and publications employed blackletter typefaces, as witnessed in the late 1920s by newspapers such as *Vorwörts*, *Die rote Fahne*, and *Frankfurter Zeitung* (which printed Walter Dexel's 1927 article "What Is New Typography?" in Gothic letters), not to mention the text of the Communist Party's election poster in 1928, designed by Heartfield, or the lettering on the covers of Kurt Tucholsky's *Deutschland, Deutschland über alles* in 1929. At the same time, certain conservative publications were using openly avant-garde typefaces such as the recent Futura. The graphic style of Hitler's movement incorporated Roman and sans serif letterforms as well as Gothic, sometimes employed side by side. What is more, some of Hohlwein's posters for the 1930s used sans serif lettering exclusively, adopting an avant-garde credo trumpeted by the New Typography, which held that these lineal letterforms embodied the proper expression of modernity. Third Reich typography incorporated a certain number of features likely to draw the eye (as previously exploited by the avant-gardes): de-centering of text, contrasts, various paths for the eye, and multiple levels of reading. Bold marks abounded—thick rules, punctuation marks, titling, and so on. However, the surface was often saturated with text and image, as distinct from the spatial dynamics sought by avant-garde artists.

Although maintaining a certain stylistic heterogeneity, the party's graphic texts (posters, newspapers, flyers, etc.) did indeed often employ Gothic lettering. As soon as they came to power, the Nazis identified Gothic lettering as the "German typeface." Gothic letterforms thus ran throughout a vast range of National-Socialist publications right from the founding of the NSDAP. Newspapers, textbooks, books, official pronouncements, propaganda messages, and so on, were often printed in blackletter typeface (several editions of *Mein Kampf* were set in Gothic). The authorities went so far as to consider replacing typewriters that didn't have Gothic letters.[22] Once Hitler came to power in January 1933, decrees mandated the use of Gothic lettering in the production and printing of all official and administrative documents. The early 1930s (and sometimes earlier) saw the development of new Gothic letterforms, in which some professional typographers were involved. Their typefaces were named, for instance, Deutschland (1933), Element (1933), National (1933), Deutsch (1936–37, Georg Trump), Grossdeutsch (literally, "Greater German," 1935, Herbert Thannhaeuser), and so on. It is worth noting that this kind of name was common for typefaces designed in Germany, as witnessed by Rudolf Koch's Deutsche Schrift, or "German Script," dating from 1910. Typefaces were also frequently named after their inventor, such as Herbert Post's Post Fraktur (1937) and Johannes Schulz's Johannes Type (1933).

The German government was not content with simply using blackletter typeface and its variants. By the mid-1930s, the Nazis had established a department of National Writing

474 Fehlet die Einsicht oben,/der gute Wille von unten,/führt sogleich die Gewalt,/oder sie endet den Streit.

476 Das deutsche Reich

475 ABCDEFGHIJK LMNOPQ RSTUVWXYZÄÖ abcdefghi jklmnopqrstuvwxyz äöüßtzch ck fffiftflssfist=(&)!?!.:,;sch 1234567890

Education (Reischslehrgänge füre Schriftschreiben) at the Jugendwaltung des Fachamtes Druck und Papier in Offenbach-am-Main. Elsewhere, various exhibitions were organized on the theme of Gothic script. In 1933, for example, the national museum of Bavaria hosted a show titled *Deutsche Schrift* (German Writing). The exhibition presented Gothic script as being the expression of a specifically German nationalism. "It is not without good reason that we sense in Gothic script the Germanic will for form to be more clearly demonstrated. Just like Gothic design in other arts, Gothic lettering appears primarily wherever virile German manhood is symbolized by fighting, creating nations, and building."[23] The man who made that comment was Fritz Helmut Ehmcke, a graphic artist, typographer, and designer of German letterforms (the object of a survey carried out by the Nazis in 1933). Another strong expression of nationalism as it related to writing came from Rudolf Koch, also a typographer, calligrapher, and typeface designer associated with 1920s modernism (he designed Kabel and Zeppelin, two sans serif faces with a geometric feel, dating from 1927 and 1929, respectively): "German script is like a symbol of the inherent mission of the German people, who, among all civilized races, must not merely defend but also act as a living model and example of its unique, distinctive, and nationalistic character in all manifestations of life."[24] A certain number of new blackletter typefaces were developed simultaneously with the rise of Nazism. Several of them—Wallau (1925–34) and Peter-Jessen-Schrift (1931), designed by Rudolf Koch—were used to typeset printed documents that conformed to Nazi directives. However, neither Ehmcke nor Koch were party members. It is nevertheless true that certain master typographers in German in the 1920s and 1930s designed letterforms used by those in power, belonging to a category of typefaces that the Third Reich first vaunted then rejected. Indeed, as it turned out, the generalized adoption of Gothic letterforms would lead to a sudden change of direction at the start of the next decade: in 1941, after having extensively used such typefaces, the Nazis suddenly outlawed them. For reasons that remain unclear, and against all historical likelihood, they henceforth claimed that Gothic script was Jewish in origin. And thus they forbad its administrative use.

Helmut Herzfeld, a.k.a. John Heartfield

In Germany, all creative graphic design dried up, apart from Nazi output in the early 1930s. Faced with the loss of their jobs, some avant-garde graphic designers turned their art into a form of resistance. John Heartfield, who had actively opposed Nazism since the start of the decade through his photomontages, was an exceptional figure. He left Berlin for Prague in 1933, emigrating once again in the late 1930s (to England), then returning to East Germany in 1950.

Born Helmut Herzfeld in Berlin in 1891, he became a hard-to-categorize artist, notably winning attention for hard-hitting photomontages that reflected his political commitment. During World War I he anglicized his name to John Heartfield as a sign of sympathy for Great Britain. Before the war, he had attended several art schools and worked as an advertising artist. He also founded the Malik publishing house in conjunction with his brother, Wieland. Heartfield joined the German Communist Party (KPD) in 1918, and initially directed his incisive imagery against the German Social Democratic Party (SPD). But with the rise of Nazism, Heartfield made National-Socialism his main target from 1930 onward. In his photomontages he frequently employed the extensive visual repertoire then current in Germany and the Soviet Union. He pilloried the Third Reich's leading figures, symbols, and

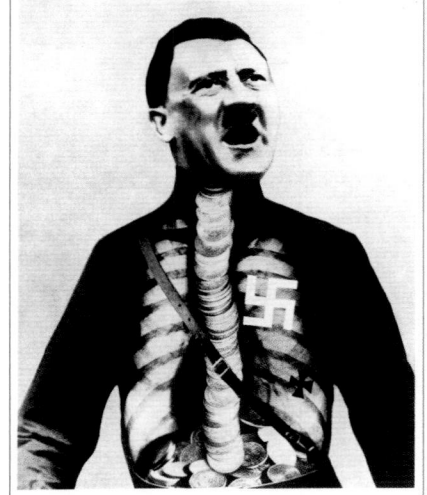

ADOLF - DER ÜBERMENSCH

SCHLUCKT GOLD UND REDET BLECH

477
John Heartfield, original photomontage of *Adolf the Superman: He swallows gold and spits tin*, published in *Arbeiter Illustrierte Zeitung* (*AIZ*) in July 1932.

478
John Heartfield, original photomontage published in *Der Knüppel* in February 1927 (entitled "*The Progress of rationalization*" in the printed version).

emblems, attacked its troubling power and ideology, and exposed the mortal threats of weapons and militarism. Heartfield's graphic output—photographs, photomontages and typography—all assailed totalitarianism in varying degrees of sarcasm, irony, dramatization, and alarm. Seeking to counter Nazi propaganda, he denounced the movement's motives and demystified its official imagery. He continued to design anti-Nazi photomontages right up to the outbreak of World War II, even after he had been exiled from Germany. Meanwhile, he founded the Malik publishing house in Czechoslovakia where he continued to publish magazines, books, and newspapers (always participating in the graphic design). Heartfield's oeuvre remains emblematic of the potential for protest through imagery—notably through the power of photomontage—and of an approach that forged a new channel of visual communication to the masses in an effort to mobilize a resistance movement.

Italy: Fascism versus avant-garde pursuits

Whereas artistic practice was brought to heel by the National-Socialists in Germany from 1933 onward, it would seem that Fascist Italy did not require the same subjection to the regime's authority. Italian leaders appeared to be less prescriptive than their Nazi counterparts when it came to graphic design, and they placed fewer restrictions on avant-garde activities. Professional graphic design was even able to expand in the Italy of the 1930s. Paradoxically, the year 1933—so critical in Germany—represented the start of new experiments and initiatives in Italy. Two major events in the realm of graphic design in fact occurred that year: the founding of Studio Boggeri and the launching of the magazine *Campo grafico*. Interest in visual communication grew, shared by industrialists and entrepreneurs as well as designers. Pre-war Italy had already played a key role in the emergence of avant-garde typography, having been the birthplace of Futurism (which then spread to Russia, Great Britain, and Mexico). Futurism was not only a movement often associated with the start of the (typo)graphic revolution, but it thrived into the 1920s and 1930s through a number of activities and publications—manifestos, reviews, artworks, exhibitions, and so on—not wholly unrelated to fascism. At the same time, in Italy as elsewhere, poster artists who remained close to a painterly register explored modernism in their own way. So once the Fascist Party came to power in 1922, graphic design took several paths. Avant-garde practitioners continued on their way, while the dictatorship adopted, in part, monumental and patriotic imagery that was partly inspired by "Roman grandeur."[25] These various paths intersected, notably because some Futurists rallied to the Fascist cause. Although the Fascists unsurprisingly exploited propaganda imagery, they sometimes also employed modernism's formal repertoire. Highly varied types of graphic design thus coexisted in Italy in the 1920s and 1930s.

Fascist imagery

After Mussolini's march on Rome in October 1922, the Fascist Party slowly developed a heterogeneous graphic output, far from Nazi-style directives designed to restrict graphic design (for example, by insisting on Gothic letterforms in the 1930s). Italian Fascists came to power a full decade before the Nazis; their movement, launched by Mussolini in 1919, was transformed into an official party during its convention in Rome in 1921. In a matter of months, between 1921 and 1922, the number of party members rose from thirty-one thousand to seven hundred and twenty thousand. In 1922, the Fascist Party entered the government and Mussolini was granted full powers by parliament. Authoritarianism steadily grew with the founding of a militia in 1923, the drawing up of a constitution that legitimized dictatorship in 1925 and 1926, and the decreeing of a single-party state in 1928. With Il Duce having grasped all the levers of power, the party was in a position to control all the major instruments of mass communication. State propaganda was henceforth channeled through all kinds of paths and media—posters, printed material (textbooks, newspapers), radio, public

479
Commemorative postcard of 1922 showing
Mussolini in his new role as head of government.

480
Palatial façade transformed into a giant
campaign poster calling for a "yes" to Mussolini,
Rome, 1934.

481
Xanti Schawinsky, *Si* (Year XII of the Fascist Era),
poster, 1934. Photomontage.

482
Xanti Schawinsky, *1934-XII*, portrait
of Mussolini, 1934. Photomontage.

parades, emblems, and other symbols (the fasces, black shirts, etc.). The lictor's fasces became the emblem of the Fascist state by the end of the 1920s, and was printed on all kinds of supports, including postage stamps. Like Hitler, Mussolini took an interest in the graphic message generated by his government, and he sometimes became actively involved. The Fascist Party stressed the need to reach the masses, adopting a policy of "going to the people" in 1932.[26] For totalitarian governments, keeping a grip over all citizens (including youth) and ideologically shaping their collective consciousness represented key goals, for which countless tools of propaganda were requisitioned, including—first and foremost—posters.

From the early 1920s until the outbreak of World War II, Fascist imagery exploited two main trends (both of which were also present in architecture): the modern path (occasionally in an openly avant-garde vein) and a return to classicism (a cross between tradition and monumentality). This stylistic eclecticism incorporated several Italian trends such as the Fascist versions of Futurism and Arte Moderne (similar to Art Deco) and even Novecento (an anti-Futurist movement that looked to the past, relying on realism to fulfill Mussolini's call for

an official state art). At first many posters drew their impact from concise styles spawned by recent (typo)graphic experiments alien to all realism (Futurism, abstraction, Art Deco, photomontage). As occurred elsewhere, official imagery was obliged to employ recurring themes and subjects: Il Duce, the military, power, grandeur, patriotic devotion, virility, commitment to the cause, and model youths (all vigorous and willing). For some fifteen years, the production of Fascist images thus exploited various formal registers, drawing its unity from a shared ideology and a shared stable of figures to be depicted. When producing posters, the regime could call upon famous designers such as Marcello Dudovich. But posters were not the only way the Fascists introduced propaganda into the street and public places. For example, vast surfaces of wall could be mobilized for Fascist imagery, such as the three-storey façade of a Roman palace, as wide as it was high, covered with the word *Si* (Yes) repeated over a hundred times, flanking a monumental picture of Mussolini's face (several yards high). Apart from Il Duce's image, other figures were sometimes represented in an idealized anonymity that allowed the figure to be repeated multiple times within the same composition.

Although images tended to dominate the text in such posters, typography nevertheless played a significant role at times, reinforcing and anchoring the message. Capital lettering seems to have been the favorite type of letterform, probably because of its monumental feel, natural rigor, and imposing, almost uniform regularity. Posters often hosted modern, sans serif typefaces, sometimes highly geometric—there are instances when the letter O is a circle, the letters A and V are triangles, C is a semi-circle, and other letters might be conveyed by original shapes: a blend of Secessionist, Futurist, Constructivist, and Bauhaus typographies. Over time, Italy's Fascist imagery lost its specificity, becoming tamer; as World War II approached, it increasingly resembled Nazi design. Yet, just like certain aspects of German visual

483
L'Italia fascista, a gathering of Italian fascist
youth in Verona, 1937.

484

484
Poster for a national convention of Fascist students, Rome, May 1929.

propaganda, Soviet design, and imagery relating to the two world wars, the Fascist visual idiom demonstrated the efficiency of employing a certain modernity of expression.

The position adopted by the Futurists

During the interwar period, the Italian graphic design scene seems to have constituted a special case. Whereas the careers of artists and designers in other countries were disrupted by the new, ruling regimes, which meant that avant-garde practices became less visible than before, Italian graphic art held its course by embracing a certain schizophrenia. On one hand it adopted the imperatives and rhetoric of Fascism, while on the other it pursued a modernist path in the early 1930s. Futurism, the path-breaking Italian avant-garde movement, had already been growing for two decades. Pursuing their intense graphic and advertising work of the 1920s, the Futurists continued to play an important role. Their attitude embodied an unambiguous avant-gardism in artistic matters, even as they adopted extremist positions in terms of political and social behavior, sometimes via extreme statements. The Futurists had become highly politicized in the late 1910s, founding their own party in 1918. The following year they were one of the groups that formed the *Fasci Italiani Di Combattimento* (which they quit in 1920).[27] Many Futurists moved closer to Fascism and joined the party when it came to power in 1922. These sympathizers included, among others, Fortunato Depero, a Futurist active in typography as well as graphic design and advertising. "Among the Futurist publications that have kept the tradition of avant-garde art alive in Italy during the Fascist years, Depero's magazines occupied a position directly linked to the historical experiment of establishing a symbiosis between Futurism and Fascism.... More specifically, a 'futuro-fascist' content, reflecting the basic axiom of the movement at that time, was expressed by Depero in his review *Futurismo 1932* .... 'Futuro-fascism' involved... the relentless assertion of an absolute complementarity between Mussolini's 'political dynamism' and Marinetti's artistic avant-garde."[28] The Futurists employed various expressive styles and media to convey their ideological and political bent, as clearly announced as early as 1909 with the publication of Marinetti's first manifesto. In 1934, Marinetti helped to inaugurate an exhibition in Berlin on "Futurist aeropainting" (sponsored, among others, by Goebbels and Göring).[29] At the same time, he published articles critical of politics in general and Mussolini in particular. Although stormy and complex, the relationship between Futurism and Fascism remained very real.

Studio Boggeri, Campo grafico, Italian industry, and graphic dynamism

Even as the relationship between Futurism and Fascism was developing, and as state propaganda was steadily expanding, modern Italian graphic design teamed up with industry, private businesses, and cultural institutions to create a particularly productive period in the early 1930s. In addition to general economic conditions, this phenomenon resulted from the convergence of various factors: the proximity of artists exiled to regions just beyond Nazi Germany, the founding of Studio Boggeri, the growing awareness of design on the part of business executives, the role of triennial exhibitions (starting in Milan in 1933), the launch of professional publications by several groups of graphic designers and printers, and the emergence of an active generation of graphic artists particularly interested in photography, typography, experimentation, and so on. Among the visible signs of this effervescence of Italian graphic awareness was the Olivetti company's decision to endow itself with a modern image. Founded in 1908, the firm created an advertising and development department in 1931 at the initiative of Adriano Olivetti (the founder's son), who was concerned with visual image as well as with product design and spatial organization. A lasting, high-profile collaboration with major designers was thus launched. Through an explicit quest for coherence and quality,

485
Deberny & Peignot, logotype for Studio Boggeri,
1933.

486
Xanti Schawinsky, cover for Olivetti,
1934.

Olivetti sought to favor "a method rather than a system, coordination rather than a plan of action."[30] Throughout the 1930s, Olivetti placed commissions with a certain number of leading figures within Italian graphic design, starting with Giovanni Pintori (hired by Adriano Olivetti himself) who would still be working for the company thirty years later. Pintori fashioned a range of fanciful and experimental visuals for Olivetti, thereby producing a number of unique posters (Pintori would also become involved in exhibition design, and in 1947 he devised a new visual image for the firm, whose advertising department he would head from 1950 to 1967). Among the other designers and graphic artists associated with Olivetti were Marcello Nizzoli (who became artistic director in 1938), Costantino Nivola, Max Huber, Xanti Schawinsky, and the Studio Boggeri team. (As was the case with Pintori, some of these collaborations would survive World War II, until the arrival of a new generation of graphic designers such as Walter Ballmer.) Olivetti was thus one of those companies—like AEG in Germany—concerned with its visual image and determined to keep in step with the graphic innovations of the day.

This example illustrates one distinctive aspect of Italian graphic design in the twentieth century—it combined high standards with a boldness and flexibility that eschewed restrictive formal constraints. Like Olivetti, other Italian firms displayed a desire to exploit the skill of graphic artists, starting in the 1930s. Campari, for instance, turned to Leonetto Cappiello, Marcello Dudovich, Fortunato Depero, and Bruno Munari. Motta sought out Cassandre and Leo Lionni. Also worth mentioning are the Einaudi publishing house, La Rinascente department stores (Albe Steiner, Max Huber), Agfa, Fiat, Pirelli (Erberto Carboni, Ezio Bonini, Pino Tovaglia, Bob Noorda), plus several pharmaceutical companies. These industrial commissions for graphic art were boosted by Italy's economic recovery of the early 1930s, which relaunched industrial mass production. Corporate bosses and decision-makers showed interest in all issues of form and presentation (of which visual advertising was just one aspect): not only the design of objects, stands, and exhibitions, but also storefronts and architecture. From this standpoint, the interaction between typography/graphic design and architecture, already apparent in the work of Depero in the 1920s, was a marked Italian trait.

Studio Boggeri represents another landmark in the history of graphic design in Italy. Founded in Milan in 1933 by Antonio Boggeri, it brought together a certain number of graphic designers, typographers, and photographers keen on modernism and the latest artistic experiments. Boggeri, himself an experimental photographer, encountered several avant-garde figures (including El Lissitzky, Piet Zwart, and Jan Tschichold) when he was working in the publishing field. He also met leading lights of the Bauhaus—Gropius, Moholy-Nagy, Bayer, and Breuer—before they went into exile. Boggeri contributed to the budding development of the role of art director by founding his own outfit, organizing and supervising his agency's work, and entering into exchanges with the numerous designers whom he brought together in original ways. Boggeri surrounded himself with many leading Italian graphic artists, including Remo Muratore, Aldo Calabresi, Ezio Nonini, Fortunato Depero, Franco Grignani, and Erberto Carboni. The people who worked with Studio Boggeri were spurred to work on all kinds of graphic forms and supports: logos, stationery, posters, press advertisements, sundry publications, window displays, etc. Design of the agency's own visual logo was awarded in 1933 to the French type-foundry Deberny & Peignot—representing an example of a commission from avant-gardist central Europe that went to French professionals—who proposed a red letter B in Didot typeface flanked by two black dots. Antonio Boggeri promoted innovative relationships not only within his own agency but also with outside businesspeople and industrialists. As with Olivetti's strategy of visual communication, it was not a question of adopting a strict line or a one-directional logic, but rather of coming up with new answers to growing corporate demands, by bringing together a collective group of designers. Here, as elsewhere, the role of both parties was crucial, beginning with the client (notably the client's awareness and use of visual communication).

257

Antonio Boggeri, familiar with avant-garde work through the publisher Alfieri & Lacroix, established professional contacts beyond the borders of Italy. Several graphic artists from Switzerland and Germany worked for his agency, beginning with Xanti Schawinsky right from 1933. A versatile artist (painter, graphic designer, photographer), Schawinsky was born in Basel, Switzerland, in 1904. He studied painting and architecture in Switzerland and Germany, and then spent a number of years at the Bauhaus, from 1924 to 1929. He then worked as a graphic artist for a few years in Germany, and also traveled to France and Spain. Schawinsky ultimately left for Italy in 1933, fleeing the Nazis and the attacks leveled at him in the press. At Studio Boggeri, he worked on projects for clients such as Olivetti, Motta, Illy Caffé, and Cinzano. An entirely different aspect of Schawinsky's oeuvre can be seen in his conception of visuals depicting Mussolini, including the propaganda poster *Si* (1934), which featured powerful typo-photomontage. Other graphic artists from outside Italy brought their experience of modernism into the country; Swiss and German designers who collaborated, from near or afar, with the famous Milan agency included Paul Renner (the creator of Futura), Imre Reiner, Herbert Bayer, Walter Ballmer, Max Huber, and Carlo Vivarelli. As a site of collective, cosmopolitan creativity, Studio Boggeri was open to experience gleaned from Futurism, the Bauhaus, photomontage, Constructivism, and New Typography, not to mention the emerging Swiss typography movement.

Studio Boggeri forged a rare synergy among the graphic traditions and experiments of Europe's avant-gardes, and has been called the first great modern graphic design agency. Although its birth coincided with an economic boom in Italy and a historic dispersal in Germany, the agency managed to remain highly active for forty years (1933–73), attesting to Antonio Boggeri's far-sightedness.

The magazine *Campo grafico* was founded in the same year—and in the same city—as Studio Boggeri. In total, sixty-six issues of this innovative, independent review were published between January 1933 and May 1939. Behind the project was a group of some twenty printers, graphic artists, technicians, and typographers—dubbed *campisti*—including Attilio Rossi and Carlo Dradi. The periodical first took its lead from the French magazine *Arts et métiers graphiques*.[31] Its very appearance displayed an attitude halfway between Futurist exuberance and a certain (typo)graphic rigor. Close in spirit to Studio Boggeri, the *Campo grafico* team wanted to promote modern and abstract art, to bring a new gaze to bear on typography, and to incorporate photomontage into the graphic arts—all on a shoestring budget greatly relying on volunteer labor, on determination, and on a spirit of experimentation. Stress was placed on recent forms of modernism and on finding an aesthetic approach that ran counter to the ambient authoritarianism; the review favored "the ideals of a European culture—as already expressed in successive avant-garde movements—over a nationalistic, authoritarian 'Kultur.'"[32] The cover of the first issue set the tone: it featured a montage of photographs in red and black. Overall, the layout of the magazine imitated certain approaches pioneered by the (typo)graphic arts of the 1920s—dynamism, systematic asymmetry, use of the four main families of letterforms, mobilization of unprinted spaces, photographic experimentation, visualization of the structure of page layout, inventive spirit, and so on. The graphic image changed from one issue to another, reflecting a wide range of visual possibilities. Many graphic artists, designers, fine artists, and photographers contributed to the magazine,

487
Luigi Oriani, cover of *Campo grafico* magazine, September 1935.

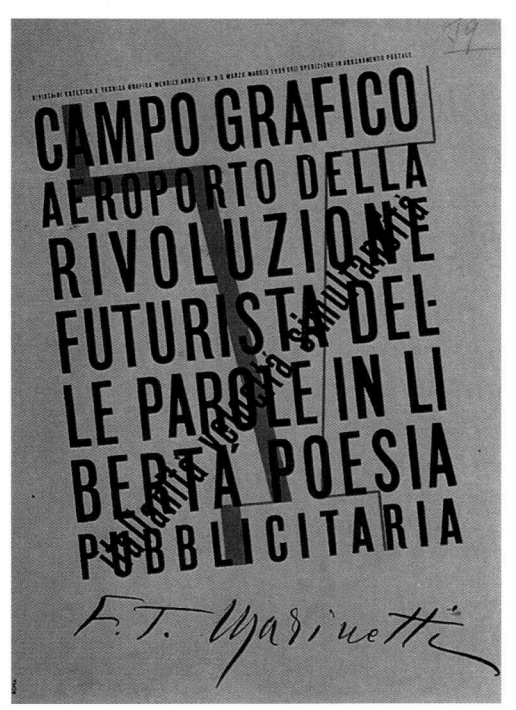

488

including Bauhaus alumni and foreigners, such as Edoardo Persico, Willi Baumeister, Friedrich Vordemberge-Gildewart, Luigi Veronesi, Enrico Bona, and Luigi Minardi. Various avant-garde idioms were featured there, in turn: the New Typography (Tschichold's *Typographisches Gestaltung* was reviewed in 1936), abstract painting, photography (Antonio Boggeri's photos were published there), photomontages, graphic productions from nearby countries, articles on typography, texts by Marinetti and Boggeri, and so on. As far as advertising pages went, the *Campo grafico* team convinced ink manufacturers to reproduce paintings by artists such as Picasso. Photography, typography, and abstract art therefore figured prominently in the magazine, alongside an innovative graphic approach. "*Campo grafico* claimed that a real renaissance could occur only if the invigorating influence of modern art and avant-garde issues were projected into the world of print."[33]

Campo grafico was one of a number of specialized periodicals that made various contributions to the applied arts in Italy (graphic arts, photography, design, interior decoration, town planning, and architecture). The team of printers behind *Graphicus,* which dated back to 1911, explored centers of interest similar to those of *Campo grafico.* Another high-profile periodical in the realm of visual communication was *Linea grafica.* Other publications, such as *Casabella* (1931), *Quadrante,* and *Domus,* helped to promote contemporary graphic design through their layouts, their subject matter, and their presentation of other fields of art. This publishing trend in favor of modern graphic style even had an impact on *Il Risorgimento grafico,* a rather conservative magazine. The dynamic thrust evident in Italy in the 1930s seems to have been the combined work of designers and printers, notably when it came to the role played by publications. As in other highpoints in the history of graphic design, the contribution of technical skills and knowledge proved crucial (as did, for example the role of lithographers in the birth of modern posters, or the collaboration of typographers and printers on the Swiss magazine *Typografische Monatsblätter*). The experiments carried out by the *Campo grafico* team remain too little known, perhaps because part of their archives were destroyed in World War II (during the bombing of the Scuola del Libro della Società Umanitaria).

Other activities and events, in addition to periodicals and graphic output, contributed to the dynamic development of visual communication in Italy. Exhibitions of decorative and industrial arts, founded at Monza in 1924, were at first biennial and later triennial. In 1933, the fifth triennial (henceforth held in Milan) was probably the first to address the issue of modern graphic design, with a special display ("Mostra dell'arte grafica") and a special German section ("Sezione grafica") devised by Paul Renner and entirely devoted to graphics. The 1936 triennial played an equally important role in the dissemination of cutting-edge foreign graphic design. The Swiss section, organized by Max Bill, shed new light on photography, graphic design, typography, letterforms, color, and so on, at a time when Switzerland, like Italy, was experiencing a boom in these fields. These two countries, for that matter, were both precocious in making the general public aware of (typo)graphic creativity, and in encouraging cooperation between businesspeople and graphic artists, thus helping to forge our modern conception of graphic design.

Taking part in the ambient dynamism, many young graphic artists, photographers, and designers emerged in the Italy of the 1930s (a similar phenomenon having occurred in Germany in

489

259

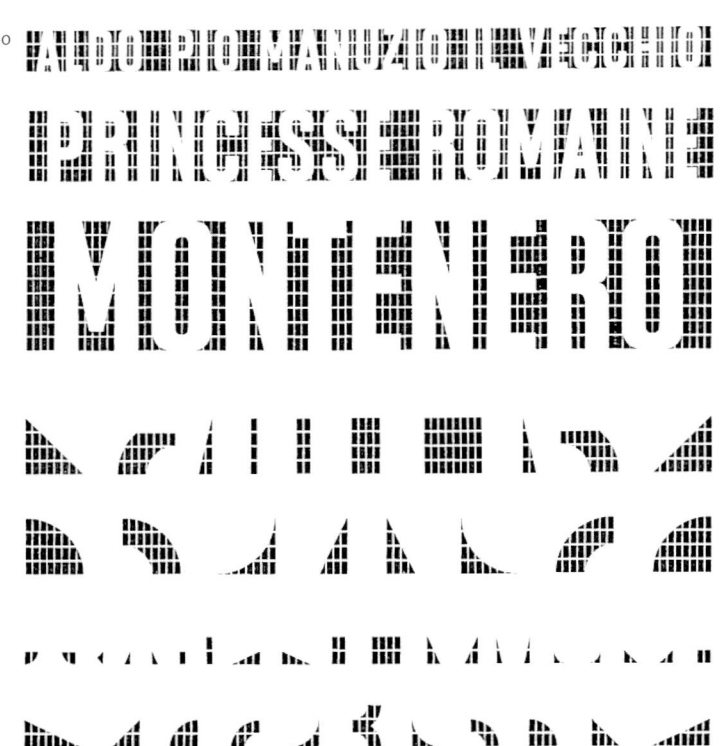

490
Guido da Milano, *Razionale* typeface,
Nebiolo foundry, 1935.

the 1920s). Many factors—publications, exhibitions, commissions, the presence of foreigners, and so on—helped to make Italy an active relay station for neighboring avant-garde movements. Milan in the north, not far from the Swiss border, became a strategic site of passage and encounters. Among the dozens of graphic artists active in Italy in the 1930s and the following decade, some of whom came from abroad, it is worth mentioning Marcello Nizzoli (born in 1887), Erberto Carboni (1889), Fortunato Depero (1892), Edoardo Persico (1900), Xanti Schawinsky (1904), Bruno Munari (1907), Carlo Dradi (1908), Franco Grignani (1908), Attilio Rossi (1909), Giovanni Pintori (1912), Remo Muratore (1912), and Albe Steiner (1913). Later, in the latter half of the twentieth century, younger generations would sustain these activities. In various ways, all contributed to the new face of graphic design. Although posters became less important to their oeuvres, some poster artists simultaneously maintained the tradition closely associated with painting and drawing, such as Leopoldo Metlicovitz (born in 1868), Marcello Dudovich (1878), and Sepo (Severo Pozzati, 1895).

The flowering of Italian graphic art in the 1930s shows that Fascism did not put a halt to the professional and modern development of this sector, since the visual propaganda issued by Italy's dictatorship itself exploited certain avant-garde techniques. Alongside the ideological and political domain, the economic situation provided a context of commissions favorable to a new generation of graphic designers and to the expression of their art. Italy thereby perpetuated the avant-garde project pursued throughout Europe in the 1920s, sustaining cultural vitality and exchanges, and favoring significant interaction between graphic art and architecture, three-dimensional spaces, exhibition design, and so on. The experiments and experience of the 1930s would encourage subsequent decades to maintain the same standard of quality, openness to spontaneity, and freedom of tone.

The Soviet Union: art vs. propaganda

As occurred in Germany, the official regime in the Soviet Union was moving towards the suppression of modernist art in the early 1930s. That art would be replaced, in part, by an authoritarian aesthetic product. In the two preceding decades Russia had been a hotbed of avant-garde activity ranging from Cubo-Futurism to Constructivism via many other "-isms." Artists and designers were often sympathetic to the Bolshevist cause, and sought to bring about a similar revolution in the arts. In this context, many of graphic design's usual supports, such as posters, became the object of constant—and sometimes spectacular—experimentation that employed typography, photography, montage, and drawings, all geared towards utmost impact. Already, the graphic idiom was incorporating a set of signs and images closely associated with the government, from symbols and emblems (both the red star of the Soviet army and the hammer-and-sickle emblem dated back to 1918) to colors (red for Bolshevists, white for czarists) to pictures of Lenin, and so on. A certain number of artists worked directly for the government, whose political line and organization they supported. Thus right from the 1920s, poster artists actively helped to promote the powerful state publishing house, Gosizdat, supported the New Economic Policy (NEP, 1921), and backed the first two five-year economic plans in 1928 and 1933 (collectivizing agriculture, promoting industry, and so on). At first, during the early part of the 1920s, Russian avant-garde movements, notably Constructivism, were able to pursue their intense creativity—an accomplishment that would soon be disparaged as "formalist" by Soviet authorities.[34] Stalin, having been elected general secretary of the Communist Party in 1922, succeeded Lenin as head of the country on the latter's death in 1924. Stalinism brought increasing disapproval of artistic modernism, ultimately resulting in the imposition of an official, realist style. As Constructivism was first castigated, then banned, some of its main practitioners shifted from creative spheres such as poster art to less constrained fields such as publishing, book illustration, interior decoration, and theater design. The innovations of Constructivist architecture were labeled "decadent."[35] When it came to graphic design the critic Yakov Tugendkhold would soon publish unadulterated criticisms of avant-garde posters, declaring in 1926 that "the more abstract a poster is, the colder it is and the less public impact it makes. That is the case with posters by our left-wing 'productivists,' which are composed of purely typographic elements: arrows, lines, question marks, exclamation marks."[36] Despite increasing repression, a creative, Constructivist approach to posters and a certain modernist design were pursued into the late 1920s (via political and advertising posters, state propaganda, film posters, etc.), and survived into the following years. Some artists such as El Lissitzky, Vladimir Mayakovsky, Varvara Stepanova, Alexander Rodchenko, and notably Gustav Klutsis, responded to government commissions by using methods such as photomontage. However, avant-garde expressiveness was never the same after the early 1930s, as the state readied itself to reject such creativity and to impose an official, immediately comprehensible style.

Stalinist imagery and the restructuring of the arts

Following Lenin's death in 1924, avant-garde artists were in danger of being stripped of their creative power, which "socialist realism" was designed to replace. Although socialist realism is normally associated with the Stalinist era, the aesthetic doctrine had already been present in the 1920s. In 1922 the Association of Artists of Revolutionary Russia (AKhRR) wholeheartedly embraced realism, proposing that a "heroic realism" replace certain avant-garde forms. In its manifesto, the group expressed its determination to depict the revolution realistically, a task in which they felt abstract art had failed. "We consider it our civic duty to reproduce, in an artistic and documentary fashion, the greatest moments of our history in their revolutionary dimension. We will depict the everyday life of the Red Army, of workers, peasants, heroes of the Revolution and of the workplace. We will show events as they truly looked, rather than through fanciful abstractions that discredit our Revolution in the eyes of the international proletariat."[37] In 1925, Stalin himself called for a "culture [that is] proletarian in content, national in form."[38] By the early 1930s, persecution of artists and writers became more marked. Official organizations controlled by the government swiftly replaced the surviving artists' groups, which were abolished by a Communist Party resolution, dated April 23, 1932, on "the restructuring of literary and artistic organizations." (An earlier resolution in 1930 had already condemned the avant-garde experiments of the 1920s.) The 1932 decree established the Union of Soviet Artists, one of several official organizations such as the Union of Architects of the USSR and—somewhat later—the Union of Painters, Sculptors, and Graphic Artists. Even prior to Germany's condemnation of modern culture, the Russian measures sought to stamp out the avant-garde, notably Constructivism and abstraction.

From 1932 onward, Stalinist imagery would conform to socialist realism, itself closely related to the government and the expression of state propaganda, in both pictorial and typographic spheres. Whereas visual communication in the Soviet Union, as elsewhere, employed its own specific images, figures, and symbols, it nevertheless displayed a number of themes and artistic approaches similar to the imagery exploited by the German and Italian regimes. Indeed, starting in the 1930s, Soviet posters presented an idealized vision of the state and leader (Lenin, then Stalin), as well as focusing

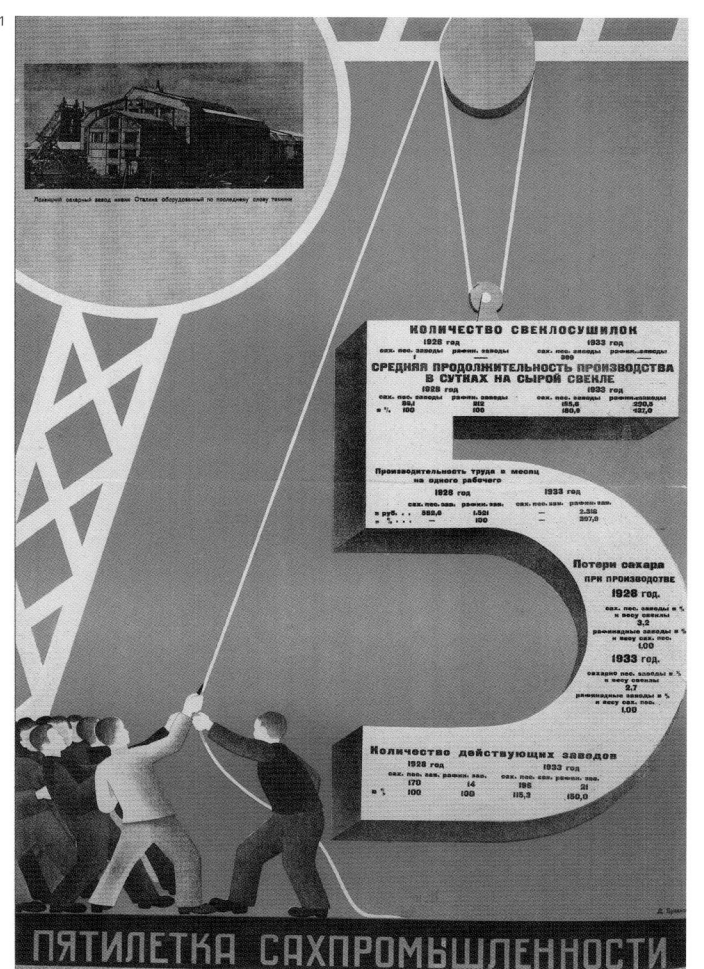

491
Dimitri Boulanov, political poster for the five-year plan for the sugar industry, 1933. Color lithograph.

491

Alexandre Samokhvalov, Soviet poster for
Komsomol (Union of Communist Youth), 1924.

493
Viktor Klimaschin, poster, USSR *Agricultural
Exhibition*, 1939.

494
Anonymous, poster supporting five-year
plans, 1930. Color lithograph.

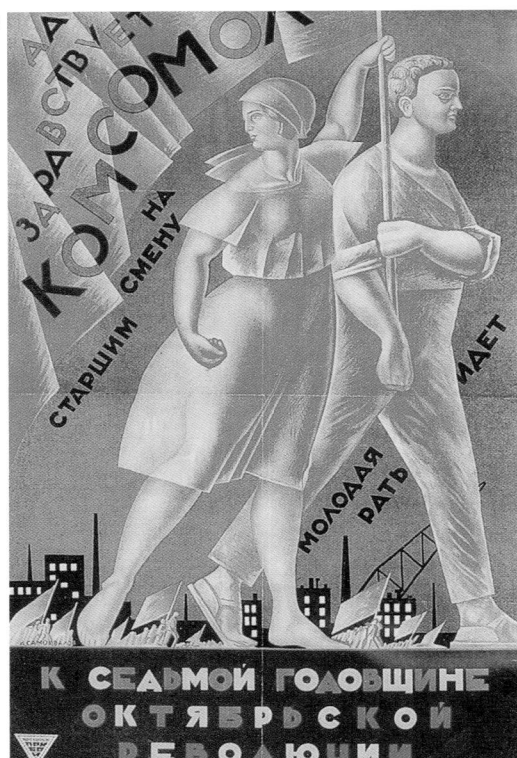

on athletes, on figures glowing with courage and commitment, on work, heroism, colossal construction projects, and so on. When it came to architecture, the outcome of the contest to design the Palace of Soviets reveals the rupture that occurred between avant-garde practices and Stalinist policies. Socialist realism marked things with its own aesthetic stamp, becoming the mandatory style in 1934. Andrei Zhdanov actively worked to make this style the sole artistic option in literature, painting, theater, cinema, music, and so on (although in fact the phenomenon did not have the same impact in every artistic sphere).

Although a new hierarchy of the arts established the preeminence of painting, graphic design—like other fields of art—continued to serve state propaganda. Posters were among the main supports targeted and monitored by the regime. At the very start of the 1930s, even before socialist realism managed to eliminate avant-garde experimentation completely, a polemic arose over a resolution on posters issued by the party's central committee. And despite the restrictions on artistic idioms resulting from the rise of socialist realism in the 1930s, photomontage and Constructivist-influenced graphic design continued to play a significant role in poster art. However, "the repeated use of photomontage, from works by Klutsis to the wall posters found in clubs and 'propaganda corners' of all kinds, ultimately turned the method into a cliché and led to a compositional simplification that went hand-in-hand with photographic naturalism."[39] An avant-garde approach to photomontage nevertheless survived into the early 1930s in opposition to socialist realism. All authoritarian regimes of the day were aware of the power of images. Everything that could be communicated or conveyed through posters (from consumer goods to industrial policy via cultural products) was henceforth associated with political, social, and economic imperatives. Eloquent slogans all converged on the same goal: "The Accomplishments of Building Socialism" (1930), "Cameras at the Service of Building Socialism" (1931), "Down with Enemies of Cultural Revolution!" (1930), "The Party's Mass Education Program in the Moscow Region for 1930–1931" (1930), "Russia's NEP will give birth to a Socialist Russia" (1930), "Let's Accomplish the Five-Year Plan in Four!" (1930), and so on.[40] Publications and exhibitions helped not only to disseminate posters but also to shape perception of them. In the mid-1920s, the Communist Academy and the Museum of the

495

495
Alexander Rodchenko, sketch, title sheet for a
History of the Communist Party in Posters, 1925.
Gouache on paper, 12 ¹/₂ × 9 ¹/₂ in. (32 × 24 cm).

Revolution commissioned a *History of the Communist Party in Posters*, a project on which Rodchenko worked. Thematic exhibitions intensified the propaganda efforts aimed at the general public, notably *Posters and Advertising Since the October Revolution* (1926) and *Posters at the Service of the Five-Year Plan* (1932).

The fate of Soviet artists

For avant-garde artists, the increasing stranglehold of the artistic style imposed from above merely added to the conflicts arising from their internal differences over modernist art. The situation was already tense in Russia in the 1920s, and subsequently became extremely difficult and oppressive. Some artists therefore went abroad. Wassily Kandinsky left for Berlin in 1921, and taught at the Bauhaus from 1922 to 1933 (even though he became a German citizen in 1928, the Nazis considered Kandinsky to be a Russian Bolshevik, so he moved on to Paris in 1933). Marc Chagall sought refuge in the United States. Others remained in the Soviet Union, such as Vladimir Mayakovsky, Vladimir Tatlin, and Kasimir Malevich, but they were forced to reconsider the modernist bent of their own work. Some were obliged to disavow publicly their own commitment to the avant-garde and were expelled from Stalinist artistic organizations. Malevich, having fallen into disgrace, was imprisoned, interrogated, and then released in 1930 (the same year that Mayakovsky committed suicide). He died in 1935, and his work would not be exhibited in the Soviet Union for a long time afterward. Such repression was ultimately fatal to the avant-garde "October" group of artists, beginning with Gustav Klutsis (arrested in 1938, then interned in a central Asian labor camp where he died in 1944) and Alexei Gan (also arrested in the late 1930s and sent to a labor camp where he died in 1942).

The goal of Stalinist decrees on art was to liquidate the avant-gardes. From the days of Russian Futurism right through those of Constructivism, passing through Rayonism and Suprematism, modern artists made major contributions to both graphic design and the "typographic revolution" in Russia (and later the Soviet Union), partly through their pioneering role in the realm of photomontage. The party imposed normative, codified imagery in the arts in the early 1930s in an attempt to eradicate avant-garde forms. Yet even though abstraction was suppressed, photomontage held its own, thanks to its visual efficiency. It could even explore surprising registers, combining socialist realism with avant-garde techniques of Expressionist or Futurist inspiration. Fashioned in the 1920s, Leninist imagery spread more extensively in the 1930s as it became Stalinist in nature. Unlike Hitler's regime, which suddenly excluded avant-garde culture (through acts such as the massive book-burnings of May 1933), the Soviet aesthetic doctrine was outlined as early as the 1920s but only really imposed over a period of years in the 1930s (notably becoming totally intransigent with the rise of Zhdanov).

In more ways than one, the imagery of socialist realism played an important role in the history of graphic design. Apart from its own merits, it was mainly—and indirectly—significant for what it helped to annihilate. Without the rise of totalitarianism, the avant-garde energy would probably have been channeled in directions difficult to imagine today. The doctrine of socialist realism, imposed in the interwar period, would eventually extend itself in time as well as space. For over a half century it eliminated all competing artistic styles, first in the Soviet Union and later in Eastern European countries. Participating in the postwar construction of Europe's Communist bloc (Romania, Poland, Hungary, Bulgaria, Czechoslovakia, etc.), socialist realism would also grip the People's Republic of China for many decades. As its internationalization proceeded apace, socialist realism was proclaimed "the world's most modern art."[41]

The United States: modernism in high gear
European graphic design in exile

At the start of the 1930s, while Europe was falling under the spell of dictators, the United States was facing a depression triggered by the stock-market crash of 1929. As the decade wore on, exiled avant-garde artists began arriving en masse in America. Some of them found it to be a country conducive to the pursuit of their artist experiments and professional careers. The United States therefore swiftly assumed an important role in the history of typography and graphic design. In both fields, creativity sometimes followed the path of nineteenth- and early twentieth-century modernism (the fine arts remaining fairly well anchored in traditional registers). In the nineteenth century, for example, very large colored posters made from sets of wood engravings were notable for their originality. Around 1900, American posters and magazine covers (including those by Edward Penfield and Will Bradley) helped to forge new forms, displaying links to Art Nouveau or revealing the influence of French and British pioneers. Subsequently, the design of letterforms underwent a major renaissance in the United States, for example through the elaboration of many sans serif typefaces (such as Franklin Gothic in 1903–12 and News Gothic in 1908, in tune with European developments). In general, however, the American visual idiom nevertheless seems to have remained aloof from European avant-garde movements. Figurative illustration was still a key feature of graphic art, far from the fashion for abstraction emerging on the other side of the Atlantic. After World War II, despite American economic prosperity during the Roaring Twenties, the fields of typography and graphic arts seemed unaware of European upheavals in those realms. As the 1930s dawned, however, the impending immigration of vast numbers of Europeans heralded important changes.

The exiled European designers seem to have received a favorable welcome in the United States in the 1930s—despite the recent depression, some of them benefited from good financial conditions and constructive professional relations, creating a context that enabled them to pursue their careers. The American print industry, which had already reached considerable size by the late nineteenth century, was undergoing constant expansion and was the object of major investments in terms of reproduction methods, mechanization, and creative products adapted to new technology.[42] Furthermore, company executives were in the habit of maintaining close contact with designers of ad campaigns—American advertising agencies enjoyed significant growth after World War II. The terrain thus seemed favorable to European designers who spent time or settled permanently in the United States. This massive flow of exiles, concentrated over just a few years—notably between 1933 and 1938—had a swift impact on the practice of graphic design. American typographers and designers were suddenly more attentive to European innovations, incorporating these developments into the process of rejuvenating styles. They quickly assimilated the various trends in modern art and design and channeled them into an innovative yet specifically American output. Exhibitions largely contributed to greater awareness of European creativity (just as the Armory Show in New York and other cities had done back in 1913). Several major shows of the 1930s thus featured some of the twentieth-century's leading movements and artists: in 1936 alone there were three such exhibitions, *Cubism and Abstract Art*, *Posters by Cassandre*, and *Fantastic Art, Dada, and Surrealism*; while in 1938–39 the Museum of Modern Art in New York presented *Bauhaus 1918–1928*, followed in 1939 by a retrospective devoted to Picasso.

European influence on graphic design was all the greater in that American pioneers and leading figures themselves reinforced the stimulating effect. The avant-garde movements having most marked typography and graphic design—Dada, Constructivism, Functionalism, the Bauhaus, and New Typography—sparked general enthusiasm in the United States, their path probably having been eased by the absence of any normative trend or any obedience to a preexisting style. But European influence on North American graphic design had begun long before the mass exile of 1933, just as intercontinental exchanges in this field had operated in

496

496
Lester Beall, cover of
PM magazine, United
States, 1937.

both directions—Edward McKnight Kauffer, for example, left America to work in England. Meanwhile, Lucian Bernhard, a pioneer of *Sachplakat*, had moved to New York in 1923, notably designing letterforms for the American Type Founders Company (ATF) from 1929 onwards. Two figures from the realm of magazine design also moved to the United States: Mehemed Fehmy Agha in 1929, and Alexey Brodovitch the following year. Both men were of Russian origin, and both had studied and worked in Paris before leaving for the United States. Keen to innovate, they revamped the function of art director at glamorous fashion magazines such as *Vogue* and *Harper's Bazaar*.

In their wake, many leading avant-garde figures left for the United States, often from central Europe. Given the multiple activities of these interdisciplinary artists, it is difficult to speak of "graphic designers" alone. Many such artists contributed, in various degrees, to the transformation of American design, whether they were, strictly speaking, architects, painters, photographers, typographers, teachers, theorists, or graphic designers. Some of them merely spent time in the United States, others remained there permanently. Among the major creative figures who spent a greater or lesser amount of time in the United States it is worth citing Josef Albers (arrived 1933), Joseph Binder and Erik Nitsche (1934), Xanti Schawinsky (1936), Walter Gropius, László Moholy-Nagy, Ludwig Mies van der Rohe, Marcel Breuer, and Gyorgy Kepes (1937), Jean Carlu, Herbert Bayer, Will Burtin, and George Giusti (1938), Ladislav Sutnar and Leo Lionni (1939), Herbert Matter (1936–46), Cassandre (the winters of 1936–37 and 1937–38), Hungarian designer Albert Kner (1940), and Saul Steinberg and George Tscherny (1941). Some of them left their home countries to escape oppressive dictatorships; others left because business had dried up. Still others lived and worked in the United States in response to professional opportunities. Many painters also made the journey, including Marcel Duchamp, Piet Mondrian, Marc Chagall, Fernand Léger, Max Ernst, Max Pechstein. Several former Bauhaus figures arrived in the United States after passing through various European countries (Gropius lived in London from 1934 to 1938, as did Breuer from 1935 and 1937; Moholy-Nagy went first to Amsterdam in 1934 and then to London in 1935; the Swiss Schawinsky, who studied at the Bauhaus, immigrated first to Italy between 1933 and 1936). Some graphic artists, such as the Frenchman Cassandre and the Swiss Matter, who was also a renowned photographer, went to America only temporarily, for professional reasons. Although they were part of the vast shift from Europe to the United States, they were not fleeing dictatorships but simply responding to foreign commissions, contributing their experience of modernism, notably to American fashion magazines, which were then undergoing a boom. Along with commercial advertising, these periodicals were among the leading American media in quest of original graphic forms (not only did such magazines seek constant novelty, but they enjoyed substantial budgets). Some periodicals undertook a radical revamping of their visual image at this time, in terms of cover and layout (major changes having already been made in the late nineteenth century); advertising, meanwhile, was turning to ever more numerous supports—posters, magazines, daily newspapers, radio—just as the manufacturing industry was embracing the concept of "corporate design."

In the United States the crash of 1929, which also affected Latin America and Europe, led to a steady economic collapse that lasted for several years. Between 1929 and 1932 the number of unemployed rose from three to twelve million as industrial output dropped by half. Franklin Delano Roosevelt, inaugurated as US president in January 1933, immediately launched the New Deal, a sweeping economic recovery program. By the mid-1930s, the government had established organizations to spur both employment and culture, such as the

Public Works of Art Project and the Works Progress Administration. Among other things, such institutions commissioned numerous posters from unemployed artists. New Deal policies led to an economic upturn, which consequently boosted the need for printed communication. The design sector therefore glimpsed the potential for significant growth. The World's Fairs of 1933 and 1939–40 gave pride of place to design and mechanization. In this changing artistic climate, the applied arts explored new stylistic registers such as Art Deco and the streamlined look. The socioeconomic recovery of the United States in the 1930s therefore coincided with the arrival of European exiles and favored the emergence of a new graphic idiom.

The contribution of European artists who arrived in the United States full of creative energy thus took place at a time that welcomed both modernism and a perpetuation of graphic tradition. Some of the new generation of American graphic artists were just starting out, and they shared the Europeans' awareness of avant-garde movements and their determination to transform visual language. At the same time, the Europeans pursued their own activities on American soil. Several former Bauhaus teachers swiftly obtained key academic posts in major art schools and universities. Other expatriate designers established fruitful professional contacts with industry, smaller firms, and publishing houses. When considering this period it seems more important to stress—as was the case with the pre-war (typo)graphic renaissance in Europe—overall trends and perspectives affecting the transformation of the applied arts, rather than to focus on specific projects or isolated productions.

Mehemed Fehmy Agha and Alexey Brodovitch

The departure of graphic designers Mehemed Fehmy Agha and Alexey Brodovitch for the United States occurred at the very end of the 1920s, somewhat prior to the main wave of European immigration. Unlike many of the exiles of the 1930s, Agha and Brodovitch left of their own free will, or upon invitation. Their careers display a number of similarities. Both were of Russian origin (born in 1896 and 1898, respectively), both began their career in graphic arts in Paris in the 1920s, and both would be become the art director of a famous American fashion magazine—*Vogue* in the case of Agha in 1929, *Harper's Bazaar* in the case of Brodovitch in 1934. Faced with conventional practices, these two advocates of the modernization of publishing styles brought a new dimension to their magazines, inspired by recent European experiments. In Europe itself, the new graphic language had already largely invaded many art and cultural reviews, those major vectors of avant-garde aesthetics. In the United States, the creativity that Agha and Brodovitch brought to the design of fashion magazines, which also addressed economic and advertising considerations, literally transformed the press and reached a readership probably quite different from the one familiar with European periodicals. It would seem that the fashion press in the United States then constituted one of the media most welcoming of photo-typo-graphic audacity—the imperatives of fashion and of regular publication both favored the search for visual originality. Inside such periodicals, the design and layout of pages welcomed effects of surprise. As already explored, in turn, by the likes of Stéphane Mallarmé, William Morris, and the Constructivists, the double-page spread could be conceived as a single entity rather than as a pair of two contiguous pages. The work accomplished by Agha and Brodovitch concerned both the role and the presence of photography, an ample use of unprinted spaces, and conspicuous typographical effects incorporated into asymmetrical compositions.

Agha took over the artistic direction of *Vogue* at the request of its editor, Condé Nast, whom he met in 1928. Agha had already worked in Germany for the German version of the magazine. Once in America in the 1930s, he strove to innovate constantly via the medium of periodicals, also contributing to the design of other publications such as *Vanity Fair* and *House & Garden*. In a swift sign of recognition of his work, Agha was named president of New York's Art Directors Club, an organization founded in 1920 to promote the quality of visual communication.

THE CONSENSUS OF OPINION

497
Alexey Brodovitch, poster *Bal banal*, March 14, 1924, Paris.

498
Alexey Brodovitch (art director), dummy for a double-page spread in *Harper's Bazaar*, undated.

499
Alexey Brodovitch (art director) and Man Ray (photographer), United States. Double-page spread for *Harper's Bazaar*, March 1936.

Also keen to experiment, Brodovitch, like Agha, was another key figure in American art direction and editorial design. Previously, he had worked in Paris (like his fellow citizens Erté and Agha) in the ten years between 1920 and 1930. His career in Paris won him a certain renown, thanks to his striking posters, stage designs, and work as artistic director of the Paris department store Aux Trois Quartiers. On arrival in the United States in 1930, Brodovitch first taught at the School of Industrial Art in Philadelphia, where he was charged with setting up an advertising design department; he also worked for the N.W. Ayer agency. He then moved to New York and became art director of *Harper's Bazaar* in 1934 at the request of Carmel Snow, the magazine's editor-in-chief. Like Agha, he experimented with the visual space of the fashion magazine. The two New York magazines, *Vogue* and *Harper's Bazaar*, were then in lively competition. Although *Vogue* enjoyed higher sales and greater distribution figures, *Harper's Bazaar* benefited from its reputation for boldness, functioning as a veritable laboratory of graphic experiments. Open to multiple sources of influence, Brodovitch was constantly in search of original visual impact. In orchestrating page layout, he accorded great importance to unoccupied spaces. And above all, he commissioned images from the greatest photographers and graphic artists, many of them European. He was determined to endow his magazine with a visual image that conveyed quality yet was open to the unexpected. The covers and pages of his magazines hosted photos by Man Ray, Erwin Blumenfeld, Henri Cartier-Bresson, Brassaï, André Kertész, Bill Brandt, Richard Avedon, Lisette Model, Irving Penn, Martin Munkacsi, and others. Brodovitch also solicited contributions from Salvador Dali, Marc Chagall, Herbert Bayer, and Cassandre, not to mention Erté (i.e., Romain de Tirtoff, a Paris-trained Russian illustrator and decorator who arrived in the United States in 1924 to work for *Harper's Bazaar*). The magazine became a platform for the promotion of recent experimentation in the fields of photography, graphic design, and the visual arts. Just as Agha had a long-lasting relationship with *Vogue*, so Brodovitch stayed with *Harper's Bazaar* until 1958. Most of the original dummies were unfortunately destroyed in a fire (destructive flames in two other countries have also robbed us of much of the archives of *Campo grafico* and the work of Werkman). As part of his graphic creativity, in 1950 Brodovitch also designed a typeface named Abro Alphabet. He spent the final years of his life in the south of France (1966–71), unwell and increasingly removed from the professional scene. His followers include Henry Wolf and Otto Storch, both of whom made their mark as artistic directors of various American magazines.

Together, Agha and Brodovitch helped to lay down the new direction of an artistic sensibility open to modernism. On both sides of the Atlantic, in radically different contexts, the years 1933–34 were pivotal. On one side dictatorships hardened, on the other economic recovery began. Through the resulting phenomenon of massive exile, European artists—including designers and typographers—transferred part of their creative activity to the United States, an activity strongly inflected by the local context (economic and commercial structures, growth of advertising and the press, education and academic training, etc.).

Bauhaus, USA

When the Bauhaus closed once and for all in the summer of 1933, some of its teachers left Germany for neighboring capitals (Paris, London, Amsterdam), while others headed to the United States. In addition to the local impact of closure, the very suddenness of the halt to Bauhaus activities—and the reasons behind that halt—encouraged the idea of reviving the school abroad. Here again, it is probably most appropriate to consider the geographical transplant of an entire artistic scene before focusing on a specific part of it (such as typography and graphic design). Combined with a repertoire of aesthetic forms that had been unusual until quite recently, a new conception of design began to spread quickly and gain broader acceptance in schools of applied arts.

Of the three successive professors of typography, graphic design, and advertising at the Bauhaus—László Moholy-Nagy, followed by Herbert Bayer and then by Joost Schmidt—the first two left Germany. Moholy-Nagy was Hungarian, for that matter, while Bayer was born in Austria. (Schmidt initially worked for the Nazi authorities, as did Bayer, but ultimately had to resign his post, and only found another job after the war.) The mass of expatriates helped to spread the Bauhaus's creative ideas everywhere, from London and Amsterdam, to major cities in the United States. Having remained in Germany, the typographer Schmidt would lose his teaching job in the mid-1930s. Such sanctions also fell upon avant-garde

500

ʌn ʌlfʌbɛt ko-ɔrdinætʃ fonɛtiks
ʌnd visʊ̣n wiḷ bɛ æ mɔṛ ɛf̣ɛktiv
tul uf kum̠unikætʃn
fɔrmd dʌrka hʌn̠ trʌnsitọ hink
ʠɛʌp sʌrp sɛrtn̠ly identikl

figures teaching in schools other than the Bauhaus; for some of these artists, political events brought an immediate halt to their careers, while for others—including some important figures—disgrace came only after a period of temporary collaboration with the Nazi regime, notably in the context of official commissions (visual design, urban planning, and so on). Their disgrace might take the form of loss of employment, allegations of "degenerate art," or removal of their work from German museums.

501

Josef Albers was one of the first members of the Bauhaus to head immediately for the United States. Appointed professor at Black Mountain College in North Carolina from 1933, he taught Bauhaus methods and pursued his experiments into optical art there until 1949. (It was around 1950, in fact, that Black Mountain College became known as a remarkably influential institution, attracting poets, artists, and musicians, and welcoming unusual, transdisciplinary experimentation.) From 1950 to 1960, Albers taught at Yale, and in 1963 he published *Interaction of Color.* His art and teaching had an indisputable influence on the evolution of the graphic idiom in the United States—chromatic effects, repetitive yet complex formal interactions, and so forth. (Victor Moscoco, a major figure in psychedelic poster art of the 1960s, studied under Albers at Yale.)

Moholy-Nagy, who was more directly involved in the graphic arts, remained in Germany for a few months after 1933, but expressed his despair in January 1934, as conveyed by the following lines written in Berlin to Herbert Read: "We are more sad than gay, and we have good reasons.... The situation in the arts around us is devastating and sterile. One vegetates in total isolation, persuaded by newspaper propaganda that there is no longer any place for any other form of expression than the emptiest phraseology."[43] So, after having left his native homeland of Hungary in 1919, Moholy-Nagy had to consider exiling himself once again, due to the rise of the Third Reich. The closing of the Bauhaus marked the start of a few difficult years in his career, moving from one city to the next. In London from 1935 to 1937 he worked as a typographer and graphic designer, pursuing his photographic and writing activities as well. He collaborated with Gropius, who was also in London at the time. During his British period, Moholy-Nagy considered the possibility of founding an art school directly derived from the Bauhaus, but the plan never came to fruition.

Gropius, meanwhile, left Great Britain for the United States in 1937. Hired by the Graduate School of Design at Harvard, he was appointed head of Harvard's architecture department the following year, charged with bringing his experience of modernism into the department. There Gropius stressed the importance of the notions of function, use, and space, rather than form in itself (recalling his rejection of style expressed in the Bauhaus context). Also in 1937, Marcel Breuer was hired to teach architecture at Harvard (thanks to Gropius), while Mies van der Rohe was asked to head the architecture unit at the Armour Institute in Chicago.[44] Their reputations and the influential posts they held enabled all three men to promote the functional dimension of architecture, in relation to the conception of space and object, on the other side of the Atlantic.

Through these different paths, the Bauhaus spirit thus resurfaced in several educational institutions in the eastern and northern United States This is the context in which plans for a New Bauhaus emerged. The Association of Arts and Industries, founded in Chicago in 1922, decided to set up an art school, and invited Gropius to become its director. He turned down the offer, but suggested that Moholy-Nagy, then in London, be approached. Moholy-Nagy jumped at the opportunity to revive the Bauhaus's educational mission and immediately left for the United States. The New Bauhaus thus opened in Chicago in September 1937. The teaching staff included several exiled Europeans such as Herbert Bayer, Xanti Schawinsky, and Gyorgy Kepes. The school modeled itself on the Dessau Bauhaus, and reinvented the foundation course (advertising art was added to the program of one of its workshops). The New Bauhaus did not survive for long, however, closing at the end of the 1937–38 academic year, even though Moholy-Nagy was extremely pleased with the work that had been done, and even though he hadn't been given notice of the decision to close. But only fifty students had registered. On being informed of the school's financial problems, Moholy-Nagy sought funding through other channels with the help of Walter Paepcke, an industrialist who was enthusiastic about modern design and whose Chicago-based company, the Container Corporation of America (CCA), had called upon French, German, and Hungarian designers—including Moholy-Nagy—in the 1930s. In January 1939, then, Moholy-Nagy managed to open a new school, the School of Design, once again in Chicago.[45] The curriculum focused on industrial design and included a course in "visual communication" that dealt with advertising and publishing. When Moholy-Nagy died in 1946, he was succeeded by Serge Chermayeff. (Visual communication is still taught there, but the institute's educational goals have since evolved, moving away from Bauhaus ideals towards the more direct needs of American society.) In addition to his educational role, Moholy-Nagy pursued his career as a graphic artist and designer in the United States, notably working for the CCA, *Fortune* magazine, and the Parker Pen company, not to mention the field of exhibition design. During his American period, Moholy-Nagy also made sculptures and took an interest in optical effects and the play of light. Having already written and published his theoretical ideas in Germany, he continued in this vein with *Vision in Motion*, published posthumously in 1947.

Like Moholy-Nagy, Herbert Bayer had taught graphic arts at the Bauhaus. He left the school in 1928 to pursue a career in the applied and graphic arts in Berlin. Born in 1900, Bayer had first studied at the Bauhaus, where he notably attended Kandinsky's workshop. Whereas Moholy-Nagy soon opted for exile, expressing a pessimistic view of the art situation in Germany in January 1934, Bayer remained in Berlin until 1938. There he ran the Dorland agency from 1928 to 1938, served as art director of *Vogue* (1928–29), produced striking covers for the magazine *Die neue Linie,* designed a typeface, and so on. Although he worked on several exhibition projects sponsored by the Nazis in the mid-

1930s, Bayer saw his own art tarred with the "degenerate" label in 1937. He immigrated to the United States the following year, remaining there until his death in 1985. Graphic design always featured strongly in his multiple activities, ranging from architecture and interior decoration to exhibition design, painting, sculpture, typography, and typeface design.

Moving first to New York, Bayer played an active role in the conception of an exhibition held at the Museum of Modern Art in 1938, *Bauhaus 1919–1928*. During his period in New York, he also held important jobs with advertising agencies J. Walter Thompson and Dorland International. Remaining faithful to his avant-garde ideals, he enriched and developed his conception of graphic design in the context of American society, constantly seeking the right relationship between artistic creativity and social environment. Bayer's American influence spread after World War II ended, when in 1946 he moved to Colorado. There Walter Paepcke would name him head of the International Design Conference in Aspen, a symposium launched in the early 1950s to address the issue, among others, of visual communication in industry. Bayer was also hired to run the design department of the Container Corporation of America. During his American period, as previously, typography was an important part of Bayer's graphic oeuvre. In Germany, he had designed the Universal typeface in 1925–26, followed by Bayer letterforms in the early 1930s. Ever an experimenter, he came up with the Fonetik Alfabet in 1958. In more ways than one, Herbert Bayer's career offers insight into the multiple facets of "visual communication," through applications simultaneously rich, complex, and ambiguous: his multidisciplinary activities enabled him to participate in avant-garde movements, work for the Third Reich, leave Germany, and pursue his career in a foreign country.

The exile of leading Bauhaus figures had a distinct influence on the development of the applied arts in the United States. Yet even though certain artists crossed the Atlantic with the idea of pursuing their European activities, once in America they had to adapt to the local context, which presented them with significant academic and professional opportunities. In the realm of graphic style, the rigorous, schematic forms associated with the New Typography had to be softened, probably as a result of the strong demand for typefaces suitable for advertising. And since exile took European artists to various parts of the United States, they were unable to reconstitute an avant-garde enclave there (although some artists managed to get together and share their experiences). Instead, they tended to adapt their ideas and practice to the projects, individuals, and society that arose from the American economy. Their exile coincided, in fact, with the start of economic recovery on the one hand, and on the other with the maturity of the New Typography (linked to a major graphic revival of earlier visual developments as well as to the recent use of photography and typo-photomontage in the print media). Expatriation to America therefore amplified the transnational scope of European movements.

The scope of European migration

For various reasons, sometimes unrelated to a need to flee Europe, many avant-garde figures either spent time or settled in the United States in the late 1930s. Among them were a certain number of graphic designers who were often artists in many disciplines, such as Herbert Matter (from Switzerland), Ladislav Sutnar (from Czechoslovakia), Leo Lionni (from Italy), Will Burtin (from Germany), Gyorgy Kepes (from Hungary), George Giusti (who was working in Zurich), Joseph Binder (from Austria), and Cassandre and Jean Carlu (from France). Cassandre and Carlu in particular were notable for their work in advertising and magazines, and both were commissioned to produce promotional visuals for the Container Corporation of America. Cassandre also worked for the N.W. Ayer agency and designed covers for *Harper's Bazaar* at Brodovitch's request. Carlu first headed to New York in the context of the World's Fair of the late 1930s; having settled in the United States in 1940, he worked during the war as a poster artist for the US Office of War Information.

502
Herbert Matter, ad for Knoll International
(produced in several languages), featuring
an armchair from Eero Saarinen's line
of molded plastic chairs, c. 1950.

502

Like them, Herbert Matter went to America without being forced to flee Europe. Born in Switzerland in 1907, he studied painting in Geneva between 1925 and 1929, and then went to Paris to study under Fernand Léger. He launched his career in Paris between 1929 and 1932, working with Cassandre and Le Corbusier as well as for the Deberny & Peignot foundry and for *Vogue*, focusing largely on graphic design and photography. On returning to Zurich in 1932, he continued to work with major graphic artists such as Anton Stankowski and Hans Neuburg, and then began a still-famous series of posters for the Swiss tourist board. In these posters he efficiently and characteristically employed differences in scale when juxtaposing images and simple typography, thereby letting photography and the impact of photomontage play a central role. The artistic freedom that accompanied this commission enabled Matter to forge an original, highly recognizable visual style, one inspired by the typo-photomontages of the 1920s yet revealing a new synthesis of avant-garde accomplishments. Hence he already enjoyed a certain renown, even in the United States. Moving to New York in 1936, he took photographs for *Vogue* and *Harper's Bazaar* (where Agha and Brodovitch were working) as well as for *Fortune*. In 1939 he worked as an interior designer at the World's Fair. Subsequently, he produced posters for the Container Corporation of America, acted as publicity adviser to Knoll International, designed the logo of the New Haven railroad line, devised the look of the publications of the Guggenheim Museum in New York, and so on. He would also make several notable films on artists (devoted to the likes of Eames and Calder), and taught graphic arts and photography at Yale from 1952 to 1976. The ads he did for Knoll International after the war demonstrate his graphic dexterity and sophistication—the furniture is either explicitly depicted or merely evoked through original, biomorphic shapes close to abstraction, not unlike graphic, handwritten marks. Although he placed special emphasis on photographic images in his advertising, the logos he devised were often inspired by typography alone by combining a few letters into a concise symbol. Matter was one of those twentieth-century graphic artists who left a striking, original oeuvre yet who remains relatively unknown. The singularity of his approach and of some of his works is probably due to the fact that he never joined a specific movement (having started work under the aegis of French painters and poster artists, even while maintaining contact with central European designers).

The Czech Ladislav Sutnar, meanwhile, headed to the United States in 1939 with the plan of designing his country's pavilion for the New York World's Fair. In the month of March of that year the Germans entered Prague, after having invaded part of Czechoslovakia. As an overt anti-Nazi, Sutnar could not imagine returning to his native land and therefore remained in the United States. Back in the mid-1920s, he had become, along with Karel Teige, one of the leading figures of the Czech avant-garde movement, which broadly aligned itself with Constructivism, the New Typography, and the idea of functional design. Once in America, Sutnar met up with several Europeans including Gropius, Matter, and Breuer. As a teacher at the Pratt Institute in New York, he actively pursued his graphic design career, specializing in the presentation of complex information and data, always seeking the right level of legibility. From 1941 to 1960, Sutnar was art director of Sweet's Catalog Service, which published information on industrial and architectural products, and called for an organized structure and meticulous arrangement of space (incorporating charts, graphics, technical and numerical data, and so on). The job therefore required sophisticated typographic expertise. Working alongside Lönberg-Holm, who was Sweet's head of Research and Development, Sutnar edited *Catalog Design* (1944) and *Catalog Design Progress* (1950), in which he discussed his concepts and his investigations into functional graphic design, where spatial management and organization became crucial. For Sutnar it was a question of simultaneously resolving issues of "function, form, and flow." He thereby made a major contribution to "information graphics" through his profound studies of how to transcribe visually complex data. Sutnar was one of those

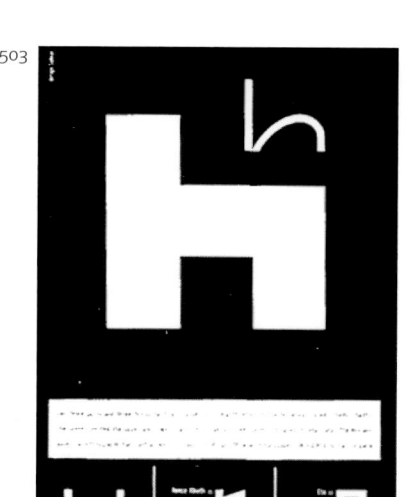

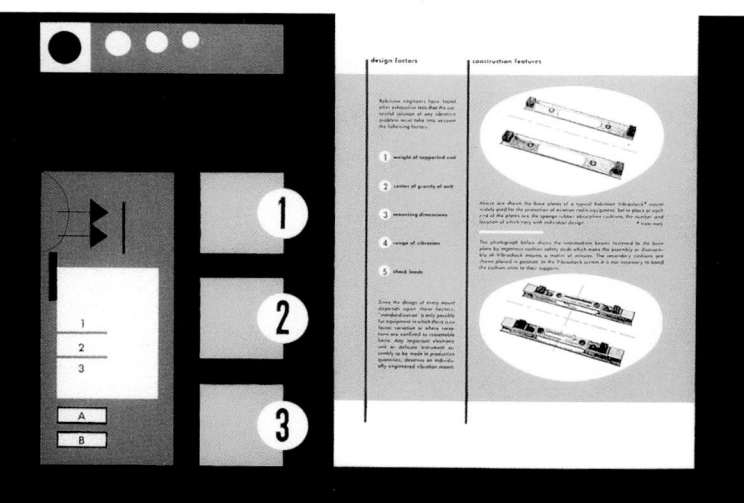

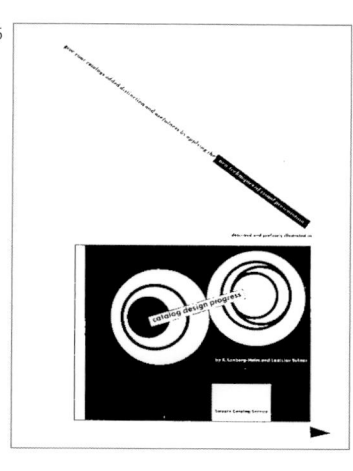

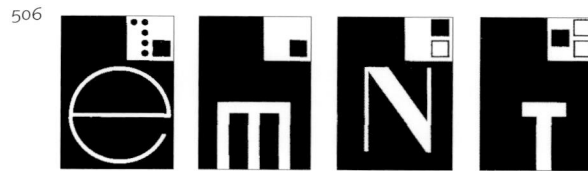

503
Ladislav Sutnar, typographic composition with
the letter "h" to promote a book, United States,
c. 1960.

504
Ladislav Sutnar and Lönberg-Holm, page from
Catalog Design Progress, 1950. 9 $^{1}/_{2}$ × 12 $^{1}/_{2}$ in.
(24 × 32 cm).

505
Ladislav Sutnar, promotional flyer for Sweet's
Catalog Service referring to *Catalog Design
Progress* (1950).

506
Ladislav Sutnar, graphics for various sections
of the *New York Art Directors Club 30th Annual
of Advertising and Editorial Art*, United States,
1951–54.

European graphic artists whose oeuvre underwent striking development in the United
States. Not unlike the approach then emerging in Switzerland, Sutnar's ideas on information
graphics and industrial design were partly based on experiments he had conducted earlier in
Europe. He felt that avant-garde movements had "provided the base for further extension
of new design vocabulary and new design means."[46] Sutnar, who started his own firm in
1951, was also successful in the realms of corporate communication and corporate image,
in which he invented strong, original, highly recognizable forms. He also published books
on his work and his conception of graphic design, notably the key reference work, *Visual
Design in Action* (1962).

Like Sutnar, other European designers had American periods that represented major
stages of their careers. Will Burtin moved there in 1938, producing most of his oeuvre in the
United States. He had studied in Germany in the 1920s, and had begun working there as a
graphic artist, including the design of exhibitions. Burtin's career path bears certain
similarities to Sutnar's: he worked on the New York World's Fair of 1939, taught at Pratt
Institute (starting in 1939), and specialized in the presentation of complex scientific and
technical information.[47] During World War II, Burtin worked for the US Air Force and the
Office of Strategic Services. He was then named art director of *Fortune* magazine in 1945,
after which he decided to devote his time exclusively to his own agency, which he opened in
New York in 1949. Burtin notably handled design commissions from the scientific, medical,
and pharmaceutical communities. His better-known works include his graphics for *Scope*,
the publication of the Upjohn pharmaceutical firm, as well as several educational
anatomical models devised for popular science exhibitions. Having won numerous awards,
Burtin became president of the American section of the CAGI and also took an active part in
organizing the International Design Conference in Aspen, Colorado.

Another noteworthy graphic artist, Leo Lionni was born in Amsterdam in 1910 but
went to school in Italy and Switzerland. Having studied economics, he decided to shift to
graphic arts and advertising early in his career in Italy. On arriving in the United States in
1939, he became art director of the N.W Ayer and Son agency in Philadelphia, and also

507
Man Ray, ad for the Container Corporation of America, 1942.

taught at Black Mountain College (where Josef Albers had been teaching since 1933). Like other European colleagues who had moved to the United States, Lionni worked as a poster artist in the first half of the 1940s on war-related output. After returning to Europe for two years, in 1949 he was named successor to Will Burtin as art director of *Fortune*. He later became head of design at the American subsidiary of Olivetti and then head of the graphic design department at the Parsons School of Design. The highly active Lionni was also one of the founders of the International Design Conference in Aspen (which also brought together Paepcke, Bayer, and Burtin), and co-edited the magazine *Print* from 1955 onwards. Finally, Lionni also wrote children's books, notably the famous *Little Blue and Little Yellow* (New York, 1959).

Where Europeans met Americans

Alongside Matter, Sutnar, Burtin, Lionni, and the Bauhaus alumni, other European designers enjoyed significant, if sometimes little-known, careers in the United States. Many of them would extend their American period beyond 1945, some of them even spending several decades there. Furthermore, the phenomenon of expatriation probably involved far more graphic artists than we realize today. Whatever their number and the extent of their presence, they certainly played a role in the development of modern graphics in the United States through their experience as avant-garde trailblazers, their writings, their lectures, their teaching, and their contribution to visual culture (magazines, books, special publications, advertising, exhibition design, logos, and so on). The sectors the hungriest for graphic input were industry, advertising, publishing, and the press, given the context of a steady boom in promotional and advertising activities. Companies were also becoming increasingly aware at this time of their image and their overall communication strategy. "Corporate design" therefore broadened the field of graphic arts in the United States, just as it did in Switzerland. In such an environment, many successful projects managed to combine quality design with a conceptual efficiency that met the client's needs.

The industrialist Walter Paepcke, among others, played a special role as a promoter and patron of graphic design. In Chicago in 1926 he founded what would become America's largest packaging firm, the Container Corporation of America (CCA). A decade later, in 1936 Paepcke decided to revamp his company's image. For that he not only appointed Egbert Jacobson as head of design, but he also turned to European artists. This initiative represents a significant example of a modern policy of public relations within a corporation and a given industry. From corporate logo to the interiors of various buildings, the CCA's entire image was reconceived. Many famous Europeans were commissioned to contribute to the firm's advertising campaigns starting in the late 1930s, including Frenchmen Cassandre (1937 onward) and Jean Carlu, and Bauhaus teachers Moholy-Nagy and Bayer, not to mention Man Ray, Fernand Léger, Herbert Matter, and Gyorgy Kepes. Paepcke's interest in graphic and visual design went far beyond the context of his own company. In 1938 he helped to raise funds to back the launch of the School of Design after Moholy-Nagy's New Bauhaus had foundered. And once the war was over, Paepcke made another key contribution by backing the International Design Conference in Aspen, a forum that would play an important role in elaborating visual culture.

The realm of visual communication thus represented a place of intersection and coexistence between Europeans and Americans. At a time when the former were moving over the to United States, a certain number of the latter made names for themselves by taking an active part in the process of modernizing their profession. There thus emerged new figures, notably including Lester Beall (born in 1903), Bradbury Thompson (1911), and Paul Rand (1914). This generation came to the fore around 1940, and some members remained active right to the end of the century. In the specific field of typeface design, several well-known figures were already at

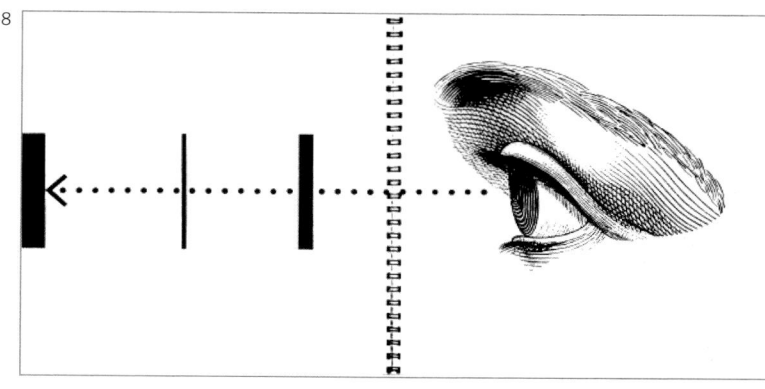

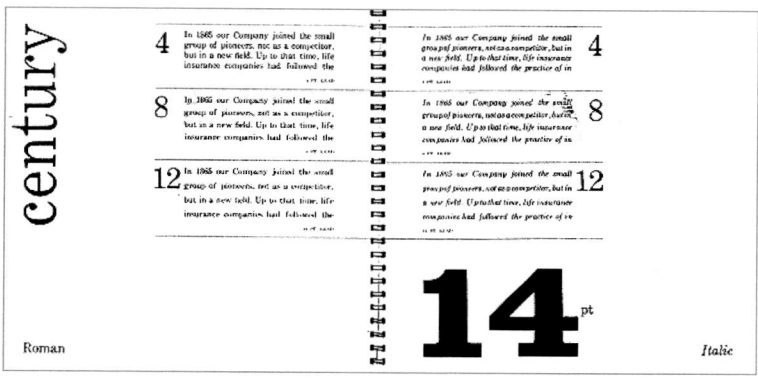

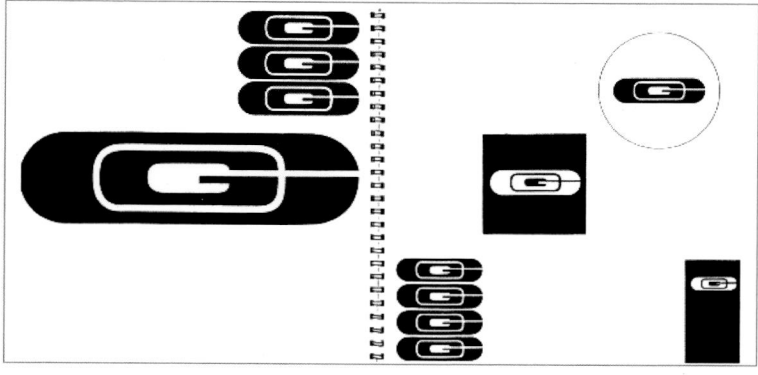

508
Lester Beall, double-page spreads from a style book for Connecticut General Life Insurance, United States, 1958.

509
Lester Beall, logotype for Titeflex Inc. (maker of flexible metal tubing), United States, 1958.

work at that time (some of them having been at it for decades), such as Frederic William Goudy (1865–1947), his disciple William Addison Dwiggins (1880–1956), and Morris Fuller Benton (1872–1948), the latter having designed Broadway typeface in 1929, as well as Franklin Gothic and New Gothic back in the early years of the twentieth century. In this sphere, the contribution of Europeans during their American sojourn was perhaps less significant, compared to their role in other realms of visual communication.

Simultaneously with this intersection of practices, visual culture in the United States was undergoing constant development, thanks not only to enthusiasm for European avant-garde ideas but also to the vitality of American graphic artists. The transition was smoothed by the interest, indeed the fascination, the latter showed in European artists and movements, whose hard-won maturity and convictions probably played a key role in the acceptance and enthusiasm they received. In the broadest sense, European applied arts benefited from a positive image in America as witnessed by the exhibitions and publications devoted to them throughout the 1930s. Between 1930 and 1935 the periodical *Advertising Arts* published the work of Brodovitch and Cassandre; Jan Tschichold's writings were known; and the small magazine PM (1934–42) took an interest in dozens of European artists, the best known of them working in the realms of typography and graphic design. Among others, PM featured the Futurists, Dadaists, a few figures from the Bauhaus (Moholy-Nagy, Albers, Bayers), Lucian Bernhard, Mehemed Fehmy Agha, Alexey Brodovitch, Edward McKnight Kauffer, Theo Van Doesburg, El Lissitzky, Karel Teige, Jan Tschichold, Paul Renner, and Herbert Matter. In addition to publications and exhibitions, several associations and organizations, founded somewhat earlier, helped to promote the arts of graphic design, advertising, and typography: the American Institute of Graphic Arts (AIGA, founded in New York in 1914), the American Association of Advertising Agencies (founded in 1917), the Art Directors Club of New York (founded 1920), the Typophiles (c. 1932), and the Society of Typographic Arts in Chicago (1927).

Given this context, the dynamics of American graphic arts simultaneously benefited from strong cultural awareness, new educational initiatives, and interest on the part of businessmen at a time when mass production was gaining ground and corporations were going international. Much graphic work of the day oscillated between informational content and advertising goal. The growth of corporate design, advertising, and information all offered scope for development in the United States, often accompanied by a quest for quality. At the same time, advertising and consumer markets were the object of new and original research and studies (communication processes, "target" analyses, assessment of reception, and so on).

Whereas avant-garde typography and graphic arts in Europe were usually part of a school or experimental movement in constant search of innovation and autonomy, the situation was very different in the United States, where there was no question of revolution or transgression. Various sources of inspiration appeared to be so many possibilities and discoveries, sparking new connections rather than complete breaks or slavish imitation. The Art Deco trend could thus extend a hand to the more sober version of New Typography (the "streamline" look being related above all to American product design). The advances made in Europe, inspired by

510
Bradbury Thompson, double-page spread in
Westwaco Inspirations 210, United States, 1958.

511
Paul Rand, brochure for the IBM Corporation,
United States, 1981.

512
Paul Rand, logotype for the Helbros Watch
Company, United States, 1944.

513
Paul Rand, poster for the New York Subways
Advertising Co., United States, 1947.

514
Paul Rand, dust jacket, United States, 1952.

515
Paul Rand, variations on the four-square
logotype for Ideo, United States.

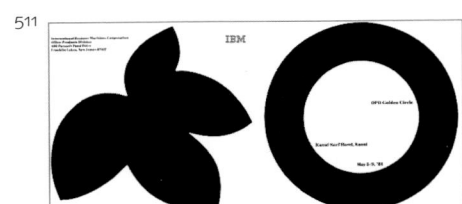

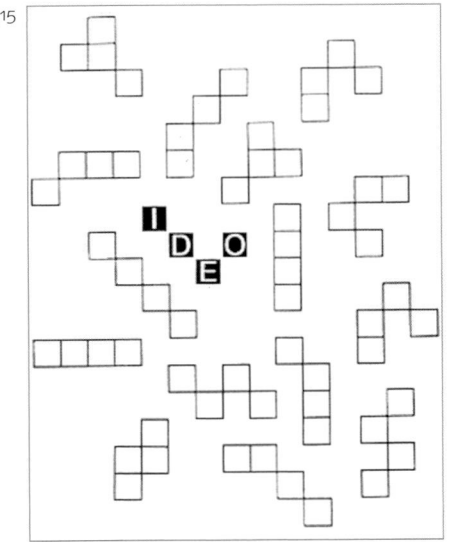

sources as diverse as Mallarmé and Jules Chéret, would have an important impact on American creativity, especially since they had followed a rich path that yielded many innovations before encountering misfortune. Having just come from a background of rupture, the Europeans apparently remained shy of joining specific "schools" in the United States, nor did they attempt to reconstitute their own shattered movements. Instead, they simply promoted a more general avant-garde influence, probably dictated by their newly far-flung locations (Chicago, New York, Philadelphia) in the vastness of the United States. Whereas the sphere of action in typography and graphic arts was reconfigured by political events in Europe (marked, for example, by Italian and Swiss creations in the 1930s), the modernist experience fed into the economic circuit in the United States in the form of a protean creativity that responded to more specialized needs and solutions. The exile of Europeans and their experiences in America thus merit special attention within the history of graphic arts, for the simultaneity of one context of repression and another of expansion—on either side of the Atlantic, as it turned out—represented a singular phenomenon full of edifying lessons. American graphic arts were able to make decisive breakthroughs starting in the 1930s, and then pursue them in the following decade when many poster artists were recruited by the government to respond to the significant needs of a country at war.

Switzerland: continuity and posterity

Up until then the theater of many avant-garde movements, Europe underwent profound changes in its aesthetic orientations during the 1930s, with the arts being hindered, if not annihilated, by the rise of governments that sought to impose total control over them. The crushing impact of Nazism on design creativity in Germany meant that neighboring countries took over, to a certain extent, by pursuing recent developments in visual communication, taking them further and making new connections. In the 1930s, then, Switzerland became a leading center of graphic design, as did Italy and the Netherlands (where Dick Elffers, Henny Cahn, Piet Zwart, and Hendrik Nicolaas Werkman, among others, were at work). Many important figures emerged in Switzerland during the interwar period, beginning with a pioneering generation of poster artists that included Ferdinand Hodler, Emil Cardinaux, Otto Baumberger, and Niklaus Stoecklin. Also making their names were the young artists and designers associated with New Typography, experimental photography, and other new artistic trends, such as typographers Jan Tschichold, Max Bill, Anton Stankowski, Hans Finsler, Herbert Matter (who left for New York in 1936), Theo Ballmer, Alfred Willimann, Ernst Keller, Walter Käch, and Richard Paul Lohse.

In those days Switzerland served to channel a wide range of past and recent influences: the conciseness of *Sachplakat* ("poster-object"), the presence of the Werkbund (1913), the rise of Dada in Zurich (1916), the frequent Swiss sojourns of El Lissitzky, and the birth of *Koncrete Kunst* (Concrete art) in Zurich, not to mention appreciation of photographic experimentation, the emergence of a Swiss school of typography, the arrival of Tschichold in Basel (1933), the impact of New Typography, the contributions of Bauhaus alumni (Max Bill, Theo Ballmer), and so on. The ambient creative spirit, whether originating in central Europe, Russia, or France (involving shared approaches to painting and drawing, plus the schools of Cubism and Art Deco), found its echo in Swiss practices. At the same time, other cultural developments and phenomena favored the Swiss rejuvenation of typography and the graphic arts in the

516
Ernst Keller, poster for an exhibition of linen fabrics and embroidery, Switzerland, 1927.

517
Ernst Keller, campaign poster *Wählt Liste 4* (Vote for List 4), Switzerland, 1935. Linocut, 4 ft. 2 3/4 in. × 3 ft. (129 × 92 cm).

516

517

1930s, namely highly active art schools, dynamic art scenes in Zurich and Basel, the founding of new associations, increased opportunities for commissions from institutions and corporations (PKZ, Bally, Binaca), the launching of specialized magazines, the skill of printers (known for their meticulous work), a lasting heritage of craftsmanship, and the impact of exhibitions such as *Neue Typographie* in 1927–28 and a photography show in 1931 (both held in Basel). Particularly worth noting is the Swiss public's awareness of—and sensitivity to—graphic design: "The Kunstgewerbemuseum, Zurich, and the Gewerbemuseum, Basel, have also done exemplary work in educating the masses through their publicity activities and by exhibitions of graphic art since the beginning of the [twentieth] century."[48] Although France remained on the sidelines when it came to certain trends in avant-garde graphics, its artistic exchanges with Switzerland continued apace. Charles Loupot, for example, began his career in Lausanne before moving to Paris in 1923. In fact, since the late nineteenth century or even earlier, many well-known Swiss graphic artists, from Eugène Grasset to Jean Widmer, had chosen to work in Paris temporarily or permanently. Similarly, numerous Swiss poster artists passed through Paris either to study or to pursue their careers and extend professional contacts. They included Baumberger, Matter (who studied under Léger and Ozenfant, and briefly worked for the Deberny & Peignot foundry), Morach, Vivarelli, Lohse, Leupin, and others. When it came to travel for study or temporary stays, some artists also looked to Germany, such as Stoecklin, Morach, Mangold, Baumberger, Bill, Brun, Willimann, and so on.

Respecting a phenomenon typical of the avant-gardes, these practices all fed into a highly interrelated dynamism, that profited from favorable circumstances. Starting in the 1920s, the particularly high-profile medium of the poster spawned significant creativity in Switzerland (as it already had in Russia, Germany, and the Netherlands), notably seen in the work of Baumberger, Stoecklin, Bill, Käch, and Keller. The Swiss *Sachplakat* movement developed as an often realist variant of German *Sachplakat*. Baumberger was one of the pioneers of this trend (as represented by his ads for clothing). Here, as elsewhere, two crucial aspects of poster art were consolidated in the 1920s—the new presence of photography and the development of posters based on avant-gardist typography. Walter Käch was allegedly the first to use photography in a Swiss poster, in 1926, an initiative followed by Herbert Matter, Alfred Willimann, Walter Cyliax, Hans Neuburg, Walter Herdeg, and Hans Finsler (who was associated with *Sachfotographie*). As to typographical posters, they might be seen as an extreme expression of the *Sachplakat* approach, the focus on text being another potential form of reduction. This conception of the medium enabled typography to escape subordination to the image even as it opened new visual spaces. The role of typographic posters (which was also significant in Germany and the Netherlands) thus represented a major aspect of the budding Swiss graphic activity.[49]

Far removed from the later cliché of "the Swiss style" (which recalled, and indeed echoed, the label of "Bauhaus style" even though both movements expressly wished to depart from the notion of "style"), the graphic arts in Switzerland were traversed by numerous influences . However, within these various registers, several trends prefigured the traits that would later characterize the postwar "Swiss school": simplification, conciseness, a sober and informative advertising tone, an extension of the aesthetics of New Typography (including the notion of a common, transnational, a-stylistic visual denominator), and an application of the concept of "basic design."

Beyond the professional sphere, Swiss graphic art was largely disseminated through education, publications, and exhibitions. Schools of arts and crafts in Basel and Zurich (the Allgemeine Gewerbeschule and Kunstgewerbeschule, respectively) offered courses in which graphic arts, photography, typography, and typeface design were taught by leading figures of the day. The Zurich school, which struck out in new directions right from the early years of the twentieth century, was perhaps the first to offer a course in typeface design, in 1916. Ernst Keller was teaching there by 1918—the Bauhaus had not yet been founded—and he

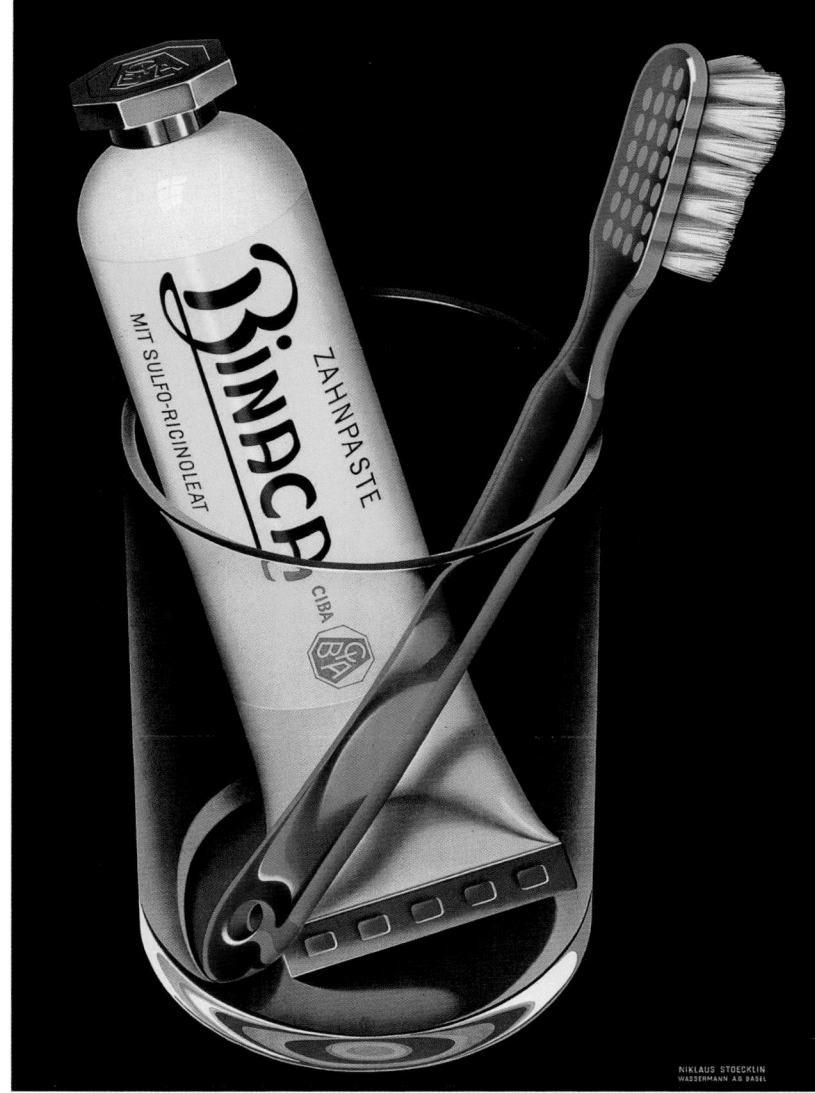

518
Otto Baumberger, poster for Remington,
Switzerland, 1918.

519
Niklaus Stoecklin, poster for Binaca toothpaste,
Basel, 1943.

520
Otto Baumberger, poster for Brak Bitter
(liqueur), Switzerland, 1937.

subsequently launched and headed the graphic arts department there (remaining at the school until 1956). Walter Käch joined the teaching staff in 1925 and Alfred Willimann in 1930. The school established a department of photography, where Hans Finsler would teach, in 1932. In 1938, Johannes Itten (a leading figure of the first Bauhaus) became director of both the school and the Zurich Museum of Applied Arts.

The Basel school, too, had links to the Bauhaus once Theo Ballmer joined its staff in 1930. The attention that the Swiss paid to education was paralleled by the publication of articles and magazines on typography and the graphic arts, beginning with the founding of the review *Typografische Monatsblätter* in Bern in 1933, and followed by Walter Herdeg's *Graphis,* published in Zurich starting in 1944 (both periodicals are still published today). These educational and editorial efforts played a crucial role in the training of graphic designers who, in their turn, would become teachers, practitioners, and authors of reference books in the late 1940s and afterward.

The new generation

As in Germany, the interwar period in Switzerland produced a significant number of active typographers and graphic artists—who were often photographers, designers, painters and/or sculptors. This generation notably yielded several highly creative, original artists, particularly around 1930. Otto Baumberger, Niklaus Stoecklin, and Ernst Keller were clear pioneers; Keller, a figure whose works (and teaching) remain too little known, notably produced a certain number of typographic posters. In so doing, he employed sans serif and uppercase letterforms, often drawing the graphic forms himself, particularly when it came to posters. Steeped in the craft tradition—and as distinct from the Bauhaus aesthetic—he favored an extension of drawn imagery over the potential use of photography. Institutional and cultural commissions encouraged him in the development of his (typo)graphical experiments.

Among the artists of the subsequent generation, all born after 1900 and some of whom studied under Keller, it is worth mentioning Anton Stankowski (born 1906), Theo Ballmer (1902), Herbert Matter (1907), and Richard Paul Lohse (1902). Stankowski, a German painter and graphic artist, studied under Max Burchartz in Germany and worked for Johannes Canis. Hired by the Max Dalang agency in Zurich in 1929, he remained in Switzerland until 1937. Ballmer, born in Basel, studied first under Keller and then at the Dessau Bauhaus in the late 1920s. Having set up as a graphic artist and photographer in Switzerland in 1930, he became known for his attention to compositional layout and construction, producing several well-known typographic posters. Bellmer also made his political feelings known (his friends included George Grosz and Hannes Meyer), and he backed the Swiss Communist Party (*Partei der Arbeit*) against the National-Socialists, resulting in a series of political posters.[50] Herbert Matter, meanwhile, worked with Cassandre and Le Corbusier in France in the early 1930s. On returning to Switzerland in 1932, he began designing his famous series of posters for the Swiss tourist board His graphics testify to an almost dizzying approach to photomontage that exploited large close-ups running into distant landscapes, creating a dynamic relationship that allowed the beholder to forget the medium and become completely caught up in the scene, as though actually part of it. A similar handling of typography usually yielded one very frontal word, harmoniously angled with the image, with a secondary word set in the middle ground, so to speak. Matter favored sans serif typefaces, fairly bold, and employed both uppercase and lowercase lettering. The upshot could be viewed as a hybrid between Constructivist principles and a fascination—also typical of Cassandre—with monumentality and capital letters. Through this series of posters, Matter made a major contribution to the then-recent use of photography as an expression of modernity.

In addition to individual artists working in Switzerland in that period, it is worth mentioning

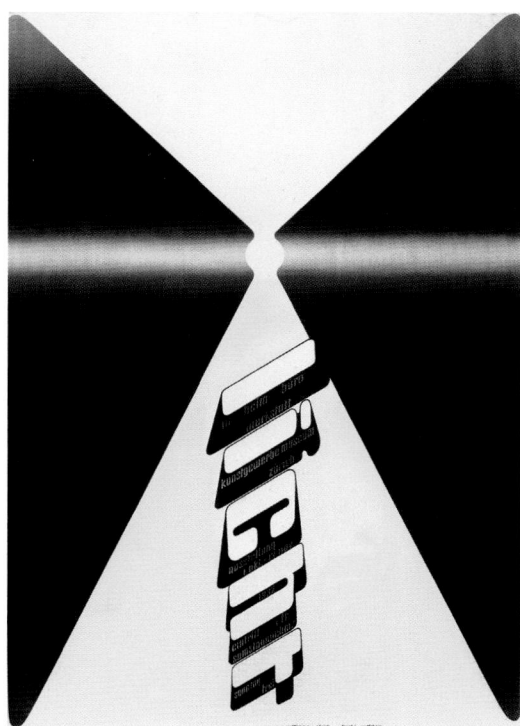

521
Alfred Willimann, poster for an exhibition, *Lighting* ("for the home, office, and workshop"), Switzerland, 1932. Lithograph.

522
Herbert Matter, poster for PKZ clothing, Switzerland, 1928. Color lithograph.

523
Alex Walter Diggelmann, poster for PKZ clothing, Switzerland, 1935. Color lithograph, 4 ft. 2 in. × 3 ft. (128.2 × 91 cm).

524
Alois Carigiet, poster for PKZ clothing, Switzerland, 1935. Color lithograph, 4 ft. 2 ¹/₂ in. × 3 ft. (128.5 × 92 cm).

525
Herbert Matter, a Czech version of his series of posters for the Swiss Tourist Board, Switzerland, 1934.

526
Herbert Matter, logotype for the city of Engelberg, Switzerland, c. 1934.

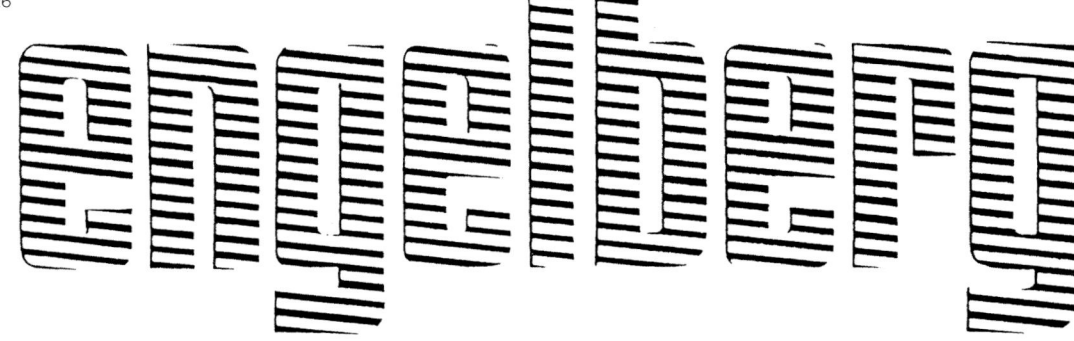

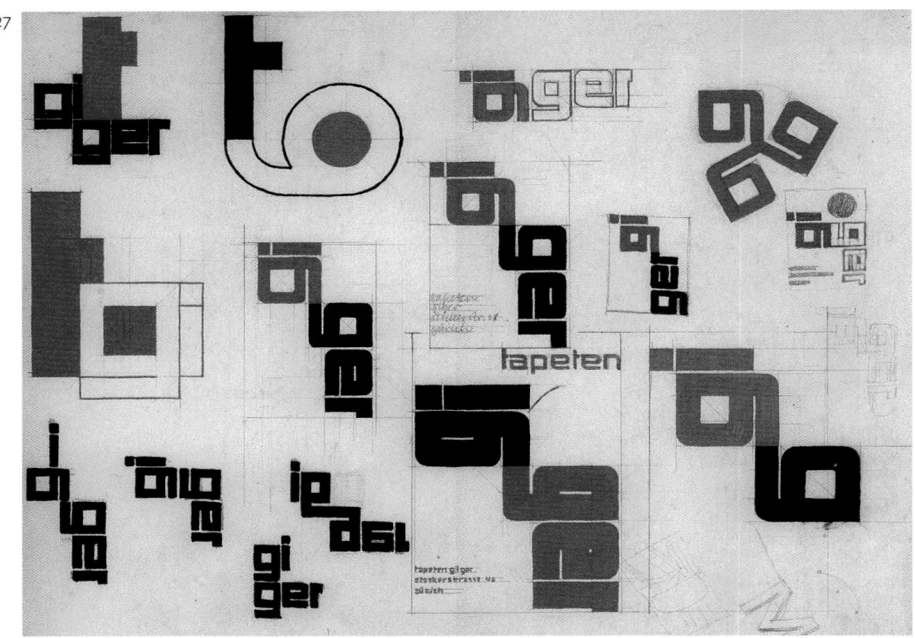

527
Theo Ballmer, sample sketches of a logotype for
Tapeten Giger wallpaper, Switzerland, 1931.

the active designers associated with the Concrete art group—notably in Zurich—such as Max Bill and Richard Paul Lohse. The very spirit and foundations of Concrete art generated strong points of convergence with New Typography and with other aspects of avant-garde graphics. Lohse had trained as an advertising artist and worked in the 1920s with the Max Dalang agency in Zurich in the 1920s (where Anton Stankowski also worked). He then set up his own outfit to handle commissions from the worlds of industry, publishing, and culture. Like Bill and many others, Lohse remained active throughout the latter half of the twentieth century thanks to a multidisciplinary career that included painting, graphic arts, and typography, thereby approaching both personal works and commissioned projects from the same visual perspective.

Max Bill and Jan Tschichold

A comparison between Max Bill and Jan Tschichold can shed useful light on differing Swiss conceptions of graphic design (ultimately leading to the men's public differences in the postwar period). Bill, born in 1908, moved to Zurich in 1929. There he studied at the Kunstgewerbeschule (School of Arts and Crafts) before heading to the Bauhaus in Dessau, where his professors included Albers, Kandinsky, Klee, and Moholy-Nagy. "At the Bauhaus [Bill] acquired knowledge of materials and a conviction of the logical need for a synthesis of the arts articulated around architecture, the arts no longer being for pleasure but having the function of contributing to the construction of spaces suited to human life and social fulfillment."[51] On returning to Switzerland, Bill continued the painting and sculpting activities he had begun in the 1920s, even as he pursued a career as a self-employed graphic designer (his main source of income during the 1930s). Although he had first envisaged concentrating on architecture, the regular commissions he received called on his skills as typographer and graphic artist— posters, publications, exhibition design and promotion, signs on buildings, and so forth.

Bill's (typo)graphic design steadily displayed greater rigor and conciseness, alongside his interest in Concrete art; it tended to be systematic, and geometric, based on mathematical order and highly structured patterns as well as on forms alien to everyday visuals. A unifying thread ran throughout his thinking and his approach to his various activities: from the Bauhaus he had learned to favor lowercase lettering, which some of his works would use exclusively; his own preferences showed a clear inclination towards sans serif typefaces (not unlike Stankowksi's preference for Akzidenz Grotesk) as well as a total commitment to the new avant-garde idiom (he abandoned figurative imagery in favor of other possibilities of visual expressiveness). Like several of his contemporaries, Bill pursued a quest for essentials, for clarity, for a functional message and a perceptual immediacy that discarded anything deemed useless. His approach was based on a reasoned strategy that aimed for greatest coherence. Whereas his earlier typographic compositions might retain a dancing quality, as his career progressed the highly constructed dimension progressively came to dominate. Like Keller, Bill worked a great deal with people from the worlds of culture and public relations. Form and context stemmed from a single, unifying logic, resulting in often sober visuals. In 1936, Bill was commissioned to design the Swiss pavilion for the Milan Triennial, where the latest trends in national typography and graphic art were to be exhibited. Although Bill's career followed a specifically professional path, he also stepped outside it, for both political and personal reasons. Allowing his

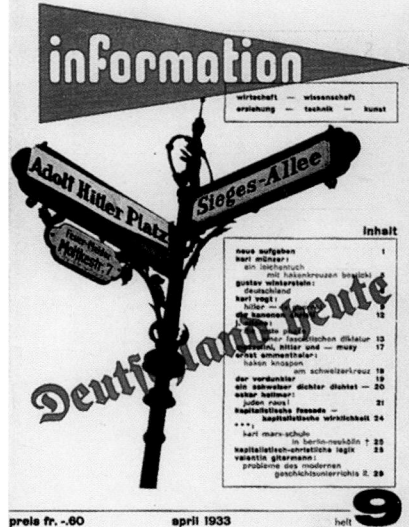

528
Max Bill, title page of the Swiss magazine, *Information*, April 1933.

529
Max Bill, poster-program for the municipal theater in Basel, Zurich, 1931. Black and rainbow-inked print.

political preferences to show in his work, he participated in the struggle against National-Socialism (as did Ballmer), notably through his graphics and layouts for the anti-fascist periodical *Information*. Furthermore, in keeping with avant-garde practices, Bill remained in touch with many artists working in neighboring countries (Bauhaus alumni, Le Corbusier, Piet Mondrian, Georges Vantongerloo, and others) and became a member of the Paris-based Abstraction-Création group in 1932 (alongside Hans Arp and Theo Van Doesburg). Bill was also one of the artists who defended their ideas in writing (leading to his polemic with Tschichold in 1946). Having pursued the ideal of tempered, functional graphics, and having served as a link between interwar artists and the younger generation, Bill became a leading figure of Swiss typography.

Jan Tschichold's approach, meanwhile, would progressively diverge from the one followed by Bill. Tschichold steadily shifted his ideas on typography as his convictions and sensibility evolved in the 1930s. Whereas he had been the spokesman for the New

530
Jan Tschichold, poster for a photography
exhibition at the Gewerbemuseum, Basel, 1938.

530

Typography, he would later go so far as to assert that he "detected most shocking parallels between the teachings of *Die neue Typographie* and National-Socialism and Fascism."[52] Meanwhile, in the spring of 1933, he had been arrested and imprisoned for several weeks, after which he left Germany for Basel. That same year, although aged only thirty, the brutality of events triggered an equally brutal rupture in his decade-long career. When he left for Basel, having recovered his freedom and lost his teaching job, the entire context in which he had forged his ideals and shaped his activity collapsed. Even so, his exile took him to a country that would soon be a famous center of Western graphic design. Whereas Tschichold might have been expected to pursue the path of New Typography in Switzerland (especially since the terrain was so conducive to it), he instead called all his earlier convictions into question. He had been hired to teach, from 1933, at Basel's school of arts and crafts (Allgemeine Gewerbeschule), but he also worked for publisher Benno Schwabe (and, later, for Birkhäuser). He continued to publish regular texts expressing his views on typography, in the form of essays, articles, and books. In *Typographische Gestaltung* (Asymmetric Typography), published by Schwabe in 1935, Tschichold pursued the idea already expressed in *Die neue Typographie* and other writings. "Each typography that is based on a preconceived form of idea—of no matter which kind—is wrong. . .. The new typography differs from the old in that for the first time it tries to develop its form from the function of the text. . .. Asymmetry is the rhythmical expression of functional design." The New Typography, claimed Tschichold, was not a mere fashion, and in pursuing its aims typographers could potentially "use all historical or non-historical letterforms, all kinds of subdivision of surfaces, any arrangement of lines." [53] Already, in certain texts written before his 1933 exile, Tschichold showed that a predilection for asymmetry and sans serif letterforms did not rule out other (typo)graphic possibilities. With time, centered compositions and serifed typefaces would resurface in his practice as well as in this theory. Perhaps this represented a revival of his early training in calligraphy and typography, anchored in traditions of the past.

Tschichold continued to stay in touch with developments abroad after 1933. He had already made contact with El Lissitzky and Moholy-Nagy as early as 1923–24, and henceforth extended his network into northern Europe, particularly Great Britain and

Denmark, traveling that way in 1935 to give lectures and show his work. In 1937–38 his book *Typographische Gestaltung* would be published in local editions in Denmark, Sweden, and the Netherlands (the Anglo-American edition would not be published until later).[54] In 1946, Tschichold went to London, where he was asked to redesign the entire typographic image of Penguin Books. His growing involvement in editorial design offers a plausible explanation for the change in his credo when it came to typography—the space of a book often calls for a certain balance and measure automatically rejected by much avant-garde experimentation.

Like Tschichold, who continued and ended his career in Switzerland, many of the protagonists of the burgeoning (typo)graphic scene there would remain active in the decades following the war. Their theories and their practice thus ensured a transition from avant-garde experiments to well-defined design and its subsequent diversification during a new boom. On foundations laid down in the interwar period, the Swiss school thus reached its heyday from the 1940s onward, at a time when the United States was also beginning to play a major role. The European countries who were at war, meanwhile, saw typography and the graphic arts abandon their artistic roots in order to pursue the path of propaganda, a path all-too-well trodden ever since World War I.

The 1930s: extinction versus revival

Within the history of typography and the graphic arts, the 1930s represented a period of profound rupture. The audacity, utopianism, and frenzy that had propelled the avant-gardes were crushed right where they had arisen. When it came to artistic activity, the crackdown was the most drastic in Germany, and less immediate in the Soviet Union; Italy, meanwhile, allowed modernist-inspired professional design to coexist alongside state propaganda. The artistic euphoria of the early decades of the twentieth century, opening new horizons or seeking new transpositions of reality (Expressionism, Cubism, abstraction, spirituality and inner subjectivity, Verism, Concrete art, etc.), did not generate expressive registers suited to the general imagery associated with dictatorships. Schools and movements such as the Bauhaus, Constructivism, and New Typography withered away if they weren't actively suppressed or abolished. Yet even when extinguished here or there, the modernization of the graphic arts and typography sprang up elsewhere. Although avant-garde dynamism could be crushed locally, its aspirations and culture could not be totally wiped out. Thus, whereas certain artists were faced with extreme hostility in the early 1930s, the movements with which they were allied found ways of continuing elsewhere. Continuity and development occurred in Italy and the Netherlands, spread into Switzerland, and blossomed in the United States. At the same time, propagandistic graphics grew apace in Germany, the Soviet Union and Italy, largely through posters but also through a number of media that the outbreak of war would increase in number and popularity. Whereas artists and designers in the interwar period aspired to help create a new world (through graphic and typographic creativity, among other means) by accepting the advent of industrialization, the dictatorial, belligerent vision called for total submission to ideological and political imperatives (which translated into socialist realism in the Soviet Union and National-Socialist painting in Germany). Like World War I, the second worldwide conflict endowed typography and the graphic arts with new powers in the realm of propaganda, thereby consolidating, in certain countries, the official imagery nurtured during the interwar period.

World War II

Propaganda imagery reaches new heights

World War II, like the first, transformed the graphic arts by placing them at the service of propaganda and the war effort. Indeed, although propaganda-driven campaigns of mass visual communication increased considerably during the period 1939–45, they had already been implemented in the nineteenth century and had undergone major development between 1914 and 1918. The difference, however, was that World War II followed the profound social rupture of the 1930s, a decade that created a double fracture in the broad graphic-design movement. Some artists pursued their careers by offering their services to the governing regimes, thereby playing an important role in the production of political and military imagery. The iconographic wellsprings of propaganda, already largely tapped by National-Socialism's brand of posters and print material, were further enriched by personality cults (or, more precisely, the cult of depicting personalities such as Hitler, Mussolini, Stalin, and Pétain.

More and more media were brought into play. In addition to visual graphics, radio expanded considerably as a channel for conveying messages and for winning hearts and minds. Because the number of homes with radios had grown substantially since the 1920s, this phenomenon assumed new scope—the airwaves were recruited to play a role that imagery couldn't fulfill. At the same time, other channels of communication and dissemination were invaded by propaganda. The leaders of countries at war became aware of the inherent potential of certain media and of their power over people—these media included illustrated broadsheets plastered on walls, photography (in posters, magazines, and other print media), leaflets, brochures, books, oral messages over public-address systems, official speeches and declarations, theatrical and musical skits, propaganda films, newsreels, street signs and displays, postage stamps, coins, insignia, rubber stamps, and so on. Political leaders also exploited the impact of large exhibitions on special themes. In France, for instance, the collaborationist Vichy government decided to imitate the major publicity events associated with the rise of the Fascist and Nazi Parties in the 1930s, namely the exhibition on the Fascist revolution held in Rome, and German shows such as *Deutsche Schrift* (German Script, 1933), *Deutschland* (Germany, 1936), *Entartete Kunst* (Degenerate Art, 1936 and 1937). The Vichy authorities therefore organized a series of exhibitions in the early 1940s with titles such as *Le Juif et la France* (Jews and France, 1941) and *Le Bolchevisme contre l'Europe* (Bolshevism versus Europe, 1942). In Great Britain, the ministry of information headed by Frank Pick established a special department in 1940, one devoted to organizing exhibitions that called upon the services of graphic artists such as Friedrich Heinrich Kohn Henrion.

The propaganda campaign employed every kind of communication technique liable to reach the masses. Posters, the major medium during World War I, henceforth became just one tool among many; paper, for that matter, was soon being rationed in Europe, along with many other products. Propaganda, however, claimed priority over the needs of advertising and publicity, and the print-runs of certain posters reached phenomenal figures even in France, despite the restrictions. Whereas Jean Carlu's famous poster, *America's Answer! Production* was allegedly printed in a run of one hundred thousand copies in the United States, in France over a million copies (and perhaps more) were made of the 1940 poster *Révolution nationale,*

531
Joan Miró, poster in support of the Spanish Republic, 1937.

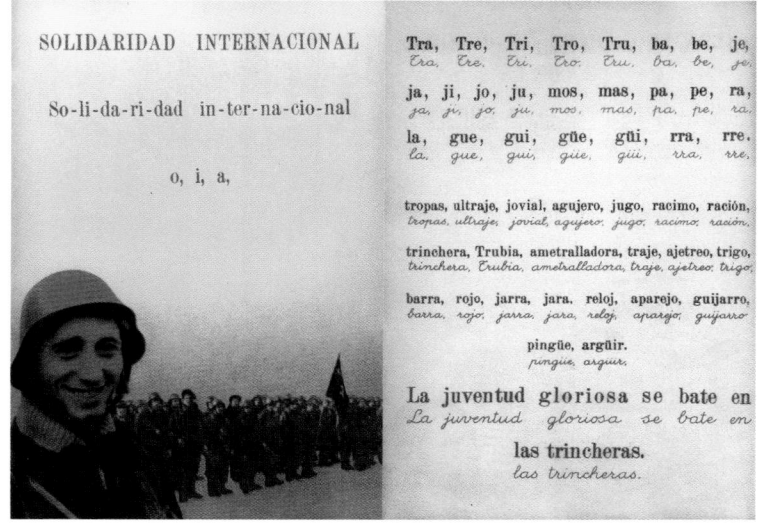

532
Mauricio Amster, double-page spread in an anti-fascist reading primer published by the Spanish ministry of information, Spain, 1937.

533
Propaganda poster for Mussolini's daily paper, *Il Popolo d'Italia* (1914–43), described as the "paper of Intervention, Revolution, Empire, People."

featuring a portrait of Pétain—and a postcard version of the same image was printed in numbers perhaps ten times as great. French posters promoting Mother's Day and Labor Day were also printed in vast quantities, the latter being reproduced in over three million copies in 1941, while other posters attained the figure of nearly one million.

Apart from the important question of numbers printed, posters from the 1939–45 period displayed a highly diversified array of visuals. They exploited all kinds of graphic and illustrative registers, ranging from realistic drawing (which had been common in World War I posters) to concise abstraction straight out of the avant-gardes, via intermediate modes of photographic montage, graphic drawings, typographic compositions, geometric shapes, and so on. Because it favored immediately understandable images accessible to a wide public, propaganda often used figurative imagery, in particular human figures (leaders, warriors, enemies, heroes, idealized versions of children and other family and social roles). Even when faced with the growing diversification of media, posters remained a key support. They were perceived instantly, were highly efficient, were cheap and easy to reproduce (and hence could be posted everywhere), and ultimately assumed a crucial role. Depending on the needs and tactics of the moment, a war poster could inspire confidence and security, provoke fear and hate, encourage patriotism, stimulate mistrust of the enemy, urge the population to increase productivity, and so on. Many posters from 1939–45 display optimistic and convincing imagery that misinformed people and largely masked the tragic reality of war by ignoring its visual horrors (except, of course, when it was a question of accusing or discrediting the enemy).

Germany

As was the case elsewhere, in Germany National-Socialist propaganda went far beyond (typo)graphic production. It was present in parades and organized gatherings where specific combinations of colors and symbols were exploited. Such events, just like the printed products of graphic design, placed crucial, determining emphasis on distinctive, emblematic signs. Marks of identification or designation such as the swastika and yellow star became ubiquitous (as early as 1933, the swastika was hoisted in front of the Bauhaus, and the yellow star became mandatory for all Jews over the age of six). When it came to printed material, the visual idiom ranged over a vast set of graphic and formal elements, from a highly drawn heroic realism to compositions that harked back to avant-garde productions of the first third of the century. Nazism's official graphic designers included not only Mjölnir (Hans Schweitzer) but also the likes of poster artist Ludwig Hohlwein, who had been a noted innovator around 1910 and then took an active part in the country's visual communication campaign during World War I. Since "politics through imagery" was a major feature of propaganda, it is probable that Hitler was personally involved in the choice of poster artists hired by the party, as well as in the selection of visuals used to convey the party's ideology in Germany and abroad (among allies and in occupied zones). Joseph Goebbels, head of the propaganda ministry founded in March 1933, also played a key role in developing the image of the Third Reich. Nazi-supplied posters in France, Poland, and Italy were designed to give Germany and Germanic culture an image of confidence, supportiveness, security. One poster in occupied France in 1940 urged the country's bereft population to have faith in German soldiers: a slogan to that effect—*Populations abandonnées, faites confiance au soldat allemand!*—was accompanied by Theo Matejko's realistic drawing of a vigorous, uniformed soldier surrounded by three children to whom he seems to be offering help and succor. In Italy, a poster encouraging Italian workers to enlist in the great cause since "greater Germany will protect you," hammered out the text in capital letters—*Operai italiani arruolativi! La grande Germania vi proteggerà*—and showed a couple emerging from the shadows, against a giant eagle and swastika.[55] Meanwhile, German soldiers and wartime populations always appeared brave and determined, whereas the enemy (whether Bolshevik or Jew) was shown to be dangerous and threatening. Posters therefore mobilized diametrically opposed visual content and tone to generate messages that could appear either benevolent or hate-mongering, as needed.

A typographic decree

Just as Nazi imagery exploited representations full of repeated themes and symbols that were instantly recognizable and produced the greatest impact on the greatest number, so the very form of printed texts came under special care and scrutiny. Decrees concerning typography were designed to regulate and prohibit, and they shed light on certain aspects of wartime typography. The Nazi regime's prime concern involved the use of Gothic—or blackletter—typeface, hinging on issues of its identity and its legibility outside of Germanic countries. As soon as the National-Socialist Party came to power (and even beforehand, in a *de facto* way), it adopted blackletter typeface as the one best suited to identify and represent it. New versions of Gothic typefaces were therefore designed, such as Deutschland, Element, and National, all dating from 1933. Yet after years of widespread use by the Third Reich, a sudden turnaround by the authorities condemned blackletter print; on January 3, 1941, Martin Bormann (soon to be appointed head of the Reich chancery, and later Hitler's private secretary) issued a "circular letter (not for general publication)" [*Rundschreiben, nicht zur Veröffentlichung*] declaring that the use of "Schwabacher-Jewish" typeface was henceforth prohibited for all administrative documents.[56] The original typescript of this circular was written on paper with the party letterhead still in blackletter typeface (a swastika topped by an eagle and flanked by the words *Nationalsozialistische Deutsche Arbeiterpartei*), suggesting that the decision was made suddenly while the only printing materials available were still in Gothic script; the decree was designated "for general notice on behalf of the Führer" (*Zu allgemeiner Beachtung… im Auftrage des Führers*), although signed by Bormann. It claimed that blackletter script was Jewish in origin, and consequently should be banned from use in any kind of printing. The circular stated that, "it is false to regard or to describe the so-called Gothic script as a German script. In reality, the so-called Gothic script consists of Schwabacher-Jewish letters. Just as they later took possession of newspapers, so the Jews living in Germany owned the printing offices at the introduction of printing and thus there came about the strong influx into Germany of Schwabacher-Jewish letters. Today the Führer… decided that Roman type [*Antiqua-Schrift*] is from now on to be designated as the standard letter [*Normal-Schrift*]. All printed products will be progressively changed over to this standard letter."

The order was clear: the Nazi Party had decided to change its typographic identity. The justification for this about-face was the alleged Jewish origin and ownership of Gothic lettering. According to people who have researched this issue, there is no historical basis for this allegation and it would appear to be a propagandistic manipulation of history. According to the wife of the leader of the Hitler Youth, "Hitler hated Schwabacher and himself designed the title of [the newspaper] *Völkischer Beobachter* in Roman letters."[57] The reason for the prohibition was probably related to the problems such script posed in countries where it had not been seen for centuries. The German armies were continuing to gain ground in early 1941, and the moment of their greatest expansion was close at hand. The Axis powers attained their largest territory in 1942, the year following Bormann's circular. Although Gothic script had remained relatively common in Germanic countries ever since the late Middle Ages (through handwriting and later typography), it had been progressively replaced by Roman typefaces since the late fifteenth century in other countries such as France, and had only appeared in countries such as Italy and Spain in its "round" form. Occupied countries were therefore unaccustomed and ill equipped to read this special script. Such a brake on reading and

534
German propaganda poster reassuring the French that "Under the SS Sign, You and Your European Comrades will Triumph," 1943.

535
Nazi poster, *Der Reichstag in Flammen* (The Reichstag in Flames), March 1933.

536
Setting up German street signs in Paris, c. 1942.

perception would certainly have raised problems for propaganda, as apparently confirmed by the final sentence of Bormann's circular: "By order of the Führer, Herr Reichsleiter Amann will first change over to the standard script those newspapers and magazines that already have a foreign distribution or whose foreign circulation is desired."

As suggested by the contradictory presence of blackletter typeface on the letterhead of this very circular, such a decision implied a colossal changeover of equipment that was difficult to execute. Just as Gothic writing had never been the sole script used by the National-Socialist Party in the 1930s, so it never completely disappeared from written and printed documents issued by Nazi authorities—late in 1944, Gothic lettering, henceforth "Jewish," was still being used on the letterhead of the Auschwitz concentration camp. Nevertheless, starting in 1941, other families of typeface began replacing blackletter in some of the Reich's typographic output. Printed material might use Roman, "Egyptian" (Mechanistic), or even sans serif faces. In 1942, the new, German-language street signs set up in Paris employed sans serif lettering. In Germany itself, whereas the production of new Gothic letterforms had continued throughout the 1930s, it suddenly fell prey to the prohibition—Gilgengart (the first typeface designed by Hermann Zapf), distributed by Stempel in 1941, vanished rapidly from circulation and was only put back on sale after the war was over.[58] For that matter, blackletter typeface would be employed less and less in Germany after World War II, even though it had been commonly used there since the thirteenth century.

Legal modernism and underground practices

As the fate of Gothic lettering shows, wartime imagery in Germany was primarily an extension of the graphic practices advocated by the regime in the 1930s. Although modernist design of the first third of the century was discouraged, it did not totally disappear from official production. For example, in the mid-1930s the government might commission graphic work in an avant-garde vein, such as the posters, catalog covers, and other documents designed by Herbert Bayer for Berlin exhibitions such as *Deutsches Volk Deutsche Arbeit* (German People, German Work, 1934, on which Joost Schmidt also collaborated), *Das Wunder des Lebens* (The Miracle of Life, 1935), and *Deutschland* (Germany, 1936). A leaflet by Bayer for this latter show combined photomontage with a Didot typeface that he himself developed in the first half of the 1930s. Inside was a short text printed in German, French, English, and Spanish. "The Führer speaks and millions listen to him. The working population, the peasants, and the regained right of self-defense are the supports of National-Socialist Germany." That same year saw Hans Vitus Vierthaler design the red and black poster for the Degenerate Art show in Munich, whose graphic appearance strongly resembled an El Lissitzky poster produced fifteen years earlier.[59] Yet whereas a certain number of officially produced graphics may have copied imagery associated with the avant-garde, the search for experimental letterforms, so keen in Germany of the 1920s (notably mixed typefaces or unique fonts), seems to have come to a halt. This raises the question of the relationship between the smallest, and theoretically most insignificant typographic sign—the letter—and the monumental and imposing dimension of dictatorial imagery. In Germany, as elsewhere, such imagery was presented above all as one of many forms within the realm of artistic output subject to ideological and political requirements. Totalitarian propaganda thus produced a rift in the use of signs and graphic supports, forcing all utopian, cultural, social, and commercial motivations to yield to politically or ideologically partisan requirements, thereby shutting down an entire sector of imagination, creativity, and expressiveness.

Over time, as official imagery developed its own strategies of communication and its own field of action, other practices nurtured new forms of underground, transgressive survival and existence (their illicit and dangerous nature probably explains our limited access to such phenomena). Clandestine graphics made it possible to express or communicate individual ideas or acts of resistance. Many documents and printed materials were improvised and cobbled together, often with modest resources or in difficult conditions. They arose from multiple needs, motives, and circumstances. For example, some documents were produced in illegal workshops, on behalf of the Resistance, as occurred in France and the Netherlands. Others were made by hand, such as the newspapers written by children in the Terezin concentration camp[60] between 1942 and 1944, yielding unique copies to be read collectively. Through a series of practices and applications as numerous as they were varied, wartime graphics seem to break down into several conflicting channels. Some were devoted to mass production in tune with belligerent governments: official, governmental, and, in some countries, dictatorial. Others served as an expression of struggle against those governments, against authoritarianism, repression and propaganda; they were produced with great difficulty, with no material security, and sometimes in the greatest vulnerability and destitution.

France

In a repeat of what occurred in Germany in the 1930s, France witnessed a massive exile of its intellectuals once the war started. The American Varian Fry notably organized the departure of some two thousand people, many of them well known, from the southern port of Marseilles.

And once a collaborationist government had been set up at Vichy, all graphic output had to serve that collaboration, when it wasn't directly imported by the Nazis themselves. But back in September 1939, the advent of war had been announced by a large poster calling for general mobilization (*Ordre de mobilisation générale*). The call came in the form of a large typographic page in black and white, with centered text beneath two crossed French flags in the patriotic colors of blue, white, and red. The text employed three distinct families of typeface: a very bold Didot, a sans serif face, and Mechanistic (Egyptian) letterforms, the main points being emphasized by uppercase letters. Everything suggests that no real graphic strategy was employed—the visual organization was nearly identical to the mobilization poster of 1914, and the approach to composition hardly differed from the official and royal announcements that had been printed and posted in France for centuries.

The establishment of the Vichy regime had a decisive impact on graphic production in France. Deciding in June 1940 that the war had been lost, Marshal Philippe Pétain asked the Germans for an armistice, which was signed north of Paris on the same spot as the German surrender at the end of World War I. He then set up a government in Vichy, a city in that part of France not under direct German military occupation. In July the French parliament granted him full powers, and Pétain became president of the French State, as it was styled. The principle of French collaboration with the German war effort was concluded at a meeting between Pétain and Hitler at Montoire on October 24, 1940. The meeting had been prepared by Pierre Laval, the vice-president of the new government and who would become increasingly influential by heading the ministries of information, of the interior, and of foreign affairs as of 1942. Right away the Vichy regime recognized the role of propaganda and began employing methods of mass communication. "Philippe Pétain... was the first leading French politician of the twentieth century to have generated such intense personal propaganda."[61] Extremely large budgets were allocated to propaganda, notably for producing posters. The Vichy government called upon many graphic designers and artists to translate its policies into images aimed at the French population. A group of professionals thus fulfilled the regime's communication needs. Among them were a few official graphic artists who enjoyed greater commissions. The commercial poster market dried up, and the visual universe of propaganda that replaced it underplayed collaboration with the Nazis and instead harped on Vichy's favorite themes and anathemas—posters thus tended to dwell on the personal cult of Pétain or to castigate Jews and communists (one poster dated 1943 was headed: "Behind Enemy Powers: Jews").

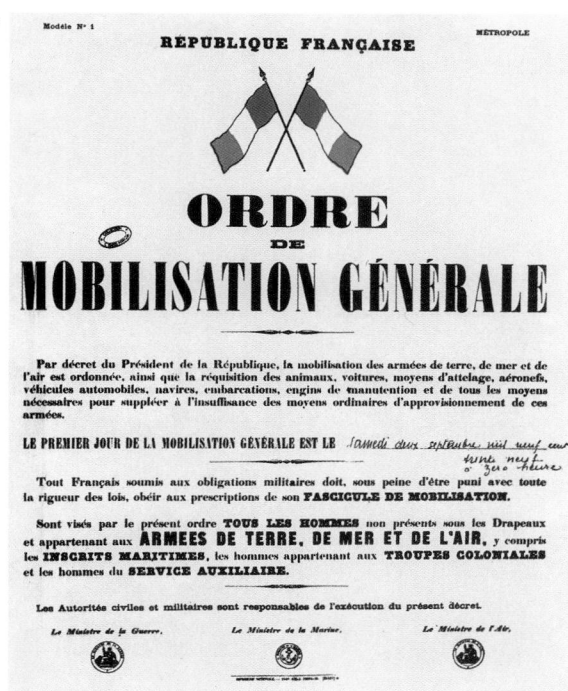

537
French government poster calling for military mobilization, hand-dated September 2, 1939.

The government's imagery was soon accompanied, in France, by the Nazis' own communication strategies. In 1940, the National-Socialists established their own propaganda office in France, called the Propaganda Staffel, which employed several hundred people and took control of a certain number of media organs and broadcast channels in the spheres of radio and press. (Part of the archives of this propaganda outfit would unfortunately be lost at the end of the war.) The Germans thus produced a large number of French-language posters. The slogans set the general tone, sometimes seeking to project a reassuring, welcoming dimension: *La puissance de l'Allemagne garante de sa victoire* (German Power Guarantees Victory), *Viens travailler en Allemagne* (Come Work in Germany), *Avec tes camarades européens sous le signe* SS *tu vaincras* (Under the SS Sign, You and Your European Comrades Will Triumph). Other printed announcements reflected the ambient tension. A "Notice" dated 1941 and signed by General von Stülpnagel announced the dissolution of the French Communist Party and decreed that "all Communist activity [is] outlawed in France" and would be punishable by death; the text appeared beneath the swastika and German eagle. Symbols and emblems occupied the high ground during this period of double propaganda—Nazi and Vichy—and typography was drafted into the war of symbols, down to individual letters: "There is a veritable battle over 'Vs.' The Germans... have raised big white flags everywhere, decorated with a monumental V, and they plastered red posters with a black V above the swastika... There are not many German Vs, but they're huge and they appear on public buildings, flags, and posters. Whereas the Vs of the Resistance are tiny, but countless—metro tickets folded in the form of a V, matches broken in the shape of a V, and so on."[62] Enormous Nazis Vs were hoisted onto the Eiffel Tower and spread across the upper part of the National Assembly building, underscored by a line of giant text, in capital letters, that read: *Deutschland siegt an* [or *auf*] *allen Fronten* (German Victory on Every Front). Furthermore, a poster magnified this V, which it presented as the sign of Germany's victory on all fronts, this phrase being set once again in uppercase letters (V, for that matter, had already been a part of the iconography of World War I).

When it came to the French themselves, official Vichy imagery was often the work of anonymous artists or was signed by little-known names. The major figures in French poster art of the interwar period suddenly vanished from the graphic landscape. Leonetto Cappiello died in 1942; Cassandre apparently gave up posters for set design and painting (and anyway, 1939 represented the end of his most enterprising works as poster artist); Charles Loupot retired to the provinces in 1940, probably for lack of work, and devoted himself primarily to painting until 1945 (although he does not seem to have remained entirely aloof from issues concerning professional organizations during the war).[63] Jean Carlu, who had left for the United States in 1940 to organize a *France at War* exhibition would remain there until 1953. (Carlu went to work for the US Office of War Information, producing a certain number of posters.) As a pacifist and anti-Nazi back in Paris in 1932, Carlu founded an Office of Graphic Propaganda for Peace, which that same year published his striking disarmament poster—*Pour le désarmement des nations*—that powerfully combined photomontage and geometric abstraction with typography. Paul Colin was one of the few major figures of that generation to design war-related posters in France: an early one (1939) for national defense bonds (*Emprunt de la défense nationale*); another one the following year, for the ministry of information, warning the population not to let the enemy overhear secret information (*Silence: l'ennemi guette vos confidences*); yet another for an event opposing dictatorship and war (*Journée internationale de la Résistance à la dictature et à la guerre*); and, towards the end, a poster designed when Paris was liberated in 1944 (untitled, marked *La Libération* on the dummy and later dubbed *La Marianne aux stigmates*). Colin had also designed some politically committed posters prior to the war, notably one in favor of the Spanish Republic and another condemning National-Socialism.

Although the best-known poster artists seemed to turn their backs on the Vichy regime, many graphic designers and illustrators did work for official organizations. The latter notably included, when it came to designing posters, Éric Castel, Michel Jacquot, Jean A. Mercier, René Peron, Bernard Villemot, and the Lyon-based collective of five illustrators, called the Alain-Fournier agency, founded in 1940 in conjunction with a local specialist in commercial posters. The collective presented itself thus: "We are determined to contribute our professional skills to the reconstruction of France... We have decided to publish, every month for a period of twelve months, two illustrated posters—one on work, the other on the family. ...[W]e feel our task would be facilitated by support from public authorities... [and] we are prepared to receive suggestions and to submit our proposals to the relevant departments."[64] Although the Alain-Fournier agency thus announced its willingness to collaborate with the regime in terms of visual communication, some of its illustrators would leave and later join the Resistance. One member of the team, Philippe Noyer, produced his very first poster, titled *Révolution nationale,* in the fall of 1940. It featured a drawn portrait of Marshal Pétain against a French flag; these two compositional elements (for which the military kepi serves as a linking device), occupy the entire upper part of the poster, while the remaining space at the bottom is filled with a rectangular block of capital letters spelling out the two words, "*Revolution nationale,*" one on top of the other. This poster, published by Vichy's General Secretariat for Information, enjoyed several print runs and swiftly reached the figure of several hundreds of thousands of copies. If reprintings in different formats—16 × 12 in., 48 × 32 in., 64 × 48 in.—are included, the threshold of one million posters was surpassed. The imperatives of propaganda not only called for reproductions in colossal quantities, they also encouraged wider dissemination through the use and adaptation of multiple media. For example, in September and October of 1940 several postcard versions of Pétain's portrait were printed in five million copies *each*. Similarly, on January 1, 1941, a large postage stamp of the marshal, still wearing his kepi, was produced in four million copies (a larger run having been prevented only by paper rationing).

Bernard Villemot was another graphic designer who worked for the Vichy government. The son of Jean Villemot and a student of Paul Colin, Villemot became famous after the war for his advertising posters for the Orangina soft drink and for Bally shoes. During the Occupation, he collaborated with the French State's official organizations for several years. In 1943, on behalf of the department of education and sport he designed a poster bearing the following text: "The athlete's oath: On my honor, I promise to practice sports with discipline, unselfishness, and loyalty, to better myself and to serve my country." That same year, Villemot designed a series of three posters based on the official motto of the French State, "Work, Family, Country," in which he combined photomontage and drawing. The third, on "Country," featured a portrait of Pétain, still wearing his kepi, who says: "Follow me! Put your trust in France everlasting!" Here the text, entirely uppercase, was composed around a central axis. Although Villement spent several years churning out such work, he would later produce graphics that supported the spirit of Resistance and anti-fascism—but only towards the end of the war, or shortly after.

Meanwhile, Maximilien Vox (whose real name was Samuel Monod) also collaborated with the Vichy regime (although in Vox's case, as in several others, this aspect of his career usually goes unmentioned). His sympathies are amply demonstrated by his persistent defense of "Latin writing," his professed nationalism, his publication of a book prefaced by Charles Maurras, and various documented sources including one asserting that "Maximilien Vox is collaborating fully."[65] Indeed, Vox reflected on and worked on various government-related projects. He wrote a chapter titled "The Graphic Arts" for a book called *Nouveaux destins de l'intelligence française* (New Futures for French Minds), in which he explained that "efforts at typographic renovation, which has been one of the healthiest aspects of the contemporary artistic movement, are now about to produce, thanks to the revamping of our institutions,

538
Jean Carlu, poster in support of
the Spanish Republic, 1937.
Photomontage.

539
Jean Carlu, poster *Pour le
désarmement des nations*
(For International Disarmament),
published by the Office de
Propagande Graphique pour
la Paix (created by Carlu in Paris),
1932. Photomontage.

540
Paul Colin, *Silence,* propaganda
poster warning against loose talk,
France, 1940.

541
Abram Games, *Your Talk May Kill
Your Comrades*, Great Britain, 1942.

542
Bernard Villemot, Vichy propaganda posters from the series on "Work, Family, Country," 1941 and 1943.

543
Philippe Noyer (Alain-Fournier collective), first version (November 1940) of the Vichy government poster calling for a "National Revolution" (later printed in various sizes and versions).

544
French version of a German poster, c. 1943, 23 1/2 × 32 1/2 in. (59.5 × 82.5 cm). An illustrated leaflet also covers the same themes.

results of national significance. At the request of Marshal Pétain's government, a department called the Office of Typographic Rationalization has been set up, its mission being to define an overall style for all material printed by the French State." Preceded by a fundamentally racist preface by Maurras, the book was published in 1942 by the regime's ministry of information and printed under the supervision of the Union Bibliophile de France, a publishing outfit founded by Vox himself in 1940. Like many others, Vox collaborated with Vichy for a limited time only—he joined the Resistance around 1943, the year his "typographical standards" for France's nationalized railroad were reissued, a charter first published in 1936 to standardize all material printed for the rail system. Vox was nevertheless one of the few leading figures in the graphic arts and typography whose collaborationist activities are well known.

In France, then, as elsewhere, all kinds of media, forms, and methods of printed production were mobilized, depending on needs and circumstances. Posters notably conveyed the themes and values for which the citizenry's support was sought: patriotism, loyalty to the supreme leader, courage, devotion, work, industry and farming, family, heroism, stoic motherhood, hygiene, health, physical condition, sports, and so on. And symbols, insignia, and attributes played a central role, as they also did elsewhere, in the form of repeated, immediately identifiable concepts, beginning with France's tricolor flag. In 1940, the Vichy government chose as its own emblem the Gallic fasces, with a double-headed axe. The symbols of German propaganda were also widespread in certain areas, notably the re-annexed region of Alsace, often crowned by a double emblem that combined the swastika with the German imperial eagle. Visual signs were displayed and disseminated everywhere, whether for purposes of collaboration, denunciation, or resistance. Jews were obliged to wear a yellow star sewn to their garments. "On May 29, 1942, a German decree stipulated that all Jews over the age of six had to wear the star in occupied French territory as of June 7, 1942.... The famous typeface founder Deberny & Peignot made the plates... [showing] the word 'Jew' in the middle of the star."[65] Meanwhile the double-barred cross known as the Cross of Lorraine, having become the symbol of the Free French, was banned as early as the month of December 1940. "Since the former general De Gaulle has chosen the Cross of Lorraine as his emblem, the Occupation Authorities have ordered that all Crosses of Lorraine be taken down immediately, wherever they appear."[67] As to "V" for victory, it was simultaneously used by the Nazis, De Gaulle, and the Resistance movements, which became particularly active in France, including among printshop workers. Damaging or defacing a poster became a form of expression and protest.

Actions and events by members of the Resistance, as well as all other kinds of illicit production or activity in the realm of graphic communication, became a means of expression in a period of repression, and today represent an important subject of study within the history of the graphic arts in times of crisis.

Great Britain

Whereas French war posters do not seem to display any specific graphic quality, the leading designers having remained aloof, in Great Britain and the United States major graphic artists were recruited by their respective governments. Britain's ministry of information, founded early in September 1939, was run from 1940 onward by Frank Pick, who had already made a reputation as an enlightened patron of the arts when he orchestrated the new designs for the London Underground system. Pick's ministry set up a department that specialized in public exhibitions, headed until 1943 by Milner Gray (who co-founded the Design Research Unit in London with Misha Black). Professional designers were recruited to help conceive such exhibitions. The ministry, the War Office, and the London branch of the US Office of War Information all commissioned top designers to guarantee high-quality printed material of all kinds for various places and uses, yet once again focusing on posters. Thus Abram Games, Ashley Havinden, Friedrich Heinrich Kohn Henrion and others made a major contribution to the development of the Allies' graphic imagery during the war.

545
Friedrich Heinrich Kohn Henrion, British propaganda poster, *Aid the Wounded*, published by the Committee for Soviet Aid, 1943–44.

As elsewhere, the authorities had specific ideas they wanted to convey to the general public. These ideas often overlapped from one country to another— posters urging people to be careful about giving away secret information flourished in Britain and the United States as well as in France. Games's impressive poster, *Your Talk May Kill Your Comrades* (1942) thus echoed Colin's French poster, *Silence...* (1940); another British poster warned that *Careless Talk Costs Lives* (1940). Americans, meanwhile, addressed this issue with the poster, *He's Watching You* (1942). In each instance, if in a different way, concise, expressive graphics produced a marked visual impact always designed to reach the beholder most efficiently. In addition to these calls for caution and discretion, British posters also urged patriotic citizens to contribute to industrial production (as did American posters and, for that matter, Soviet posters during the 1930s in an effort to support the Communist Party's five-year programs). People were also invited to contribute to the war effort in more personal ways: *Your Courage, Your Cheerfulness Will Bring Us Victory*. Propaganda posters were variously aimed at soldiers, women, workers, and plain passersby, all attracted, in turn, to these expressive images. Certain material constraints sometimes limited printed output—a lack of paper hit Britain particularly hard, not only during the war but afterward (just as clothing and food would continue to be in short supply long after victory).

The United States

The United States entered the war against the Axis powers somewhat later, after Pearl Harbor was attacked in December 1941. As occurred in other warring countries, government organizations in charge of information developed strategies of visual communication that induced them to turn to professional graphic designers and illustrators. Several government departments, including the Office of War Information, organized competitions and awarded targeted commissions, sometimes handling production and printing themselves. Like the British approach, American imagery displayed a concern for quality graphics and modern expressiveness (even if only applied to a certain proportion of overall output). Federal authorities called upon not only American artists but also Europeans resident in the United States—this appeal to various nationalities was a singular phenomenon within the general context. To varying degrees, American propaganda was the work not only of Norman Rockwell, Ben Shahn, Edward McKnight Kauffer, and John Atherton, but also of Jean Carlu, Leo Lionni, Herbert Matter, Joseph Binder, Henry Wolf, and Henry Koerner (who arrived from France, Italy, Switzerland, and Austria, respectively). The transatlantic migration of the 1930s created special circumstances in so far as some of the exiles had already carved out a space for themselves as teachers or designers, painters, architects, and graphic artists. Through them, the European avant-garde movements strengthened American connections that had already been initiated before the war. Such channels enabled European design of the interwar period to influence wartime imagery in the United States, right from 1941 onward. This influence can be seen in several well-known posters such as Joseph Binder's *Air Corps US Army*, Leo Lionni's *Keep 'em Rolling*, Herbert Matter's *American Calling*, and Carlu's *America's Answer! Production*.

Carlu's famous image was the winner of an official competition, and was printed in roughly one hundred thousand copies to be distributed in industrial plants and workplaces. Here typography, taking the form of picture-words, becomes a key element of composition, whereas many war posters stressed above all the figurative or symbolic image, assigning a secondary role to the space reserved for text. Following this initial breakthrough, Carlu began doing regular work for the Office of War Information, where he was also appointed an artistic advisor. Another Carlu poster, *Gift Packages for Hitler* (1943, executed for the Container Corporation of America), reveals his dexterity in handling montage and contrast of scales in an explicitly modernist idiom. Such a poster would have been unimaginable during World War I a quarter of a century earlier, if only for its use of photography. Like other designs, this poster shows the extent to which the spirit and resources of photomontage helped to transform graphic design by forging brand new visuals. In 1944, Carlu—still in the United States—produced a poster for France, to be distributed by American forces after the D-Day landing. Titled *Entre le marteau . . . et l'enclume* (Between Hammer and Anvil),[68] the image is composed of powerful symbols: a swastika in the middle is being crushed between a hammer composed of the British, American, French, and Soviet flags, while the anvil is struck with the Cross of Lorraine, symbolizing the French Resistance. The whole composition is organized around a central, vertical thrust, set between the two parts of the slogan running horizontally across the top and bottom of the poster (a technique already highly prized by the avant-gardes of the 1930s and largely borrowed by Nazi posters as well). Other designs stressed the impact of existing emblems or signs, vastly enlarged so as to constitute the focal point of attention. It was a competition like the one won by Carlu that spurred Joseph Binder in New York to design *Air Corps US Army*, in which the graphic composition transforms an airplane wing with Air Corps emblem into a nearly abstract composition that makes an extremely concise statement (whereas most propaganda imagery of the day relied on figurative imagery).

In the United States as in other countries at war, posters constituted a central tool of the propaganda effort, along with many other types of printed material such as leaflets, handbooks, catalogs, and so on. Some of these materials were even dropped from airplanes into foreign countries (an approach that recalls the Futurist tactic of throwing leaflets from planes, tall buildings, and cars). American propaganda posters came in a wide range of types and styles, many employing a register close to popular illustration, going so far as to produce an only slightly modified version of James Montgomery Flagg's famous *I Want You for the US Army* poster, already extensively used during the World War I. Other posters were more in step with avant-garde aesthetics, such as those by Lionni, Binder, and Carlu. America's wartime graphic idiom thus adopted various forms of expression. A modernist approach was disseminated and probably nurtured popular receptivity to a new kind of visual communication, which would enjoy significant expansion in the 1940s thanks to the work of Paul Rand, Lester Beall, Henry Wolf, Herb Lubalin, Bradbury Thompson, and many others.

546
Jean Carlu, American-produced poster destined for post D-Day France, (Between Hammer and Anvil), United States,1944, 3 ft. 11 in. × 2 ft. 6 in. (115 × 78.5 cm).

547
American-produced poster for liberated France (a similar one with the colors of the Belgian flag was produced for the liberation of Belgium), U.S. Office of War Information, 1944–45, 3 ft. 3 in. × 2 ft. 5 in. (100 × 76 cm).

548
Charles Coiner, American propaganda poster, *Give It Your Best!* published by the Office of War Information, Washington, 1942.

549
Jean Carlu, propaganda poster, *America's Answer! Production*, United States, 1941–42.

550
Leo Lionni, photomontaged propaganda poster, *Keep'em Rolling!* published by the Office for Emergency Management, 1941.

551
Albe Steiner, Italian underground poster
criticizing "Mussolini's war," 1943.

Despite the almighty authority of official imagery and its power for widespread propagation in public spaces, war-torn Europe nonetheless mounted reactions of protest, resistance, and opposition. Several mass media were employed to these ends, including leaflets, books, radio, and of course posters (which meant defacing or slashing official posters as well as producing new ones). Charles de Gaulle, of course, made his famous call for resistance on June 18, 1940, over the airwaves from his base in London; in refusing to accept defeat, he declared that, "whatever happens, the flame of French resistance must not be extinguished and will not be extinguished."[69] At the same moment, a typographic poster was printed, bearing the colors of the French flag and a heading that appealed "To All Frenchmen" (*À tous les Français*). The text itself began with the famous phrase—not actually uttered by De Gaulle on the radio—"France has lost a battle, but she has not lost the war!" Signed by De Gaulle, the poster urged the French to continue fighting the Axis powers (as had his radio speech). Classic in composition, this public notice was designed along the same graphic lines as the official call to general mobilization issued in September 1939. This "call to the French" proclaimed its identity through a pair of crossed flags at the top and through a patriotic blue-white-red border. The poster, distributed in London, was actually bilingual, with an English translation of the text appearing in the lower left. The written version corroborated the radio broadcast of June 18—although the French Resistance had few resources, it knew how to exploit those resources as efficiently as possible.

Graphic material began to be produced underground, often in modest printshops or with highly limited materials, as a reaction to established governments and their propaganda. Although this phenomenon was restricted not only by shortages of paper and by the risk inherent in such activities, expressions of resistance grew over time and adopted unusual channels. New groups sprung up to organize actions and publications. In Italy, the Netherlands, and France, movements coalesced to produce specific printed materials. Due to lack of means, many of these illicitly printed documents placed less emphasis on images and allocated greater importance to text. Symbols, emblems, and other effective signs nevertheless played a significant role, as they did in official documents, even though the types of subjects and values extensively promoted by established governments were incompatible with the spirit of the Resistance.

The Netherlands

The Dutch Resistance seems to have been particularly active when it came to producing material based on printing, typography, and the graphic arts. Invaded by Germany in May 1940, the Netherlands remained under German occupation until 1945. Artistic practices there came under the control of Nazi authorities, and the group known as the Netherlandish Organization of Artists (Nederlandse Organisatie van Kunstenaars), of which typographer Jean François van Royen was a member, was dissolved in 1942. Some well-known typographers and graphic artists continued to work in the Netherlands during the war, pursuing their personal oeuvre and joining the Resistance, a phenomenon that seems to have assumed unusual scope

552
A. A. Balkema, double-page spread from *Zehn kleine Meckerlein* (Ten Little "Indians"), an anti-Nazi rhyme smuggled out of a concentration camp, 1943.

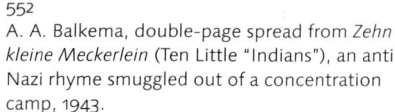

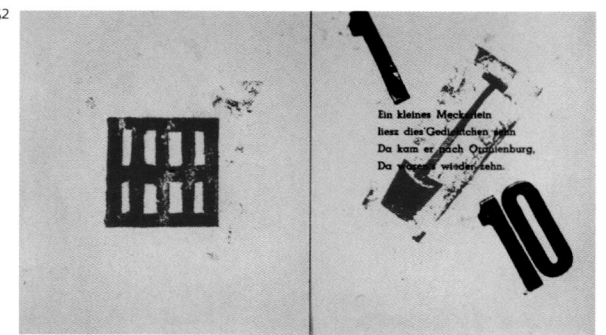

there. Between 1940 and 1945, clandestine (typo)graphic design and production generated extensive output, some of it significant. All kinds of media were used illicitly, ranging from the publication of literary texts to research into experimental effects. In several Dutch cities, small printshops remained active throughout the early 1940s—Amsterdam, Groningen, The Hague, Utrecht, and elsewhere. Often, conditions dictated highly limited print-runs, which therefore restricted the impact of distribution.

Some printed material appeared on the fringes of official publications, giving birth to contemporary aesthetic forms of visual culture incompatible with the occupier's expectations. In the sphere of literature, over one thousand clandestinely published

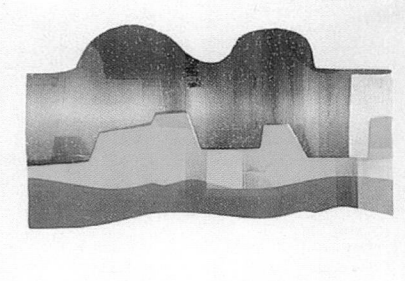

Holland

Boven mijn hoofd hebt gij uw lucht gebreid,
een hemel, rijk van zon en wijd van wind,
terwijl ik juichend door de ruimten schrijd,
of aan uw borst lig als een drinkend kind.

553
Hendrik Nicolaas Werkman, underground
publication of the poem, "Holland,"
the Netherlands, 1942.

554
Hendrik Nicolaas Werkman, cover for an
underground publication dedicated to
"the unknown soldier" who died in 1940,
the Netherlands, 1942.

555
Hendrik Nicolaas Werkman,*Gesprek*
(Conversation), cover of issue 9 of *De Blauwe
Schuit* magazine, Groningen, 1942.

books have been documented, which is a significant—and perhaps underestimated—number, given the production conditions. Some covers and title pages were designed by the likes of Hendrik Nicolaas Werkman, Friedrich Vordemberge-Gildewart, and Jan Bons. Other artists and designers known to be active in Dutch Resistance circles and the illicit circuit included Willem Sandberg, Otto Treumann (born in 1919, and usually associated with the postwar generation), and Wim Brusse. Working alone in Groningen, Werkman pursued his highly unusual experiments in typography, already begun in the interwar period. At the same time, Sandberg, now known for having headed the Stedelijk Museum after the war, was forging identity cards for members of the Dutch Resistance; yet he, too, pursued his autonomous graphic research during the war, notably via a series of eighteen *Experimenta Typographica*. Although Werkman and Sandberg were highly committed to such experimentation, this kind of work was risky and called for courage on the part of those who dared to pursue it. They were knowingly working against official, authorized culture, in order to carve out potential spaces of action and expression for themselves. Some of them were arrested and convicted for daring to express such attitudes, spending time in prison. Others paid with their lives—the typographer Jean François van Royen died in a concentration camp in 1942. Clandestine activity also cost the lives of certain printers, such as Frans Duwaer, who notably worked with several well-known designers. The same tragic fate awaited Hendrik Nicolaas Werkman, who had developed an original, avant-garde style in the 1920s; just when the country was on the verge of liberation, Werkman and his printshop were discovered on March 15, 1945. The next month he and nine other prisoners were shot by the Nazis, just a few days before Groningen and the rest of the Netherlands were liberated.

France

In France, the Resistance movement's graphic activities were directly related to the march of events. Initially irregular, output of illicitly printed documents increased significantly by the end of 1943. As in the Netherlands, this counter-production simultaneously covered rebellious pamphlets, small publications, clandestine literature, and so on. "In 1943, as the extent of the Maquis grew, intellectual resistance to the Germans underwent terrific development. Tons of paper, purchased and shipped thanks to marvelous courage and ingeniousness, were transformed into thousands of leaflets, brochures, poems, and news reports notably published by the 'Bibliothèque Française' in the southern zone."[70] Typographers and printers were particularly mobilized, despite the vast disproportion in resources available to them compared to state propagandists.

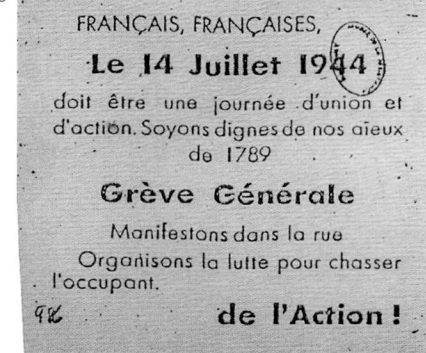

556
French underground leaflet calling for an uprising in 1944.

557
A Phoenix press in an underground printshop in Paris in the Champs de Mars quarter; the trapdoor giving access to the printshop was hidden by a piece of furniture. Photograph part of a series (reconstitutions) by Robert Doisneau, taken between the end of 1944 and the beginning of 1945 to illustrate the publication *Imprimeries Clandestines*, March 1945.

558
Poster featuring titles of underground newspapers, Algiers, 1943. 28 × 22 in. (71.5 × 55.5 cm).

Given those conditions, and probably also the risks involved, the Resistance produced relatively few posters, and those they printed were small in size. However, Jean Carlu designed two posters for the Free French in 1942. More common were other media such as roneotyped and printed leaflets, fliers, stickers, broadsheets, pamphlets, books, newspapers, and other printed material, usually text-based and frequently produced on modest equipment. Among other roles, these documents were often designed to coordinate the organization of public gatherings, strikes, protest movements, uprisings, and so on. As in the Netherlands, French printers, designers, typographers, and layout artists who worked for the Resistance, whether professional, amateur, or anonymous, were taking enormous risks. They might be arrested, imprisoned, and even sent to a concentration camp, as happened to Roger Lescaret, who began printing leaflets as early as 1940 and who was arrested, jailed, and sent to a camp, yet survived to take up his clandestine activities once he was freed.

When it came to printed material and imagery, resistance could take forms other than production. Defacing official imagery and the occupier's propaganda was another way of expressing opposition, one that required minimal resources. Many posters were thus defaced, slashed, or even subverted by graffiti. Autonomous graffiti also sprouted, scrawled in chalk on blank walls. Given tight monitoring by the occupier and the lack of legal methods for expression, alternative techniques had to be invented. Thus certain public notices were subject to entirely unanticipated rituals: "No sooner were announcements of death sentences posted than they were slashed. Police officers were therefore stationed nearby, but the police could hardly prevent Parisians from piously setting bouquets of flowers at the foot of the posters. In certain neighborhoods, flowers completely covered the pavement."[71] The defacing of posters became so widespread that the authorities adopted punitive measures. In January 1942, the Vichy regime decreed that the slashing of government posters would be punishable by a fine and prison. Although the context was highly specific, these strictures and restrictions distantly recall the ones that have targeted printed material throughout its history, testifying to the power of the medium, especially in the case of propaganda posters, here posited as irrefutable and untouchable. By attacking official posters, the destructive action of members of the French Resistance sought to desanctify the symbolic and public presence of the occupying forces. And in so doing, they were visibly demonstrating not only the role and importance of printed posters, but also their fragility.

559
Paul Colin, design for a poster, titled
La Libération, made during the Liberation
of Paris, 1944.

560
Paul Colin, printed version of the same poster,
untitled (but known as *La Marianne aux
stigmates*, Marianne with Stigmata) August 17,
1944.

Graphic arts faced with requisitioning and restrictions

World War II represented a new phase in the history of typography and graphic design, one that was significant, expressive, tragic. The authority and power of visual communication were once again asserted. Although some forms of modernist expression were tolerated by state propaganda, the period 1939–45 seems to have quashed the principle of graphic experimentation that had driven and enlivened the avant-garde movements of preceding decades. Such practices became extinct in certain places, converting themselves into a tool of propaganda. Some designers, in radically varying contexts and either in a personal capacity or in response to official commissions, nevertheless managed to continue working in a vein consistent with their earlier efforts, as witnessed by experiments in typography and publishing in the Netherlands, plus commissions from Allied governments to well-known professionals such as Abram Games, Friedrich Heinrich Kohn Henrion, Jean Carlu, Herbert Matter, Joseph Binder, and others. At the same time, another whole range of graphic output remained more conventional yet still exploited its ability to make an impact. Within such imagery, typography and graphic design would underscore a given facet dictated by political and ideological goals laid down by a government, indeed a dictatorship. Governments and imperatives made their presence felt visually through posters, emblems, and slogans. World War II amplified the scope and intensity of mass communication. Messages might be conveyed through the press, over the airwaves, via exhibitions, through demonstrations and parades, by rhetorical speeches, by monumental inscriptions, by frequent posters, and so on. The (typo)graphic aspect of communications thus came to occupy a key place in the public sphere. Leaders, dictators, governmental organizations, and military chiefs swiftly seized control of these means (long before war was actually declared, when it came to Italy and Germany). In striking proof of this power, letterforms themselves were sometimes put into play, from Mussolini's vast façade covered with the single word *Si* to the gigantic letter V displayed in France by the victorious occupier, not to mention formations of humans lying on the ground to create giant capital letters. Furthermore, the fate of blackletter typefaces under Hitler provided dramatic proof of the stakes invested in typography, as well as the concepts potentially projected onto it.

Typography and graphic design were thus extensively redirected and channeled. In certain instances they came under strict control from conception to display or use. It was not until the war was over that the graphic arts recovered their vitality, their freedom of expression, and their raison-d'être in normal peacetime activities—business, industry, culture, publishing, logos, signage, and so on.[72] Once the grip was loosened, the second half of the twentieth century permitted a phenomenal new blossoming and revival of (typo)graphic expressiveness and activities. The ruptures and repressions of the 1930s and early 1940s were replaced by a renewed dynamism and intense diversification in creativity that had long been suppressed (see notably the "visual jokes" in postwar posters). Histories of typography and design often pass quickly over the graphic idiom and visual propaganda associated with periods of war, or indeed ignore them altogether (as often exemplified by encyclopedia entries, biographies, and even exhibitions on given designers). Yet from every standpoint, such imagery belongs—*de facto* and *de jure*—to that history, often revealing and underscoring certain fundamental aspects of it. Furthermore, such graphic works function as important gears of transmission and transition: often produced during pivotal periods, they make it possible to recognize "before" and "after." The static graphic images of the two world wars, literally part of the international dimension of those respective conflicts, bear in themselves the specific mark of the twentieth century (whereas, at the dawn of the third millennium, during this new era of massive, instantaneous transmission of information on a planetary level, a medium such as the poster probably no longer draws the eye in the way it did just fifty years ago). Finally, when it comes to the human level, far from any artistic considerations, we should not forget that, during times of war, any work in typography, printing, or graphic design outside of official channels could lead to a loss of liberty, indeed of life.

NOTES

1 "Fascisme," *Le Petit Robert 2* (Paris: Dictionnaires Le Robert, 1980), 640.

2 Ibid., 640.

3 M. Jimenez, *Qu'est-ce que l'esthétique?* (Paris: Gallimard, 1997), 354.

4 P. Fleury, *Les Feuillets,* (Paris: École Nationale Supérieure des Arts Décoratifs, 1994), IV.

5 J.–M. Palmier, *Weimar en exil* (Paris: Payot, 1988), 1: 9–10.

6 The book-burnings organized by the Nazis notably included Tucholsky's titles. He committed suicide in exile in 1935.

7 Adolf Hitler, *My Struggle,* trans. anon., vol.1, chap. 10, accessed in November 2005 at http://www.hitler.org/writings/Mein_Kampf.

8 Quoted by A. Rowley, "Nazisme et culture," in Jacques Bertoin, *L'Art dégénéré* (Paris, 1992), 29.

9 Hitler, *My Struggle,* vol 1. chap. 6. op. cit.

10 Within the context of the history of book publishing, printing, and typography, the burning of these books recalls the censorship that occasionally cost Humanist printers their lives during the Renaissance—Antoine Augerau was sentenced to be burned at the stake on Place Maubert in Paris in 1534, while Étienne Dolet was hanged, then burned on the same spot in 1546—not to mention the fate reserved for certain typesetters and printers who operated secret presses during World War II (Frans Duwaer and Hendrik Nicolaas Werkman).

11 L. Richard, *Encyclopédie du Bauhaus* (Paris: Aimery Somogy, 1985), 127.

12 Philippe Dagen, "Il y a 70 ans, le bref été du Bauhaus," *Le Monde* (Sept. 19–20, 1993), 2.

13 "Architecture et Etat au XXᵉ siècle," *Encyclopaedia Universalis* (Paris, 1996), 2: 876.

14 Jan Tschichold, "Glaube und Wirklichkeit" (1946), reprinted in *Typografische Monatsblätter. RSI 1* (1995), 10.

15 The similarities between these two posters have been established by both historians and poster specialists. See, for example, L. Ferverau, *Terroriser, manipuler, convaincre! Histoire mondiale de l'affiche politique* (Paris: Somogy, 1996), 75 and 77.

16 Hitler, *My Struggle,* vol. 1, chap. 10. op. cit.

17 Quoted in Bertoin, *L'Art dégénéré,* 69.

18 Ibid., 140.

19 Christopher Burke, *Paul Renner: The Art of Typography* (London: Hyphen Press, 1998), 148. The American artist Sam Maitin (now deceased), who had met with Bayer and discussed the subject with him, reported that Bayer claimed he never worked for the Nazi regime (personal interview, 2002).

20 Some sources vary the name of Hans Schweitzer, one author spelling it Schweitze, another giving him the first name of Franz.

21 G. Badia (ed.), *Histoire de l'Allemagne contemporaine* (Paris: Messidor/Éditions sociales, 1987), 308.

22 Similarly, "the minister of propaganda encouraged the production and distribution of a 'people's radio' …that could only receive broadcasts from the main German stations… and not from foreign broadcasters. In 1933 alone, 1,500,000 of these inexpensive radios were sold." Badia, *Histoire de l'Allemagne contemporaine,* 307.

23 Friz Helmut Ehmcke, quoted by Y. Schwemer-Scheddin, "Broken Images," in P. Bain and P. Shaw (eds), *Blackletter: Type and National Identity* (New York: The Cooper Union for the Advancement of Science and Art, 1998), 59. Some of the information in this major source of typography under National-Socialism has been used here; equally valuable is chapter six of Burke, *Paul Renner: The Art of Typography.*

24 Rudolf Koch, quoted by H. P. Williberg, "Fraktur and Nationalism," in Bain and Shaw, *Blackletter,* 43.

25 "Fascisme," *Le Petit Robert 2,* 640.

26 M. Palla, *Mussolini et l'Italie fasciste* (Paris: Castermann/Giunti, 1993), 87.

27 The *Fasci Italiani di Combattimento* was a grouping that Mussolini organized in order to launch the Fascist movement.

28 Giovanni Lista, "Depero et le futurisme," *Revues de Depero, 1931–1933: Numero unico* (Paris: Éditions Jean-Michel Place, 1979), 9–10.

29 According to Palmier, *Weimar en exil,* 46.

30 Giovanni Anceschi, cited in G. Iliprandi, *Languaggio grafico* (Milan: Editoriale A–Z, 1966), 18.

31 Founded by Charles Peignot in 1927, *Arts et métiers graphiques* was published in France up till 1939.

32 A. Rossi, *Campo grafico 1933–1939* (Milan: Electa, 1983), 9.

33 Ibid., 10.

34 Quoted by S. Zadora in S. Fauchereau (ed.), *Moscou 1900–1930* (Paris: Seuil, 1988), 103.

35 P. Cabanne, *L'Art du vingtième siècle* (Paris: Aimery Somogy), 95.

36 Yakov Tugendkhold, quoted in E. Barkhatova, *Affiches constructivistes russes* (Paris: Flammarion/Moscow: Avant-Garde, 1992), 7.

37 Zadora, in Fauchereau, *Moscou 1900–1930,* 103 and 106.

38 R. Lomme, "La formation du modèle soviétique," *Encyclopaedia Universalis,* vol. 21 (Paris, 1995), 145.

39 Barkhatova, *Affiches constructivistes russes,* 8–9.

40 These slogans are all found in Barkhatova, *Affiches constructivistes russes.* op. cit.

41 A. Baudin, *Les Arts plastiques et leurs institutions* (Bern: Peter Lang, 1997), 2.

42 Investment in the printing industry continued throughout the twentieth century, ranging from photocomposition to computer technology.

43 Quoted in Krisztina Passuth, *Moholy-Nagy* (Lonon: Thames & Hudson, 1985), 61.

44 The Armour Institute would later become the Illinois Institute of Technology.

45 In 1949 the School of Design, renamed Institute of Design, merged with the Illinois Institute of Technology.

46 Quoted in S. Heller, "[Sutnar]," *Eye* 13 (1994), 47.

47 Note the similarities with the careers of Agha and Brodovich.

48 *Who's Who in Graphic Art* (Zurich: Amstutz & Herdeg Graphis Press, 1962), 438.

49 In the final decades of the twentieth century and the early years of the twenty-first, typographic posters still represented a major part of the oeuvre of Swiss poster artist Niklaus Troxler, some of whose work has been purchased by the Museum of Modern Art in New York.

50 On Bellmer's political posters, see *Typografische Monatsblätter,* RSI 3, (2001), 1–11.

51 *Dictionnaire Bénézit,* volume II (1976), 35.

52 Quoted in R. McLean, *Jan Tschichold: Typographer* (London: Lund Humphries, 1990), 69.

53 First quotation from Jan Tschichold, *Typographische Gestaltung,* cited in E. M. Gottschall, *Typographic Communications Today,* (Cambridge, Mass./London: MIT Press, 1989), 41; second pasage from Jan Tschichold, "Qu'est-ce que la nouvelle typographie et que veut-elle?" in *L'Image des mots* (exh. cat., Paris: APCI / Centre Georges Pompidou / Alternatives, 1985), 113–114.

54 First published in English in 1967 as *Asymmetric Typography.*

55 Both of these anonymous posters are reproduced in M. Gallo, *L'Affiche: Miroir de l'histoire, miroir de la vie* (Paris: Robert Laffont, 1989), 188.

56 Excerpts from the Martin Bormann circular are quoted in French (in "L'image a besoin de caractères," proceedings of the symposium, *Typografische Monatsblätter.* RSI/Érb-a Valence 5 (1999), 3 (ill. nº. 8), trad. P. Keller. Schwabacher is a late Gothic typeface that appeared around 1480 and subsequently became very widespread. The term *Antiqua-Schrift* in Bormann's circular, denoting the typeface that was to replace Schwabacher, is generally translated in English as "Roman." For an English translation of the circular letter, see Bain and Shaw, *Blackletter…,* 48.

57 Henriette von Schirach, from a letter to *Die Zeit* (1976), quoted in P. Luidl, *Die Schwabacher: Den Schwabacher Judenlettern auf der*

Spur (no city or publisher, 2002), 54.

58 P. Shaw, "The Calligraphic Tradition in Blackletter type," *Scripsit* (Summer 1999), vol. 22: nos. 1 and 2; on Gilgenart, see pages 33 and 36. Much later, Hermann Zapf would design the famous Zapf Dingbats (1978), now commonly used in digital technology.

59 See note 15 above.

60 Northwest of Prague, Czech Republic.

61 L. Gervereau, *Un siècle de manipulations par l'image* (Paris: Somogy, 2000), 89.

62 J. Guéhenno, *Journal des années noires* (July 25 and August 17, 1941), quoted in S. Marchetti, *Affiches 1939–1945* (Lausanne: Edita, 1982), 66.

63 See M.-E. Chessel, *La Publicité: Naissance d'une profession* (Paris: CNRS, 1998), 210. The published material on Loupot generally indicates that he did little work as a graphic artist during the war.

64 Marchetti, *Affiches 1939–1945*, 14.

65 Catherine Bédarida, "La guerre de cinq ans des graphistes de Vichy et de la Résistance," *Le Monde* (February 11, 2000), 27.

66 Michel Wlassikoff, *Signes de la collaboration et de la Résistance* (Paris: Autrement, 2002), 104.

67 Order issued to local mayors by the deputy prefect of Boulogne in December 1940, quoted by A. Apaire and B. Sinais, "La série 'Francisque'," *Timbres Magazine* (January 2001), 46.

68 As in English, the French expression "caught between hammer and anvil" means being exposed to blows from both sides.

69 Quoted in Marchetti, *Affiches 1939–1945*, 55.

70 Forestier, according to notes by Claude Morgan, quoted in R. Chatelain, "Les typos de la Résistance," *Typografische Monatsblätter. RSI* 5 (1998), 9.

71 Madeleine Gex-Leverrier, quoted in Marchetti, *Affiches 1939–1945*, 56.

72 A peacetime context obviously doesn't automatically exclude the possibility of compromise, manipulation, disinformation, exploitation, or submission to ideological, political, and economic constraints. On this subject see, for example, Gervereau, *Un Siècle de manipulations...*; M. Lavin, *Clean New World: Culture, Politics, Graphic Design* (Cambridge, Mass.: MIT Press, 2001); P. Jobling and D. Crowley, *Graphic Design: Reproduction and Representation since 1800* (Manchester/New York: Manchester University Press, 1996); and P. Fresnault-Deruelle, who states in *L'Image placardée: Pragmatique et rhétorique de l'affiche* (Paris: Nathan, 1997), that "as soon as images acknowledge manipulation, they become the theater of semiotic and rhetorical machinations that invite appearances to come to the aid of the sensory impressions affecting us" (88).

Part 5
Contents

Postwar economic boom

Characteristics and horizons

"Today everything is stylistically allowable."

Karl Gerstner[1]

A fresh start—eclecticism, professionalism, connections

The aftermath of World War II spawned a renaissance in graphic design free from the demands of wartime propaganda—whether ideological, political, or militaristic. Depending on context and strategy, such propaganda had been defensive or offensive in tone, protective or hostile, reassuring or alarming, celebratory or spiteful, invigorating or insistent. Once the war ended, however, graphic creativity could reenter the circuits of economic production, readopting the pattern of commissions and orders from business, industry, institutions, and cultural entities. Sociopolitical upheavals and the launch of the "postwar economic boom" allowed graphic design to make a fresh start, even as it revived connections with certain avant-garde movements of the interwar period. The year 1945, which saw the deaths of Hitler, Goebbels, and Roosevelt, thus seems to be another pivotal date in the history of graphic design. Although war did not bring a halt to typography and the graphic arts, it obliged them to withdraw from their usual spheres and to adopt an active role in the international conflict; this transition occurred in a particularly marked way in certain countries such as Germany and France. With the collapse of the Third Reich, the graphic arts could return to their modern ways and designers could recover the maneuvering room they had lost in the early 1930s due to major perturbations caused first by exile and then by war. Along the way, World War II shed light on one crucial phenomenon, namely the behavior of typographers and graphic designers when they suddenly found themselves confronted with an extreme political situation, given that their skills and profession made them particularly useful in the sphere of visual propaganda.[2]

561

561
Saul Steinberg, untitled, originally published in *The New Yorker,* July 29, 1961. Ink on paper.

After having traversed—and left its mark upon—a particularly dark period of history, graphic design would experience a thorough change in situation in the decades following the war. Strong economic growth in the United States and Western European countries was probably the leading factor in the resurgence and stimulation of the graphic arts in the latter half of the century. Yet this factor was soon joined by sweeping technological changes that led to the demise of movable metal type some five hundred years after Gutenberg (and just three decades before the digital revolution). The period that was dawning thus produced highly shifting attitudes toward graphic practices. Designers of the early decades of the twentieth century clearly flaunted their social or political priorities (whether utopian or idealistic), displayed great interest in a multidisciplinary approach, were open to experimentation, and were willing to reflect upon the role of technology and mechanization (clearly visible in the forms they adopted),[3] indeed they often expressed spiritual goals or took an oppositional stance (often from the standpoint of trying to build a new society). The postwar graphic idiom would tend to embrace not only mass production but also the development of certain spheres of design—signage, for instance—all the while retaining a concern for quality and an awareness of its own rich history. The consumer-society economy would offer considerable, and sometimes highly original, opportunities for work in the realms of advertising, graphic design, and typography. The phenomenon was particularly noticeable in the United States, where the boom in mass media, art, and culture increased the sources of influence on which graphic style could draw. A

306

562
Armin Hofmann, poster for a Henry
Moore/Oskar Schlemmer exhibition at the
Kunsthalle, Basel, 1955. Linocut, 4 ft. 2 in. × 3 ft.
(128 × 90 cm).

563
Henryk Tomaszewski, poster for a Henry Moore
exhibition, 1959. 2 ft. 1 ¹/₂ in. × 3 ft. 1 in.
(65 × 94 cm).

great number of factors thus fed into the visual expression of the day, reinforcing its
ubiquitous presence: strong industrial and economic growth, a striking rise in advertising, an
unrivaled volume of printed output, the development of television as a mass medium (in the
1950s and 1960s), and the movies—all against a background of the steadily accelerating pace
of the perception of time in society.

On the threshold of the second half of the twentieth century, during a brief period between
the numerous and highly varied disruptions of the previous decades and the consolidation of a
propitious new environment, typography and graphic design adopted and adapted to
changing rhythms, protean applications, and increasing professionalization. Indeed, graphic
design seems to have become an autonomous art at this time. Whereas much previous
(typo)graphic experimentation had been the work of versatile artists seeking tentative links to
industry (at least the emergent sector of industry that valued artistry), the significance of
graphic design became henceforth widely accepted in the world of business, industry, and
administrative institutions. In striking fashion, companies and cultural institutions began
expressing a strong concern for their visual image and for graphic communication (a concern
that became even more intense in the latter half of the century). As also occurred in the
nineteenth century on the heels of the Industrial Revolution, the media and supports available
to typography and graphic design enjoyed a famously expansive and diversified phase that
continually highlighted their new potential. This expansion was closely related to the
economy, the media, and technology—in the United States, for example, an ongoing boom in
the magazine trade reinforced a desire for expressiveness, modernity, and graphic quality.

On the technical level, one fundamental culmination in the realm of typography occurred
right at the end of the war.[4] The "letters of light" made possible by the system of
phototypesetting—or photosetting—represented a decisive break with Gutenberg's method,
thereby rendering the whole process of typesetting and printing much more flexible and less
cumbersome.[5] Although the use of machines had already accelerated and mechanized the old
method of hand-setting considerably, the arrival of photosetting removed distinct material
weight from the system of reproducing text: a simple photosensitive support could henceforth
replace all those metal letters and all the cases for storing them, even as it eliminated the work

564
Herbert Leupin, poster for Suze (aperitif), 1955.

of redistributing letters in cases for subsequent manual setting. The new system would itself prove temporary, however, since in a matter of decades it would be replaced by computer technology.

Apart from its renewed contact with technical possibilities and economic opportunities, postwar graphic design inherited an impressive avant-garde past and grew up in a highly stimulating artistic context. It situated itself in a direct line with the movements of the early part of the century—Cubism, Expressionism, Futurism, Dada, Constructivism, De Stijl, the Bauhaus, and New Typography (with their various methods of collage, photomontage, "typophoto," and typo-photomontage, and their techniques of editing, structuring, and destructuring). All these still-vibrant traditions provided a terrific launching pad for creative graphics. When it came to typography and graphic design, the example of early twentieth-century attitudes simultaneously encouraged a broad acceptance of technology and industry, a reevaluation of craft methods, an affirmation of the links with mass production, a constant search for an aesthetic dimension, a determination to contribute to human well-being and lifestyle, and the pursuit of ever-greater modernity in everyday forms. These trends, added to the legacy of tradition, created a heterogeneous base conducive to a revival of the artistic interconnections disrupted by authoritarian coercion and wartime oppression. The postwar artistic landscape, then, by reinventing these sources of creative design, had the effect of nurturing new ramifications in art and new growth in design, yielding Abstract Expressionism, the Cobra group, Art Brut, Art Informel, geometric abstraction, Op Art, kinetic art, Pop Art, and later artist's book, and so on. Such concepts, themes, and concerns as the exploration of the notion of movement, the liberation of the physical gesture of making art, the wholesale acceptance of advertising and media imagery, and the mechanical reproducibility of artworks were all shared by (typo)graphic artists. The latter continued to cross boundaries and to assert their transnational dimension (as witnessed by the movement called the International Typographic Style), thereby following in the footsteps not only of the restless avant-garde movements of earlier decades but also in those of certain forms of nineteenth-century modernism, notably Art Nouveau.

AGI, ATypI, and Icograda: the role played by associations

The new development and changes in typographic art were accompanied by the founding of new organizations and associations of graphic designers. What characterized these groups was their international scope and their increasing professionalization. The plan to set up the Alliance Graphique Internationale (AGI) was drawn up in Paris in 1951 at the initiative of three Frenchmen (Jean Colin, Jacques Nathan-Garamond, and Jean Picart le Doux) and two Swiss (Donald Brun and Fritz Bühler), all of whom had met in Basel. The association, which was contemporaneous with the Aspen International Design Conference in Colorado, was incorporated and registered in Paris in November 1952. Its goal was to support high-quality graphic design through various means—exhibitions, publications, annual meetings of members, and so on. Right from 1952, the association's original statutes stipulated that, "The goal of the Association is to enable member artists to defend the material, moral, and legal interests of the profession of graphic arts by: 1) creating contacts and cultivating friendships between artists of different countries who share aesthetic affinities and who have an international reputation in the realm of applied graphic arts; 2) contributing, in collaboration with local organizations in each country, to the advancement of the profession and the protection of its interests...; 6) organizing exhibitions of the graphic arts, in each member country in turn, in order to promote the work of artists from neighboring countries...; 8) potentially publishing a bulletin, in three or four languages, that will bring the goals and activities of the Association to the

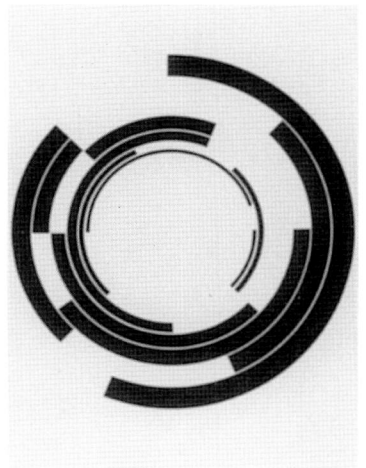
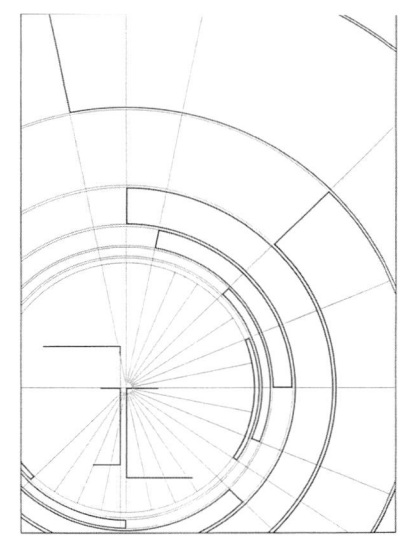

565

beethoven

tonhalle grosser saal
dienstag, den 22. februar 1955,
20.15 uhr
4. extrakonzert
der tonhalle-gesellschaft

leitung carl schuricht
solist wolfgang schneiderhan

beethoven ouverture zu «coriolan», op. 62
violinkonzert in d-dur, op. 61
siebente sinfonie in a-dur, op. 92

vorverkauf tonhalle-kasse, hug, jecklin,
kuoni
karten zu fr. 3.50 bis 9.50

565
Josef Müller-Brockmann, studies and designs for
a poster for a concert at the Tonhalle in Zurich,
1955. Sketches, grid, and printed poster.

awareness of graphic design professionals."[6] These goals and concerns testify to a desire for cultural exchange and communication that is clearly a direct heir to the avant-garde spirit and ambiance. From an entirely different standpoint, the fact that this text, written in post-war Paris, immediately mentioned the "moral and legal interests" of the profession inevitably resonates, if only indirectly, with the shift in direction and practice of certain designers on behalf of wartime propaganda.

After the AGI was founded, another wide-ranging, international organization appeared on the scene. Also established in the 1950s, it was yet another Franco-Swiss initiative. The Association Typographique Internationale (ATYPI) was founded in Lausanne, Switzerland, in 1957 by Charles Peignot.[7] Devoted exclusively to typography, the organization sought to promote creative quality in the field of lettering and typeface design, also addressing the issue of legal protection. And it still brings together industry leaders, experts, and professionals every year. It was ATYPI, for that matter, that official adopted in 1962 the typeface classification system known as Vox-ATYPI, initially composed of nine families of face as proposed by Maximilien Vox, plus two further families that were added at the time of official acceptance.[8] This classification constituted a significant development, pursuing the idea suggested by Francis Thibaudeau in 1921 and testifying to the need for consistent nomenclature in the face of ever-increasing diversification.

Sharing the same international aspirations as the AGI and ATYPI was the International Council of Graphic Design Associations (Icograda), founded in London in 1963. This new association was behind the idea of promoting quality, techniques, and professional skills and exchanges through a major series of publications, seminars, and conferences. It brought together many existing associations and institutions devoted to graphic design and visual expression.[9] Within the space of a decade, then, three major professional organizations were launched— AGI, ATYPI, and Icograda—all of which have continued to thrive and grow for roughly the past fifty years. One crucial, noteworthy point is that all three henceforth incorporate non-Western practices, demonstrating that t his movement can transcend traditional geographic boundaries and can reach out to other cultures.

566

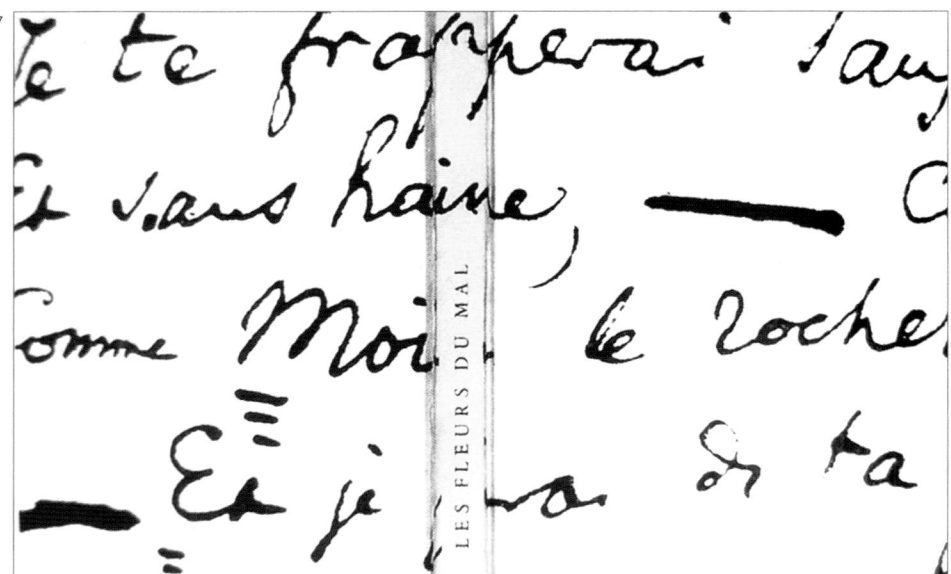

567

566
Franco Grignani, poster for Alfieri & Lacroix
(publisher of art books, based in Milan),
1967–68.

567
Pierre Faucheux, binding for Baudelaire's *Les
Fleurs du mal*, 1948.

568
Herb Lubalin and Tom Carnase, logotype for
Mother & Child, a proposed magazine that was
never published, United States, c. 1965

568

M⊕THER

New burst of creativity

The determination to organize, structure, and valorize skills and practices contributed to a growing professionalization of typography and graphic design in the postwar period. And this trend was accompanied by a new burst of creativity. Early in that period, experimentation in the realm of graphics occurred in many countries and in extremely diversified contexts and ways. Graphic design enjoyed significant development in the United States, Switzerland (where the war had not halted previous practices), Poland, the Netherlands, France, Germany, and Italy. The Soviet Union, however, was henceforth mired in socialist realism and strict surveillance, and so remained generally aloof from these developments. In the West, however, the spirit of the prewar avant-garde was revived and eclecticism was again on the agenda, visibly present in practice as well as in sources of inspiration. In 1956, not long before Karl Gerstner proclaimed that, "today everything is stylistically allowable" (1963), British designer Ashley Havinden, whose career dated back the 1930s, perceived and described the situation as such: "To solve each problem the mature designer will draw on any period of expression, and will mix these periods if necessary—if, by so doing, the aptness, speed, and conviction of communication are thereby enhanced. His sole criterion is his own good taste and artistic integrity towards his work. He feels free to draw on classical antiquity; Bauhaus functionalism; eighteenth-century symmetry; Renaissance realism; Cubist experimentation; early Victorian quaintness; Surrealist dream images; engineering blueprints; the space divisions of abstract art and modern architecture; the typography of the fifteenth century; X-ray photography; wood engravings; statistical diagrams; the new typography of Tschichold; fantastic decorated display letters, etc., etc."[10]

While many of the historical avant-garde practices in typography and graphic design were spawned in central and Eastern Europe, their offspring seemed to migrate to vaster, more dispersed realms. The diversification of expressive idioms in a fairly distinct spatio-

310

temporal sequence (defined by a succession of "-isms") gave way to post-war practices that emerged everywhere, simultaneously, and insisted on a great freedom of expression. Every country and every region seemed to offer specific possibilities for the historical development of graphic design, depending on the immediate effects of the war, the economic situation after the war, local developments in other arts (notably painting), attitudes toward earlier trends, and the individual designers actually working on the spot. In the early 1950s, graphic developments observable in the United States, Switzerland, Poland, or France, for example, reflected practices that no longer seem influenced so much by neighboring trends as by national, indeed local, factors (New York, Zurich, Basel, Paris, San Francisco, etc.). At the same time, there coexisted approaches that might be complementary (as explicitly demonstrated by Swiss and Polish practices), or divergent, or even diametrically opposed. Graphic designs were being invented and reinvented from extremely varied repertoires that became uncategorizable. A graphic landscape composed of hybrid elements in constant movement was henceforth surfacing in the West, inspired by varied, composite sources, and ultimately impossible to summarize or clearly categorize, yet nevertheless including phenomena such as the International Typographic Style, Polish poster art, American (typo)graphic expressionism, the Swiss school, notions of corporate identity, concepts of system and integral design, signage, artists' posters, joke posters, publishing experiments (books and periodicals), popular graphics, psychedelic graphics, punk graphics, and so on. Graphic expression during the post-war economic boom was generally most closely linked to the commercial context, only to a lesser extent reflecting individual artistry (in terms of critical comment, social commitment, political conviction, or the urge for transdisciplinary experimentation), at least until the advent of the protest movements of the 1960s.

Creativity and trends country by country

The United States

The United States, especially New York and the west coast, became a major center of typography and graphic design in the 1950s and 1960s. Like Switzerland, which had remained aloof from World War II, the United States offered favorable terrain for visual expression. The country emerged from the war having suffered fewer human and material losses than did its European counterparts. President Harry Truman claimed that the United States would enter the post-war world as the most powerful nation in history.[11] The post-war economic boom, with its business expansion, audiovisual explosion (with the swift spread of television in the 1950s), and generalized growth resulted in steady commissions for graphic work. As in Europe, graphic design tended to become an autonomous field and an increasingly professional trade, as witnessed here and there by the founding of professional associations, by the nature and volume of commissions, and by increasingly specialized training.[12] Given this context, certain media and certain graphic forms stood out, such as magazines, advertising, and corporate imagery, to which should be added typeface design.

Composite landscapes

While the interwar period accentuated a sharp juxtaposition of trends and influences (resulting, along the way, in the European exile of the 1930s), and while wartime graphics in the United States maintained a modern outlook, the subsequent period was notable for its sustained diversification of sources and practices (which also occurred in many other countries). The middle of the twentieth century was characterized by an unusual heterogeneity not unlike certain aspects of the graphic arts in the nineteenth century. Countless creative approaches all seemed to gain acceptance, favoring the emergence of varied (typo)graphic styles. Since the late 1920s—even during the war years—graphic artists of various origins had been making names for themselves in the United States, such as Mehemed Fehmy Agha, Alexey Brodovitch, Lester Beall, Bradbury Thompson, and Paul Rand. They all participated in the ambient modernization, and often shared a familiarity with European art (in which some of them, like the Russian-born Agha and Brodovitch, actively participated). Whereas American assimilation of European movements in the early decades of the century seems to have occurred rapidly and unreservedly, the later period adopted a more aloof approach, intent on adding a personal flavor to the movements that had previously procured the liberation of forms of visual expression.

The unique phenomenon of European artistic migration to America, plus the welcome given to avant-garde ideas, helped to dynamize the United States in general and inspired the next generation of artists who would become famous in the United States (Jackson Pollock, Willem de Kooning, Robert Motherwell, Philip Guston, Mark Rothko, Barnett Newman, Ad Reinhardt, Ellsworth Kelly, Frank Stella, Kenneth Noland, Jules Olitski, Morris Louis, and others). In an echo of "the New York school of painting" and of "abstract expressionism," American historians of graphic design began referring to the "New York [graphic] school," "graphic expressionism," "typographic expressionism," and even "American typographic expressionism."[13] The link between (typo)graphic design and the visual arts (painting, collage,

571
Paul Rand, logotype for the Westinghouse
Electric Corporation, United States, 1960.

572
Paul Rand, press release for Westinghouse.

573
Paul Rand, leaflet for IBM, 1973.

574
Paul Rand, rebus-poster for IBM
(eye, bee, M), United States, 1981.

assemblage, etc.) nevertheless seemed less tangible than before, when it had been an integral part of major experimental trends and stemmed from a cross-disciplinary oeuvre. Although correspondences between the various artistic fields were no longer of quite the same kind, they nevertheless remained active and important. From expressionist drip paintings to Pop Art via hard-edge paintings, the variety of painterly and visual styles probably influenced the potential expressiveness of the graphic arts from the 1950s onward, just as, inversely, the specifically graphic idiom of mass imagery would influence certain schools of painting (Pop Art in the United States, Nouveau Réalisme in France).

Graphic designers were active on both the east and west coasts of America. Starting in the 1940s, and becoming more pronounced in the 1950s and 1960s, New York grew into a major center of graphic design. It was home to the Art Directors Club of New York, founded in 1920, as well as Raymond Loewy's design agency. Some of the largest advertising agencies also had their headquarters there (many of them on Madison Avenue), and New York firms alone accounted for half of all advertising investment made by American companies. New

York was where various sectors of the visual communications industry could display their dynamism, notably when it came to logos and corporate identity. In general, American graphic design placed special emphasis on typography, apparently free from any restrictive framework. Japanese designer Ikko Tanaka expressed a certain fascination with this approach. "In the history of design, the phrase 'American typography' may not exactly be recognized yet. Nevertheless, from the mid-1950s to the latter part of the 1960s amazing developments occurred in typographic design on the east coast of the United States, particularly in New York.... American typography displayed great strides in the fields of everyday advertising and magazines for mass audiences, rather than along educational lines, the path followed in Europe.... The artists who embodied this phenomenon were Herb Lubalin, Lou Dorfsman, and Henry Wolf."[14]

The west coast was equally active, notably in the context of the various protest movements—including the beat generation of the 1950s and the hippie movement of the 1960s—and in conjunction with musical trends: pop, rock, and psychedelia spawned their own particular graphic identities that were clearly unconventional and nonconformist. Even as these tendencies were emerging on both coasts of the United States, schools and universities were setting up high-level professional courses, sometimes thanks to the protagonists of the interwar period (such as László Moholy-Nagy at the New Bauhaus and Josef Albers, Herbert Matter, and Paul Rand at Yale). East-coast art schools such as the Rhode Island School of Design consolidated their design courses and even the Massachusetts Institute of Technology set up, in the 1950s, special services to provide local help with design issues (the Office of Publications and the Design Services Office would notably hire the likes of Ralph Coburn, Jacqueline Casey, and Muriel Cooper).

Mass design, unique creations, and pluralism

Within educational institutions, new forms of graphic design enjoyed wide dissemination through their reproduction in mass-produced form, a phenomenon that also affected professional circles and even the general public; this dissemination differed significantly from that of the historic avant-gardes, whose graphic design work enjoyed major outlets through exhibitions and reviews yet never reach the same level of recognition and popularity.[15] In the post-war United States the figure and role of art director assumed unique importance, particularly in the realm of magazine publishing, where the job began to go to famous creative designers. Design-conscious periodicals included *Apparel Arts, Arts and Architecture* (some of whose covers were the work of Ray Eames in the early 1940s), *Charm, Eros, Esquire, Fortune, Harper's Bazaar, Holiday, Life, Look, Mademoiselle, Saturday Evening Post, Seventeen, Show, Time, Vogue, Westwaco Inspirations*, and so on. They hired distinguished art directors from all generations, namely Alexey Brodovitch, Cipe Pineless, Bradbury Thompson, Lester Beall, Paul Rand, Leo Lionni, Will Burtin, Henry Wolf, George Lois, Allen Hurlburt, Art Kane, George Giusti, Herb Lubalin, Sam Antupit and Otto Storch. Some art directors theorized about the fundamental question of the role of graphics within overall advertising design. Many designers, for that matter, actively worked in the field of advertising and made various types of contributions to it; worth mentioning are Paul Rand, Henry Wolf, Herbert Matter, Herb Lubalin, Saul Bass, Gene Federico, Leo Lionni, Helmut Krone, Robert Brownjohn, and Bob Gage. The advertising agencies reputed to be particularly concerned with visual quality included Young & Rubicam, Doyle Dane Bernbach (DDB) and Sudler & Hennessey. As head of the Container Corporation of America (CCA), Walter Paepcke commissioned a series of posters—by Herbert Bayer, among others—on the theme of "Great Ideas of Western Man," which became a design landmark at the time. In addition to advertising, magazines, and the specialized press, American design also invaded the spheres of corporate identity and visual communication. Paul Rand worked for IBM and Westinghouse (alongside Charles Eames and Herbert Bayer), William Golden was commissioned by the CBS

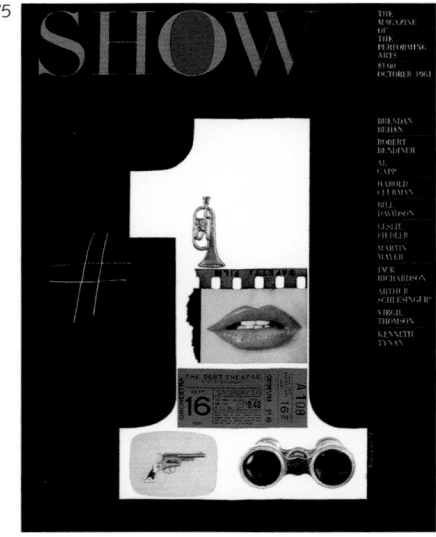

575

575
Henry Wolf, cover for *Show*, "The Magazine of the Performing Arts," October 1961.

576

576
Rudolph de Harak, clock dial, undated.

577
Rudolph de Harak, the publisher's logo for
McGraw-Hill paperback editions, United States,
c. 1960.

577

broadcasting network, Herbert Matter worked for Knoll and the New Haven Railroad
(whose trains were designed by Marcel Breuer), while Herb Lubalin executed commissions for
various clients.

The broad tendencies and general media employed by American graphic design yielded a
number of projects that have gone down in history. Thus in the early 1950s Herbert Bayer
was asked to design the *World Geographic Atlas,* a book that was praised for the quality and
originality of its graphics, which contributed to the conveying of information. Similarly, Saul
Bass won attention for his outstanding credit-sequences for Hollywood films of the 1950s,
such as *The Man with the Golden Arm* (1955) and *Anatomy of a Murder* (1959), both by
Otto Preminger, and *Psycho* (1960) by Alfred Hitchcock. Rudolph de Harak, meanwhile, was
doing remarkable, and perhaps unique, work in book design in the early 1960s, designing
some three hundred and fifty covers for paperbacks published by McGraw-Hill, devising
graphics that were simultaneously consistent, experimental, daring, demanding, and lavish
(this work bears comparison with the bold publishing ventures done by post-war French
designers such as Pierre Faucheux and Massin).

A great number of striking (typo)graphical projects were thus generated in the United
States between the end of the World War II and the late 1960s, a full quarter of a century.
There steadily emerged a new ambiance of eclecticism in design, practice, and execution that
challenged all the traditional reference points. Whereas Western graphic design had remained
fairly identifiable in terms of individuals and movements from the late nineteenth century
through the 1930s, American design of the second half of the twentieth century assumed such
scope that it is hard to isolate specific directions or ramifications, as acknowledged by the
protagonists themselves. This phenomenon was exacerbated by the multiplicity of sources
already being exploited by the mid-1950s, as described by Ashley Havinden.[16] Setting apart
special cases such as de Harak's book designs and Bass's film credits, it would seem more
appropriate to identify general tendencies (along with specificities of execution, configuration,
and contribution) rather than focus on the work of a few leading designers, of whom there
were many. Two of the main protagonists of the day were Paul Rand and Herb Lubalin,
whose works are frequently reproduced and are therefore among the most visible and
familiar.[17] Yet in one way or another many designers active at that time, although not enjoying
the same notoriety, also left their mark on the history of graphic design: Alex Steinweiss, Alvin
Lustig, Arnold Saks, George Tscherny, Walter Allner, Erik Nitsche, Louis Danziger, Ivan
Chermayeff, and Thomas Geismar.[18] Rather than displaying distinct lines or directions,
American graphic design perhaps primarily reflects the merging of an assimilation of earlier
experiments with an exploratory attitude permitted by a specific (and favorable) new context.
For designers this meant simultaneously insisting on quality, seeking to retain or extend

578

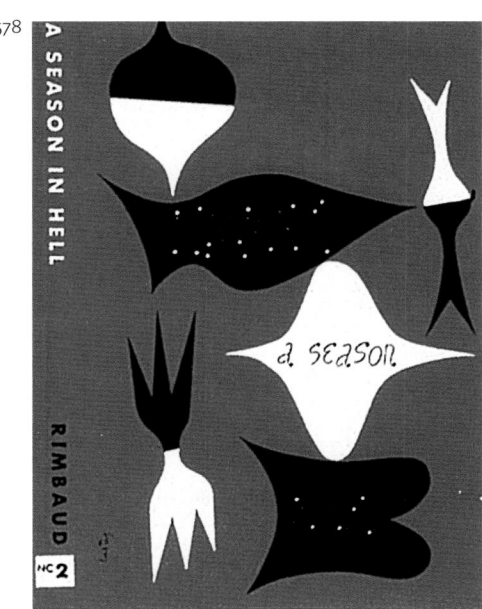

578
Alvin Lustig, cover for Arthur Rimbaud's
A Season in Hell, 1945.

personal expressiveness, consolidating the profession's status, and developing partnerships (with advertising directors, with other designers and architects working on transversal projects, etc.). Perhaps harking back to the advertising boom of the late nineteenth century, modern graphics left the haven of artistic creativity to enter a shared world of mass communications, becoming more intimately involved in the economy, the consumer society, the mercantile system, and the vision and style of everyday life.

Rifts with advertising

While American designers of the post-war period enjoyed abundant commissions, this situation perhaps ultimately led to a lively schism between certain aspects of graphic art and advertising design. It may seem paradoxical that such a split should have occurred where advertising and commercial graphics displayed such remarkable concern for (typo)graphic quality. Yet right from the mid-1950s, Paul Rand himself expressed great reservations about his own work in the advertising field. As art director of the William H. Weintraub advertising agency since 1941, he had noted over the previous fifteen years a fundamental incompatibility between his own work and the changing needs of ad agencies. "It's not possible to work with advertising agencies. The politics in the agency I was with were just too overwhelming. The agency was sold, and the people who bought it were marketing people. There was no point in my staying. So I left."[19] From within the agencies themselves, echoes of another divergence could be heard. Bob Gage and Helmut Krone, two art directors at Doyle Dane Bernbach (DDB, founded in 1949), were particularly critical in their comments on graphic design and typography. "Design is cold," said Gage, "it doesn't move people." Whereas Krone claimed that, "The thing about DDB was that designers were like poison. Somebody who knew how to draw was poison. A guy who was too good a typographer—we didn't want him." Krone explained that, "We knew about the Bauhaus, but we weren't after design, we were after advertising. We were interested in reaching people. That's *all* we were interested in."[20]

Thus a clear distinction was perceived between a certain notion of graphic design and advertising design, a distinction noticeable not only in the field but also in the classroom—courses in graphic design at Yale, for instance, where Rand taught, ignored advertising imagery completely.[21] This gap widened with the advent of the protest movements of the 1960s, and also became apparent in Europe. On the one hand, advertising became associated with commercial imagery whose budgets and goals targeted a vast audience and hence were subject to economic restraints, whereas on the other hand "design" willingly leaned toward the institutional and cultural sectors (allowing for the fringe development of the notion of personal or politically committed design).

This post-war distinction between advertising and a certain idea of graphic design had not truly arisen prior to that point. Some European avant-garde designers, for that matter, had incorporated advertising into the full range of expressive forms that they embraced (graphic, typographic, spatial, architectural, and so on). They were motivated not only by financial considerations but by a

579
Saul Bass, *That's Entertainment. Part II.*

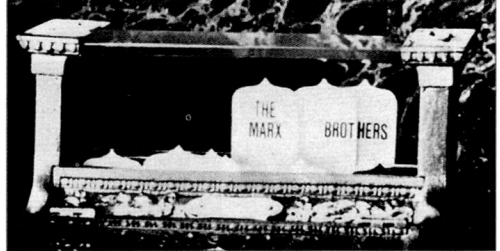

That's Entertainment Part II
ザッツ・エンタテイメント・パート II

The film is a compendium of well-loved pieces of old MGM films. The title logically was a recreation of many of the old, well-loved title devices that were used in by-gone days for forgotten films : names on wood, on the sand, formed by a marching band, etc.

映画は好評をはくした古いMGM映画の集すいである。タイトルは論理的に古いタイトルの焼き直しで、昔の忘れられた映画で使われた好評のタイトル制作法によるもだった。砂や木に書かれたキャスト、行進するバンド、あるいは巻物に書かれたキャスト、などなど……。

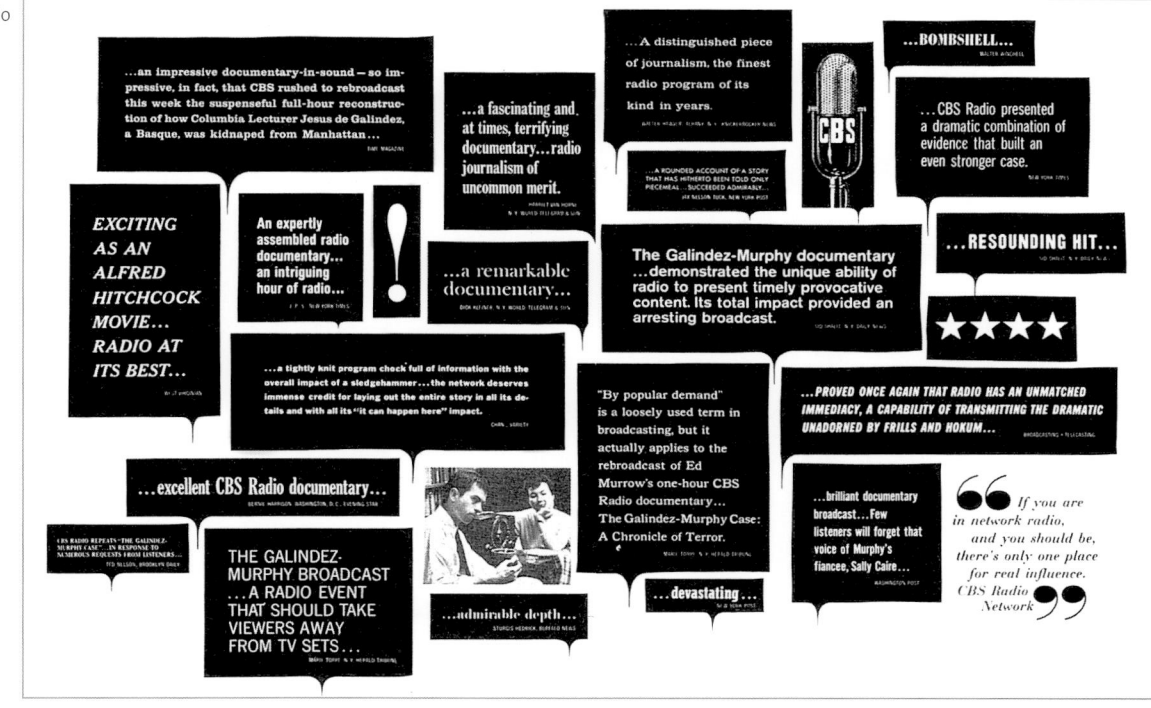

desire to revamp the visual and publishing spheres to the widest extent possible, going so far as to express great interest in experimental advertising (not to mention the numerous draftsmen, illustrators, painters, and designers, from Jules Chéret to Lucian Bernhard, who worked in the realm of the visual promotion of mass-consumer products). It was from this perspective, for instance, that Kurt Schwitters founded Ring Neuer Werbegestalter (New Advertising Designers' Society), or NWG, an association that brought together "German artists and advertising specialists" in the goal of "bringing modern forms of expression to advertising design."[22] The link between the arts and the multidisciplinary aspirations of the interwar period in fact sought, among other concerns, to reach out to industry and mass production, thereby incorporating reproducible, printed imagery and commercial or semi-commercial material into the vast field of visual expression in which artists were seeking their way.

Dissemination, eclecticism, and disappointment

Furthermore, the advertising side of graphic design in the United States was prospering in a climate that favored it. The earlier impact of European avant-gardes was still being felt, and many designers expressed their interest in the movements of preceding decades. Lester Beall, for example, discovered several avant-garde schools early in his career. Similarly, Rand, having studied under George Grosz, was familiar with European phenomena in painting and other spheres, which fueled his notions of design. Both men had steeped themselves in the New Typography. Exhibitions and other means of dissemination had played a role in that familiarity, such as the exhibitions of the works of French poster artists from the 1930s. Alexey Brodovitch, who came from Europe to dynamize American magazine design, passed on his experiences by teaching in the 1940s and 1950s; Henry Wolf and Otto Storch were among his students. Meanwhile, Victor Moscoco—who would become known for his psychedelic posters in the 1960s—studied under Josef Albers at Yale. Within this vast network of influences and dynamic relationships, a veritable culture of graphic design was forged in the United States. That culture focused on the two preceding centuries and was transmitted through schools and universities by teachers who were experienced, high-profile practitioners themselves. It also benefited from the concretization of a certain number of initiatives aimed at developing knowledge of graphic design in all its forms, through symposia, professional associations and publications, open

582
Seymour Chwast and
Milton Glaser, letterforms.

583
Seymour Chwast, cover of *Holiday*
magazine (Frank Zachery, art director),
September 1968.

584
Seymour Chwast, double-page spread for a
Hallmark book (Harold Peter, art director).

582

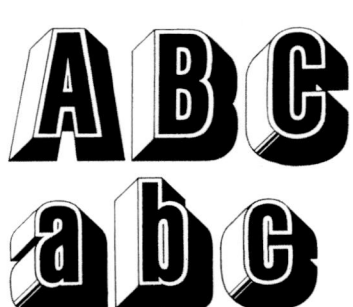

583

584

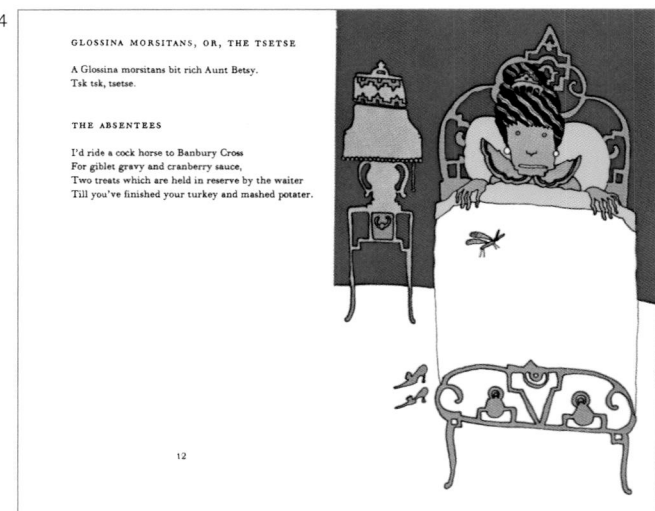

competitions, exhibitions of typography and graphic design, and so on. In the 1950s and 1960s, Aaron Burns, a member of the Type Directors Club, was particularly active in this area, organizing lectures, conferences, and exhibitions devoted to American and European typographic design; in 1960 Burns founded the International Center for the Typographic Arts.

The eclecticism of design immediately after the war expanded and extended into the 1950s and 1960s. Trends ranged from "early-1940s modernism" through advertising graphics, book and periodical design, corporate imagery, and revival tendencies, on to humorous and playful design, the casual Push Pin Studio look, the rise of "rebel causes," the influence of the Swiss school and the New Wave, right up to the protest and psychedelic cultures of the 1960s. A considerable number of art directors emerged in the spheres of advertising and magazines (such as Otto Storch, Henry Wolf, Will Burtin, George Lois, etc.). At the same new, new approaches to graphic design were surfacing, epitomized by Herb Lubalin's (typo)graphic work and the Push Pin Studio. Co-founded in New York in 1954 by Milton Glaser, Seymour Chwast, Edward Sorel, and Reynold Ruffins, Push Pin Studio fully participated in the new vitality sought by American graphic artists. A long way from the International Typographic Style that derived from New Typography, Push Pin Studio became famous for its willfully expressive, funny, and lavish designs characterized by a nonconformist approach. The group favored certain supports, such as record jackets, book covers, posters, little promotional or cultural ads,

585

586

585
Wes Wilson, poster for
the Fillmore concert hall
(Grateful Dead and others),
San Francisco, 1966.

586
Bonnie MacLean, poster for the
Fillmore concert hall, San
Francisco, 1967.

587
Bill Henry, poster for the Avalon
Ballroom, San Francisco, 1968.

588
Peter Max, poster, *1, 2, 3, Infinity*,
United States, 1967.

587

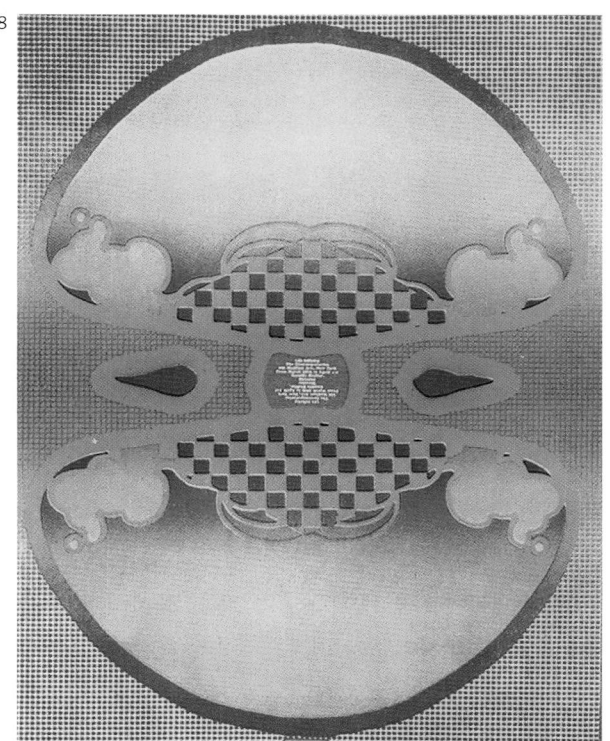

588

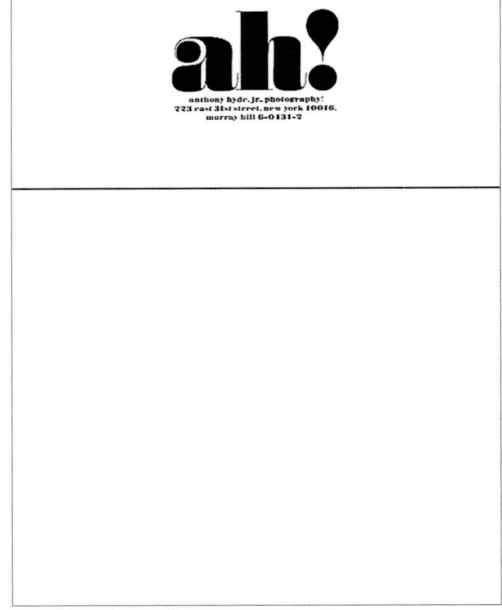

590

591

589
Herb Lubalin, prototype (rejected)
for a new can of dog food, United States.

590
Herb Lubalin, announcement of an anti-war
poster competition, *Avant Garde* magazine,
United States, c. 1968.

591
Herb Lubalin, letterhead for photographer
Anthony Hyde, based on the client's initials
(ah), United States.

and illustrations. This graphic spirit was a forerunner to the psychedelic movement of the 1960s with its stunning posters, perhaps most developed on the west coast around San Francisco but equally present in New York, Seattle, Chicago, and Dallas.[23] Visibly inspired by Art Nouveau, this swiftly emerging yet fleeting movement glorified flowing, extravagant typography and design on the verge of illegibility, displaying a willfully marginal, fantastical, and striking artistry. Eccentricity and boldness intertwined in imagery whose highly stylized visuals generated an enigmatic sense of strangeness. The leading designers in this field included Victor Moscoco, Wes Wilson, Stanley Mouse, Rick Griffin, and, in New York, Peter Max. Emblematic of highly original and literally impressionistic visual experimentation, their designs were singularly efficient even though light years away from any functionalist approach. The phenomenon would be short-lived, however, and was soon prey to commercial recuperation.

All of these ambient tendencies in visual expression nurtured a thriving graphic landscape that also welcomed the technological developments of the day. When it came to typography, photosetting steadily replaced the age-old methods of typesetting—and their mechanical extension—in the 1960s. As to imagery, the growing use of photography invaded the world of illustration in terms of both design and methods of reproduction. At the same time, the phenomenal growth of television helped to configure an environment in which the role of mediatized images—primarily based on photography—was in the ascendant. The broadcast media henceforth rivaled posters and wall displays. And when it came to typography, technological developments stimulated new methods for designing and employing letterforms. Contemporaneous with the new possibilities afforded by photosetting, the International Typeface Corporation (ITC) was founded in New York in 1970 by Aaron Burns, Herb Lubalin, and Edward Rondthaler. The faces they devised, revamped, or revived for ITC were presented in *Upper and Lower Case* magazine (*U&lc*), which began publishing in 1973 and was edited by Lubalin until 1981. Among the typefaces offered by ITC, sometimes developed in highly extensive sets of fonts, were American Typewriter, Avant Garde Gothic, Souvenir, Eras, and Kabel.

American graphic design thus blossomed in the decades following the war, as is witnessed by the admiration felt by Japanese designer Ikko Tanaka on arriving in the United States in early 1960s.[24] However, by the early 1970s, just when ITC was founded, certain disappointments and profound criticisms were being expressed, just at a critical time when social, political, and economic events were taking an unfavorable turn (a series of protest movements, the Vietnam quagmire, and an economic slowdown). It would indeed seem that, after a long period of expansion, graphic design finally experienced harder times. The boom in advertising and the press that had lasted throughout the 1950s and 1960s no longer sparked the same enthusiasm. Henry Wolf, a leading art director (and one of Brodovitch's successors at *Harper's Bazaar*), claimed that "everything came to an end in the late 1960s and early 1970s. Publishers wanted to make money rather than have beautiful magazines."[25] Corroborating Wolf's feeling, if from another standpoint, Herbert Bayer complained about the lack of consideration paid to graphic design and its social role. In a text published in New York in 1967, he lamented the lack of awareness and recognition of this sphere of activity, outside a tiny circle of people. "In the United States, the art of typography, book design, and visual communication in general, in its many aspects is being classed among the minor arts. It has no adequate place of recognition in our institutions of culture. The graphic designer is designated with the minimizing term 'commercial,' and is generally ignored as compared to the prominence that is accorded by the press to architecture and the 'fine arts.' Visual communication made revolutionary strides and real contributions to the contemporary world picture. Yet the artist-typographer represents a small number of typography producers compared to the output of the nation."[26]

American graphic design nevertheless benefited from a long period of growth that lent it crucial solidity, as witnessed by the creativity associated with certain media and certain graphic forms (corporate logos and design, periodicals, advertising, and so on). Furthermore, even though they seemed to pass through a difficult period around 1970, American trends in graphic design bequeathed to posterity their crucial experience of eclecticism, heralding the major developments of the last third of the twentieth century, such as the New Wave and digital design.

Switzerland

Switzerland's graphic design activities were not disrupted by the war. Indeed, it was during the 1940s that businesses, industry, and cultural institutions began making increasingly extensive use of graphics. By remaining free from wartime demands, the Swiss could pursue the experiments launched earlier by a number of pioneers. Already a highly developed sense and awareness of visual culture had been nurtured there in the early decades of the twentieth century. Zurich had been the birthplace of Dada in 1916; poster artists had long developed a specifically graphic and (typo)graphic repertoire alongside the more painterly tradition; several designers, such as Ernst Keller, Niklaus Stoecklin, and Otto Baumberger were producing works that heralded a stylistic renewal; great emphasis was placed on technical details as well as on methods of fabrication and reproduction; the teaching of graphic arts, which had acquired new importance, was open to avant-garde developments; and finally there was direct Bauhaus input from the likes of Max Bill and Theo Ballmer, while the Basel sojourn of Jan Tschichold in 1933 brought the New Typography and related trends to Switzerland. All these phenomena and situations were conducive to the stimulation of modern graphic design, lending it great vitality. The cities of Basel and Zurich in particular were two lively centers of graphic design in the 1940s, not only from the standpoint of practicing artists but also in terms of teaching and public awareness (thanks to farsighted museum policies of collection, conservation, and exhibition). Furthermore, many books, articles, magazines and other publications reinforced local culture and knowledge of the graphic arts, often in multilingual editions that further enhanced the possibility of dissemination.

Concrete art and "Swiss" typography and graphic design

592
Donald Brun, poster for Elna (sewing machines), 1946. 4 ft. 2 in. × 2 ft, 11 in. (128 × 90 cm).

593
Robert Büchler, poster for a typography show at the Gewerbemuseum in Basel, 1960. Black and white, 4 ft. 2 in. × 3 ft. (128 × 90.5 cm). The spatial layout and visual appeal is based on the distinction between vowels and consonants, and upper- and lowercase letters in Akzidenz Grotesk typeface.

594
Max Bill, poster for Concrete art show, Switzerland, 1960. 4 ft. 2 in. × 2 ft. 11 ^{1}/$_2$ in. (127.8 × 90.5 cm).

Marked by the spirit of Constructivism and New Typography, the trend that would become known as "Swiss typography" was closely associated, right from the start, with the rise of Concrete art (*Konkrete Kunst*), especially in Zurich. Richard Paul Lohse and Max Bill (born in 1902 and 1908, respectively), two major representatives of that movement, were both painters as well as graphic designers (and the same could be said of a leading figure of the next generation, Karl Gerstner, born in 1930). Adopting the typically versatile avant-garde attitude of the inter-relatedness of all the arts, all three men succeeded simultaneously as pioneers of Concrete art and as designers who worked in a parallel vein. As was the case with László Moholy-Nagy, El Lissitzky, Kurt Schwitters, Theo Van Doesburg, and many others, these artists were drawn to typography and graphic design as a source of visual possibilities and supports for their conception of art, allowing it to develop and find new expression—not to mention as a source of income (as some of their predecessors had also discovered). Affinities between the fine and applied arts reemerged, asserting the open, transversal links already present in the Vienna Secession, in Art Nouveau, and among fin-de-siècle poster artists (and regularly renewed since that time). With Concrete art, close connections were established between choice of imagery, visual idiom, and (typo)graphic style typical of the day. Rigor, geometry, mathematical logic, precision, structure, orchestration, the concept of series, visualization of the spatial layout, use of a grid, the search for quintessential forms—all the bywords of Concrete painting provided the foundations for a highly constructed, constructive, constructivist design that acknowledged the accomplishments of earlier decades.

Developments in typography and graphic design in Switzerland between 1940 and 1960 represented not only the extension of certain earlier trends (De Stijl, Constructivism, the second Bauhaus, and New Typography), but also the affirmation of a considered, didactic approach that favored straightforward expressiveness, well-ordered rather than unrestrained forms, and a special sense of poetry and intuition. Even so, it is worth stressing that Swiss graphic design was not solely limited to the stylistic connotations often associated with it (see, for example, the work of Donald Brun and Herbert Leupin).[27] Seeking a fluidity of message through the use of a simple and even somewhat ascetic style, designers elaborated a visual repertoire that could meet

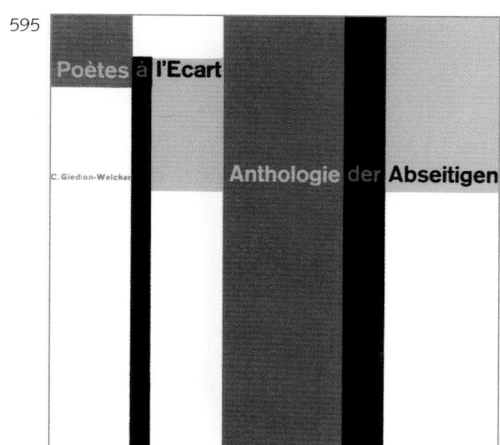

595

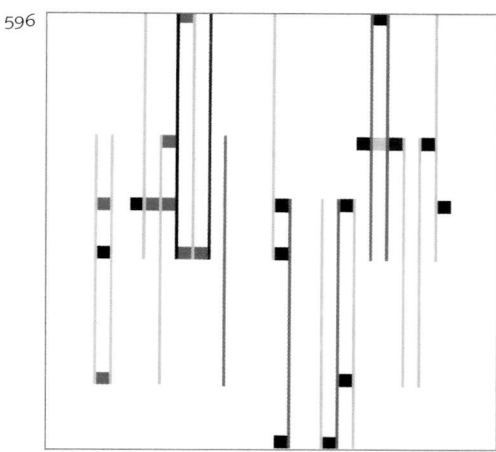

596

595
Richard Paul Lohse, cover for the book *Poètes à l'écart* (Carola Giedion-Welcker), 1946.
7 3/4 × 7 3/4 in. (19.5 × 19.5 cm).

596
Richard Paul Lohse, *Konkretion I*, 1945–46.
Oil on Pavatex, 27 1/2 × 27 1/2 in. (70 × 70 cm).

these needs. Hence their quest resulted in a central role for lettering and text, in the importance of a template not only as an organizational tool but also as a visible and tangible element, in a propensity for sobriety (a clear preference for sans serif faces, the frequent suppression of non-linear space, the limited range of typefaces, fonts, and so on), not to mention the importance accorded to photography. Compositions placed increasing stress on nonprinted surfaces and zones of flat color, as well as on the arrangement of various elements on the support. Many of these tendencies derived from the New Typography, some of them being taken further. Work on lettering was always meticulous and focused ever- greater attention on detail, refining the notion of microtypography.[28] From this standpoint, and within these aesthetics, the valorization of typography and legibility—alongside questions of composition, tension, and balance—yielded a delicate dynamism and measured elegance. A specific, overall synthesis resulted from a liberation of space and a concentration on the content to be conveyed. The concept of graphic "image" was enriched with abstract elements such as letters, signs, initials, words, unusual lettering and other forms, elevating typography to a visual sphere often reductively restricted to non-text imagery.

One highly present aspect of Swiss design was the notion of grid[29] (or at least the division of space) as inscribed by the act of writing itself, already evident in the ruled lines of medieval manuscripts and the earliest systems of writing. An exploration of the space and organization of a page was typical of Swiss typography. Since several languages are spoken in Switzerland, it seemed obvious that numerous multilingual publications should favor a reflection on the allocation of space and the use of grid systems. In contrast, the historical avant-gardes, although already concerned with the construction and surface area of a page, had tended to place stress on structure and on composition (or decomposition) rather than on the underlying grid itself. The Swiss template, mainly designed to provide a coherent organization for a series of double-page layouts within a printed medium, could also be used for a poster, or a series of posters, for book covers, or for variations on a logo or visual image. This visualization of structure and organization would seem, moreover, to have been explored in graphic work of earlier periods, for it is apparent in certain compositions associated with the Vienna Secession, the Wiener Werkstätte, De Stijl, the Bauhaus, the New Typography, and even magazine and newspaper graphics. The same could be said of the book by Hans Arp and El Lissitzky, *The Isms of Art,* and of the poster by Theo Ballmer, *Norm,* as well as of Bauhaus books, of the arrangement of texts in some of Schwitters's compositions, and so on. In other, related contexts, a grid was an essential tool, if generally invisible in the completed work, in both page layout and typeface design (x-height, proportions of ascenders and descenders, thickness of main strokes, and other elements of construction). The history of typographic characters offers, for that matter, an extreme example of the use of a grid in designing a face, namely *romain du roi* (also known as Grandjean, designed in the late seventeenth century for Louis xiv), which was based on a grid made up of over two thousand tiny squares. (Some time before, the blackletter face called Textura had been decomposed in modular fashion, as demonstrated by Dürer's work, published in 1525.)

Concerned with numerous aspects of typography, Swiss graphic design boasted a bevy of representatives and leading figures, as did American design. They included certain people who had been active during the interwar period, plus the Concrete art group, as well as the new generation of graphic designers. Many worked in Basel or Zurich. Those who came to the fore, over time, included Niklaus Stoecklin, Ernst Keller, Theo Ballmer, Jan Tschichold, Max Bill, Walter Herdeg, Herbert Matter, Max Huber, Richard Paul Lohse, Hans Neuburg, Emil Ruder, Josef Müller-Brockmann, Armin Hofmann, Carlo Vivarelli, Karl Gerstner, Nelly Rudin, Donald Brun, Herbert Leupin, Siegfried Odermatt, Marcel Wyss, and Carl Graf. It is worth noting that at least half of them combined their design business with a teaching or writing career. The wealth of publications seemed to confirm the importance of the Swiss typographic movement, bequeathing history with countless documents, information, theories, and accounts (many of these books, often written and designed by the artists themselves, remain highly useful tools today).[30]

Typographic controversy and culture

Jan Tschichold appears to be the key transitional figure between the historical avant-gardes and Swiss typography. Once a fervent defender of New Typography, Tschichold came to adopt a distinctly different line. Clear dissension erupted between him and his spiritual heirs, beginning with Max Bill, who published *Über Typografie* (On Typography) in 1946. This brief essay was a reaction to Tschichold's turnaround and it offered a redefinition of typographic practice. Bill started out by contesting Tschichold's shift of position. "Not long ago, one well-known theorist of typography [Tschichold] declared that the New Typography, which had enjoyed growing favor in Germany from roughly 1925 to 1933, had been destined primarily for advertising and was now outmoded." Bill continued with a description of his own vision of typography. "Typography is the design of textual compositions not unlike the way in which modern, concrete painting is the design of surface rhythms. These compositions are constituted of letters arranged in words. The relationships and differences in size of characters, and the various fonts, are all precisely determined. No other professional sector of applied arts comprises such a quantity of precise design conditions as typography. This particular raw material determines the nature of typography."[31] This argument must be set in the context of Bill's protean activities (which, for that matter, distinguished him from his opponent), which included painting, sculpture, architecture, design, typography, writing, and publishing. His essay underscored the role of typography within Swiss graphic design and stressed the specificity of typographic expression. Bill's reaction to Tschichold's new line sparked an immediate response from the man himself. Tschichold thus published his own text, which began with a refutation of Bill's arguments. "The article by the Zurich painter and architect Max Bill... seems to have been prompted by my lecture on 'The Constants in Typography.' ...Bill was not in the audience. His quotations from my lecture, half understood and clumsily reported, must therefore be second or third hand.... As a matter of fact, I stated...: 'The New Typography is probably not outmoded but, as has been demonstrated, it is only suited to advertising and short texts. For books, and in particular for literature, it is totally unsuited in most cases.'" Adding to the polemics, Tschichold went on to complain about the New Typography's "ascetic simplicity and extreme emotionalism," accusing it of "an intolerant attitude... [exemplified by] its military-style determination and its claims of dominance, those troubling aspects of German nature that are behind Hitler's rise to power." Tschichold's initial enthusiasm had thus given way to bitter disillusionment, couched almost in "Arts and Crafts" terms: "Finally, I discovered that New Typography was in fact just the culmination of what nineteenth-century typography had advocated with its infatuation with progress.... Machine production has caused heavy, almost fatal loss of the values of a worker's experience—so placing it on a pedestal is totally misguided." From the standpoint of book design, Tschichold added that "it testified... to an overly juvenile zeal for throwing the old rules overboard with disdain... for wanting to be different and 'modern.'"[32] The issues raised by Bill and Tschichold are still pertinent today. In order to understand and appreciate their respective positions, they should probably be seen as representatives of attitudes that are simultaneously complementary and divergent, the product of the context of the times and the personal history and convictions of each man (Tschichold being a figure impossible to ignore, given his role in the original avant-garde movements and the changes in his life and career wrought by the rise of Nazism, not to mention his global professional output).

The debate over typography triggered by Bill and Tschichold remains instructive and intriguing today. Some graphic designers in post-war Switzerland would follow the line defended by Bill (and originally formulated by the young Tschichold), an approach that would be extensively discussed, explained, and shared in the 1940s. For that matter, the theory and practice of graphic design converged in a lively culture created by numerous publications, often documented and illustrated. Both books and reviews abounded, as they had among the earlier avant-garde movements. In 1953, Bill published his famous book, *Form*, after having organized an exhibition titled *Die gute Form* for the Swiss Werkbund in 1949. Tschichold, meanwhile, continued to publish articles regularly, never hesitating to sharpen his critical axe. "On the Use of Print Characters in Advertising" was the title of a text that appeared in 1946–47, in which he argued that "Today, as in the past, foundries can deliver such a variety of faces to anyone who wants them that we're spoiled for choice. A novice, or an amateur, will often choose the most extraordinary typefaces over the most appropriate ones, because he places too much importance on distinguishing his text from all others... It is nevertheless incontrovertible that certain kinds of print material, notably texts without illustration, constantly call for new letterforms in order to draw the reader's attention." Tschichold concluded his article with the following observation. "What we need is not a greater variety of typefaces, but a much greater number of professionals who really know how to exploit what already exists."[33] Since that time, the design of typefaces has constantly grown and produced such a phenomenal eclecticism that Tschichold's comments—some fifty years after they were made—still raise challenging questions about layout and use of space, even as they themselves are challenged by digital design.

Cultural awareness, publications, and education

Confirming the importance of the stakes and questions symptomatically raised by Bill and Tschichold just after the war, several Swiss typographers and graphic designers working in the 1950s and 1960s became deeply involved in publishing activities—as did some fine artists, such as Karl Gerstner—including the production of a certain number of professional publications. The phenomenon was not totally new, since the leading professional review *Typografische Monatsblätter*, founded in 1933,[34] having merged in 1947 with *Revue suisse de l'imprimerie* (and still publishing under the joint title *TM/RSI*), regularly published crucial articles, devoted special issues to major designers, and kept abreast of typographic developments; the magazine was as curious about recent creativity as it was concerned with tradition. Monographs and textbooks also abounded during those two decades, alongside articles and reviews. Many of these publications addressed fundamental issues (including ones that remain relevant today). Emblematic of this literature was the trilingual *Neue Grafik/New Graphic Design/Graphisme actuel*, edited by Karl Gerstner, Richard Paul Lohse, Hans Neuburg, and Carlo Vivarelli from 1958 onward. Eighteen issues were published in all, coming to an end in 1965. Heir to the spirit of highly constructed design and New Typography of the 1920s, the magazine immediately targeted an international readership, determined as it was to promote developments in Swiss typography and to document the culture from which it stemmed.

Founded some fifteen years earlier, *Graphis*—another trilingual magazine—began publishing even before World War II ended, in 1944. Published by Walter Herdeg in Zurich, *Graphis* welcomed the unusually wide range of contemporary subjects being addressed in the 1950s (including Polish poster design and Swiss typography). In 1959, the magazine published an article by Emil Ruder on "Ordnende Typographie" (Ordered Typography), in which the author set out what he felt was the role that typography should fulfill. "First principle: the text must be clearly legible. The 'mass of text' on the page must be measured to make it possible for the reader to take it in without undue effort... The spaces between words, between letters, and between lines must be carefully proportioned. The issue of form only arises once this basic condition has been met. Of course, these rules in no way constitute a limitation on artistic freedom; it is not a closed, rigid system to be followed. Typography... is basically a question of ordering and precision."[35] Ruder's text, as its title makes clear, articulated certain trends and options adopted by Swiss typography. The movement encouraged reflective analysis on the subject, as witnessed by the scope of publications that

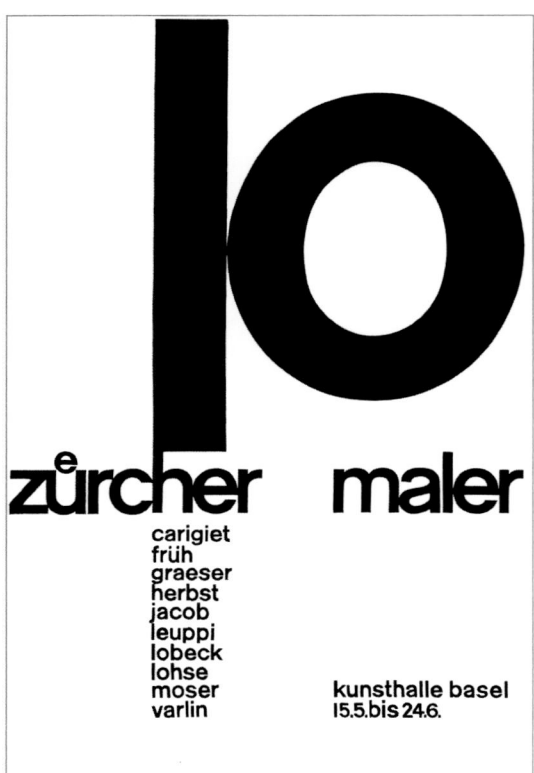

597
Design for a book cover with a visible use of leading. Reproduced in Emil Ruder's *Typographie/Typography* (1967), featuring the work of Ruder and the Basel school.

598
Emil Ruder, poster for an exhibition of ten Zurich painters at the Kunsthalle in Basel; reproduced in Ruder's *Typographie/Typography* (1967).

599
Print obtained from an assembly of lead typographic elements not usually visible; reproduced in Ruder's *Typographie/Typography* (1967).

addressed it. From this standpoint, written culture seemed to be an inherent part of typography and graphic design in Switzerland. It clarified positions, defended sometimes divergent ideas, and attempted to define typography, typographic presuppositions, and the issues that were at stake during the upheavals of the first half of the century.

These specialized reviews were joined, during the period in question, by a number of major essays, articles, and books. Such efforts blossomed in the late 1950s with the publication of, among other titles, Jan Tschichold's *Zur Typographie der Gegenwart* (1957, published in English by New Laboratory Press, Pittsburgh, in 1961 as *Contemporary Typography*) and Markus Kutter and Karl Gerstner's *Die neue Graphik /The New Graphic Design/Le Nouvel art graphique* (published by Arthur Niggli in 1959). In their book Kutter and Gerstner recount twentieth-century typographic design, in which both men took an active part. Tschichold, meanwhile, continued to express his reservations about certain innovations; he was committed to discreet letterforms and argued for historically validated criteria of quality. His book opened with the comment that typography is a goal in itself, namely to make the message to be conveyed easily accessible to the reader's mind. The first condition for a handsome page, he argued, is a legible, well-employed typeface. Yet he claimed that he had recently come across many everyday examples of typography that were unconsciously—or perhaps consciously— ugly, and therefore hard to read. He thus felt that the taste of the day was swinging from one extreme to another.[36] At the same time, several typographers and graphic designers imitated Karl Gerstner by publishing books—often multilingual and usually well illustrated—on their own practice. Such publications not only functioned as manuals full of references and information of various kinds, but might also dwell on certain aspect of modern design. Thus in 1961 Josef Müller-Brockmann published *The Graphic Designer and His Design Problems*, followed in 1971 by *A History of Visual Communication* and *History of the Poster*, and in 1981 by *Grid Systems/Raster Systeme*. Armin Hofmann, meanwhile, published his *Graphic Design Manual* in 1965 and Emil Ruder edited *Typographie/Typography* in 1967. Gerstner's publications, meanwhile, displayed a strong determination to include pictorial as well as

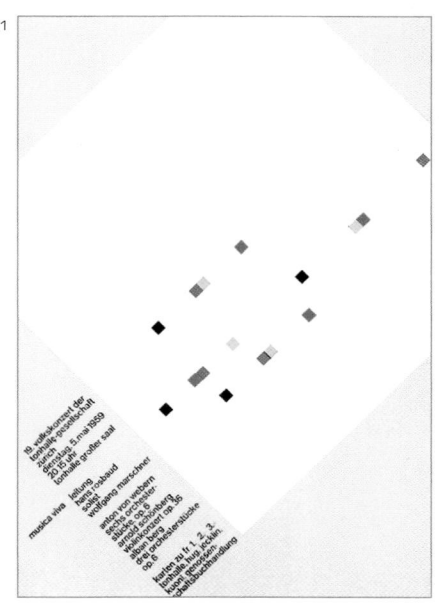

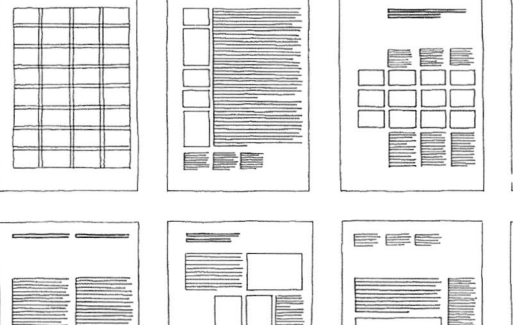

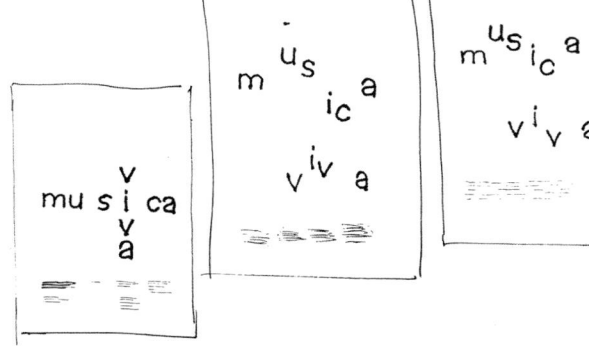

600
Josef Müller-Brockmann, experimental photograph, c. 1950s.

601
Josef Müller-Brockmann, posters for concerts at the Tonhalle, Zurich, 1950s.

602
Josef Müller-Brockmann, designs for layouts based on a thirty-two-square grid; reproduced in Müller-Brockmann's *Grid Systems in Graphic Design*.

603
Josef Müller-Brockmann, sketches for a series of posters for concerts in Zurich, c. 1970–72.

typographic research into his oeuvre, as witnessed by *Kalte Kunst?* (1957), *Programme entwerfen* (1963), *Kompendium für Alphabeten* (1972), etc. All these major books by practitioners and teachers made it possible to appreciate and grasp a theory that had a direct hold on the reality of its subject.

These publications still offer insight into the full scope of Swiss typography of the 1950s and 1960s in terms of its intentions as well as its actual output. Often described as sober and austere—and therefore somewhat limited—it nevertheless evokes a certain visual poetry, a mixture of rigor and experimentation, a personal quest for ways in which to attract the eye or encourage it to read. A return to sources makes it possible to appreciate the convictions held at the time, to grasp the spirit in which they were expressed and executed. In his introduction to his 1965 textbook, Hofmann asked readers "to accustom [themselves] to the idea that [their] mental and vocational equipment must be constantly refurbished," because, as he had explained a few paragraphs earlier, "whereas a few years ago the activities of the graphic designer were mainly restricted to the creation of posters, advertisements, packaging, signs, etc., his work has now expanded to embrace virtually every field of representation and design."[37] Such comments incited readers to retain an open mind.

In the 1950s and 1960s, the typographic work being done in Switzerland met with a favorable reception even as it adopted various paths. Often bilingual or even trilingual, literature on the subject was easy to disseminate on an international level. Ideals of objectivity and efficiency, plus a taste for visual experimentation within measured forms, suggested numerous directions to be explored by the movement's leading figures. Some Swiss designers were not only respected practitioners but also influential teachers. The transmission of their convictions and methods through training institutions would have a decisive impact. From this standpoint, the Kunstgewerbeschule (School of Arts and Crafts) in Zurich seems to have been the first outstanding institute, right from the interwar period. Ernst Keller, who worked there from 1918 to 1956, notably taught Theo Ballmer and Armin Hofmann, while Emil Ruder was a student of both Alfred Willimann and Walter Käch. (In earlier days, students at the Kunstgewerbeschule had included Richard Paul Lohse and Max Bill in the 1920s, Carlo Vivarelli in the late 1930s, and Carl Graf in the early 1940s.) A new generation of teachers then steadily rose within the schools in Zurich and Basel. Ruder taught typography at Basel's Allgemeine Gewerbeschule starting in 1942, and by 1965 was not only director of the school but also head of the Gewerbemuseum (Museum of Arts and Crafts), two posts that he would hold until his death in 1970. Hofmann also began teaching in Basel in 1947. Müller-Brockmann, meanwhile, gave classes in the Zurich school from 1957 to 1960. Swiss educational influence spread outside the country itself, for Max Bill was co-founder in 1950 of the Hochschule für Gestaltung (College of Design) in Ulm, Germany, and served as its first rector from 1951 to 1957. Hofmann, in addition to his regular teaching duties in Basel, gave courses at Yale starting in 1966, as well as at Philadelphia's College of Art and the National Institute of Design in Ahmedabad, India. Müller-Brockmann, too, performed teaching stints in Germany, the United States, Canada, and Japan.

Max Bill, Emil Ruder, Josef Müller-Brockman, and Karl Gerstner

From the 1940s to the 1960s, Swiss graphic design displayed a number of facets and variations depending on the designer involved. From a fine-arts angle, Richard Paul Lohse and Max Bill stand out as the two main representatives of a style directly related to Concrete art. Born in 1902 and 1908, respectively, both belonged to the Allianz group (founded in 1937), both were active in various fields of the applied arts, and both were concerned with more than mere practice. Lohse was editor-in-chief of the architectural review *Bauen+Wohnen* from 1947 to 1955, and was subsequently an editor of *Neue Grafik* from 1958 to 1962. From the early 1940s onward, the visual and graphic vocabulary of Lohse's paintings increasingly affirmed orthogonal structures and the quest for a new type of equilibrium. His purely (typo)graphic oeuvre—the product of commissions from industry and cultural institutions—followed the same formal logic as his paintings. Faithful to the ideals of Swiss typography, Lohse did not think advertising work was alien to other kinds of graphic design, but was simply a support calling for clear and informative presentation, as were other media such as book covers and corporate imagery.

Max Bill, meanwhile, became a well-known graphic artist after studying at the Bauhaus. In Zurich in the 1930s he made his living from graphic design and advertising work. Displaying keen interest in typography, Bill also worked, like Lohse, in the broader realm of design and architecture. For Bill, as for Ruder, notions of order and rigor were crucial right from the very conceptual stage. A protean artist, Bill always paid particular attention to letterforms, visible in his lettering as well as in his typeface experiments; in the early 1960s, for example, he designed a face whose letters and words sought to provide a visualization of their aural form. In addition to his work as artist and designer, Bill was a political activist— in the early 1930s he contributed his graphic skills to the struggle against National-Socialism and fascism through his work for the Swiss periodical *Information*. He also had a real political career when he was elected a member of the Zurich city council and of Switzerland's federal parliament.

The generation that emerged in the 1940s was epitomized by Emil Ruder and Josef Müller-Brockmann, both theorists and teachers as well as practitioners. Ruder's typographic oeuvre entailed "a tension between the fundamental and the experimental."[38] His book *Typographie/Typography* (first published in 1967 with the English subtitle of *A Manual of Design*) was particularly demanding in terms of the concept of legibility. "Typography has one plain duty before it, and that is to convey information in writing. No argument or consideration can absolve typography from this duty. A printed work which cannot be read becomes a product without purpose." Ruder then went on to supply the definitions

604

605

604
Armin Hofmann, poster for an exhibition on
the Japanese temple and tea-house, Basel, 1955.

605
Armin Hofmann, poster for the exhibition
Die gute Form (Good Form), Basel, 1954.

606
Armin Hofmann, poster for a Fernand Léger
/Alexander Calder show at the Kunsthalle,
Basel, 1957.

and recommendations that characterized his philosophy, shedding light on the movement behind it:

"A line of more than sixty characters is hard to read; too little space between lines destroys the pattern they make, too much exaggerates it.... With an enormous range of typefaces available, thin or thick, large or small, [modern typography] is a question of selecting the right one, composing the copy with these faces and interpreting it.... Unlike the Renaissance, when the unprinted blank was merely a background for what was printed thereon, contemporary typographers have long recognized the empty space of the unprinted surface to be an element of design.... And in the twentieth century in particular, artists have again become alive to the significance and power of rhythm in design."[39]

Ruder's convictions and methods—based on notions of order, clarity, and rigor articulated in a spirit of experimentation—placed him at the very heart of Swiss typography.

Müller-Brockmann, meanwhile, pursued similar ideals and enjoyed similar recognition for his many-sided activities. He was noted in particular for his series of posters for a Zurich concert hall, the Tonhalle, beginning in 1951 (these visuals were often reproduced in various forms, just like Herbert Matter's posters for the Swiss tourist bureau). By conjugating a vocabulary of simple yet dynamic forms, Müller-Brockmann's designs functioned as visual

607

607
Karl Gerstner, double-page spread from Markus Kutter's *Das Werk der Zukunft*, Basel, 1959.

608
Karl Gerstner, title page of Markus Kutter's *Schiff nach Europa*, Basel, 1956.

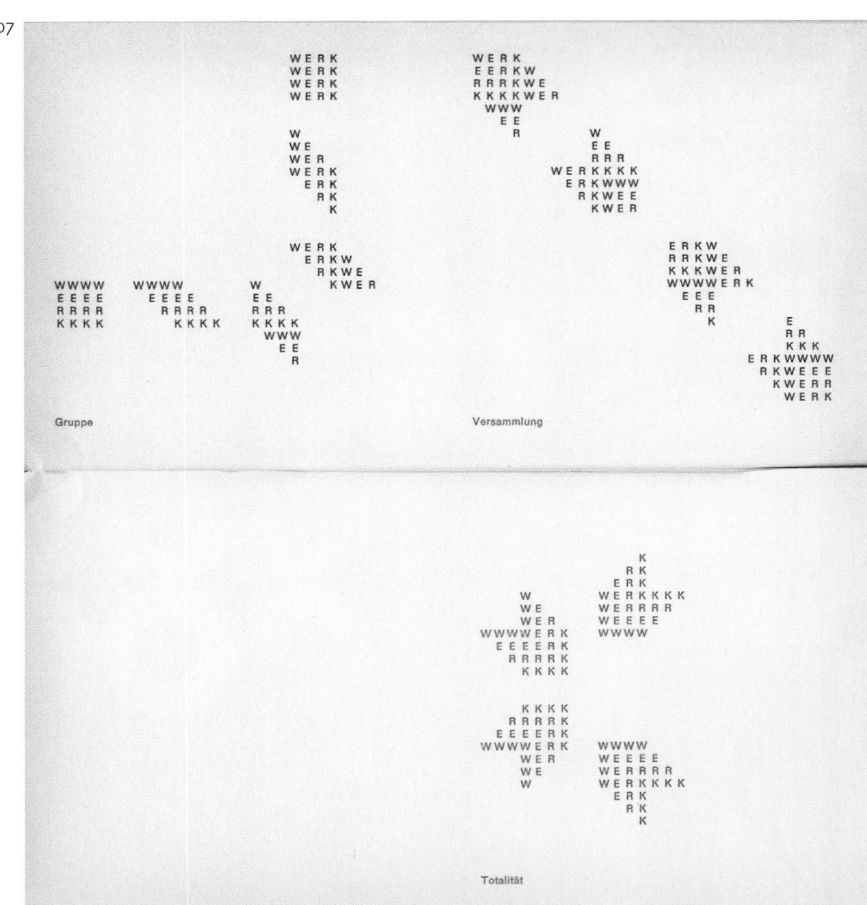

Gruppe

Versammlung

Totalität

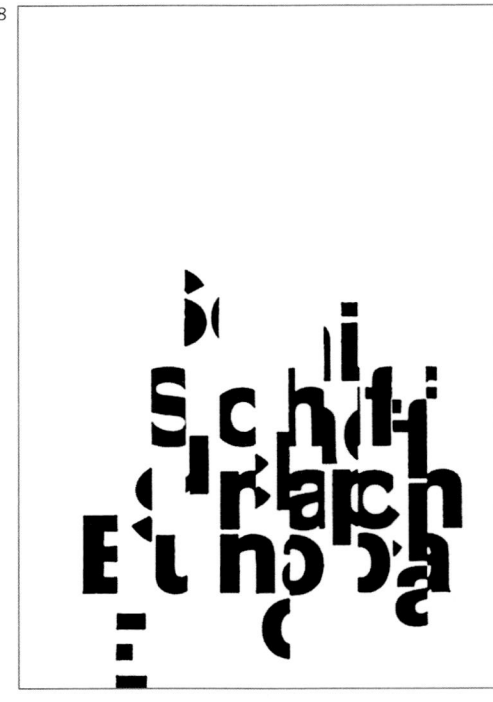

609
Karl Gerstner, some early sketches of IBM Original typeface (on which Gerstner Original was based), 1980s. "I had a new typeface in mind, without the traditional roots that make Berthold's Akzidenz so handsome."

610
Karl Gerstner, poster for a Kurt Schwitters exhibition at the Centre Georges Pompidou in Paris (1994–95).

transcriptions of the aural impact of musical sounds. His posters could be seen as a suite in which abstract rhythmic forms progressively gave way to text alone—sans serif faces in a limited number of fonts—exploring and affirming typographic poster art through an ever-renewed equilibrium; they now represent fine examples of the aesthetic ambiance of the day. For Müller-Brockmann, formal resolution was the product of an analysis of communication needs, one that moreover required a sufficient knowledge of context and terrain. A designer should "use the resources of science and technology to provide a clear view of the interior structure of things and the basis of their specific meanings. The optical, acoustic, kinetic, and spatial aspects of these possibilities in composition are novel and fascinating. The verbal text [should be] given a convincing and interesting pictorial support."[40] Hence both Müller-Brockmann and Ruder—both of whom were born in 1914—epitomized the arrival of a generation directly issued from the tradition of historical avant-gardes.

Coming behind them was the figure of Karl Gerstner, born in 1930. Having studied under Ruder and Hofmann, Gerstner was part of the second wave of Swiss typography. In 1959, he co-founded the Gerstner & Kutter agency with Markus Kutter (later redubbed Gerstner, Gredinger & Kutter), specializing in graphic design and advertising. Gerstner's work challenged the (typo)graphic preferences of his predecessors (such as their marked predilection for sans serif letterforms, asymmetry, and left-aligned compositions), thereby underscoring the potential diversity and scope of stylistic idioms acceptable at the time. Although adopting a certain distance from the conventional rigor, Gerstner's oeuvre displays direct links with the visual culture he inherited. Like Lohse and Bill, he became known as a painter and artist, his graphic and typographic work being just one facet of an interdisciplinary approach.[41]

Typographic choices and the design of typefaces

When it came to choice of lettering and use of typefaces, Swiss typography and graphic design in the 1950s and 1960s continued to stress the lineal forms (i.e., sans serif) advocated by the New Typography. For that matter, the 1950s witnessed the design of Folio, Univers, and Neue Haas-Grotesk (soon renamed Helvetica), the first one published in 1954 and the latter two in 1957. At the same time, Hans Eduard Meier got down to designing Syntax—begun in 1955 (and finally completed in 2000)—a sans serif face whose refined, skillful letterforms are inspired by Renaissance Humanist scripts. A decade later, and from a different perspective, Tschichold developed Sabon between 1964 and 1967—this Roman face was inspired by sixteenth-century models, notably Garamond—and was therefore a long way from the experimental typefaces he designed back in the 1930s.[42] An entire wing of Swiss typography adopted sans serif letterforms. Going even further, ever faithful to a spirit of rigor and perhaps a certain asceticism, some designers favored or advocated the use of one special typeface in particular. Müller-Brockmann, for example, strongly favored Akzidenz Grotesk, a late nineteenth-century typeface that also happened to be Anton Stankowski's preferred choice. Ruder, meanwhile, used and unreservedly advocated Univers,[43] a face based right from the start on a serial principle, comprising twenty-one variations. Similar typographic preferences reflected a methodical approach as well as a spirit of moderation and consideration for a lightened, informative communication.

The practices forged in Switzerland in the mid-1940s and developed over the next quarter century—whether involving specific typographic trends, the design of typefaces, the pursuit of the phototypographic approach or of other, parallel methods—represent a striking phase in the history of Western visual expression. Although the movement waned somewhat when new transitions got underway, it continued to influence activities abroad—particularly in the United States, France, and Japan—and played a fully-fledged role in the ambient eclecticism. Viewed retrospectively, from the standpoint of digital technology, the Swiss conception of typography appears to be not only a historical landmark but also an unending source of inspiration.

Poland

Whereas Swiss typography could be seen as the direct heir to the trends developed during the interwar period, Polish graphic design of the same period was marked by an originality that defies any direct comparison. From the 1940s to the 1960s, Swiss and Polish creativity incarnated two highly different approaches, reflecting distinct attitudes and constituting complementary examples on the historical level. Here again, political and socioeconomic factors were of prime importance. The devastating consequences of war meant that Poland was obliged to rebuild itself. The country was invaded in September 1939 by German and

611
Tadeusz Trepkowski, anti-war
poster, *Nie!* (No!), 1952.
Color lithograph,
3 ft. 3 in × 27 $^1/_2$ in. (100 × 70 cm).

612
Waldemar Swierzy, poster for
the Beatles, 1964.

then Soviet troops, and its geographic map was redrawn once the war was over. The conflict provoked much human and material damage, resulting in over six million dead, numerous cities to be rebuilt, and an extremely weakened industry. Graphic design thus confronted a difficult economic situation at the close of the war. And yet Poland was the site of unique experiments, notably in the realm of posters. Indeed, this particularly fertile movement became known as "Polish poster art." In the decades following the war there sprung up an innovative trend that represented one of the highpoints of graphic design of the day. Whereas many Swiss designers were fond of notions of construction, clarity, and typographic meticulousness, Polish artists sought above all a personal graphic idiom that often involved traces of a physical gesture. Heirs to an avant-garde tradition that showed a marked taste for uninhibited, unconstrained experimentation, the Poles elaborated spontaneous imagery—completely liberated from conventional principles—in their search for original forms of expression and for a visual creativity far removed from the concerns of microtypography.

Striking originality

When compared to a dominant trend in the West, Polish graphic design maintained a notable distance from the world of business and commercial imagery associated with product identification and marketing. Instead, it more closely reflected the cultural sphere. Aware of the role and power of posters, the government set up an organization called Wydawnictwo Artystyczno-Graficzne (WAG), which acted as an intermediary between official commissions and the most sought-after graphic designers. Posters were a key feature of sociocultural events, filling public streets and squares with images of movies, theater, opera, circus, the arts, and so on. Flaunting a strikingly original style, color, and tone, Polish posters won widespread recognition. Far removed from functionalist or objective tendencies, and equally distant from

613

614

613
Henryk Tomaszewski,
circus poster, *Cyrk*, 1963.

614
Jan Lenica, circus poster,
Cyrk, 1976. Color offset,
3 ft. 2 ¹/₂ in. × 2 ft. 2 ¹/₂ in.
(97.7 × 67.2 cm).

615
Henryk Tomaszewski,
poster for Jan August
Kisielewski's *Caricatures*,
Narodowy Theater, 1976.

613

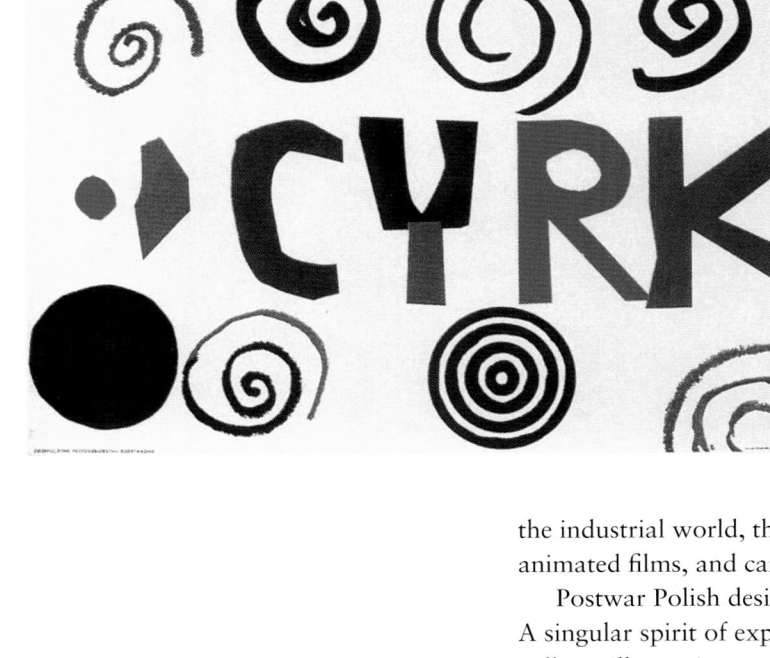

615

the industrial world, they seemed to have more in common with paintings, illustrated books, animated films, and cartoons.

Postwar Polish design employed highly varied approaches and sources of inspiration. A singular spirit of experimentation was constantly at work, calling upon photomontage, collage, illustration, and painterly techniques, alluding to Surrealist tactics, handwritten forms, and folk art. Many designers (often poster artists) became famous, sometimes inspiring disciples. Although the movement appears to have germinated in the interwar years, international recognition for many did not come until after the war. Tadeusz Gronowski, active in the 1920s, was retrospectively hailed as a precursor. Also well known at that time were Wladyslaw Strzeminski and Henryk Berlewi, co-founders of the Blok group in Warsaw. Surprisingly, post-war Polish poster art showed little interest in the Constructivist tendency epitomized by Berlewi.

Among the emerging generation it is worth noting Tadeusz Trepkowski, Henryk Tomaszewski (both born in 1914), and Eryk Lipinski. They would be joined by many graphic artists, most born around 1930, such as Jan Lenica (born in 1928), Jan Mlodozeniec (1929), Franciszek Starowieyski (1930), Roman Cieslewicz (1930), Jerzy Flisak (1930), and Waldemar Swierzy (1931), not to mention Mieczyslaw Berman, Wojciech Fangor, Julian Palka, Maciej Urbaniec, and Wojciech and Stanislaw Zamecznik. Some of these designers worked for the state agency, WAG, which was headed by Josef Mroszczak.

Their visual explorations yielded a series of bold, unique, highly characteristic images. From certain late nineteenth-century works they borrowed a powerful expressiveness and a certain economy of means. Among other features—and not unlike a similar French trend— Polish posters exploited a graphic and visual register that eschewed a simple, straightforward use of photography. Whereas the explosion of media, the propagation of audiovisual material, and the development of new techniques of reproduction all favored a strong role for photography within graphic design (as notably evident in the realm of advertising), Polish practices stuck to images that retained a strong sense of the role of montage, of manual intervention, of physical gesture, of plasticity, of spontaneity, of hand-lettering, of a visual

poetry that was neither mechanical nor geometric. Henryk Tomaszewski produced some of the most characteristic and best-known posters in Poland; another often-reproduced work is Tadeusz Trepkowski's *Nie!* (No!), which dates from 1952 and represents a call for peace in the form of a bomb that dominates most of the surface area, yet in which appears a fragment of a ruined building and capital letters spelling out the protest slogan *Nie* (accompanied by a resounding exclamation point).

Henryk Tomaszewski, Jan Lenica, and Roman Cieslewicz

Henryk Tomaszewski set up as a graphic designer after the war, having studied at the Academy of Fine Arts in Warsaw in the years preceding the outbreak of fighting. His posters are emblematic of the Polish school, many of them pitched in a pleasant tone tinged with humor, and are often designed to promote cultural events and performances (theater, circus, marionette shows, exhibitions of art or posters, and so on). Using limited resources, Tomaszewski developed a lively, spirited imagery by imbuing all aspects of his composition with intense optical value. The lettering—whether handwritten, typeset, or cut out—adopted a playful or informative role, depending on requirements, and sometimes constituted the primary visual element, as typified by *Moore* (1959) and *Cyrk* (1963). His oeuvre also exploited techniques of collage, illustrative drawing, and arrangements of flat zones of color.

Another leading designer of the day, Jan Lenica, also produced posters as well as illustrations, humorous newspaper cartoons, animated films, and theater sets. In a somewhat Surrealist vein, his graphics often employed figures presented either in thick black outline (as Alphonse Mucha also did in his day and his own manner), in silhouette, or in fragments. Equally renowned was Roman Cieslewicz, even though he did not remain in Poland itself for very long. Having graduated from the Academy of Fine Arts in Krakow in 1955, he notably won recognition for his designs of posters and other graphic material for the cultural sector, including a stint as art director of the monthly magazine *Ty i Ja* (You and I). His designs reflect an aspect of the Polish idiom in which the incorporation of photomontage and technical features of photography play a central role (for example, his recurring use of the motif of a highly enlarged and highly visible half-tone screen). The creative work of Tomaszewski, Lenica, and Cieslewicz constitute distinctive oeuvres, each of which conveys a particular graphic personality marked by idiosyncrasy. They produced many of the most famous works of the Polish school, which enjoyed its own distinctive overall style, one not really comparable with any prior or contemporary movement, and clearly aloof from the trends being followed in countries such as Switzerland, the United States, France, and so on.[44]

619
Wojciech Fangor and Henryk Tomaszewski,
poster, *May 1st Peace*. Color lithograph, 1960.

The influence of the Polish school

The leading figures of the Polish movement enjoyed international recognition and impact in the postwar years. In Poland itself, the education offered by art schools helped to spread and reinforce the phenomenon. Just as the schools in Basel and Zurich had been particularly active from the 1940s to the 1960s, so the quality of the teaching provided by the fine art schools in Warsaw and Krakow played a crucial role in training up-and-coming generations. Warsaw enjoyed a wide reputation, for that is where Tomaszewski and Josef Mroszczak—who was art director at the state agency, WAG—both taught. (The city of Poznan, for that matter, also had a reputable art school.)

The impact of the Polish school abroad was the result not only of the practice and dissemination of its graphic output, but also of its pedagogical exports. Franciszek Starowieyski taught in East Berlin and New York, while Lenica worked not only in Poland but also in France and West Germany. Cieslewicz moved to Paris in 1963, where he became a teacher. At the same time, specialist international reviews began covering the work of Polish graphic designers, especially poster artists, who were included in a number of exhibitions. Cultural events and operations reinforced the scope of the movement. The first International Poster Biennial was held in Poland itself in 1966, and shortly afterward, in 1968, a museum entirely devoted to poster art—Muzeum Plakatu—opened in Wilanow, not far from Warsaw.

Given its originality and lively impact, Polish poster art managed to hold out for several decades against normative principles that sought to impose a limiting coherence or restrictive theorization on visual graphics. Born of a spontaneous, gestural expressive idiom, determined to retain great freedom of tone and composition, it combined the immediate boldness and dispersed eclecticism of Futurist graphics with the concision and efficiency of *Sachplakat* and Constructivist photomontage. Unconstrained by any putative aesthetic, the movement could call upon various means of expression, from a lively stroke of the painter's brush to the meticulous assembly of photographic fragments. The range of Polish output reveals a rejection of all conformism. Through its enduring dynamism, the movement managed to sustain its historical thrust and initial originality right into the 1970s. It was particularly influential in the 1960s, including abroad (having an impact, for example, on the future founders of the French group, Grapus). Retrospectively, Polish graphic design of the post-war decades still bears the mark of a highly original approach. (For that matter, Czechoslovak design of the same period, although apparently little known, discussed, or illustrated, also produced numerous noteworthy works and artists.)

Italy

As in Poland and France, the post-war period in Italy marked the start of a resurgence in graphic design. The country made a significant contribution to the expansion of visual communication that occurred in many places from the 1940s onward. Thanks to the sustained impact of Futurism, Italy had already enjoyed a heyday in visual graphics even prior to World War I. This was continued the 1930s with the work of Studio Boggeri, the review *Campo grafico,* and the work commissioned by the Olivetti firm. After the war, Antonio Boggeri continued to hire many of the leading graphic designers of the day, from Germany and Switzerland as well as Italy (including Max Huber, Walter Ballmer, and Bruno Monguzzi). The professional links established between Olivetti and graphic artists also survived—Giovanni Pintori worked steadily for the firm for several decades, starting in the 1930s, designing or supervising corporate graphics of rare quality.

During the war years themselves, graphic design in Italy, as elsewhere, had to bend to the needs of propaganda even as it continued to work, underground, in favor of the Resistance— as demonstrated, for example by the posters and leaflets produced by Albe (Alberto) Steiner, who was politically active in the Resistance movement. But the burdensome consequences of war were followed by resurgence and reconstruction in the late 1940s, partly thanks to the

620
Franco Grignani, poster for Alfieri & Lacroix
(publisher of art books, based in Milan), Milan,
1962–63. One of a series of small posters based
on the ampersand symbol (&). 8 × 11 $^3/_4$ in.
(21 × 29.7 cm).

621
Franco Grignani, cover for the British magazine,
Typographica, London, 1963. 8 × 10 $^3/_4$ in.
(21 × 27.5 cm).

Marshall Plan. Economic recovery, which encouraged growth in all spheres of business, also favored graphic design. Italian creativity began to flourish alongside the economic boom in the years following the war. Milan, as a financial and business center surrounded by zones of industrial activity, played an especially important role in the recovery (as it had in the 1930s). More and more businesses were commissioning designers to fulfill their needs for advertising, promotion, and corporate identity, so advertising agencies and design studios enjoyed solid growth. As in the United States and Switzerland during those same years, the advertising sector became receptive to design, a phenomenon sure to favor the production of high-quality, indeed artistic, commercial imagery. Here, too, the profession began to organize itself, structure itself, and insist on professional standards as demand continued to grow. Many industries, firms, and organizations of all kinds wanted to hire leading designers, who could guarantee the quality of the corporate image thus conveyed. The firms that regularly commissioned graphic work—because highly attentive to their visual image—included Olivetti, Fiat, Pirelli, RAI (the national radio and television corporation), the Rinascente department store, the Einaudi and Feltrinelli publishing houses, and the Milanese printer and publisher Alfieri & Lacroix.

Given this context, many designers emerged in Italy in the period extending from the 1940s to the 1960s, including Franco Grignani, Giovanni Pintori, Luigi Veronesi, Bruno Munari, Massimo Vignelli, Erberto Carboni, Carlo Dradi, Pino Tovaglia, Ilio Negri, Giulio Confalonieri, Michele Provinciali, Armando Testa, and Bruno Monguzzi. In addition, a certain number of Swiss-trained graphic artists went temporarily or permanently to Milan to work there, enriching the Italian context with their own background. These designers included Max Huber, Walter Ballmer, Carlo Vivarelli, and Imre Reiner (a Hungarian national who studied in Germany and moved to Switzerland in the early 1930s). Bob Noorda, another leading light of Milanese design, originally came from the Netherlands. As a center of graphic design in the post-war era, the city of Milan became a crucible where the traditions of Europe's avant-garde movements could be forged with a determination to develop new styles with new sparkle.

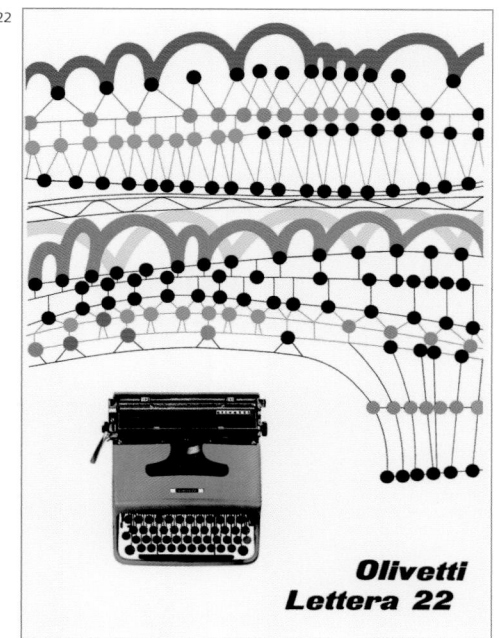

Franco Grignani, Giovanni Pintori, Albe Steiner, and Max Huber

As in Warsaw, New York, Zurich, and Basel, many Italian designers were able to elaborate outstanding oeuvres. They included Franco Grignani (born 1908), Giovanni Pintori (1912), Albe Steiner (1913), and Max Huber (1919). In the specific domain of typeface design it is worth mentioning Aldo Novarese (born in 1920), who began working at the Nebiolo type-foundry in Turin in 1936 and remained there until 1975, proving to be highly prolific throughout his long career.

Grignani, meanwhile, began his design career in the 1930s, after having studied architecture. First active as a Futurist painter, he soon taught himself—and subsequently concentrated on—graphic design, typography, and experimental photography. His work was notably distinctive for its exploration of optical phenomena and effects, inhabited by figures characterized by deformations, contractions, multiplications, and distortions (somewhat evoking Expressionism). Sometimes, Grignani limited his palette to black and white. Part of the expressive language and boldness of Grignani's innovative graphic work was due to his origins as a Futurist painter, if on a distinctly different register. He explained his motivations as follows: "My interests, spurred by creative necessities, have ever been addressed—experimentally—towards a new vision-exciting typography at the service of commercial communication.... Signs [gain] humanization and almost become sound in the extension of their space values."[45] Among Grignani's best-known works are his posters for printers and publishers Alfieri & Lacroix. These posters played on typographical experimentation and transformation, surprise, alliteration, and visual serendipity. The evolution of his career confirmed Grignani's interest in a resonant typography, as confirmed by another passage from the same text, dealing with the way typography might reach the optical senses:

My own research, gradually developed since 1953 in this field, has been devoted to the projection of alphabetic signs through optical filters creating distortions. There was no need of anything new but the analysis of the conditions of typographical reading affected by the mechanical speed of locomotive means, by interference due to transparent partitions in architecture, or by resort[ing] to forms as reflected by bent or specular surface.... Today typography may be the subject and could replace figuration.

Although quite personal, Grignani's taste for text and the way it might be visualized (color, timbre, sonority, and so on) recalls, in certain respects, contemporary work by American designer Herb Lubalin and Swiss designer Josef Müller-Brockmann. Although not very well known, Grignani played an important role around 1960 and should perhaps be considered a precursor of future developments, given his ability to abandon the principle of visual rigor in a quest for optically intriguing configurations. Works by Grignani are owned by a certain number of museums, for that matter, including the Museum of Modern Art in New York, the Stedelijk Museum in Amsterdam, the Victoria & Albert Museum in London, and the Warsaw museum.

Giovanni Pintori was another figure who made an original mark on the history of graphic design, displaying a similarly inventive spirit and freedom of tone. His more than three-decade career working for Olivetti represents a key part of his contribution to visual expression. As a student of advertising graphics in the 1930s at the Instituto Superiore per le Industrie Artistiche (ISIA), near Milan, Pintori took courses taught by the likes of Marcello Nizzoli (who became Olivetti's art director in 1938) and Edoardo Persico (a contributor to the review *Campo grafico*). In 1936, Pintori began working on Olivetti's graphic image, and he would continue to work for the firm until 1967. Over the decades, on behalf of Olivetti, he designed numerous posters, brochures, leaflets, and advertisements, also working on exhibition design and revamping the company's visual image in 1947. He was named the firm's art director in 1950. His most typical Olivetti design included the posters *Lettera 22* and *Lexicon* (1952–54). His graphic style tended to combine simple abstract shapes suggesting the parts or mechanism of a typewriter, along with typographic elements and materials, all in a visual atmosphere that was often lively, dynamic, and pleasant (a trait shared by Grignani's oeuvre). Although letters and numbers thus play an important role in Pintori's compositions, his posters sometimes featured very concise texts, often limited to the name of the brand and the specific item, somewhat in the *Sachplakat* spirit. When his work with Olivetti came to an end, Pintori opened his own design studio in Milan. Like Grignani, he enjoyed an international reputation and his works were shown in design exhibitions held in Milan, Lausanne, London, Paris, New York, and Tokyo.

Like Pintori and Grignani, Albe (Alberto) Steiner belonged to the generation that began working in the 1930s, and largely made its reputation after World War II had ended. Steiner was special, though, in having established links with the anti-fascist avant-garde and in working for the Italian Resistance as a graphic designer during the war years. Subsequently his clientele notably included Olivetti, Agfa, and Pirelli, as well as the Piccolo Teatro. He also served as art director, successively, of a political review, of the Rinascente department store, and of the Milan publishing house Feltrinelli; meanwhile, he continued to produce work that reflected his political convictions, notably by doing the layout and design of newspapers and periodicals such as *L'Unità* and *Il Politecnico*. Considered to be highly cultured, Steiner maintained his view, even after the war, that graphic design must remain a responsible form of expression and creativity. According to German-British designer Friedrich Heinrich Kohn Henrion, "He loved to experiment and innovate in two and three dimensions. He saw design as a way of life and as a way of influencing the environment."[46]

Similarities with Steiner's situation can be seen in the work and career of Max Huber. Although born in Switzerland in 1919, Huber spent most of his working life in Milan. He was a student at the Kunstgewerbeschule in Zurich from 1935 to 1938, studying under Alfred Willimann, learning about photomontage, and meeting the likes of Müller-Brockmann and Vivarelli. In 1940 he left for Milan, where he began working with Studio Boggeri. He brought his experience of the nascent Swiss school to his work with local Milanese designers (including Steiner, Pintori, and Munari), and also attended classes at the Accademia di Brera. When Italy entered the war in June 1941, Huber decided to return to Zurich that year. There he collaborated with Max Bill on exhibition design and also did graphic work with a

625

625
Giovanni Pintori, construction for Olivetti, Milan, c. 1950.

626
Max Huber, wrapping paper for La Rinascente, Milan, 1951–52.

627
Max Huber, logotype for the Italian department store, La Rinascente, 1950, using Bodoni Italic and Gill Sans bold faces.

628
Max Huber, poster for fabrics from La Rinascente, 1952.

629
Max Huber, poster for the Italian department store, La Rinascente, Milan, 1951–52.

627

626

628
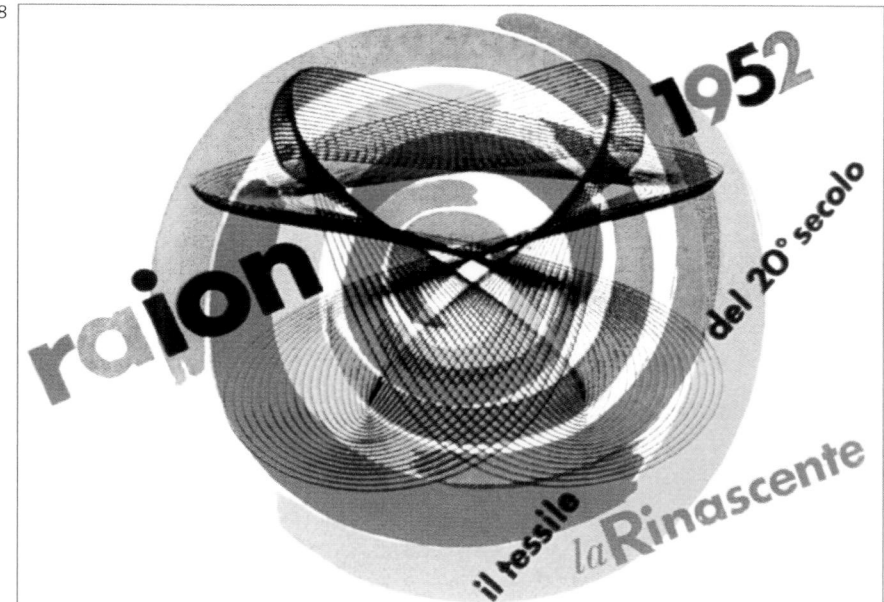

629

sociopolitical bent. Once the war ended in 1945, Huber moved back to Milan. Like his higher-profile colleagues, he was approached by major clients such as the Einaudi publishing house (for whom he designed all promotional graphics), the Rinascente department store (corporate logo, window displays, etc.), and the state-owned broadcasting service, RAI. Huber's optically powerful graphic style revealed an amazing ability to combine a demanding formal rigor with an experimental quest for dynamism that typified Milanese design of the day. He explored the superimposition of text and image, effects of transparency, qualities of light and movement, and the impact of color. He developed a strong graphic idiom based on no restrictive principle by combining visual lavishness with conceptual simplicity. Like certain poster artists and designers from the New York school, Huber treated (typo)graphic forms as potential stimuli liable—if sufficiently original—to reinvigorate the act of perceiving. He was also keen to maintain a link between painterly and design activities, becoming a member of the Swiss Allianz group in 1944 and joining Milan's Concrete art movement (Movimento Arte Concreta) as early as 1949. Huber's works, like those of Pintori and Grignani, were selected for many exhibitions abroad—in Europe, the United States, and Japan—and would be acquired by certain museums in Zurich, Amsterdam, Warsaw, and New York.

Devising specialized training

As in neighboring Switzerland, the dynamism of Italy's graphic scene was also indebted to the active participation of the educational and cultural sectors (in the form of exhibitions, and so on). It would nevertheless seem that special courses in graphic design were established in Italian art schools somewhat later than elsewhere. Local typographers and graphic designers often studied painting or architecture at school, a circumstance that in fact favored a multidisciplinary approach, and perhaps explains why several of the leading designers also practiced photography, interior decoration, or urban planning (which was also true well before the war). Although this lack of specialized training seems to have persisted, a few educational initiatives were launched in the post-war period.

Prior to the war, however, in the 1920s and 1930s, it would seem that the Instituto Superiore per le Industrie Artistiche (ISIA) in Monza supplied most of the training in the field of graphic communication. Founded in 1921 under the name of the Università delle Arti Decorative, probably inspired by the Bauhaus model, ISIA would close in 1939. But its student body included Giovanni Pintori in the early 1930s and its teaching staff included Edoardo Persico and Marcello Nizzoli (whose pro-fascist posters were rejected for reproduction in *Campo grafico* by the magazine's editor-in-chief, Attilio Rossi).

In the post-war period, Milan's Scuola Umanitaria probably played the key role. That is where several leading figures on the graphic scene taught, such as Pino Tovaglia, Ilio Negri, Michele Provinciali, Massimo Vignelli, and Albe Steiner. Training in graphic design subsequently enjoyed significant growth as new courses in visual communication were instituted in the 1960s in places like Rome, Florence, and Venice. Also worth noting were schools in Urbino and Monza, as well as the Scuola Politecnica di Design in Milan (where Max Huber would teach in the 1970s).

Despite the limited range of specialized training in the 1930s and 1940s, the practice of graphic design created a rich landscape inherited simultaneously from the avant-gardist tradition (through the works of Tommaso Marinetti and Fortunato Depero, for example); from the presence of German and Swiss artists (such as Xanti Schawinsky, Max Huber, and Walter Ballmer); from an openness to experimental photography (Antonio Boggeri, Luigi Veronesi); from the central, crucial catalyst of major clients (industrialists, businessmen, publishers); and from the model presented by the founding of Studio Boggeri in 1933. In certain ways, post-war graphic design in Italy shared traits with its American counterpart: strong dependence on economic context, familiarity with earlier movements and the Swiss school, a search for increased expressiveness, and an aloofness from other norms. Apparently removed from the gestural, artisanal quality of Polish poster art, Milanese design adopted reproduction technology and methods, all the while maintaining a liveliness of form and content (which employed superimposition, deformation, distortion, repetition, and so on). It might be argued that this graphic style represented, in relation to the two contemporary schools in Switzerland and Poland, a third, somewhat intermediate path. Italian graphic initiatives of the 1940s and 1950s, even as they displayed strong connections with pre-war trends, pointed the way forward to later developments in graphic design.

France

France represented a special situation in typography and graphic design as the first half of the twentieth century drew to a close with the end of World War II, notably in comparison with other countries that resolutely shared a modernist culture in this domain. Graphic creativity largely vanished from France during the war years due to the rise of visual propaganda, both French and German, and also due to the departure of some of its leading representatives. Yet France had not previously participated very extensively in the vast (typo)graphic movement occurring in central Europe, in which, for that matter, it had not shown a particular interest. While fervent Italian Futurism was spreading into Russia and elsewhere, while De Stijl was cozying up to Dada, while Constructivism was bouncing around the Bauhaus and environs, and while American design was waking up to European developments, the graphic arts in France were primarily characterized by a few lone figures; the protagonists of French typography were notably professionals associated with the Deberny & Peignot type-foundry.

Having long ignored most avant-garde (typo)graphic developments despite a few exchanges and initiatives, France finally seemed to open up somewhat in the 1950s. And even then there persisted certain reservations, largely within the typographic community and largely directed against German practices. Henceforth, however, France would awaken to the general design trends in the West, would display new curiosity, and would accept the eclectic repertoires and heritage of all the "-isms." It thereby combined domestic creativity with acceptance of foreign developments, as witnessed by the arrival and subsequent success of Swiss designers such as Albert Hollenstein and Jean Widmer. Visual communication enjoyed a new impetus in the fields of publishing, advertising, periodicals, and typeface design as many new trends and creations began to spring from the soil of French typography and graphic design. The many striking postwar developments included a major revamping of the book-publishing sector by Pierre Faucheux and Massin,[47] followed by other designers; in the sphere of posters, a light, witty vein emerged with the rise of Bernard Villemot, Raymond Savignac, Jacques Nathan-Garamond, Jean Colin, Jean Picart le Doux, and André François (not to mention designers active before the war, such as Jean Carlu and Charles Loupot); when it came to typeface design, Adrian Frutiger was joined by Albert Boton, Roger Excoffon, Marcel Jacno, and José Mendoza y Almeida. If there was a marked vitality in graphic design at the time, that was partly because, as elsewhere, real needs were being felt: the change in lifestyle and the growth of a society of mass production and mass consumption meant a constantly growing need for imagery, signage, and typographic content in the spheres of commerce, advertising, logos, news, publishing, and so on.

630

630
Charles Loupot workshop, advertising panel for Saint-Raphaël (aperitif), Paris, 1957.

Artistic, professional, and technological dimensions

In its way, the ambient artistic and literary scene contributed to the upheaval in (typo)graphic styles. An interest in geometric abstraction probably favored acceptance of a highly constructed graphic idiom (associated with the New Typography and related trends). At the same time, Art Informel, Art Brut, and lyrical abstraction opened the field to other forms of expression

631
Raymond Savignac, poster for *Het laatste Nieuws*, 1948–52. Color lithograph, 5 ft. 2 in. × 3 ft. 10 in. (158 × 117 cm). Initially designed for a French evening newspaper that was never published.

632
Raymond Savignac, poster for Cinzano (aperitif), 1951. 2 ft. 6 in. × 3 ft. 5 in. (77 × 105 cm).

633
Bernard Villemot, poster for Perrier, 1977.

634
Bernard Villemot, poster for Gitanes (cigarettes), 1958.

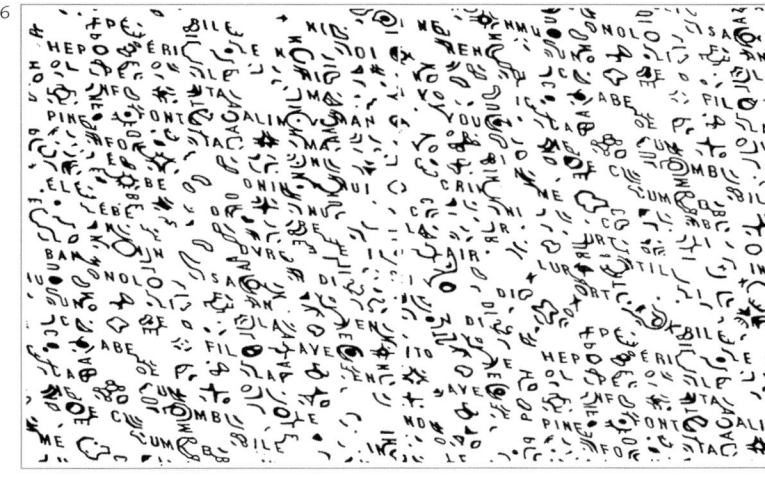

635
Raymond Hains, untitled, 1950.

636
Raymond Hains and Jacques
Villeglé, *Hépérile éclaté,* a
hypnogogic vision of Camille
Bryen's poem "Hépérile" (1950)
as projected though reeded glass,
France, 1953.

637
Raymond Hains, *Venice Biennale,*
1970.

638
Maurice Lemaître, *Ce qu'il faut dire
de ma peinture* (What Should
Be Said about My Painting), 1960.
Oil and collage on canvas,
5 ft. 3 3/4 in. × 4 ft. 3 in.
(162 × 130 cm).

centered on physical movement and the gesture of writing. The diversity of expressive registers in the artistic sphere also held for typography and graphic design, where initial reliance on a limited repertoire gave way to varied approaches and practices. A number of links between art and graphic design were created or reopened, as artists and painters demonstrated their interest in design, printed works, typography, and letterforms. Auguste Herbin would go so far as to invent his own "visual alphabet," developed and employed from 1942 onward as the compositional basis of his paintings; his alphabet was composed of color combinations of basic geometric forms such as the circle, semi-circle, square, and triangle. The future Nouveaux Réalistes, meanwhile, turned their attention to printed imagery and lettering as found in public spaces—starting in 1949, Raymond Hains and Jacques Villeglé produced many artworks based on torn and lacerated posters. Hains was also interested in the visual potential of the written word, and in 1952 viewed Camille Bryen's poem "Hépérile" through reeded glass, creating strange deformations that served as the basis for Hains's artwork *Hépérile Éclaté* (Exploded View of "Hépérile"), generating what he called "ultraletters." In working on these hard-to-decipher textual and alphabetical forms, Hains referred to the "giddy feeling [he had] on seeing letters go from legible to illegible," and of the "pleasure of hearing a language spoken without trying to understand the meaning or sense."[48] (In a completely different context, if from a related and contemporaneous perspective, Italian designer Franco Grignani was experimenting with the deformation and distortion of letters and texts in his quest for new visual stimuli.) As to the Lettriste movement, launched in Paris in 1946 by Isidore Isou, it placed its main artistic focus on language, writing, letters, characters, and so on (see its concepts of "letter-poetry," "lettrist poetry," "metagraphics," "hypergraphics," "post-writing," and "super-writing"). Meanwhile, the founding of the Collège de Pataphysique in 1948 (whose members included Max Ernst, Man Ray, Jean Dubuffet, Raymond Queneau, Jacques Prévert, Marcel Duchamp, and Michel Leiris) contributed yet another literary and artistic dimension to these games of language and typography, as demonstrated by the group's publications. All these movements and initiatives would cultivate, from mid-century onward, a taste and a visual penchant for work on letters and characters at the intersection of the realms of art, writing, and literature.

At the same time, that is to say the early 1950s, a series of events took place in the fields of typography and graphic design that consolidated interest in the historical development and international scope of those sectors. New forms of professional contact became possible in 1952 with the founding, in the same year, of the Alliance Graphique Internationale (AGI) and the Rencontres de Lure, two organizations that are still active today. The AGI's objective was "the unification of persons in the whole world active in the field of graphic design who, in the exercise of their profession, command high respect in their country or internationally... the enhancement of the international reputation of graphic design as a means of communication, information and education... [and the] encouragement of all efforts directed towards the training and promotion of young talented graphic designers."[49] Since that time, members of the AGI have met annually in different countries. The forum known as the Rencontres de Lure also takes place once a year, always in the same village in southern France. Over the years, the forum has hosted speakers as varied as Jean Giono, Eugène Ionesco, Michel Butor, Victor Vasarely, Hermann Zapf, Massin, Gérard Blanchard, and Raymond Savignac. Furthermore, one of the co-founders of the forum, Maximilien Vox, was behind the famous "Vox Classification."[50]

Another significant development in the professional world of typography concerned the technological invention of phototypesetting (or photosetting). It meant that hot-metal setting, whether manual or mechanical, could be replaced by a photosensitive surface (film or bromide) on which the type could be inscribed through a photographic process. Experiments with this kind of system, actively sought since the late nineteenth century, began bearing fruit in the 1930s. A machine that promised the first industrial use of photosetting was finalized in 1944 by two French engineers, René Higonnet and Louis Moyroud. Locally, however, the technique did not obtain sufficient backing to reach the marketing stage. "Once again, the French printing industry failed to grasp the importance of the existence of true photosetting technology, with the exception... of the Deberny & Peignot company."[51] Turning to American industrialists, Higonnet and Moyroud managed to produce a prototype of the machine, called Photon, in 1946. But it was not until 1954, six years after it was invented, that the first photosetting machine, manufactured in the United States and dubbed Lumitype, was imported into France, at the request of Charles Peignot. Although Peignot would go on to make a few of the machines in France, most were manufactured in Anglo-American or Germanic countries. The first text in Europe "to be set with this photographic setting machine" was thus published in 1954 and represented "a historic event for the print industry" since "it appears that this ingenious machine is likely to revolutionize typesetting techniques."[52] This remarkable method would be the first to eclipse completely the techniques developed by Gutenberg (late nineteenth-century typesetting machines being merely a mechanization of those techniques). One wonders why France showed so little interest in two successive phenomena that, while not really comparable, impinged heavily on the world of typography, namely developments in European graphics in the first third of the century and then the crucial invention, in the mid-1940s, of a technique that would transform the reproduction of texts and would dominate the history of typesetting until the advent of the computer age.

Original design for the publishing trade—Pierre Faucheux and Massin

Following the end of World War II, a certain number of initiatives, plans, and projects emerged in France's graphic design sector, attesting to a vitality and modernity conducive to a renewal of local practices and an openness to foreign influence. It would seem that, unlike what occurred in Germany, much of France's printing equipment survived the war unscathed, so that its material infrastructure could be used as it had in the past. Soon after hostilities ceased, a striking phenomenon arose on the French design scene. A major revamping of book design was triggered at the initiative of Pierre Faucheux, soon followed by Massin, Robert Delpire, Jacques Darche, and Jacques Daniel. The movement first surfaced as early as 1946 among book clubs—that is to say, the system of mail-order sale of books, based on similar German and American models—which required members to buy at least four books a year, each title being the object of distinctive graphic packaging. The originality of the idea, combined with a thirst for reading material at the end of the war, guaranteed the success of these book clubs and of the publishing industry in general (twelve thousand new titles were issued in France in 1947). By the 1950s, book clubs boasted up to seven million members. For designers whose creativity was solicited by the clubs, this meant reinventing the book as a veritable object that would not merely be read but that would please the eye, stimulate curiosity, and cry out to be handled. As Massin told it, "a volume was no longer this thick, rectangular block as dead as a brick, but a living thing into which we struggled to inject a third dimension, whereas the printed surface usually has only two. So we made holes in the bindings, and encrusted objects into the covers."[53] These experiments involved layout as well as covers, interior as well as exterior. Such conceptions of the published form of book-as-object recalled the bold Futurist experiments in this realm, undertaken in Italy and Russia in the 1910s.

Pierre Faucheux, born in 1924, pursued his career as typographer-designer even as he continued his multifarious activities in other applied arts. He studied at the prestigious Parisian school of graphic and industrial arts, the École Estienne, and started out as a typographer in

639
Pierre Faucheux, collage of tissue papers used to prepare a dummy, 1965.

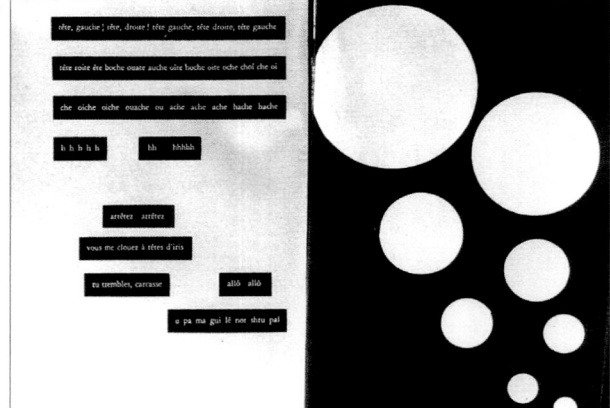

640
Pierre Faucheux, dummy book cover, 1947.

641
Pierre Faucheux, cover of the poetry magazine,
K, no. 3, France, 1947. The back part, on the
right, could be detached and used as a
bookmark.

642
Pierre Faucheux, inside pages from Henri
Pichette's *Les Épiphanies*, published by *K*, 1948.

1942. Once the war was over, he moved into the forefront of a major revamping of the French publishing scene. His work with book clubs began in 1946 with the Club Français du Livre, the first of its kind in post-war France. Acting as the club's art director from 1946 to 1954, he was responsible for some seven hundred titles. He then held the same post at the Club des Libraires de France, for whom he designed roughly five hundred books. The popularity of book clubs meant that his graphic experiments encountered a broad public, and inspired a certain number of designers to follow in his footsteps. For Faucheux the task meant not only setting the text and laying out the page, but setting the scene, generating the space; he wanted to bring the writing to life through formal inventiveness and thereby turn the book into a dynamic object (a far cry from the meticulous feel of Swiss microtypography). He rendered forms tangible as well as visible, breathing life into text and typography, violating formats and unleashing space. He thus redrew the map of book design, which traditionally respected very discrete boundaries. In this respect, Faucheux reenacted countless avant-garde experiments of earlier decades, giving great freedom to typographic expression by breaking the frames, redistributing space, picturing contents and feelings, and dispersing, multiplying, and shattering all compositional elements. Reaching further back in history, this approach also invoked the literary experiments of Laurence Sterne, Coqueley de Chaussepierre, and Stéphane Mallarmé. By exploiting changes of scales, visual intensity, eclectic typefaces and formats, unexpected shifts and layouts, and surprise effects, Faucheux's work came across above all as a recasting of the material nature of the book, for which prior knowledge of the contents was indispensable. Thus, each of his

643

644

645

creations was inventive, offering a specific interpretation of the text through his expressive graphic style. Massin paid tribute to Faucheux by explaining his fertile lack of inhibition. "Everything was usable—outmoded faces, old equipment, the whimsies and insights of the 1930s; he used multiple columns and justifications, broke up titles as though he was composing shaped verse, played with the white and black spaces in the text. No one in those days showed so much startling inventiveness and visible jubilation in typography; for while Faucheux could be as rigorous as the Germanic Swiss and the last survivors of the Bauhaus, he also had a whimsy that they lacked. It was thanks to him that I learned my trade, and that I came to realize that there are no ugly letterforms, only people who don't know how to use them."[54]

Faucheux's editorial graphics would influence not only his peers but also the desires of publishers themselves. In 1962 he founded his own studio, Atelier Pierre Faucheux, to specialize in designing graphics for publishing houses (he would ultimately employ a staff of fifteen). Noteworthy designs that came after his book-club heyday included his covers for the Libertés imprint (published by Jean-Jacques Pauvert, 1964–68), with their immense, black uppercase letters on kraft paper, and another series of covers for the Point imprint (published by Le Seuil, 1969), whose visual look has remained unchanged. Concerning the Libertés books, the publisher recalled: "I was naturally looking for an out-of-the-ordinary appearance. Clearly inexpensive. Lettering on very cheap paper, with block letters on the cover, like something just tossed onto the publishing market. I discussed the project with Pierre Faucheux, who was immediately enthusiastic, and understood that it wasn't a question of technically innovative, sophisticated exploits, but of remaining provocatively simple. It was Faucheux, I think, who had the idea of the format and the cover of kraft paper. As well as the Didot typeface inside, which I liked instantly."[55] Mainly known for his inventive designs in the realm of publishing, Faucheux also worked as an architect (in collaboration with Le Corbusier), an interior designer (for museums, exhibitions, galleries, and bookstores), and a furniture designer.

Massin, meanwhile, born in 1925, was one of the main figures to follow Faucheux's path. Son of a stone engraver who showed him how to carve before he could even read and write, Massin taught himself typography through contact with the professional scene, working in turn as journalist, author (of novels, essays, and monographs), graphic designer, and typographer. It is worth noting that Massin's graphic work was done in particular contact with literary circles, an inter-relationship generally cultivated by avant-garde movements. Hired by the Club Français du Livre in 1948, Massin learned typography in a matter of weeks from an Italian typographer, and there discovered the work of Faucheux. It was for the book club, in 1949, that Massin designed his first hard-bound book, a volume of Rimbaud's poetry, representing the start of a long career mainly devoted to book design. He pursued this work in the 1950s with the Club du Meilleur Livre. As he recalled, "several of us—Faucheux, Daniel, Bonin-Pissaro, Darche, and others—created a real revolution. Before we arrived, books with soft covers, designed to be leather-bound [after purchase, by their owners], were produced without thought. We handled these covers in a modern, dynamic way, the exact opposite of lavish, moribund editions. I'd say that we borrowed cinematic methods to do page layout."[56] In 1958 Massin was hired to be an art director with Les Éditions Gallimard, with whom he remained for roughly twenty years. In 1961 he designed the covers for Gallimard's Idées imprint. Ten years later, in 1972, he developed the overall design of the new Folio imprint: an illustration against a white ground, title printed top left in Baskerville Old Face ("a timeless typeface… which gives a very fine black, simultaneously elegant and strong, halfway between Elzevir and Didot").[57] Some two thousand Folio covers were produced under his supervision, requiring approximately two hundred illustrators. Like Faucheux's 1969 design for the Points imprint, Massin's solution has stood the test of time: the cover designs of both popular series of paperbacks have remained unchanged for over three decades.

Massin also produced some original typographical interpretations of literary texts such as Raymond Queneau's *Cent mille milliards de poèmes* (A Hundred Thousand Billion Poems, 1961) and *Exercices de style* (Exercises in Style, 1963), as well as Eugène Ionesco's *Cantatrice chauve* (The Bald Soprano, 1964), and *Délire à deux* (Delirium for Two, 1966), all published by Gallimard. Subsequently, Massin worked with other major French publishers (Hachette, Denoël, and Albin Michel). In addition, he would publish, among other things, a certain number of reference works on lettering and imagery, notably *La Lettre et l'image* (Letter and Image, 1970), *Les Cris de la ville* (Town Cries, 1978), *L'ABC du métier* (A Trade Primer, 1988–89), and *La Mise en pages* (Page Layout, 1991). Massin thus produced a major corpus of theory that analyzed his professional practice. This contribution is not only worth stressing but also makes Massin one of those Western designers of the second half of the century—such as Paul Rand, Josef Müller-Brockmann, and Jan Tschichold—who extended their careers into the realm of the transmission and sharing of their skills and ideas through substantial publications (textbooks, theoretical volumes, essays, articles, analyses, historical insights, critical perspectives, and so on).

Swiss designers in France—Adrian Frutiger, Albert Hollenstein, and Jean Widmer

Alongside the explorations being carried out by French graphic artists in the field of book design, a completely different phenomenon was about to burst on the post-war design scene in France. The arrival of several typographers, typeface designers, and graphic artists from Switzerland brought an experience directly related to earlier avant-gardes—and to traditional practices—with which France still seemed unfamiliar. Starting in the 1950s, Swiss designers helped to introduce notions of basic design and microtypography into France. Some of them

646

646
Adrian Frutiger, signage for Roissy-Charles de Gaulle airport, Paris, 1970–71. The brief was to design a typeface suited to the function and architecture of the airport. French words, in black, and English words, in white, both appear on an orange background to allow equal legibility of black and white characters.

648
Adrian Frutiger, signage for the Paris Métro (Métro typeface, early 1970s). Characters used in blue on a white background for directional signs, and in white on a blue background for information concerning stations. Legibility tests were first used to determine the space between the words and the lines, then the space left around the edge of the sign.

649
Adrian Frutiger, Métro typeface (semi-narrow), signage for the Paris Métro, early 1970s. (Each character has a guide to the width of letter in order to ensure the satisfactory composition of texts.)

647
silhouette   silhouette
silhouette   silhouette
silhouette   silhouette
silhouette   silhouette

647
Adrian Frutiger, legibility tests for the signage for Roissy: normal characters on the left, airport characters on the right. The study of the legibility of text at a distance formed an increasingly important area of typography in the latter half of the twentieth century.

settled permanently in Paris right from the start of their careers, while others only stayed temporarily. Those who arrived between 1948 and 1953 included Hans Eduard Meier (born in 1922, who left again in 1950 to teach in Switzerland), Adrian Frutiger (born 1928), Jean Widmer (1929), Albert Hollenstein (1930), and Peter Knapp (1931). Widmer would play an important role in the field of visual design within cultural institutions, and Knapp would likewise in magazine publishing. Frutiger, Hollenstein, and Meier, meanwhile, more specifically represented the sectors of letterform design and typography. As members of a generation situated between the historical avant-gardes and the end of the millennium, Frutiger, Hollenstein, and Meier all studied at the Kunstgewerbeschule in Zurich, then headed by Johannes Itten, a leading figure of the first Bauhaus.

Frutiger, known primarily for his prolific activity as a designer of typefaces, studied under Alfred Willimann and Walter Käch in Zurich. Invited by Charles Peignot to work at the Deberny & Peignot type-foundry, he moved to Paris in 1952. Whereas the first letterforms he developed for the company were mere exercises for him, by 1954 he had developed his first major face—Meridien. That same year, responding to Charles Peignot's request to produce a sans serif face for the Lumitype machine (the first photosetting equipment available in France), Frutiger recommended research he had begun as a student, which ultimately produced the famous Univers typeface (initially called Monde), presented to the public in 1957.[58] Designed to be used for both hot-metal and photosetting techniques, Univers was also adapted for transfer-lettering applications. As head of Deberny & Peignot's design studio, Frutiger was also responsible for adapting classic faces to the photosetting method, including Garamond, Baskerville, and Bodoni.

648

649
ALPHABET MÉTRO
ABCDEFGHIJKLMNOPQR
STUVWXYZ   LA LT TT
Â É È Ê Ç Ü   .,'-_.
1234567890 AOÛT 1973

In 1968, he redesigned the original Optical Character Recognition typeface (OCR-A, devised by engineers in 1966), which became OCR-B and was adopted as the international standard for electronic machine reading. His major contributions to the realm of letterform design, often the product of teamwork, included several faces specifically created for signposting in Paris transportation facilities. Thus he devised the signage and lettering for two Paris airports (Orly in 1959, followed by Roissy / Charles de Gaulle in 1970–71; the latter, with slight revisions, would become the typeface called Frutiger in 1973–76). At the same time, he did the same for the Paris Métro system, resulting in the Métro face. In all, Frutiger designed several dozen typefaces, including Sérifa (1967), Avenir (1988, similar to Futura), and Vectora (1991).

Hollenstein, meanwhile, was particularly active in spreading and popularizing typefaces. Initially employed by a French book club, he opened his own studio in 1956. In 1958 he conceived Brasilia, a sans serif block face designed by Albert Boton. Starting in 1959, he issued his own catalog of faces, *Hollenstein Phototypo*. The first edition introduced Neue Haas-Grotesk, later called Helvetica, invented in Switzerland just two years earlier. It was notably through Hollenstein's catalog that Helvetica, an exact contemporary of Univers, became known in France (both faces are now modern classics). Pursing his activities in design and in the importation of foreign type, Hollenstein started introducing specifically American faces in 1966, presented in a catalog titled *American Type Shop* (which included, among others, Franklin Gothic and News Gothic, both designed by Morris Fuller Benton back in the first decade of the twentieth century). Sensitive to the unusual appearance of these typefaces with their original letterforms, Hollenstein managed to make them popular among professional circles. At the same time, his studio promoted a whole range of cultural activities, hosting and organizing various seminars on typography in the form of courses, public screenings, exhibitions, and so on. He was particularly keen on audiovisual media and announced his attention to focus on them, but his accidental death in 1974 brought his career to an untimely end.

Like Hollenstein, Jean Widmer was sensitive to cultural cross-currents. "For me, like Knapp and Frutiger, Paris in the post-war period provided a whole new typographical spirit. A full-page ad was still unthinkable in Switzerland—we took advantage of the positive side of France's Latin spirit."[59] Because Widmer encountered Johannes Itten early on in Zurich and then met Max Bill in Paris, and subsequently conveyed his own vision and conception of modernism through a long teaching career, he now appears to have been a key bridge spanning pre-war dynamism, the emerging Swiss school of the 1940s, and French design of the latter half of the twentieth century. For a while highly active in the advertising sector, he worked as art director of the Galeries Lafayette department store in Paris from 1959 to 1961, then performed the same job for the magazine *Jardin des modes* in the 1960s. In 1970 he founded his own agency, later known as Visuel Design/Jean Widmer. Throughout the last three decades of the twentieth century major institutional commissions gave Widmer, flanked by his team, the opportunity to forge his own vision of graphic design—efficient, modest, and modern. He explained his approach in a straightforward way: "I never tried to disguise or transform the material or subject, I just wanted to enhance it."[60] He notably developed, first on his own and then through his agency, a striking series of posters launched in 1969 for the Centre de Création Industrielle (CCI). Visuel Design/Jean Widmer Studio was also responsible for a major system of highway signage (including the design of hundreds of pictograms), and for the corporate logo and visual image of many institutions, cultural or otherwise, which often included an entire range of printed materials and systems of signposting (in Paris alone, such commissions came from the Centre Pompidou, the Conservatoire National Supérieur de Musique et de Danse, the Institut du Monde Arabe, the Galerie Nationale du Jeu de Paume, and the Musée d'Orsay, this last designed in collaboration with Bruno Monguzzi). Through his conception of graphic design, through the dissemination of his work, and through his teaching (a forty-year stint at the École Nationale Supérieure des Arts Décoratifs), Widmer

350

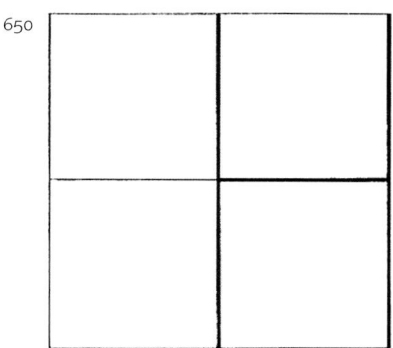

650
Albert Hollenstein, logotype for his studio.

651
Albert Hollenstein, *Hollenstein 74* catalog.

652
Albert Hollenstein, cover of *Hollenstein Phototypo*, 1970.

653
Jean Widmer, posters for exhibitions at the Centre de Création Industrielle, Paris, 1970. Silkscreen, 25 1/2 in. × 19 3/4 in. (65 × 50 cm).

654
Jean Widmer, studies for a poster for the exhibition "La Rue" at the Centre de Création Industrielle, Paris, 1970. Sketches in marker pen on tracing paper.

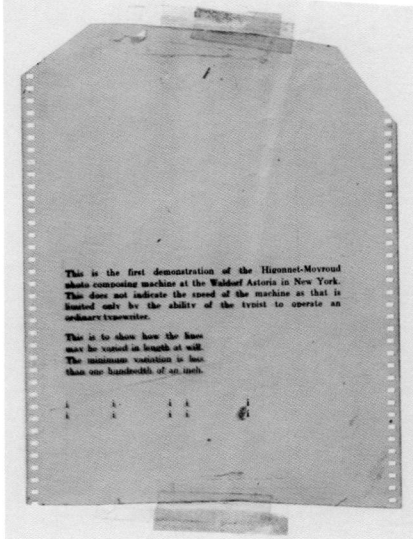

655
The first bromide film of a text phototypeset with the Lumitype machine, New York, April 26, 1949.

656
The film matrix disk of the Lumitype-Photon phototypesetting machine, Paris, late 1950s.

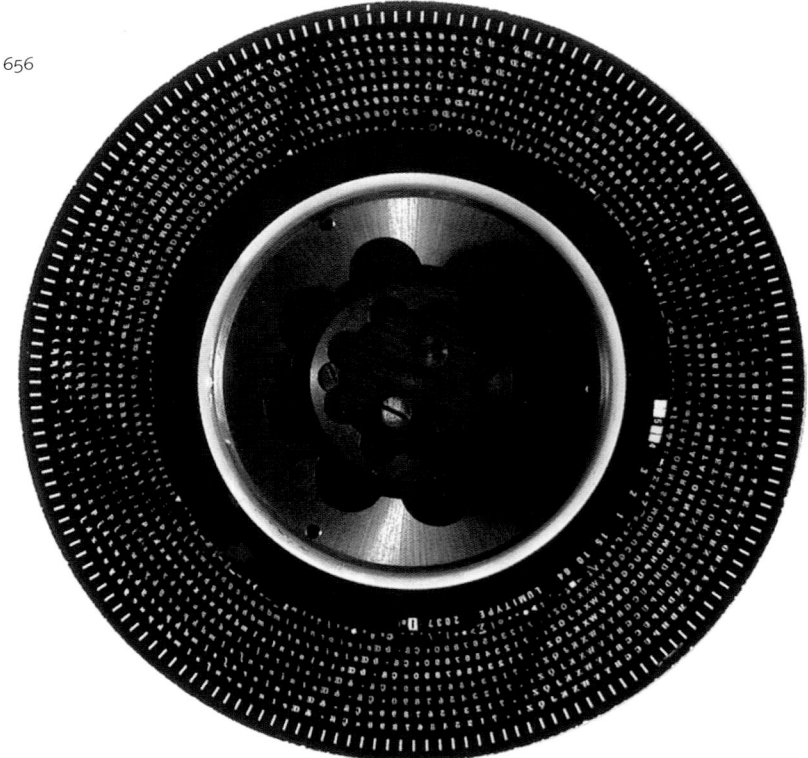

helped to train several generations of designers and to bring to a wider public certain approaches to modernism that had been little known in France prior to the 1950s and 1960s. "Proper tribute to Jean Widmer is long overdue. He continues to promote a rational modernism and he appeals to the greatest number in the name of progress. It's time to readopt his taste for the lasting, social usefulness of graphic design, far from the petty bustle of seductive advertising imagery plastered everywhere on a grand scale. His elegant inventiveness is highly civil. It respects *others* and demands that the right to information be imbued with constant creativity—it embodies a kind of trust."[61]

Designing typefaces

Affected by post-war developments in typography and graphic design in the West, the specific activity of creating new letterforms suddenly assumed unusual, extraordinary scope. It would seem that the latter half of the twentieth century displayed, above all, a striking eclecticism in the matter (an eclecticism already evident during the Victorian era). The mass production and consumption of type was accompanied by a multifarious renewal of its many forms. Several trends emerged or were consolidated within this vast panorama: the development of a new generation of sans serif faces, a new infatuation with forms typical of the nineteenth century, a demand for characters destined for a highly specific use (for a given company, institution, or system of signage), letterforms designed for electronic methods of display and recognition, a renewed interest in script faces, and so on. These various trends, as well as the sustained interest in typefaces for body text, continued to call for extremely precise skills, quality designs, and careful balancing acts—all geared towards meeting the time-honored challenge of coming up with new, original forms (as expressed in extreme fashion in the 1960s with the swirls, curves, and twists of psychedelic lettering).

657
Colin Brignall, Countdown typeface, perhaps the first original drawing for Letraset (adhesive transfer letters), c. 1965. The face was also used for signage. Colin Brignall first worked as photo technician for a typeface design studio (1964), then went on to become a letterform designer and ultimately director (1980) of the Letraset studio. He created over one hundred typefaces, including Aachen (1969, Letraset).

On the technical level, this general evolution was driven by the effective transformation of typesetting methods and technologies, in particular the development of photosetting (which was nevertheless accompanied by other, related, phenomena such as the mass-marketing of transfer-lettering products). Photosetting equipment spread significantly in the latter part of

a B C D e
F G H I J K
L m n O P
Q R S T U
V W X Y Z

● Upper-case design is used for these characters
● Lower-case design is used for these four characters
● Only one design exists for these seven characters

neu
Jlphjbet

j   een   une   eine
pobbibility   godelijkheid   pobbibulithé   godlichteut
for   door   pour   fur
the   de   le   due
neu   nieuwe   deueloppement   neue
deueLoppent   onthytobeLung   noudeu   enfytobtlung

Jn
introduction
for
J
prodrjnned
hypodrjphy

658
Bradbury Thompson, Alphabet 26, a single
upper- and lowercase face that eliminated
ascenders and descenders (with the exception
of J and Q). The typeface was first presented in
issue 180 of *Westwaco Inspirations* magazine,
1950.

659
Wim Crouwel (Total Design), cover of the
brochure presenting the New Alphabet,
"an introduction for a programmed typography,"
Amsterdam, 1967. Kwadraat-Blad (Quadrat-
Print), 10 × 10 in. (25 × 25 cm). The Kwadraat-
Blad were a series of printing experiments,
coordinated by Pieter Brattinga, "in the realms
of graphic arts, fine arts, literature, and music."

the 1950s and was in general use by the 1960s. The bulk and weight of lead had thus given way to a method based on photographic techniques (though only a quarter of a century before the advent of digital technology). The cost of manufacturing and using type was thus substantially reduced, in a trend similar to the mechanization that had vastly increased output in the late nineteenth century. There was a total transformation in access to and use of typesetting equipment—lighter, more accessible technology led to a diversification in the design and production of typefaces, ranging from the revival of Victorian letterforms to the conception of new faces via the reinvestigation of a rich tradition.

Because the second half of the twentieth century unflaggingly sustained this expansion of the visual universe, many typeface designers were able to earn a certain renown in countries such as the United States, Switzerland, France, Germany, the Netherlands, and Italy. They included Ed Benguiat, Max Bill, Albert Boton, Roger Excoffon, Adrian Frutiger, Marcel Jacno, Herb Lubalin, Hans Eduard Meier, Max Miedinger, Aldo Novarese, Imre Reiner, Bradbury Thompson, Jan Tschichold, and Hermann Zapf. Some of them produced only a limited, specific, identifiable set of designs while others, such as Novarese, Benguiat, Zapf, and Frutiger, were particularly prolific, producing new typefaces by the hundreds. According to Japanese designer Ikko Tanaka, at the time there was an unusual enthusiasm and taste for type and for characters themselves. "In the 1950s... lettering manifested a brilliant show of independence in European and American design. Letters possessed the meaning of words themselves. They had beautiful abstract shapes.... Awareness of the magnificent qualities of the letter was keenly expressed in graphic design. That is what lay at the heart of the typography movement in Europe and the United States in the 1950s."[62] Although he stressed the pronounced Western enthusiasm for letters in the latter half of the century, Tanaka emphasized the timeless links between typography, alphabetic characters, and graphic design. This infatuation was reinforced by the determined resumption of the early twentieth-century spirit of experimentation (which in the meantime had given birth to several unreleased typefaces often geared towards research and exploration rather than production and profitability). Over the decades there appeared a succession of unusual designs that followed on from interwar initiatives. Bradbury Thompson, for example, designed Monalphabet in the 1940s, then Alphabet 26, presented in *Westwaco Inspirations* magazine in 1950—a type with a single alphabet that combined uppercase and lowercase forms and was practically devoid of descenders and ascenders, so that capital letters differed from lowercase letters only in size. Max Bill, meanwhile, decided in the 1960s to design an alphabet "for our times" that combined Kurt Schwitters's "optophonetic" research of the late 1920s with the additional goal of elaborating machine-readable lettering. Similar concerns were evident in Wim Crouwel's 1967 Nieuw Alfabet (New Alphabet), a "proposal for a new kind of letter" to be used for televisual display and based on an orthogonal grid, thereby offering "possibilities for new development."

Apart from experimental designs, which often remained in the trial stage, many new typefaces were produced with a view to release and commercialization. Many trends emerged, some faces having already joined the repertoire of major types. The 1950s were marked by, among other things, a significant phase of revamping sans serif faces. Folio, designed by Konrad Bauer and Walter Baum, was realized in 1954, while 1957 saw the release of both Univers and Helvetica, emblematic designs of their day that have since become part of our typographic heritage—always highly prized, sometimes openly criticized. Univers features optimal overall homogeneity. Because uppercase height does not differ radically from lowercase height, Univers capitals produce uniform typographic color useful for setting texts in various languages. The goal of this type was to supply an alternative to the various generations of sans serif models such as they had been developed since the late nineteenth century. Taking optical effects into account, Univers combines a clean line with a great coherence of forms, based on a vertical orchestration. Frutiger explained the existence of sans serif face as an extension of ancestral forms dictated by techniques of inscription and epigraphic engraving. Letters without serifs, he argued, essentially reflect engraved or incised forms. Their rigor and purity can be explained by the resistance of the material to the tool that cuts it: the greater the resistance, the more the forms of the sign will be simplified.[63] Attesting to the lively enthusiasm sparked by Frutiger's Univers, Emil Ruder would make it his preferred typeface, calling it a "masterpiece of coordination and logical thinking."[64] In contrast, other people, such as Karl Gerstner, criticized the slick, uniform neutrality of Univers, devoid of any surprise and tending to eliminate the special features of a character and to reduce the overall color. (The same complaint would be made of Helvetica, which remained highly prized by certain typographers, including some in Switzerland itself.) Univers would nevertheless be a huge hit, notably in the realm of advertising in both Europe and America.

Just as certain graphic designers maintained long-running relationships with corporate clients who relied on their services, so some type designers had lasting connections with foundries. Such was the case, in France, with Adrian Frutiger's collaboration with Deberny & Peignot—the designer's substantial oeuvre was thoroughly marked by his skill and his ability to design characters for specific uses (such as signage in major public facilities where there is a massive, sometimes international, flow of people). At the same time, forms reflecting an entirely different spirit were being created in France. This is exemplified by the exuberant and gestural faces designed by Roger Excoffon, including Choc and Mistral script types (1953),

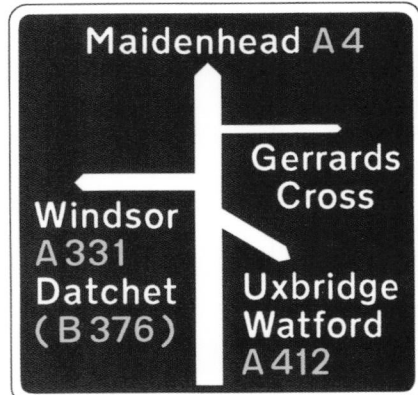

660

Calypso (1968), Banco (1951–52), and the famous Antique Olive (1962). In fact, French design was characterized not only by a quest for a certain neutrality but also by a renewed interest in handwritten forms and a taste for exuberance. Like Frutiger at Deberny & Peignot, several type designers spent much of their careers working with the same typeface publisher. That was notably the case with Hermann Zapf (who worked with the German firm Linotype) and Aldo Novarese (who worked with the Italian foundry Nebiolo). In Germany, Zapf's tradition-steeped dexterity as a calligrapher was wedded to a need to be in tune with his time, resulting in a vast repertoire of types that most famously include Palatino (1950), Melior (1952), and Optima (1958). He was also the designer of the notorious Zapf Dingbats (1978), a set of special, whimsical signs, decorations, and patterns assembled in the form of a typeface ("dingbat" being not only the technical, typographical term for unspecified signs but perhaps also suggestive of antipodean slang for "crazy" or "eccentric").[65]

When it came to typeface design in Italy, Aldo Novarese was a particularly productive inventor. Some of his best-known work, Microgamma (1952) and Eurostile (1962), display a geometrically inspired construction. While Novarese, Zapf, and Frutiger were highly active figures in this sector, many other contemporary designers in the West devised types that have become noteworthy or even famous in the post-war period; some of them were professional type designers, but others were engineers or totally anonymous individuals.[66] Examples include E13B (an anonymous design dating from 1958, composed of a series of signs meant to be read optically); Jan Tschichold's Sabon (1967); Frutiger's Serifa (1967), OCR-B (1968), and Frutiger (1976); Hans Eduard Meier's Syntax (first sketched in 1955, first released in 1968, and finally definitively completed in 2000); Albert Boton's Eras (1969 and 1976); Colin Brignall's Aachen (1969); Ed Benguiat's Souvenir (1970); and Herb Lubalin's Avant-Garde Gothic (1970–71). An overview of the designs of this period reveals ever-renewed differences and similarities, at the level of application as well as creation.

As was the case in the nineteenth century, the production of new type after the hiatus of World War II contributed to a typographic and economic boom. Once again the need to categorize and list the existing mass of letterforms was strongly felt. As Francis Thibaudeau had suggested thirty years earlier in his book *La Lettre d'imprimerie* (Printing Typefaces),[67] in

660
Jock Kinneir and Margaret Calvert, model of highway signpost, Great Britain, early 1960s. Painted on panel, 8 ft. 4 in. × 15 ft. 5 in. (255 × 470 cm). This design was adopted for the entire British road system.

661
Jock Kinneir, highway signpost, Great Britain, c. 1970.

662 Antique Olive

abdcefghijklmnopqrstuvwxyz
ABCDEFGHIJKLMNOPQRSTUVWXYZ
1234567890

665 manuaires

Humanes
Garaldes
Réales
Didones
Mécanes
Linéales
Incises
Scriptes

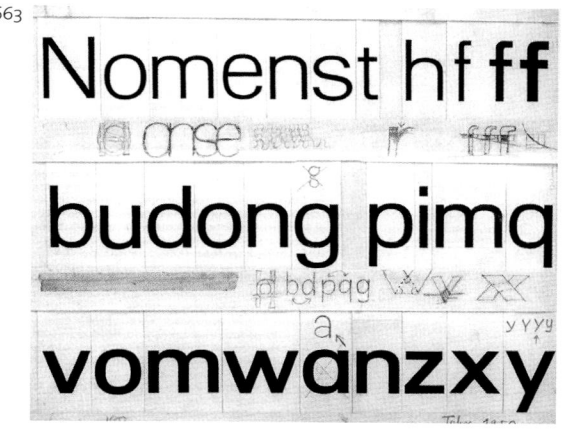

666 UNIVERS

abcdefghijklmnopqrs
ßtuvwxyz
ABCDEFGHIJKLMNO
PQRSTUVWXYZ
1234567890

667 HELVETICA

abcdefghijklmnopqrs
ßtuvwxyz
ABCDEFGHIJKLMN
OPQRSTUVWXYZ
1234567890

662
Roger Excoffon, Antique Olive typeface,
Olive foundry, 1962–66.

663
Adrian Frutiger, research into a sans serif
typeface, done under Professor Walter Käch,
Zurich, 1950–51.

664
Adrian Frutiger, research into a sans serif
typeface, École des Arts et Métiers, Zurich
(under Professor Walter Käch), 1950–51.
According to Frutiger, the teaching of this
school follows the line that "the design of each
letter, including the uprights, should be done
entirely freehand, which gives a good sensitivity
to the lines and a pleasing aspect to the texts
composed with it."

665
The French version of the nine families of
typeface in the Vox Classification system,
officially adopted by the Association
Typographique Internationale (ATYPI) in 1952.
The English equivalents are: Manual,
Humanistic, Garaldic, Transitional, Didonic,
Mechanistic, Lineal, Incised, and Script.

666
Adrian Frutiger, Univers typeface designed
for Deberny & Peignot, Paris, 1957.

667
Max Miedinger, Helvetica typeface designed
for Haas, Basel, 1957 (originally called Neue
Haas-Grotesk).

1952 Maximilien Vox drew up a classification system that comprised nine distinct families, labeled Humanistic, Garaldic, Transitional, Didonic, Mechanistic, Lineal, Incised, Script, and Manual. The usefulness of this system led to its adoption—once complemented by two other families, Blackletter and Non-Latin—by the ATYPI in 1962. This breakdown thus became the international standard in geographic zones that use the Latin alphabet. Whereas Thibaudeau in 1921 identified "four major classic families" (after four centuries of movable type technology), the ATYPI classification recognized eleven, almost three times as many. The profusion of typefaces that began in the nineteenth century, and has continued to grow ever since, thus favored the development of analytical tools and grids that make it possible to grasp and categorize the colossal volume of typefaces now employed and available. Just as the expansion and boom in typographic production was an integral part of the consumer society and of rapidly changing fashions, so eclecticism, which logically followed from this process of constant diversification, would triumph in spectacular manner once computer technology arrived in the mid-1980s.

Such diversification profitably enlarged the scope of creativity and engendered much enthusiasm. Tempering this exuberance, some leading professional typographers nevertheless expressed strong reservations about this phenomenon. They counseled a certain moderation. Hollenstein, for one, argued that true talent and fame in the realm of type design remain rare. "How many really famous innovators have there been? Maybe one or two per generation up to 1900, and two or three per decade since that time. That's not a lot."[68] The many critical comments made by typographers down through the decades, reflecting the wealth of material and corresponding debate, include some that directly challenge entire classes of type. Similar

668

abcdefg 12345

abcdefg 12345

670 Auch der Bildschmuck der Frühdrucke knüpft an die Illustrationen der Handschriften an. Am Ende des Mittelalters ga abcdefghijklmnopqrst uvwxyz & 1234567890 ABCDEFGHIJKLMNO PQRSTUVWXYZ

668
Hans Eduard Meier, Syntax typeface, Switzerland. Top: first proposal, 1955. Bottom: final release version.

669
The first five fonts of Syntax typeface: normal, Italic, semi-bold, bold, extra-bold. 1968 and later.

670
Hans Eduard Meier, Syntax typeface, initial proposal of 1955.

671
Comparison of four typefaces (top to bottom): Futura (1927), Gill (1928), Helvetica (1957), and Syntax (first sketched in 1955, produced 1968–2000).

672
The digital versions of Syntax (top) and Sabon (bottom), the faces used for the titles and running text of this book.

673
Jan Tschichold, Sabon typeface, 1967. Digital version. This is the face used for the running text of this book.

669
ABCDEFGHIJKLMNOPQRSTUVWXY
Zabcdefghijklmnopqrstuvwxyzß&123
4567890.,:;!?()[]§†*''""‹›«»--—
ABCDEFGHIJKLMNOPQRSTUVWXY
Zabcdefghijklmnopqrstuvwxyzß&123
4567890.,:;!?()[]§†*''""‹›«»--—
ABCDEFGHIJKLMNOPQRSTUVWXY
Zabcdefghijklmnopqrstuvwxyzß&123
4567890.,:;!?()[]§†*''""‹›«»--—
ABCDEFGHIJKLMNOPQRSTUVW
XYZabcdefghijklmnopqrstuvwxyz
ß&1234567890.,:;!?()[]§†*''""‹›
«»--—
ABCDEFGHIJKLMNOPQRSTUV
WXYZabcdefghijklmnopqrstuv
wxyzß&1234567890.,:;!?()[]§†*
''""‹›«»--—

671
abc 123
abc 123
abc 123
abc 123

672
jmprs
jmprs

673
abcdefghijklmnopqrstuvwxyz

ABCDEFGHIJKLM
NOPQRSTUVWXYZ

ABCDEFGHIJKLM
NOPQRSTUVWXYZ

1234567890
1234567890

observations by people as different as Tschichold and Massin display concern with general perception and longevity. In 1946, Tschichold questioned the future of "Antique" (sans serif) and Egyptian type, two of the four families identified by Thibaudeau. "Vestiges of the nineteenth-century's star letterforms, Antique and Egyptian faces, have recently enjoyed renewed popularity, but who knows how long that will last?"[69] Independently, Massin also queried Thibaudeau's list. "While I'll admit that there exist typefaces with a universal, timeless appeal—the Elzevirs—I couldn't be so sure about the Didots, whose style is too heavily pronounced."[70] In the way they cut across each other, these comments point to the questions raised by the broad issue of eclectic letterform design, which has been so much a part of visual practice and culture ever since the nineteenth century and which now heralds the future

674

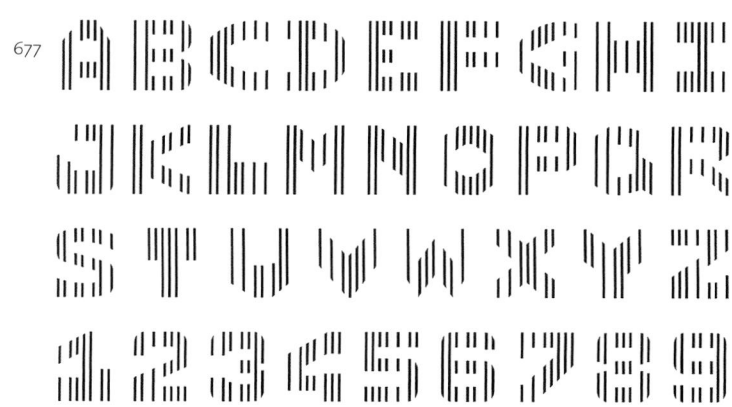

675

676

677

678

679

674
Left: Examples of letters and numerals revealing the formal characteristics of version A of OCR (Optical Character Recognition, devised by ECMA engineers in 1966). Right, top: OCR-A typeface. Right, bottom: OCR-B, designed by Adrian Frutiger in collaboration with ECMA, 1968. Typeface adopted in 1973 as international standard.

675
Timothy Epps and Christopher Evans, machine-readable typeface, National Physical Laboratory, Division of Computer Science, Great Britain, 1969.

676
Max Bill, studies for a typeface to be read by the human eye as well as by machines, 1960s.

677
CMC7 (Caractère Magnétique Codé 7 Bâtonnets), a seven-bar magnetic-ink typeface devised in the 1950s to be read by special machines; adopted as a standard in France and other European countries in 1962.

678
Maxim Zhukov, Meander typeface, Moscow, 1972.

679
Hermann Zapf, Zapf Dingbats typeface, 1978.

Professionalism and expansion

Other centers of graphic design

After the war, geographical mobility and transnational influence recovered the importance they had enjoyed in the early decades of the twentieth century. They continued to function through highly diverse channels: multilingual publications, traveling exhibitions, itinerant designers, foreign teachers, and highly international schools (nearly half of the students and teachers at the Ulm School of Design came from abroad—Europe, the Americas, Japan—representing a total of over one hundred and fifty nations).[71] More and more countries were making a splash on the international graphic design scene as the field spread, multiplied, and reinvented itself in diverse centers of activity. In addition to the United States, Switzerland, Italy, Poland, and France, major developments in the realms of typography and graphic design took place in the Netherlands, Great Britain, Germany, Mexico, Cuba, and Japan. Interest in visual expression was moreover accompanied by an increased awareness and knowledge of non-Western design, which led to a more open, appreciative attitude toward it.[72]

The Netherlands

Throughout the twentieth century, Dutch graphic design consistently demonstrated its vitality, professionalism, and presence in everyday life. The specific realm of typeface design was equally fertile. The postwar scene in the Netherlands benefited from a significant avant-garde heritage (the De Stijl movement, the New Typography trend, and unclassifiable and original tendencies such as the work of Werkman). Preeminent designers of the day included Willem Sandberg, Wim Crouwel, Jan Bons, Pieter Brattinga, Otto Treumann, and Dick Elffers (of this group, Treumann had frequented Piet Zwart, while Elffers was an assistant, in turn, to Paul Schuitema and Piet Zwart in the 1930s).[73] Sandberg (born 1897), a leading designer in the postwar period, had already been appointed a curator at the Stedelijk Museum in 1937; during the war years, he continued his activities in underground fashion, publishing eighteen of his *Experimenta Typographica* and working for the Dutch Resistance (by forging identity papers, among other things). He produced a number of posters and exhibitions for the Stedelijk, ensuring long-term faithfulness to a coherent, modest, yet recognizable style (often identifiable through the use of rough shapes torn from paper). As to Crouwel (born in 1928), he belonged to a later generation that did not emerge until the 1950s. In 1963 Crouwel co-founded the influential Total Design studio, which adopted a versatile approach to graphic design; in 1965, for instance, the studio would be commissioned to design the signage for Schipol Airport in Amsterdam. A keen typographer, Crouwel's significant graphic output included the Nieuw Alfabet (New Alphabet), specially designed in 1967 to be displayed on television screens. His work led him to the conclusion that "typography is the foundation of graphic design."[74] Expressing distinct reservations over contemporary type design, even before the arrival of computer technology he declared that "much of the so-called experimental typography is just another form[al] exercise within the framework of a certain modern trend; only some of these experiments are fundamental and create a basic discussion on typography."[75]

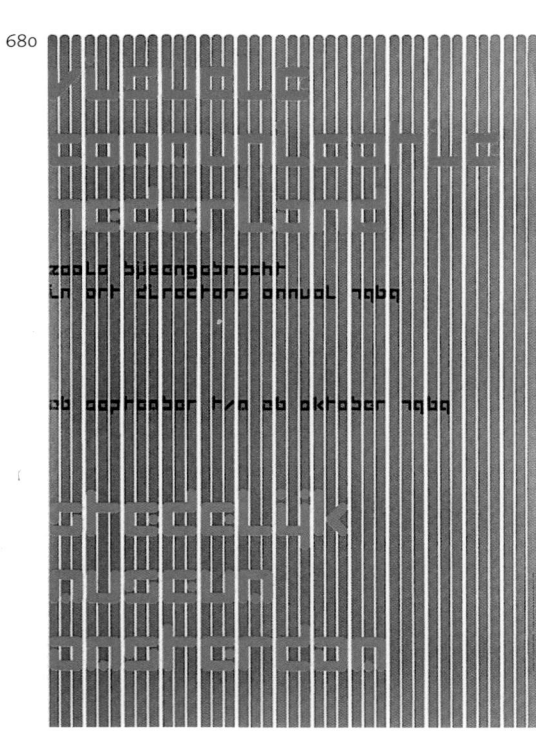

680
Wim Crouwel, poster for a show on visual communication in the Netherlands at the Stedelijk Museum, Amsterdam, 1969.
3 ft. × 2 ft. 1 in. (95 × 64 cm).

Great Britain

The British graphic design scene was also active following World War II. Jan Tschichold lived in England between 1947 and 1949, having been asked to supervise the typographic revamping of Penguin Books' various imprints. Similar research into book design was then underway in Germany and France, if in highly different directions. In addition to Tschichold's temporary presence, two other figures in Britain stood out from the crowd in the late 1940s—Herbert Spencer and Anthony Froshaug (born in 1924 and 1920, respectively). Both were steeped in the typographical renaissance and were teachers at London's Central School of Arts and Crafts. Froshaug also taught at Germany's Ulm School of Design in the early 1960s, then went on to the Royal College of Art. Spencer, meanwhile, devoted part of his career to the publishing world. He had long-standing professional ties with Lund Humphries, starting in 1950, and was involved in various publications that documented and promoted an avant-garde culture. In 1949 he founded the famous magazine *Typographica* (which ceased publication in 1967), thereby affirming his commitment to modernism. His taste for an expressive typography and for an avant-garde attitude can also been seen in his publication of several reference books, *The Visible Word* (1968), *Pioneers of Modern Typography* (1969), and *The Liberated Page* (1987), the latter being an anthology of experimental typography in the twentieth century as reflected in the pages of *Typographica*.

The British design world was marked by other initiatives, trends, and creations in the 1960s, ones that not only harked back to the avant-garde tradition of the interwar period but also pointed to new developments in visual expression. American designer Bob Gill moved to London in 1960, and two years later joined up with Alan Fletcher and Colin Forbes to found the Fletcher, Forbes & Gill agency, itself the forerunner of the famous Pentagram design consultancy (which was established in 1972 and eventually opened branches in the United States). Another sign of the times was the extensive design—in Britain as elsewhere—of signage systems required by transportation facilities, public services, and sites of mass transit

681
Anthony Froshaug, layout of the book, *Typographic Norms*, London, 1964. 8 × 11 3/4 in. (21 × 29.7 cm).

682
Painted wall on Carnaby Street, London, late 1960s.

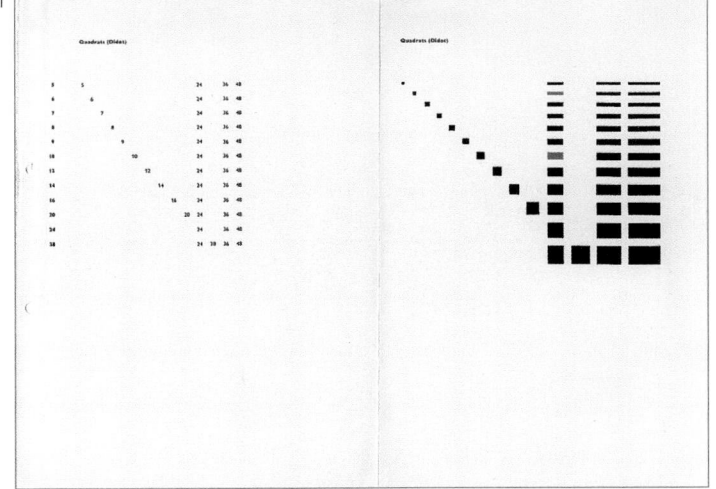

or heavy traffic (subway systems, airports, highways, hospitals, etc.). Nearly a quarter of a century after Edward Johnston's pioneering work for the London Underground, Jock Kinneir played a major role in defining the graphics of information through his work on vast signage projects. He was first commissioned to do the signposting for Gatwick Airport, just outside London; then, in the early 1960s, in conjunction with Margaret Calvert he produced one of his most familiar designs—the road signs for all of Britain's motorway system. Like some of his contemporaries who also focused on a particular aspect of visual communication, Kinneir recorded his experiences in a book, *Words and Buildings* (1980). This record contributed, as did the writings and publications of Spencer and Froshaug, to a better understanding of developments in—and the culture of—graphic design in Britain in the second half of the twentieth century.

Germany and the Ulm School

Compared to other countries, post-war Germany was confronted with a recent past that was particularly weighty and complex. Whereas avant-garde design had flourished extensively there prior to the war (as it had in the Netherlands and the Soviet Union), Germany was also the country where it had subsequently encountered the greatest obstacles and sternest censorship. After this long phase of constraint, German design finally began reviving around 1950. The better-known graphic designers of the dawning new period included Anton Stankowski (who returned from Zurich in 1937 and who had known Max Burchartz and Johannes Canis in the 1920s), Herbert Kapitzki (who studied under Willi Baumeister), Almir Mavignier (an artist from Brazil who studied graphics at Ulm), Pierre Mendell, and Willy Fleckhaus. In the specific domain of typeface design, the names of Georg Trump, Hermann Zapf, and Günter Gerhard Lange come to the fore. Stankowski (born in 1906) spent decades exploring the links between his pictorial concerns and his graphic experiments, while his typographic work revealed a strong penchant for Akzidenz Grotesk. He used this sans serif face, in fact, when developing the city of Berlin's visual image in the 1960s (the city's logotype dates from 1969). As to Fleckhaus (born in 1925), he made a noteworthy contribution to book and magazine design, particularly for the Suhrkamp publishing house and *Twen* magazine. At the same time, a certain number of major German publishers began paying greater attention to typography in the 1950s and 1960s, in terms of both cover and text, notably when it came to paperback books.

One of the key events in postwar Germany was the founding of a school of graphic design in Ulm. Although the Hochschule für Gestaltung, internationally known as the Ulm School of Design, was above all famous for its training in industrial production and design, courses were also given in "visual communication," one of the four main departments of the school. The important role played by the Hans and Sophie Scholl Foundation in setting up the school partly explains the anti-fascist attitudes and sociopolitical tendencies that influenced design theory at Ulm.[76] Plans for the school were first laid in the early 1950s, then Max Bill was appointed to be its first director in 1954, and its doors officially opened in 1955. A certain number of leading figures contributed to the program at the School of Design, offering high-quality teaching that soon made the school's reputation. Walter Peterhans organized the basic course right from 1953 (he had been head of the photography department at the Bauhaus from 1929 onward). Between 1954 and 1958, Bill's secretary was none other than Eugen Gomringer, one of the founders of Concrete poetry not long before. Guest instructors included Josef Albers, Walter Gropius, Mies van der Rohe, Charles Eames, Josef Müller-Brockmann, Karl Gerstner, and Buckminster Fuller. Coursework in visual communication, meanwhile, was broken down into one section devoted to the typographic realm (including graphic design, photography, and exhibition design) and another devoted to film and television. The department's staff included Otl Aicher, Anthony Froshaug, Herbert Kapitzki, and Friedrich Vordemberge-Gildewart. As early as 1950 the school's curriculum clearly announced its mission:

The Visual Design section will train specialists in the entire realm of advertising, including layout artists for books, designers for exhibitions, and so on. It therefore aspires to train specialists whose background will not limit them to one specific activity such as typography, graphic design, or photography, but who will master all these fields and can interrelate them....

Understanding among peoples today is largely conveyed through graphic messages, for example photography, posters, and drawings. Giving these messages a form that corresponds to their function and forging methods of implementation that coincide with the needs of our day constitute the goal of the Visual Communication department. That is why graphic design,

683

684

685

Bauaufsicht | BERLIN

Der Senator für Bau- und Wohnungswesen sucht für den Fachbereich Haus- und Gesundheitstechnik einen

Mitarbeiter

Erwünscht sind Bewerber mit abgeschlossenem Studium an einer Technischen Fachhochschule (Heizungs-, Lüftungs- und Gesundheitstechnik), praktischen Erfahrungen auf diesen Gebieten und Kenntnissen des Bauaufsichtsrechts.
Zu den Aufgaben des Mitarbeiters in der für die Bau- und Wohnungsaufsicht zuständigen Abteilung (I) gehören schwierige Einzelentscheidungen auf dem Gebiet der Haus- und

Flüssigkeiten, Bearbeitung von Widersprüchen aus dem Aufgabengebiet und Zustimmungen gem. § 99 Bauordnung (BauO) Bln.
Die Position — Vgr. IV a BAT — ist sofort zu besetzen.
Zusätzlich bieten wir zahlreiche soziale Leistungen wie Beihilfen, Kinderzuschläge, Essenzuschuß, Weihnachtszuwendung und zusätzliche Altersversorgung. Wir haben gleitende Arbeitszeit.
Bewerbungen werden unter Angabe der Kennziffer **73 285** mit den üblichen Unterlagen bis zum 21. Dezember 1973 an den Senator für Bau- und Wohnungswesen — ZB 23 —,

683
Willy Fleckhaus, graphic rendering of the word "hippies" for *Twen* magazine, 1967.

684
Anton Stankowski, monogram, 1927.

685
Anton Stankowski, typographic image for the city of Berlin, c. 1960s.

686
Otl Aicher Studio, study for a standardized
system of pictograms for use in international
contexts (airports, Olympic Games, trade fairs,
major exhibitions, etc.), published in 1976.

687
Otl Aicher, title sequence for a German TV
program, *Länderspiegel*, Germany, 1974.

686
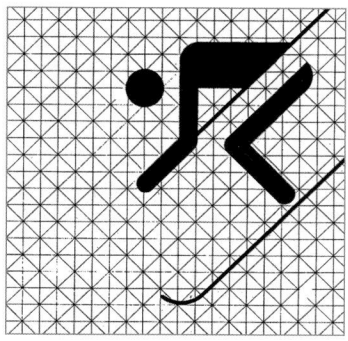

687
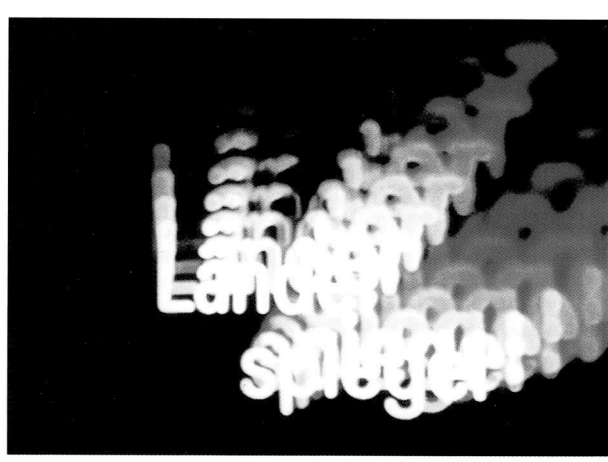

688

688
Pierre Mendell and Klaus Oberer,
packaging for Chat cough
medicine, Munich, 1964.

689
Hartmut Kowalke (a student in
Tomas Maldonado's course at the
Ulm School of Design), proposal
for a jacket for the record *Round
Midnight*, 1962–63.

689
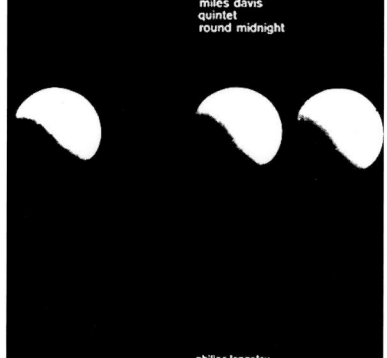

690
Friedrich Friedl, development of a typeface with variable dynamics, text by Carlos Fuentes, India ink on cardboard, Germany, 1966.

690

photography, typography, and exhibition design will be handled as a unit to which film and television will later be added.... Research within the department will seek, through experimentation and analysis, to make visual expression fit its goal as closely as possible and to define its significance. In so doing, we will call on new scientific discoveries made in recent years in the theory of perception and meaning.[77]

At first, teaching at Ulm followed the general lines laid down at the Bauhaus. Courses were quick to embrace the communications industry and to turn to mass graphic design, developing an approach to typography similar to that of the Swiss style. The institution was also concerned to enrich education in design with a series of theoretical considerations on the issues of semiotics, systems theory, ergonomics, information theory, and perception. It wanted to broaden students' minds through a combination of practical training and theoretical reflection, thereby redefining the function and position of the profession of designer into one that entailed a responsible, critical, and social role. "In its day, Ulm managed to convince society that cultural values were important not only in the home but that they had to be incorporated into schools, offices, factories, hospitals, and transportation. Some of its projects were truly pioneering...."[78] After fifteen years of existence (barely longer than that of the Bauhaus) and subject to many difficulties and disputes, the Ulm School of Design closed its doors in 1968 at the decision of the Stuttgart government, its main source of funding. During its lifetime, Ulm's Hochschule für Gestaltung trained some six hundred and fifty students, developed an international network of exchanges, and inspired other institutes of design, notably in India and Brazil.

Japan

While the post-war period saw the resumption or pursuit of graphic design in areas where an avant-garde practice had previously existed (Germany, the Netherlands, and so on), a clearer view of design could perhaps be had in non-Western countries and cultures. Among other influential movements, central European work inspired designers across a vast geographic range that included the United States, Japan, Scandinavia, and Spain. Many zones of visual communication, sometimes geographically very distant, generated interest and

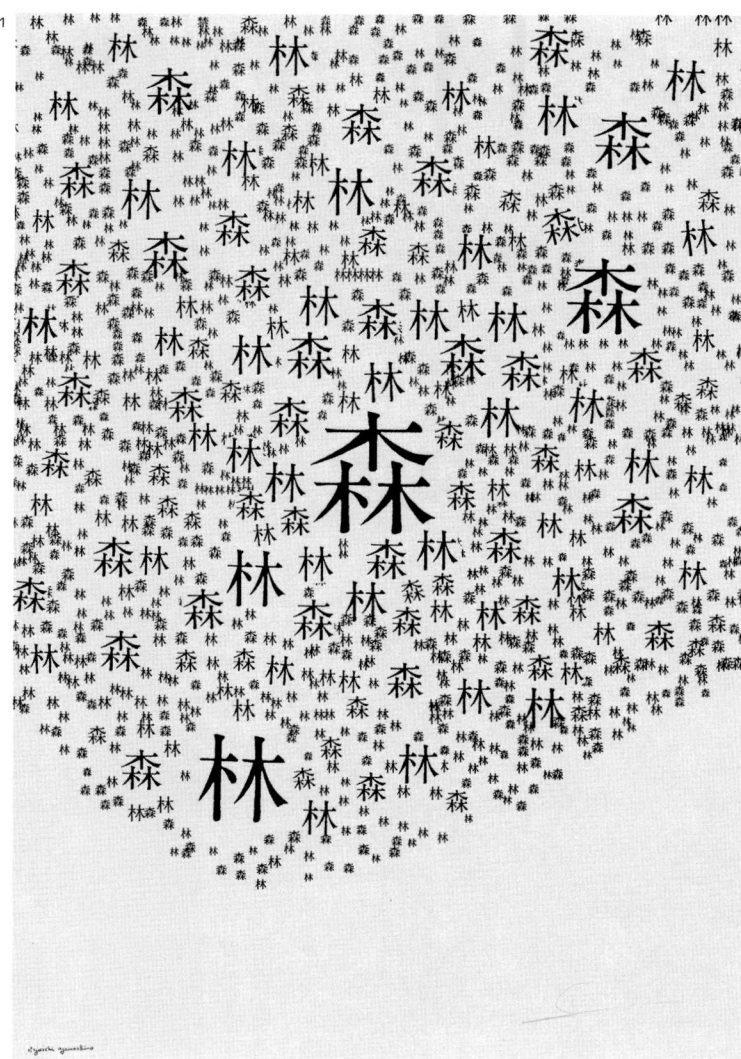

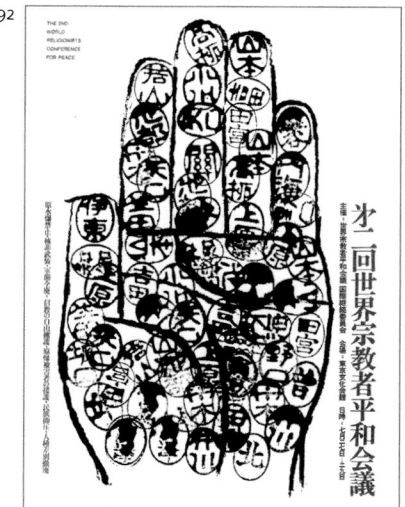

acknowledgment in the field of graphic design. Such was the case in Japan, where the art of printmaking had considerably influenced the birth of modern posters one hundred years earlier. Among the leading figures of Japanese graphic design in the post-war period it is worth mentioning Yusaku Kamekura (born in 1915, a key protagonist of the post-war resurgence), Ryuichi Yamashiro (1920), Kiyoshi Awazu (1929), Kazumasa Nagari (1929), Ikko Tanaka (1930), Shigeo Fukuda (19332), and Tadanori Yokoo (1936). Japanese design soon attained international recognition and impact.[79] Many other countries outside of Europe and North America would progressively emerge or reemerge, asserting and even imposing their skill at Western techniques of modern graphics, and confirming the wide-open nature of artistic practices, the variety of possibilities, and above all the recognition and assimilation of different approaches.

Exuberance versus reservations

The second half of the twentieth century heralded greater visibility for typography and graphic design. The successive events and upheavals of the 1930s and 1940s culminated in a period of recomposition, perhaps all the richer and more energetic for having to throw off recent memories of obstruction, restriction, and requisition. A certain number of factors contributed to the context in which graphic design took shape in the second half of the century, beginning with the growth of mass media. This explosion accompanied the rise of a consumer society and the enduringly favorable conditions of the post-war economic boom enjoyed by industrialized nations. Given this context, issues of social or political commitment were no longer of prime concern to designers. Instead, stress was laid on professionalism in both training and practice, and on the development of certain spheres of visual expression (such as corporate image, book and magazine publishing, and advertising). There was a clear desire to present the beholder with designs that were witty, relaxed, playful or even jubilant. Furthermore, technological changes and developments had a major impact on visual communication in the decades following the war, in terms of the flexibility of production, artistic choices, and practical organization; such developments included the transition to phototypesetting, an intensive use of photography, the impact of offset printing methods, and so on. Hence, as had always been the case, typography and graphic design were partly determined by the socioeconomic, technological, material, artistic, and historical context in

691
Ryuichi Yamashiro, poster for a campaign to encourage people to plant trees, 1955. Silkscreen, 3 ft. 4 1/2 in. × 2 ft. 4 3/4 in (103 × 72.8 cm). A visual play on the ideogram for "grove" (written with two characters) and forest (written with three characters).

692
Kiyoshi Awazu, poster for the Second World Religionists Conference for Peace, (Tokyo), Japan, 1964. Offset, 3 ft. 4 1/2 in. × 2 ft. 4 3/4 in. (103 × 72.8 cm). Illustration designed 1961, showing a hand covered with seals of names.

693
Koichi Sato, poster for the Ohara School of Ikebana, 1985. 3 ft. 4 1/2 in. × 2 ft. 4 3/4 in. (103 × 72.8 cm).

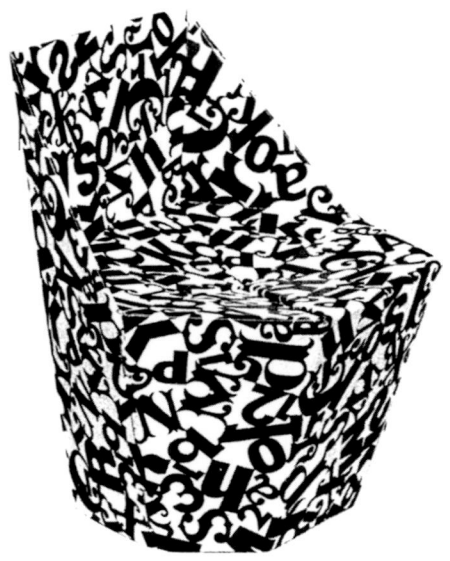

694

694
Peter Murdoch, *Chair Thing*, folding cardboard chair for children, Great Britain, mid-1960s.

695

695
Salvador Dalí, design of a logotype for Chupa Chups lollipops (marketed by Enric Bernat in 1958), c. 1969.

which they found themselves, even as they continued to reflect the innovations and directions directly initiated by designers.

Supplanting the successive series of "-isms" in the days of the avant-gardes, numerous expressive styles emerged simultaneously in the West and elsewhere. Already transnational during the interwar period, movements and influences went international in an ambiance of pluralism, diversification, and heterogeneity. In parallel fashion, changes in perception and sensibility occurred. Tendencies intersected, overlapped, straddled, or subsumed one another. The rapid pace of fashion and the coexistence of disparate registers encouraged the tolerance of complementary attitudes and, above all, seriously challenged rigid positions by blurring traditional landmarks. Some creative styles favored a personal touch, an artistic approach, and subjective expression through painterly, gestural graphics; others pursued the ideal goal of an objective, clear, neutral form at the service of its content. Already explored by the avant-gardes of the first decades of the century, these two approaches would enjoy a fertile heritage and, although in theory quite distinct, they could sometimes meet, connect, and interbreed. While the Polish and Swiss schools were heading in markedly different directions, designers in Milan and New York were inventing their own creative recipes from historical ingredients derived from fundamentally diverse sources. Thus even as designers such as Tomaszewski, Lubalin, Pintori, and Grignani were exploring new visual possibilities, several members of the Swiss school were refining a broad set of concepts into a didactic, communicable form (one that would ultimately have numerous applications and international repercussions).

The realm of graphic design experienced an ever-swifter proliferation of movements and an acceleration of international influences in the latter half of the twentieth century. The 1950s and 1960s were a time when certain professional phenomena spread from country to country—major associations of graphic artists were founded here and there, while agencies and studios were launched to bring lone designers together. Worldwide, authorities were henceforth paying special attention to signage in public spaces, especially airports and other transportation facilities: the Milan subway in 1963–64 (Bob Noorda), the British motorway system in 1964, the New York subway in the early 1970s (Massimo Vignelli), the Paris Métro in 1973, Amsterdam's Schiphol Airport in 1965, airports in Paris in 1959 and 1970–71, and so on. Meanwhile, tensions arose between graphic design and advertising (particularly tangible in the United States and the Netherlands); elsewhere, design had to cope with the massive arrival of color photography; and in the meantime, new attempts were made to establish international organizations devoted to typography and graphic design (the International Design Conference in Aspen in 1951, the AGI in 1952, ATypI in 1957, Icograda in 1963, etc.). All these phenomena helped graphic design to become an object of growing interest and attention as it increasingly invaded the public sphere.

To all this should be added an impression of generosity and euphoria that arose from or spurred the multiplicity and intersection of all these forms of expression. In the space of just a decade or two, approaches alternately rigorous or extroverted occupied the field: the International Typographic Style, the Swiss and Polish schools, psychedelic design, playful tendencies, refined Oriental aesthetics, revival trends, imagery borrowed from the 1960s protest movements (and, later, from the punk movement), and so on. Although this eclecticism often met with enthusiasm, notably on the part of younger generations (who have continued to profess it), some leading figures—of all ages—expressed reservations about the direction in which they felt typography and graphic design were headed. In 1964, for example, Ashley Havinden expressed a certain pessimism in the *Times*, claiming that the creativity of poster and layout artists had been sadly cut short since true graphic design was completely disappearing from billboards to the benefit of blown-up photographs.[80] Havinden's pessimism anticipated a series of critical comments—which would continue to be heard throughout the last three decades of the century—such as the one made by Herbert Bayer in an article published in 1967. He expressed his concern over what he felt was a lack of understanding, or

696

696
Niklaus Troxler, poster for a Joe McPhee Trio
concert at Willisau (Switzerland), 1975.

ignorance of the role of letters within typography: "Moreover, the typographical revolution
was not an isolated event, but went hand in hand with a new social and political
consciousness and consequently with the building of new cultural foundations.... It must
unfortunately be remembered that we live in a time of great ignorance and lack of concern
with the alphabet, writing and typography."[81] These brief examples reveal that the wealth of
(typo)graphic design in the post-war period met with reservations and interrogations as well
as with exuberance. These varying attitudes also prefigured, in their way, the issues that have
accompanied graphic design in recent decades.

NOTES

1 Karl Gerstner, *Programme entwerfen* (1963), quoted in E. M. Gottschall, *Typographic Communications Today* (Cambridge, Mass./London: MIT Press, 1989), 51.

2 Bernard Villemot, for instance, discussed his activities during the war, as quoted in Jean-François Bazin, *Les Affiches de Villemot* (Paris: Denoël, 1985), 37–38. "At the time I had no political ideas and no commitment whatsoever.... These commissions seemed like a boon, because we lacked everything and were starving to death.... I thus decorated a National Charity exhibition-railcar for [Pétain].... which allowed us to eat some sweets and vitamin biscuits.... Little by little, things began to evolve. In 1944 I learned about—I became aware—of the Resistance. So in the printshop we began to forge identity papers." Bazin goes on to comment, "After the Liberation, there was no witch hunt among poster artists worthy of the name and the profession. For that matter, Robert Aron's hefty, four-volume history of the post-war purges in France doesn't contain a single word on this subject. Many illustrators... depicted Marshal Pétain. A few poster artists were criticized for their work during the Occupation yet [some of them] went on to enjoy fine careers "(39–40).

3 When it comes to the paths adopted by designers faced with various technologies in the 1920s, a comparison between the oeuvres of Cassandre and Jan Tschichold is revealing. They began their careers at the same time, when photography was just beginning to appear in posters. Yet each took a distinct path that would be crucial in defining his work of that period: Cassandre hardly ever employed photography, preferring to draw and paint in the tradition of late nineteenth-century poster artists, whereas Tschichold accorded photography a key role in the development of a new graphic idiom.

4 See below, the section devoted to France, notably to René Higonnet and Louis Moyroud.

5 Robin Kinross used the expression "letters of light" as a subheading in his *Modern Typography* (London: Hyphen Press, 1992), 115. It also echoes, if somewhat indirectly, Moholy-Nagy's use of the term "typophoto."

6 Article 2, statutes of the Alliance Graphique Internationale as registered at the Prefecture de Police, Paris, on November 3, 1952.

7 Peignot was then president and CEO of the Deberney & Peignot type-foundry.

8 See note 50 and text, below.

9 Icograda currently boasts nearly one hundred member associations from some fifty countries.

10 Ashley Havinden, *Advertising and the Artist* (London: The Studio, 1956), 15.

11 Dictionnaire *Le Petit Robert 2* (Paris, 1980), 622.

12 The United States seem to furnish a particularly enlightening example of the way in which the history of graphic design can be propagated by a few pioneers who addressed the subject in art schools and universities, such as Alvin Eisenmann at Yale and Louis Danziger in California (the latter actively participated in the 1970s in consolidating the field of the history of graphic design through his long-term teaching at, among other places, Cal'Arts).

13 For the terms "New York school" and "American typographic expressionism," see notably P. B. Meggs, *A History of Graphic Design* (New York: John Wiley & Sons, 1998), 337 and 355.

14 Ikko Tanaka, "The Age of American Typography," *Transition of Modern Typography* (Japan: Ginza Graphic Gallery, 1996), 66. Tanaka went to the United States in 1960, where he met Herb Lubalin, Lou Dorfsman and Aaron Burns, all of whom made a great impression on him.

15 The exception to the European situation was a certain number of works and publications that did enjoy unusual popularity and impact, such as the 1925 publication of "Elementare Typographie," Tschichold's special issue of *Typographische Mitteilungen*.

16 See note 10, above.

17 On Rand, see his own books plus S. Heller, *Paul Rand* (London: Phaidon, 1999).

18 Many American designers remain little known in France, outside of specialist circles and professionals of the same generation. This applies to all periods, not just the one under discussion, the exception being designers who have benefited from the publication of a monograph.

19 Paul Rand, quoted in N. Polites, "Advertising design, graphic design, and what's the difference?" *Print* XLIV: vi, 53.

20 Ibid., 53–54.

21 "Danziger... thinks the schism was exacerbated by the design schools, which in the 1970s became both more powerful and more removed from the world of design practice." While Rand notes that "at Yale, where he teaches graphic design, nobody ever talks about advertising, regarding it as too commercial, too demeaning." Ibid., 53.

22 *Das neue Frankfurt* (1928), quoted by K. Matschke, "Der Ring...," in S. Lemoine (ed.), *Kurt Schwitters* (exh. cat., Paris: Centre Georges Pompidou/RMN, 1994), 201.

23 See *Off the wall: affiches psychédéliques de San Francisco 1966–1969* (Paris: Thames & Hudson, 2004).

24 See passages above (note 14) and below (note 62).

25 Quoted in S. Heller, "Big ideas that built America," *Eye* 22 (1996), 77.

26 Herbert Bayer, *Painter, Designer, Architect: Visual Communication* (New York: Reinhold, 1967), 75. Bayer's original text was deliberately set in lowercase, as he also stipulated for exhibition catalogs (see two Paris exhibitions, *Section allemande* [Grand Palais, 1930] and *Bauhaus 1919–1969* [Musée National d'Art Moderne /Musée d'Art Moderne de la Ville de Paris, 1969], both designed by Bayer and both set exclusively in lowercase letters).

27 In spoken French, the expression "Swiss typography" often carries a pejorative connotation of an overly restrained style (sometimes the mere adjective "Swiss" has the same connotation).

28 See chapter 1, note 67.

29 See J. Müller-Brockmann, *Grid Systems in Graphic Design: A Visual Communication Manual for Graphic Designers, Typographers, and Three Dimensional Designers* (Switzerland: Niggli, 1981).

30 See, below, the passage concerning the writings of Tschichold, Bill, Gerstner, Lohse, Herdeg, Müller-Brockmann, Ruder, and Hofmann. Also see H. E. Meier, *Die Schriftentwicklung/The Development of Script and Type/Le Développement des caractères* (Switzerland: Syntax Press, 1994 [1959]). It would be worth taking a closer look at the phenomenon of combining interest in (and practice of) typography with its extensions in display, writing, explanation, theorization, and publication.

31 Max Bill, "Über Typografie," *Schweizer Graphische Mitteilungen* 5 (1946, Sankt Gallen); translated into French and reprinted as "Sur la typographie," *Typografische Monatsblätter. RSI* 1 (1995), 3–4.

32 Jan Tschichold, "Glaube und Wirklichkeit," *Schweizer Graphische Mitteilungen* 6 (1946, Sankt Gallen), translated into French and reprinted as "Foi et réalité, "*Typografische Monatsblätter: RSI* 1 (1995), 9–12.

33 Jan Tschichold, "À propos de l'emploi de caractères d'imprimerie dans la publicité," *Publicité et arts graphiques* (1946–47), 69–74.

34 *Typografische Monatsblätter* and *Campo grafico* were thus founded the same year, 1933, in Switzerland and Italy, respectively. This date was also crucial in German history and the repercussions of that history on typography.

35 Emil Ruder, "Ordnende Typographie," *Graphis* 85 (1959), 405.

36 Jan Tschichold, "Vue cavalières sur le modernisme en typographie [Zur Typographie der Gegenwart], French translation (Paris: Société anonyme Monotype, 1961), 5.

37 Armin Hofmann, *Graphic Design Manual* (trilingual) (Switzerland:

Arthur Niggli, 1965), 40 and 38.

38 Hans-Jürg Hunziker, *L'Affiche typographique suisse* (exh. cat., Villeurbanne, France: Maison du livre, de l'image et du son, 1995), 18.

39 Emil Ruder, *Typographie/Typography* (Teufen, Switzerland: Niggli, 1967), 6, 14, 16, 18.

40 Josef Müller-Brockmann, *Graphic designers en* [sic] *Europe*, vol. 1 (Freiburg: Office du Livre, 1971), 62.

41 On Lohse, Bill and Gerstner, see, for example: C. Bignens and J. Stürzebecher, *Richard Paul Lohse: Konstruktive Gebrauchsgrafik* (Ostfildern-Ruit: Hatje Cantz, 1999); C. Bignens, H. R. Bosshard, and G. Fleischmann, *Max Bill: Typografie, Reklame, Buchgestaltung* (Zurich: Niggli Verlag, 1999); K. Gerstner, *Karl Gerstner: Review of 5 × 10 Years of Graphic Design*, edited by M. Kröplien (Ostfildern-Ruit: Hatje Cantz, 2001).

42 This book is set in Sabon (running text) and Syntax.

43 See below, note 64.

44 On Tomaszewski, Lenica, and Cieslewicz, see, for example, T. Sarfis and E. Maruszewska (eds.), *Henryk Tomaszewski: Graphismes et pédagogie* (Paris: Somogy, 1995); *Jan Lenica: Plakat- und Filmkunst* (exh, cat., Berlin: Frölich und Kaufmann, 1981); M. Rouard, *Roman Cieslewicz* (Paris: Thames & Hudson, 1993).

45 Franco Grignani, "Critical essay on current typography," in H. Schmid (ed.), *Typography Today* (Japan: Shigeo Ogawa, 1980), 106–107.

46 Quoted in Gottschall, *Typographic Communications Today*, 153.

47 Massin's full name was Robert Massin but he preferred to be known by his family name alone.

48 Interview with Raymond Hains, quoted by C. Schlatter, "La formation des avant-gardes françaises à partir de 1945," in B. Blistène and V. Legrand (eds.), *Poésure et peintrie* (exh. cat., Marseille: Centre de la Vieille Charité, Musées de Marseille/Réunion des musées nationaux, 1993), 267 and 269.

49 Alliance Graphique Internationale, English version of the 1977 statutes accessed at http://www.a-g-i.org/about/statutes.php on December 14, 2005.

50 Vox's initial system in 1952 called for nine families of typeface: Humanistic, Garaldic, Transitional, Didonic, Mechanistic, Lineal, Incised, Script, and Manual. Two new families were added when ATYPI officially adopted the classification in Verona, Italy, in 1962: Black Letter ("Gothic") and Non-Latin (Arabic, Hebrew, etc.). Now becoming an international standard, the names of these families have official translations in French and German.

51 J.-C. Faudouas, *Dictionnaire des grands noms de la chose imprimée* (Paris: Retz, 1991), 91.

52 See J. Robert, *Les Avatars du caractère* (Paris: Kodak-Pathé), 18.

53 Interview with Massin, *L'ABC du métier* (Paris: Imprimerie nationale, 1988–89), 77. On Massin, see his own books as well as the three-volume catalogue raisonné of Massin's typographic oeuvre (City of Chartres, 1998, 1999, and 2001).

54 Ibid., 49.

55 Quoted in C. Devarrieux, "Diable Pauvert," *Libération* (March 25, 2004), IV. On Faucheux, see F. Caradec, P. Faucheux, M.-C. Marquat, and Pierre Faucheux, *Le Magicien du livre* (Cercle de la Librairie, 1995).

56 Quoted in M. Braudeau, "Massin, l'œil de la lettre," *Le Monde* (March 14–15, 1999), 12.

57 Ibid.

58 Cf. the German name "Universal" for a face designed by Herbert Bayer in 1925–26.

59 Jean Widmer, interviewed by F. Job, "Jean Widmer: la culture à la lettre," *Création* 72 (November 1991), 50.

60 François Barré, *Jean Widmer* (exh. cat., Maison du livre, de l'image et du son /Les Éditions du Demi-Cercle, 1991), 5.

61 Ibid.

62 Tanaka, "The Age of American Typography."

63 Adrian Frutiger, *Type Sign Symbol* (Zurich: ABC, 1980),15.

64 Emil Ruder, quoted in Schmid (ed.), *Typography Today*, 52. Typographer Helmut Schmid, having studied under Ruder in Basel before moving to Japan, also demonstrates this sustained interest in Univers, right down to his current designs.

65 See also other types published by Emigre such as Thingbat, Whirligig, and ZeitGuys (1993 and 1994).

66 For the period 1960–90, see L. Wallis, *Modern Encyclopedia of Typefaces 1960–1990* (London: Lund Humphries, 1990).

67 In his book, Thibaudeau proposed the following breakdown: "Didot, Antique, Egyptian, [and]… Elzevir constitute four highly characteristic families." *La Lettre d'imprimerie* (Paris: Bureau de l'édition, 1921).

68 Albert Hollenstein, "La création de caractères aujourd'hui," *Communication et langages* 9 (March 1971), 55.

69 Tschichold, "À propos de l'emploi de caractères d'imprimerie…," 71.

70 Massin, *L'ABC du métier,* 149.

71 The Bauhaus had already adopted such an international approach, with many of its students coming from Hungary, Czechoslovakia, Scandinavia, the United States, and Latin America. When the institution moved to Berlin, thirty-three of its one hundred and sixty-eight students came from abroad.

72 Although the history of typography and graphic design in the West remains underdeveloped and under-represented, the non-Western dimension and history of these fields, often linked to other methods of writing and reproduction and especially to other conjunctures and contexts, seems to be even more poorly known (apart from certain phenomena that have been the subject of specific research, namely in the history of writing and book publication). The first edition of *Who's Who in Graphic Art* (Amstutz & Gradeg, 1962) listed some fifty countries, including Argentina, Brazil, Chile, India, Israel, Japan, Mexico, Norway, Sweden, Uruguay, and Venezuela. The 1994 edition of *Who's Who in Graphic Design* (Benteli-Werd) reproduced works from Argentina, Brazil, Chile, Colombia, Croatia, Egypt, Iran, Iceland, Israel, Korea, Morocco, Portugal, Sweden, Tunisia, Turkey, Venezuela, and Zimbabwe.

73 On Dutch typography and graphic design in the twentieth century, see: P. Brattinga and D. Dooijes, *A History of the Dutch Poster 1890–1960* (Amsterdam: Scheltema & Holkema, 1968); K. Broos and P. Hefting, *Dutch Graphic Design* (London: Phaidon, 1993); A. W. Purvis, *Dutch Graphic Design 1918–1945* (New York: Van Nostrand Reinhold, 1992); J. Middendorp, *Dutch Type* (Rotterdam: Editions 010, 2004). On Wim Crouwel, see: F. Huygen and H. Boekraad, *Wim Crouwel: Mode en module* (Rotterdam: Editions 010, 1997); *Kunst + design Wim Crouwel: Preisträger der Stankowski-Stiftung* (exh. cat., Cantz, 1991, German-English).

74 Crouwel, in reponse to a questionnaire, quoted by M. Paris, *Questions sur la typographie,* thesis (Paris: École Nationale Supérieure des Arts Décoratifs, 1989).

75 Quoted in Schmid, *Typography Today,* 18. op. cit.

76 Hans and Sophie Scholl were executed by the Nazis in 1943 for their Resistance activities.

77 Excerpted from the proposed curriculum, Hochschule für Gestaltung [HfG], 1950, and from HfG-Info, 1955 as reprinted in *L'École d'Ulm: Textes et manifestes (*exh. cat., , Paris: Centre Georges Pompidou, 1988), 45.

78 Comment by Herbert Lindinger, Ibid., 7.

79 See for example, the texts and bibliographies in *Design japonais 1950-1995* (exh. cat., Paris: Centre Georges Pompidou, 1996), and R. S. Thornton, *Japanese Graphic Design* (London: Laurence King, 1991).

80 Cited in A. Weill, *L'Affiche dans le monde* (Paris: Aimery Somogy, 1991), 315.

81 Bayer, *Painter, Designer…*, 75.

**Part 6
Contents**

The final decades of the twentieth century

Pre-digital graphic design: context and overview

The final phase of the history of pre-digital graphic design straddled the decade of the 1970s. This phase actually began in the late 1960s and lasted for nearly a generation, ending in the mid-1980s with the advent of new technology. The proliferating protest movements of the late 1960s were suddenly confronted by a reversal of economic conditions in the West following the oil shock of 1973. New changes thus loomed on the horizon after the long-term expansion that resulted from twenty-five years of steady growth in production and in the consumer society that went with it. The new situation required a series of profound restructurings (very different, however, from those that followed the total economic collapse of the 1930s), resulting from rising unemployment along with rising inflation. The economy began to go through cycles of growth and recession. The long post-war economic boom had created a context that was highly favorable to the development of design in industrialized countries. And in spite of the economic instability of the final decades of the century, the fields of typography and graphic design managed to sustain a significant level of activity thanks to—among other things—their henceforth ubiquitous presence in mass culture, their new-found popularity, and the eventual arrival of digital technology. Even before the phenomenal technical innovations of the 1980s, the social, economic, and cultural environment heavily influenced the scope and organization of the graphic design sector. Many sociocultural phenomena would interact or resonate with design practices in one way or another, ranging from the political activism and the demands of the 1960s and 1970s to the consolidation of counter-cultures and of "youth culture" via ongoing artistic experiments and the steady expansion of the media.

Subjectivity and disparity

The picture of dominant trends was being redrawn. The post-war decades had represented a revitalized eclecticism in (typo)graphic forms and design; whereas adherence to distinct stylistic principles or to an identifiable trend had previously been fairly clear, the realm of possibilities was constantly enlarging, encompassing the revival of earlier styles as well as the development of the most recent methods and techniques, resulting in countless forms of expression (individual or collective, either based on the past or on a total rejection of it). At the same time, many age-old concerns were being seriously reconsidered once again, such as the notion of legibility (spurring typographers and contemporary practices to look again at Roman letterforms of the late fifteenth century), the quest for an avant-garde functionalism, the search for "objective" graphics, the concept of "good forms,"[1] and the idealizing goal of clear, efficient communication. These various concerns were explored, challenged, reappropriated, and revamped, often from the standpoint of greater freedom of expression and autonomy.

Although cracks in the idea of adhering to a specific principle or model widened in the last three decades of the twentieth century, they could already be perceived in graphic design of the 1950s and 1960s, as exemplified by Push Pin Studio and the hybridization of visual vocabularies. Typography and graphic design became involved in the protest movements and counter-culture of the 1960s, fragmenting and juxtaposing various approaches that ranged from whimsy and humor to retrospection and ambiguity, by way of kitsch, extravagance, and more. Concepts such as these generated great enthusiasm and challenged the precepts of clear,

697
Tania Mouraud, *City performance no. 1*, France, 1977–78. Urban installation, silkscreened poster, 9 ft. 10 in. × 13 ft (300 × 400 cm).

698
Tania Mouraud, *NI (Nor)*, France, 1988. Acrylic on canvas, 2 ft. 4 ³/4 in. × 4 ft. (73 × 120 cm).

ordered communication. A marked predilection for pleasing or subjective forms provided an important counterweight to the issue of immediate usefulness or functionality.

Starting in the 1970s, perhaps inspired by the fine arts, the major trends and tendencies in visual communication became ever more multifarious and amplified. The difficulty in identifying and categorizing the specific creative directions stems above all from the proliferation of repertoires, approaches, attitudes, media, influences, material possibilities, and so on. Vast sections of visual culture were invaded by graphic design, including the imagery associated with the consumer society. Whereas the nineteenth century had borne the first wave of (typo)graphic design aimed at the masses, the 1960s represented a new stage in this expansion, working not only through the press, advertising, and publishing industries, but also through movies and television. At the same time, leisure, pleasure, entertainment, and consumption were becoming ever larger aspects of social life, of attitudes, and of behavior, nurturing a frame of mind that was very influential on methods of visual communication. The visual media themselves began to evolve, to a certain extent, into objects of consumption, finding ever more niches in which to play a role in the so-called information and communication society. All of these design phenomena—like many other creative activities—were accompanied by a progressive abandonment of reliance on earlier models and references. Instead, they expressed renewed interest in—among other things—mass culture. Around 1970, then, unexpected and unusual developments were occurring in both research and production of typographic and graphic design, ranging from New Wave to punk and Pop Art and all the imagery associated with protest movements and the counter-culture. From this standpoint, 1968 represents a moment of transition, particularly in Europe, lasting from the student uprisings in Paris in May 1968 to the closing of the Ulm School of Design in November.

The role of visual communication in art

Graphic design and typography were not only beginning to suggest their own new ramifications, they could also be viewed from the perspective of the visual transformations occurring in other realms of art, architecture, and interior decoration. Kinetic art, Pop Art, minimalist art, Nouveau Réalisme, New Figuration, Fluxus, land art, Arte Povera, body art, video art, conceptual art, Supports/Surfaces, hyper-realism, and so on, were all schools and movements that not only altered the horizons of art but also encouraged the design world to reinvent, reorient, and refresh itself. Some trends in art reestablished close, indeed crucial links with (typo)graphic supports, objects, and forms, recalling the Cubists' and Dadaists' interest in letters, words, print, and brand names. Pop Art revisited advertising and media imagery, along with popular signs and objects lifted from the retailing and consumer circuits. The most ordinary graphic features—so common that they often escaped conscious notice—thus became the focus of a selective attention that reappropriated elements of mass visual culture from the merchandise itself. In France, meanwhile, the Nouveaux Réalistes were bringing a new eye to printed graphics. Their practice of slashing and unsticking posters turned theoretically ordinary shreds of advertising imagery into works of art.

Various approaches thus indicated that urban signs and everyday landscapes—which included much graphic design—were becoming once again a major source of artistic inspiration. Artists would remove such material from its context and insert it into reality via methods of subversion, sampling, and transformation, thereby reinvigorating the context in which such material could be perceived and received. Many art trends of the 1960s and 1970s cultivated a special relationship with letters and lettering. The Fluxus movement broadly incorporated typographic output, for example in the form of leaflets and posters. Conceptual art, meanwhile, hinged on language, allotting a major role to the visualization of text and typography (through typewritten pages, enlargements of fragments of printing, lists of words, telegrams, file cards, neon-tube lettering, etc.). Pop, in its broadest sense, seems to have been one of the movements most open to exchanges with graphic culture (which went on to develop its own idiom). Record jackets, magazine covers, and posters all displayed a shared aesthetic with pop music and other fashionable events. Highly typical of the London of the 1960s, the movement had a major impact on various sectors of design, which spread rapidly from Great Britain into various industrialized countries in the West, along with pop music itself. The quest for clarity and efficiency thus found itself seriously challenged and shaken by the values of the emerging youth culture.

Architecture, design, and typography: "anything goes" versus radicalization

Since the 1960s, profound changes had been underway in the realms of architecture and design. Even as the influential International Style was being consecrated in an exhibition hosted by the Museum of Modern Art in 1972—titled, precisely, *The International Style*— new directions were emerging, along with a search for new paths. Architect Phillip Johnson declared in 1966 that there were no longer absolute rules or certainties; there was only an impression of wonderful freedom.[2] Functionalism and rationalism were unable to fulfill people's needs and expectations, so other approaches emerged and became dominant. Shapes, colors, and materials adopted strange and fanciful dimensions, sometimes startling, sometimes irregular, or else modular, ambiguous, mobile, open. The architecture soon known as "postmodern" perfectly reflected this general trend, as seen in the work of Robert Venturi, Charles Moore, and Michael Graves. Similarly, the world of design reacted to new impulses, including an explosion in the use of plastic materials and bold colors. The Italian scene, especially in Milan, became highly inventive in the realm of design starting in the mid-1960s. An alternative, "radical design" movement spawned a number of well-known collective practices, from Archizoom Associati and Superstudio in Florence (both founded in 1966) to Memphis in Milan (1981). In quest of new horizons, greater freedom, and original forms, the explosion of design, architecture, and the graphic arts in the mid-1960s harked back to the avant-garde phenomenon of the early decades of the twentieth century, with the notable difference that the earlier designers could boast a greater professional versatility. Whereas Jan Tschichold, as a specialist, seemed to be the exception among artists of the interwar period, by the end of the century designers and typographers were often identified with a specific sphere of creativity. This situation seemed to reinforce the specificity of graphic design practices, as suggested by the question raised by Max Bill as early as 1964: "How did we arrive at the strange situation of a specialized field [graphic design] that cannot be completely classified either as an art or as objective information"?[3]

Starting in the 1960s, and becoming even more pronounced in the last three decades of the century, the landscape of Western typography and graphic design became fairly complex. Movements, individuals, and trends flaunted their diversity, yielding phenomena that were often disparate, fundamentally heterogeneous, reactive, and sometimes rebellious. From an overall standpoint, the most visible centers of activity and the most dynamic countries in the 1970s were Switzerland, the Netherlands, the United States, Great Britain, and Japan, along with Germany and France. Just as these new waves gained momentum, the sudden and massive tide of technology in the mid-1980s would sweep everything before it, pushing the possibilities of typography and graphic design ever further. The photosetting equipment that supplanted traditional typesetting machinery in the 1960s therefore had a relatively short lifespan. Nevertheless, by anticipating the arrival of computer technology, the flexibility introduced by photographic methods made a major contribution to the genesis of contemporary forms.

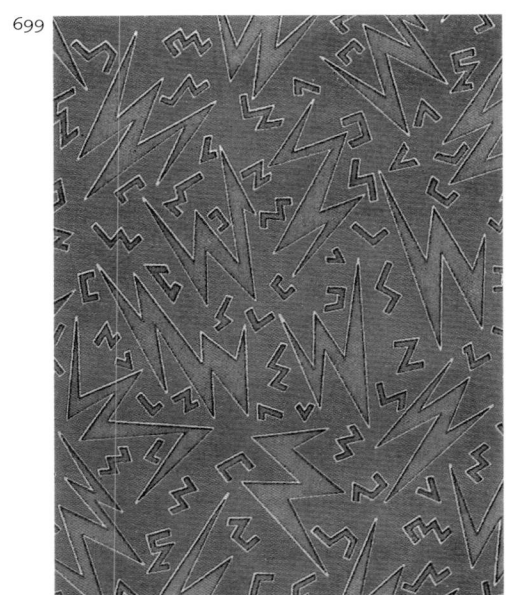

699

699
Nathalie du Pasquier, Memphis design group (Milan), design for a printed fabric, 1983.

700

701

700
Lust (a group of Dutch designers), restoration of
a 1928 building by Jan Buijs, The Hague,
Netherlands, c. 1990s.

701
Studio Dumbar, examples of the environmental
application of new signage for the Dutch post
office (PTT), 1988–89.

702

702
Joan Brossa (1909–1999), *Visual-Walkable-Poem
in Three Parts,* Velòdrom d'Horta, Barcelona
(municipal commission), 1984.

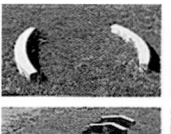

An overview of the major trends of the 1970s
Creative designers

Some of the designers working in the post-war period remained active into the 1970s and even beyond, just when the next generation was emerging, having benefited from training steeped in the past yet resolutely turned towards inventiveness. Among the individuals and collectives that came to the fore, promoting ever more diverse influences, were Louise Fili (born in 1951), Dan Friedman (1945), Werner Jeker (1944), Barbara Kruger (1945), Katherine McCoy (1945), Bruno Monguzzi (1941), R.D.E. Oxenaar (1929), Woody Pirtle (1944), Jamie Reid (1940), Paula Scher (1948), Niklaus Troxler (1947), Jan Van Toorn (1932) and Wolfgang Weingart (1941), as well as agencies such as Tel Design (founded in 1962), Odermatt + Tissi (1968, Siegfried Odermatt and Rosmarie Tissi, born in 1926 and 1937, respectively), Visuel Design/Jean Widmer (1970), the Grapus group (1970), and Studio Dumbar (1977). As part of the generation born in the 1940s, most of these designers began to make their breakthroughs in the relatively brief period between the advent of photosetting and the arrival of digital technology.

Another noteworthy aspect of the 1970s was the arrival of women among the leading figures of graphic design (their integration into the realm of typeface design would not come until later). Up till that point, the vast majority of protagonists in the design field had been men, with only a few women who managed to make a place for themselves and acquire a certain renown. Of the women who made a mark on the history of design, a significant number were the companions of famous male artists, while others came from related fields rather than issuing directly from the professional design corps. Women who contributed to modern (typo)graphic design, education, and/or culture thus included, among others, Ethel Reed, Sonia Delaunay, Varvara Stepanova, Käthe Kollwitz, Käte Steinitz, Hannah Höch, Ellen Auerbach and Grete Stern (the "ringl + pit" advertising studio), Beatrice Warde (who used the nom-de-plume of Paul Beaujon for her articles in *The Fleuron*), Cipe Pineless, Nicolete Gray, Muriel Cooper, Jacqueline S. Casey, Mary Vieira, Gudrun Zapf-Hesse, Nelly Rudin, Rosmarie Tissi, Ursula Hiestand, Katherine McCoy, Sheila Levrant de Bretteville, April Greiman, Paula Scher, Zuzana Licko, Ellen Lupton, Clotilde Olyff, and Irma Boom.[4]

703
Women's Graphic Collective, *Woman is Rising*, United States, 1975. Silkscreen, 18 1/2 × 18 in. (47 × 46 cm).

704
Nicolaus Ott and Bernard Stein, poster-calendar for 1991, Germany, 1990.

705
Uwe Loesch, poster for the Forty-first Convention of German Historians, Munich, 1996.

Experimentation revived

The main directions followed by graphic design in the 1970s pointed down vastly different if complementary paths, ranging from strict functionalism to an anarchic, untrammeled

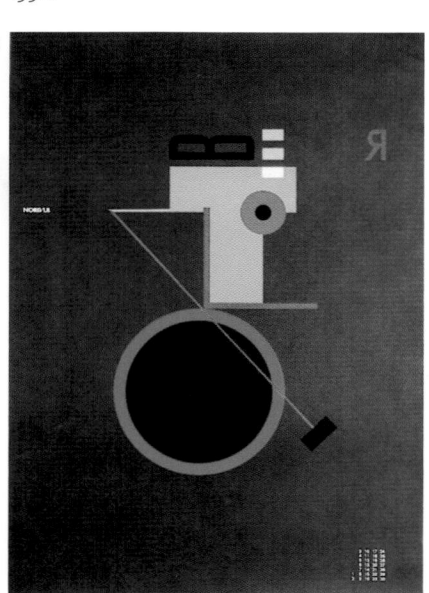

expressivity reminiscent of the avant-garde repertoire of the first half of the twentieth century. Some designers and trends were clearly determined to maintain a moderate approach, eschewing spectacular effects and demonstrating a certain historical—sometimes even scholarly—sophistication. Respecting the tradition of modernism in their own way, such designers emerged in the United States, the Netherlands, Great Britain, Switzerland, Italy, and France (the same countries as in the immediate postwar period), and their main representatives included Wim Crouwel, Bruno Monguzzi, Massimo Vignelli, and Jean Widmer. Their oeuvres visibly constituted an extension of the avant-garde idiom, each in its own way and in the style of its day.

Yet equally typical of the 1970s was an entirely different path, one that clearly sought to transcend and

706
J. Abbott Miller, Design/Writing/ Research, *Brick Book*, limited edition, Andrea Rosen Gallery, New York, 1997 (installation). Books made in the size and shape of bricks were stacked in the gallery in various configurations.

escape all prior and existing movements. Several major trends participated in this phenomenon, which was particularly strong in Switzerland, the United States, Great Britain, and the Netherlands. They manifested themselves above all in their quest for a renewed expressiveness that, far from being a simple break with functionalism, appeared as the logical successor to the long pursuit of objectivity (itself sometimes experienced as—or at least, labeled—a hindrance, yet clearly a useful springboard, if only in counterpoint or as a countervailing impulse). Favoring innovation, these initiatives might be perceived as heirs to the forms, if not the spirit, of movements such as Futurism, Cubo-Futurism, Dada, Constructivism, and the dynamic graphics that came out of Poland, Italy, and the United States in the post-war period, not to mention psychedelic influences.[5]

The various trends and experiments that provided impetus to the 1970s included the New Wave, pioneered by Wolfgang Weingart in Basel, and the "deconstruction" phenomenon in the United States, which developed initially at the Cranbrook Academy of Art in Bloomfield Hills, Michigan, where Katherine McCoy taught. The movement constituted a lively episode in the realm of graphic design, and students who benefited from its stimulating environment in the 1970s and 1980s included Jeffery Keedy, Edward Fella, David Frej, and P. Scott Makela. The respective contributions of Weingart and McCoy largely hinged on their teaching activities, which spurred an important evolution in the graphic arts of the day. Weingart began teaching in the typography department of Basel's Kunstgewerbeschule (School of Arts and Crafts) in 1968; McCoy began her career at Cranbrook in 1971, co-chairing the department of graphic design. Both helped to make their schools important centers of graphic art in the 1970s (although the Basel school had already enjoyed a good reputation for some time), and both had a notable influence on their students. Some of those students would go on to achieve recognition and to win teaching posts of their own. Furthermore, the spirit they instilled soon spread to other places and would have numerous visible repercussions in the final decades of the century. Like the Bauhaus and the Royal Academy of Fine Arts in The Hague, certain centers of graphic design were thus able to provide core art training and to have a significant impact at the level of education thanks to the charisma and involvement of individuals who either taught or made their mark there.

Punk was a contemporaneous yet distinct trend, also driven by a determination to forge an out-of-the-ordinary visual image. Spawned in England and fully established by the mid-1970s, the punk scene generated a great deal of graphic creativity, largely indebted to Dada and an anarchist spirit. Although many of the printed artifacts and items produced by the movement remain anonymous, the work of Briton Jamie Reid figures prominently. Revisiting the techniques of cut-out and confrontational collage, punk design required only modest resources to generate a rowdy and disturbing creative product. As was the case with some Pop and psychedelic design, punk graphics were above all the visual correlate of a new musical form that arose from street culture, urban life, and the burgeoning youth movement; they therefore favored specialized supports such as record jackets, posters, fliers, graffiti, tee-shirts, tattoos, and so on. Punk's radical creativity, which advocated a raw, anarchic style, would ultimately have multiple influences on graphic design, first through the impact of the movement on continental Europe and the United States in the 1980s, then through a more general, diffuse effect.

Even as punk was putting its distinctive brand on things, deconstruction and other New-Wave type approaches were also having their impact in Western countries, as seen in the work of individual designers and collective groups. Certain posters by Gert Dumbar in the Netherlands, for example, display a serious desire to shake up conventional, functional forms. The generous, surprising work of Niklaus Troxler in Switzerland, meanwhile, also shared—and showed—a need to set itself apart from tried-and-true practices. Troxler was notably a tireless producer of highly personal, diversely influenced posters and other publicity material for the Willisau Jazz Festival in central Switzerland (an event he himself founded in 1975). His work also fit into the experimental tradition of exploring correspondences between graphics and

707
Niklaus Troxler, poster for a Dave Holland
Quintet concert in Willisau, Switzerland, 1983.

708
Niklaus Troxler, black-and-white poster for a
jazz concert by Ellery Eskelin and Han Bennink,
Willisau, Switzerland, 2000.

709
Niklaus Troxler, poster for a jazz concert by
Miniature, Willisau, Switzerland, 1990.

710
Niklaus Troxler, poster for an exhibition, *Typo
Plakate* (Typographic Posters), Willisau,
Switzerland, 1996.

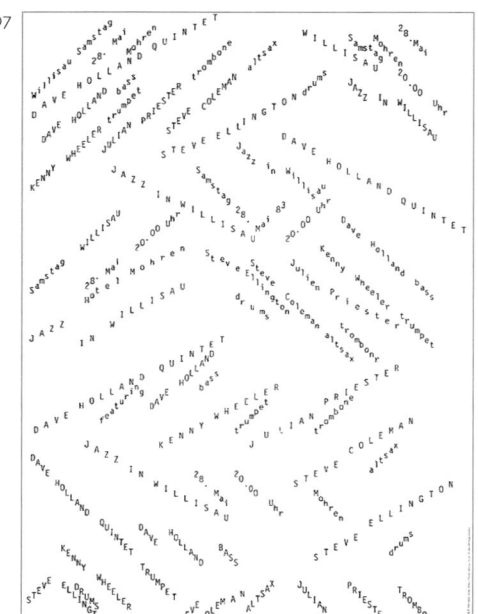

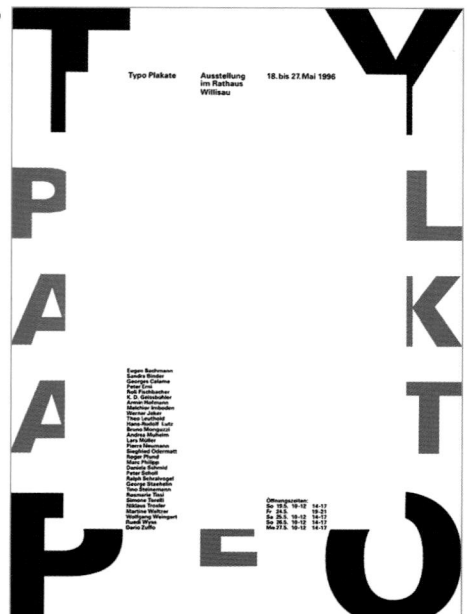

music, between visual and aural perception. Such correspondences were at the heart of designs
as varied as those by the punk movement and by Josef Müller-Brockmann for concerts of
classical music.[6] When it came to inter-relationships between (typo)graphic forms and artistic
practices—which had been particularly strong ever since the Cubists took an interest in
lettering, typography, and printed material—both fine artists and so-called creative designers
continued to cultivate such connections. Letters, words, and typography once again became a
frequent and common component of artworks (even though the professional versatility
displayed by painters and artists in the first half of the twentieth century, which enabled many
of them to enjoy parallel careers in the sphere of typography and graphic design, did not seem

711
Barbara Kruger, *Your Comfort is My Silence*, 1981.

712
Barbara Kruger, *You pledge…*, installation,
Mary Boone Gallery, New York, 1991.

to survive in the same form). So true was this phenomenon that the apparent distinction between the sphere of art and the more specific sphere of graphic design or visual communication no longer seemed very obvious. The role of typography, text, and/or graphic design was a particularly expressive one, for example, in conceptual art (Joseph Kosuth, Lawrence Weiner, Robert Barry, Art & Language, etc.) and in the work of Barbara Kruger and Jenny Holzer. For some artists, the very form and means of graphic and typographic expression even represented the main material elements they used (as had been the case for certain Dada artists). At the same time, graphic designers were displaying a keen need to experiment, something that had already been felt in the days of the historic avant-gardes (see the likes of Wladyslaw Strzeminski and Hendrik Nicolaas Werkman). Weingart's explorations, for instance, were highly representative of this attitude, which seemed to have waned somewhat during the immediate post-war boom, perhaps due to the increasing professionalization of the graphic arts and their adaptation to economic and media expansion, not to mention the growth of the industrial and corporate sector's needs for visual communication.

An ever-expanding graphic scene

As had been the case for several decades—and also for part of the nineteenth century—the dynamics of graphic design in the 1970s stemmed from a determined quest for renewal, which encouraged the spread of certain international trends. Also noteworthy was the stronger presence of European countries that had previously been left on the sidelines, plus a greater awareness of non-Western practices thanks to specialized reviews, publications, exhibitions, exchange programs, conferences and seminars, and international professional organizations. From this standpoint, Japan occupied an increasingly important position after the war, even as other countries began to attract notice for their graphic design (in the sense that modernist Western art defined the practice)—notably Argentina, Brazil, Canada, Chile, China, India, Iran, Israel, Mexico (already on the map), Norway, Spain, Sweden, Uruguay, and Venezuela. This enhancement of geographic visibility—still recent, yet already apparent in the 1970s and reinforced in subsequent decades—made it possible to call upon a broader graphic repertoire and to draw influence from local or national cultures that were little known—or totally unknown—in the West (whether folk, vernacular practices, or singular, highly skilled crafts). Over the decades, many countries thus enjoyed a certain recognition—on the international level—for their graphic design. Design was now an international affair, with important output from northern and southern Africa, the Middle and Far East.

Experimentation in the 1970s

The New Wave

The New Wave trend was part of a rejuvenation of Swiss design that began around 1970, and had a major impact on graphic expression in the United States and Europe in the following decade—and even beyond, when it came to creativity inspired by the new digital technology. New Wave theory seemed above all to represent a reaction to the spirit of the Swiss school as it had developed in the 1940s and subsequently spread to the international scene. By the 1960s, the concerns typified by Emil Ruder and Josef Müller-Brockmann—namely, a combination of the functionalist concerns of the first third of the century with the more recent influence of Concrete art plus the meticulous approach of microtypography—had reached such a culmination and such a status that newer aspirations inevitably sought to supersede them, some of which would succeed in attaining recognition. Retrospectively, it would seem that the meticulous approach of Swiss typography, hardly conducive to exuberant or spectacular expressiveness, almost naturally encouraged a reaction destined to transcend it by relaunching new visual experimentation. In this respect, it is highly significant that the New Wave's first impulse was given by Wolfgang Weingart, who studied in Basel before becoming a teacher there himself. Yet this perspective also suggests that, rather than being a movement that sought to oppose prior practices, New Wave was fundamentally a newer, further offshoot of those practices. Other individuals in Switzerland actively pursued the renewal of graphic design. Forerunners included Siegfried Odermatt and Rosmarie Tissi, who were somewhat older than Weingart, being born in 1926 and 1937, respectively. The former was self taught, the latter studied at the Kunstgewerbeschule (School of Arts and Crafts) in Zurich. Together, the pair founded the Odermatt + Tissi studio in Zurich in 1968. Like Weingart, they adopted a certain distance from the visual approach advocated by the International Typographic Style, which by then had apparently reached a certain stage of maturity.[7] In so doing, Tissi and Odermatt favored graphic and typographic solutions that were simultaneously freer yet heavily structured, therefore unusual and intuitive, sometimes downright surprising, and clearly in search of an original idiom open to techniques of montage and assemblage. Weingart himself paid tribute to their work and their research. "Odermatt and Tissi... viewed old typefaces in a new light, could find plenty of ideas in a box of rubbish, and turned unassuming forms into vigorous ones—square or circular, ragged or stepped. It was playful in appearance only, because these two fellows—one of whom is a woman—deliberately took risks, namely the risk of constantly calling oneself into question, challenging oneself as well as the medium or the client. They renounced the familiar, the routine, the easy money-spinner; they embraced discovery, invention, surprise. Odermatt and Tissi were driven not only by a quest for originality, but also by conviction. ... They were living testimony to the fact that convincing graphic ideas emerge from an individual temperament rather than from a school of thought. ... Their oeuvre therefore represented a truly exotic curiosity in little old Switzerland."[8]

713
Odermatt + Tissi (Siegfried Odermatt and Rosmarie Tissi), design for the promotion of a printshop, Switzerland.

714
Odermatt + Tissi (Siegfried Odermatt and Rosmarie Tissi), typeface, Switzerland, 1972.

Wolfgang Weingart's contribution

Born in 1941, Weingart enrolled as a student in Basel's school of arts and crafts in 1964; by 1968 he was a teacher there. Around 1970, he began challenging the assumptions of Swiss graphic design, bringing his own approach to it and launching a career that centered on the notion of typographic experimentation. At first, Weingart focused basically on typography, but by the mid–1970s he was incorporating photography, half-tone screens, and collage into his work. Calling upon intuitive methods rather than logical, rigorous ones, he invented and elaborated highly unusual visual stimuli. This meant boldly playing with a set of procedures and skills, in a highly personal way, which explored the formal potential of typography and its ability

715
Wolfgang Weingart, experimental typography, published in *TM/RSI*, Switzerland, 1972–73.

716
Wolfgang Weingart, page of experimental graphic work, published in *TM/RSI*, no. 12, 1976.

to communicate emotionally—strong, irregular letter-spacing, underlined text, alternation of bold and Italic fonts, unusual juxtapositions and superimpositions, bizarre accumulations, positive-negative interplay, free composition (eschewing horizontal as well as orthogonal layout), random arrangements, and so on. All these techniques created optical surprises and stimulated the eye in ways quite different from the ones advocated by functionalism or by the belief that visual communication needed to focus on clarity and efficiency.

Right from the early 1970s, Weingart's work came to represent an alternative graphics that sidestepped the rigor of the methods associated with his own country. The boldness of his research set an influential example for the up-and-coming generations. The repercussions of his work would be felt as far away as the west coast of the United States. Weingart was one of the harbingers of the typographical trends of the final decades of the century, for he seriously challenged the age-old notion of legibility as he sought to replace any loss in ease or speed of reading with a distinct gain in visual appeal. Indeed, many typographers, typeface designers, and graphic artists would soon be skirting the edge of legibility, when they weren't actually going far beyond it or even ignoring it completely.

Dan Friedman and April Greiman

Among the people who met Weingart or went to study under him at Basel, were the noteworthy figures of Dan Friedman and April Greiman, who achieved recognition in the 1980s. Born in 1945 and 1948 respectively, both left their native America to study in Europe, and once they returned home they became teachers as well as graphic designers. Friedman began his education in the United States (studying under Ken Hiebert, who himself had studied under Armin Hofmann in Basel), continued it at the famous Ulm School of Design, and then attended Basel's Allgemeine Gewerbeschule in the late 1960s, where he met Weingart. On returning to the United States in 1970, Friedman taught first at Yale University and then, from 1972 to 1975, at the School of Visual Art in New York City. In 1972 he invited Weingart to come to the United States so that his work and methods could be appreciated first-hand.

Friedman's career and philosophy present viewpoints and critical analyses that are extremely interesting for the light they shed on graphic design of the second half of the twentieth century. He argued that "graphic design has always defined its focus in narrow terms—in ways that may stimulate designers into a frenzy but mean nothing to the rest of society."[9] In the 1970s, he worked on major corporate design programs and became associated with the Pentagram group. Realizing by the 1980s that his design work no longer matched his ideals, he effected a major shift. "In the 1960s I saw graphic design as a noble endeavor, integral to larger planning, architectural, and social issues. What I realized in the 1970s, when I was doing major corporate identity projects, is that design had become a preoccupation with what things look like rather than with what they mean.... Modernism forfeited its claim to a moral authority when designers sold it away as corporate style."[10] Friedman thus left Pentagram in the 1980s, and adopted a certain distance from commercial and institutional design. He began to advocate the concept of a "Radical Modernism," one that would return to "the idea that design is something that can help improve society and people's condition. Radical Modernism, therefore, is [a] reaffirmation of the idealistic roots of our modernity, adjusted to include more of our diverse cultures, history, research, and fantasy."[11]

April Greiman, who became one of the cult designers of the late twentieth century, also studied in Basel in the early 1970s, under Hofmann and Weingart. On returning to the United States, she first worked and taught on the east coast, later moving to California. By the 1980s her work was earning widespread recognition. Greiman's place in the history of graphic design takes on particular significance as she was one of the very first women to achieve such international renown in the field. Proof of her importance can be found in publications (including her own) and exhibitions devoted to her work, in the seminars and symposiums that discuss her designs, and in her role and influence in the sphere of education.

April Greiman's graphic style yielded unusual designs based on intuition and the unexpected. Having familiarized herself with the art world between 1966 and 1971, she was

717
April Greiman, poster for the *Pacific Wave: California Graphic Design* show at the Fortuny Museum, Venice, 1981.

718
Page from a catalog of work by April Greiman, reproducing her poster for the *Graphic Design in America* show at the Walker Art Center of Minneapolis, Minnesota, 1989.

719
April Greiman, postage stamp commemorating the 19th Amendment 1920–1995, commissioned by the US Postal Service, 1995.

717
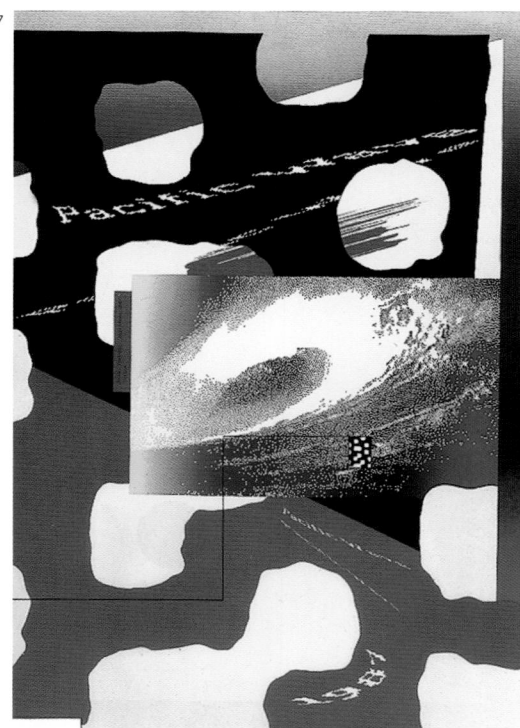

718

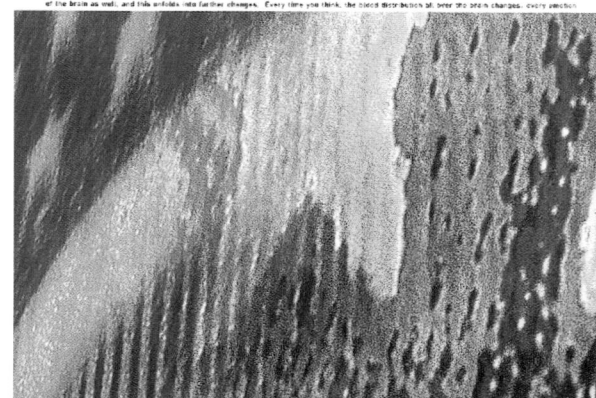

719

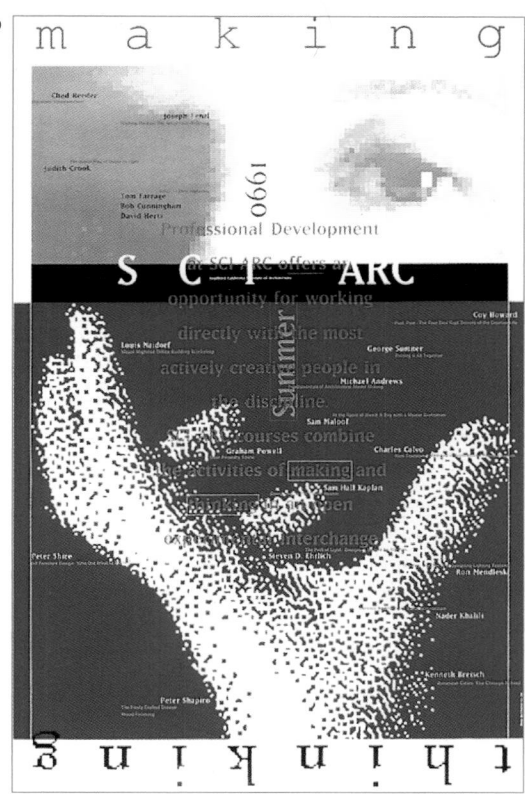

part of the generation that was well placed to profit, in turn, from a new educational impetus and a booming design scene (further spurred by two successive technical revolutions, photosetting and digital technology). Often described as emblematic of Californian New Wave design, her work displays a singular handling of forms (made explicit by the title of her 1990 book, *Hybrid Imagery: The Fusion of Technology and Graphic Design*). Typography, photography, and graphics often combine to lend uncommon depth to the imagery in her compositions, rich with a highly original visual density. Juxtaposition, repetition, twinning, scrambling, superimposing, layering, random dispersion, density, fragmentation, unanchored space: Greiman's extensive formal repertoire betrays her determination to experiment, take risks, and innovate.

The 1980s and 1990s brought her renown in Europe as well as the United States. From 1982 to 1984 Greiman headed the graphic design department at the California Institute of the Arts (the famous school better known as Cal'Arts). In the mid-1980s she was immediately drawn to digital technology, the use of which reinforced effects of fragmentation, multiplication, and pixelation already present in her work. Around these techniques there emerged the idea of "technological design," whose forms acknowledged their origin in computer technology. Greiman was therefore one of the pioneering typographers and designers who adopted digital technology right from the start, making it an integral part of their creative process, philosophy, and output. Other precursors included Rudy VanderLans and Zuzana Licko (who founded the review *Emigre*, and were also based in California), plus certain Dutch graphic artists and typeface designers (such as the Studio Dumbar team and Erik van Blokland and Just van Rossum), and British designer Neville Brody.

720
April Greiman, poster, *Making Thinking*, Southern California Institute of Architecture, 1990.

The extent of creativity: countries, trends, and individuals

The trajectory from Switzerland to California sketched a high-profile line in the history of contemporary graphic design, from the innovations launched by and developed around Wolfgang Weingart to a generation of artists influenced by, among other things, the constantly accelerating, dynamic oeuvre of April Greiman. As occurred in the mid-1930s (if in a completely different context), new typographic initiatives in German-speaking countries would find an echo in the United States, leading to major developments. In Switzerland itself, many other typographers and designers began—or continued—doing distinguished work in the 1970s and 1980s and beyond, both within Weingart's movement and outside it. These figures include Jost Hochuli (born in 1933), Werner Jeker (1944), Roger Pfund (1943), Hans Rudolf Bosshard, Hans-Rudolf Lutz, and Ernst and Ursula Hiestand. Significantly, some of these designers authored major books on typography or graphic design, thereby sustaining a tradition begun by their predecessors, participating in turn in the dissemination of their design skills and culture. Depending on how history has been written and/or construed, the New Wave phenomenon (sometimes vaguely conflated with postmodernism) may or may not include other figures of the 1970s and 1980s. Whatever label is used, the general trend it reflects embraced a good number of individuals and agencies in the last three decades of the twentieth century, all of whom sought to produce intriguing graphics. They favored a strong, often spectacular visual impact and were little inclined to employ neutral, sober effects. In various forms and to various degrees, this broad, revived aspiration for originality surfaced simultaneously in Switzerland, the United States, the Netherlands, Great Britain, and France.

If in the United States the deconstruction school inspired by Katherine McCoy was leading the way in 1970s design, in the Netherlands, innovation was being pursued by several groups. These included the Total Design group (founded in 1963, notably including Anthon Beeke and Frans Lieshout), Tel Design (founded at the same time, in which Gert Dumbar worked from the mid-1960s to 1977), the famous Studio Dumbar (founded in 1977 by Dumbar, who recruited numerous designers), and individuals such as Jan van Toorn and R.D.E. Oxenaar. Like Total

This is a RECORD COVER. This writing is the DESIGN upon the record cover. The DESIGN is to help SELL the record. We hope to draw your attention to it and encourage you to pick it up. When you have done that maybe you'll be persuaded to listen to the music - in this case XTC's Go 2 album. Then we want you to BUY it. The idea being that the more of you that buy this record the more money Virgin Records, the manager Ian Reid and XTC themselves will make. To the aforementioned this is known as PLEASURE. A good cover DESIGN is one that attracts more buyers and gives more pleasure. This writing is trying to pull you in much like an eye-catching picture. It is designed to get you to READ IT. This is called luring the VICTIM. But if you have a free mind you should STOP READING NOW! because all we are attempting to do is to get you to read on. Yet this is a DOUBLE BIND because if you indeed stop you'll be doing what we tell you, and if you read on you'll be doing what we've wanted all along. And the more you read on the more you're falling for this simple device of telling you exactly how a good commercial design works. They're TRICKS and this is the worst TRICK of all since it's describing the TRICK whilst trying to TRICK you, and if you've read this far then you're TRICKED but you wouldn't have known this unless you'd read this far. At least we're telling you directly instead of seducing you with a beautiful or haunting visual that may never tell you. We're letting you know that you ought to buy this record because in essence it's a PRODUCT and PRODUCTS are to be consumed and you are a consumer and this is a good PRODUCT. We could have written the band's name in special lettering so that it stood out and you'd see it before you'd read any of this writing and possibly have bought it anyway. What we are really suggesting is that you are FOOLISH to buy or not buy an album merely as a consequence of the design on its cover. This is a con because if you agree then you'll probably like this writing - which is the cover design - and hence the album inside. But we've just warned you against that. The con is a con. A good cover design could be considered as one that gets you to buy the record, but that never actually happens to YOU because YOU know it's just a design for the cover. And this is the RECORD COVER.

721
Hipgnosis (collective founded in London in 1968), text and design for the cover of the XTC album *Go 2*, 1978. The text begins, "This is a RECORD COVER. This writing is the DESIGN upon the record cover. The DESIGN is to help SELL the record."

722
Pentagram Agency, rebus of the word Pentagram.

723
Alan Fletcher (Pentagram Agency), Pentagram Calendar, collage of ephemera such as a cigarette packet, train ticket, movie ticket, etc., Great Britain, 1993.

Design in the Netherlands, the British design agency Pentagram (founded in 1972) continued to rack up major accomplishments, employing people such as David Hillman, Woody Pirtle, Peter Saville, Dan Friedman, and Paula Scher. In Britain, after the influence of punk in the 1970s, the 1980s saw the emergence of Neville Brody (who began his career at the start of that decade) and the partnerships 8vo and Why Not Associates (founded in London in 1985 and 1987, respectively).

In France, design took directions clearly distinct from the paths followed elsewhere. The 1970s and 1980s were notably marked by Roman Cieslewicz (who moved from Poland to Paris in 1963) and by two studios founded in the early 1970s: Visuel Design/Jean Widmer (Widmer having immigrated from Switzerland) and Grapus (a highly politicized group founded by Gérard Paris-Clavel, Pierre Bernard, and François Miehe). These designers remained emblematic of two tendencies long perceived and experienced in France as opposing or contradictory.

The Cranbrook Academy of Art

The movement known as "deconstruction in design" emerged from the Cranbrook Academy of Art in Bloomfield Hills, Michigan, which from the 1970s to the early 1990s hosted one of the most radical reconsiderations of typographical precepts inherited from earlier periods. It entailed a singular approach to graphic theory by a group centered on Katherine McCoy. Cranbrook already enjoyed a high reputation for teaching architecture and design thanks to the presence of creative people such as Charles Eames, Eero Saarinen, Harry Bertoia, and Daniel Libeskind. At the time, Cranbrook boasted an autonomous department of graphic design, to which Katherine McCoy was appointed co-chair in 1971. Influenced by Swiss practice and skills, her work steadily evolved towards less forthright notions open to complexity, fuzziness, and sometimes total saturation. According to McCoy, "graphic design is now seen as a visual language.... Images are to be read and interpreted, as well as seen; typography is to be seen as well as read."[12] Within this academic institution, text and images were subject to investigations that sought to revalorize the evocative, expressive, and eloquent potential of typography and graphic design even as visual materialization was underscored. In a register quite different from the one developed by Weingart and other Europeans, although clearly sharing certain goals, the Americans were challenging the idealist model of slick,

724
Visuel Design/Jean Widmer (competition winner), original logo for the Centre Georges Pompidou, Paris, 1974–77. Still in use today.

725
Visuel Design/Jean Widmer, poster for an exhibition, *Inhabiting Europe*, at the Centre de Création Industrielle, Paris, 1989–90.

726
Ernst Hiestand and Jean Widmer (competition winners), Manual setting out the principles of signage for the Centre Georges Pompidou, Paris, March 1976.

727
Visuel Design/Jean Widmer, entry for a competition to design a logo for the city of Berlin, 1993. The leaf of the Linden tree is not only a symbol of peace and freedom, but also recalls the famous Berlin avenue called Unter den Linden, laid out in the seventeenth century.

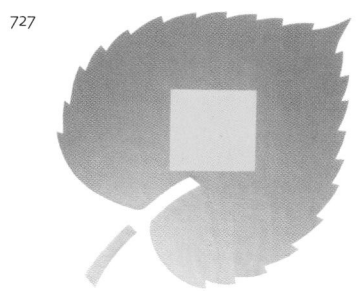

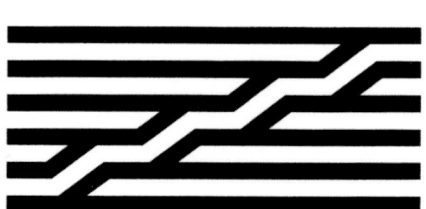

728
Why Not Associates, double-page spreads from the book *Steelworks,* Why Not Publishing, Great Britain, 1990.

729
Edward Fella, recto/verso poster, *Morris Brose: A Sustained Vision*, also used as a mailing, Detroit Focus Gallery, Michigan, 1987.

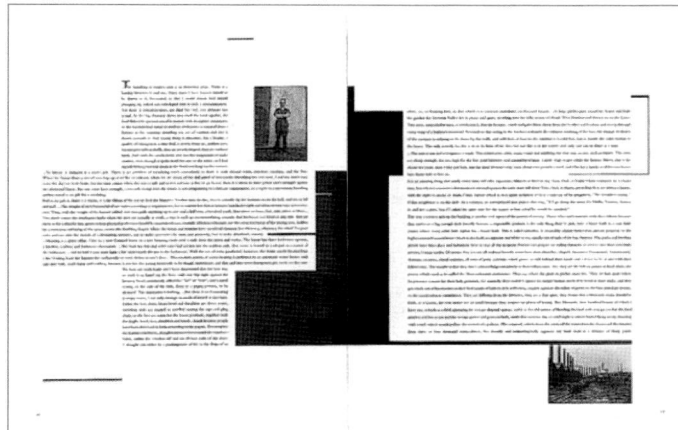

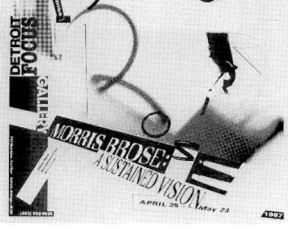

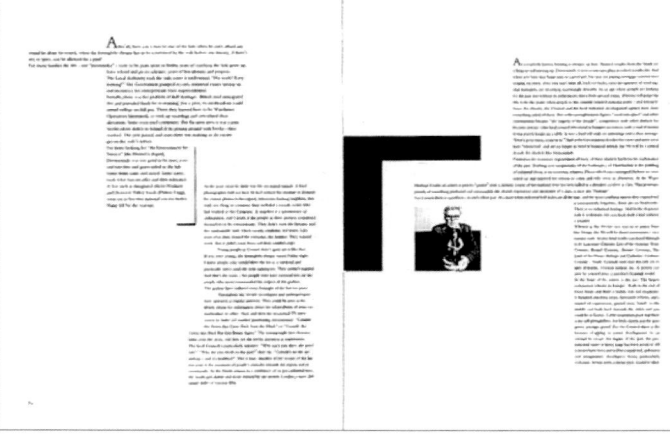

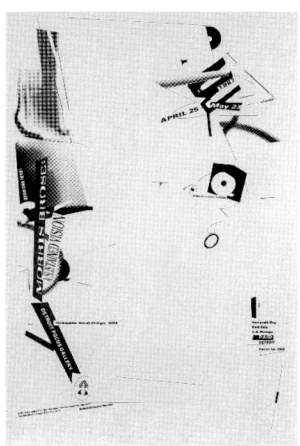

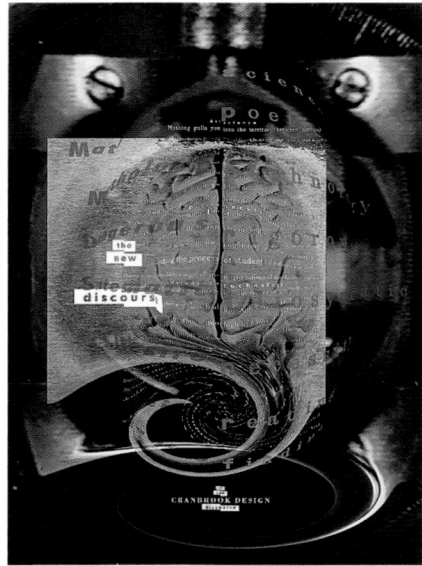

730
P. Scott Makela, poster, *The New Discourse: Cranbrook Design*, Cranbrook Academy of Art, Michigan, 1990.

accurate, clearly organized visual communication that aspired to a state of perfection. This new perspective was stimulating—by definition—for it adhered to the philosophy that language, message content, and processes of communication were in no way transparent, straightforward, immediate, or clear. They were all a weave of many layers of meaning. A (typo)graphic transposition of this perspective took the path of hybridized elements, of interferences, of mysterious cross-sections and plans, of multiple, strangely interlinked levels of reading, and of vibrations and unexpected occurrences; such explorations recalled the exuberance and cacophony of Futurist and Dada typography. The philosophy of design developed at Cranbrook furthermore invoked literary and semiotic theories that reflected the polysemic nature of language, meaning, and communication.

Sometimes described as a formalist or decorative movement, the school that sprung up around McCoy produced graphic work that involved original registers of visual expression, providing design with new impetus. The trend would turn out to be highly influential not only in the United States but also, somewhat later, in Western Europe. Designers who studied at the Cranbrook Academy of Art notably included Jeffery Keedy, Edward Fella, Lorraine Wild, David Frej, Lucille Tenazas, and P. Scott Makela.

Directly or indirectly, many American and European typographers and graphic designers would draw major inspiration from the ideas promoted at Cranbrook. The trends that derived from deconstruction sometimes seemed to avoid asking the question of the extent and ways in which a delight in forms can weigh on meaning, a question that also raises the issue of the remit of graphic design, including its social and environmental role (in the broadest sense), its reception, and the people it targets (or concerns), not to mention the responsibility of the designer.

Dutch graphic design

Given the country's sustained involvement in (typo)graphic culture and practice, the Netherlands constitutes a particularly interesting case study throughout the twentieth century. Starting with the experimentation at the dawn of the century and the founding of the De Stijl movement in the late 1910s, typography and graphic design have consistently generated remarkable activity there. In the last three decades of the century, leading graphic artists have included Gert Dumbar (following in the footsteps of predecessors such as Willem Sandberg, Wim Crouwel, and others). Born in Jakarta, Indonesia, in 1940, Dumbar studied first at the Koninklijke Academie voor

731
Studio Dumbar, posters for the Zeebelt Theater, The Hague, 1993 (photo: Lex van Pieterson).

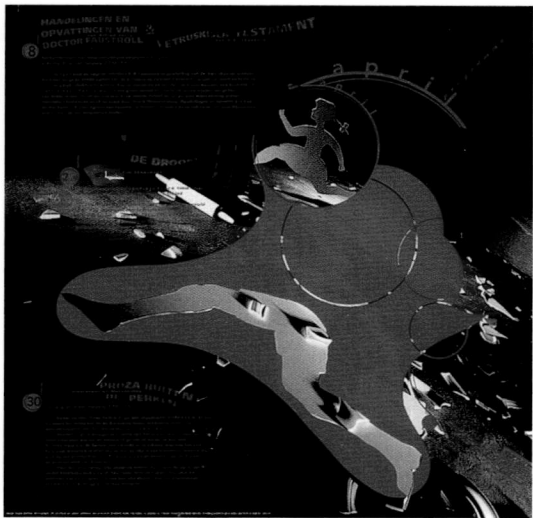

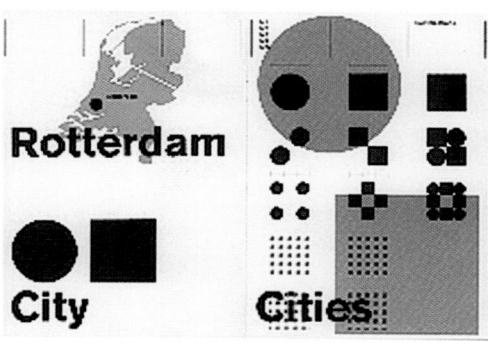

732
Koweiden Postma (design), Hans Verschuuren (photograph), poster for a dance event, *Tiga*, the Netherlands, 1990.

733
Mevis + van Deursen (Armand Mevis and Linda van Deursen), winning entry in a competition to devise the image of Rotterdam as European Capital of Culture in 2001.

Beeldende Kunsten (Royal Academy of Fine Arts) in The Hague, and then at the Royal College of Art in London, from which he graduated in 1967. He subsequently joined Tel Design in The Hague, where the country's graphic tradition and culture were perpetuated. He played a major role in the vast project to redesign the image of the Netherlands' national rail system (Nederlandse Spoorwegen). In 1977, Dumbar founded his own outfit, Studio Dumbar, to which he recruited numerous designers. His studio specialized in graphic design work for institutional and government clients, as well as cultural organizations and industry, garnering a range of commissions to which designers such as Zwart, Kiljan, and Schuitema contributed. In conjunction with the Total Design agency, Studio Dumbar notably revamped the visual image of the Dutch postal service. Heirs to a rich graphic tradition, Dumbar and his team came up with strikingly diverse proposals, able to range from a constructive rigor to an expressively profuse idiom not far from New Wave design and deconstruction (Dumbar, for that matter, would visit the Cranbrook Academy of Art). Meanwhile, throughout his career Dumbar addressed media aimed at all kinds of applications and contexts, from hospital signage to theater posters. Having become the leading figure of Dutch graphic design in his day, Dumbar, along with his team, explored bold typographic and visual repertoires often based on surprise, intuition, and graphic experimentation, always in a playful tone. Dumbar claims he wants to employ visual materials "whose only function is that they don't function,"[13] a comment revealing the same attitude and spirit as other contemporary quips such as "form follows fun," "form follows fiasco," "less is a bore," and "less is more, more or less."[14]

Numerous designers in various cities also left their mark on graphic design in the Netherlands, benefiting from an extensive reliance on design in the public sector and from the rich culture that resulted. While The Hague and Amsterdam appeared to be the country's two major centers, new initiatives also arose in Rotterdam, which was home, for example, to an agency and a review called Hard Werken (1978–80). Among these designers, R.D.E. Oxenaar is worth singling out—starting in 1966 he designed Dutch bank notes, to which he managed to impart a surprising freshness and graphic quality (all the more remarkable in that most countries at the time clung to the centuries-old appearance of money).

Great Britain: the punk movement and Neville Brody

Like the Netherlands, Switzerland, and the United States, Great Britain made a major contribution to graphic design in the 1970s and 1980s. Some of the more visible events were the rise of the punk movement, followed by the Neville Brody phenomenon. Deliberately out of phase with the other trends of the day, punk was a distinctive graphic image. It emerged powerfully in the mid-1970s among London's rebel youth. Because it was so closely linked to a musical style, punk imagery recalled—if on a radically different visual register—the psychedelic phenomenon in the United States in the 1960s (which also produced a stream of posters outside all typographic convention, based on optical effects). Punk's visual repertoire was most likely inspired by the underground publications associated with London's counter-culture movement in the 1960s, notably IT (*International Times*) and OZ (founded in 1966 and 1967, respectively). Indirectly, it also harked back to the graphics of the French student movement of May 1968, not only in terms of a swift, spontaneous, apparently artless technique but also in terms of its call for social change, its rejection of conventional codes, and its flagrantly inexpensive and improvised methods.

Punk creative design came across as a distant cousin of Dada. It shared the same vehemence, same anarchic spirit, same subversive aspect and same chaotic approach—to which it added the raw expression of aggression and destructiveness. Photomontage, recycling, and collage were henceforth abetted by photocopying technology. Leaflets, fliers, record jackets, fanzines, and fashion communicated punk design to a group of people in the know, thereby establishing new relationships between signs of recognition and belonging that were both visual and aural,

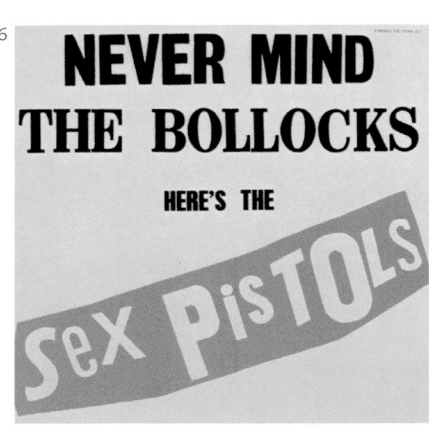

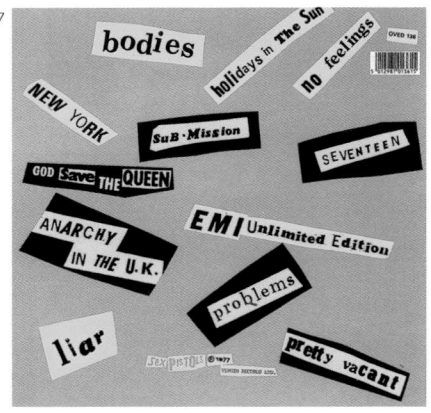

graphic and musical. Designs combined high-contrast black-and-white photographs with expressive drawings, cut-out lettering, and occasionally hand-written texts. Strong color contrasts (back-white, white-black, red-black, yellow-magenta, white-yellow, etc.) were accompanied by a profusion of elements interrupted by sudden tears or cuts, by traces of manual gestures, by marks of amateur production, by collage techniques, by an avoidance of horizontality in favor of freer, livelier compositions, and by a strong imbrication of text and images. The movement came to the attention of the general public through the Sex Pistols, a group whose graphic image, created by Jamie Reid, has remained emblematic of this trend even as it became part of a widely shared visual culture. Punk creative design in London in the 1970s, like Wolfgang Weingart's efforts at renewal in Basel, actively shaped Western Europe's graphic landscape. Although the movement did not survive in its original form for very long (a matter of a few years), it had repercussions in the United States, especially New York and the west coast, as well as in other parts of Europe around 1980. Punk graphics were also picked up by alternative fashion magazines (such as *i-D*) and then recycled, indeed recuperated, by commercial circuits that considerably softened the rawness of the original imagery.

Just when the punk movement was spreading to other Western countries, around 1980, Neville Brody launched his career in Britain. He soon became an important figure on the

734
Jamie Reid, leaflet advertising the Sex Pistols, *Punk Special* [at the] *100 Club*, Great Britain, 1976–77. 14 1/2 × 11 1/2 in. (37 × 29 cm).

735
Jamie Reid, poster for the Sex Pistols' *Never Mind the Bollocks*, Great Britain, 1977. 3 ft. 5 in. × 2 ft. 4 in. (105 × 71 cm).

736
Jamie Reid, record cover for the Sex Pistols' *Never Mind the Bollocks*, London, 1977. 12 1/2 × 12 1/2 in. (31.5 × 31.5 cm).

737
Jamie Reid, reverse of record cover for the Sex Pistols' *Never Mind the Bollocks*, London, 1977.

738

739

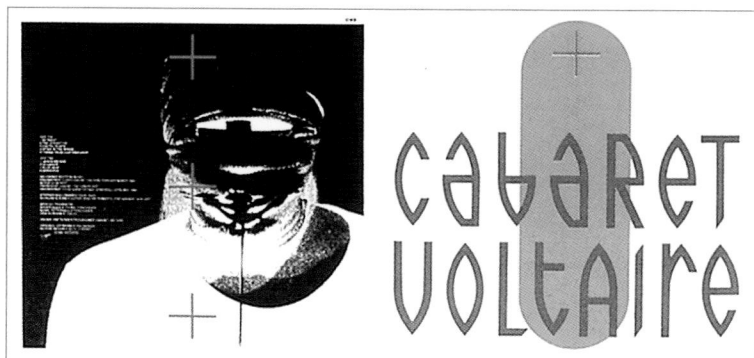

740

abcdef

abcdef

abcdef

738
Neville Brody, cover and liner of the record
Micro-phonies, 1984.

739
Neville Brody, double-page spread in issue 59
of *The Face*, Great Britain, 1985.

740
Neville Brody, three versions of the Blur
typeface: light, medium, bold; Great Britain,
1992. (FontShop)

741
Neville Brody, Gothic typeface, Great Britain,
1992. (FontShop)

741

aбcдeFghiᴣklⱞⱺⱺⱣrstuᵥᵥᵥxyᵹ[ɜⱺ]

ABCDEFGHIJKLMNOPQRSTUVWXYZ

1234567890[.,::?!$6-*]{ÄÖÜÅØÆŒÇ}

design scene, being part of the new generation of cult designers whose work remained highly
fashionable for a decade or two (a cycle that now seems to be getting shorter at the dawn of
the twenty-first century). Brody thus achieved a level of international recognition probably
comparable to that of April Greiman (the same recognition that would later be attained by the
likes of David Carson and John Maeda. It is worth noting that all of these individual successes
were accompanied by widespread publications in the United States and several European
countries).

Born in 1957, Brody studied at the London College of Printing (1976–79) and swiftly
made a reputation as a graphic and typeface designer. His career should probably be
understood in the context of the ambient visual culture, described as young, Pop, punk,
alternative, urban, and so on. Much of his creative output in the 1980s was done for the
music industry, notably posters and record jackets (right from the early 1980s), as well as
for magazines. Some of his works bear distinctive features related to his way of using a
letter, word, logo, or title, all designed by himself. His typography and graphics therefore
always retain a personal touch, visible in his special way of combining straight lines with
curves, of playing on somewhat geometrical constructions, of repeating certain specific
shapes such as the mandorla. The typographic elements designed by Brody seem to provide
the keystone to his oeuvre, lending it identity, originality, and continuity. He belonged to a
pivotal generation in his field, highly aware of notions of balance and proportion yet
simultaneously concerned to leave a subjective imprint on his designs. He combined rigor
with randomness, precision with surprise, predictability with accident; he thereby

incorporated and reinvigorated, in his own way, certain aspects of the history of graphic design in the twentieth century. His noteworthy contributions include his work as art director (1981–86) of *The Face* (a magazine devoted to fashion, music, and art, founded in 1980 and aimed at a young readership), and his graphic work for other magazines such as *City Limits* and *Arena*. He also designed several typefaces, notably Industria (1990), Insignia (1990), Typeface 4, 5, and 7 (1991), and Gothic (1992).[15] His work ultimately had a visual impact on, among other things, magazines for the general public, fashion glossies, and alterative urban publications, all representative of an important aspect of developments in typography and graphic design.

Although Brody's career, right from the start, coincided with a pivotal period corresponding to the swift spread of computer technology, his oeuvre must also be situated in the context of the heritage of British (typo)graphic design. That heritage ranges from Tschichold's presence in England in the late 1940s to the punk movement of the 1970s, incorporating along the way Herbert Spencer's work (visual, written, and editorial), Jock Kinneir's redesign of public signage systems, developments on the educational front by Anthony Froshaug and Michael Twyman, publishing activities (e.g., the magazine *Typographica* and Studio Vista's books on graphic design), the founding of agencies such as Henrion Design Associates and Pentagram, the business and industrial world's growing interest in visual image, the launching of magazines such as *i-D* and *The Face* (with page layouts designed to appeal to the youth culture of fashion and music), and the rise of individuals and outfits such as 8vo, Why Not Associates, and Brody himself.

France: May 1968 and the Grapus collective

Many countries in the industrialized West were able to broaden the foundations of typography and graphic design in the second half of the twentieth century, thanks to better education and to ever-expanding commissions (from public and private institutions,

businesses, cultural organizations, etc.), not to mention the role of publications and exhibitions and the founding of professional agencies and associations. The world of typography and graphic design henceforth encompassed all of these activities, to varying degrees. In France, in addition to the work of earlier pioneers and accomplished designers (such as Cassandre, Loupot, Faucheux, Massin, Frutiger, Widmer, and Cieslewicz), the design scene continued to be characterized by original phenomena and unique oeuvres, design that is hard to compare to work being done elsewhere in the West even though often related to international trends. Indeed, the designs of Cassandre in the 1920s and 1930s, like those of Faucheux after the war (and like the work, elsewhere, of Werkman and Sandberg) succeeded as independent visual forms on the fringes of dominant trends, different from other contemporary styles. Similarly, the output of the Grapus group from 1970 to 1991 yielded an uncommon, lively, and thrusting graphic style indebted to the Polish school and the spirit of May 1968.

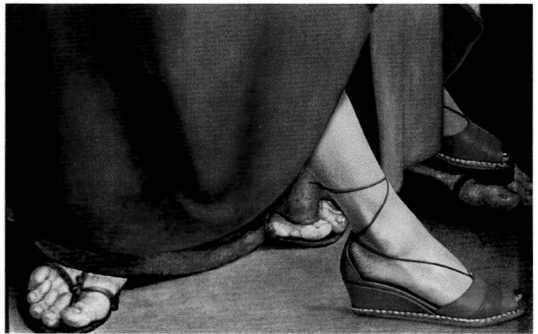

742
Roman Cieslewicz, poster for Franco-Polish solidarity, *liberté = wolnosc*, 1981.

743
Roman Cieslewicz, photomontage, Charles Jourdan shoes, 1982.

744
Atelier Populaire, *Capital,* Paris, May 1968.
Silkscreen, 3 ft. 2 $^1/_2$ in. × 29 $^1/_2$ in. (98 × 75 cm).

745
Atelier Populaire, *Oui Usines Occupées*
(Yes to Occupied Factories!), Paris, May 1968.
Silkscreen, 27 × 20 in. (69 × 52 cm).

746
Atelier Populaire, *Non,* (No to Capitalist
Factories!), Paris, May 1968. Silkscreen,
26 × 17 $^3/_4$ in. (66 × 45 cm).

747
Asger Jorn, *Pas de puissance d'imagination sans
images puissante* (No Power of Imagination
without Powerful Images), France, 1968.
Lithograph, 19 $^1/_2$ × 12 $^3/_4$ in. (49.5 × 32.5 cm).

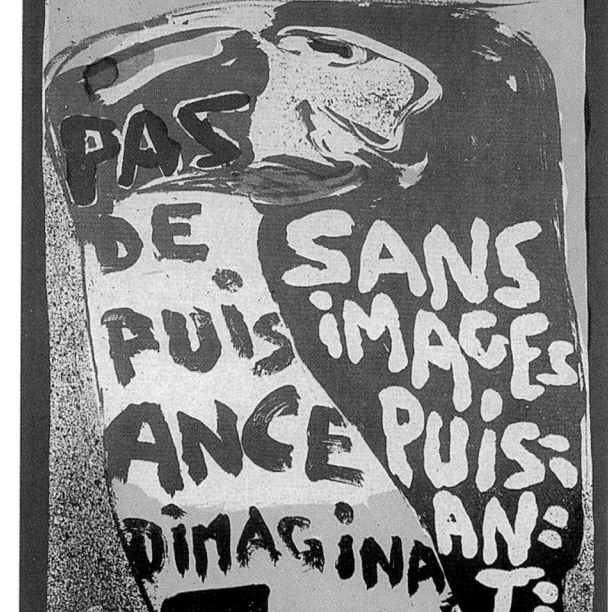

In France itself, 1968 bought two successive events that marked the history of graphic design: first, the mass demonstrations of May, which engendered new visual developments, then the loss—through suicide—of a defining individual, Cassandre. These events created an explosion of political posters, leaflets, and wall displays, produced in the hectic months of May and June. It has been estimated that some six hundred thousand posters went up in Paris and around during those two months alone. Simple yet striking, created hastily and often, with limited resources and a limited range of colors, these supports resonated with the social protest and upheaval then underway. When it came to techniques and methods employed, the protesters relied on, in the words of one commentator: "a 'people's printshop' [*atelier populaire*] [that] mainly used lithographic and silk-screening processes on an artisanal level. For lithographed posters, the only material and equipment available was to be found at the École des Beaux-Arts [School of Fine Arts], so it was geared for artistic use (hand presses, small print-runs). Silkscreening, which didn't require much equipment, proved to be the easiest method for everyone and was the most productive—roughly sixty copies an hour. Three or four presses in a people's printshop equaled 1,000 posters a day if you worked day and night! ... Some posters were done by linocut or stenciling (the large ones). Since offset was more expensive.... only posters of major import were printed that way.... The paper used was usually newsprint (offcuts salvaged from the printshops of the daily newspapers), and butcher paper was bought by the reams."[16] One widely distributed leaflet gave detailed explanations to the uninitiated of the method for making a silkscreened poster. Several hundred different posters were designed and printed by these "people's printshops," the most famous images being the ones produced by the above-mentioned *atelier populaire* in the École des Beaux-Arts. Many of these posters, often done anonymously, were cranked out by students themselves. Graphic designs reproduced in this way were soon visible all over the streets, alongside the "mural newspapers" also occupying the walls.

In June, an article in *La Cause du peuple* (The People's Cause) described this phenomenon with warmth and enthusiasm:

Ever since the École des Beaux-Arts has been occupied, progressive students and artists have been contributing their skills, in total anonymity, to the struggles being carried out each day by workers. This is no experimental lab—workers come to provide their slogans, discuss things with students and artists, and criticize the posters or distribute them outside.... Thus outmoded bourgeois methods of work have completely disappeared: posters are planned collectively after a political analysis of the day's events or after discussions at the factory gates, then are presented democratically to the General Meeting at the close of the day. This is how they are judged: "Is the political idea right?... And does the poster convey that idea?" Designs that are accepted are then silkscreened or lithographed by teams that work day and night. Dozens of teams of poster-stickers are then organized, joined by other teams from the local Action Committees and the Strike Committees at occupied factories, all of whom share their experiences in discussions with the people. Recently, people's poster workshops have been set up in various Action Committees in Paris and the suburbs, while others are springing up in the provinces in order to strengthen the links between students, workers, and peasants. THE STRUGGLE GOES ON.[17]

Posters and other printed material generated by the events of May 1968 favored concise, shortened forms that would catch the eye of passersby and make an immediate impact. They were often entirely hand-drawn in a single color, making little use of photography, and they combined lettering, symbols, and schematic figures in a recognizable style (thus distantly evoking nineteenth-century posters made before the arrival of color lithography). Produced by groups of students, laborers, and working-class activists, these graphics display the particularity of being made in a hurry, on immediate behalf of a social or political cause; they thereby belong to a special class of graphic design. The texts and slogans on the posters, often in a handwritten, gestural style using capital letters, set the tone even as they loudly proclaimed their own status. *Non !* (No!), *Refusez l'intoxication* (Don't Be Duped), *Presse ne pas avaler* (The Press: Do Not Swallow), *Information libre* (Free Information), *C'est trop* (Enough is Enough!), *Frontières = répression* (Borders = Oppression), *Bas les masques* (Off with the Masks), *À bas la société spectaculaire-marchande* (Down with the Biz-Showbiz Society), *L'art au service du peuple* (Art for the People), *Unité ouvriers paysans* (Worker–Peasant Unity), *Usines universités union* (Factory University Union), *À bas les cadences infernales* (Down with the Hellish Pace of Work), *À nous de parler* (Our Turn to Speak Up). The graphic style of May 1968 remained aloof from contemporary formal concerns (such as the imminent New Wave, and so on). Furthermore, it was a powerful illustration of political commitment and the expressive power of certain graphic supports at a time when the specifically social (and political) role of graphic design in the West was being dampened by the economic impact of business, industry, and official institutions (hence far from the revolutionary aspirations proclaimed and pursued in Europe in the 1910s). Outside France, 1968 also saw graphic design mobilized for purposes of protest in other circumstances—students in Prague notably produced a series of posters following the invasion of Czechoslovakia by Warsaw Pact troops in August.

Other phenomena surfaced in France itself in the wake of the events of May 1968 and related protests. The boldest and most original expression of the experiments that challenged and visibly refashioned the practices of preceding decades was undoubtedly the work of the Grapus collective. Founded in 1970 by Gérard Paris-Clavel, Pierre Bernard, and François Miehe, the group shared and displayed a strong desire for a sociopolitical renaissance. Two members of the group had studied under Henryk Tomaszewski at the Academy of Fine Arts in Warsaw. Their work was thus influenced by the Polish model: a spontaneous and unusual visual appearance featuring handwritten lettering and gestural marks and traces that made a striking impact. Although Grapus worked for cultural institutions, it immediately acknowledged its political loyalties by accepting commissions from the French Communist Party and from Communist-run municipalities and organizations; Grapus claimed that it wanted "to produce propaganda in a professional and collective manner."[18] Through its

748
Grapus, poster for a musical event, *Chansons dans la Ville*, 1977–78.

749
Grapus, poster, *La Nature de l'Art*, for an exhibition of land art at La Villette, Paris, 1988. 4 ft. × 2 ft. 7 in. (120 × 80 cm).

748

749

singular graphic repertoire, the group openly supported and served sociopolitical causes in a highly original style. Images and texts played an important role in the collective's productions—colors were lively, the imagery often employed symbols, and words were subject to all kinds of manipulation: misalignment, enlargement, superimposition, plays on language and on the shapes of symbols, contrasts between hand lettering and typography, impact of scrambling, and so on. Grapus came up with emphatic, immediately graspable visual ideas, as though directly transposed from spoken language. In the opinion of designer F.H.K. Henrion, "the results perfectly combined words and writing, sometimes playing on puns and visual or verbal ambiguities, yet never sacrificing the clarity of the message."[19]

The group's original political commitment was complemented by its visual design work in the cultural sphere, which came from commissions or competitions. In the 1980s, designers associated with Grapus won contests to devise the visual image of the La Villette museum complex (1984) and the Louvre (1988). After recruiting numerous designers, the group finally split into three different entities in 1991 (the very year the group was awarded France's Grand Prix des Arts Graphiques). The most important aspect of Grapus's contribution perhaps resides in its careful selection of thoughtful and thought-provoking imagery that reflected a social as well as a political commitment. Such designs employed writing and typography as iconic material, not as a potential realm for the design of letterforms (unlike Neville Brody, for example, whose worked is strongly marked by the style of his own typefaces). Furthermore, the work of Grapus testifies to the scope of potential repertoires, notably compared to the output of the Visuel Design/Jean Widmer agency (both firms having been founded at the same time, one heir to the Polish school, the other to the Swiss school). This bipolar situation attested to the henceforth accepted coexistence, in Western countries, of distinct—indeed diverging—trends that share only a desire to update visual language.

The vitality of protest and spectacular effects

As we have seen, in France and elsewhere, visual communication continued to display vitality throughout the second half of the twentieth century once had it recovered from the serious setbacks inflicted by totalitarian governments and World War II. Across numerous countries, each new decade ushered in new trends or specificities generated by the active presence of designers committed to their work and stimulated by international exchanges on the professional level. The generations that emerged in the 1970s asserted the need to transform or transgress the (typo)graphic forms then familiar or in favor, which they did by destructuring institutionalized practices; they rejected conventional rigor and promoted themselves as a potential alternative—for certain applications, at least—to the International Typographic Style and the Swiss school. Graphic design of the 1970s reflected a quest for new compositions via a rearrangement of components on the page or in space (which often resulted in a fragmentary, shattered, dispersed, or piecemeal effects). The goal was clearly to catch the eye—as it always had been—at the expense of the supposed clarity of the message. This need for personalization and particularization probably represented a natural, liberating reaction to various tendencies including the International Typographic Style, which had become fairly commonplace and seemed to be aging rapidly. Although certain (typo)graphic forms and experiments of the 1970s and 1980s may seem like radical gestures that represent a profound break, in fact they were preceded by the explorations conducted throughout the earlier part of the previous century. The new trends that emerged at the end of the post-war economic boom could in fact call on an immense visual repertoire, one that might be appropriated in various ways and to various degrees, whether alluding to Cubist collage or Pop and psychedelic imagery, or harking back to Marinetti's "typographic revolution" and Dada, or favoring certain aspects of Constructivism, or merely acknowledging the singular work of designers like Werkman and Grignani.

The various types of new impetus that arose in the 1970s have been given all kinds of labels, but these terms do not define movements with clear borders or simple descriptions.[20]

Many designers of the 1970s were seeking originality, aspiring to transcend acquired skills. Kurt Schwitters' famous advice of 1924, exhorting typographers to strive for originality — "always do otherwise than others" — clearly still had appeal.[21] The contemporary attitude towards deconstruction was therefore related to the upheaval advocated by avant-garde movements dating back to the early twentieth century and even earlier. This attitude nevertheless focused more on fueling innovation than on assessing its relationship to the historical material that had been crucial in authorizing and generating a good deal of the creative design of the day. Those designs adopted an approach that reactivated the beholder's rapport with the tenets of visual communication by challenging legibility, toying with clarity, teasing the beholder-reader-viewer-consumer, increasing involvement in the process of perception, intervening in the very construction and transmission of the message, and so on. Such tendencies, adopting the pace of the fashion world, perhaps leaned more heavily towards aesthetic considerations as they distanced themselves from social ones. It is worth noting that whereas these new directions were particularly suited to certain media and applications, sometimes addressing themselves to a specific, initiated audience in a given cultural code, they remained aloof from other sectors of graphic and typographic communication.

Far from occupying the crossroads of acquired applications, graphic design of the 1970s set off in quest of new paths and visual possibilities that would prove stimulating at the level of reception as well as creation. The most visible part of ambient creative design included the schools of deconstruction and/or extreme expression. Many designers in both Europe and the United States worked in these directions, and each new trend or variant enjoyed an impact and notoriety all the swifter for being heavily mediatized — the ability to visually impress the public was a highly important initial criterion.[22] At the same time, the elaboration of a clear, discreet, and modest typography, seeking a different type of efficiency, retained its own validity in cases that called for rapid, functional, or immediate understanding (not to mention the fact that such an approach represented an autonomous form of expression that some designers professed with great conviction). The landscape of graphic design thus offered a weave of highly diverse and distant approaches, displaying a remarkable heterogeneity (as did other areas of visual art at that time).

Graphic artists, designers, and architects set the tone. In 1985, Milton Glaser (who anticipated the post-war transformations), summed up this ineluctable openness, then becoming accepted more officially. "All that stuff about revealing structure and reducing things to their simplest forms — I couldn't go for that. I guess the revolutionary thing we did was to take the position that there is no single voice capable of expressing every idea, that romance is still necessary, ornament is necessary, and simplification is not better than complexity."[23] In a similar vein, Ettore Sottsass, a co-founder of the Memphis group, argued that artists had "a duty ... to blaze trails of fantasy, surprise, independence."[24] Architect Robert Venturi, meanwhile, concisely expressed the attitude of his own day:

I like elements which are hybrid rather than "pure," compromising rather than "clean," distorted rather than "straightforward," ambiguous rather than "articulated," perverse as well as impersonal, boring as well as "interesting," conventional rather than "designed," accommodating rather than excluding, redundant rather than simple, vestigial as well as innovating, inconsistent and equivocal rather than direct and clear. I am for messy vitality over obvious unity.... A valid architecture evokes many levels of meaning and combinations of focus: its space and its elements become readable and workable in several ways at once.[25]

When it came to the realm of graphic design, the most diverse visual registers could coexist in the final decades of the twentieth century, especially once digital technology arrived. The boldness and experimentation that preceded the computer age therefore largely laid the groundwork for "technological design" that immediately embraced notions of randomness, hybridization, modulation, interchangeability, ambiguity, dispersion, spatial layering, depth, and so on.

393

The advent of digital design

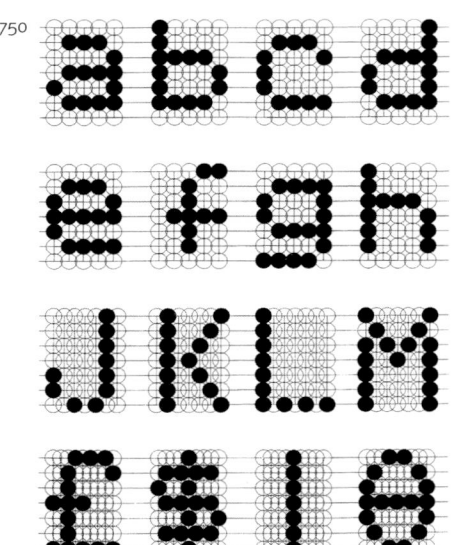

750
Olivetti, typeface for the first generation of office printers (based on a grid of 35, 49 or 63 dots), Italy, 1972.

Often seeking personalized or liberating forms of expression, the trends in typography and graphic design in the 1970s and early 1980s preceded the computer revolution by just a few years. In a way, they were also harbingers of the spirit that governed early digital design. Henceforth, the dominant movements and individuals would be partly conjugated through the syntax—and pace—of fashion design. The tendency to valorize vivid forms and to encourage competitive escalation governed a considerable portion of the then-emerging output and culture of design, as well as the history of design then being written. Designers who favored a certain moderation or particular attention to detail—working from a long-term perspective, for instance, rather than from one of immediate appeal—did not seem to enjoy the same visibility. Some of them adopted that path through personal choice, others through necessity (dictated by the nature of the typographic or design work involved), for it was more suited to certain sensibilities and to certain types of application such as the presentation of purely informative texts in given situations, the layout of substantial volumes of published text, and signage systems with specific requirements (that said, new trends are always a potential trigger of unexpected transformations). Yet it is likely that this aspect of graphic design, despite its distinct presence and interest, has been under-represented and underestimated in recent decades, a phenomenon that has probably become more extreme at the dawn of the third millennium (given the globalization of media imagery, the all-digital craze, the role of moving images in [typo]graphic design, accelerating rhythms and "real-time" expectations, and so on).

Dealing with new methods and new data

The mid-1980s heralded a major turning point in the history of graphic design practices and professions—digital technology would revolutionize methods of creativity and production, encompassing moving images and sounds as well as static pictures and texts. The swift arrival and development of cutting-edge technology, although requiring exceptional transformations, was just one of a long series of inventions that have changed these professions, from Gutenberg's success in devising a system of movable type in the fifteenth century, to the progressive mechanization and automation of this system in the nineteenth century, accompanied by the massive arrival of lithographic techniques, followed by the incorporation of photography early in the next century, and right up to the important, if short-lived, breakthrough represented by photosetting technology. Quite apart from production methods, the possibility of displaying images on a computer screen gave graphic design and typography a whole new medium with which to play, one with enormous potential. Digital tools (notably word processing, image editing, and the personal on-line publication of scripto-visual or other information) forced all users to deal with typographic data themselves, leading to a popularization of practices that had previously been unavailable to the uninitiated (with the exception of simple typewriters and transfer-lettering techniques).

751
Susan Kare, design of icons for Apple's Macintosh computer, United States, 1983-84.

752
Letterforms designed for use with personal digital assistants (PDAS). c. 1990s.

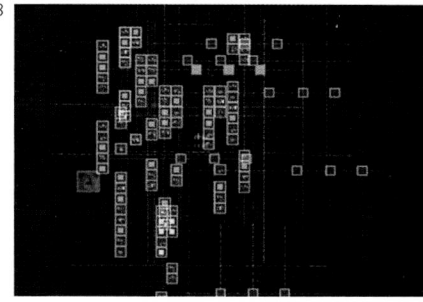

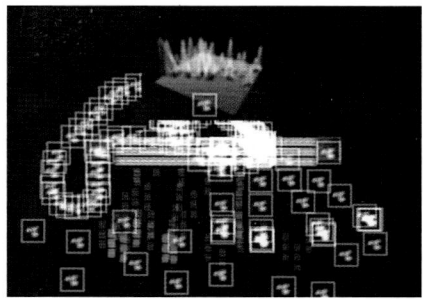

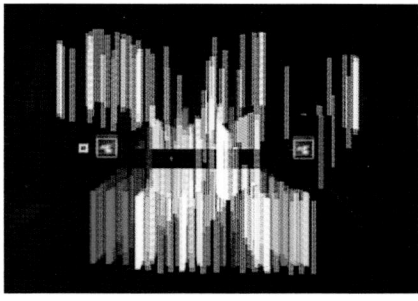

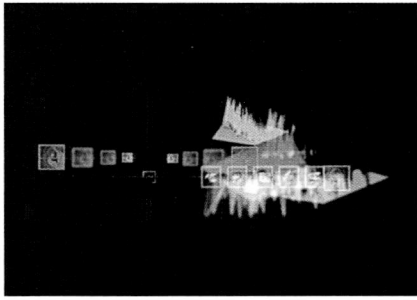

753
Andrea Tinnes and Chris Selby, under Professor
Michael Worthington, proposal for *The Elements
of Print Typography*, digital design, California
Institute of the Arts, United States, 1997.

The digital extension of graphic design began around 1984 with the launch of Apple's new home computer, Macintosh. It was the first microcomputer with such user-friendly features as a mouse and a graphic interface employing icons and windows. Although not the very first personal computer (IBM had begun selling a PC in 1981 that predated modern microcomputers), the Macintosh was the first to enter successfully the professional world of typography and graphic design. (Back in 1978, the Massachusetts Institute of Technology [MIT] had already hosted a demonstration of interactive media.) The arrival of computers on the scene of visual communication implied profound changes that functioned on various levels. They provided design with a brand new foundation and context for work, being simultaneously a tool, a means of expression and production, a medium, a place of storage (libraries of typefaces, etc.), a new system of generation and display (pixels, vectors, resolution, numbers of colors), a site of interactivity, and operating system and programs (including special—and defining—software). As far as the chain of graphic production went, a printer became one of the most important peripherals. Very distant descendents of the printing press (which required an operator), the early printers of the 1980s offered poor resolution with visible dots. Although this technical limitation inspired a certain (typo)graphic creativity in the mid-1980s, by the approach of the third millennium printers attained a nearly perfect level of resolution, at least from the standpoint of normal visual perception, thanks to a palette of 16,581,375 colors (255 × 255 × 255).

The combination of screen display with all kinds of binary-coded data (text, static and moving images, sound, 3-D imagery, video, etc.) paved the way for new possibilities of expression, exploration, and exploitation of forms and material. The computer screen, a vertical, luminous surface requiring neither pigment nor paper, carved out an entire new space for graphic design. It could serve, in turn, as a tool for initial conception, then for preview, for production, and for reception. This mode of display was adapted to various kinds of formats—including horizontal—from portable screens small enough to fit in the palm of the hand (a surface that had already been determining in the birth of writing, for example, in the form of cuneiform tablets, and one that still survives in the shape of paperback books) to a projection on giant screens, not forgetting the usual format (slightly larger than a standard sheet of paper). Hence screens are used for electronic publishing and for accessing all the data on the Internet as well as for retrieving all other kinds of digital storage and archive.

The conjunction of multifarious kinds of digital data with the notion of hypertext created truly new conditions for typography and graphic design, favoring ongoing extensions of means of expression as well as changes (or metamorphoses) in methods of display. As had occurred in the past, technological changes once again had a major impact on the processes associated with visual communication. Computer technology also brought with it the crucial notion of interactivity, which turned a reader, beholder, or spectator into a potentially reactive, active, indeed creative participant who interacts with the machine. Whereas the history of printing progressively led to eclectic combinations of typography, color, and photography applied to traditionally static supports, digital technology actually imparted movement to typography and graphic design (a phenomenon anticipated earlier by certain avant-garde film techniques, such as credit sequences by Saul Bass and the films of Norman McLaren, not to mention televisual imagery). The closing years of the twentieth century pointed visual communication in the direction of broad, new, relatively unexplored horizons involving movement, animation, time-based factors, sequencing, and linking, all of which called for new approaches. While at the dawn of the third millennium it is difficult to assess the full scope and implications—both direct and indirect—of the still-recent digital phenomenon, considerable transformations have already occurred on the levels of the creation and reception of (typo)graphic forms and possibilities, as well as professional needs and sources of information, not to mention the constitution, elaboration, and dissemination of graphic culture itself.

The 1980s and 1990s: unprecedented transition, digital profusion

The advent of digital technology in the mid-1980s occurred in the context of a constantly expanding design universe and thus further multiplied spaces and forms of creativity even as it transformed creative processes. Often presented as the agent of a revolutionary break with the past, in fact the computer contributed to a renaissance of graphic design right from the outset. It would nevertheless seem inappropriate to set these transformations on the same plane as the most radical accomplishments in the visual history of typography and graphic design, such as the making of medieval illuminated manuscripts, the birth of Roman (and, later, sans serif) lettering, poetic innovations in typography (such as those associated with Mallarmé), and the most original aspects of Futurist and Dada compositions (all phenomena unrelated to technological developments). Digital typography and graphic design brought to the surface a certain number of recurring features, notably including the deconstruction–reconstruction obtained by pixelation, multiple repetition of a single element, effects of superimposition and transparence, a play on half-tone screens and lines, a juxtaposition of different formal registers, the use of ready-made filters on photographic images, and a penchant for scrambling and complexity, all of which reflected a need for stylistic pluralism and raised new questions to which rigid forms and responses provided no answers.

The last fifteen years of the second millennium represented a transitional period during which computer use became extremely widespread, although not universal. Indeed, whether through choice or through difficulty in adapting to new methods that differed from the old (therefore requiring new technical training), some designers carried on in their traditional ways. This attitude has even survived into the early years of the twenty-first century, notably among the generation born during the interwar period and in the context of senior design management. As far as the conceptual phase goes, the practically universal adoption of digital technology raises the question of the role still played by hand-drafting and drawing faced with techniques of direct, on-screen display. From this standpoint it would be interesting to reconsider the birth, use, and spread of major techniques such as collage and photomontage, the offspring of specifically manual techniques, yet still so important in the context of digital design (copy, cut, paste, paste in front, paste behind, paste inside, copy-and-merge, collage, etc.).[27]

As the third millennium dawns, the frontiers of typography and graphic design continue to expand and disperse in a creative environment always on the lookout for innovation and inventiveness. However, despite the coexistence of countless formal registers, one quite distinct aspect of contemporary design stands above all others, tempering this perception of profusion: of the considerable volume of (typo)graphic output that is produced in mass-consumer societies every day, every hour, only a very tiny part is the object of real creative work, of profound conception and reflection (an observation that was also true of other periods).[28] A good part of it is simply popular graphic culture and output. Another part is caught up in the need for swift cost-cutting, respecting the quantitative logic of commercial productivity. Yet another part seems to be totally unaware of the accomplishments and potential of visual communication. Endless examples of these phenomena can be seen, for instance, in the presentation of data on the Internet.

To a large extent, the current historical view of the closing years of the twentieth century seems to favor the most media-steeped designers, whose work was amenable to presentation in the form of exhibitions, catalogs, articles, and lectures accompanied by projected imagery, or other public events (all quickly publicized and disseminated by an international milieu). The rise to fame often depended on the need—and the ability—to put together a set of a dozen or so visual items (in which posters might still feature prominently) liable to attract the attention of a general public not only accustomed to high-speed perception, sustained scrolling, visual surfing, and constant browsing, but also comfortable with everything ephemeral and fleeting. From this standpoint, the recent period echoes certain phenomena typical of the nineteenth century and Victorian design. While it is becoming increasingly complicated to define notions of quality—visual, formal, artistic,

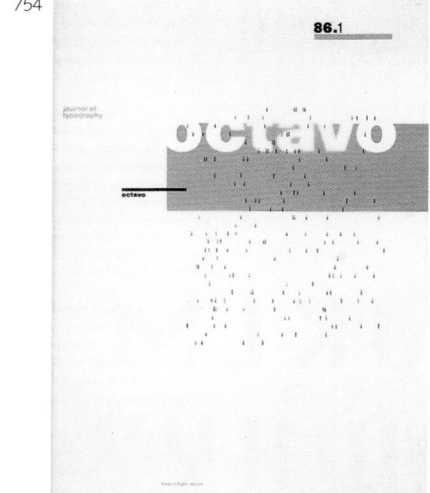

754
8vo, cover of the first issue of *Octavo, Journal of Typography* (designed and published by 8vo), Great Britain, 1986.

755
8vo, screens of the eighth and final issue of *Octavo, Journal of Typography*, published in digital form, Great Britain, 1992.

756

756
8vo, poster for the Boymans-van
Beuningen Museum, Rotterdam, 1989.

757
8vo, poster for the Flux Music Festival in
Edinburgh, 1997.

757

758
Müller + Hess, posters for an exhibition of the
work of Richard Paul Lohse, Zurich, 1999.

759
John Maeda, *Flora*, interactive calendar for
Shiseido, 1997.

760
Paul Elliman, posters for a series of lectures
at Princeton's School of Architecture, 1999 and
2000.

758

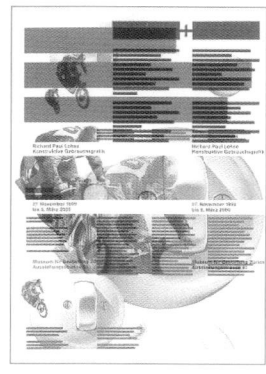 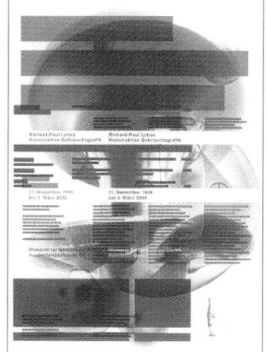 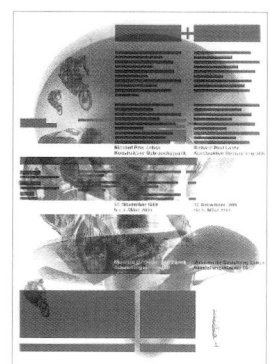

759

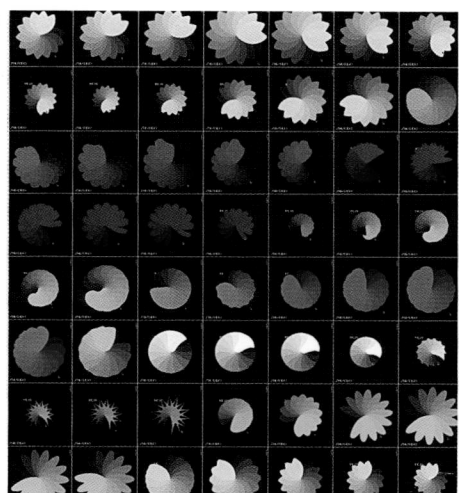

760

 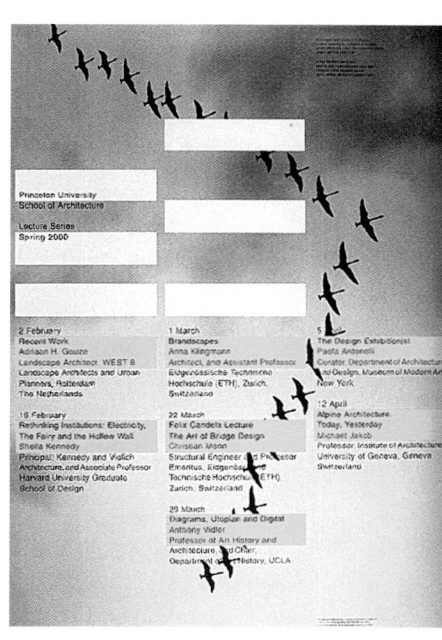

761

conceptual—or even merely to define different practices, ambient culture strongly amplifies the emerging figures and striking phenomena of Western typography and graphic design of the moment, now that the spread of culture via Internet has assumed major proportions.

The intersection of a well-established eclecticism with digital technology in the 1980s favored graphic and typographic experimentation that triggered a new visual curiosity and new visual needs. Getting a jump on the medium, the designers who first based their graphic explorations or output on computer methods and data are now considered pioneers (such as the founders of Emigre). Some of them immediately viewed computer technology as a driving force behind a complete revamping of their practices. New hardware brought with it new freedom and new possibilities, thanks to its flexibility of use and its integration of the whole design chain. Although history shows that technology does not always revolutionize visual forms (Gutenberg's printshop began by imitating handwritten manuscripts, and the main visual lines of Mallarmé's *Coup de dés* can be seen in his autograph version),[30] the emergence of digital technology transformed graphic design in terms of practices, forms, processes, and applications. The use of a computer became mandatory by the 1990s (in agencies, among independent designers, and in schools, firms, and offices that had design departments). Computer technology can nevertheless be used in widely varying ways by typographers,

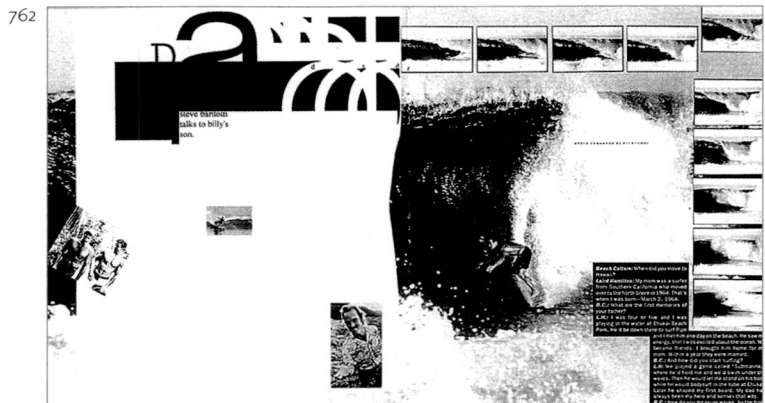

762

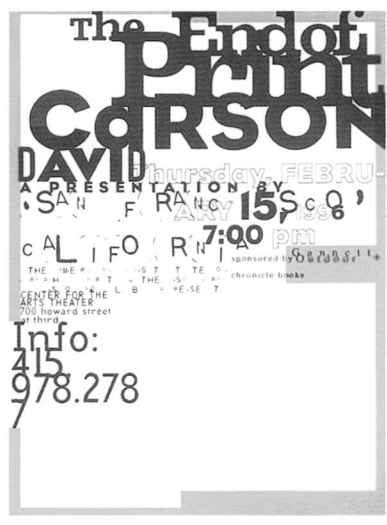

763

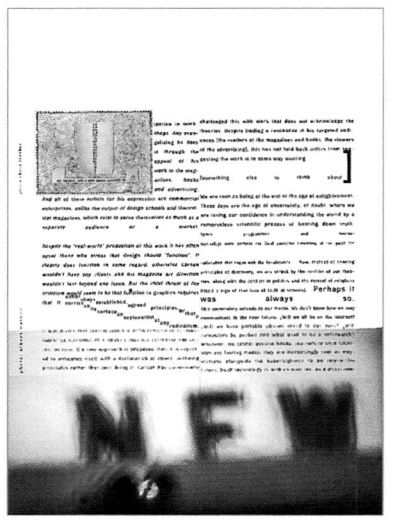

764

761
David Carson, *Orbs Products*, poster for the new launch of Ray Ban sunglasses in Australia, Young & Rubicam Agency.

762
David Carson, double-page spread from *Beach Culture*, 1991 (photo: Art Brewer).

763
David Carson, poster for his lecture, "The End of Print," San Francisco, 1996.

764
David Carson, page from *The End of Print: The Grafik Design of David Carson*, 2nd edition, 2000.

typeface designers, and graphic artists. Some perceive it as an instrument of exploration and a stimulus to imagination, while others see it as a straightforward production tool.[31]

Typographers and graphic designers

The arrival of digital methods coincided with the overlap between the generation of designers working since the 1970s (sometimes since the postwar period and, more rarely, the interwar period) and the generation whose careers began with the new technology. The former, who were still numerous, pursued their work while the latter inaugurated a new era of technological eclecticism. Spanning the generations, individuals worth citing include Wim Crouwel (born in 1928), Gert Dumbar (1940), Edward Fella (1938), April Greiman (1948), Karel Martens (1939), Bruno Monguzzi (1941), Peret (Pere Torrent, 1945), Gunther Rambow (1938), Paul Rand (1914—1996), Niklaus Troxler (1947), Anton Stankowski (1906), Wolfgang Weingart (1941), and Jean Widmer (1929). The new trends, individuals, agencies, and groups that surfaced in the final decades of the century brought to the fore such names as Wild Plakken (founded 1977), Ott + Stein (1978, Nicolaus Ott and Bernard Stein, born in 1947 and 1949), *Emigre* magazine (co-founded in 1984 by Rudy VanderLans, originally from the Netherlands, and his wife Zuzana Licko, who also run an agency of the same name),

MetaDesign (founded in 1979 by Erik Spiekermann, born in 1947), 8vo (1985) and *Octavo* magazine (1986–92), Why Not Associates (1987), Fontshop (1989), Tomato (1991), and Vorm Vijf. At the same time a number of individual designers surfaced, notably Tibor Kalman (1949–1999), Javier Mariscal (1950), Neville Brody (1957), David Carson (1957, famous for *Ray Gun* and *Beach Culture* magazines), Phil Baines (1958), Siobhan Keaney (1959), Allen Hori (1960), Barry Deck (1962), Cornel Windlin (1964), and Nick Bell (1965).

Like the broader field of graphics, the specific sector of typeface design became particularly active with the advent of digital technology. An ever-growing choice of samples, catalogs, and publishers became accessible. New designs defied traditional classifications, often challenging old conventions of longevity and even legibility, adapting themselves to current fashions for fanciful alphabets. Among the countless typefaces published in the 1980s and 1990s, a few are noteworthy for their originality or popularity. Well-known international publishers such as Emigre, Fontshop, and Linotype are particularly representative of the trend. (For that matter, individual designers can now market their own work directly on-line.) For example Emigre, based in California, publishes faces designed by Jonathan Barnbrook, Barry Deck, Edward Fella, Jeffery Keedy, Zuzana Licko, Just Van Rossum, and Rudy VanderLans. Noteworthy Emigre fonts include Oakland and Emperor (1985), Oblong (1988), Keedy Sans (1989), Template

765
Rudy VanderLans, pages from issue 37 of *Emigre* magazine, California, 1996.

766
Collective work, double-page spread from the "Heritage" issue of *Emigre* magazine, 1990, California.

767
Elliott Peter Earls, lettering and double-page from an Emigre brochure on his work, California, 1998.

768
Stephen Farrell, double-page spread from issue 38 of *Emigre*, 1996, California.

765
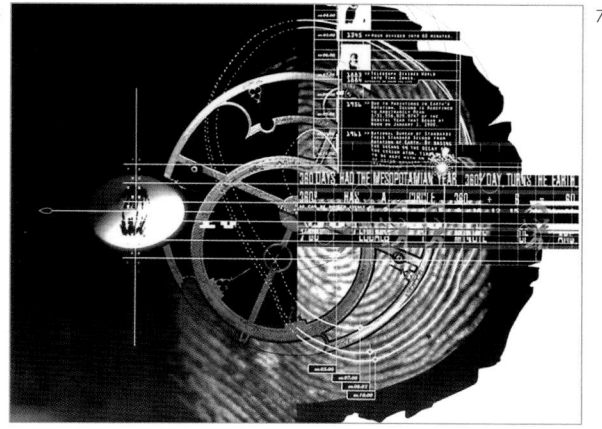

766

767

768

ABCDEFGH

769
Page from the 1996 Emigre catalog featuring Emperor typeface, designed in 1985 by Zuzana Licko for low-resolution screens and printers.

770
Mark Andresen, Not Caslon typeface, 1995. (Emigre)

771
Max Kisman, Fudoni typeface (a cross between Futura and Bodoni), the Netherlands, 1991. (FontShop)

772
Matthew Carter, Bell Centennial typeface, designed for the AT&T telephone directory, 1978. Typeface designed between 1975–78. It lent optimal legibility to small print.

773
Pierre di Sciullo, Minimum-Bong typeface (FontShop). Top to bottom: light, medium, and noir. 1993–95.

Gothic (1990), Dead History (1990), Remedy (1991) and Not Caslon (1995). From Germany, Fontshop offers the work of numerous designers such as Phil Baines, Erik Van Blokland, Neville Brody, Max Kisman, and Just Van Rossum. The FontFonts catalog, meanwhile boasts Beowolf (1990), Dirty Faces, Meta and Thesis (1990s), Fudoni, Trixie and You Can Read Me (all 1991), Blur and FF Gothic (1992), Disturbance (1993), and Minimum (1993–95).

The breaking down of barriers between practices, strongly favored by digital technology, spurred a major number of designers to work simultaneously on graphics, typography, letterform design, and lettering.[31] The recent vitality of typography and graphic design is obvious in many ways, for example through magazines that feature such work, through the fame of cult designers (David Carson in the 1990s and John Maeda in the early years of the twenty-first century), and through the heady pace of change as it tries to keep up with fashion. Despite all the enthusiasm and current approval for (typo)graphic design, the overall trends and interests of the current period continue to remain aloof from any overt acknowledgement of historical precedents.

Critical attitudes and reflections

Given the developments linked to digital technology, the dawn of the new millennium coincided with extreme mutations in graphic design. Although computerized tools held many promises (offering great flexibility to designers, ease of use to everyone, and new methods as well as a new medium itself), their impact and reception have not always been positive. The natural fascination that they trigger has also been accompanied by critical reactions. Digital technology, by increasing the pace of creative work and by constantly expanding the potential visual repertoire, can also lead to the impression of a loss of bearings. The widespread adoption of computer-aided design in the late twentieth century thus spawned a broad school of skepticism: while the

774 Wxhrend die Schriftzeichen ihre Bedeutung nie xndern, sind ihre Formen steter Wx... Et 1234567890 Lapidar Text

775 abcdefghijklmn
abcdefghijklmn

776 #1234567890°_
@&é"'(§è!çà)-
AZERTYUIOP¨*
azertyuiop^$
QSDFGHJKLM%£
qsdfghjklmù`
>WXCVBN?./+
<wxcvbn,;:=
•¤ë"{¶«¡Çø}Ÿ
´„"'[å»ÛÁØ]–
æÂê®†Ú°îœñô,
ÆÅÊ€™Ÿªïœ∏Ô¥
‡Òð ƒ fiÌÏÈ¬µÙ@
ΩΣ∆·flÎÍË|Ó‰#
≤‹≈©◊ß~∞…÷≠
≥›/¢√∫1¿•\±

CCC

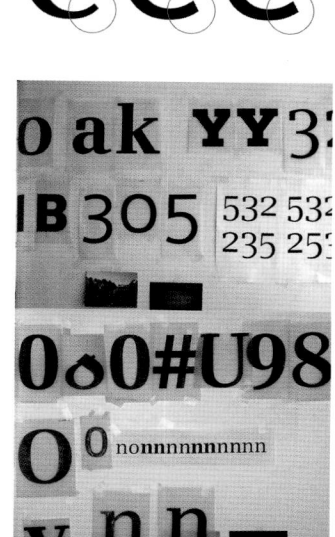

777 CORNELIVS·LVCI
VS·SCIPIC·BARBA
TVS·CNAIVOD·PA
RYFHQVCXKMZ

778 FF Gethic One One
FF Gothic One Two
FF Gethic Two One
FF Gothic Two Two
FF Gethic One One Condensed
FF Gothic One Two Condensed

774
Hans Eduard Meier, sans serif version of Lapidar typeface, Switzerland, 1995. This face was inspired by ancient stone inscriptions (see 777).

775
Erik Spiekermann, Meta+ typeface, 1993. (FontShop)

776
Hans-Jürg Hunziker, typeface for the Siemens corporation (used for all internal and external communication), France, 2000–02. Left: Siemens Serif. Top: Comparison of three fonts—Siemens Serif, Seimens Sans, and Siemens Slab. Bottom: Studies and trials.

777
Example of a Roman inscription in stone (second century BCE) that inspired Hans Eduard Meier in his design of Lapidar (1995, see 774).

778
Neville Brody, Gothic typeface, six variations, 1992. (FontShop)

new technology is often praised for its benefits and the convenience it offers, some designers have expressed strong reservations about it. They question not only specific techniques but also the general ambiance of playful eclecticism. Such considerations have been expressed by people concerned to defend their idea of modernism, such as Paul Rand and Massimo Vignelli, who adopted their positions in a sometimes categorical way, not unlike Tschichold before them.

Peret, a Spanish designer born in 1945, made the following comments in the French daily *Le Monde* in 2002. "It's obvious that computers have radically altered the practice of graphic design. But their splendid images are often hollow and meaningless. Where has the poetic sensibility of Cassandre gone? Where's the caustic tone of Grapus? Or the humor of Glaser, or the power of Cieslewicz? This new mannerist, virtuoso imagery lacks soul. But graphic designers have moral and ethical responsibilities, because they address society."[33] John Maeda, an American of Japanese stock, born in 1966, and highly involved in MIT's Media Lab, claimed that very same year that, "technology is designed to improve technology, not real life.... Technology for technology's sake is hampering creativity... the very image of this whole culture needs changing, it should be directed toward a certain ecology of expression... What's the real spirit of the information era? How can we put some cultural meaning into this revolution?"[34] Such comments are all the more telling in that they come from one of the most famous representatives of digital design in the West today, working in a cutting-edge experimental institution whose historical impact on typography and graphic design is likely to be great, since it was there in MIT's Media Lab that, in the closing years of the twentieth century, "electronic ink" was invented, aimed at making possible, among other things, electronic books that may one day rival paper books. While these reservations may dampen some of the enthusiasm for digital technology, their real interest lies in their critical import: seeking a new balance, they insist on once again acknowledging—whether out of necessity, legitimate desire, or nostalgia—natural factors such as physical gestures, the role of the hand, a certain sense of poetry, a considered moderation.

Right from the start, computer technology inspired graphic and typographic experiments directly related to the machine, its potential, and its specificities (computing power, software component, interface, programming, coding, matrix image, interpolation, picture resolution and print resolution as measured in pixels[35] or dots, and so on).[36] But the general enthusiasm for computer technology has been countered by critical assaults that directly address the realm of (typo)graphic design. Emigre provides an excellent example of this phenomenon. It rapidly became a highly valued opinion-shaper in the West, and the young generation adored *Emigre* magazine, a showcase for new experiments in digital design. However, both the agency and its periodical were the object of merciless criticism from the likes of Massimo Vignelli (born in 1931, hence a figure of the post-war economic boom), who described them as a "typographic waste factory."[37] Fernand Baudin, writing in *Communication et langages* in 1991, noted the significance of Emigre in the design world—despite it being completely unknown in his own country of origin: "*Emigre* is a quarterly publication aimed at graphic designers the world over. It will soon publish its twentieth issue. I came across it by chance... in Brussels... and I was interested in finding out more about its publishers. I mentioned it whenever I ran into people in Paris, Mâcon, Brussels, Lurs—never getting the least reaction. Whereas in New York, Boston, San Francisco, London, and Berlin the entire graphic design community knows *Emigre*."[38] A reaction like Vignelli's focuses and reflects interesting divergences of opinion on typography and graphic design, and more particularly on typeface design and page layout. While some people demand and defend great freedom to experiment, others express serious reservations based on the age-old forms of letters. Thus, the extreme caution of someone like Tschichold, who declared that "the feeling of our times has nothing to do with the straightforward act of reading in itself—people today read exactly as readers did in 1540,"[39] would be countered by the audacity and vision of Emigre, who claimed that "type styles that we perceive as illegible today may well become tomorrow's classic choices."[40] Between those two extremes, Josef Müller-Brockmann expressed a more moderate position that nevertheless looked to the future: "Roman typefaces... convey the spirit of a bygone age."[41]

The advent of digital technology thus exacerbated inevitable divergences within the various approaches to typography and graphic design. The differing conceptions projected onto these practices were probably largely inherited from the nineteenth and twentieth centuries. Henceforth typographers are irresistibly tempted by the idea of disrupting legibility and the possibility of disturbing a complacent reading; this phenomenon has markedly increased since the arrival of computer technology but it was already heralded by New Wave experiments and even earlier, minimalist explorations of letterform design by Wladyslaw Strzeminski, Bruno Munari, Cassandre, and others. Although they are sometimes perceived as major innovations, such trends indeed had precedents. We can even find traces of them in the very origins of writing several thousands years ago. "A strange struggle took place right from [antiquity] between a letter's usefulness and its beauty, between legibility and artistry, between an effort to render visible and a desire to remain secret."[42]

Increased expansion and ubiquity

The practices and techniques now being employed in the early twenty-first century suggest a major expansion of the definition of typography and graphic design. Although this has drawn criticism from some design practitioners, design continues to stress high-quality forms, market demands, relevant choices, in-depth work on new media (and a reassessment of other media), synergy with other fields of art, adaptation of certain historic skills and accomplishments, and so on. Employing the concepts and possibilities of conjugation, hybridization, modulation, flexibility, elasticity, and variability, there have been determined efforts since the 1990s to escape any monolithic approach, any rigidity, any overly restrictive system. This attitude is exemplified, in the realm of typography, by the development of "extended-family" designs (conjugating sans serif, serifed forms and sometimes semi-serif into one system, for instance Stone [1987] and Rotis [1988–89]), of "random" typefaces (Beowolf, in which the appearance of each character changes according to a computer program of composite designs such as Fudoni (a cross between Futura and Bodoni) and Prototype (derived from ten different letterforms); it is also reflected by research into typographic transposition of vocal intonation or architectural input, not to mention Matthew Carter's modular type for the Walker Art Center in Minneapolis, Minnesota, which includes five kinds of "snap-on" serif and over- or

779
One of a series of postcards from the FontShop type publisher, featuring Alessio Leonardi's Baukasten face.

779

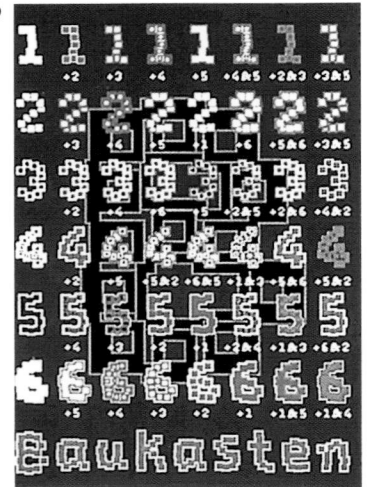

780

abcdefghijklmno
ABCDEFGHIJKLM
1234567890[.,;:?!$£*]

abcdefghijklmno
ABCDEFGHIJKLM
1234567890[.,;:?!$£*]

abcdefghijklmno
ABCDEFGHIJKLM
1234567890[.,;:?!$£*]

781

printing and type. In the process, due to economic and commercial considerations, much vitality was lost. We believe that the computer, although considered by many to be cold and impersonal, can bring back some of these lost qualities.

782

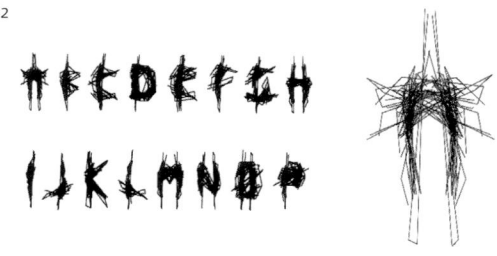

783

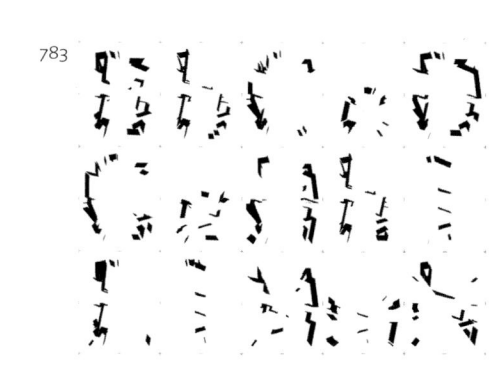

784

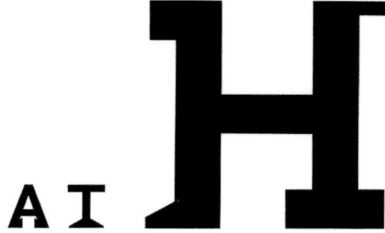

WALKER, A TYPE DESIGNED FOR THE GRAPHIC IDENTITY OF THE WALKER ART CENTER, HAS FIVE DIFFERENT KINDS OF "SNAP-ON" SERIF THAT CAN BE ADDED TO LETTERS AT WILL BY THE USER.

WALKER
WALKER-UNDER
WALKER-OVER
WALKER-BOTH
WALKER-ITALIC
WALKER-ITALIC-UNDER
WALKER-ITALIC-OVER
WALKER-ITALIC-BOTH

780
Zuzana Licko, three versions of the Emigre typeface (Emigre 8, Emigre 15, and Emigre 10). Typeface designed for low resolution screens and printers, 1985. (The numbers refer to the number of pixels that compose the capital height.)

781
Erik Van Blokland and Just Van Rossum, Beowolf typeface, a "random font" in which a character appears differently each time it appears, based on a computer program, the Netherlands, 1990.

782
Sara Maconkey, Exist typeface, "a personalized digital font" based on her own DNA sequence, 1999.

783
Ralph Steinbrüchel, typographical interpretation of an architectural structure (based on the plans for the Victoria & Albert Museum extension in London), 1999.

784
Matthew Carter, typeface with five different kinds of serifs, designed for the Walker Art Center of Minneapolis, Minnesota, 1995. Top: sample of variable serifs.

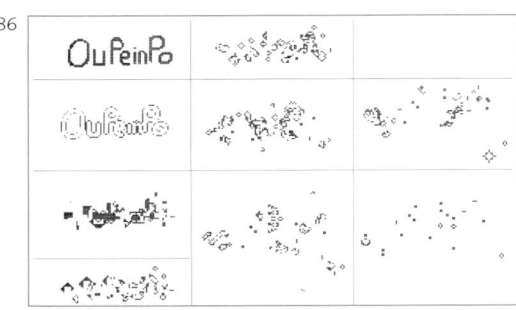

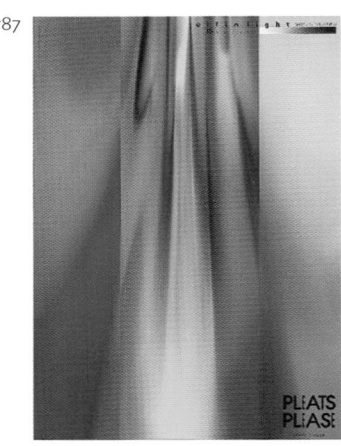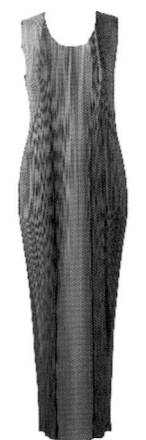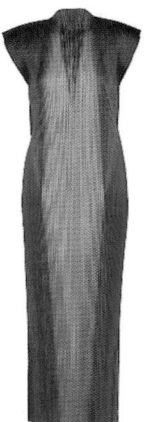

785
Ralph Schraivogel, poster, *Cinema Africa*, Switzerland, 1991.

786
Brian Reffin Smith (who became a member of OuPeinPo in 1999), *Degeneration of the Word OuPeinPo According to John Conway's Rules of Artificial Life*. Generations 1, 2, 3, 5, 10, 100, 200, 300, and 600. "Life occurs on a virtual checkerboard [with] squares called cells [that exist] in one of two states: alive or dead. Each cell has eight possible neighbors, the cells which touch its sides or its corners. If a cell on the checkerboard is alive, it will survive in the next time step (or generation) if there are either two or three neighbors also alive. It will die of overcrowding if there are move than three live neighbors, and it will die of exposure if there are fewer than two." The resulting patterns can be amazing.

787
Mitsuo Katsui, graphic textures for garments from Issey Miyake's "Pleats Please" line, digital creation, Tokyo, 1997.

under-lining that create a corporate identity even as they offer a ready-to-use modular system. This propensity for handy, interactive features can also be seen in graphic design itself, through unconventional objects ("brick books"), animated graphics, interactive electronics (including motion and sound), specific digital artworks (such as those by John Maeda), designs related to environmental concerns or destined for outdoor sites, artistic works and messages designed for public places (often advertising space), etc.[43] As the third millennium dawns, typography and graphic design continue to move ahead, reinventing themselves through individual and collective initiatives, keeping up with technological advances and economic necessities, reacting to events on the ever-changing art scene.

The mass spread and public deployment of typography and graphic design that was unleashed in the nineteenth century now constitutes a major part of our visual environment, notably in cities. This phenomenon has been further reinforced by the fact that with "microcomputers, communication between user and machine is done mainly through graphic means."[44] The ubiquity of graphics turns them into something that is perceived automatically or unconsciously. Just as in other realms of design—and as architecture does somewhat erratically—graphic design (and marketing) makes a significant contribution to the way living spaces are fashioned, determining and influencing our vision of the environment; this entails the capacity to convey information, to serve and ease—or not—the flow of traffic, to project extremely varied messages to a mass public, to shape or train habits of reading and perception, to influence behavior, to inculcate stereotypes and reflexes, to generate surprise, and so on. "Today design sits at the intersection of cottage-industry cultural production, corporate sponsorship, and mass-distribution systems such as magazines or the Internet, which are dominated by the visual."[45]

788

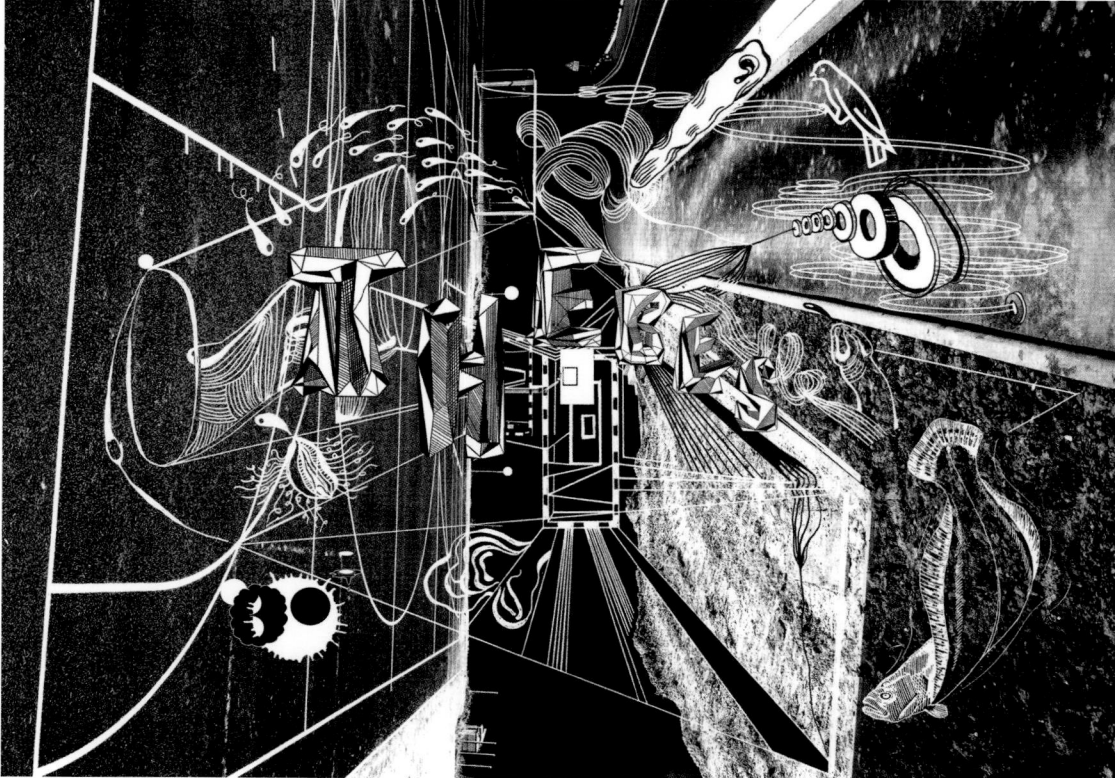

789

790

788
M/M (Paris), *The Alphamen—Boris X*, 2004. One of a series of twenty-six silkscreens done from photographs by Inez van Lamsweerde and Vinoodh Matadin, 25 $^{1}/_{2}$ × 19 $^{3}/_{4}$ in. (65 × 50 cm). Twenty-six signed copies, lettered A to Z, printed by Eric Linard, co-published by Éric Linard Éditions and CNEAI, 2004.

789
M/M (Paris), *Antigona (Billboard)*, 2004. Silkscreened poster, 13 ft. × 9 ft. 10 in. (400 × 300 cm), based on the set devised by M/M (Paris) for Tommaso Traetta's 1772 opera, *Antigona* (conducted by Christophe Rousset, directed by Éric Vigner).

790
M/M (Paris), *Witness Screen/Écran témoin*, 2002. Silkscreened poster, 4 ft. × 5 ft. 10 in. (120 × 176 cm), produced for a film by François Curlet.

791
Stefan Sagmeister, poster for the release of the Lou Reed album, *Set the Twilight Reeling*, United States, 1995–96.

791

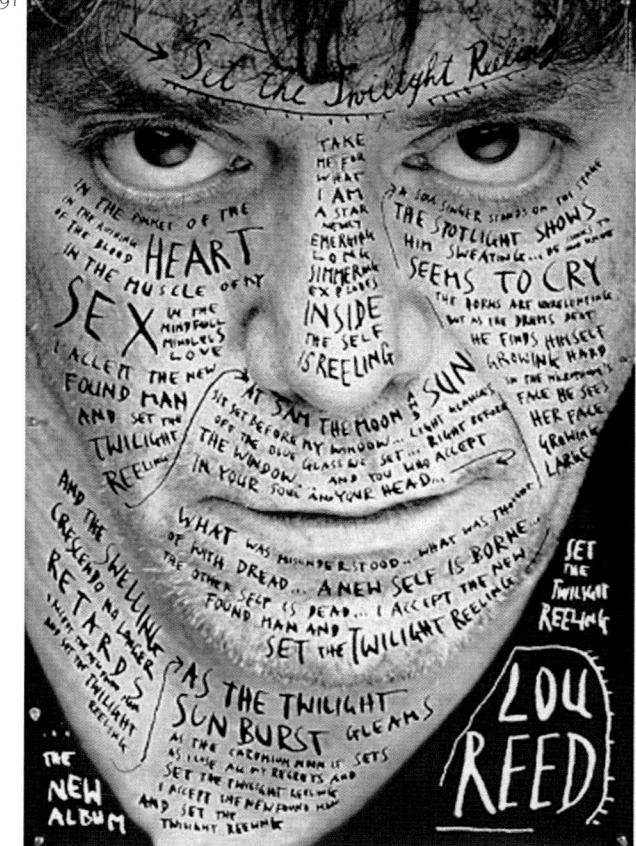

792

792
Jaap van Triest, Karel Martens, double-page
spread from the book, *Karel Martens: Printed
Matter\Drukwerk*, the Netherlands, 1996
(published by Hyphen Press, London).

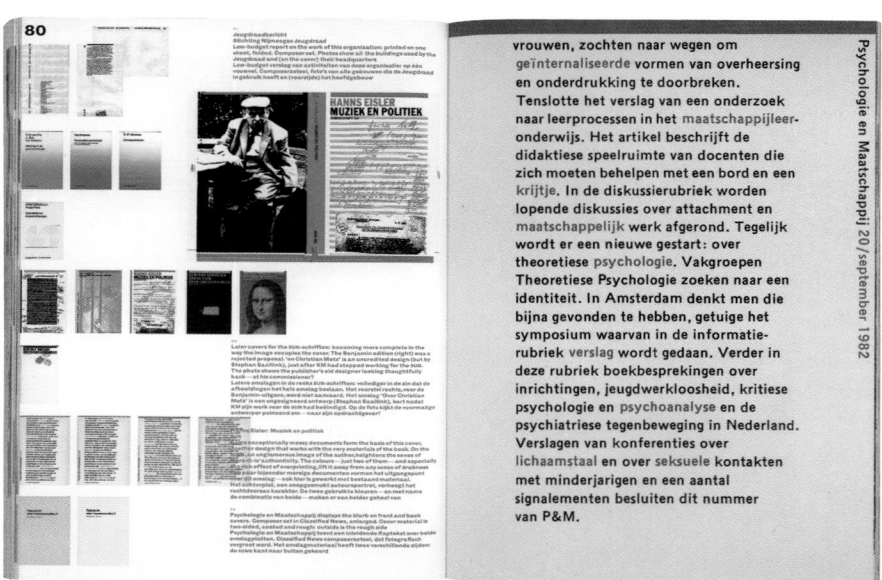

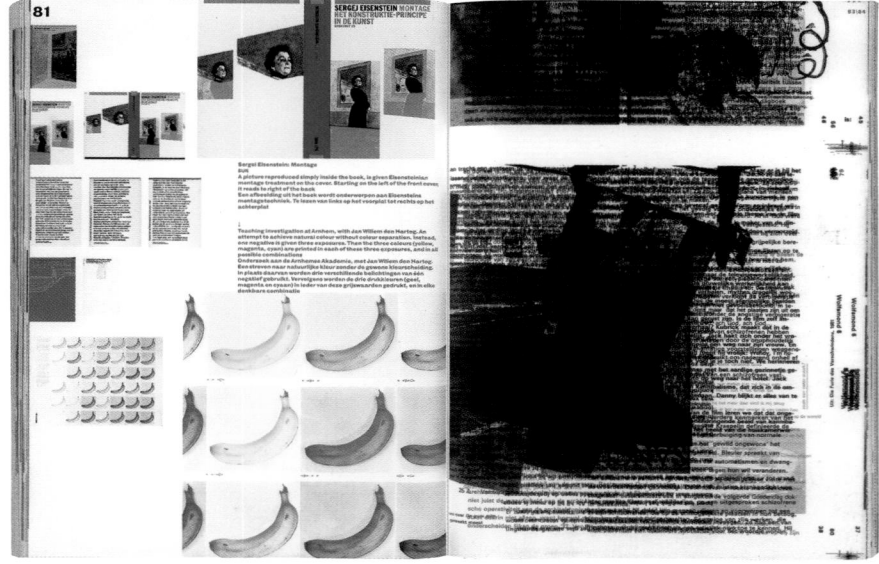

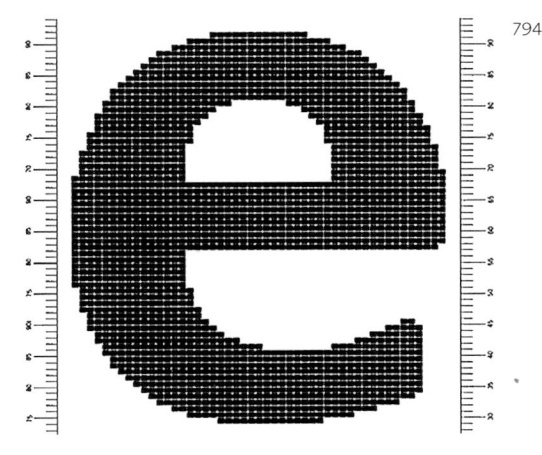

793

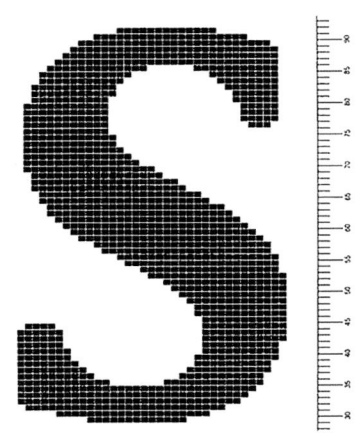

794

795

796

800

797 abcdefghijkl

798 abcdefghijkl

799 abcdefghijkl

793
Gerard Unger, Praxis typeface
(a sans serif alternative to Demos),
the Netherlands, 1976

794
Gerard Unger, Demos typeface,
one of the first digital fonts.
Commissioned by the Hell
Company (Germany),
the Netherlands, 1976

795
Gerard Unger, signage for the
Amsterdam subway system
in M.O.L. typeface (the Dutch
equivalent of "mole"),
the Netherlands, 1974

796
Gerard Unger, signage based
on the Vesta typeface,
the Netherlands, 2001

797
Gerard Unger, Swift 2.0 typeface,
the Netherlands, 1995.

798
Gerard Unger, Vesta typeface,
the Netherlands, 2001.

799
Gerard Unger, Gulliver typeface,
the Netherlands, 1993

800
Gerard Unger, signage for
the Dutch highway system.
Commissioned by ANWB,
the Netherlands, 1997.

Widespread freedom

801
Roland John Goulsbra, Agrafie and Alexie
typefaces, Germany, 1994 (Linotype and
TakeType).

Issues and redefinitions

The transformation of design practices and issues triggered by the digital upheaval have amplified the potential scope of typography and graphic design, underscored the diversity of existing attitudes, and revived divergences and dissensions largely inherited from the profuse activity of the preceding two hundred years. Once again, technology and media come across as two crucial dimensions in the history of visual communication. Just as reproducibility became significantly more feasible once Gutenberg invented his system of printing with movable type, enhanced by the widespread use of paper, so color lithography considerably transformed the landscape of nineteenth-century graphics, even prior to the mechanization of typesetting and printing techniques. Similarly, in the twentieth century, photographic and, more recently, digital techniques have altered the picture. When it comes to this last development, the current scene seems to confirm the shattering of all stylistic forms, reference points, and supports. This context welcomes an extraordinary wealth of creative design, if at the risk of producing a uniformity of styles and values in an environment relatively devoid of historical knowledge and appreciation.

The expansion of approaches and the dispersal of references raise the question of the definition and situation of graphic design, given the henceforth global—and instantaneous—circulation of texts, signs, images, advertising, news, games, music, and so on. The issues raised by contemporary practices call for a glance back at the very origins of graphic design and what that term might cover. For some people, it emerged with the very first marks, lines, signs, symbols, images, and texts produced by human hands long before the modern era. For others, it began with Gutenberg. Often, the term is associated with urbanization and industrialization (production, standardization, centralization, specialization, working methods, notion of progress, and so on). The narrowest view, which associates the birth of graphic design with the historical avant-garde movements, would limit it to the twentieth century. Each of these putative starting points corresponds to an important stage in the historical development of graphic design taken in its broadest sense (for who knows what archaic forms might have existed prior to the ones we know and label as "the earliest"?).

Henceforth, in the so-called leisure-consumer-information society, approaches to graphic design reflect a whole range of new possibilities and attitudes. The dematerialization that is accompanying digital technology and the decades-long quest for new types of subjective expression have now been joined by a huge popular access to typography and the graphic arts, combined with a partial de-professionalization, such that it is probably easier for the general public to cite a few typefaces—Arial, Times New Roman, and Helvetica having practically become household names—than it is for students or practitioners to cite landmarks in design history.[46] This truly new and salutary phenomenon has enabled people in industrialized countries to engage in activities previously limited to a professional milieu.[47] Countless individuals now own computer equipment that induces them to make (typo)graphic choices of their own. The drawback of this situation—if it is a drawback—is that, in principle, the practice of graphic design now means nothing more than learning how to use a computer.

This extraordinary breakthrough seems to have intensified the positive and negative aspects it incarnates. On one hand the visual sphere is constantly expanding and feeding off ever-changing influences and contributions, the fashion trend having liberated unprecedented creative energy and design flexibility.[48] On the other hand, from the standpoint of professionalism, know-how, and historical appreciation, typography and graphic design are undergoing profound upheavals. Often linked to demands for innovation, efficiency, immediacy, visibility, and popularity, design also suffers from the constant flux of media imagery associated with advertising and publicity—high-tech, fleeting, playful, euphoric. This context blurs the distinction between high-quality design (fully developed imagery) and images for general consumption (reflecting the technical and economic requirements of mass culture).

The evolution of forms and centers of typographic and graphic design in the twentieth century once again raises the issue of modernism. From the historic perspective, the modernist era dates back to, among other things, the invention of movable type in the mid-fifteenth century. When it comes to graphic design, the accession to modernism is usually attributed to its adoption of the principle of change, renewal, and discontinuity, as spearheaded by artistic and literary movements in the nineteenth century and continually reinvoked ever since. More specifically, historian Robin Kinross suggests dating the emergence of modern typography to the early eighteenth century, corresponding to a reorganization and new division of labor.[49] Historically, for both typography and graphic design, certain phenomena that first occurred or intensified in the nineteenth century are now perceived as crucial—beginning with the early mass production and expansion of media (such as the popular illustrated press), the development of new types of public images (soon in color), the ensuing transformation of the urban landscape, the possibilities raised by the invention of lithography and photography, the process of mechanization and automation, rising literacy, and more specifically the appearance of new families of typeface and the spread of non-book typography. Although typography and graphic design often diverged from their previous models in the twentieth century, the characteristics of their evolution were sometimes associated with minimalism, simplicity, sobriety, austerity, and functionalism, going so far as to be described as "inflexible and restrictive"[50] and even "non-poetic." That was the standpoint from which the final three decades of the century sought a new, "postmodern," path, turning towards a mélange of influences, an openness to complexity, to metaphor, individualism, emotion, ornamentation, the vernacular, borrowings, reiteration, and so on. All these directions can indeed be found in recent design practices, even if some of them also existed previously.[51]

802
Phil Baines, poster for the first issue of the typography magazine *Fuse*, Great Britain, 1991. It used the You Can Read Me font to spell out, "can you & do you want to read me?"

803
Brian Coe, "an alphabet designed as part of an experiment to determine how much of each letter of the lowercase alphabet could be eliminated without seriously affecting legibility," c. 1965–1968.

804
Phil Baines, You Can Read Me typeface, Great Britain, 1991. (FontShop)

802

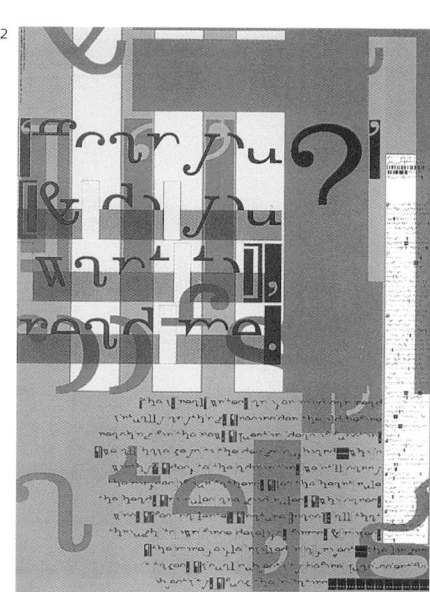

803

804

Creation/reaction—a generational rift

The highly visible developments in late twentieth-century graphic design sparked highly varied reactions, from unquestioning delight to harsh criticism (though not necessarily in equal proportions). In a sign of the times, the reactions are often linked with a generational effect.[52] While expressions of enthusiasm and fascination are very pronounced (and very easy to find), so are the objections. These objections target both the formal aspects of design and the role played by designers. Often it is typography that receives most comment. Many of the severest critics are also leading figures in the design world, such as Paul Rand, Wim Crouwel, Adrian Frutiger, Massimo Vignelli, and Max Caflisch. Some have expressed themselves in harsh terms. Paul Rand, for instance, deplored a "lack of humility and originality and an obsession with style [that] seem to encourage these excesses.... [T]he goal ought not be what is *new* (original), as Mies put it, but what is *good*.... 'Form is not the goal but the result of our work.'"[53] Massimo Vignelli, meanwhile, complained that, "in the new computer age, the proliferation of typefaces and type manipulation represents a new level of visual pollution threatening our culture. Out of thousands of typefaces, all we need are a few basic ones, and trash the rest."[54] And Wim Crouwel lamented that, "with all our efforts in this age of renewal and innovation, the bulk of visual output is below zero."[55] Adrian Frutiger pointed out that, "mankind possesses letterforms that have been perfected over the past five hundred years.... Why change them now? It's normal for designers to conduct experiments, but their trial runs won't survive. The destruction of typefaces that we're seeing today is just a passing moment."[56] Or, as Max Caflisch argued: "If typography is just a more or less experimental pastime in which the text is rendered almost unrecognizable and unintelligible, the jumble that results... will in any case seem silly once it's a question of showing them to an uninitiated public. Communication in the sense of the free exchange of ideas and knowledge should be a bridge that links the past to the future.... A system that should not be dictated by any formalism but that favors access... to the meaning of the text.... Writing and lettering play an important, indeed preponderant, role in conveying ideas."[57] All these reactions come across as uncompromising condemnations that reflect a dissenting viewpoint, one that rejects noncritical consumption of an "anything goes" approach to visual design. At the same, these opinions offer a powerful reflection of the destabilizing effect of recent phenomena, and hence the profound interest that they have managed to arouse.

Role, responsibility, commitment

These off-the-cuff reactions ultimately point to profound questions concerning the scope, essence, function, issues and even sites of typography and graphic design. Which in turn raise once again the issue of a designer's social role, extending beyond professional circles or artistic communities.[58] Reviving an old divergence, some commentators in the early twenty-first century are calling for designers to show greater responsibility, indeed greater commitment, whereas others want to defend artistic autonomy, oeuvre, and approach. Rand, for example, claimed that, "even though common decency implies continuing concern for human needs, social issues are not aesthetic issues, nor can they be the basis for aesthetic judgments."[59] His advice was intended for practitioners as well as teachers.

Concerned to address this issue of commitment, several historians, critics, and practitioners have emphasized the social role of a designer. Their viewpoint stresses the fact that designers are in a position of significant power given their ability to produce combinations of text and images destined for mass consumption. Furthermore, some twentieth-century

805
Niklaus Troxler, poster conceived as a reaction to the apathetic reaction of bystanders during violent mugging in downtown Zurich *Gewalt Halt!* (Halt Violence!), Switzerland, 1993.

805

806 conditionnement

807

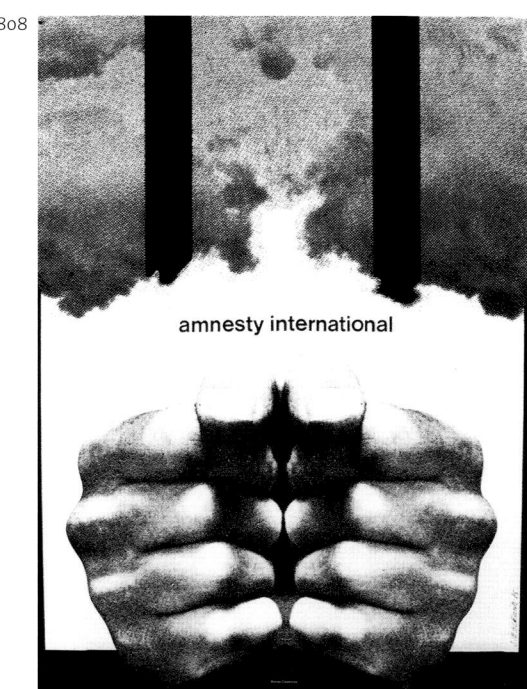

amnesty international

808

809

806
Roman Cieslewicz, double-page spread on "packaging" in the first issue of the artist's magazine, *Kamikaze*, 1976. 19 3/4 × 12 1/2 in. (50 × 32 cm) (page). IRA mask on left, facial-care mask on right.

807
Grapus, multilingual poster, *Peace!*, France, 1989. Silkscreen, various formats ranging from 23 1/2 × 31 1/2 in. to 9 ft. 10 in. × 13 ft. (60 × 80 cm to 300 × 400 cm); several editions.

808
Roman Cieslewicz, poster for Amnesty International, 1975. 33 × 24 in. (86 × 63 cm). Amnesty International USA commissioned posters from eighty international artists.

809
Special "design anarchy" issue (37) of *Adbusters* magazine, 2001.

810
Kristine Matthews and Sophie Thomas, *No Shop*, collective contribution to International Buy Nothing Day, a four-day installation in London, November 1997. Double-page spread of the installation published in *Eye* 27, 1998.

810

artists have literally seized upon this expressive power and ability to generate meaning from the methods and tools employed by the graphic arts (photography, typography, and drawing; symbols, signs, and other graphic elements used in collage, juxtaposition, superimposition, etc.). In this respect, if in radically different contexts, works by John Heartfield in the 1930s and by Barbara Kruger in recent decades reveal the dimension of protest or criticism that graphic forms may assume when they address social, political, and/or economic issues. These examples strongly demonstrate the ability of (typo)graphic forms to express, signify, share, resist, combat, disobey, or denounce—that is to say, "to inform" in the etymological sense of "giving form to" or "fashioning." They can thus convey and transmit a personalized, creative view of the state of society, reacting to political, economic, and other questions.

Back in 1964, Max Bill asserted that "it is a graphic designer's knowledge and conception of the world, as well as the scope and rigor of his conscience, that ultimately decides the measure of responsibility he will assume."[60] While some people admitted, and still admit, the crucial role of a designer's social responsibility, recent analyses and criticisms continue to lament the lack or complete absence of any commitment. In the 1990s, one leading British periodical in the field, *Eye*, reflected such positions in its pages. In 1991, for instance, an article claimed that, "Typography is powerful and typographers should wake up to their responsibilities, not at the obvious level of aesthetics... but social responsibility."[61] Another piece, also published in 1991, asked whether "graphic designers [can] actually do something to change the world," and replied "'Yes ,' if one disregards the fact that there are very limited outlets for this kind of work, and accepts the fact that being socially responsible means taking the initiative oneself, dealing rationally with issues, and having a commitment to a specific cause."[62] In 1994 yet another article argued that, "if... there is no rigid boundary between private life and mass culture, personal memory, and public record, then the graphic design profession occupies a privileged and responsible position which it has neither recognized nor attended to."[63] Whether from a critical or a constructive perspective—both of which sometimes converge—various writers attributed graphic design with a distinct power to change society and the environment for the better, an idea formerly expressed with idealistic confidence by Friedrich Heinrich Kohn Henrion, "Design is a structuring activity... a way of reducing chaos... It is truly an invitation to participate in the creation of new things and to improve the quality of life."[64]

History, culture, practices

The set of questions being raised in the contemporary period also concerns the roles and positions of criticism, analysis, history, and theory. Alongside actual practice, these disciplines offer a space of reflection and knowledge, making it possible to adopt a certain distance or perspective, and thereby possible to explain, to compare, and so on. Furthermore, the importance placed on history and theory also reflects the scope and stakes of typography and graphic design, doubly informing us of its significance within the weave of historical events (touching upon culture, technology, art, media, communications, society, economics, politics, etc.). A somewhat amazed Roland Barthes made the following observation in "Variations sur l'écriture," a text written in 1973: "Scholars have fully studied only ancient writing, for the study of writing has only one name, *paleography*...; so there is nothing on modern writing— paleography ends in the sixteenth century. Yet how can we fail to realize that an entire historical sociology... would emerge from a 'neography' that does not exist.... Indeed, from nineteenth-century writings, or even those of our own century? As soon as it becomes modern, writing is repressed.... Writing is always linked too closely to history and its social stakes—for a very long time it has been.... a property of class."[65]

In fact, typeset writing and graphic designs are research topics of great interest that remain to be explored (as evidence of visual communication, as forms of advertising, as artistic or popular forms of expression, and so on, depending on context). In recent years—indeed, recent decades—this question of the role assigned (or not) to history, theory, culture, and criticism has been raised regularly by major scholars and practitioners in various countries.[66] In 1992, Rand could still write that, apart from "familiarity with a few obvious names and facts about the history of painting and design, history is a subject that is not taken seriously.... Experience in the workplace and a thorough knowledge of the history of one's specialization [are] indispensable."[67] From a different standpoint, Friedrich Friedl observed in 1986 that, "although today's oppositions are similar to the ones of the past... there is hardly any solidly based, thoroughly debated discussion on questions of graphic design."[68]

On the other hand, design's unflagging, self-vaunted openness has enabled it, like the fine arts, to reinvent itself ceaselessly, to transform itself, to occupy unusual terrain, to envisage original interactions, to generate new modes of reception, and to reactivate the gaze and perception in different ways. Rejecting all stasis, it constantly questions its own definition. Although the current period calls for a certain distancing, it constantly reasserts the freedom acquired in the realms of typography and graphic design in the nineteenth century, largely glorified and explored by the historical avant-garde movements and never forgotten since. This outlook dislodges or reshapes notions of creativity and know-how, rupture and continuity, heritage and genre, thereby interrogating the very limits of graphic design, its role, its professional scope, and so on, further underscoring the need for historical insight and understanding of the issues. Digital technology, computer screens and programs henceforth constitute the crucial resources of (typo)graphic production. Accessible to the general public, they have now triggered an unprecedented explosion of individual, self-taught design that may be amateur, independent, subjective, nonconformist, fringe, or whatever. Such designs partly lie outside the "professional" sphere traditionally marked by apprenticeship and acquired skills (schools, training programs, etc.), by shared know-how and technical information, by special realms of application, and by professional institutions and encounters (and rivalries), as well as by—if perhaps in less explicit fashion—codes, presuppositions, tacit criteria, and the whole package of existing culture, behavior, and heritage. This shifting perspective is complicated by still other phenomena, making the contours of graphic design even less stable and certain, such as the ubiquitous nature of visual communication through overwhelming advertising imagery and the incessant flow of media. Faced with the current scene's lack of certainties, it would seem essential to acknowledge, to the best of one's ability, the very numerous aspects of various design practices and to consider them in their broadest possible scope, always open and conducive to instability, always liable to spark unexpected ramifications, repercussions, mutations, and turnarounds.

811
Tania Mouraud, *SEEINGYOURSELFSEEING*, France, 1992. Rough plaster on wall.

812
Tania Mouraud, *Black Continent: "Point"* (playing on the counterforms of the letters of that word), France, 1991. Acrylic on canvas, 7 ft. 2 1/2 in. × 13 ft. × 8 in. (220 × 400 × 20 cm).

"...to grasp what's really happening today"

The extreme diversity of practices should suffice to legitimize the promotion of historical knowledge and a corresponding curiosity. Raising the question of the history of typography and graphic design leads us to consider several crucial components of the subject, beginning with its definition, its origin, its reality, its contents, its changes, its impact, its implications, its limitations, and its horizons (to the extent that they exist and can be described). Adopting a synoptic viewpoint[69] makes it possible to elicit the vitality of both typography and graphic design, revealing many of the countless facets through overall analysis. It also favors a highly profitable encounter with the many views on these spheres and on the wide range of positions adopted towards them (in terms of practical works and theoretical writings, both past and present). It thereby becomes possible to approach the various forms of (socio)cultural convictions represented by those positions. A broader view also favors a transversal grasp of the subject and reveals underlying threads. It notably suggests, through historically remote comparisons, inter-relationships and convergences that might contribute unusual insights, indeed challenge conventional positions or viewpoints.

The parallel examination of history and contemporary developments is one of the most propitious methods for understanding the notion of graphic design and the various faces of typography. In addition to the promise of discoveries revealed by general research in this area, such a history offers the possibility of developing transdisciplinary approaches suited to the cultural and socioeconomic foundations of graphic design. Styles, supports, trends, and individuals all contribute to a defining background that combines experience, techniques, visual imperatives, working methods and traditions, interests, profits, economy, and so on. To this should be added various under-explored aspects of graphic design, notably including the situation on other continents (practices, histories, training methods, distinctive features), folk and anonymous graphic arts, the role of the beholder, the impact of digital technology and the repercussions of visual communication on lifestyles, behavior, and physical constitution. When placed in this very broad framework, the existence of graphic design supposes, if not the question of personal commitment (construction of meanings, public impact, environmental concerns, social awareness, etc.), at the very least the issue of participation in a form of creativity in the given period, system, and sociocultural space in which visual codes are played out.

While it reflects certain manifestations of the fascination with formal and conceptual concerns, history should also record, simultaneously, the tragic side of various phenomena, whether due to social upheaval, expatriation, war, death, truncated careers, or frustrated hopes. This dark side of the past is not always given the place it deserves and is sometimes overlooked altogether,[70] except when a given subject inevitably invokes it (such as a study of Heartfield's work). Worthy of consideration are events and facts as varied as, for example, the executions of Antoine Augereau and Étienne Dolet in the sixteenth century, incidents of collaboration and exile in the 1930s and 1940s, the risks run by printers during World War II, the murder of Hendrik Nicolaas Werkman in March 1945, and the suicide of Cassandre in 1968.

Another unresolved, if more general, issue concerns the status of historical knowledge in the context of active practice. Several paradoxes surround the theme of the constitution of an autonomous branch of history devoted to typography and graphic design. First, the very development of those practices are inextricably correlated to major periods of history (see the birth of writing in antiquity, or the emergence of printed books for the modern era); writing and typography are hence naturally and continually at grips with history. Next, from another point of view, graphic forms and signs are so inscribed in our daily environment and living space that they seem unavoidable, which means it might be worth asking to what extent such presence—ordinary and familiar—might paradoxically thwart attention and dull interest.

A living history can contribute to a better definition, perhaps even a better use, of the power and potential of typography and graphic design. It also affords a better grasp of the dispersion and contradictions of their actual practice. It offers a path towards understanding, enlightenment, foresight.[71] Faced with the heterogeneity of the current situation, it is also a way to acquire a form of experience that prepares the way for an uncertain future, especially in so far as "the present is not only what is contemporary. It is an effect of tradition and the outcome of a series of transformations that must be reconstituted in order to grasp what's really happening today."[72]

This field of knowledge is all the more worth exploring in that it is conducive to interaction with many other spheres, given its natural openness to transdisciplinarity and exchange, and given its implication in a vast context. In addition to the insight it might bring to artistic, cultural, and social issues, it suggests many convergences with numerous established fields of research (the information and communication sciences, the history of technologies, media, and the press, specialist fields of advertising, propaganda, photography, writing, book publishing, literary creation, visual poetry, design, urbanism, visual arts, semiology, popular culture, and so on). These interactions are also inevitable because (typo)graphic creativity in the twentieth century was no longer the work of specialists alone (graphic and poster artists, typographers, typeface designers, printers), but was also enriched by contributions from painters, designers, versatile artists, writers, photographers, architects, publishers, theorists, engineers, and even anonymous individuals.

It is probably a double dimension that best suits the perspective of the history of typography and graphic design. On the one hand, it comes across as a veritable bridge, establishing numerous zones of overlap with other spheres, while on the other hand, the objects of its study present numerous singularities. The etymology of typography ultimately reminds us that this history also means writing about writing.[73]

813

813
Saul Steinberg, drawing, 1970.

Notes

1 The notion of "good form" alludes to gestalt theory and, in this specific design context, to a traveling exhibition, *Die Gute Form*, organized by Bill in 1949 (the show went to Switzerland, Germany, the Netherlands, and Austria). There Bill developed the idea that "the aesthetic impulse which stimulates the emergence of good practical forms is always a basically moral one. That is why we resent having to buy repulsive-looking goods which only serve to debase the cultural level of our epoch. We indignantly repudiate a state of affairs which allows the diffusion of so much rubbishy hideousness… There is no rhyme or reason in all this camouflage ornamentation and we utterly reject it, old and new alike. And against it… we set the simple straightforward ideal of good forms, honest designing, for everything… from plastic tea-cups to the planning of better towns…." On this subject see Max Bill, *Form: A Balance Sheet of Mid-Twentieth-Century Trends in Design* (Basel: Karl Werner, 1952), 11.

2 Quoted in P. Cabanne, *L'Art du vingtième siècle* (Paris: Aimery Somogy, 1982), 291.

3 From a paper given by Max Bill at Icograda ("Art et graphisme, graphisme et art," September 1964), quoted in M. Rouard-Snowman (ed.), *Jean Widmer graphiste, un écologiste de l'image* (Paris: Centre Georges Pompidou, 1995), 18.

4 Reference works reflecting various aspects, analyses, and viewpoints on the role of women in graphic design, book publishing, and the arts, include: E. Lupton, "Women Graphic Designers," in P. Kirkham (ed.), *Women Designers in the USA: 1900–2000* (London: Yale University Press, 2000); M. Lavin, *Clean New World* (Cambridge, Mass.: MIT Press, 2001), 42–43, 50–67, 104–105, 108–143; E. M. Thomson, "Women in Graphic Design History," in *The Origins of Graphic Design in America, 1870–1920* (New Haven/London: Yale University Press, 1997); E. Lupton and J. A. Miller, *Design Writing Research* (London: Phaidon, 1999), 178–179; J. Middendorp, *Lettered: Typefaces and Alphabets by Clotilde Olyff* (Ghent: Druk, 2000); Y. Johannot, "Homme-et-livre, Femme-et-enfant," in *Tourner la page: Livre, rites et symboles* (Grenoble: Jérôme Millon, 1994), 191–196; R. Arbour, *Les Femmes et les métiers du livre: 1600–1650* (Paris/Chicago: Garamond Press/Didier Érudition, 1997); J. Tombeur, *Femmes & métiers du livre,* Typographic Convention (Paris: Talus d'approche, 2004); "L'Image des femmes dans la publicité (report to the French Undersecretary of Woman Rights and Professional Training, Paris: La Documentation Française, 2002); P. Krémer, "Publicité, clichés, dignité," *Le Monde* (February 8–9, 2004), 36–37; B. Remaury, "Les images du corps féminin," in *Le Beau sexe faible: Les Images du corps féminin entre cosmétique et santé* (Paris: Grasset/Le Monde, 2000), 21–85; G. Duby, M. Perrot *et al., Images de femmes* (Paris: Plon, 1992); P. Jobling and D. Crowley, *Graphic Design: Reproduction and Representation since 1800,* (Manchester/New York: Manchester University Press, 1996), 95–101; K. Mulvey and M. Richards, *Decades of Beauty: The Changing Image of Women, 1890–1990* (New York: Octopus Publishing, 1998); C. Quiguer, "L'Inflation des images féminines," in *1900* (exh. cat., Paris: Grand Palais, 2000), 255–265); G. Duby and M. Perrot, *Histoire des femmes en Occident* (Paris: Plon, 1991–1992); *Féminisme, art et histoire de l'art,* Symposium at École Nationale Supérieure des Beaux-Arts, Paris; J. Attfield, "Form/Female Follows Function/Male: Feminist Critiques of Design," in J. A. Walker, *Design History and the History of Design* (London: Pluto Press, 1989), 199–225; C. Buckley, "Made in Patriarchy: Toward a Feminist Analysis of Women and Design," in V. Margolin (ed.), *Design Discourse* (Chicago: The University of Chicago Press, 1989, 251–262; J. Rothschild (ed.) *Design and Feminism: Re-visioning Spaces, Places, and Everyday Things* (New Brunswick: Rutgers University Press, 1999).

5 Cf. the labels "supermannerism," "supergraphics," and "ornamental and mannerist postmodern design styles," in Ph. B. Meggs, *A History of Graphic Design* (New York: John Wiley & Sons, 1998), 432 and 447. See also various terms along the lines of "undesign," "anti-design," and "anti-form."

6 It would moreover seem that this correspondence between visual graphics and musical sound, already evident in the transdisciplinary approach of the historic avant-gardes, has been a constant of visual communication in recent decades, reinforced in the digital age of multimedia by new consumer items destined for auditory appeal.

7 On the International Typographic Style, see Alan and Isabella Livingston, *Dictionary of Graphic Design and Designers* (London: Thames & Hudson, 2003).

8 Wolfgang Weingart, "Odermatt & Tissi ," *Graphis* 241 (vol. 42, 1986), 51.

9 Dan Friedman, interviewed by P. Rea, "Dan Friedman," *Eye* 14 (1994), 11. It is interesting to compare Friedman's comment with one—cited later in this chapter—by Max Caflisch, who came from a completely different typographical background. "If typography is only a more or less experimental pastime where texts are made pretty unrecognizable and unintelligible, the results they produce…will seem in any event silly once they are shown to an uninitiated public."

10 Ibid., 11.

11 Ibid., 16.

12 Katherine McCoy, quoted by E. Lupton, "The Academy of Deconstructed Design," *Eye* 3 (1991), 58.

13 Gert Dumbar, quoted in Penny Sparke *et al., Design: Le livre* (Florilège, 1990), 205.

14 "Form Follows Fun" is the title of the first chapter of *New American Design* by Hugh Aldersley-Williams (New York: Rizzoli, 1988), 38. *Form Follows Fiasco* is the title of a book by Peter Blake (Boston: Little, Brown & Co., 1974). "Less is a bore," was famously uttered in the early 1970s by Robert Venturi, quoted in Sparke, *Design: Le livre,* 193.

15 These typefaces, some of which have encountered notable success, are published by Fontshop.

16 François Mésa, *Mai 68: Les Affiches de l'atelier populaire de l'ex-École des beaux-arts* (Paris: S.P.M., Paris, 1975), 8.

17 *La Cause du peuple* 11 (June 6–7, 1968), reprinted in Mésa, *Mai 68,* 7.

18 Interview with the founder of Grapus, "Le groupe Grapus," *Bon à tirer* 7 (September 1978), 8.

19 F.H.K. Henrion, quoted in Josée Chapelle, "Grapus," *À la lettre: Aspects de la création typographique en France* (exh. cat., Paris: CCI/Centre Georges Pompidou, 1989).

20 On postmodernism see, for example, P. Jobling and D. Crowley, *Graphic Design: Reproduction and Representation since 1800* (Manchester/New York: Manchester University Press, 1996), chapter 9; R. Kinross, *Modern Typography: An Essay in Critical History* (London: Hyphen Press, 1992), chapter 12.

21 Kurt Schwitters, "Thesen über Typographie," *Merz (Typoreklame)* 11 (1924), quoted by S. Lemoine, "Merz, Futura, DIN et cicéro," in S. Lemoine (ed.), *Kurt Schwitters* (exh. cat., Paris: Centre Georges Pompidou/Réunion des musées nationaux, 1994), 189.

22 For a selection of most recent creative design, see, for example: Christian Küsters and Emily King, *Restart: New Systems in Graphic Design* (London: Thames & Hudson, 2001). Their book presents thirty-seven of the world's most experimental studios at the dawn of the third millennium. See also I. Ramonet, *La Tyrannie de la communication* (Paris: Gallimard, 2001), 272–275 and *passim.*

23 Quoted E. M. Gottschall, *Typographic Communications Today* (Cambridge, Mass.: MIT Press, 1989), 8.

24 Quoted by Brigitte Fitoussi, *Memphis* (Paris: Assouline, 1998), 4.

25 Quoted by Y.-A. Bois, "Éclectisme,

architecture," *Encyclopædia Universalis* (Paris, 1996), Thesaurus-Index, 1156, from Venturi's *Complexity and Contradiction in Architecture*, which Vincent Scully rightly described as "the most important writing on the making of architecture since Le Corbusier's *Vers une Architecture* of 1923."

26 Jan Tschichold, *Vues cavalières sur le modernisme en typographie* (Paris: Société Anonyme Monotype, 1961).

27 Emigre catalog (California, 1996).

28 These functions are now standard in word-processing, desktop-publishing, and image-editing software as well as in some operating systems.

29 This observation also concerns the boundaries generated by the perception, projection, and inculcation of the dividing line between the "fine" and "applied" arts, between "popular" and "high" culture, etc.

30 Some major advances and developments were not the direct product of technology, although perhaps related to it.

31 Some designers complain, moreover, of the comparison of the screen to a "page."

32 This phenomenon is distinct from the multidisciplinary approach of certain artists in the early decades of the twentieth century.

33 Peret [Pere Torrent], quoted in M. Champenois, "Peret, le Catalan, et ses mousquetaires," *Le Monde* (April 20, 2002), 31.

34 John Maeda, quoted by A. Rivoire, "Maeda médite," *Libération* (January 25, 2002), 32.

35 Pixel is an abbreviation of "picture element" and refers to the smallest discrete component of an image—usually a dot—that is recorded and potentially transmitted by a computer.

36 Edmond Couchot, "Art numérique," *Encyclopædia Universalis* (CD-Rom, vol. 9). "Digital art is dependent on a highly complex technology based on computers, also known as the science of automated information processing. It is necessary to grasp the originality of this technology in producing images, sounds, and texts in order to understand what

has changed and what has survived in artworks derived from it. When it comes to images, two basic characteristics of digital pictures emerge, stemming from the automatic computation done by the machine, and both can be acted upon by the creator and/or the beholder of that image.... A pixel is a kind of exchanger between the tangible reality of the image and its virtual counterpart. It yields two consequences: the matrix-structure of the image makes it possible to access every single element and to control all of them totally; the methods for making an image change radically. A picture is no longer the product of an impact on a surface...but the result of a computation. Digital pictures are no longer image-traces, they are image-matrices. From a more general standpoint, sound processing and, to a certain extent, word processing also follow the same logic. Thus image, sound, and text, stripped of their tangible supports and reduced to pure information, are open to transformations, manipulations, and combinations that are impossible—indeed unimaginable—with traditional techniques."

37 Massimo Vignelli (1993), quoted by N. d'Harcourt, "Jusqu'où peut-on être illisible?" *Bon à tirer* 159 (January 1994), 23.

38 Fernand Baudin, "Emigre, les 'nouveaux primitifs' du graphic design," *Communication et langages* 89 (Paris: Retz, 1991), 61.

39 Jan Tschichold, *Vues cavalières sur le modernisme en typographie* (Paris: Société Anonyme Monotype, 1961), 7–8.

40 Emigre catalog (California, 1996), 50.

41 Josef Müller-Brockmann, *The Graphic Designer and His Design Problems* (Niederteufen, Swiss.: Arthur Niggli, 1983), 21.

42 A. Berthier and A. Zali (eds.), *L'Aventure des écritures: Naissances*, (Paris: Bibliothèque nationale de France, 1997), 15.

43 Some of these examples are illustrated in Küsters and King, *Restart*.

44 Jacques Hebenstreit, "Compactage

de données," *Encyclopædia Universalis*, Thesaurus-Index, (Paris, 1996), 832.

45 Lavin, *Clean New World,* 7.

46 As Steven Heller put it, "Despite all its accomplishments, the contemporary design world is afflicted by a deep vacuousness. Most students and many practitioners cannot even list or describe the field's milestones or pioneers." See "Design History," *Print* (September–October, 2003).

47 The impact of typewriters and transfer-lettering was hardly comparable to that of computer technology, although photocopying technology did play an important role.

48 This phenomenon has also facilitated the assimilation of formal repertoires that had been uncommon, whether non-Western, traditional, local, vernacular, fanciful, folk, amateur, etc.

49 Kinross, *Modern Typography.*

50 Rich Poynor, *Typography Now: The Next Wave* (Booth-Clibborn, 1995), 8.

51 See the work of Push Pin Studio, for example.

52 This point is also discussed earlier in the text.

53 Paul Rand, "From Cassandre to Chaos," *Design Form and Chaos* (New Haven/London: Yale University Press, 1993), 210 and 213.

54 Massimo Vignelli (1991), quoted by J. Keedy, *Eye* 11, 1993, 54.

55 Wim Crouwel, from a talk given at the annual ATypI conference in 1996, partially published as "Divided They Fall," *TypoGraphic News: The Newsletter of the International Society of Typographic Designers* 78 (Winter 1997), 4.

56 Adrian Frutiger, quoted in M. Vermersch, "Affreux, sales et durs à lire," *Bon à tirer* 160 (February 1994), 23.

57 Max Caflisch, *La typographie a besoin des caractères*, speech given in Lausanne in 1977 for the twentieth anniversary of the founding of ATypI (n.p., n.d.), 31.

58 See the manifesto *First Things First*, originally drafted in 1964 by Ken Garland in London and signed by twenty-two colleagues; then updated as *First Things First Manifesto 2000* and published in

numerous reviews in North America, Great Britain, the Netherlands, and Germany, notably *Eye* 33 (1999), 26–27, with thirty-three signatories, including several famous names. See also Rick Poynor, *Obey the Giant* (London: August Media, 2001).

59 Paul Rand, "Confusion and Chaos: the Seduction of Contemporary Graphic Design," in Steven Heller and Marie Finamore (eds.), *Design Culture* (New York: Allworth Press, 1997), 123.

60 Max Bill, "Art et graphisme, graphisme et art," talk given at ICOGRADA in September 1964, reprinted in M. Rouard-Snowman (ed.), *Jean Widmer graphiste: Un écologiste de l'image* (Paris: Centre Georges Pompidou, 1995), 18.

61 Michèle-Anne Dauppe, "Get the Message?" *Eye* 3 (1991).

62 Steven Heller, "Guerilla Graphics," *Eye* 4 (1991), 6.

63 Rob Dewey (quoting Ellen Lupton), "Facing up to the Reality of Change," *Eye* 14 (1994), 5.

64 Quoted in Gottschall, *Typographic Communications Today*, 153.

65 Roland Barthes, "Variations sur l'écriture," in *Le Plaisir du texte—* proceeded by *Variations sur l'écriture* (Paris: Le Seuil, 2000), 32 and 33. Although published posthumously, the text was written in 1973.

66 See, for example, Steven Heller, "Design History," *Print* (September–October 2003).

67 Rand, "From Cassandre to Chaos," 213.

68 Friedrich Friedl, "La trajectoire de Jan Tschichold," *Typografische Monatsblätter: RSI* 4 (2001), 13. Friedl also co-authored the trilingual book, *Typographie: Quand, qui, comment/Typographie: Wann, wer, wie/Typography: When, Who, How* (Cologne: Könemann, 1998). On Friedl's graphic oeuvre, see F. Friedl, *Exakte Gestaltung: Frei Arbeiten von 1964–1994* (Frankfurt: Amt für Wissenschaft und Kunst, and Mainz: Hermann Schmidt, 1994).

69 For lack of sufficiently detailed studies and research in this domain.

70 On this issue, see notably chapter 4.

71 As Herbert Spencer—the British
typographer, born in 1924, who
founded and edited the magazine
Typographica—put it in a speech
to the Type Directors' Club
Silvermine Seminar in 1958:
"Tradition is a living, active, and
vital force in creative activity."
Quoted in Gottschall, *Typographic
Communications Today*, 235.

72 Robert Castel, "Présent et
généalogie du présent [...]," in
Dominique Franche *et al* (eds.),
Au risque de Foucault (Paris:
Centre Georges Pompidou, 1994),
161.

73 The etymology of "type" is from
Late Latin *typus* (type), from
classical Latin *typus* (figure,
image), from Greek *tupos* (a blow
impression); graphic comes from
Greek, *graphikos* (a writing or
drawing), from *graphein* (to
write). See *The American Heritage
Dictionary of the English
Language*.

Appendices

Index

Bold face page numbers represent illustrations.

425

Bibliography

General works: graphic design, visual communication

Andel, Jaroslav, *Avant-Garde Page Design 1900–1950*, New York: Delano Greenidge, 2002, (German-English-French edition)

Baroni, Daniele, *Art graphique design*, Paris: Chêne, 1987 (French translation; 1st ed. 1986)

Booth-Clibborn, Edward and Daniele Chêne, *Art graphique*, Paris: Fernand Nathan, 1980

Chwast, Seymour and Steven Heller, *Graphic Styles. From Victorian to Post-Modern*, London: Thames & Hudson, 1994 (1st ed. 1988)

"Design graphique," *Les Cahiers du Musée national d'art moderne*, no. 89, Paris: Centre Georges Pompidou, 2004

Gerstner, Karl and Markus Kutter, *Die neue Graphik /The New Graphic Art/Le Nouvel Art graphique*, Teufen: Arthur Niggli, 1959

Gervereau, Laurent, *Les Images qui mentent. Histoire du visuel au xxe siècle*, Paris: Seuil, 2000

Gervereau, Laurent, *Un Siècle de manipulations par l'image*, Paris: Somogy, 2000

Heller, Steven and Georgette Ballance (eds.), *Graphic Design History*, New York: Allworth Press, 2001 (anthology)

Hollis, Richard, *Graphic Design in the 20th Century*, London: Thames & Hudson, 2001 (1st ed. 1994)

Jean, Georges, *Langage de signes. L'écriture et son double*, Paris: Gallimard (Découvertes), 1989

Jobling, Paul and David Crowley, *Graphic Design. Reproduction and Representation since 1800*, Manchester/New York: Manchester University Press, 1996

Kitts, Barry and Liz McQuiston, *Graphic Design Sourcebook*, Boston: Little Brown, 1987

Lavin, Maud, *Clean New World. Culture, Politics, Graphic Design*, Cambridge Mass./ London: MIT Press, 2001

Livingston, Alan and Isabella Livingston, *Graphic Design + Designers*, London: Thames & Hudson, 1992

Looking Closer. Critical Writings on Graphic Design, Looking Closer. Classic Writings on Graphic Design, New York: Allworth Press, 1994, 1997, 1999, 2002 (four-volume anthology)

Meggs, Philip B., *A History of Graphic Design*, New York: John Wiley & Sons, 1998, 3rd ed. (1st ed. 1983)

Müller-Brockmann, Josef, *Geschichte der visuellen Kommunikation/A History of Visual Communication*, Switzerland: Arthur Niggli, 1986

Remington, Roger and Barbara Hodik (gen. eds.), *The First Symposium on the History of Graphic Design. Coming of Age*, Rochester Institute of Technology, 1983

Weill, Alain, *Le Design graphique*, Paris: Gallimard (Découvertes), 2003

Thematic works: graphic design, visual communication

Bouvet, Michel, *East Coast West Coast*, Paris: Textuel/Mois du graphisme d'Échirolles, 2002 (French-English)

Broos, Kees and Paul Hefting, *Dutch Graphic Design*, London and Oxford: Phaidon, 1993

Cassandre, A. M., "Publicité," *L'Art international d'aujourd'hui*, no. 12, Paris: Éditions d'art Charles Moreau, 1929

Cranbrook Design. The New Discourse, New York: Rizzoli, 1990

Delangle, Philippe and Michel Wlassikoff, *Signes de la collaboration et de la Résistance*, Paris: Autrement, 2002

Dupuis, Pascal, *Ego, lutte, image*, Paris Université I, 1994 (thesis supervised by Marc Jimenez)

Enamel Icons. 1895–1935 (exh. cat.), Macao: The Macao Museum of Art, 2002 (English-Chinese-Portuguese)

Fern, Alan M., *Word and Image*, New York: The Museum of Modern Art, 1968

Fossati, Paolo and Roberto Sambonet, *Lo Studio Boggeri, 1933–1973*, Cinisello Balsamo (Milan): Pizzi, 1974

Fournier, Édouard, *Histoire des enseignes de Paris*, Paris: E. Dentu, 1884

Garland, Ken, *Mr. Beck's Underground Map*, London: Capital Transport, 1994

Gerstner, Karl, *Designing Programmes*, Switzerland: Arthur Niggli, 1964 (English translation)

Gibbs, David (ed.), *Pentagram. The Compendium*, London: Phaidon, 1993

Gourevitch, Jean-Paul, *L'Imagerie politique*, Paris: Flammarion, 1980

Graphistes autour du monde. Graphic Artists around the World, Paris: Textuel/Mois du graphisme d'Échirolles, 2000

Heller, Steven, "Big ideas that built America," *Eye*, n°. 21, vol. 6, autumn 1996

Heller, Steven, *Merz to Emigre and Beyond: Avant-Garde Magazine Design of the Twentieth Century*, London: Phaidon, 2003

Henrion, Friedrich Heinrich Kohn, *AGI Annals*, Zurich: Alliance Graphique Internationale, 1989

Hofmann, Armin, *Methodik des Form-und Bildgestaltung/Manuel de création graphique/Graphic Design Manual*, Switzerland: Arthur Niggli, 1965 (1st ed.)

Klein, Naomi, *No Logo*, London: Picador, 2002 (1st ed. 2000)

Küsters, Christian and Emily King, *Restart: New Systems in Graphic Design*, London: Thames & Hudson, 2001

Leclanche-Boulé, Claude, *Le Constructivisme russe. Typographies et photomontages*, Paris: Flammarion, 1991 (1st ed. 1984)

Lupton, Ellen and J. Abbott Miller, *Design Writing Research. Writing on Graphic Design*, London: Phaidon, 1999

Massin, *L'ABC du métier*, Paris: Imprimerie nationale, 1988–1989

Massin, *La Lettre et l'Image*, Paris: Gallimard, 1973

Middendorp, Jan, *Ha [...]. Kroniek van het grafisch ontwerpen in Den Haag 1945–2000*, Rotterdam: 010, 2002

Müller-Brockmann, Josef, *Graphic Design in IBM. Typography, Photography, Illustration, IBM Europe*, Paris, 1988

Müller-Brockmann, Josef, *Grid Systems in Graphic Design. A Visual Communication Manual for Graphic Designers, Typographers, and Three-Dimensional Designers*, Switzerland: Arthur Niggli, 1981 (German-English)

Müller-Brockmann, Josef, *The Graphic Designer and His Design Problems*, Niederteufen: Arthur Niggli, 1983 (German-English-French; 1st ed. 1961)

Pastoureau, Michel, *Figures de l'héraldique*, Paris: Gallimard (Découvertes), 1996

Poynor, Rick, *The Graphic Edge*, London: Booth-Clibborn, 1993, new ed. 1995

Poynor, Rick, *Obey the Giant*, Basel: Birkhauser, 2001

Purvis, Aston W., *Dutch Graphic Design, 1918–1945*, New York: Van Nostrand Reinhold, 1992

Rand, Paul, *A Designer's Art*, New Haven: Yale University Press, 1985

Rand, Paul, *Design Form and Chaos*, New Haven/London: Yale University Press, 1993

Rand, Paul, *Thoughts on Design*, London: Studio Vista, 1970

Rhodes, Anthony and Victor Margolin (eds.), *Propaganda: the Art of Persuasion, World War II*, London: Angus & Robertson, 1976

Rossi, Attilio, *Campo grafico 1933–1939*, Milan: Electa, 1983

Rouard-Snowman, Margo, *Museum Graphics*, London: Thames & Hudson, 1992

Snyder, Jerome and Henry Wolf, *The Push Pin Style* (exh. cat.), Paris: Musée des Arts Décoratifs/Communication Arts Magazine, 1970

Sutnar, Ladislav, *Visual Design in Action*, New York: Hastings House, 1961

Tantet, Marie, "La stratégie publicitaire de Benetton," *Communication et langages*, n°. 94, 4th trimester 1992

Thornton, Richard S., *Japanese Graphic Design*, London: Laurence King, 1991

Tufte, Edward R., *Envisioning Information*, Cheshire, Conn.: Graphics Press, 1990 (reprinted 1995)

Tufte, Edward R., *The Visual Display of Quantitative Information*, Cheshire, Conn.: Graphics Press, 1983 (reprinted 1997).

Tufte, Edward R., *Visual Explanations. Images and Quantities, Evidence and Narrative*, Cheshire, Conn.: Graphics Press, 1997

Visual design. Fifty Years of Production in Italy, Idealibri, s.l., 1985

Waibl, Heinz, *The Roots of Italian Visual Communication*, Como: Centro di Cultura Grafico, 1988 (English-Italian).

5 × Berlin, Paris: Pyramyd, 2006 (French-English)

General works: typography, writing, scripts, layout, printing, the book

Audin, Marius, *Le Livre. Son architecture, sa technique*, Forcalquier: Robert Morel, 1969 (preface by Henri Focillon), (1st eds. 1921 and 1924)

Auger, Daniel, *La Typographie*, Paris: Presses universitaires de France (Que sais-je?), 1980

Barthes, Roland, *Variations sur l'écriture*, in *Œuvres complètes*, vol. 2, Paris: Seuil, 1994 (text written in 1973)

Baudin, Fernand, *L'Effet Gutenberg*, France: Cercle de la Librairie, 1994

Biasi, Pierre-Marc de, *Le Papier. Une aventure au quotidien*, Paris: Gallimard (Découvertes), 1999

Blackwell, Lewis, *Twentieth Century Type,* London: Calmann and King, 1992

Blasselle, Bruno, *Histoire du livre*, Paris: Gallimard (Découvertes), 1997, 1998 (two vols)

Caflisch, Max, *Schriftanalysen*, St. Gallen: Typotron, 2003, (two vols.)

Calvet, Louis-Jean, *Histoire de l'écriture*, Paris: Plon, 1996

Carter, Sebastian, *Twentieth Century Type Designers*, London: Lund Humphries, 1995 (1st ed. 1987)

Catach, Nina, *La Ponctuation. Histoire et système*, Paris: Presses universitaires de France (Que sais-je? n°. 2818), 1996 (1st ed. 1994)

Christin, Anne-Marie (ed.), *A History of Writing. From Hieroglyph to Multimedia* (translation D. Dusinberre), Paris: Flammarion, 2002

Christin, Anne-Marie, *L'Image écrite ou la Déraison graphique*, Paris: Flammarion, 1995

Druet, Roger and Grégoire Herman, *La Civilisation de l'écriture* Paris: Fayard/Dessain et Tolra, 1976 (preface Roland Barthes)

Dusong, Jean-Luc and Fabienne Siegwart, *Typographie. Du plomb au numérique*, Paris: Dessain et Tolra, 1996

Étiemble, René, *L'Écriture*, Paris: Gallimard, 1973

Gottschall, Edward M., *Typographic Communications Today*, Cambridge Mass./London: MIT Press, 1989

Gray, Nicolete, *A History of Lettering*, Oxford: Phaidon, 1986

Gürtler André, "Die Entwicklung der lateinischen Schrift/L'Évolution de l'écriture latine/The Development of the Roman Alphabet," in *Typografische Monatsblätter*. RSI, Dec. 1969

Heller, Steven and Louise Fili, *Typology. Type Design from the Victorian Era to the Digital Age*, San Francisco: Chronicle Books, 1999

Heller, Steven and Philip B. Meggs (eds.), *Texts on Type. Critical Writings on Typography*, New York: Allworth Press, 2001 (anthology)

Jean, Georges, *L'Écriture, mémoire des hommes*, Paris: Gallimard (Découvertes), 1987–2001

Johannot, Yvonne, *Tourner la page. Livre, rites et symboles*, Grenoble: Jérôme Millon, 1994 (1st ed. 1988)

Kapr, Albert, *The Art of Lettering. The History, Anatomy, and Aesthetics of the Roman Letterforms*, Munich: Saur, 1983 (1st ed. 1971, in German)

Kinross, Robin, *Modern Typography. An Essay in Critical History*, London: Hyphen Press, 1992 (reissued 2004)

Kunz, Willi, *Typografie : MaKro- und MikroästhetiK. Grundlagen zur typografischen Gestaltung*, Switzerland: Niggli, 1998

Lawson, Alexander, *Anatomy of a Typeface*, London: Hamish Hamilton, 1990

Martin, Henri-Jean, *La Naissance du livre moderne*, Paris: Cercle de la Librairie, 2000

Mediavilla, Claude, *Calligraphie*, Paris: Imprimerie nationale, 1993

Meier, Hans Eduard, *The Development of Writing*, Zurich: Amstutz & Herdeg/Graphis Press, 1959 (reprinted 1994 as *The Development of Script and Type*) (German-English-French)

Monnet, Nathalie, *Chine: l'Empire du trait. Calligraphies et dessins du ve au xixe siècle* (exh. cat.), Paris: Bibliothèque nationale de France, 2004

Olson, David R., *L'Univers de l'écrit. Comment la culture écrite donne forme à la pensée*, Paris: Retz, 1998 (1st ed. 1994, English)

Peignot, Jérôme, *De l'écriture à la typographie*, Paris: Gallimard, 1967

Schmid, Helmut, *Typography Today*, Japan: Yuichi Ogawa, 2003 (1st ed. 1980)

Thibaudeau, Francis, *La Lettre d'imprimerie. Origine, développement, classification*, vol. 1, Paris: Bureau de l'édition, 1921

Les Trois Révolutions du livre (exh. cat.), Paris: Musée des Arts et Métiers/Imprimerie nationale, 2002

Wolgensinger, Jacques, *L'Histoire à la une. La grande aventure de la presse*, Paris: Gallimard (Découvertes), 1989

Zali, Anne (gen. ed.), *L'Aventure des écritures. La page*, (exh. cat.) Paris: Bibliothèque nationale de France, 1999

Thematic works: typography, writing, scripts, layout, printing, the book

À la lettre. Aspects de la création typographique en France, Paris: Centre de Création industrielle/Centre Georges Pompidou, 1989

Bain, Peter and Paul Shaw (eds.), *Blackletter. Type and National Identity*, New York: The Cooper Union for the Advancement of Science and Art, 1998

Baur, Ruedi, *La Nouvelle Typographie*, Paris: Centre national des arts plastiques (Actualité des arts plastiques), 1993

Belleguie, André, *Le Mouvement de l'espace typographique. Années 1920–1930*, Paris: Jacques Damase, 1984

Berthier, Annie and Anne Zali (gen. eds.), *L'Aventure des écritures. Naissances*, (exh. cat.) Paris: Bibliothèque nationale de France, 1997

Blanchard, Gérard, *Pour une Sémiologie de la typographie*, Belgium: R. Magermans, 1979

Bosshard, Hans Rudolf, *Technische Grundlagen zur Satzherstellung, Mathematische Grundlagen zur Satzherstellung*, Bern: BST, 1980, 1985

Bosshard, Hans Rudolf, *Der Typografische Raster/The Typographic Grid*, Switzerland: Niggli, 2000

Breton-Gravereau, Simone and Danièle Thibault (gen. eds.), *L'Aventure des écritures. Matières et formes*, (exh. cat.) Paris: Bibliothèque nationale de France, 1998

Le Cabinet des poinçons de l'Imprimerie nationale, Paris: Imprimerie nationale, 1963 (3rd ed.)

Caflisch, Max, *Typographie braucht Schrift/Typography needs type/La typographie a besoin des caractères* (Speech, Lausanne, September 29, 1977, 20th anniversary of the foundation of the ATypI), published with support from the firm of Dr. Ing. Rudolf Hell (Kiel) (no publication details)

Carter, Rob, *American Typography Today*, New York: Van Nostrand Reinhold, 1989

Christian, Arthur *Origines de l'imprimerie en France*, Paris: Imprimerie nationale, 1900 (lectures)

Damase, Jacques, *Révolution typographique. Depuis Stéphane Mallarmé*, Geneva: Motte, 1966

Duplan, Pierre and Roger Jauneau, *Maquette et mise en page*, Paris: Usine nouvelle, 1982

"Écriture et typographie en Occident et en Extrême-Orient," *Textuel*, n°. 40, 2001 (Centre d'Étude de l'écriture, Université Paris VII)

Écritures. Graphies, notations, typographies (exh. cat.), Paris: Fondation Nationale des Arts Graphiques et Plastiques, 1980 (exhibition organized by Jérôme Peignot and Marc Dachy)

Elam, Kimberley, *Expressive Typography*, New York: Van Nostrand Reinhold, 1990

Étiemble, René and Paul-Marie Grinevald, *Les Caractères de l'Imprimerie nationale*, Paris: Imprimerie nationale, 1990

Febvre, Lucien and Henri-Jean Martin, *L'Apparition du livre,* Paris: , Albin Michel, 1971

Fleischmann Gerd (ed.), *Bauhaus. Drucksachen, Typografie, Reklame*, Stuttgart: Oktagon, 1995 (1st ed. 1984)

Frizot, Michel and Jérôme Peignot, *L'Œil de la lettre. Les rapports de la lettre et de la photographie des origines à nos jours*, Paris: Centre National de la Photographie/Ministère de la Culture, 1989

Fröhlich, Godi and Ruedi Rüegg, *Bases typographiques*, Zurich: ABC, 1972

Frutiger, Adrian, *Des Signes et des hommes*,

Lausanne: Delta & Spes, Denges, 1983 (1st ed. 1978)

Gerstner, Karl, *IBM Bodoni Manual* (internal *IBM* publication) n.p. n.d. (c. 1975)

Gerstner, Karl, *Kompendium für Alphabeten*, Teufen: Arthur Niggli, 1972

Goudy, Frederic, *The Alphabet and Elements of Lettering*, New York: Dorset Press, 1942

Hochuli, Jost and Robin Kinross, *Designing Books. Practice and Theory*, London: Hyphen Press, 1996

Hochuli, Jost, *Detail in Typography* Wilmington (Mass): Compugraphic, 1987

Hostettler, Rudolf, *Type. A Selection of Types/Une sélection de caractères d'imprimerie/Eine Auswahl guter Drucktypen*, Switzerland: Arthur Niggli, 1958 (2nd ed.)

Iliazd (Zdanevitch Ilia), *Ledentu le phare*, Paris: Allia, 1995 (1st ed. 1923)

L'Image des mots (exh. cat.), Alternatives, APCI/Paris: Centre Georges Pompidou, 1985

Jost Hochuli: Printed Matter, Mainly Books/Jost Hochuli: Drucksachen, vor allem Bücher, Zurich: Niggli, 2002

Kinross, Robin, *Unjustified Texts. Perspectives on Typography*, London: Hyphen Press, 2002

Kuitenbrouwer, Carel, *Typographie hollandaise* (exh. cat.), Villeurbanne: Maison du livre, de l'image et du son, 1991

Labuz, Ronald, *Typography and Typesetting. Type Design and Manipulation using Today's Technology*, New York: Van Nostrand Reinhold, 1988

Laliberté, Jadette, *Formes typographiques. Historique, anatomie, classification*, Quebec: Les Presses de l'université Laval, 2004

Laliberté, Jadette, "La typo moderne. Conséquence de la révolution industrielle?" in *Communication et langages*, n°. 72, 2nd trimester 1987

Lehner, John and Eduard Mader, *Authentic Art Nouveau Lettering and Design*, New York: Dover, 1989

Lewis, John, *Typography: Basic Principles. Influences and Trends since the 19th Century*, London: Studio Books, 1963

Lista, Giovanni, "Depero et le futurisme," *Revues de Depero. 1931–1933. Numero unico […]*, Paris: Jean-Michel Place, 1979

Lista, Giovanni, *Le Livre futuriste*, Modena: Panini, 1984

Meehan, Bernard, *The Book of Kells*, London: Thames & Hudson, 1994

Meggs, Philip B., Rob Carter, and Ben Day, *Typographic Design. Form and Communication*, New York: Van Nostrand Reinhold, 1985, (reprinted 2002)

Middendorp, Jan, *Dutch Type*, Rotterdam: 010, 2004

Middendorp, Jan, *Lettered. Typefaces and Alphabets by Clotilde Olyff*, Ghent; Druk, 2000

Mœglin-Delcroix, Anne, *Livres d'artistes*, Paris: Centre Georges Pompidou/Herscher, 1985

Mœglin-Delcroix, Anne, *Esthétique du livre d'artiste*, Paris: Jean-Michel Place/Bibliothèque

nationale de France, 1997

Mukai, Shutaro and Ikko Tanaka, *Transition of Modern Typography. Europe & America 1950s–'60s*, Japan: Ginza Graphic Gallery, 1996

Nesbitt, Alexander, *Decorative Alphabets and Initials*, New York: Dover, 1959

Ornamented Types. Twenty-Three Alphabets from the Foundry of Louis John Pouchée, I.M. Imprint/London: St. Bride's Printing Library, 1992

Paillard, Jean, *Claude Garamont. Graveur et fondeur de lettres du roi François Ier*, La Courneuve: OFMI-Garamont, 1969 (1st ed. 1914)

Paris, Muriel, *Petit manuel de composition typographique*, France, 1999 (published with the aid of FIACRE/DAP)

Pedersen, Kim and Anders Kidmose,*[sort på hvidt]/[in black & white]*, Den Grafische Højskole/The Graphic College of Denmark, 1993

Peignot, Jérôme, *Du Calligramme,* Paris: Chêne, 1978

Peignot, Jérôme, *Du Chiffre*, Paris: Jacques Damase, 1982

Peignot, Jérôme, *Typoésie*, Paris: Imprimerie nationale, 1993

Perfect, Christopher and Gordon Rookledge (revised by Phil Baines), *Rookledge's International Typefinder. The Essential Handbook of Typeface Recognition and Selection*, London: Sarema Press, 1990

De Plomb, d'encre et de lumière. Essai sur la typographie & la communication écrite, Paris: Imprimerie nationale, 1982

Poynor Rick and Edward Booth-Clibborn (eds.) *Typography now. The Next Wave*, London: Booth-Clibborn, 1995 (1st ed. 1991)

Poynor, Rick (éd.), *Typography now two: Implosion*. London: Booth-Clibborn, 1996

Richaudeau, François, *La Lisibilité. Langage, typographie, signes… lecture*, Paris: Denoël, 1969

Rothenstein, Julian and Mel Gooding (eds.), *Alphabets and other signs*, London: Redstone Press, 2003

Ruder Emil, "Ordnende Typographie/La typographie de l'ordre," *Graphis*, no. 85, 1959

Ruder, Emil, *Typographie*, Switzerland: Arthur Niggli, 1982 (1st ed. 1967), German-English-French

The Russian Avant-Garde Book. 1910–1934, New York: The Museum of Modern Art, 2002

Shaw, Paul, "The Calligraphic Tradition in Blackletter Type," *Scripsit*, vol. 22, nos. 1 and 2, summer 1999

Solo, Dan X., *Art Nouveau Display Alphabets, Special Effects and Topical Alphabets, Stencil Alphabets, Victorian Display Alphabets*, New York: Dover, 1976, 1978, 1988, 1976

Spencer, Herbert, *The Liberated Page*, London: Lund Humphries, 1987

Spencer, Herbert, *Pioneers of Modern Typography*, London: Lund Humphries, 1969 (reprinted

1982)

Spencer, Herbert, *The Visible Word*, London: Lund Humphries, 1969

Tolmer, Alfred, *Mise en page. The Theory and Practise of Lay-out*, London: The Studio, 1931 (English with a summary in French)

Tory, Geofroy, *Champ Fleury*, Geneva: Slatkine Reprints, 1973 (1st ed. Paris, 1529)

Tschichold, Jan, *Asymmetric Typography*, New York: Reinhold Publishing Corporation, 1967 (1st ed. 1935, in German)

Tschichold, Jan (Ivan, Iwan), "Elementare Typographie", special number of *Typographische Mitteilungen* (*Zeitschrift des Bildungsverbandes der deutschen Buchdrucker Leipzig*), Leipzig, October 1925

Tschichold, Jan, *Livre et typographie*, Paris: Allia, 1994 (French translation)

Tschichold, Jan, *The New Typography. A Handbook for Modern Designers,* Berkeley/Los Angeles/London: University of California Press, 1995 (introduction Robin Kinross) (English translation; 1st ed. 1928)

Tschichold, Jan, *Vues cavalières sur le modernisme en typographie*, Paris: Société anonyme Monotype, 1961 (French translation)

Wallis, Lawrence W, *Modern Encyclopedia of Typefaces, 1960–1990*, London: Lund Humphries, 1990

Walton, Roger (ed.), *Typographics 1. The Art of Typography from Digital to Dyeline*, New York: Hearst Books International, 1995

The Poster

Ades, Dawn, *Posters. The 20th Century Poster. Design of the Avant-Garde*, New York: Abbeville Press, 1984

Appelbaum, Stanley, *The Complete Masters of the Poster*, New York: Dover, 1990

Arnold, Friedrich, *Anschläge. Politische Plakate in Deutschland 1900–1970*, Ebenhausen: Langewiesche-Brandt, 1972

Barkhatova, Eléna, *Russian Constructivist Poster*, Paris: Flammarion, 1992

Brattinga Pieter and Dick Dooijes, *A History of the Dutch Poster 1890–1960*, Amsterdam: Scheltema & Holkema, 1968

Fresnault-Deruelle, Pierre, *L'Éloquence des images. Images fixes III*, Paris: Presses universitaires de France, 1993

Fresnault-Deruelle, Pierre, *L'Image placardée. Pragmatique et rhétorique de l'affiche*, Paris: Nathan, 1997

Gallo, Max, *L'Affiche. Miroir de l'histoire, miroir de la vie*, Paris: Parangon, 2002 (reprint)

Gervereau, Laurent, *La Propagande par l'affiche*, Paris: Syros-Alternatives, 1991

Gervereau Laurent, *Terroriser, manipuler, convaincre! Histoire mondiale de l'affiche politique*, Paris: Somogy, 1996

Hillier, Bevis, *Posters*, London: Weidenfeld &

Nicolson, 1969

Hunziker, Hans Jurg, *L'Affiche typographique Suisse* (exh. cat.), Villeurbanne: Maison du livre, de l'image et du son, 1995

Hutchinson, Harold F., *The Poster. An Illustrated History from 1860*, London: Studio Vista, 1968

Kellenberger, Éric and Anne-Claude Lelieur, *Objets, réalismes, affiches suisses 1905–1950*, Paris: Bibliothèque Forney, 1982

Marchetti, Stéphane, *Affiches 1939–1945*, Lausanne: Édita, 1982

Margadant, Bruno, *L'Affiche suisse, 1900–1983*, Basel: Birkhäuser, 1983

Marx, Roger, Jack Rennert, and Alain Weill, *Les Maîtres de l'affiche, 1896–1900*, Paris: Chêne, 1978

Mésa, François, *Mai 68. Les affiches de l'atelier populaire de l'ex-École des beaux-arts*, Paris: S.P.M., 1975

Metzl, Ervine, *The Poster. Its History and its Art*, New York: Watson-Guptill, 1963

Müller-Brockmann, Josef and Shizuko Müller-Brockmann, *Geschichte des Plakates/Histoire de l'affiche/History of the Poster*, Switzerland: ABC, 1971; reissued: Paris: Phaidon, 2005

Rademacher, Hellmut (sic), *L'Art de l'affiche en Allemagne et ses maîtres* Leipzig: édition Leipzig, 1965 (French translation)

Le Spectacle est dans la rue. Album d'affiches de Cassandre, Paris: Draeger Frères, 1935 (preface by Blaise Cendrars)

Weill, Alain, *L'Affiche dans le monde*, Paris: Aimery Somogy, 1991

Monographs, creators, personalities

Adrian Frutiger, son œuvre typographique et ses écrits (exh. cat.), Villeurbanne: Maison du livre, de l'image et du son, 1994

A. M. Cassandre (exh. cat.), Paris: Galerie Janine Hao, 1966

A. M. Cassandre (exh. cat.), Geneva: Galerie Motte, 1966

A. M. Cassandre (exh. cat.), Paris: Musée des Arts Décoratifs, 1950

Apeloig Philippe, entretien avec Michel Rozenberg, Au cœur du mot. Inside the Word, Switzerland: Lars Müller, 2001

Bargiel, Réjane and Christophe Zagrodski, *Steinlen affichiste, catalogue raisonné*, Lausanne: Grand-Pont, 1986

Baudin, Fernand, *Dossier Vox*, Belgium: Association des Compagnons de Lure, Rémy Magermans, 1975

Baur, Ruedi and Pippo Lionni, *Design: Ruedi Baur et Pippo Lionni*, France: Integral concept, 1991

Bazin, Jean-François, *Les Affiches de Villemot*, Paris: Denoël, 1985

Bechtel, Guy, *Gutenberg*, Paris: Fayard, 1992

Berry, John D., "William Caslon," in *U&lc*, vol. 25, n°. 3, winter 1998

Berthold, Wolpe. *A Retrospective Survey*, London:

Victoria & Albert Museum/Faber & Faber, 1980

Bignens, Christoph, Hans Rudolf Bosshard, and Gerd Fleischmann, *Max Bill. Typografie, Reklame, Buchgestaltung/Max Bill: Typography, Advertising, Book Design*, Zurich: Niggli, 1999 (German-English)

Bignens, Christoph and Jörg Stürzebecher, *Richard Paul Lohse. Konstruktive Gebrauchsgrafik*, Ostfildern-Ruit: Hatje Cantz, 1999

Blackwell, Lewis and David Carson, *The End of Print. The Grafik Design of David Carson*, London: Laurence King, 2000 (revised ed., 1st ed. 1995).

Blei, Franz, *Aubrey Beardsley*, Paris: Futuropolis, 1979 (1st ed. 1977)

Bradley, Will, Clarence P. Hornung and Roberta W. Wong, *Will Bradley, his Graphic Art*, New York: Dover, 1974

Broido, Lucy, *The Posters of Jules Chéret*, New York: Dover, 1992

Broos, Kees, *Piet Zwart 1885–1977*, Amsterdam: Van Gennep, 1982

Brown, Robert and Susan Reinhold, *Cassandre. Catalogue intégral des affiches*, Paris: Hubschmid et Bouret, 1981 (1st ed. 1979, English)

Brown, Robert K. and Reinhold Susan, *The Poster Art of A. M. Cassandre*, New York: E. P. Dutton, 1979

Burke, Christopher and Paul Renner, *The Art of Typography*, London: Hyphen Press, 1998

Cappiello, Paris: Réunion des musées nationaux, 1981

Caradec, François, Pierre Faucheux, and Marie-Christine Marquat, *Pierre Faucheux. Le magicien du livre*, France: Cercle de la Librairie, 1995

Cohen, Arthur A., *Herbert Bayer. The Complete Work*, Cambridge Mass./London: MIT Press, 1984

Colle-Lorant, Sylvia, *A. M. Cassandre affichiste*, Paris Université I, 1982 (thesis supervised by Marc Le Bot)

Devynck, Danièle, *Henri de Toulouse-Lautrec. Les affiches (collection du musée Toulouse-Lautrec)*, Odyssée, 2001 (English-French)

Engen, Rodney K., *Walter Crane as a Book Illustrator*, London: Academy Editions, 1975

Ernst, Keller. Graphiker, 1891–1968. Gesamtwerk, Zurich: Kunstgewerbemuseum, 1976

Evans, David, *John Heartfield AIZ/VI, 1930–38*, New York: Kent Fine Art, 1992

Every Face of the Great Master Cassandre (exh. cat.), Japan: Suntory Museum, 1995

Friedl, Friedrich, *Exakte Gestaltung. Freie Arbeiten von 1964–1994*, Frankfurt/Mainz: Amt für Wissenschaft und Kunst/Hermann Schmidt, 1994

Gaëtan-Picon, Geneviève and Alain Weill, *Charles Loupot*, Paris: Musée de l'Affiche, 1979

Gerstner, Karl and Manfred Kröplien (eds.), *Karl Gerstner. Review of 5 x 10 Years of Graphic Design etc.*, Ostfildern-Ruit: Hatje Cantz, 2001

Graphic designers aux États-Unis, n°s. 1, 2, 3, Paris:

Office du livre, 1971, 1972

Graphic designers en Europe, n°s. 1, 2, 3, 4, Paris: Office du livre, 1971, 1972, 1973

Les Graphistes associés, Creil: Les Graphistes associés, Dumerchez, 2000

Greiman, April and Aris Janigian, *April Greiman, réflexions créatives. Essai philosophique sur le graphisme numérique*, Paris: Pyramyd, 2001 (preface Lewis Blackwell) (French translation; original title *Something from Nothing*)

Grundberg Andy, *Brodovitch*, New York: Harry N. Abrams, 1989

Gustav Klucis, Stuttgart: Gerd Hatje, 1991

Haley, Allan, "John Baskerville of Birmingham. Letter-founder and Printer," in *U&lc*, vol. 11, n°. 4, February 1985

Heller, Steven, *Paul Rand*, London: Phaidon, 1999

Henri, Pierre, *La Vie et l'Œuvre de Louis Braille*, Paris: Presses universitaires de France, 1952

Henrion, Friedrich Heinrich Kohn, "A little scandal in the street," in *The Penrose Annual*, vol. 63, 1970

Henrion, Friedrich Heinrich Kohn, *Top Graphic Design*, Zurich: ABC, 1983

Hodik, Barbara and Roger Remington, *Nine Pioneers in American Graphic Design*, Cambridge, Mass.: MIT Press, 1989

Hoek Els (ed.), *Theo Van Doesburg. Œuvre catalogue*, Utrecht/Otterlo: Kröller-Müller Museum/Centraal Museum, 2000

Hollis, Richard, "Pierre Faucheux Permanent Innovation," in *Eye*, n°. 19, vol. 5, winter 1995

Huber, Max, *Projetti grafici 1936–1981*, Milan: Electa, 1982

Huygen, Frederike and Hugues Boekraad, *Wim Crouwel. Mode en module*, Rotterdam: 010, 1997

Iliazd, Paris: Centre Georges Pompidou, 1978

Jan Lenica. Plakat- und Filmkunst (exh. cat.), Berlin: Frölich und Kaufmann, 1981

Jammes, André, *Les Didot. Trois siècles de typographie et de bibliophilie* (exh. cat.), Paris/Lyon: Bibliothèque historique de la Ville de Paris/Musée de l'Imprimerie de Lyon, 1998

Jazz Blvd. Niklaus Troxler Posters, Switzerland: Lars Müller, 1999

Jean Carlu (exh. cat.), Paris: Musée de l'Affiche, 1980–1981

Jean Widmer, Villeurbanne: Maison du livre, de l'image et du son/Les Éditions du demi-cercle, 1992

Jean Widmer. A Devotion to Modernism (exh. cat.), New York: Herb Lubalin Study Center of Design and Typography, 2003

Kapr, Albert, *Johann Gutenberg*, Aldershot: Scolar Press, 1996 (English translation; 1st ed. 1986)

Kinross, Robin et al., *Karel Martens. Printed Matter\Drukwerk*, London/Netherlands: Hyphen Press, 1996

Kunst + Design Wim Crouwel. Preisträger der Stankowski-Stiftung (exh. cat.), Cantz, 1991 (German-English)

Lars Müller (ed.), *Josef Müller-Brockmann. Gestalter,*

Switzerland: Lars Müller, 1994

László Moholy-Nagy (exh. cat.), Marseille/Paris: Musées de Marseille/Réunion des Musées Nationaux, 1991

Lavrentiev, Alexandre, *Varvara Stepanova. Une vie constructiviste*, Paris: Philippe Sers, 1988

Lemoine, Serge (gen. ed.), *Kurt Schwitters* (exh. cat.), Paris: Centre Georges Pompidou/Réunion des Musées Nationaux, 1994

Lorquin, Bertrand, *Toulouse-Lautrec. L'art de l'affiche*, Paris: Gallimard (Découvertes hors série), 2002

Maeda, John, *Maeda@media. Journal d'un explorateur du numérique*, Paris: Thames & Hudson, 2000 (preface Nicholas Negroponte)

Margerie (de) Anne, *J. B. Bodoni. Typographe italien 1740–1813*, Paris: Jacques Damase, 1985

Maximilien Vox. Un homme de lettre, Paris: Mairie de Paris, Direction des Affaires Culturelles/Bibliothèque des Arts Graphiques, 1994

McLean, Ruari, *Jan Tschichold: Typographer*, London: Lund Humphries, 1975

Mouron, Henri, *A. M. Cassandre. Affiches, arts graphiques, théâtre*, Geneva: Éditions d'Art Albert Skira, 1985

Néret, Gilles, *Aubrey Beardsley*, Cologne: Taschen, 1998

Niklaus, Troxler. Affiches de jazz, Germany: Oreos, 1991

Niklaus Troxler. Graphic Designer's Design Life, China: Wang Xu, 1999

Noguez, Dominique and Annick Lantenois, *Tout est politique. Claude Baillargeon*, Paris: Adam Biro, 1997

Passuth, Krisztina, *Moholy-Nagy*, Paris: Flammarion, 1984 (1st ed. 1982)

Peckolick, Alan and Gertrude Snyder, *Herb Lubalin. Art Director, Graphic Designer and Typographer*, New York: American Showcase, 1985

Poynor, Rick, "This signifier is loaded. Zurich designer Cornel Windlin [...]," in *Eye*, n°. 22, vol. 6, autumn 1996

Reminiscor (pseudonym), "Jan Tschichold: typographe," in *Communication et langages*, n°. 25, 1975 (1st ed. 1972, German)

Rouard, Margo, *Roman Cieslewicz*, Paris: Thames & Hudson, 1993

Rouard-Snowman, Margo (gen. ed.), *Jean Widmer graphiste, un écologiste de l'image*, Paris: Centre Georges Pompidou, 1995

Sarfis, Thierry and Ewa Maruszewska (gen. eds.), *Henryk Tomaszewski. Graphismes et pédagogie*, Paris: Somogy, 1995

Savignac, Raymond, *Affichiste*, Paris: R. Laffont, 1975

Schmidt-Friderichs, Bertram, *Pierre-Simon Fournier (1712–1768)*, Paris: Jacques Damase, 1991

Vox Maximilien, *A. M. Cassandre. Peintre d'affiches*, Paris: Les Éditions parallèles, 1948

Weill, Alain, *Cassandre. Les Maîtres de l'affiche*, Paris: Bibliothèque de l'image, 1995

Weingart, Wolfgang, *Weingart: Typography/My Way to Typography/Wege zur Typographie*, Switzerland: Lars Müller, 2000

Wichmann, Hans (éd.), *Armin Hofmann. His Work, Quest and Philosophy*, Basel, Boston and Berlin: Birkhäuser Verlag, 1989 (German-English)

Willett, John, *Heartfield contre Hitler*, Paris: Hazan, 1997 (French translation)

Wozencroft, Jon, *The Graphic Language of Neville Brody*, London: Thames & Hudson, 1988

Zagrodski, Christophe, *Loupot*, Paris: Le Cherche-Midi éditeur, 1998

Other works

Ades, Dawn, *Photomontage*, London: Thames & Hudson, 1976

Apollinaire, Guillaume, *Calligrammes, poèmes de la paix et de la guerre*, Paris: Gallimard (reprinted 1966)

Arp, Hans, El Lissitszky (eds.), *Die Kunstismen/Les Ismes de l'art/The Isms of Art*, Zurich: Eugen Rentsch, 1925 (reprinted Baden: Lars Müller/Fondation Jean Arp et Sophie Taeuber-Arp, Switzerland, 1990)

Palmier, Jean-Michel and François Aubral et al., *L'Art dégénéré. Une exposition sous le IIIe Reich*, Paris: Jacques Bertoin, 1992

Art & publicité 1890–1990 (exh. cat.), Paris: Centre Georges Pompidou, 1990

Art grandeur nature 2004 (Contemporary Art Biennale, Seine-Saint-Denis, France), Saint-Ouen: Synesthésie éditions, 2004

Bandini, Mirella, *Pour une Histoire du lettrisme*, Paris: Jean-Paul Rocher, 2003

Barbara Kruger, Los Angeles, Museum of Contemporary Art, 1999–2000 (accompanying an exhibition)

Barthes, Roland, *The Degree Zero of Writing* (translation A. Lavers and C. Smith), New York: Farrar Strauss Giroux, 1976

Baudrillard, Jean, *The System of Objects*, London: Verso, 1968

Bauhaus 1919–1969 (exh. cat.), Paris: Musée National d'Art Moderne/Musée d'Art Moderne de la Ville de Paris, 1969 (set by Herbert Bayer)

Benjamin, Walter, "The Work of Art in the Era of its Mechanized Reproduction" (1936), in *Illuminations,* New York: Random House, 1985

Bill Max, *Form. A Balance Sheet of Mid-Twentieth-Century Trends in Design*, Basel: Karl Werner, 1952 (German-English-French)

Blistène, Bernard and Véronique Legrand (gen. eds.), *Poésure et peintrie. D'un art l'autre* (exh. cat.), Marseille/Paris: Centre de la Vieille Charité, Musées de Marseille/Réunion des Musées Nationaux, 1993

Bois, Yve-Alain, "Modernisme et postmodernisme," in *Encyclopædia Universalis. Les Enjeux*, Paris, 1990

Cahiers Dada Surréalisme n°. 3. Dada et la typographie, Paris: Lettres modernes, 1969

Central European Avant-Gardes. Exchange and Transformation, 1910–1930, Los Angeles County Museum of Art/MIT Press, 2002

Chalumeau, Jean-Luc, *Les Théories de l'art. Philosophie, critique et histoire de l'art de Platon à nos jours*, Paris: Vuibert, 1994

Champigneulle, Bernard, *Encyclopédie de l'Art Nouveau*, Paris: Somogy, 1981

Clair Jean (gen. ed.), *Vienne 1880–1938. L'Apocalypse joyeuse* (exh. cat.), Paris: Centre Georges Pompidou, 1986

Coke Van Deren and Jean-Michel Palmier, *Avant-garde photographique en Allemagne, 1919–1939*, Paris: Philippe Sers, 1982

De l'Écriture à la peinture, exh. cat., Saint-Paul: Fondation Maeght, 2004

Design "Le livre," Paris: Florilège, 1990 (French translation; 1st ed. 1986)

Dormer, Peter, *Design since 1945*, London: Thames & Hudson, 1993

L'École d'Ulm: textes et manifestes, Paris: Centre Georges Pompidou, 1988

Ewig, Isabelle, Thomas W. Gaehtgens and Matthias Noell (eds.), *Das Bauhaus und Frankreich/Le Bauhaus et la France. 1919–1940*, Berlin: Akademie Verlag, Centre allemand d'histoire de l'art, 2002 (texts in German or French)

Fahr-Becker, Gabriele, *Wiener Werkstätte. 1903–1932*, Cologne : Taschen, 1993 (English translation)

Fitoussi, Brigitte, *Memphis*, Paris: Assouline, 1998

Focillon, Henri, *Vie des formes*, Paris: Presses Universitaires de France, 1996, (1st ed. 1943)

Gervereau, Laurent, *La Disparition des images*, Paris: Somogy, 2003

Guidot, Raymond, *Histoire du design*, Paris: Hazan, 2000

Histoires de blanc & noir (exh. cat.), Musée de Grenoble/Réunion des Musées Nationaux, 1996

Hulten, Pontus (gen. ed.), *Futurism and Futurisms*, London: Thames & Hudson, 1986

Ionesco, Eugène, *La Cantatrice chauve*, Paris: Gallimard, 1964 (Design by Massin)

Jimenez, Marc, *Qu'est-ce que l'esthétique?* Paris: Gallimard, 1997

Larkin David and June Sprigg, *Shaker. Life, Work and Art*, London: Cassell, Paris, 2000

Lemoine, Serge, *Art constructif*, Paris: Centre Georges Pompidou, 1992

Lemoine, Serge, *Dada*, New York: Universe Books, 1987

Lemoine, Serge, "Le grand passage," in *Art concret suisse: mémoire et progrès* (exh. cat.), Musée des Beaux-Arts de Dijon, 1982

Leroi-Gourhan, André, *Le Geste et la Parole. Première partie: technique et langage*, Paris: Albin Michel, 1964

Lipovetsky, Gilles, *L'Empire de l'éphémère. La mode et son destin dans les sociétés modernes*, Paris: Gallimard, 1987

Lipovetsky, Gilles, *L'Ère du vide. Essai sur l'individualisme contemporain*, Paris: Gallimard, 1983

Lorenz, Otto, *Art Nouveau. Les femmes*, Paris/Germany: Imprimerie des arts et manufactures de Paris/Berghaus, 1989

Loze, Pierre, *L'Art Nouveau*, Paris: Flammarion, 1999

Lupton, Ellen and J. Abbott Miller (eds.), *The ABCs of [triangle, square, circle]: the Bauhaus and Design Theory*, London: Thames & Hudson, 1993

Mallarmé, Stéphane, *Un Coup de dés jamais n'abolira le hasard. Poème*, (A throw of the dice never will abolish chance) Paris: Gallimard, 1993 (Paris: Gallimard, 1914; 1st ed. May 1897, review, *Cosmopolis*)

Margolin, Victor (gen. ed.), *Design Discourse. History, Theory, Criticism*, Chicago/London: The University of Chicago Press, 1989

Margolin, Victor, *The Struggle for Utopia. Rodchenko, Lissitzky, Moholy-Nagy, 1917–1946*, Chicago/London: The University of Chicago Press, 1997

L'Œil éphémère. Œuvres de Jirí Kolár, Musée des Beaux-Arts de Dijon/Réunion des Musées Nationaux, 2002

Paris–Berlin 1900–1933. Rapports et contrastes France–Allemagne (exh. cat.), Paris: Centre Georges Pompidou, 1978

Peyré, Yves, *Peinture et poésie. Le dialogue par le livre*, Paris: Gallimard, 2001

Pierre, Arnauld, *Tania Mouraud*, Paris: Flammarion, 2004

Pionniers du XXe siècle. Guimard, Horta, Van de Velde (exh. cat.), Paris: Musée des Arts Décoratifs, 1971

Ramonet, Ignacio, *La Tyrannie de la communication*, Paris: Gallimard, 2001

Roh Franz and Jan Tschichold (eds.), *Foto-Auge/Œil et photo/Photo-Eye*, Stuttgart: Wedekind & Co., 1929 (reprinted Tübingen: Ernst Wasmuth, 1973)

Rouard, Margo and Françoise Jollant Kneebone (gen. eds.), *Design français 1960–1990* (exh. cat.), Paris: APCI/Centre Georges Pompidou, 1988

Stähli, Christoph and Sandra Hoffmann, *Stadtplan: Dreiundvierzig Typographische Bauprojekte*, Basel: n. p., 1995 (text Peter Gisi)

Sterne, Laurence, *Life and Opinions of Tristram Shandy, Gentleman*, in D. Grant (ed.) *Sterne*, London: Rupert Hart-Davis, 1950 (1st ed. 1759–1767, Great Britain)

Theo Van Doesburg 1883–1931 (exh. cat.), Nuremberg and Basel: Kunsthallen, 1969

Wingler, Hans Maria, *The Bauhaus. Weimar, Dessau, Berlin, Chicago*, Cambridge Mass./ London: MIT Press, 1986 (1st ed. 1962)

Zweig, Stefan, *The World of Yesterday* (translation H. Zohn), University of Nebraska Press, 1994

Dictionaries, lexicons, glossaries, guides

L'ABCdaire des écritures, Paris: Flammarion/Bibliothèque nationale de France, 2000

Barré-Despond, Arlette (gen. ed.), *Dictionnaire international des arts appliqués et du design*, Paris: Éditions du Regard, 1996

Catalogs, periodicals and publishers' samples: Adobe, Agfa, Berthold, Emigre, Fontshop, Linotype, Monotype, Scangraphic, etc.

Dreyfus, John and François Richaudeau (gen. eds.), *La Chose imprimée*, Paris: Retz, 1977

Faudouas, Jean-Claude, *Dictionnaire des grands noms de la chose imprimée*, Paris: Retz, 1991

Folsom, Rose, *The Calligrapher's Dictionary*, London: Thames & Hudson, 1990

Friedl, Friedrich, Nikolaus Ott, and Bernard Stein, *Typographie. Quand, qui, comment/Typographie. Wann, wer, wie/Typography. When, who, how*, Cologne: Könemann, 1998

Guide du typographe, Lausanne: Association suisse des typographes, 2000 (6th ed.)

Hostettler, Rudolf, *The Printer's Terms*, St. Gallen: Rudolf Hostettler, 1969 (1st ed. 1949) (German-English-French-Italian-Dutch)

Lexique des règles typographiques, Paris: Imprimerie nationale, 1990

Livingston, Alan and Isabella Livingston, *Dictionary of Graphic Design and Designers*, London: Thames & Hudson, 1998

Makhoul, Michel Hanna and Roger Remington (gen. eds.), *Directory of Graphic Design Archives. Collections and Resources*, Rochester, New York: National Graphic Design Archive, 1994

Mediavilla, Claude, *L'ABCdaire de la calligraphie*, Paris: Flammarion, 2000

Paput, Christian, *Vocabulaire des arts graphiques, de la communication, de la PAO […]*, France: T.V.S.O., 1997

Richaudeau, François, *Manuel de typographie et de mise en page*, Paris: Retz, 1989

Thompson, Philip and Peter Davenport, *The Dictionary of Visual Language*, Harmondsworth: Penguin Books, 1982 (1st ed. 1980) (preface George Lois)

Who's Who in Graphic Art. Répertoire illustré des artistes graphiques, illustrateurs, typographes et caricaturistes de classe internationale, Zurich: Amstutz Herdeg/Graphis Press, 1962

Who's Who in Graphic Design, Zurich: Benteli-Werd, 1994

Magazines, periodicals

Affiche (Netherlands)
Arts et métiers graphiques (France, 1927–39)
Azimuts (France)
Baseline (Great Britain)
Communication et langages (France)
Creative Review (Great Britain)
Design Issues (United States)
Emigre (United States, 1984–2005)
Étapes (France)
Eye (Great Britain)
Graphis (founded in Switzerland in 1944)
Idea (Japan)
Novum (Germany)
Print (United States)
Signes (France, 1991–98)
TipoGráfica (tpG; Argentina)
Typografische Monatsblätter/Revue suisse de l'imprimerie (TM/RSI; Switzerland)
Typographica (Great Britain, 1949–67)
U&lc ("Upper and lower case"; United States, 1973–99)

Translated from the French by
David Radzinowicz (Chapters 1–3)
and Deke Dusinberre (Chapters 4–6)
Copyediting: Lindsay Porter
Jacket design: Peter Keller
Typesetting: Thomas Gravemaker
   (Anne-Lou Bissières for the original edition)
Proofreading: Penelope Isaac
Color Separation: Artisans du Regard, Paris

This book was typeset in Sabon and Syntax
(see illustrations on page 356).

Sabon, which Jan Tschichold began designing in 1964, was first released in 1967. It was specifically commissioned to fulfill the special requirement of maintaining the same appearance when used in three different systems of typesetting, whether by hand setting (movable type) or machine (matrixes for Linotype and Monotype). The design of the face was based on sixteenth-century roman type, notably Garamond. It was named after Jacques Sabon, a sixteenth-century type engraver and founder. Syntax also has a rich history. Hans Eduard Meier sketched an initial design in 1955, but only put his final touches to it in 2000, the first release version dating from 1968. Thus half a century passed between the designer's original concept and ultimate culmination, testifying to the intention to develop a lasting form. Syntax displays the particularity of wedding the simplified structure of sans serif letterforms with the features and proportions of Renaissance scripts (Italian humanistic scripts from the early Quattrocento and roman typeface from the last third of the fifteenth century). One special feature is the very slight slope of its verticals, of roughly one degree, which stems from the involuntary movement of the first drawings done by hand, an aspect that was deliberately retained in the final version.

Distributed in North America
by Rizzoli International Publications, Inc.

Originally published in French as
Graphisme, Typographie, Histoire
© Flammarion, Paris, 2005

English-language edition
© Flammarion, Paris, 2006

06 07 08 4 3 2 1
FC0523-06-X
ISBN-10: 2-0803-0523-9
ISBN-13: 9782080305237
Dépôt légal: 10/2006

Printed in Singapore by Tien Wah Press.

Photo Credits

The numbers correspond to the figures

Austria Vienna: Thonet Brothers AG 226; MAK-Austrian Museum of Applied Arts/Contemporary Art 244, 246, 247. Canada Musée des Beaux-Arts du Canada/Musée Canadien de la Photographie Contemporaine 161. France Albi: Musée Toulouse-Lautrec 203, 204; Aurillac: Archives du Cantal 83; Issy-Les-Moulineaux: Collection MFCJ/Jean-Loup Charmet 59 ; Lyon: Musée de l'Imprimerie 165; Nancy: Musée de l'École de Nancy/Studio Image 197; Paris: AKG 184, 206, 218, 219, 252, 267, 482, 548, Archives Flammarion 20, 24, 50, 156, 331, Archives Serge Lemoine p. 6, Bibliothèque des Arts Graphiques/Mairie de Paris 263, Bibliothèque Doucet/Michel Nguyen 413, Bibliothèque Forney 181, 182, 210, 212, 255, 433, 529, 547, 579, 643, Bibliothèque. Historique de la Ville de Paris/Jean-Loup Charmet 303, Bibliothèque Nationale de France p. 10, 29, 32, 48, 51, 69, 89, 91, 96, 104, 127, 150, 543, Bridgeman Art Library 77, 87, 130, 153, 190, 199, 270, Bruno Scotti 28, 60, 75, 103, 105, 113, 221, 222, 224, 278, 279, 280, 281, 282, 287, 290, 292, 295, 298, 299, 300, 308, 334, 337, 344, 356, 389, 390, 392, 393, 394, 407, 410, 452, 461, 478, 492, 499, 501, 502, 503, 532, 535, 560, 561, 639, École Nationale Supérieure des Beaux-Arts 163, Galerie Lara Vincy 644, 645, 646, Les Arts Décoratifs, Musée de la Publicité/Laurent Sully Jaulmes 191, 208, 319, 419, 431, 432, 434, 435, 437, 439, 546, 556, 557, Médiathèque de l'École Nationale des Ponts et Chaussées 183, M/M Paris-Galerie Air de Paris-CNEAI 810, 811, 813, Didier Moiselet 312, 313, 314, 364, 395, 398, MOURON/CASSANDRE 421–430, Réunion des Musées Nationaux 11, 17, 41, 305, 311/M. Beck Coppola 1/Franck Raux 16/Margarete Büsing 18, 40/Ravaux 54/Philippe Migeat 306/Gérard Blot 417, Rue des Archives 185, 475, Société Française de Photographie 157, 160; Villeneuve d'Ascq: Musée d'Art Moderne de Lille Métropole/Philip Bernard 271. Germany Berlin: Bauhaus Archiv 383; Bühl: Lingner und Fischer GmbH 264; Essen: Museum Folkwang 411. Italy Archivio Storico Olivetti 631, 632; Florence: Scala 327; Naples: Fotografia Foglia 19; Macao Museu de Arte 250, 253. Netherlands Amsterdam: Gerard Unger 814–822. Switzerland Willisau: Niklaus Troxler 715–718, 807; Zurich: Hoshchule Gestaltung und Kunst-Museum für Gestaltung 523, 524, 525, 526, 527, 528, 531, 537, 571, 613, 614, 615. United Kingdom Glasgow: Glasgow Museum of Art 215, Glasgow School of Art, 216; London: British Library 56, 234; Retrograph Archiv, DACS 461; Oxford: M. R. Dudley 236. United States Michigan: Randall Bytwerk 469, 470, 471, 473, 476; New York: Mary Boone Gallery 720, The Museum of Modern Art/Scala, Florence 268; wolfgangsvault.com 594
For all figures not quoted above: all rights reserved.

Places of conservation:
France Biot: Musée Fernand Léger 417; Paris: Bibliothèque Centrale du Muséum d'Histoire Naturelle 60b, Bibliothèque Mazarine 60c, Bibliothèque Municipale de Tours 60d, Bibliothèque Nationale de France 60a, Collection Michel Brodovitch 502, Giovanni Lista, Musée Guimet 11, 54, Musée du Louvre 16, Centre Georges Pompidou Musée National d'Art Moderne 306, 310, 311, 393, 412; Saint-Germain-en-Laye: Musée des Antiquités Nationales 1; Tours: Bibliothèque Municipale 60d. Germany Berlin: Staasbibliothek 18, 40; Munich: Artothek Staatsgalerie Moderne Kunst 414. Italy Milan: Collection Calmanini 281; Rome: private collection 492. Japan Tokyo: The National Museum of Modern Art 269. Netherlands Amsterdam: Stedelijk Museum 299; The Hague: Gemeentemuseum 350, 357; Otterlo: Kröller-Müller Museum 351. Russia Moscow: Tretiakov Gallery 298; St Petersburg: Russian State Museum 300. Switzerland Basel: Öffentliche Kunstsammlung 75, 87, 103, 105; Zurich: Museum für Gestaltung 333. United Kingdom London: British Library 234, 235, 237, 291, British Museum 222, 224, Victoria & Albert Museum 221. United States Collection Vince Aletti 503; Collection June & Elaine Leibowits 561; Collection Elaine Lustig Cohen 308; Collection Susan Pack 332, 334

"Cosmic call", message sent out by radio in 1999 towards four stars 50 to 70 light years away from the Earth. The first of 23 pages of a document made up of universal signs—starting with the definition of figures, mathematical operations, and going on to pages dealing with physics, astronomy, mankind, etc. Designed by Canadian physicists Yvan Dutil and Stéphane Dumas. *"Every page is outlined with a frame of one pixel in thickness […]. The characters were generated by computer with the intention that they be as different as possible from each other, whichever way round they are viewed […] we calculated that even if a degradation of 10 % occurred after a voyage of 100 light years, the characters would still be legible."*